THE PREMIER SEE

VII DIE   JULIO
MDCCC   VI
IESI   ET   MARIAE
NOM   INE

AB
REVERENDISSIMO
JOHANNO CARROLL
EPISCOPO BALTIMORII

The Premier See

A History of the Archdiocese of Baltimore, 1789–1994

THOMAS W. SPALDING

THE JOHNS HOPKINS UNIVERSITY PRESS
BALTIMORE AND LONDON

This Softshell Books edition has been brought to publication with the generous assistance of a grant from the Xaverian Brothers.

Softshell Books edition, 1995
04 03 02 01 00 99 98 97 96 95   5 4 3 2 1

The Johns Hopkins University Press, 2715 North Charles Street,
Baltimore, Maryland 21218-4319
The Johns Hopkins Press Ltd., London

Library of Congress Cataloging-in-Publication Data

Spalding, Thomas W.
   The premier see: a history of the Archdiocese of Baltimore,
      1789–1994 / Thomas W. Spalding.
         p.   cm.
   Bibliography: p.
   Includes index.
   ISBN 0-8018-3857-6 (alk. paper)—ISBN 0-8018-5215-3 (pbk. alk. paper)
      1. Catholic Church. Archdiocese of Baltimore (Md.)—History. 2. Baltimore (Md.)
   Region—Church history.   I. Title.
BX1417.B3S65   1989   89-2645
282'.752—dc20   CIP

Frontispiece: Detail from the Resurrection Window of the Co-Cathedral of the Assumption showing Bishop John Carroll at the laying of the cornerstone of the church, July 7, 1806. Photograph by Denise Walker.

Contents

Preface and Acknowledgments

IN THE LAST YEARS of his administration as archbishop of Baltimore, Cardinal Lawrence Joseph Shehan decided it was time the oldest Catholic see in the United States had a history. At the recommendation of Monsignor John Tracy Ellis, I was asked to write it. I agreed and was given full freedom to tell the story of the archdiocese as I saw it. There was no contract. To the research and writing I devoted two full years and almost a dozen summers. Even then I was not able to examine all the original sources—the archives of most of the religious orders that served the archdiocese, for example, or the papers of many bishops and other significant people whose lives impinged upon those of its archbishops—nor all the published material that touched in some way the development of the oldest archdiocese. The principal sources were the archives of the archdiocese of Baltimore, the archdiocesan weekly (and earlier monthly), and the more important secondary works, which include scholarly biographies of all the archbishops through Cardinal James Gibbons.

Though in many ways the history of the premier see is mirrored in the development of others, it is in many ways unique. The oldest see is the place of origin and of nurture for what I, and others, have called the Maryland tradition in American Catholicism. It is a tradition that was often in tension with the immigrant church roughly of the period 1830 to 1960, which also had its counterpart in the archdiocese of Baltimore. The history of the premier see is unique certainly in that it is, in great part, a history of the Catholic Church in the United States up to the death of Cardinal James Gibbons in 1921. Until then its archbishops were chosen—some willingly, most not—to be the principal conduits for decisions taken by the pope and the Roman curia or by the American bishops in council. For this reason primarily, I decided at the start that the archbishops must serve as the focus of the history and their administrations provide its organizational framework. The unique character of the oldest archdiocese, I also decided, could not be indicated or appreciated without attention to the national role assigned—or assumed by—the archbishops of Baltimore.

To attempt the history of any American diocese without due reference to its bishops would be to examine the spokes of a wheel apart from the hub. At the same time, I have tried to examine as many spokes as the principal sources allow. Beyond the inescapable task of constructing a traditional administrative and institutional history for a diocese that has never had one, I have endeavored to incorporate those developments that figured prominently in the growth of lay Catholicism. The story is told, therefore, from the vantage point of both the editorial and the archiepiscopal desk. It reflects to no small degree what was of interest to the editor of the diocesan weekly as well as to the archbishop. The former was exceedingly generous in the attention he accorded parish societies and activities, reflecting attitudes ranging from political to pious. These are areas that will increasingly, I am sure, command the attention of the historians of American Catholicism as episcopal biography is exhausted. How well the two vantage points have been interwoven I must leave to the reader to decide.

At the same time, a caveat must be entered. Those who take up this history with the expectation of finding the story of a particular parish or biography of a certain pastor or member of the laity (aside from a Carroll, a Taney, or a Bonaparte) or even mention of every religious order that has served the archdiocese will be disappointed. It is hoped nevertheless that this history will stimulate, as well as serve as background for, accounts of such people, institutions, and organizations.

Over the long course of reconstructing the two-hundred-year history of the oldest see—as well as a prediocesan period of more than a hundred and fifty years reduced from three ample chapters to a brief prologue for reasons of economy and emphasis—I have incurred innumerable debts of gratitude.

Cardinal Shehan continued in his retirement to show an avid interest in the progress of the history. It is a matter of regret that it was not finished for his reading. Archbishop William D. Borders, his successor in Baltimore, has also been unfailing in his interest and encouragement as well as in the financial assistance that has made the research, writing, and publication of the history possible. Both Cardinal Shehan and Archbishop Borders were also extremely generous in the time they gave to my many questions.

I now count among my friends the three archivists who have in turn provided both kind and competent assistance to the many scholars who have examined the voluminous archives of the archdiocese of Baltimore while I was working on them: Rev. John J. Tierney, Sister Mary Felicitas Powers, RSM, and Rev. Paul K. Thomas. Sister Felicitas's searches are particularly appreciated. I am also grateful to Mr. Thomas L. Hollowak, Baltimore City archivist, especially for sharing his knowledge of Baltimore's

Polonia, and to Rev. Peter E. Hogan, SSJ, archivist of the Josephite Fathers, for his insights into the black Catholic community. My gratitude extends likewise to Dr. Wendy Schlereth, archivist, her assistants, and the librarians of the University of Notre Dame, as well as to the librarians of the Catholic University of America and Maryland Room of the Enoch Pratt Free Library. The Cushwa Center for the Study of American Catholicism awarded a grant that covered much of the expense of the research at the University of Notre Dame. Almost without exception the archivists, librarians, and custodians of special collections whom I asked for scholarly assistance, as well as those approached for interviews, were unstinting in their response to the unconscionable demands I placed upon them. Many of those who granted interviews are indicated in the footnotes, but not all. To attempt to name all would inevitably result in regrettable omissions.

I must thank the many who read at least portions of the manuscript as it took shape and responded with corrections and suggestions. At the risk of offending others, I must mention Rev. John Bowen, SS, Rev. Michael J. Roach, Dr. Christopher J. Kauffman, Dr. Jay P. Dolan, Dr. Philip Gleason, Mr. Louis Mercorella, and Ms. Terry Schutz. Father Bowen has helped in other ways as have Robert Emmett Curran, S.J., and Rev. Robert O. McMain. I am also grateful to Father Roach and to Mr. Jacques Kelly for their help in the search for and selection of illustrations for the history.

I am particularly grateful for encouragement and assistance to the administration and faculty of Spalding University, where I teach, and the Xaverian Brothers, the religious congregation to which I belong. Here I must mention Sister Miriam Therese Olabarrieta, SCN, and Brothers Dionysius Recktenwald, James Kendrick, Declan Kane, Conrad Callahan, and James McCarthy.

Finally I must express a special gratitude to Rev. G. Michael Schleupner, former chancellor of the archdiocese of Baltimore, to Rev. William A. Au, and to others at the Catholic Center of the same city, namely, Mrs. Jeanne Trexler, Mrs. Constance Supro, and Miss Mary Elizabeth Sweeney, and to Mary Lou Kenney and Henry Y.K. Tom of the Johns Hopkins University Press.

Thomas W. Spalding, C.F.X.
Spalding University

THE PREMIER SEE

Prologue, 1634–1789

IN THE 1570S THE RIM of Christendom as defined by His Catholic Majesty rolled as far north as the Chesapeake Bay, where Spanish Jesuits established a short-lived mission.[1] The future of the Catholic Church in the United States, however, lay not with these members of the Society of Jesus, who were destined for martyrdom, but with the English Jesuits and their fellow passengers who would sail into the Chesapeake some sixty years later. They would be menaced not by the native Americans they called Indians but by other Englishmen professing different Christian creeds. The resulting tension would constitute the basic reality for Roman Catholics in English-speaking America for three hundred years and more.

The religious wars of Europe had reached their bloodiest phase when George Calvert had his vision of Catholics and Protestants living in peaceful communion in a small corner of the New World. However striking in its similarity to Thomas More's fabled Utopia, where all religions were equally tolerated, Calvert's ideal community was a speculative product not of Renaissance humanism but of a child of the Counter-Reformation's perception of the destructiveness wrought by a century of warring theologies. Elizabeth I had justified her persecution of Catholics on the grounds that a nation state could not endure the strain of two religions within its borders.[2] A generation later, Calvert had come to believe that the forcing of a conscience could be even more destructive of the common weal.

The victim himself of such an effort, George Calvert in 1624 at the height of a promising career had returned to the faith in which he had been baptized. He had cast his lot with a minority that counted hardly more than 5 percent of the English population, a minority sorely tried in spirit if not in body by the penal laws and the oaths designed to test its loyalty to the crown. Almost of necessity English Catholics had developed peculiar modes of discipline and worship: fluid congregations dependent on a patron, a clergy that shared the life of the laity, at least of the gentry, a sacramental life reduced to its simplest forms. Accommodations to time and place had come easier to second-generation "papists" in England.[3]

The Catholics who came to Maryland carried much of this cultural equipage, as Evelyn Waugh, after a visit to southern Maryland in 1948, observed. "The old Catholic families of [the archdiocese of] Baltimore have much in common with the old Catholic families of Lancashire. The countryside round Leonardtown has the same tradition of Jesuit missionaries moving in disguise from family to family, celebrating Mass in remote plantations, inculcating the same austere devotional habits, the same tenacious, unobtrusive fidelity."[4]

Calvert's plan derived from a body of Catholic opinion taking shape in England. Many, perhaps most, English Catholics now accepted the fact that they would constitute but one among many churches, that the Catholic Church would never again represent the religion of the state, that if it was to survive it would have to support the king and not the pope in political affairs. Religion was a private matter that should not affect one's civil or social status. The proper concern of the state, on the other hand, was to preserve public harmony, not to coerce religious belief. "Conversion in matters of Religion," read a Maryland colonization tract, "if it bee forced, should give little satisfaction to a State of the fidelity of such convertites, for those who for worldly respects will breake their faith with God, will doubtless doe it, upon fit occasion, much sooner with men."[5]

For George Calvert and his son Cecil, to whom fell the task of carrying out the master plan, the "pious enterprise" in Maryland was as pragmatic as it was visionary. The colony was meant to be more than a haven for persecuted Catholics. It would be a feudal domain from which the lord proprietor would derive both power and profit. The Calverts could hardly hope to people their "palatinate" with Catholics alone. A neutral state in matters religious was essential to the success of their plan. The religious freedom and separation of church and state they espoused would become a part of the Maryland tradition. At the same time, they envisioned an aristocracy of Catholic gentlemen to whom they could entrust the governance of their colony. The existence of such an elite with a sense of public service would constitute still another feature of that tradition.

The seventeen gentlemen, mostly Catholic, some two hundred laborers and servants, mostly Protestant, and three Jesuits who stepped off the *Ark* and the *Dove* on March 25, 1634, onto St. Clement's Island would represent the starting point. For sixty-five years, under the second and third barons of Baltimore, Cecil and Charles Calvert, the experiment would be tested. It would be twice undone and twice remade before the conclusive repudiation of 1689 at the time of the Glorious Revolution. But its shape and rationale would remain a part of the memory of the Catholic community as a goal whose restoration was devoutly to be wished.

   In the first ten years of testing, the Jesuits posed the most serious threat to Calvert's master plan. Though they had agreed to enter the colony and take up land on the same terms as lay adventurers, they soon demanded the recognition that canon law accorded clerics in Catholic Europe. Father Andrew White, the first superior, was content to restrict his labors to the conversion of Indians—ultimately wasted effort as the colonists in Maryland, as elsewhere, pushed the natives beyond the fringe of the settlement. Father Thomas Copley, however, arrived in 1637 determined to advance the interests of the Society of Jesus in matters temporal as well as spiritual.

   When in 1638, the colonists rejected the first code of law the lord proprietor had fashioned for them, Copley insisted that the Jesuits had in no way influenced their action. The Assembly had, in fact, taken no measures to "shew any favor to Ecclesiasticall persons, or to preserve for the church the Immunitye and priviledges, which she enjoyeth every where else," he complained. The baron should "ponder well the Bulla Coenae," a papal bull excommunicating anyone who violated church liberties or the rights of the Holy See.[6] A struggle, it would seem, between a clerical party, the supporters of the Jesuits, and a proprietary party produced a compromise body of laws in 1639 that contained a grammatical absurdity: "Holy Churches within this province shall have all her rights and liberties."[7] The word "immunity" was dropped from a previous draft.

   Of the Jesuit provincial in England Cecil Calvert demanded that his Maryland subjects accept no land from the Indians or trade with them without his permission, that they recognize the laws of the Assembly as equally binding on all, cleric as well as lay, and that they agree to testamentary and matrimonial cases being heard by lay officials rather than ecclesiastical tribunals as in Europe, the *Bulla Coenae* notwithstanding.[8] The provincial took the Jesuits' case to the Roman authorities, who proved reluctant to enter into the controversy. The most determined struggle was over land given the Society of Jesus by the Indians. This resulted in Lord Baltimore's application of the English statutes of mortmain in Maryland, whereby no religious society could as a body hold title to property. Thereafter the Jesuits were compelled to hold land individually or through lay trustees.

   The Puritan threat in Maryland brought the controversy to a close, the Jesuits and their supporters recognizing that they could ill afford the luxury of intramural bickering while their very existence was in question. While Baltimore's refusal to recognize Jesuit claims precluded the development of a special status under the law in English-speaking America that future churchmen might cite as precedent, the Jesuits' stand forestalled the growth of a tradition of unquestioning subservience to the state on the part of the church itself. The principles of separation and of free exercise were alike strengthened by the controversy.

Thereafter the Jesuits restricted themselves to the spiritual ministrations of the Catholic minority or to an active proselytizing of the non-Catholic majority that a later age would call evangelization. The determination of policy within the Catholic community they left to the leaders of those Catholic families who would constitute the Catholic elite in Maryland.

The experiment may have worked had not affairs in the mother country intruded themselves into those of the colony at critical points in its development. Imitators of the Puritan revolution in England attempted, unsuccessfully, a similar revolution in Maryland in the 1640s and another in the 1650s. The second was instigated by Puritans whom Lord Baltimore had invited into his colony to escape persecution in Virginia. One of the strategies employed by the proprietor and his supporters to deflect such a course was the Act concerning Religion of April 21, 1649, the first legislative grant of religious toleration in the New World.[9] It articulated, however, a policy that had been operative since the beginning.

The collapse of the Puritan movement ushered in the golden age of Catholic aristocracy in Maryland. As in Virginia in the period after the Restoration of 1660, the triumph of the Cavalier was complete. In Maryland most of the families that climbed into the charmed circle of social and political prominence were Catholic and were related to the Calvert family. The Carroll, Brent, Darnall, Digges, Brooke, Sewall, and Neale families would retain their wealth and social position even after the loss of political power at the time of the Glorious Revolution, the Whig triumph in Great Britain, in 1689.[10]

As important as the Catholic elite, because more prolific, were the other Catholic clans whose progenitors appeared in Maryland before 1689. Between the lordly planter and the lowly farmer stood an intermediate group of families—the Fenwicks, Matthews, Greens, Boarmans, Gardiners, and Jenkinses, to name but a few—who established family ties both up and down the social ladder and provided in the process a high degree of cohesion to the Catholic body. Catholics as a whole, even those who came in as indentured servants, fared better than their Protestant neighbors.[11] John Shercliffe, for example, was brought over in 1638 and prospered to the degree that he was able to return to England and bring back servants at his own expense. Among the latter, in 1657, was a teenage kinsman of Shercliffe's named Thomas Spalding, the ancestor of a future archbishop of Baltimore. Though few Catholics came to Maryland of their own accord after 1689, and heavy fines kept the number of Irish servants low, papists remained about 12 percent of the population throughout the colonial era. That they could maintain this ratio in the face of sizable immigration was due in great part to the success of the proselytizing efforts of the Jesuits.

This success was partly responsible for the harshness of penal laws aimed at papists in Maryland after 1689. To an even greater degree were harsh penal laws a repudiation of the ambitions of certain Catholic leaders who plotted a return to power. Foremost among the latter was Charles Carroll the Immigrant, who had come to Maryland on the eve of the Glorious Revolution. His struggle with Governor John Hart, who told his Catholic subjects they could live at peace if they would cease their agitation, resulted in disfranchisement of Catholic Marylanders in 1718.[12] Already they had been denied the right to hold office, restricted in their worship to private residences, and discriminated against in testamentary and guardianship laws. In the future they would be made to pay a double tax.[13] Not all of the harshness, however, could be blamed on the Catholics themselves. The passage and enforcement of anti-Catholic penal laws occurred most often when the mother country was at war with the Catholic powers in Europe. Antipopery would peak in the French and Indian War (1754–63), which reached to the backlands of Maryland itself.

Despite frequent threats, the full force of the penal laws in England was never unleashed in Maryland, and those on the books were honored more in the breach than in the observance. No Maryland Catholic went to the gallows or to prison for his religious beliefs. None suffered the confiscation of his estate. Quite the contrary, the largest Catholic fortunes were built in the penal years. Until his death in 1749, a leading Puritan's Catholic grandson, Richard Bennett III, was thought to be the richest of His Majesty's subjects in America, as well as one of the most generous.[14] Thereafter the first fortune in Maryland could be claimed by Charles Carroll of Annapolis, son of the Immigrant. The Catholic aristocrats were, on the whole, not only wealthier but better educated than their Church of England counterparts. Yet Catholics suffered the ignominy of second-class citizenship in Maryland, of being branded disloyal and subversive. They were denied not only the benefits but also the satisfaction of public service. For the Catholic aristocrats, that was pain enough.

With the Treaty of Paris of 1763, which erased the French presence from North America, conditions improved appreciably for Maryland papists. Bishop Richard Challoner, vicar apostolic of the London District and episcopal superior of Maryland, reported to Rome: "In Maryland, the laws are opposed to [the Catholic Church] as in England; however, these laws are rarely put into execution and usually there is a sort of tacit toleration." There were, he claimed, some sixteen thousand Catholics in Maryland, about half of whom approached the sacraments. They were served by twelve Jesuits. "These religious manifest great zeal and lead edifying lives."[15]

By 1763 the Jesuits had five large estates in Maryland totaling over twelve thousand acres: St. Inigoes and Newtown in St. Mary's County, St. Thomas Manor in Charles County, White Marsh in Prince George's County, and Bohemia in Cecil County. There was also Priest Neale's Mass House at Deer Creek in Harford County. Immediately after the war, there was a burst of construction. Churches and residences were built for new Jesuit centers at Tuckahoe on the Eastern Shore and at Frederick Town in Frederick County. Smaller churches were erected for the congregations at Pomfret, Leonardtown, Medley's Neck, and Bushwood in southern Maryland. Larger buildings were raised at St. Inigoes and St. Thomas Manor and a church at Newtown (still standing). On June 4, 1764, George Hunter, the Jesuit superior, purchased from Charles Carroll of Annapolis Lot 157 on Saratoga and Little Sharp Streets in Baltimore for the purpose of building a church.

In 1763 two-thirds of the Catholics of Maryland could still be found in the southern counties: St. Mary's, Charles, and Prince George's. As early as the 1710s, however, Catholics from these counties started to move into Harford County and in the 1740s began to make the even more daring leap to the foothills of the Catoctin Mountains in Frederick County. John Digges, who had acquired ten thousand acres in what proved to be Pennsylvania near Conewago, laid in the 1730s a wagon road from his land to the town of Baltimore, incorporated in 1729, and built a warehouse there. In 1756 the Jesuits began to say mass regularly for exiled Acadians in a house on the northwest corner of what are now Calvert and Fayette Streets in Baltimore. In 1770 they began a church on the land acquired from Squire Carroll.[16] The future of the Catholic Church in Maryland lay in this budding port and in the counties to the north and west.

Soon after the Peace of Paris in 1763, Bishop Challoner and the Congregation of the Propaganda Fide in Rome laid plans to send one or more bishops to the American colonies. The leading Catholic laymen of Maryland drew up a remonstrance to prevent so "fatal and pernicious" a step. Squire Carroll, in a separate letter, told Challoner that a vicar apostolic would undermine the peace and harmony that had existed between Jesuits and laity in Maryland for over 130 years.[17] The prospect of an unwanted bishop soon paled by comparison with an even greater threat to the Jesuits. As early as 1759 Catholic monarchs began the process that eventually led to the brief of Pope Clement XIV, *Dominus ac Redemptor*, dated August 16, 1773, whereby the Society of Jesus was dissolved throughout the world. From Bruges, Father John Carroll wrote his brother Daniel in Maryland: "I am not, and perhaps never shall be, recovered from the shock of this dreadful intelligence. The greatest blessing which in my estimation I could receive from God, would be immediate death."[18] All nineteen Jesuits in Maryland and Pennsylvania signed the form sent by Bishop Challoner that made them secular priests. Challoner named the former Jesuit superior, John Lewis, his vicar general for English-speaking America. The "tea party" in Boston that December conspired to delay the question of a bishop, raised once again, for another decade.

In Maryland, as in the other colonies, a revolutionary ferment had been at work since the passage of the Stamp Act in 1765. In 1773 Charles Carroll of Carrollton, the son of Charles Carroll of Annapolis, propelled his fellow Catholics in Maryland irrevocably into the patriots' camp. After sixteen years of study abroad, the twenty-seven-year-old Carroll had returned to Maryland in 1764 with a conviction that "America is a growing country; in time it will and must be independent."[19] In Maryland he examined the political terrain carefully and concluded that the Catholic community should do a volte-face.

Maryland Catholics had never accepted the principles of a Glorious Revolution that had brought them only shame and powerlessness. Having lost faith in the cause of the Catholic Stuarts, however, they had anchored their hopes in the court party in Maryland, the adherents of the Protestant Lord Baltimore, and had placed their security in the hands of the upper house. Carroll was repulsed by these proprietary placemen, whose days, he felt, were numbered. He cultivated, therefore, the friendship of the new leaders of the country, or popular, party in the lower house, whom most Catholics looked upon as their enemies. Under the pen name of "First Citizen," Carroll challenged the defense of proprietary power by the leading spokesman of the court party, Daniel Dulany. In the process he not only established himself as a "flaming Patriot" but was able to lay to rest for half a century the anti-Catholic prejudice that Dulany had sought to exploit. Carroll's decision to place the fate of Maryland Catholics in the hands of the popular movement was "one of the most significant developments on the road to minority rights, not only in Maryland, but in America generally."[20]

Charles Carroll of Carrollton was elected to the Revolutionary Convention that met in Annapolis soon after. The convention voted enthusiastically that all differences concerning religion "cease and be forever buried in oblivion."[21] On the county committees of observation Catholics found a place in surprising numbers. In the Continental Army and in the state militia from which they had been excluded in the French and Indian War they were also well represented.[22] On July 4, 1776, Charles Carroll was elected a member of the Maryland delegation to the Continental Congress, the first Catholic to hold national office. He proceeded to Philadelphia to be the only Catholic to sign (on August 2) the Declaration of Independence.

On February 27, 1776, Charles Lee of Virginia had written to John Hancock of Massachusetts: "I should think that if some Jesuit or Religeuse of any Order (but he must be a man of liberal sentiments, enlarged mind and a manifest friend of Civil Liberty) could be found out and sent to Canada, he would be worth battalions to us. . . . Mr. Carroll has a relative who exactly answers this description."[23] The relative was Father John Carroll. His acceptance of the assignment to accompany a delegation to Canada represented his first exercise of public service.

Born January 8 (or 19), 1736, at Upper Marlboro, the fourth child of Daniel and Eleanor Darnall Carroll, John had gone with his cousin Charles from the Jesuits' school at Bohemia to their school at St. Omer in Flanders in 1748. On September 7, 1753, he had entered the Jesuits and on February 14, 1761, had been ordained in the episcopal chapel at Liège.[24] Like a moth drawn to a flame, he had arrived in Rome, as tutor to a young English aristocrat, as the "fatal stroke" was about to be dealt his hapless Society. "What a revolution of ideas," he wrote a Jesuit friend, "do all these proceedings produce in a mind accustomed to regard this city as the seat of Religion."[25] Soon after, he returned to his native Maryland to become a part of another revolution.

He was not overjoyed to be a part of the mission to win the French Canadians to the Revolutionary cause, believing that ministers of religion should not embroil themselves in political affairs and sensing that the mission was doomed to failure in any event. The friendship that developed on the journey between himself and Benjamin Franklin, however, would play an important part in his advancement. He was delighted also to see a number of Catholics elected to the Maryland Assembly under the new state constitution, including his brother Daniel, who was also sent to the Congress of the Confederation.[26]

The war had broken ecclesiastical as well as political ties with the Old World. As it drew to a close, Carroll became increasingly concerned about the future of the orphaned band of former Jesuits in America. Early in 1782 he wrote to Charles Plowden, a close friend and former Jesuit in England:

"The clergymen here continue to live in the old form: it is the effect of habit." Carroll bemoaned the "ignorance, indolence, delusion (you remember certain prophecies of reestablishment) and above all the irresolution of Mr. Lewis" that prevented any form of administration from being adopted "which might tend to secure to posterity a succession of Catholick Clergymen, and secure to these a comfortable subsistence."[27] Carroll himself took the initiative in drawing up a plan of organization. He and five other ex-Jesuits met at their plantation at White Marsh in June 1783 to enlarge upon the plan and draft a constitution that would create a chapter of elected representatives from three districts. Spiritual matters remained in the hands of the superior, Father John Lewis, but temporalities were entrusted to a procurator general, Father John Ashton. Otherwise, there would be complete equality in terms of status, benefits, and responsibilities.[28]

An unspoken reason for the organization was to keep the former Jesuit estates intact until the anticipated restoration of the Society. For the ex-Jesuits in America, the Sacred Congregation of the Propaganda Fide in Rome charged with the superintendence of all missionary lands posed the greatest threat to their properties. Alluding to information Plowden had volunteered regarding the Propaganda's designs, Carroll stated emphatically: "For they may be assured, that they will never get possession of sixpence of our property here, & if any of our friends could be weak enough to deliver any real estate into their hands, or attempt to subject it to their authority, our civil government would be called upon to wrest it again out of their dominion. A foreign temporal jurisdiction will never be tolerated here."[29]

At a second meeting of the chapter in November—not long after another Treaty of Paris granted international recognition to the United States as a sovereign nation—an address to the pope was drafted requesting that the superior, Father Lewis, be granted the power to impart faculties to new priests, to administer confirmation, and to bless oils, chalices, and altar stones.[30] The rationale for the request was set forth by Carroll in what was apparently a covering letter to a curial official in Rome. "You are not ignorant," he wrote, "that in these United States our Religious system has undergone a revolution, if possible, more extraordinary, than our political one." In all of the states toleration had been granted to Christians of every denomination. In Pennsylvania, Delaware, Maryland, and Virginia, "a communication of all Civil rights, without distinction or diminution, is extended to those of our Religion. This is a blessing and advantage, which is our duty to preserve & improve with the utmost prudence, by demeaning ourselves on all occasions as subjects zealously attached to our government & avoiding to give any jealousies on account of our dependence on foreign jurisdictions, more than that, which is essential to our Religion, an acknowledgement of the Pope's spiritual Supremacy over the whole Christian world."[31]

When he learned that the Propaganda had made overtures to the Congress of the Confederation on the propriety of establishing a vicar apostolic in America, Carroll penned his strongest animadversion on the Sacred Congregation. "But this you may be assured of," he told Plowden, "that no authority derived from the Propag[an]da will ever be admitted here; that the Catholick Clergy & Laity here know that the only connexion that they ought to have with Rome is to acknowledge the pope as the Spir[itua]l head of the Church; that no congregation existing in his states shall be allowed to exercise any share of his Spir[itua]l authority here; and that no Bishop Vicar Apostolical shall be admitted; and if we are to have a Bishop, he shall not be in partibus (a refined political Roman contrivance), but an ordinary national Bishop, in whose appointment Rome shall have no share: so that we are very easy about their machinations."[32]

Carroll was perturbed that the Propaganda had proceeded in its negotiations without consulting the American clergy. In the time-honored channels of papal diplomacy, it had worked through the court of France to sound out the American ministers there on the feasibility of a vicar apostolic for the United States.[33] Congress instructed Franklin to notify the papal nuncio in Paris that the Roman proposal, "being purely spiritual, is without the jurisdiction and the powers of Congress, who have no authority to permit or refuse it."[34] Roman diplomacy had no ready answer for this strange new doctrine. The authorities would have to deal directly with the American clergy.

Still eager to satisfy the American government, however, the Propaganda bestowed the powers sought by the American clergy not on John Lewis but on John Carroll, whose appointment would, the cardinal prefect of the Propaganda explained, "please and gratify many members of the Republic, and especially Mr. Franklin." In his letter of June 9, 1784, Cardinal Leonardo Antonelli named Carroll "Superior of the Mission in the thirteen United States."[35]

In thanking the cardinal, Carroll insisted that the United States was not yet ready for a bishop. He appended, however, a report requested by the Propaganda. There were in Maryland, he claimed, 15,800 Catholics and in Pennsylvania 7,000. There were others scattered throughout the nation, perhaps as many as 1,500 in New York, but they were destitute of all religious services. There was also an unknown number of French-speaking Catholics in the West. There were nineteen priests in Maryland and five in Pennsylvania.[36]

Carroll's attitude toward Rome was dictated partly by his desire to see the church in the United States accepted by non-Catholic Americans. When a kinsman and former Jesuit, Charles Henry Wharton, became an Episcopal minister and penned an explanation of his conversion that was critical of the Catholic Church, Carroll felt obliged to rebut, in the longest work he would ever write, those contentions that made his church appear repressive and alien to liberty-loving Americans. Not even the hope of vindicating the faith, Carroll concluded, could have induced him to engage in controversy "if I could fear that it would disturb the harmony now subsisting amongst all christians in this country, so blessed with civil and religious liberty; which if we have the wisdom and temper to preserve, America may come to exhibit a proof to the world, that general and equal toleration, by giving a free circulation to fair argument, is the most effectual method to bring all denominations to an unity of faith."[37] It was one of Carroll's strongest statements of belief in the missionary role of his native land.

In researching the rebuttal, Carroll was taken by the work of an English priest named Joseph Berington and the "reasonable system of universal Forbearance, and Charity amongst Christians of every Denomination" it advanced. There were two subjects Carroll urged Berington to pursue: the extent of the spiritual jurisdiction of the Holy See and the use of Latin in the liturgy. "I consider these two points as the great Obstacles, with Christians of other Denominations, to a thorough union with us . . . particularly in N. America." The use of the vernacular, Carroll believed, "ought not only to be solicited, but *insisted* on."[38]

When certain English priests with advanced views espoused not only the vernacular in the liturgy but also the abandonment of clerical celibacy, Carroll wrote Plowden: "Is it really true, that any are so bold, as to avow the latter sentiment; or even assert, that any single Bishop may alter the language of the liturgy, without the approbation of the Holy See, & a general concurrence of at least other national Bishops? I should be indeed sorry, if the few words of my letter to Berington should be tortured into such a meaning."[39] Archbishop John Thomas Troy of Dublin wrote Carroll that the question of the vernacular was also being agitated in Ireland, and he had written a pastoral letter against it.[40] Thereafter Carroll gave no public encouragement to the use of English in the liturgy.

At the same time, Carroll remained unflagging in his advocacy of religious liberty and the separation of church and state. When in November 1784 a law was introduced in the Maryland Assembly to lay a general tax for the support of ministers of all religions, Carroll put himself in opposition. To Plowden he explained that "we, as well as the Presbyterians, Methodists, Quakers· and Anabaptists are induced to believe, that it is calculated to create a predominant and irresistible influence in favour of the Protestant Episcopal Church . . . and therefore we shall all oppose it with might and main. We have all smarted heretofore under the lash of an established church and shall therefore be on our guard against every approach to it."[41] There can be little doubt that Catholic opinion weighed heavily in the defeat of the tax bill.

The following year, however, Carroll informed Cardinal Antonelli that there was a move afoot to tax properties of the Catholic clergy in Maryland. "As soon as the laws of England were abrogated," he explained, "freedom of religion was established, and we sought in every way to form a corporate body and to hold property in common. . . . So far we have made no progress because of the prejudice against the acquisition of property by ecclesiastics, or as they say, by mortmain."[42] In December 1788 the Maryland Senate finally passed a general act of incorporation that specifically exempted the former Jesuit estates from the two-acre limitation set on church holdings by the Maryland Declaration of Rights. The House of Delegates rejected the bill on the grounds that there was not enough time to consider it.[43] It was probably the question of the Jesuit lands that delayed a general incorporation act in Maryland for another fourteen years.

Catholics in New York, however, had taken advantage of a general incorporation act of 1784 to become a corporate body and build a church. When one of the factions in a dispute that developed claimed the right to choose and dismiss the pastor, Carroll declared that if such a principle were accepted, "the unity and Catholicity of our Church would be at an end."[44] When the pastor originally appointed, however, left the congregation in disgust, Carroll decided to recognize his rival. "I know and respect the legal right of the Cong[regatio]n," he told him. "It is as repugnant to my duty and wish, as it exceeds my power to compel them to accept & support a Clergyman, who is disagreeable to them."[45] In Philadelphia the Germans, against Carroll's wishes, broke away from St. Mary's Church to build a church of their own. Carroll allowed them to have the pastor they wanted but without conceding their right to choose him.[46]

Back in New York, the trustees turned against the second pastor. His supporters, however, denied Carroll admittance to the church when he went to New York to attempt a reconciliation. Carroll ended by advising the trustees to take the troublemakers to court.[47] He returned to Maryland convinced that the time had come to ask for a bishop. In a petition to Pope Pius VI, dated March 12, 1788, John Carroll, Robert Molyneux, and John Ashton asked that a diocese coextensive with the American mission be established immediately under the pope and that the choice of its bishop, "at least in this first instance," be left to the clergy.[48]

Greater authority was needed to deal with the growing number of troublesome priests who drifted in from different parts. A desperate need for pastors, however, determined Carroll to accept the services of some. In 1788 he gave faculties to three in order to provide for small Catholic congregations in Norfolk, Charleston, and Boston. The one assigned to Norfolk soon wandered off, and the one at Boston behaved so outrageously that Carroll was obliged to suspend him. He was also obliged to suspend the German pastor in Philadelphia. The only recent arrival who succeeded in shattering Carroll's remarkable equanimity, however, was a Rev. Patrick Smyth from Ireland, who published a work depicting the ex-Jesuits in America as greedy, indolent, pleasure-seeking, cruel, and incompetent.

"O poor Jesuits!" Carroll wrote to his friend Plowden, "when shall we have you again." Whenever the "medley of clerical characters" feel aggrieved, he explained, "they proceed to bring in Jesuitism, & to suggest, that everything is calculated by me for its restoration." At the same time, some of the former Jesuits thought him "too irresolute and indifferent" on the matter of revival.[49] Carroll had, in fact, discouraged a precipitate movement toward a union with a small group of Jesuits who had survived under the protection of Catherine the Great in Russia. Would not, he asked his confreres, "the very measure, we are now pursuing for the establishment . . . of a Diocesan Bishop, be deemed an artifice to promote the restoration of the Society?"[50] Eventually the attacks of clerical malcontents would make their way to Rome, and Carroll would be informed of Cardinal Antonelli's "being haunted with fears of the revival of the Society in America." To Plowden he would confide: "I think it providential, that his alarms have been raised since the issuing of the bull for erecting the See of Baltimore. I suspect that otherwise it would have been refused."[51]

In February 1789 Carroll had received a letter from Antonelli telling him that the Holy Father had responded favorably to the earlier petition for a bishop. Carroll was instructed to consult the clergy to determine where the see should be located and whether it should have an ordinary or titular bishop. The clergy could then proceed to an election.[52] Baltimore, where Carroll had taken up residence in 1786, was the unanimous choice for a site, "this being the principal town of Maryland," Carroll explained to

Plowden, "& that State being the oldest & still the most numerous residence of true Religion in America."[53] Quite naturally, the preference was
for a bishop with ordinary jurisdiction rather than a vicar apostolic. The
votes were collected in each of the three districts stretching from Pennsylvania to southern Maryland and carried to White Marsh, where on May 11
the third General Chapter of the clergy convened. "We then proceeded to
the Election," Carroll told Plowden, "the event of which was such as de-
prives me of all expectation of rest or pleasure henceforward, and fills me
with terror, with respect to eternity."[54] To Carroll went twenty-four of the
twenty-six votes.

I

The Carroll Church

Bishop John Carroll 1789–1808

Archbishop John Carroll 1808–1815

Archbishop Leonard Neale 1815–1817

Archbishop Ambrose Maréchal 1817–1828

Archbishop James Whitfield 1828–1834

The history of the archdiocese of Baltimore would be shaped by two traditions that were often in tension: the Maryland tradition, largely the legacy of John Carroll, and the immigrant tradition, one that would develop later in response to the coming of millions of poor Catholics from different nations. The Maryland tradition would find its fullest expression in the episcopacy of Carroll and his immediate successors in Baltimore. The immigrant tradition, though originating under Archbishop Samuel Eccleston, would find its fullest expression in the episcopacy of Archbishop Michael J. Curley in the twentieth century. In between a valiant effort would be made to revivify the Maryland tradition by Baltimore's first cardinal, James Gibbons. A more successful restoration would come with Vatican Council II and Baltimore's second cardinal, Lawrence J. Shehan.

This schema is, of course, simplistic. A tradition fashioned by Carroll in a largely southern milieu could hardly be the same as that operative in an urban and industrial setting, no more than could the immigrant church of the antebellum years be fully identified with that of the jazz age. Nor were the two traditions antithetical in every respect. In some of their manifestations—an ardent patriotism and an acceptance of American political principles, for example—they were remarkably alike. Yet in the openness of the one and the exclusivity of the other—the social and cultural engagement of the Maryland tradition, on the one hand, and the ghetto building of the immigrant tradition, on the other—they differed as night from day.

The Carroll church that embodied the Maryland tradition had its roots in the vision of the Catholic Calverts. It presupposed a neutral state based upon the principles of religious freedom and separation of church and state. The embracement of these two principles was the first of the building blocks with which Carroll would construct the classic edifice that would serve as a model for many of his successors. Reinforcing the first were several others: an ardent patriotism born of Revolutionary ferment, an appreciation of the democratic processes and structures these principles called forth, and a conviction that the new republic was destined to play a missionary, even messianic, role in promoting such principles, procedures, and structures.

There were other building blocks. As important to Carroll as to the Calverts was the broad ecumenism that persuaded Catholics and Protestants (Jews would be encompassed later) to live in peace and to their mutual benefit. An expression of this ecumenism was a civic sense that found an outlet in public service, a community spirit that brought the religious and public spheres into a productive relationship. With its roots in the Calverts' concept of a Catholic elite, however, it was a community spirit born of an aristocratic sense of noblesse oblige and of a belief in the leadership of those born to lead. In no diocese would the Catholic families of wealth and power persist with such self-assurance. In a changing church they would become the most dependable guardians of that ecumenical outlook and sense of public service that Carroll had inherited from the Calverts.

Another building block Carroll would attempt to set in place was a measure of autonomy in the relationship of the local church to the Holy See. This stemmed in part from his unhappy memories as a Jesuit but was dictated also by the need to adjust to American realities. It would be supported by the Gallicanism of the priests who would conduct his seminary, the Sulpicians. At the same time—and despite the contempt in which he held the pope he called by no other name than Ganganelli—Carroll had a great reverence for the person of the Roman pontiff and the throne he occupied as a symbol of unity.

The church that Carroll raised would share also the five basic continuities the historian Martin Marty has perceived in the American religious tradition as a whole: pluralism, experimentalism, scripturalism, enlightenment, and "voluntaryism."[1] Catholics of the Maryland tradition would accept the pluralities of religious witness as a part of the American landscape. These early Catholics would, as much as the enterprising Protestants, attempt the untried in their search for workable procedures and structures. Though not as quick, perhaps, to quote chapter and verse as their Protestant neighbors, they could claim a greater familiarity with the Bible than could a later and less literate generation of Catholics. Their acceptance of the principles of the Enlightenment as articulated in the new nation would be as solid as was the aversion of the Catholics in Europe toward the implications of the Enlightenment there. American Catholics accepted the premise that religious affiliation was a voluntary affair that carried with it financial obligations. In all these ways Carroll's fellow Catholics resembled their Protestant compatriots more than their coreligionists across the Atlantic.

Of the five continuities, experimentalism would, perhaps, claim with greatest insistence a place in the Maryland tradition. While there would always be a tendency to replicate European prototypes and patterns, Carroll's generation would be just as ready to look closer to home for its models. Maryland Catholics had little appreciation of the majestic changelessness that European Catholics attributed to their church. The resilience, flexibility, and versatility that were marks of the Carroll church would persist.

Carroll would not, of course, consciously begin his episcopacy by chiseling building blocks and setting them in place. The major task of the first bishop was to respond to the immediate needs of a widely scattered flock. The most pressing of these were priests and churches. The clerical force that Carroll would build would prove a disappointment throughout his twenty-five episcopal years, both in quantity and quality, and in some ways work the greatest harm upon the Maryland tradition. But churches would multiply rapidly, and they would be owned by laymen. Carroll encouraged lay ownership as being in accord with American law and democratic practices. The development of the trustee arrangement would be the closest his church would come to a "movement to accommodate Catholic ecclesiastical structures and practices to the democratic élan of the age."[2] It would also be the first of the building blocks to be rejected and the last to be rediscovered.

One of the major achievements of the Carroll years would be the restoration of the Society of Jesus in the United States. It was a goal and in time a fact that would color almost every decision taken and assignment made. It would be for Carroll a source of joy and discomfort by turn, of discomfort largely because of the esteem he would come to entertain for the Society of St. Sulpice, whose plans would not always coincide with those of the Society of Jesus but would be more in tune with the Maryland tradition. In the end Carroll would favor the Sulpicians and set the course of his diocese in a direction quite different than what it would have taken under Jesuit aegis.

Given the magnitude of the task entrusted to him, that of organizing an infant church as large as the nation itself and then reproducing it in smaller units, it is amazing that his missteps were not more frequent and more painful. He would begin the process of ecclesial mitosis with a courage and a calm that would be a source of inspiration for the host of hierarchs who would follow. In particulars he would have to sacrifice the "republican blueprint" he is said to have drawn.[3] Yet he would never betray the larger vision of a church attuned to the American ethos, a vision that derived largely from the Revolutionary experience itself. He would pass from the scene with the Maryland tradition he had carefully crafted largely intact.

The Maryland-born successor and former Jesuit Leonard Neale would weaken the edifice substantially by an attack upon the trustee system. His rule, however, would be brief, and the next three archbishops would be Sulpician or Sulpician trained. A part of the tradition of St. Sulpice was a moderate Gallicanism that placed the needs of the local church above those of the papacy. Another part dictated an assumption of the coloration of the culture in which the Sulpicians found themselves.[4] As the Sulpicians became more American and more a part of the Maryland tradition, the Jesuits would become less American in membership and spirit and increasingly ultramontane. The French-born Sulpician Archbishop Ambrose Maréchal would effectually deflate the power of the Jesuits in the oldest archdiocese.

Under Maréchal and his English-born protege, Archbishop James Whitfield, Maryland Catholics would continue to enjoy the respectability Carroll had won for them. Mostly Anglo-American in leadership and basic constituency, the local church would remain miniscule in numbers, possessed of a minimum of institutions, its members hardly distinguishable from their non-Catholic neighbors. The French and earlier Irish would be easily assimilated. French abbés would give tone to the church. Irish merchants would lend solidity. Its problems would continue to be internal: defiant trustees and a demanding suffragan, John England, heading the list of vexations. All would change, however, when the last of the Sulpician archbishops, Samuel Eccleston, ushered in a new era.

1 Founding Father

THE BRIEF *Ex hac apostolicae* naming John Carroll the first bishop of the first diocese of the United States was dated November 6, 1789. It was an original document; there was no model to follow in the official correspondence of the Holy See.[1] Carroll received unofficial word in February. The brief arrived in April. Despite invitations and intimations that he be ordained bishop in such places as Quebec, Dublin, Paris, or some city in the Low Countries, Carroll decided the ceremony should take place in the private chapel of Thomas Weld at Lulworth Castle in Dorset, England, where his friend Charles Plowden was chaplain.

The bishop-elect disembarked in London on July 22, 1790. His arrival coincided with the deepening of a division between English Catholics who favored an oath of loyalty to the government and those who opposed.[2] Though pressed by both sides, Carroll sidestepped commitment with consummate tact. It could not have gone unremarked, however, that he had chosen to be consecrated by Charles Walmesley, the vicar apostolic most opposed to the oath, and that the sermon would be preached by Carroll's friend Plowden, another outspoken opponent. Nevertheless, Carroll commended Lord Robert Petre, a leader of the accommodationists, for his efforts to deliver Catholics from the "cruel bondage" that had so long enslaved them. No government, he told the nobleman, could support such oppression once it came to know "the justice and political advantages of not only a free toleration, but of extending equal rights to the professor[s] of all religions. The daily advantages arising to America from this policy should be a lesson to Britain."[3]

No hint of the controversy intruded upon the ceremony at Lulworth Castle that raised John Carroll to episcopal rank on August 15, 1790. "Glorious is the day, my brethren," Plowden declaimed, "for the church of God which sees new nations crowding into her bosom." The orator saw in the recent revolution, which had "dismembered the great British Empire" and given birth to "a new empire in the West," the designs of Providence for restoring the purity of the faith planted by Augustine of Canterbury among English-speaking people. Carroll, "the first Father and Bishop of the new church," was "another Austin."[4] With Plowden and the Rev. James Porter as his assistants, Bishop Walmesley laid his hands on the head of the American and then applied the sacred oils liberally.

Before his return to America, Bishop Carroll had an auspicious meeting with a visitor from France, the Abbé Charles-François Nagot. The Society of St. Sulpice, Nagot explained to Carroll, was ready to establish a seminary in Baltimore at its own expense.[5] Though Carroll believed the time was not ripe, it was an offer he could hardly refuse. His joy, however, was tempered by the "melancholy reflection," as he told Plowden, "that we owe so great a blessing to the lamentable catastrophe in France."[6] The Sulpician superior, Jacques-André Emery, had divined the destructive character of the Revolution launched in 1789. The Civil Constitution of the Clergy of 1790 led inevitably to an exodus of priests unwilling to be servants of the state and to the execution of many who remained, including several Sulpicians. The nascent church in America would be well served by the emigré priests.

The Beginnings

After a disagreeable voyage that may have determined him never to see Europe again, Bishop Carroll disembarked at Baltimore December 7, 1790. Five days later, on a Sunday, the nation's first Catholic bishop was installed in St. Peter's church, now his cathedral. From an unimposing throne he received "the obeisance of the Clergy, & some of the laity in behalf of the rest."[7] In his sermon he described the "more burdensome" responsibilities that befell him in a land "where every thing is to be raised, as it were, from the foundation": the establishment of a uniform discipline, the creation of schools, the training of priests, the preservation of the faith among a widely scattered flock, and the cultivation in the hearts of the faithful of "a warm charity and forbearance towards every other denomination" but without "that fatal and prevailing indifference" found in America. "Ah! when I consider these additional duties, my heart sinks almost under the impression of terror which comes upon it."[8] The terror he described was hardly a figure of speech. Few bishops had faced demands of such magnitude.

In May, when the roads were passable, he made the long journey to Boston to lay the law down to two priests and their clamorous factions. He remained for three weeks, confirming, preaching, and socializing. "It is wonderful to tell, what great civilities have been done to me in this town," he wrote Plowden, "where a few years ago a popish priest was thought to be the greatest monster in creation."[9] To one of his hosts, Governor John

Hancock, he explained that the favors lavished upon him had "both astonished and confounded me."[10] Carroll discovered that he enjoyed the deference paid this curiosity in America—a Catholic bishop. He rarely disappointed the curious, playing his role with becoming dignity and just that touch of the exotic expected in a Roman prelate. Though he failed to heal the breach in Boston immediately, in 1792 he would persuade one of the most able of the emigré priests, Francis Matignon, to take charge of the church there. In 1796 Matignon would be joined by an equally able emigré, John Cheverus, and together they would make the small Catholic congregations of New England models of tranquility and progress.[11]

In Baltimore awaiting Carroll's return were four Sulpician priests and five seminarians, who had arrived in July. The priests were Charles Nagot, John Mary Tessier, Anthony Garnier, and Michael Levadoux. Of the seminarians, two were English, one French, one Canadian, and one American. Two Marylanders soon joined them. A three-story brick building called One Mile Tavern on Hookstown Road (now Pennsylvania Avenue) was purchased, and here on October 16 St. Mary's Seminary officially began with Nagot as rector and superior of the Sulpician community.[12]

A month and six days later the first student, William Gaston, a boy of thirteen, was enrolled at Georgetown College, a project Carroll himself had urged upon the chapter of the clergy as early as 1786. Its promoters were eager to put to use a building begun in 1788 despite the fact that the college had as yet no president—a "terrible inconvenience," Carroll told Plowden.[13] Robert Plunkett, an ex-Jesuit, would soon arrive from England to take charge of this first Catholic college in the United States.

The First Synod

Between these two beginnings the first diocesan synod in the United States was held November 7–10, 1791, at the cathedral. Twenty-four priests in all were able to attend. The twenty-four decrees enacted concerned themselves mostly with the uniform administration of the sacraments. Hymns or prayers in English, for example, were allowed during mass and the performance of the sacraments. Priests were obliged to dress in black ordinarily and to wear the cassock at mass. A deviation from a norm was usually justified by citing an earlier synod, that of Lima, Peru, for example, for exempting slaves from the necessity of religious instruction before marriage.[14]

Carroll sought to reassure the cardinal prefect in his first full report to the Propaganda as bishop. "There are no innovations in these decrees—

everything was copied from former synods. Nor did we attempt to legislate on all subjects, but only on those that are most pressing. When I see that these statutes are duly carried into execution the others will follow."[15] No other synod was held in Carroll's lifetime. He sent no copy of the 1791 decrees to the Propaganda, in fact, until reminded to do so in 1793. Nor did he ever publish them. They remained in Latin except for those translated for the benefit of the laity in the pastoral letter Carroll issued some six months after the synod. These concerned financial support.

Carroll realized that among the fundamental ways the Catholic Church in America would differ from that in Europe would be a dependence upon the voluntary offerings of the faithful for the support of its priests and places of worship, even in Maryland. "This duty [to contribute]," he admitted in the pastoral, "has been insisted on so little amongst us, as long as the assistance of the faithful was unnecessary for the maintenance of their pastors, that many will hardly conceive it to be a duty." No longer, Carroll said plainly, could Catholics take the consolations of religion for granted. He called his readers' attention to the decrees stipulating that at each mass an offertory collection would be taken up by two or three curators (trustees) chosen by the pastor or by the congregation itself and that the receipts would be divided three ways—one-third for the support of the pastor, one-third for the relief of the poor, and one-third for the upkeep of the church.[16]

A reason for Carroll's reluctance to hold another synod may have been the complex and delicate problems that required in the new nation a modification of universal norms. More was doubtless said and understood at this first synod than found its way into Latin, and the decrees themselves may have been qualified by episcopal commentary or clerical debate. Such was possibly the case in the enactment of the decree concerning the use of the vernacular. In 1794 a former Jesuit, Charles Sewall, would write to Carroll that he had heard "that in consequence to Mr. Garnier's convincing arguments, you no longer administer any of the sacraments in English. I cannot believe it."[17]

Such may also have been the case as regards the decree requiring a promise in a mixed marriage that all children be raised in the Catholic faith. In 1802 Carroll himself would concede the possibility of a child's choosing his or her own religion at a competent age after having been instructed by the Catholic spouse and presumably also by the non-Catholic one.[18] It would appear, moreover, that no censure fell on couples who continued the practice of raising the sons in the faith of the father and the daughters in the faith of the mother.[19]

The synod afforded Carroll the opportunity to express himself on many aspects of the inchoate church to which the clergy as a whole looked to him for guidance. One such area is suggested in a letter to Plowden shortly before he issued the pastoral. "I am I own, principally sollicitous [*sic*] to form establishments, which will be lasting. To pass thro' a village," he contended, "where a Roman Catholic Clergyman was never seen before; to borrow of the parson the use of his meeting house, or church in order to preach a sermon; to go or send about the village, giving notice at every house, that a priest is to preach at a certain hour, and there to enlarge on the doctrines of our Church; this is the mode adopted by some amongst us for the propagation of religion. But I would rather see a priest fixed for a continuance in the same place, with a growing congregation under him; than twenty such itinerant preachers."[20] Despite the scattered condition of his flock, Carroll did not envision a circuit-riding clergy in the manner of the Methodists, who were spreading rapidly throughout Maryland.

Corporation of the Roman Catholic Clergy

For Carroll the American model was the settled parish of the Protestant Episcopal Church with its elected vestry, which accorded better to the needs of the gentry than of the backland farmers. It also accorded well with his desire to secure church property. There would seem to be little doubt that Carroll encouraged parochial congregations in Maryland, and elsewhere, to form vestries, or bodies of trustees, and to seek incorporation as legal bodies under the laws of the state. The former Jesuits of Maryland, under Carroll's direction, set the example.

On December 23, 1792, they finally won from the Maryland legislature an act that created a corporation for the Roman Catholic clergy of the state. The corporation was to be a board elected by representatives of the clergy. In the corporation was vested title to all former Jesuit estates as well as to Georgetown College. Carroll and twelve other ex-Jesuits met on October 4, 1793, to draw up the bylaws. These provided for triennial elections to fill a five-member board to be officially known as the Corporation of the Roman Catholic Clergy of Maryland. The following February the elected trustees met to determine the membership of the Select Body of the Clergy, those "entitled to a share of the profits arising from the estates secured by law." The Select Body was initially limited to twenty-six. All were former Jesuits or alumni of the Academy of Liège, the old Jesuit scholasticate under a new name, with but one exception: Louis de Barth, a German of noble birth.[21]

The bishop was not even mentioned in the act of incorporation. Un-

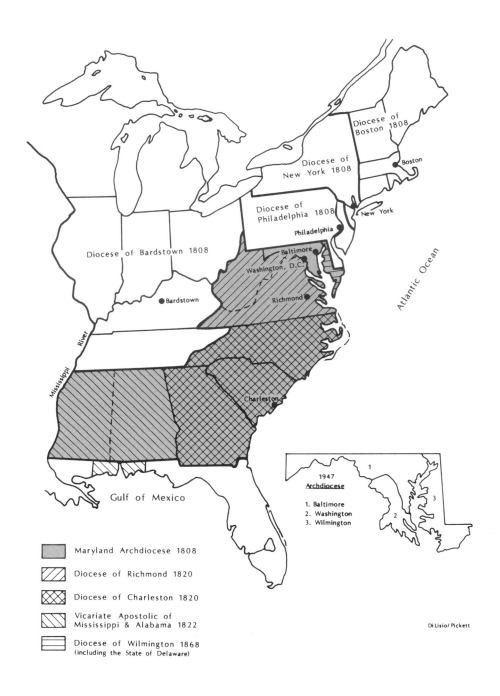

Diocese of Boston 1808

Diocese of New York 1808

Boston

Diocese of Philadelphia 1808

New York

Philadelphia

Diocese of Bardstown 1808

Baltimore

Washington, D.C.

Bardstown

Richmond

Atlantic Ocean

Mississippi River

Charleston

Gulf of Mexico

1947
Archdiocese

1. Baltimore
2. Washington
3. Wilmington

Maryland Archdiocese 1808

Diocese of Richmond 1820

Diocese of Charleston 1820

Vicariate Apostolic of
Mississippi & Alabama 1822

Diocese of Wilmington 1868
(including the State of Delaware)

Di Lisio/ Pickett

Map 1. Reductions of the Diocese of Baltimore, 1808–1947

der the bylaws the decision to expel a member for immoral conduct was left to the board, but the member could appeal to a joint meeting of the bishop and representatives of the Select Body. A priest not a member of the Select Body might share in the benefits of the estates at the recommendation of the bishop. The "Bishop of Baltimore, and his successors for the time being, shall be entitled to the salary as now established, of £ Curr[cn]cy 210 per annum, provided that the future bishop not be appointed without the free election of the clergy of this diocese, or of a part of them selected for this purpose."[22]

As a bishop, Carroll's role in relation to the Select Body differed little from that accorded him as superior in the constitution of the clergy of 1783, which Carroll himself had drawn. Presumably the Corporation could still claim the powers granted by the constitution to the former chapter. Among them was the right to fill vacancies after having made "application" to the "Superior in *spiritualibus*."[23] Carroll had assured the fretful ex-Jesuits of the southern district in 1788 that it would never be in the power of the future bishop to frustrate their designs for the restoration of the Society, "particularly as he is secluded [excluded] from all share of Government in our temporal affairs."[24] As a member of the Select Body, he could have been elected to the five-member board. Those chosen, however, were James Walton, John Ashton, Leonard Neale, Robert Molyneux, and Charles Sewall. Until 1802 he attended none of the meetings of the board, nor was he invited. Until 1802 Carroll made a conscientious effort to distinguish between matters spiritual and temporal and to restrict his actions with regard to the Corporation, which controlled the majority of priests in Maryland, to matters spiritual. What caused him to modify this policy will be considered later.

Trustees and Churches

Carroll was ready to admit the same distinction between the spiritual role of the pastor and the temporal role of the people legally charged with the governance of parochial congregations, that is, the trustees. Though by 1811 Carroll would insist that it was a universal practice that the pastor be ex-officio president of the board of trustees or vestry, he raised no objections to earlier acts of incorporation, such as that of the congregation of Norfolk of 1804, which not only excluded the pastor from the board but laid upon him strict obligations.[25] Neither did he insist that the pastor have a veto over the decisions of the vestry. Nor did he rule out entirely the possibility of lay patronage, the right of a congregation to choose its own pastor, particularly the right of lay benefactors to do so. But because he was unsure of the degree to which canonical right of patronage in Europe applied to the United States, he was unwilling to submit such cases to the Propaganda.[26] In most instances Carroll tried to respect the wishes of a congregation for a particular pastor.

THE CATHEDRAL CONGREGATION

The "Roman Catholic Congregation of Baltimore-Town" was in 1795 the first Catholic parish incorporated by the Assembly of Maryland. St. Mary's in Bryantown was in 1796 the second, to be followed by the Catholic Congregation of Cobb Neck in Charles County in 1799 and that of St. Joseph in St. Mary's County in 1801.[27] In 1802 the Assembly finally passed "An Act to Incorporate certain persons in every Christian Church or Congregation in the State." This general incorporation act required only that the trustees file with the county clerk a statement indicating the times of meeting and the manner of choosing trustees. Reflecting a fear as old as that of the Calverts of church property held in mortmain, the act limited the number of acres a congregation could possess to two and the annual revenue to $2,000.[28]

Carroll left it up to the congregations whether to avail themselves of the provisions of the act or not. A study of the county records would probably reveal that most did, but some apparently formed boards of trustees without seeking legal incorporation at the court house. It never occurred to these early Catholic communities that there was any other way of doing business. The first task of a new congregation was to raise a church, and for this trustees were deemed indispensable.

The 1795 act of incorporation for the Catholic congregation of Baltimore, in effect for the cathedral congregation, provided for a board consisting of the bishop, the "senior pastor," and seven lay trustees elected by the pewholders. The pewholders had to be adult males who contributed no less than the equivalent of three bushels of wheat a year. Elections were to be held every Monday after Whitsunday. Neither bishop nor pastor was given a veto over the decisions of the board, but the bishop had to be president and the rector, or pastor, who was Rev. Francis Beeston, vice president.[29] The first meeting was held December 29, 1795, only five days after passage of the act. The trustees proceeded to address the most pressing need: a cathedral worthy of the premier see.[30]

The see city's growth outraced the dreams of the city fathers. Its 8,000 inhabitants in 1782 had expanded to 15,000 in 1795. By 1800 it would count 26,500 and by 1810 46,500. In 1795 it was already the third largest city in the nation. Besides its busy port and shipbuilding yards, it boasted sugar refineries, rum distilleries, tobacco factories, shoe and boot factories, tanneries, roperies, paper mills, and cotton mills. To the north a hill owned by Colonel (later General) John Eager Howard presided with a pleasing dignity over the city. Across the marshes was Fells Point, growing at a faster pace than Baltimore itself.[31]

Catholics were attracted to Baltimore from many parts. In the early 1790s the sons of Michael Jenkins of Long Green in Baltimore County— Thomas Courtney, William, Edward, and Michael— moved to Baltimore to learn trades and lay the bases for small fortunes in leather, saddles, and furniture.[32] The Irish-born Luke Tiernan moved in from Hagerstown in 1795 to become the first Baltimore merchant to engage in shipping trade with Liverpool.[33] He was one of the original seven elected to the cathedral vestry. The other six were the Irish-born James Barry, a banker, Robert Walsh, a merchant, and Charles O'Brien; the German-born Charles Ghequierre, a merchant, and George Rosensteel; and the Scottish-born convert David Williamson, a merchant and banker. From southern Maryland would come Edward Neale and William Spalding and from western Maryland Arnold Livers and Basil Elder, all to find a place among the cathedral trustees in the late 1790s or early 1800s.

The cosmopolitan character of Maryland's largest city was due in great part to its Catholic residents. A sizable portion of the Germans, who constituted about a tenth of its population, was Catholic. With the coming of the refugees from the French colony of Saint-Domingue, a significant part of the city's blacks, who made up a fifth of its population, was also Catholic. The revolt in Saint-Domingue (now Haiti) in 1791 sent boatloads of French-speaking Creoles to Baltimore in 1793, giving it a decidedly French cast and providing a range of services sought by the wealthy: hairdressers, perfumers, milliners, wine merchants, confectioners, dancing masters, French teachers, and even a fencing instructor.[34]

Baltimore before 1790 was the city of organization not only for the Roman Catholic Church in the United States but also for the Methodist Episcopal (and later Methodist Protestant) Church and the United Brethren. It would soon be the home of the first Swedenborgian church in the country, the seat of the Episcopal Diocese of Maryland, and the site of the first Unitarian Church south of the Mason-Dixon line.[35] In 1790 at least four out of nine of the city's 13,500 souls were churchgoers, higher than the national average. Episcopalians numbered about 8.3 percent of the city's population; Methodists, German Lutherans, and Catholics about 7 percent, or some 950 members, each. The Methodists, however, had by 1790 built four churches, while the other eight denominations had only one each.

During the 1790s the Catholic population tripled, and by 1810 it was Baltimore's largest denomination with about 12 percent of the population, or well over 4,000 members. Only the Methodists kept pace.[36] The cathedral parish register, which counted 74 baptisms and 13 marriages in 1784, numbered 330 baptisms and 57 marriages in 1800, and this after two other Catholic parishes had been created.[37] Despite the well-to-do adherents who made Baltimore their home, the Catholic Church, more than any other in the city, embraced the lower class. While white-collar proprietors, professionals, and public servants were more often Presbyterians or Episcopalians and skilled artisans Methodists or United Brethren, Catholics were unskilled laborers. The percentage of unskilled, however, would gradually decline as the number of white-collar members increased.[38] A Catholic elite would develop in Baltimore as elsewhere.

Because of the small number of wealthy Catholics in the city initially, the task of raising a cathedral proved more formidable than the bishop or the trustees had anticipated.[39] When subscriptions fell well below expectations, the trustees decided to conduct one of the most ambitious lotteries in the history of the state.[40] In 1803 they won from the Maryland Assembly permission to sell 21,000 tickets at $10 each. Fifteen percent of the proceeds, or $30,000, would go to the building of the cathedral, the rest to prizes. No one seemed the least amazed when the bishop himself won first prize. This $20,000 award was, of course, turned over to the building fund. Fifty thousand dollars was a good start.

Next came the problem of the site. Land was purchased in 1796 at the present Pratt and Exeter Streets, but the center of population was already shifting northward. Carroll and the trustees wanted to relocate over the old cathedral cemetery and an adjoining lot on Charles Street. Many, however, including the Sulpicians, were in favor of accepting the offer of General Howard of a tract on his hill just over the city line. The trustees finally agreed when the general reduced the asking price to $20,000.[41]

Then there was the problem of the architect. Wanting nothing but the best, the trustees chose the man the United States Congress had hired to design the national Capitol, William Thornton. When Congress dropped Thornton in favor of Benjamin Henry Latrobe, however, the trustees did the same. Latrobe submitted two plans, one Gothic, one Roman. A modified version of the latter was finally chosen.[42] On July 7, 1806, the cornerstone was laid with appropriate solemnity. Bickering among the architect, superintendent, and chairman of the building committee caused vexing delays. It took until 1809 to finish the foundations and begin work on the superstructure. Hard times occasioned by the Embargo of 1807 and the War of 1812 would bring a complete suspension of construction. As with so many of his plans, Carroll would not live to see the completion of his cathedral some fifteen years and $225,000 after the first stone was laid.

The trustees in the first decade of their existence gave most of their business meetings over to the lottery, land transactions, and the building of the cathedral. They were, nevertheless, compelled to deal with a variety of matters. At the second meeting, for example, they debated the Spanish consul's agreement to surrender his pew "rather than expose the Congregation to behold a scandalous riot in the Church."[43] For several years the cathedral trustees assumed responsibility for what would become the second and third parishes in Baltimore. In 1797 they sought a deed for the lot and church of St. Patrick in Fells Point and fixed a salary for the priest who would attend the German Catholics of the city.[44] In 1805 the cathedral trustees surrendered control of St. Patrick's so that a "separate parish" might be established. The bishop gave his consent.[45]

ST PATRICK'S OF FELLS POINT

Originally not a part of the city, the Point, as it was often called, had a better harbor and attracted a sizable population. To serve the Catholic community there, largely Irish, a Sulpician professor, Anthony Garnier, began to say mass in 1792 on the third floor of a building on Bond and Fleet Streets. In 1796 he undertook the construction of a boxlike church in Apple Alley, which Carroll dedicated in 1797 and entrusted to John Floyd. One of the original seminarians from England, Floyd had been ordained in 1795. Before his first year at St. Patrick's was out, he was felled by that periodic scourge of port cities, yellow fever, and Garnier took charge again until another seminarian, Michael Cuddy, was ordained in 1803. Cuddy died also of yellow fever a year later. His place was taken by John Francis Moranvillé, an emigré who would enjoy a productive pastorate of twenty years at St. Patrick's.[46]

Moranvillé began by begging door to door for funds to build a larger church. Within a year the subscription list reached $20,000. The cornerstone was laid the same month as that of the cathedral on land acquired from Robert Walsh on Market (now Broadway) and Bank Streets. In November Moranvillé created a board of trustees to direct the project and to provide for the needs of the church when finished. A constitution, filed January 30, 1807, under the terms of the general incorporation act, provided for a board consisting of the pastor and six elected laymen. Though the trustees had to be pewholders, any adult male who had contributed $2.00 or more to the church the previous year could vote in the annual elections.[47] The church, 106 feet by 64 feet, was blessed by Carroll on November 29, 1807. To the Sulpician Ambrose Maréchal, then in France, he wrote soon after that Moranvillé had "succeeded beyond all expectations in constructing the largest and most beautiful church in the city." It would eventually be surpassed by the Cathedral, Carroll added, but with the confession that the latter had been undertaken "on too grand and costly a plan."[48]

"From the outset," observed an historian of the parish, "the trustee system worked admirably in St. Patrick's, and the harmony between [the trustees] and the pastors was always of the highest order."[49] The same could be said of Carroll's relationship with the trustees of St. Peter's Cathedral. In striking contrast were his dealings with the German congregation that came to be called St. John the Evangelist.

THE GERMAN PARISH

The German parish had an ignoble beginning with a wandering friar named John Baptist Causse. Because of the need for German-speaking priests in Pennsylvania, Carroll, with great misgivings, had granted him faculties and then suspended him in 1791 for insolence and insubordination. The defiant priest came to Baltimore and on February 17, 1792, placed in the *Maryland Journal* an announcement: "The German Roman Catholics will open next Sunday for the first time Divine Services in their *own language* at the house of John Brown, near Centre Market."[50] That Sunday (February 19) Carroll delivered a fearful sermon, excommunicating Causse and all who continued to resort to him.[51] Causse moved on.

At the beginning of 1797, a German Franciscan, Frederick Cesarius Reuter, appeared in Baltimore with respectable credentials and was employed by Carroll to attend the still small German Catholic community. At the same time, however, Carroll pronounced excommunication again upon two priests in Philadelphia, John Goetz and William Elling, who had nudged the Germans there into schism. Soon after, Reuter left for Europe under false pretenses and proceeded to Rome, where he lodged charges against the bishop of Baltimore. Carroll, he claimed, scorned the Germans, allowed no sermons or instructions in their native tongue, and excommunicated those who violated his prohibitions. Reuter returned to Baltimore at the beginning of 1799 and triumphantly placed in Carroll's hand a letter from the Propaganda critical of his treatment of the Germans.[52]

Furious, Carroll wrote the acting prefect, Cesare Brancadoro, emphatically denying all charges except that of refusing to allow Reuter to publish a catechism he had written in German. Carroll thought it "entirely out of place for the supreme power of the Apostolic See to be interposed by you to the weakening of the ordinary jurisdiction of the episcopal see" and all without consultation or even warning. "For if this jurisdiction perish there will remain no bridle with which to control the conduct of clergy or laity." It was Carroll's strongest letter to Rome.[53] He nevertheless granted Reuter conditional faculties and permission to build a chapel of ease dependent on the cathedral church. He directed the Germans to choose representatives to work out arrangements with himself.[54] Trustees were apparently elected, but no incorporation was sought at Annapolis. Hardly was construction begun before Reuter set off a second time for Europe, on this occasion armed with appeals from the German Catholic congregations of both Philadelphia and Baltimore. The latter was represented by fifty-three trustees! Together they complained of Carroll's actions and requested separate German parishes and a German bishop.[55] This time Reuter received a stern rebuke. He returned to Baltimore somewhat chastened.

With the collapse of the schism in Philadelphia in 1802, Carroll allowed Reuter to assume charge of the German congregation in Baltimore and the trustees to conduct a lottery to pay the debts contracted in the building of the church. In October 1802 he blessed the church of St. John the Evangelist. At the same time, he promised to grant it parochial status in a year if Reuter and the congregation behaved themselves. It proved a vain hope. At the settlement of the lottery, wealthy subscribers were reimbursed, poorer ones not. An affluent trustee insisted that a shed be built for his horse and chair, and in the quarrel that ensued Carroll sided with the trustees and Reuter with those who opposed the demanding parishioner. At this point another parishioner, told that his wife had been intimate with Reuter, assaulted the priest. Reuter took him to court but was awarded damages of only one cent by an unfriendly jury.[56]

Carroll suspended Reuter for "scandalous conduct" and appointed in his stead Rev. Francis X. Brosius. Reuter refused to be dislodged. In May 1804, at Carroll's direction, Brosius sought a court order to remove him. Before it could be served, a riot broke out in the church itself between the supporters of Reuter and those of Brosius. In May 1805 the court finally decided in Brosius's favor. When Reuter left town, Carroll relieved Brosius, replacing him with Rev. John Mertz, who, as Carroll anticipated, eventually tamed the turbulent members of the German Catholic community.[57] As late as 1814, however, Carroll would have occasion to note Mertz's "painful situation with respect to his *Jacobinised* Trustees."[58]

In Maryland, nonetheless, the trustee system worked well in all but St. John's, but it did not, as some historians have claimed, promote democracy at the parish level. If anything, it served to reinforce the aristocratic character of Maryland Catholicism, which might have been the reason why it worked so well in the oldest diocese. The poor could not vote. The richest members of the parish were elected trustees. In Baltimore they were among the wealthiest 10 percent of the Catholic community.[59] The same was probably true of the incorporated parishes of southern Maryland. At the cathedral only a few electors would show up annually to rubber stamp the nominations proposed by the board itself.[60]

Pewholding would constitute the principal source of revenue for parishes in Maryland throughout the nineteenth century. Pews were sold at auction to the highest bidder, and rents were scaled according to the pew's proximity to the altar.[61] The wealthy did not in the least mind the walk down the aisle to the front of the church. Stole fees and stipends also assured a more ample share in the ministrations of the church for the well-to-do. At the beginning of Carroll's episcopacy, the "rate of retribution" for a low mass was set at thirty-three cents, for a high or requiem mass at one dollar, for each wax candle three cents, and for a funeral sermon four dollars.[62]

CHURCHES IN THE DISTRICT OF COLUMBIA

Catholic aristocrats were also conspicuous in the development of the church in the District of Columbia. The Church of Rome, in fact, figured prominently in the history of the national capital. From near the White House to the Capitol ran a stream named the Tiber by a man named Pope, whose tract was patented as "Rome."[63] The claims of the Carrolls of Duddington, the Youngs, and the Brents, all closely related to the bishop, to the choicest lands in the District would assure them a prominent place in Washington society.[64] Daniel Carroll, the bishop's brother, was the most active of the three commissioners named by the president in 1791 to superintend the construction of the new city and curb the zeal of its Catholic architect, Pierre L'Enfant.[65] Robert Brent, the bishop's nephew, would be named by President Thomas Jefferson the first mayor, a position he would hold for a decade. James Hoban, the Catholic architect of the White House and other public buildings, brought Irish laborers to the capital as well as the priest who would found the city's first parish.

The first Catholic church in the District of Columbia, however, was Holy Trinity in Georgetown, built by the Rev. Francis Neale in 1791–94 for those who attended mass in the chapel of Georgetown College. In 1794

Neale would also open a church in Alexandria, Virginia, then a part of the district.[66] The first Catholic church in the city of Washington itself was erected by Anthony Caffrey (or Caffry), a Dominican fresh from Ireland. In 1794 Carroll allowed Caffrey to have the two lots at F and 10th Streets Northwest, originally sold by the commissioners at a reduced rate for a Catholic church, deeded to himself.[67] There Caffrey raised the small frame church he named for St. Patrick, the first of any denomination in the capital. In 1804 he was replaced by William Matthews, who began his fifty-year pastorate in Washington by building a larger church. In 1806 Carroll blessed the new St. Patrick's, and in 1810 an organ was installed.[68] In the eastern part of the city Catholics attended the family chapel of James Barry at Greenleaf Point.

OTHER CHURCHES IN MARYLAND

In Maryland new congregations sprang up as if by magic in Carroll's early years as bishop, and all with little urging from the bishop himself. Carroll had no desire to multiply parishes for which he had no priests. Rarely, in fact, were these parochial congregations called parishes; strictly speaking they were not, as the Propaganda reminded Carroll in 1803.[69] Most often they were called congregations or missions and their pastors, rectors or missionaries.

The growth of Catholic congregations in western Maryland was phenomenal, especially in Washington and Allegany Counties and adjoining areas of Virginia and Pennsylvania, where the Catholic Church gained a foothold for the first time. The founder of the church in that rugged part of Maryland was Denis Cahill, a "man of powerful nerve and hearty faith," as the prince-priest Demetrius Gallitzin would characterize him.[70] Cahill had come from Ireland in 1788 with no credentials and was immediately swallowed up in the backwoods. In 1795 he wrote to Carroll from Hagerstown, some seventy miles away, to tell him that he had brought together congregations at Hagerstown and Cumberland, another seventy miles distant, as well as at Martinsburg, Shepherdstown, and Winchester in Virginia, and Chambersburg in Pennsylvania. Lots had been given for churches in most of these places, and within a year he hoped to have four churches built.[71] A church had already been raised in Hagerstown in 1794 with the help of Charles Carroll of Bellevue and Luke Tiernan.[72] One of the lots donated in or near Cumberland was the gift of John Logsdon, a prominent member of the Catholic congregation at Mount Savage, called Arnold's Settlement, some ten miles northeast of Cumberland. Until Mount Savage built a church of its own in 1818, that and the Cumberland congregation worshiped together in the church Cahill erected in Cumberland about 1795.[73]

In Frederick County a church was begun in the town of Emmitsburg in 1793 by Rev. Matthew Ryan on land bestowed by James and Joseph Hughes.[74] John Dubois, an energetic emigré who had arrived in Virginia in 1791 with letters of introduction from the Marquis de Lafayette to the leading citizens of that state, agreed in 1794 to take charge of the former Jesuit mission in Frederick Town. Sometime before 1798 he began a new church that was still unfinished in 1804, when a lottery was conducted to complete it.[75] In the meantime, he also took charge of the church at Emmitsburg and began another a few miles south for the Catholics of Elder Station. It was his hope, he told Carroll in 1807, to incorporate the two churches as one congregation under the name of Mary and Joseph.[76] Dubois also attended other small congregations near Frederick Town, one that had grown up at Maryland Tract, the estate of Governor Thomas Sim Lee, a convert, and another on Carrollton Manor, the estate by which Charles Carroll identified himself. In 1807–8 he built a brick church for the congregation at Barnesville in Montgomery County.[77]

In that part of Frederick County that would become Carroll County in 1836, churches were built for congregations at Taneytown and Westminster. In 1797 the trustees of Taneytown told Carroll they had finished their church and needed a pastor.[78] Gallitzin visited both congregations until Carroll found a priest to reside at Taneytown, the Roman-born Nicholas Zocchi. In 1805 Zocchi built a church for the congregation at Westminster.[79]

To the northeast of Baltimore in Harford County a church was completed at Hickory in 1792 on land purchased in 1779 for the congregation that had used Priest Neale's Mass House at Deer Creek.[80] This constituted the easternmost of a string of churches stretching from the Chesapeake to the western end of the state. In this northern tier of counties lay the future of the oldest diocese.

Ex-Jesuits and Sulpicians at Odds

Though encouraged by the indices of a growing and vital faith, Carroll was disheartened by the inability of his two favorite projects, the college and the seminary, to take root and flourish. His frustration was matched by the gloom that had displaced the buoyant hope of both the aging ex-Jesuits and the newly arrived Sulpicians.

In 1792 six members of the Society of St. Sulpice joined the original four: Benedict Joseph Flaget, John Baptist David, and John Baptist Chicoisneau in March; Gabriel Richard, Francis Ciquard, and Ambrose Maréchal in June. Only one was kept at the seminary. Michael Levadoux, Flaget, and Richard were sent to the French-speaking villages in the Illinois country, Ciquard to the Indians in Maine, David to Bryantown, and Maréchal to Bohemia. Even the four who remained at the seminary—Nagot, Tessier, Garnier, and Chicoisneau—spent as much time in parochial work as in teaching.[81]

St. Mary's Seminary did not produce the clergy Carroll needed. Of the five seminarians brought over in 1791, only two were ordained for the diocese of Baltimore: John Floyd died soon after his ordination in 1795, and John Edward Mondésir returned to France three years after his own in 1799. The first priest to be ordained by Carroll, on May 23, 1793, was Stephen Theodore Badin, one of two seminarians brought over in 1792. Badin had finished most of his studies in France. A bright spot was the enrollment in 1792 of Augustine Smith, an alias for Prince Demetrius Gallitzin.[82] Already well educated, he finished his theological studies in 1795 and was ordained. In 1797 William Matthews, an alumnus of the Liège Academy, entered and was ordained March 29, 1800, the first native son raised by Carroll to the priesthood. He was the fourteenth enrolled but only the fifth to be ordained for the diocese. When he left, the seminary was empty again.[83]

At the same time, prospects worsened for the former Jesuits. A restoration seemed yearly more remote. In the decade following the incorporation of the Roman Catholic Clergy, half of the twenty former members of the Society of Jesus died, prompting Charles Sewall to write woefully to Carroll: "I find it at least a sorrowful meditation to reflect that we are going off the stage fast, to leave those estates, which we have so long kept for the good of religion, to others whom we know not."[84] In the same period the Corporation of the Roman Catholic Clergy found it necessary to admit at least five members who had had no ties with the Jesuits.

The need for competent teachers and administrators at Georgetown College made the Corporation look to the Sulpicians for assistance. The vice presidency in 1795 was offered to Benedict Flaget and the presidency in 1796 to "Mr. DuBourg, a French clergyman of abilities & most pleasing character," as Carroll described him to Plowden.[85] William Louis Valentine DuBourg was not a wise choice, it turned out. Born in Saint-Domingue but reared in France, where he attended both the Seminary of St. Sulpice and the Sorbonne, DuBourg fled the Revolution in 1792, coming to America in 1794 and joining the Sulpicians the following year. Though a man of immense charm, energy, and imagination, his unconcern for details and debts annoyed the directors of the college. Even more, perhaps, did his nationality when a wave of anti-French feeling swept the country in 1798 as a result of the XYZ Affair.[86] DuBourg resigned at the end of 1798 and went to Cuba to join Flaget and another Sulpician in the foundation of an academy there. A few months later, the Corporation demanded the return of Bohemia, whose management and revenues had been entrusted to the Sulpicians when their financial aid from France had been cut off.[87]

The school in Cuba died aborning, and DuBourg returned to Baltimore in 1799 to found an academy there. Perceiving a rival college in embryo, the directors of Georgetown protested its opening to Carroll. To Carroll's objections Nagot responded: "How is it that in a country where equal liberty is the basis of political government, we are blamed for taking this course?"[88] The Sulpician superior knew just the right arguments to use with Carroll. The bishop apologized. "It would have been more fitting," he acknowledged, "to leave you in the full exercise of your rights which every inhabitant has in the United States, of opening a school and receiving as many students as he pleases."[89]

In apparent retaliation for the establishment of the Baltimore academy, the Corporation at a meeting in July 1800 decided to offer courses in philosophy at Georgetown for the seven students who had been earmarked for St. Mary's Seminary. Carroll was outraged. Among the former Jesuits, he confided to Plowden, were some "whose violence will listen to no lessons of moderation; & others, whose knowledge and observations are too confined to comprehend that anything useful can be learned beyond what they know." He saw the action of the board as "evidently an attempt to wrest from the Bishop the government & superintendence over the studies and education of his Clergy."[90]

Carroll was also upset when some of the ex-Jesuits held a secret meeting in November at St. Thomas Manor to consider affiliation with a pseudo-Jesuit society called the Fathers of the Faith. Explaining to the bishop why he had not been invited to the meeting, Sewall said plainly that it appeared "that your affection for us was much cooled, that your heart was now fixed on the Sulpicians of Baltimore in preference to all others; insomuch that you wished them to be legal successors to our Estates."[91] Carroll simply did not believe that this was the wisest road to restoration and wanted a greater voice in plans to revive the Society of Jesus in the United States.

Another problem arose in the spring of 1801, when the conduct of John Ashton, which will be considered later, made it necessary to remove him from the management of White Marsh. Carroll himself, after suspending Ashton's faculties, ordered him to surrender the Corporation's most pro-

ductive estate. Then he wrote to the board of trustees that he had proceeded in the matter "farther perhaps, than properly belonged to my peculiar duty, as limited to spiritual matters; yet sensible at the same time, that
these are so often blended with matters temporal, that it is impossible to
move in the former, without touching the latter." Carroll concluded: "There
is too much reason to fear, that there is something radically wrong or defec-
tive in our present system."[92]

Carroll had abstained from temporal affairs to the extent of not even
allowing property to be vested in himself as bishop.[93] The action of the
former members of the Society to which he had been so devoted, however,
led Carroll to alter the perception he had entertained of his role as bishop
and to take a more active part in decisions touching temporalities. When
the next triennial election of the Corporation, or board of trustees, was
held at Georgetown in August 1802, Carroll had himself elected to the
board.

Sensing a radical change in ecclesial policy, twelve members of the Select Body of the Clergy complained to the former board that the election
had been "improper, if not illegal, null and void, also plainly subreptitious,
as being planned and carried on by two of the Representatives without the
knowledge and consent of the other members." One of the two who had
obtained Carroll's election was doubtless Francis Beeston, rector of the Baltimore cathedral.[94] Another election was held on October 2, 1802. Carroll,
Leonard Neale, his coadjutor, two former Jesuits, and the priest who had
replaced Ashton at White Marsh were elected to the five-member board.
On this occasion Ashton was the only one to submit a formal complaint.
He reminded the members that Carroll himself had admitted to having "no
power of intermeddling with our temporalities" and that the "compenetra-
tion of offices" created a "monster with two heads."[95] Carroll and Neale,
nevertheless, would continue to be elected to the board for the rest of their
lives.

This enlargement of episcopal power did not immediately solve the
problems that had arisen. Faced with an empty seminary in Baltimore and
the antipathy of the Corporation, the Sulpician superior in Paris, Jacques-
André Emery, decided to recall his subjects to France, where the political
climate had improved appreciably and teachers were needed for seminaries.
Carroll had pleaded with Emery, claiming that the withdrawal of the Sulpicians "would be one of the greatest misfortunes which could happen to this
diocese."[96] Emery wavered for a time but, when conditions did not improve, began in 1803 to recall his subjects in America. The first were teachers

at the seminary: Garnier, Levadoux, and Maréchal. Illness prevented Nagot's recall. Ultimately, it was the success of DuBourg's academy that kept the Sulpicians in the United States.

Until 1803 the Sulpician school in Baltimore took in only French- and Spanish-speaking students. In that year, and with Carroll's blessing, it opened its doors to "Americans" and began an ambitious building program. In 1805 St. Mary's College obtained a charter from the state to grant degrees and in 1806 authorization to conduct a lottery to pay its debts with the proviso that it would remain in operation for thirty years.[97] Carroll readily attributed the success of the college to DuBourg, "an active and towering genius." It counted more Protestants than Catholics in its student body, he told Plowden. "Some of the rigid Sulpicians shake their head at this (to them) seeming departure from their Institute, but I believe the general effect will be beneficial."[98]

In contrast, Carroll was distressed at the lack of progress at Georgetown College. Leonard Neale had moved from Philadelphia in 1799 to assume the presidency. Under Leonard and his brother Francis the reputation of the college continued to decline. Leonard's elevation to the episcopacy as Carroll's coadjutor in 1800 did not help. While the number of students at St. Mary's College passed the hundred mark, the number at Georgetown fell to nearly twenty. The Neales blamed St. Mary's College. Carroll blamed the Neales. Not only were they overly strict, running the college like a seminary, but they had, in Carroll's view, little of the intellectual and cultural endowments expected of the president and vice-president of a college.[99] Both Carroll and the Neales hoped that the revival of the Society of Jesus would save the college on the Potomac.

The Jesuit Restoration

When it was learned in 1802 that the pope had the year before given permission to the remnant of the Society in Russia to aggregate former members in other countries, Carroll agreed to make application to the Russian general, Gabriel Gruber, in behalf of the ex-Jesuits in the United States.[100] The unsettled condition of Europe delayed the arrival of the positive response until 1805. Carroll gave permission to all former members to renew their vows as Jesuits.

As it turned out, only five of the ten former members of the Society still living reentered the order: Charles Sewall, Charles Neale, Robert Molyneux, John Bolton, and Sylvester Boarman. Carroll explained to the Jesuit superior in England that the American Jesuits would be better served by his and Neale's retention of their episcopal powers than by their reentry into the Society.[101] A Jesuit historian has claimed, however, that Carroll chose not to rejoin "partly because of lingering distrust of the papacy, partly because of serious misgivings about the Society's ability to adapt to the modern world that the intellectual and political revolutions were making."[102]

Carroll named Molyneux superior. Though somewhat lazy and irresolute, he was in Carroll's opinion the most sensible of the five and the one most likely to look to him for direction. On September 20, 1805, Carroll and Molyneux signed an agreement acknowledging the Jesuit superior's right to choose managers for the estates of the Corporation and to exclude pastors that the bishop might appoint to congregations attached to them from residence upon the estates, in effect a veto. At the same time the annuity allowed the bishop from the estates was to continue "perpetual & inalienable."[103] The following year the Corporation transferred to Carroll the revenues of Bohemia in lieu of the annual subsidy of $800 he received.[104]

The claim of the Society upon the estates of the Corporation did not go well with at least one member of the Select Body, who had no previous ties with the Jesuits. William Pasquet, the manager at Bohemia, pointed out to Carroll that religious priests had heretofore been refused admittance to the Select Body on the grounds that they had no will of their own. By renewing vows as Jesuits, Pasquet insisted, Molyneux and the others had, in effect, severed their ties with the Corporation.[105] Though Carroll's answer is not preserved, it is certain he disagreed.

Though the restoration in America was effected with only five members, a novitiate was opened in October 1806 with Francis Neale, an alumnus of Liège, the brother of Leonard and Charles, and now fiscal agent of the Corporation as both novice and novice master. Candidates were not wanting. In 1808 four who had gone to St. Mary's Seminary for theology would be ordained as Jesuits, the brothers Enoch and Benedict Joseph Fenwick among them. In 1806–7 five Jesuits were sent over by the Russian general to see the American mission off to a good start.[106]

Carroll, nevertheless, was unhappy with half measures. In 1806 he instructed his Dominican agent in Rome, Richard Luke Concanen, to approach the pope quietly for formal approbation of the American revival. There is reason to believe that Concanen obtained papal approval but that the documents to this effect were lost or destroyed.[107] In view of the Propaganda's refusal to recognize the papal permission for aggregation to the Russian remnant in the case of the English Jesuits, Carroll made not a single mention of the restoration of the Society in the United States in his correspondence with the Sacred Congregation in Rome.

To the resolution of the problem of the restoration of the Society of Jesus and a consequent improvement in the affairs of Georgetown College could be added an upswing in the fortunes of the Society of St. Sulpice in America. Not only was the Baltimore college flourishing, but, to a more modest extent, the seminary was also. In 1808 seven would enter St. Mary's Seminary to bring the total enrollment to twenty-three.

The Problem Priests

Carroll's preoccupation with the seminary and the Society of Jesus derived in large measure from a wish to be rid of problem priests. Of all the emotionally and physically draining difficulties with which he had to contend, none was so painful. Carroll had to shape a clergy in a land where there were no established patterns of conduct for Catholic priests and where freedom of action and opportunities for ease and enrichment abounded. He had to mold a clergy from an assortment of exiles and castoffs, an ethnic mix of disparate temperaments, and a medley that ranged from the under- to the overzealous. None of his successors, perhaps, could claim a greater number of the simply troublesome, those adept at wars of attrition over unwanted assignments or those who provoked endless complaints on the part of unhappy parishioners. There were no periodic conferences that allowed him to instruct them collectively. He was compelled to mold them individually and often through tedious correspondence.

To the overzealous Gallitzin in the mountains of Pennsylvania he wrote in 1798: "I have already admonished you . . . to try to win the affections of your congregations, to lead them by mildness, even here and there, to overlook things which are not precisely as they should be, that afterwards you may correct them by gentle persuasian, instead of at once making use of authority, and to carry that authority to its utmost limits."[108] The approach that Carroll pressed upon the prince-priest was precisely the one he used most often with his clerical subjects, not only the simply troublesome but even those whose behavior was outrageous by any standard.

Carroll could take stern measures when he deemed them necessary, especially in the case of open defiance of episcopal authority. In three such instances he used the ultimate weapon in his arsenal: excommunication. As it happened, all three victims—Causse, Goetz, and Elling—were German, leading to charges of national prejudice. For this reason, perhaps, he used this weapon no more. For instances in which no act of public defiance was involved, he was patient, even compassionate. His forbearance in the face of unexampled provocation is best seen in the cases of three clergymen each unique in his own way: Denis Cahill, John Ashton, and Simon Felix Gallagher.

Cahill, the pioneer priest of western Maryland, though remarkable for his zeal, was no one's man. Partly for that reason, trustees were not so plentiful in the west as in other parts of Maryland. When it seemed to him in 1796 that Carroll was trying to give the congregation of Hagerstown to another, Cahill lashed out at him in one of the most vicious letters Carroll preserved. He accused the bishop of "jealousy," of "cruel injustice," of endeavoring by his "venemous breath to blast the fruits of my labor." He charged him also with buying the miter from his fellow Jesuits. He threatened to expose such scandals as Rev. John Ashton's "tasty arrangem[en]t with his doll Sukey" and Ashton's claim that Carroll himself had fathered children in Virginia. Cahill demanded $300 as the price of silence.[109]

Carroll calmly demanded a retraction and apology and waited four months. The delay he explained by "an almost invincible reluctance to push matters to an extremity" and demanded that Cahill appear in Baltimore for an ecclesiastical trial.[110] The priest ignored the summons. Finally in 1803 there arrived in Baltimore an apology of sorts. On the letter Carroll wrote "not satisfactory" because there was no retraction. "But I shall leave him to the suggestions of his own conscience," he added.[111] Cahill is said to have returned to Ireland in 1806.

Like Cahill, John Ashton was accustomed to having things his own way. Unlike Cahill he was not a recent arrival of uncertain antecedents but a former Jesuit who had served the Maryland mission and the nascent diocese well. When the "arrangement" mentioned by Cahill caused the Corporation to dismiss him from the management of White Marsh, Carroll relayed the decision. "What authority has John of Baltimore," Ashton raged, "to dispossess me of White Marsh," a post he had held for twenty-eight years? "Let me cut my bread in peace or I will disturb the peace with a vengeance," he threatened.[112] Shamed by the moderation of Carroll's response, Ashton expressed regret for having written as he had but turned his ire upon Bishop Neale in such slanderous terms that Carroll withdrew his faculties.

Carroll imposed no further censures, however, even though Ashton continued to "disturb the peace" for the next eight years. "There is something not right in the heads of the Neales," he wrote Carroll in 1806 concerning the principal targets of his wrath. "What a woeful thing it would be to have a crazy Bi[sho]p."[113] When the Society of Jesus was restored, Ashton claimed to have documentary proof that it had no right to the estates given by donation or bequest, such as White Marsh, a claim that a future archbishop of Baltimore would use to advantage.[114]

In 1809 Ashton threatened to sue Bishop Neale for slander and declared publicly that he had been attacked by nuns in men's clothing. (Both Leonard and Charles Neale directed convents.) Bishop Neale, who deplored "the lenity hitherto shewn" Ashton, wrote Carroll in exasperation: "For God['s] sake do something to correct the Monstrous evil which flows in on us from this unhappy man."[115] Carroll's response may be deduced from a letter Ashton wrote him two months later: "I know how well disposed you are to relieve the distress of the afflicted, and how much more prompt you are to forgive than to inflict punishment."[116]

Though not the only one to deplore Carroll's "lenity," Leonard Neale was, perhaps, the most persistent in urging investigations and punishments. As early as 1795, he called Carroll's attention to the delinquencies of Rev. Simon Felix Gallagher. This talented alcoholic appeared in Baltimore in 1793 with a letter of recommendation from Archbishop Troy of Dublin attesting his learning and eloquence. Though suspicious, Carroll assigned him to Charleston, South Carolina. In 1795 Neale wrote from Philadelphia that he had heard that Gallagher was a Freemason, that he drank, that he accepted a challenge to a duel, and that he had taken liberties with a married woman.[117] It was not until January 1797, however, that Carroll warned Gallagher that he had heard from several sources of his "undisguised intemperance" and neglect of duties.[118] Gallagher's promise of reform was belied by excesses committed in Baltimore in 1801.

It was probably at this point that Carroll instructed Bishop Neale to conduct an investigation. "I am determined," he explained, "to discard from the service of the altar and the care of souls every intemperate priest. My past forbearance has perhaps increased the evil."[119] There is no evidence that an investigation was held. Instead, Carroll suggested to Gallagher that he surrender his church and devote full time to teaching. Calling Carroll's letter "an instrument of ecclesiastical suicide," the pastor wrote directly to the pope, complaining of Carroll's "order" for him to resign.[120] When he left Charleston, ostensibly to pursue his case in Rome, Carroll seized the opportunity to send another priest to Charleston. The Irish trustees, however, would have nothing to do with him because he was French. Gallagher returned to Charleston to play an ambiguous role until the death of the French priest in 1806. On the advice of Edward Lynah, Carroll's most trusted confidant in Charleston, Carroll reinstated Gallagher as pastor. He had, said Lynah, for the last three years led a new life and had regained "his former respectability in Society."[121]

From this point on, Carroll's letters to Gallagher were friendly, even flattering. It was Carroll's intention nonetheless to effect the priest's removal to a place where he could be watched more closely. In 1808 he suggested New York, "not to seduce you from Charleston, which would be in an uproar for losing you," but for his health's sake. He also opened the possibility of a transfer to Washington.[122] But Gallagher would not be budged.

In all of Carroll's dealings with the Irish priest, Gallagher never crossed the line into outright insubordination.[123] For that reason he was one of the most difficult of the problem priests to deal with. As bishop, Carroll had no set solution for resolving such cases, but mildness characterized his course of action toward all but the most reprobate. Whether Carroll would have had greater success by adopting the hard line urged upon him by Bishop Neale may be judged when we find Neale in a position to do as he proposed.

The presence of problem priests affected Carroll's policies profoundly. For one thing, he was obliged to have recourse to the Congregation of the Propaganda more often than he probably wished and to become increasingly dependent on it for support. At the time of the Reuter controversy, he wrote the acting prefect: "Generally speaking, since I became bishop I have always experienced the great kindness of the very eminent fathers of the Sacred Congregation. They have demonstrated such trust in me that I would wish to be guided by their counsels, and should feel safe under their protection. . . ."[124]

Time-Honored Procedures

"Generally speaking," the more difficulties he encountered, the more the first bishop fell back on traditional forms and time-honored procedures in the church. Whatever inclinations he may have had to tread new paths and reshape the local church to harmonize with the American scene—as he had evidenced in his preference for a vernacular liturgy, the election of bishops, and arrangements at the parish and diocesan levels that looked to American models—he found greater safety and stability in European patterns. Problem priests played an important part in such decisions as to exclude the second order of the clergy from the choice of bishops after the selection of Leonard Neale, a point still to be considered.

Problem priests, however, were not the only factor pulling Carroll back from the risks of innovation. Those to whom he looked most often for advice and support were not Americans but Europeans, like his friend

Plowden in England or Anthony Garnier of the seminary before the latter's recall in 1803, a departure that induced in the bishop a fit of depression.

There can be no question that Carroll contributed to the Europeanization of the American church. He played, a recent historian has claimed, reversing previous estimates, "a decisive role in this shift from [his] republican blueprint of the 1780s to a more traditional model of Roman Catholicism."[125] Though Carroll's "blueprint" was sketchy at best, it is incontrovertible that from a church of simple forms and features and democratic tendencies that were the legacies of the colonial and Revolutionary period, as well as a certain autonomy in its actions and decisions, it would become in its future course increasingly baroque in its liturgy, hierarchical in its governance, and ultramontane in its theology. And yet, it could hardly have been otherwise. Carroll's inherent conservatism surfaced more and more as the destructive character of the French Revolution became increasingly and painfully apparent to devout Catholics. It would, moreover, be unfair to expect of Carroll an immunity from the universal tendency of authority to become more cautious with mounting responsibilities. He was a guardian, not a prophet.

At the same time, Carroll was, more than any other, the principal architect of the Maryland tradition in the oldest diocese and in the American church as a whole. This contribution will be the focus of still another act in which he stands at the center of the stage.

2   *Metropolitan*

FROM THE MOMENT HE GRASPED the episcopal reins, John Carroll knew that a single bishop would never do for a diocese coextensive with one of the largest nations in Christendom. Carroll did not like travel. Though he journeyed as far north as Boston twice, there is no record that he ever ventured farther south than Norfolk or farther west than Frederick County. One of the reasons he had called his first and only synod in 1791 was to consult his priests on the question of another bishop.

The Suffragan Sees

In his first report to Rome as bishop, Carroll had asked that a second diocese be created at New York or Philadelphia, or at least that a coadjutor with right of succession be granted him. So as not to give offense to the government, he explained, he would like the coadjutor to be elected by the American clergy. Carroll wanted fifteen priests—the ten oldest and five chosen by himself—to make the choice, the Holy See reserving the right to reject the person so chosen.[1] At the time, the Propaganda judged it too early to dissolve the unity of the American church but consented to a coadjutor. It would not allow him to be chosen by election; Carroll's election was to remain the only exception. Carroll could propose a candidate after consultation with his priests. The consultation in May 1793 nonetheless took the form of an election. The choice fell upon Lawrence Graessel, a former Jesuit and Carroll's vicar general for Philadelphia.[2]

The Propaganda made it clear in letters to both Carroll and Graessel that the Holy Father was to decide when new sees were needed, and this even should Carroll be "unreasonably" opposed.[3] Autonomy was not to be granted readily to the church in the new republic. While concordats negotiated in a Europe of dramatically altered power relations placed the choice of bishops with monarchs or cathedral chapters, the Holy See was forced to find another way to choose a bishop for a local church that had no chapters and no connections with the government. In the procedure it devised for the United States, Rome would become accustomed to making the choice itself.[4]

In the report requesting the right to elect the next bishop, Carroll indicated his intention of creating "a group of priests to serve as a chapter."[5] When the right of election was refused, Carroll made a formal request that he be allowed to organize the ten or twelve priests in charge of the principal congregations into "a sort of chapter," which in turn would choose its own dean. While he did not ask that this quasi-chapter have the right to choose his successor, Carroll did request that it have the power to rule the diocese during a vacancy.[6] The right to nominate was doubtless a role that Carroll saw as coming in time.

Carroll's plan for a chapter would become a casualty not only of the breakdown in communications with Rome occasioned by the European conflict but also of Carroll's increasingly unhappy relationships with his own clergy. The antics of such men as Reuter, Cahill, Gallagher, and Ashton, plus his inability to find good pastors for even a dozen of the principal parishes before 1808, could only have suggested the dangers and difficulties of entrusting episcopal selection to the clergy. The possibility of the Baltimore Sulpicians' constituting at least the greater part of a cathedral chapter was precluded by the jealousy of Jesuits in their process of resuscitation.

In July 1793 Graessel died before he could be raised to the episcopacy, a victim of the periodic epidemics of yellow fever that claimed some of Carroll's best priests. In his place as coadjutor Carroll recommended Leonard Neale to Rome. The fact that Neale was hardly the man Carroll most admired suggests that this choice was also the outcome of an election, another Carroll chose not to mention in his Roman correspondence. The War of the First Coalition, the captivity of Pope Pius VI by Napoleon in 1798, and the pope's death the following year prevented the brief of Neale's elevation, dated April 17, 1795, from reaching Baltimore until the summer of 1800. Another epidemic of yellow fever caused the episcopal ordination, Carroll's first, to be postponed until December 7. Though remarkably devout, Neale was not the assistant Carroll needed so badly as his burdens multiplied. As a close friend, James Barry, confided: "There is no danger of Neale setting the Potomac on fire."[7]

In the period of disrupted communications with Rome, problems arose almost monthly in one or another part of the extensive diocese. Only in New England, where Francis Matignon and John Cheverus worked well in tandem, was there relative peace. The healing of the schism in Philadelphia in 1802 brought a temporary lull in the affairs of that city. But in New York the flawed character of the clergy and factious character of the

faithful became daily more pronounced. In the widely scattered and sometimes obstreperous congregations that stretched from the Potomac south
to the Spanish border, it proved almost impossible to keep a priest for long
except in Charleston, where Gallagher remained firmly entrenched.

Of particular concern to Carroll was the rapidly developing church on
the frontier. Kentucky fever had swept the Catholic counties of southern
Maryland, sending more than a fourth of all the Catholics in that most
Catholic part of his diocese to the land beyond the mountains.[8] Lured by
cheap acreage, they had settled in tight-knit farming communities along
the creeks in central Kentucky in the hope of attracting priests. Not until
1793, when he sent the newly ordained Stephen Badin there, did Carroll
find a priest with staying power. Badin was joined in 1805 by the hardy
Fleming, Charles Nerinckx, a group of Dominicans, and a colony of Trap-
pists. Problems of another sort developed when Nerinckx sided with the
Jansenistic Badin and the Dominicans with the fun-loving frontierspeople,
whose purported excesses Badin had sought to curb. It was not easy to keep
the peace six hundred miles away.[9] Above the Ohio surplus Sulpicians had
served French-speaking settlements, but by 1808 only Gabriel Richard remained at Detroit.

As if a diocese that stretched from the seaboard to the Mississippi were
not enough, Carroll was saddled with the administration of remote areas,
one as large as the original diocese. Though his care of the Louisiana Territory, which fell to him in 1804, was to have lasted only until a bishop or an
administrator could be found, prospective candidates were reluctant to take
on a formidable Capuchin named Antonio de Sedella, or Père Antoine, rector of the cathedral in New Orleans and a law unto himself. Not until 1812
would William DuBourg, the founder of St. Mary's College, arrive as administrator of the diocese of Louisiana.[10] In 1804 Carroll was both "surprised and alarmed" when the Propaganda named the bishop of Baltimore
administrator also of the Danish West Indies, or Virgin Islands, as well as
the Dutch and British islands of the Antilles that fell under no special episcopal jurisdiction. Carroll named an Irish secular priest there as prefect and
a French Sulpician as vice prefect and hoped for the best.[11]

As early as June 1802 the Propaganda itself suggested not a second diocese but the subdivision of the sprawling republic into four or five suffragan sees. Carroll was asked to recommend appropriate sites and worthy
priests to be their bishops.[12] Difficulties in communication prevented an
authentic copy of the request from reaching him until 1806. Immediately he
returned a letter proposing sees at Boston, New York, and Philadelphia.
For Kentucky he suggested Lexington, Frankfort, or Bardstown, the last

because it was closest to the concentration of Catholics in that state. Seven months later, after a round of correspondence, he recommended that John Cheverus be named bishop of Boston because Francis Matignon absolutely refused the burden. As bishop of Philadelphia he proposed a Franciscan, Michael Egan. For Kentucky he submitted four names: Badin; Nerinckx; Benedict Flaget, who had ministered in the West; and Thomas Wilson, the Dominican prior. For New York he could find no one to recommend. He suggested that the diocese be placed under Cheverus until a suitable candidate could be found.[13]

Rome acted promptly on the recommendations. On April 8, 1808, Baltimore was raised to metropolitan status. At the same time suffragan sees were created at Boston, New York, Philadelphia, and Bardstown. Cheverus was named bishop of Boston, Egan bishop of Philadelphia, and Flaget bishop of Bardstown. For New York the Holy See itself chose Richard Luke Concanen, a Dominican living in Rome and Carroll's agent there. On April 24, 1808, Concanen was raised to the episcopacy by Michele Di Pietro, cardinal prefect of the Propaganda since 1805, and entrusted with the briefs of the bishops-elect as well as the pallium for Carroll. War prevented his sailing for America. In June 1810 he died in Naples, a prisoner of the French.[14] Flaget had succeeded, however, in reaching France in a vain attempt to escape the episcopacy and in August returned to Baltimore with copies of the briefs. Egan was the first to be ordained bishop, on October 28, at St. Peter's Cathedral, then Cheverus on November 1, in the same church, and finally Flaget, on November 4, in St. Patrick's Church at Fells Point. Neale and one or another of the new bishops or bishops-elect acted as Carroll's assistants.[15]

Metropolitan Burdens

The bishops remained in Baltimore a few weeks to plan the future of the new province. They formulated a series of regulations in "as strict conformity with the universal Church as our peculiar situation . . . will allow" and published those that pertained to the laity. Baptisms and marriages had to be performed in church. Theatergoing, dancing, and the reading of books harmful to faith and morals, especially novels, were deprecated. Freemasons were to be denied the sacraments.

Most of the regulations, however, pertained to the bishops and their clergy. A provincial council was to be held in two years. Frequent synods and annual episcopal visitations were judged impractical, but bishops were expected to visit all parts of their dioceses. Should the Holy See permit, the

nomination to vacant sees was reserved to the archbishop and his suffragans. Religious priests engaged in the ministry should not be removed
by their superiors against the will of the bishop. The entire mass and essential parts of the sacraments should be said in Latin. And there were others
of less consequence.[16]

The provincial council was never held. Nor were Carroll and his suffragans allowed to fill vacant sees. Nor did Carroll visit all parts of his diocese. The observance of some of the other regulations would cause difficulties. The problems of an infant church in America were hardly solved by
the creation of a province.

The bishops also issued a pastoral protesting the recent imprisonment
of Pope Pius VII by Napoleon. Then they composed a report to the pope
explaining their decision to proceed with the establishment of a metropolitan province despite the failure of the pallium, the symbol of archiepiscopal power, to arrive. They asked the pope for any special instructions
he might have, referred to the need for a procedure to fill vacant sees, and
requested all necessary faculties.[17]

This report and the American bishops' subsequent actions suggest
that in November of 1810 they decided to deal directly with the pope in the
future. When there was no response to the report and the requests included, Carroll wrote to the Propaganda for the faculties requested. But it
was the only communication of an American bishop with that body from
the end of 1810 until the end of 1814.[18] In 1813 the archbishop and his suffragans addressed another letter to the pope, touching again the matter of
vacant sees and requesting routine faculties.[19] Again there was no response.
Carroll was told that the pope had received the bishops' communications
but was unable to respond. The chaotic affairs of the Old World frustrated
an apparent attempt to bypass the Propaganda. When the pope was finally
freed in 1814 by the fall of Napoleon, a crisis in the nomination of American
bishops, which will be considered later, plus the Propaganda's complaint of
Carroll's failure to keep it informed, compelled the archbishop to resume
contact with that Roman body.

The suffragan sees, it seemed, only added to Carroll's burdens. As
metropolitan he was still obliged to play an appellate role in the conflicts of
priests and bishops. With no precedents to fall back on, moreover, the new
bishops quite naturally looked to Carroll for counsel and support. Boston
and Bardstown posed few problems. Under Flaget, in fact, the latter produced a variety of churches and institutions that rivaled those of Baltimore.
New York and Philadelphia, however, proved as worrisome as in the days
of a single diocese.

No attempt was made during the pope's imprisonment to fill the see of New York. Carroll appointed one of the Jesuits sent from Russia, Anthony Kohlmann, administrator. It was a wise choice. Among other things, Kohlmann began a college for boys and brought Ursulines from Ireland to open an academy for girls. Carroll gave as a reason for assigning Kohlmann to New York the extension of the Society of Jesus, "a thing much to be desired."[20] He soon perceived, however, the impossibility of its operating two colleges with the resources at hand. "Which of the two must be abandoned?" he asked the Jesuit superior at Georgetown. "Here there can be no hesitation."[21] The New York college was suppressed, much to the chagrin of Kohlmann, who believed strongly that the Jesuits' center of gravity in America should shift from the Potomac to the Hudson.

In Philadelphia the difficulties Bishop Egan encountered with both the trustees and the co-pastors of the cathedral parish, William Vincent Harold and James Harold, nephew and uncle, not only drove him to distraction but literally to the grave despite Carroll's efforts at peacekeeping.[22] Finding a successor for Egan would prove as protracted and distressing as finding one for Concanen in New York.

In New Orleans DuBourg won less than a victory in his first tilt with the redoubtable Sedella. Something of what he was up against can be seen in the fact that when he went abroad to seek help in 1815, the Propaganda instructed Carroll to tell Sedella that he must obey the man DuBourg had left in charge.[23] In the Virgin Islands a predominantly Irish population refused to accept the French priest Carroll had named to replace the Irish prefect who had died in 1814. Reluctantly Carroll granted faculties to the priest favored by the Irish, Jeremy O'Flynn (or Flynn), a Trappist who had left his monastery without permission.[24]

Other Worries

Closer to home, Carroll was frustrated in his attempt to complete his cathedral. An act for a second lottery had passed in 1811, but the War of 1812 intervened. Additional parishes were needed in both the capital and the see city. In Washington Daniel Carroll of Duddington and Nicholas Young donated land in the eastern part of the city for a church and a cemetery, and the Barrys, Brents, Carrolls, and other families subscribed generously. But the project bogged down in details.[25] In Baltimore two wealthy Irishmen, Luke Tiernan and John Walsh, proposed a parish largely for the Irish and named two Irish Dominicans in Philadelphia, William Vincent Harold and John Ryan, as possible co-pastors. In 1813 Carroll gave a guarded consent.[26]

With Egan's death, however, the two Dominicans entertained other plans. At St. Mary's College DuBourg had built in 1806–8 a gem of a church, and its *chapelle basse* served a mixed congregation of English-speaking whites, French-speaking whites, and French-speaking blacks, mostly the dispossessed of Saint-Domingue.

There were also French-speaking parishioners at St. Mary's in Charleston, South Carolina. Partly for their sake and partly to keep Gallagher in line, or possibly to ease him out, Carroll sent Joseph-Pierre Picot de Limoelan de Clorivière. Before his escape to America in 1803, Clorivière had been an officer of the King's Guard and a member of the "Infernal Machine" that had plotted Napoleon's assassination. In 1808 he entered St. Mary's Seminary and in 1812 was ordained. In Charleston, however, he drove French Bonapartists and Irish republicans into such a frenzy that the former threatened to kill him at the altar. With the restoration of his beloved Bourbons in 1814, Clorivière defused a powder keg by returning to France, a move he would later regret.[27] Gallagher used his departure as an excuse to request an assistant, an Irish Augustinian, Robert Browne. Though Browne was badly needed at Savannah and at Locust Grove in Georgia, where a colony of Marylanders had settled, Carroll acquiesced, in the process lighting the fuse for an explosion under his successor.

Trouble with the Jesuits

Carroll's later years were troubled most, perhaps, by the differences that developed between himself and the Society of Jesus after the death of Molyneux in 1808. Charles Neale, Molyneux's successor, went out of his way to demonstrate his independence. He reassigned members without consulting Carroll. Carroll in turn called a young Jesuit, Enoch Fenwick, to take the place of Francis Beeston, who had died in 1810, as his secretary and rector of the cathedral. Neale objected loudly that it was a violation of his right. "I hope that your Rev[eren]ce from a Friend, will never turn prosecutor," he wrote.[28] He also protested the bishops' regulation of 1810 that a religious superior could not reassign one of his subjects without the ordinary's consent.[29] Carroll's complaints to the general in Russia resulted in Neale's being replaced by John Grassi, whom the general had sent over the previous year.

In the beginning Grassi proved as deferential as Carroll could wish. He also assumed the presidency of Georgetown College, with "great improvement," as Carroll noted, "in the number of students and course of studies."[30] But Carroll soon had reason to complain of, and to, Grassi. The new superior was overly anxious for the Society to gain complete control of the properties of the Corporation, and thus antagonized members of the Select Body who had no ties with the Jesuits. One was Germain Barnaby Bitouzey, Ashton's successor at White Marsh. Bitouzey railed against the invasion of the "Russian Association" when Grassi sent the Jesuit novices to White Marsh without prior agreement. "Should those who choose not to swear obedience to a foreign master," he asked Carroll, "be deprived of equitable and legal rights?"[31] Carroll warned Grassi against stirring up "anti Jesuitical clergymen" by moving too fast. He also warned against the presumptuous language and premature "pretensions" of some of his associates, and by implication of Grassi himself.[32] Until a full restoration was effected, Carroll told the Jesuit superior in England, he considered members of the Society secular priests and subject to the bishop.[33]

Even when he received word in December 1814 of the complete restoration by a papal bull dated August 7, 1814, Carroll congratulated Grassi but added: "The restoration of the Society to its antient [sic] perfect state must be the effect of time."[34] On the one hand, Carroll was fearful that the Jesuits from abroad were not sufficiently acquainted with the American mind and method. On the other, he was well aware that American Jesuits had imbibed but imperfectly the spirit and constitutions of the Society. Francis Neale, the novice master, had never been a novice in the Society himself, and Charles Neale, who would three times be chosen superior, had been no more than a novice at the time of the suppression and knew so little of the laws of the Society that he owned property till the day he died and willed it to his family.[35]

Neither the native-born nor the alien members of the Society could appreciate Carroll's caution. When Grassi accused him of coldness to the Jesuits, Carroll retorted that his feelings had risen "almost to indignation." He reminded Grassi that he alone had taken the necessary steps to save the Jesuit estates, that he alone had raised Georgetown College for the Society, that he alone had exercised the constant vigilance needed to preserve both, and that he alone had negotiated the affiliation with the Russian remnant.[36] Not alone, perhaps, but his efforts in behalf of the Jesuits were of such magnitude that there may well have been no Society in America without them.

Carroll's communications with Grassi, nevertheless, had always fallen somewhere between advice and mandate. Since he believed none of the Jesuits from Europe "discerning enough to estimate the difference between the American character; and that of the Countries, which they left," he intended to continue his direction.[37] Grassi, on his part, was eager to have a clearcut determination of the properties, powers, and privileges of the Society. He pressed the archbishop to fix the congregations that would in the future be exclusively committed to the Society. "To do this correctly," Carroll answered evasively, "requires a joint conference with Bp. Neale, you and some more of the Brethren."[38] Such a conference was not held in the six months of life left the first archbishop.

Sulpician Growth

Like the Jesuits, the Sulpicians had grown steadily. Convinced that neither St. Mary's College nor Georgetown College could be depended upon as feeders for the seminary, however, Charles Nagot, the superior, had accepted the loan of a farm called Pigeon Hill near Conewago in Pennsylvania and with a fellow Sulpician, John Dilhet, began a preparatory seminary with ten teenagers, mostly sons of nearby farmers. In 1807 DuBourg, ever the man of great enterprises, had offered all that remained of his patrimony, nearly $3,000, to build a permanent *petit seminaire* on land that John Dubois had purchased near Emmitsburg. Dubois, who had long wanted to join the Sulpicians, was delighted. As DuBourg's agent he began the construction. In April 1809 eighteen students from Pigeon Hill and Baltimore were lodged in the new building on the mountain. A second was begun, but DuBourg withdrew from the project when his patrimony was exhausted. Simon Bruté de Remur arrived in 1812, and from then until Dubois's elevation to the episcopacy in 1826 Mount St. Mary's, as the seminary was called, was a two-man operation.[39]

Economic necessity created the college associated with the seminary. From the beginning, Dubois accepted students whose vocation to the priesthood was dubious at best. The military threat to Baltimore during the War of 1812 proved a boon to the inland college. Brothers of the girls at Mother Seton's academy nearby were enrolled in increasing numbers. By 1815, when Mount St. Mary's Seminary was granted a degree of autonomy by the Sulpician superior in Paris, it was plain that the archdiocese had its third college for young men.[40]

The Sisterhoods

Even more spectacular than the growth of the Jesuits and Sulpicians and their colleges was the development of religious communities of women and Catholic academies for girls.

Carmelites from Hoogstraet in Flanders had planted the first convent in the United States at Port Tobacco in Charles County in 1790. Native to the county were the superior, Mother Bernardine Matthews, and her two nieces, who were also nieces of Leonard, Charles, and Francis Neale. Vocations to this strictly cloistered community were never wanting. In 1793, with no prior consultation, Carroll obtained an indult from Rome for the nuns to teach. Their spiritual director, Charles Neale, refused to permit this deviation from their contemplative rule.[41] Carroll would have to look elsewhere for religious teachers for girls.

Carroll had hoped to induce English or Irish sisters to come and open academies, but the first school for girls was begun at Georgetown in 1799 by Poor Clare Sisters from France. When their superior died in 1804, the others sold all they had to Leonard Neale and returned to France. Neale entrusted the school to a group of pious ladies who had followed him from Philadelphia in the hope of being formed into a religious congregation. The uncertainty as to the kind of sisters they would be ended with the discovery of the rule of the Sisters of the Visitation among the books left by the Poor Clares. Attempts thereafter to nudge them in other directions were unavailing.[42]

While the Carmelites were strictly cloistered and the Visitation Sisters, or Visitandines, semicloistered, the Sisters of Charity of Emmitsburg enjoyed all the flexibility of their counterparts in France. The Emmitsburg sisterhood had its beginning with the appearance of a small, frail widow and her three daughters (two sons were at Georgetown) at St. Mary's Chapel the day it was dedicated, June 16, 1808. William DuBourg had persuaded Elizabeth Ann Bayley Seton to break with Protestant relatives in New York and open a school near the seminary in Baltimore. In a house still standing on Paca Street she began classes with seven pupils in September. "It is expected that I shall be the mother of many daughters," she wrote her sister-in-law in October.[43]

DuBourg fashioned the sisterhood. On June 1, 1809, Mother Seton and four companions put on the habit, in effect, the widow's weeds Elizabeth had worn since the death of her husband in 1803, two years before her own conversion to the Catholic Church. Toward the end of June, Mother Seton herself led the first group to Emmitsburg, where land had been acquired by one of the persons who had fallen under her spell, and the next month the rest followed Sister Rose Landry White, herself a widowed mother, a native of Baltimore, and the ablest of Mother Seton's associates. They called themselves the Sisters of Charity of St. Joseph and followed a rule close to that of the Daughters of Charity that Flaget had brought from France. There was the prospect of eventual union with the French body, but the mother made it clear that her children would always come first, a priority accepted by her Sulpician directors.[44]

Elizabeth Seton, however, was not happy with the direction of John Baptist David, the Sulpician placed over her sisterhood after the departure of DuBourg. She complained often to Carroll, who, caught in the middle, urged resignation. In 1811 David left with Flaget for Kentucky. In time the mother came to recognize the virtues of the rough-hewn John Dubois, David's successor, and thus began a long and fruitful association between the Mountain and the Valley, as their respective institutions were familiarly known. Together the two ran a first-rate school for girls.[45]

Academies for the well-to-do were not part of the original plan. As Carroll had explained to his own sisters in the spring of 1809, the sisterhood soon to be organized was "to aid the poor by their work and industry, to nurse the sick and perform for them all kinds of necessary attention and care."[46] Five years later he wrote to David in Kentucky that it had been necessary to depart from the model, the Daughters of Charity in France, in a number of essentials, such as care of the sick.[47] Debts had to be paid. At the academy, opened in 1810, was a segregated class for poor girls in the neighborhood, which historians have been pleased to call the first parochial school, but the principal energies of the sisters were perforce directed toward the Carroll, Harper, Brent, and Barry girls. In 1814, however, the sisters at Emmitsburg were invited to staff an orphanage begun by the Catholics of Philadelphia. Under Sister Rose White a small colony took charge of this first of many institutions devoted wholly to the poor.[48]

A Changing Elite

Maryland Catholics were still thought to be wealthy, and many were. Of the nine Marylanders who owned 150 or more slaves at the time of the first federal census (1790), five were Catholics. Charles Carroll of Carrollton with 316 slaves headed the list. Daniel, the bishop's brother, had only 53. A quarter or more of those owning 50 slaves were of the bishop's faith— almost double the percentage of Catholics in the total population.[49] By the time of the War of 1812, the old Catholic aristocracy, whose activities now centered as much in town houses as in manor houses, had absorbed new strains. The Carrolls, Darnalls, Digges, Brents, Brookes, and Neales welcomed from Ireland the Barrys, Walshes, and Tiernans and from France or Saint-Domingue the Pascaults, Chatards, and Ducatels.

The position of the Catholic aristocracy was enhanced even more by its marital alliances with the European nobility. In 1803 Carroll had, with some misgivings, united in marriage Jerome Bonaparte, brother of the Emperor Napoleon, and Elizabeth Patterson, whose brother had married one of the daughters of Charles Carroll. Though the emperor had the marriage annulled for reasons of state, Madame Bonaparte, though not a Catholic, had the bishop baptize her and Jerome's son, also Jerome, and she raised him in the faith of his father.[50] Three of the beautiful Caton granddaughters of Charles Carroll would find suitable husbands in the British peerage, while the fourth, Emily Caton McTavish, would stay home to marry the British consul in Baltimore and become an even greater benefactor to the church than her grandfather was.

The Catholic aristocrats of Maryland and the District of Columbia continued to play a commanding role in the church in a number of ways. In the public positions they continued to fill, for example, they were not only able but eager to counsel, to promote, and to safeguard the interests of the church. Wealthy families continued to build and maintain chapels for the Catholics in their neighborhoods. The Carroll chapels at Doughoregan Manor and in Annapolis were the most notable, but in addition to the Boone's and Queen's chapels that survived the colonial era, the Digges, Young, Waring, Reeve, Barry, and other families provided houses of worship in the Revolutionary and early national periods. In other ways they proved generous benefactors. James Barry, for example, donated the pews for St. Patrick's in Washington in 1810.

In the early national period the distinction between a layman and a clergyman was not as clearly drawn as it would be in a later period. In their street apparel they were hardly distinguishable. Secular priests were called "Rev. Mr." or sometimes simply "Mr." Until a decade or so before the Civil War, only religious priests would be addressed as "Father." Priests were considered "gentlemen," a term used sparingly before the Age of Jackson.

The Catholic aristocracy that promoted the Maryland tradition was rooted in Whiggery, the belief in property as a social separator and in a government of and for the people but not by the people. The landowning Catholic aristocrats of Maryland were Federalists to a man, as was their archbishop. A handful of Catholic merchants, however, such as John Hillen and Luke Tiernan of Baltimore were Jeffersonians.[51] Whether Federalist or Jeffersonian Republican, Maryland Catholics were thoroughly convinced that theirs was a land blessed by God.

Architect of the Maryland Tradition

"Divine Providence," Carroll declared in one of his early sermons, "has so directed the course of human affairs . . . that now, agreeably to the dictates of our own consciences, we may sing canticles of praise to the Lord, in a country now become our own, & taking us into her protection."[52] About the time he became bishop, Carroll composed a prayer invoking divine guidance upon civil authorities from the president down that would, except for the Civil War years, continue to be said in the Catholic churches in Maryland.[53] So devoted was Carroll to American principles, especially religious freedom and separation of church and state, that until his dying day he lost no opportunity to exalt them. Alluding to the British system of government at the time of the heated question of Catholic emancipation in England, Carroll wrote Archbishop Troy of Dublin in 1808: "Our Executive never interferes in the discipline, doctrine, or regulations of any religious society. They were not consulted nor took any part in the appointment of our Bishops, or the Church of England, or Methodists."[54] Carroll never doubted the wisdom of such a course.

Bishop Carroll's panegyric on George Washington, a statesman "supereminent and unrivalled in the annals of mankind," at the time of the president's death was matched by few.[55] The willingness of Protestants to live at peace with Catholics was due in no small part to the respect they had for Carroll, "well known for his community spirit and ardent nationalism."[56] His patriotism remained above suspicion even during the War of 1812, when he made no attempt to hide his dislike for Napoleon. There was "a remarkable disinclination" among Protestant ministers, whether Republican or Federalist, "to associate the flock of John Carroll with its doomed leaders across the sea."[57]

No minister of religion contributed more to the ecumenical spirit that pervaded Maryland in the early national period than did Carroll. This he accomplished primarily by the leadership he exerted in promoting civic enterprises.[58] As early as 1782 he accepted a position on the original board of trustees of St. John's College in Annapolis and was elected its president in 1788. In his see city he played a leading role in the founding of the Library Company of Baltimore in 1795, the Baltimore Female Humane Association, the first charity school of the city, in 1798, the Maryland Society for Promoting Useful Knowledge in 1800, the Humane Impartial Society for the relief of indigent women and the Baltimore General Dispensary in 1802, and others. When not the president of these bodies, he served on their boards, which often met in the cathedral rectory. In 1803 he was elected chairman of the board of trustees of Baltimore College. Not long after the University of Maryland was rechartered in 1812, Carroll was elected provost but declined this honor because of his age.[59]

Carroll sat with other clergymen on these boards, with the leading Episcopal and Presbyterian ministers on that of the Library Company, for example, and with United Brethren, Lutheran, and Methodist ministers on that of the Female Humane Association. He developed warm friendships with several of them, particularly Rev. William Bend, rector of St. Paul's Episcopal Church. At the latter's demise in 1812, Carroll wrote the rector of St. Peter's Cathedral: "With you I lament most feelingly the death of our excellent neighbor and companion, not expecting we shall ever meet with any one in his station, with whom we shall communicate with such entire freedom, and so much concur in sentiment in all the intercourse of society."[60]

Carroll's favorite project was the Library Company of Baltimore because, he told Plowden, reading was "always my favourite employment."[61] With Bend and Rev. Patrick Allison of the First Presbyterian Church, he drew up the constitutions and was elected first president. To this position he was returned for the rest of his life. Carroll was allowed to name the librarian and, it would seem, to determine the acquisitions.[62] For most of his presidency the librarian was Rev. George Perrigny, a refugee from Saint-Domingue who also served as chaplain to Doughoregan Manor.

Fellow Catholics followed Carroll's example. What he did for Baltimore, William Matthews did largely for Washington. Pastor of St. Patrick's for fifty years, Matthews was one of the capital's best-known and most honored citizens. In 1811 he was co-founder of the city's first public library and later its president for thirteen years. In 1813 he was elected to the public school board and was for thirty years thereafter one of its most active members.[63] Catholic laymen were no less prominent in civic and philanthropic enterprises. Charles Carroll of Carrollton assumed at least honorary positions at the drop of a hat.

In 1796 the Baltimore Benevolent Society was founded, the first such Catholic organization in the United States. Its purpose was to provide, through monthly dues, insurance and retirement benefits for practicing Catholics.[64] It did not represent, as did later Catholic benevolent societies, an attempt to isolate Catholics. Baltimore's members of the Church of Rome, reflecting the pervasive spirit of civic charity, were simply imitating the other religious denominations of the city in providing for their poor, elderly, and infirm.[65] The same was true of the school established by the Abbé Moranvillé at St. Patrick's in Fells Point in 1815. The latter was, nevertheless, the first true parochial school in the archdiocese. More typical, however, were the cooperative ventures mentioned above as well as the Hibernian Society founded in 1803 through the joint efforts of Irish Catholic and Presbyterian merchants. German Catholics and Protestants also associated easily in the German Society founded some years before.

There was in Baltimore more contention within churches than between them, and the principal antagonisms between them were between high- and low-church bodies, the latter espousing the "new measures" of revivalism, or between the mainline Episcopalians and Presbyterians and the more radical Swedenborgians and Unitarians. Such differences distracted Protestants from their quarrels with Roman Catholics, who generally found high-church or mainline denominations more congenial in their beliefs and practices.[66]

Only one serious altercation between Catholics and Protestants occurred in the Carroll years. In 1811 the Maryland Presbyterians issued a pastoral letter warning Protestant parents about the proselytizing activities at St. Mary's College. DuBourg answered it in a piquant pamphlet that elicited a defense of the pastoral. DuBourg and Simon Bruté collaborated on a second satirical response, which the Presbyterians left unaddressed.[67]

In their defense of the pastoral, the Presbyterians were careful to state: "We readily acquit the present Venerable Superior of the Catholic Church for these States of any aim of insidious encroachment. Protestants within all denominations, in this native state, have long borne witness to his liberal and dignified deportment in the walks of social intercourse, in every respect congenial with the constitution, under which we all participate in equal rights." Their quarrel was with "the proprietary zealots of St. Mary's College."[68]

The Sulpicians and Jesuits were responsible for the first confraternities and sodalities in the archdiocese. It was mostly for the French-speaking blacks served at the *chapelle basse* of St. Mary's Chapel that the earliest pious confraternities were organized. Carroll himself, however, was recorded as founder of the Confraternity of Mount Carmel in 1796, but it was Flaget who established the Confraternity of the Holy Rosary in 1802, and Tessier the Confraternity of Our Lady of Good Help in 1815.[69] The first sodality was established for the students of Georgetown College about 1810. The earliest sodalities were usually organized at boys' colleges or girls' academies, such as Georgetown Visitation.[70]

Devotional societies, however, were rare in the early national period. Catholic piety was quiet and personal, of the kind imbibed from Bishop Challoner's *Garden of the Soul*.[71] Even the public liturgy of the Catholic

Church had a Protestant ring. Next to the "Eucharistical Sacrifice," a Catholic hymnal declared that "singing praises was the noblest employment of a Christian."[72] In *Masses for the Use of the Catholic Churches in the United States,* published in Baltimore in 1805, could be found the following prayer:

> Save O Lord the Commonwealth. Let the people's rights prevail.
> Let Columbia trust in thee to whom she owes her liberty.
> Voice of praise let us raise. Great Jehovah praise to thee.
> We are free thanks to thee. Father of our liberty.[73]

Catholics read their Bibles almost as much as Protestants did. Carroll himself served as agent for the dissemination of the Bibles published by Matthew Carey of Philadelphia. Catholic piety often bore a striking resemblance to that of Protestants.

Carroll did not wish Catholic worship, or the display of Catholic piety, to be a source of dissension. When "Mr. Moranvillé's fondness for pomp and shew" spilled into the streets of Fells Point for the celebration of Corpus Christi in 1811, Carroll complained to the rector of the cathedral: "We should enjoy our rights of conscience & worship, with fortitude, gratitude to God, & respect for our fellow citizens: but surely it was rash, & might have been the occasion of a riot, to go beyond his own limits, and exhibit in a public street the most Ven[era]ble Sacrament."[74] Carroll's aversion to theatergoing, particularly on Sunday, mirrored the prevailing mores sustained by almost every pulpit in Baltimore. On lotteries the churches divided, but most, including the Catholic Church, approved.[75]

Carroll wished the local church to blend imperceptibly into the social fabric. He governed a church with a minimum of institutions and organizations and had no urge to multiply strictly Catholic ones. Unlike most of his successors in Baltimore, he took no delight in the compilation of statistics. After his report to the Propaganda in 1785, he never mentioned in his correspondence the number of Catholics, churches, or priests under his jurisdiction.

Carroll soon rid himself of the fear of giving offense to the government by allowing Rome to make appointments and decisions. To a degree, it was a pretext for keeping the Propaganda at arm's length. The measure of autonomy that Carroll wished to win for the American church derived in part from a distrust of Roman authorities, particularly the Propaganda, on the part of the American Jesuits dating from the suppression. Carroll's Gallicanism may have gone deeper. Alluding to the Organic Articles of 1682 in a letter to Garnier, Carroll insisted that "if truth be, as it should, the object of Theological investigation, even those articles should be left to free inquiry, where the general voice of the Church has not determined it."[76]

The Sulpicians needed no convincing. To the United States they brought a moderate Gallicanism exemplified in the French church by Emery. It was, as Christopher Kauffman, an authority on the Sulpicians, has described it, a Gallicanism "that stressed the movement of the Holy Spirit in the *particular* national context rather than in the *centralized* authority structures of the papacy."[77] In their cautious approach to the Holy See, the earlier American Jesuits and the French Sulpicians found a common ground. The Sulpicians would prove the more consistent guardians of an attitude that Carroll incorporated into the Maryland tradition. At the same time, America's first bishop instilled in his spiritual children a deep and genuine loyalty to the person of the pope as a symbol of unity. In 1814 on the occasion of the liberation of the pope, he composed a pastoral as rhapsodic as his panegyric to Washington and ordered the Te Deum sung in all Catholic churches.[78]

Not unrelated to the Maryland tradition was the classic restraint exercised by the Catholic aristocracy of Maryland. Carroll's cultivated reserve, as one of his acquaintances noted, "restrained in others all propensity to indecorum."[79] Outside his family there was no one, except, perhaps, James and Joanna Barry, with whom he was truly intimate, and even to them he did not disclose his deepest thoughts. These he guarded jealously. At the same time, Carroll was approachable. His door was open to the mighty and the lowly alike. Even during the long hours he spent at his writing desk, he did not discourage interruptions. In the course of a letter to Mrs. Seton, he paused to hear a drunken sailor tell him of a revelation he had had to write a book. "When it comes from the press," Carroll wrote in one of his rare flashes of humor, "you will allow me to send you a copy."[80]

The Troubled Last Year

The last year of Carroll's life was perhaps his busiest and most unpleasant. His health deteriorated rapidly, causing him to decline the kind of invitations he had readily accepted, such as to open the dedicatory ceremonies for the Washington Monument in Baltimore. Management problems developed at Bohemia, his principal source of income. His relations with the Jesuit superior worsened. A resumption of correspondence with the Propaganda proved disagreeable. Though happy to report progress in Boston, Bardstown, and New York to Plowden, he added sadly: "I am the only sluggard, & do no good."[81]

The most upsetting development was a crisis in the selection of bishops for New York and Philadelphia. Carroll was startled by a letter from Archbishop Troy announcing the appointment of John Connolly, an Irish Dominican who had resided many years in Rome, as bishop of New York. To Plowden he confided: "I wish this may not become a very dangerous precedent, fruitful of mischief."[82] Soon after, he received official word from Cardinal Lorenzo Litta, prefect of the Propaganda, who also revealed that the Dominican William Vincent Harold had been recommended as Bishop Egan's successor in Philadelphia. Litta asked for Carroll's opinion on this possible appointment.[83]

After a falling out with Egan, Harold had returned to Ireland accompanied by his fellow Dominican and friend John Ryan. There they had spread "glaring falsehoods" about Carroll and his Jesuit associates, as Carroll himself had reported indignantly to Plowden in 1814, not the least of which was the Jesuits' trafficking in Negroes.[84] Carroll believed that Troy, James Harold (the uncle), and Ryan had all connived to win the bishopric of Philadelphia for William Harold. "I deprecate his appointment," Carroll wrote heatedly to Plowden, "which would be the signal of rancour religious and political; religious between the friends of the holy deceased Bp. & partisans of Harold; political, between the opponents of furious democracy, and [those who favor] innovations upon established governments, or rather those, who are always ripe for innovations, glossed over with fair pretexts of *rights of the people*."[85]

Of Archbishop Troy, Carroll asked pointedly: "Would it not be resented as a very improper interference, if we the Bps. in the U.S. should presume to suggest to the Holy See the persons to be appointed to fill Vacant Sees in Ireland?"[86] To Litta Carroll insisted that the American bishops were "greatly disturbed" by the rumors of Harold's appointment, which would arouse the "gravest dissension" in America.[87]

Carroll was not without blame in the matter of the choice of bishops for New York and Philadelphia. Though the American bishops had asked the pope in 1810 to allow vacant sees to be filled at their recommendation, Carroll had taken no action on the matter of a successor for Bishop Concanen of New York. This would undoubtedly have been on the agenda of the provincial council scheduled for November 1812. The council, however, had not been held, primarily because of the inability of Bishop Cheverus to attend. A month after the death of Bishop Egan in July 1814, however, Carroll had written Neale, Cheverus, Flaget, and the administrators of New York and Philadelphia to seek their recommendations for the bishopric of Philadelphia.[88] The majority had proposed John Baptist David, then director of the seminary in Kentucky. Carroll had not asked them for recommendations for New York because, as he later explained to Cardinal Litta, it was known that Bishop Concanen had proposed the Sulpician Ambrose Maréchal as his coadjutor. At the end of November Carroll had finally broken his long silence with the Propaganda and, among other things, forwarded to Litta the recommendations of the bishops.[89]

In the fall of 1815 there was still no word of the appointment to Philadelphia. Nor had Bishop Connolly, though raised to the episcopacy the previous November, set foot in New York, where he was badly needed. Carroll believed he was waiting to sail for America with Harold as bishop. Carroll died without knowing whether his protests to Litta had deflected such a course.

Toward the end of October, Carroll suffered a spell of bad health from which he knew he would not recover. On November 22 Bishop Neale came from Georgetown to help him draw his will and settle accounts. For two weeks thereafter Carroll endured the steady stream of visitors who came for a last good-bye. He died December 3, 1815, at age seventy-nine, on the feast of the great Jesuit missionary St. Francis Xavier.

"All Baltimore honored his memory," Simon Bruté informed the Sulpicians in Paris. "The public papers were bordered in black . . . as when Washington died."[90] His funeral, the *Baltimore Telegraph* reported, "brought together a greater crowd than we have ever witnessed on a similar occasion. The great and the rich, the poor and the lowly . . ."

"The Liberality of his character," the *Telegraph* also claimed, "and his Christian charity endeared him to his Protestant brethren, with whom he dwelt in brotherly love. He was a patriot and loved his native land; nor should Americans forget that his exertions and benedictions, as a man and a Christian prelate, were given to the cause of the independence of his country. His manners were mild, impressive and urbane. The various stores of knowledge came from his lips with uncommon classical grace and richness. . . . His charities were only bounded by his means, and they fell around him like the dews of heaven, gentle and unseen."[91]

3   *That Pernicious System*

"I AM AN OLD MAN OF seventy and my strength is exhausted by reason of the forty years I have spent in missionary labors," Archbishop Neale explained to Cardinal Litta two months after Carroll's death. "Hence, not wishing to excuse myself, for I desire to be sacrificed wholly in the opus Dei, I am compelled to ask for a coadjutor who will sustain me in my old age and be my aid in this great work."[1] Neale knew he would not rule the archdiocese long.

Born October 15, 1746, near Port Tobacco, Neale was not quite seventy years old. He had spent three years in the jungles of South America before returning to Maryland in 1783. In 1798, his last year in Philadelphia, he had joined the ranks of the clerical victims of yellow fever. When the Society of Jesus was reestablished in 1805, he surrendered not only the presidency of Georgetown College but also his cubicle opposite the college chapel, where each morning his bed was folded into a cupboard. He moved into a small house next to the Sisters of the Visitation, the principal focus of his interest and energies until the assumption of his archiepiscopal role. As Carroll's coadjutor he was entrusted, more or less, with the episcopal supervision of the southern counties of Maryland. Neale traveled even fewer miles than Carroll, leading an almost eremitic life. When he succeeded Carroll on December 3, 1815, he was a feeble recluse. He remained in his hermitage in Georgetown, visiting his see city no more than two or three times in the one year, six months, and fifteen days left to him. Bishop Cheverus bestowed the pallium on the second archbishop on November 19, 1816, in Holy Trinity Church in Georgetown because Neale was unable to travel to Baltimore.[2]

Though Neale sought a coadjutor at once, he did not live long enough to know if Rome had approved the man upon whom all had finally agreed. His first choice was Cheverus, but Cheverus did not wish to leave Boston. The Propaganda itself suggested Ambrose Maréchal, who had begged that his appointment as bishop of Philadelphia be rescinded.[3] Neale accepted the suggestion with "great joy" and named Maréchal his vicar general in January, 1817. "I formerly told you that you would be damnatus ad bestias," he told Maréchal, "& now you see it verified. Be not disturbed if A[lmighty] God has chosen you for trials. He tries those he means to favor."[4]

Sterner Measures

On February 4, 1816, Neale sent a circular to his priests, the closest he came to a pastoral letter, on the observance of Lent. He took the occasion to exhort them to lead truly priestly lives, to avoid frequent contact with seculars, and not to neglect daily meditation, spiritual reading, the study of theology, and the instruction of children. He condemned the "many" priests who had abandoned the sacerdotal life as a disgrace to the church and a scandal to the faithful.[5] The exhortation betokened a different kind of episcopal leadership from Carroll's.

Despite his debility Neale proved a decisive administrator. In his first days as ordinary he moved to remedy the abuses Carroll had tolerated. Two priests in Maryland notorious for drunkenness he called to account. A church allowed by its congregation to fall into disrepair he interdicted.[6] Determined to replace clergymen of dubious character with worthy priests, in distant parts of his jurisdiction he designated three new French pastors of largely Irish congregations. In each instance the change proved disastrous.

At St. Croix he revoked the faculties Carroll had granted the popular O'Flynn and replaced him with the Abbé Matthew Herard. To Norfolk, where the congregation had worked in relative harmony with its pastor, Michael Lacy, for twelve years before his death in 1815, Neale sent a young priest recently arrived from France, James Lucas, who barely spoke English. Joseph Clorivière, the Bourbon partisan, had repented his return to France and had come back to reclaim the pastorate in Charleston. In Gallagher's absence Neale named Clorivière the sole pastor and instructed Robert Browne, the Augustinian, to return to Augusta. When Gallagher counseled Browne to stay in Charleston, Neale expelled Browne from the archdiocese and suspended Gallagher on charges of drunkenness. Evidence for this he had quickly gathered from several sources, including Maréchal. The repercussions, as Neale doubtless expected, were not long in coming.[7]

The Irish members of the three congregations complained bitterly not only of the nationality of their new pastors and their inability to preach but also of their cupidity. They also objected, though not to Rome, to their politics. Irish Jeffersonians and French royalists of the Bourbon persuasion mixed like oil and water. A supporter of Clorivière complained to Neale that Browne was not only a "Democrat" but a "Bonapartist."[8] Finally, none of the three priests chosen by Neale had what could be called winning personalities.

The Trustees Fight Back

Neale was determined not only to rid his diocese of priests he deemed unworthy but also to eliminate the trusteeism that nurtured them. "Your uncouth reception & treatment from the trustees," he consoled Lucas, "are nothing but harsh mementoes of the impropriety of lay trusteeship which I have always been inimical to, & henceforward as far as I can prevent that pernicious system, I shall not fail to do it, *as I stand fully convinced that great evils must eventually flow from it, wherever it is established.*"[9]

In Norfolk Neale provoked a formidable antagonist, not an Irishman but a learned Portuguese physician, Dr. John Francis Oliveira Fernandez. The latter put pen to paper and produced, among other things, a *Letter Addressed to the Most Reverend Leonard Neale, Archbishop of Baltimore.* By an appeal to church history and Febronian principles, the doctor sought to invest the Norfolk trustees in particular and trustees in general with all the rights of *jus patronatus*, the power to choose and in matters temporal to control the pastor.[10] The *Letter* was, according to one historian, "the most theoretical assertion of the rights of laymen over the clergy that appeared during the trustee controversy."[11] Upon its rationale the trustees obtained a court injunction against the use of the church building by Lucas and his supporters. Neale instructed Lucas that his opponents were to be treated as schismatics and their church interdicted. At the same time, he chided the pastor for acts of imprudence and cautioned him to "avoid all bickerings & disputes."[12]

In the meantime, Browne from Charleston and O'Flynn from St. Croix had gone to Rome to plead their respective causes. In Browne's absence Gallagher wavered and went finally to Georgetown to seek a reconciliation. Neale persuaded him to go first to New York to make a retreat under Bishop Connolly, after which he would absolve him from censure. In January 1817, however, Gallagher traveled to Georgetown and triumphantly laid in Neale's hand a letter from Cardinal Litta that Browne had forwarded from Rome. Neale was instructed to send all documents concerning the case of Gallagher and Browne to the Propaganda, to remove Clorivière, and to reinstate Gallagher and Browne in Charleston while the case was pending. The cardinal prefect also informed Neale of the complaints from St. Croix and admonished him to lay aside his pro-French bias and send Irish or American priests to the islands.[13]

Bewildered and angry, Neale sent first a long complaint to the pope. "Most Holy Father, is it thus the faith is propagated?" he asked. "I can scarcely believe that such an order emanated from the Holy See, or surely if it did emanate, it must have been obtained surreptitiously: for by this course the door is opened for every rebellion in this distant country, and means are given, as I think, for the destruction of religion. . . . "[14] A week later he wrote Litta in like vein. The trustees of Charleston, he insisted, were for the most part men of lax lives imbued with a false spirit of democracy that recognized no authority but their own. Rebellious Catholics were saying that they could obtain anything they wished from the Propaganda because the archbishop of Baltimore was not in favor there. Neale declared boldly that his conscience would not allow him to obey this mandate from the Holy See. He suggested, in addition, that the Virgin Islands be assigned to the archbishop of Dublin. A packet of supporting documents accompanied his twelve-page letter.[15]

Neale instructed Clorivière to remain in Charleston and refused to reinstate Gallagher and Browne until he received a response from Rome. He persuaded the Jesuit superior, Anthony Grassi, to go to Rome to plead his case and asked the other American bishops and the administrator of the diocese of Philadelphia to write in his behalf to the Propaganda. All but Connolly complied.[16]

Some two months later Lucas relayed to Neale the news from Clorivière that the Norfolk trustees had contacted those of Charleston in the hope of obtaining a priest through Gallagher or Browne. A coalition between the two groups was taking shape.[17] Soon after, the vestrymen of Norfolk sent directly a *Petition to the Holy See*. It alluded to the trouble in the Virgin Islands and South Carolina occasioned by "the wild extravagance and incorrigible obstinancy of the present Archbishop of Baltimore" and added the afflictions of Norfolk to the "tide of universal complaint." Irishmen, the vestrymen contended, constituted the great majority of Catholics in America and had contributed more than their share to the growth of the church. Yet, ambitious French priests, whose audacity had been held in check by the "mild disposition of Archbishop Carroll," were now forced upon them and the rights of patronage denied them. The vestrymen asked that Virginia be made a diocese and that Thomas Carbry, a Dominican priest in New York, be named its bishop.[18] The petition was taken to Rome by two Norfolk trustees, who carried also an elaborate plan of government that included a representative assembly of pastors and laymen. Both petition and plan were obviously the work of Dr. Oliveira Fernandez, who sent along a personal letter to Cardinal Litta with a request for a private chapel.[19]

In the meantime, both pope and Propaganda had responded to the archbishop's letters of complaint. Neale was at liberty, said the pope, "to proceed with full discretionary powers against the said Gallagher and his associate Robert Browne, for we have resolved to approve and maintain whatever measures you have adopted."[20] Though apologetic, the Propaganda pointed out to Neale that he had failed to send the report it had requested on the condition of his diocese.[21] The two missives would not reach Neale before his death. The apparent triumph, moreover, would be seriously diminished under his successor by Rome's response to the Norfolk petition.

While he moved with vigor against the troublesome trustees in distant parts, Neale ignored the peaceful ones in his own state. The cathedral trustees, in fact, enjoyed a freedom of action unknown before or since. Unlike Carroll, Neale attended none of the meetings of the board of trustees, of which he was a legal member. Presumably he gave his distant blessing to its plans to resume construction of the cathedral and open free schools, but the minutes contain no reference to his views. With contracts renegotiated, the building recommenced in the spring of 1817. For two schools separate boards of men and women launched subscriptions at the beginning of the year. The girls' school was opened in February and the boys' in December 1817.[22]

The Neale-Grassi Agreement

Unlike Carroll, Neale was disposed to grant the Jesuits anything they wanted. On April 3, 1816, Neale and Grassi, the Jesuit superior, signed "an arrangement . . . regulating the Missions of the said Society within this Diocese." It encompassed all the Jesuit estates of southern Maryland and the Eastern Shore and their outlying missions as well as St. Ignatius in Harford County. Frederick Town and its dependent missions were restored to the Society. The congregations of Georgetown and Alexandria, St. Patrick's in Washington City, and the congregations of Queen's Chapel and Rock Creek were also "assigned and given to be permanently in the spiritual care of the Religious of the Society of Jesus, according to their Institute." If no Jesuits were available for these missions, the superior would employ secular priests. And if these could not be found, application would be made to the archbishop to determine what means could be taken to meet the needs of the missions in question.[23]

A list was drawn by Neale and Grassi that enumerated thirty-two congregations in Maryland and the District of Columbia and fourteen in Pennsylvania. The latter, of course, were outside Neale's jurisdiction.[24] Omitted were the Harford congregation and Frederick Town and its dependencies. These, however, as well as a considerable number of other churches in western Maryland appear in a catalogue of the Society of Jesus representing the conditions in 1817. An almost identical list was preserved by the archbishop.[25] From the three lists it can be determined which congregations and missions the Jesuits claimed as their own in Maryland and the District of Columbia in consequence of the Neale-Grassi agreement.

White Marsh and missions (Prince George's County):
1. White Marsh
2. Annapolis [Carroll Chapel in Anne Arundel County]
3. Young's Chapel
4. Boone's Chapel
5. Digges' Chapel
6. Piscataway
7. Mattawoman

St. Thomas Manor and missions (Charles County):
1. St. Thomas Manor
2. Pomphret
3. Cornwallis Neck
4. Cedar Point (no church)
5. Chickamuxen (no church)
6. Newport
7. Cobb Neck
8. Upper Zachia [Waldorf]
9. Lower Zachia [Bryantown]

Newtown and St. Inigoes and missions (St. Mary's County):
1. Newtown
2. Our Lady of Medley's Neck
3. St. John
4. St. Aloysius [Leonardtown]
5. St. Joseph
6. Sacred Heart
7. Trans-Patuxent mission [Calvert County]

8. St. Inigoes
9. St. Nicholas
Georgetown College missions (District of Columbia):
   1. St. Patrick
   2. Queen's Chapel
   3. College Church [Holy Trinity]
   4. Alexandria
   5. Rock Creek
Bohemia and mission (Eastern Shore):
   1. Bohemia
   2. St. Joseph[26]
Harford County
   1. St. Ignatius
Frederick Town and missions (Western Maryland):
   1. Frederick Town
   2. Carroll Manor
   3. Hagerstown
   4. Cumberland and Arnold's Settlement
   5. Maryland Tract [Petersville]
   6. Fifteen Mile Creek [Little Orleans]
   7. Libery Town "et aliae"[27]

Apparently all had churches except the two in Charles County designated in the Neale-Grassi agreement as churchless and three or four of the dependencies of Frederick Town. It is doubtful also that Calvert County had a church. These worshiping communities, where mass was said in private homes, would come to be called stations.

By Neale's death in 1817 only eleven congregations in Maryland and the District of Columbia would remain officially outside Jesuit control:

Baltimore:
   1. Cathedral
   2. St. Patrick
   3. St. John
   4. St. Mary's Chapel
Emmittsburg:
   1. St. Joseph
   2. Mountain Church
Doughoregan Manor: St. Mary's Chapel
Taneytown: St. Joseph
Westminster: Corpus Christi

Barnesville: St. Mary
Rockville: St. Mary

Though on paper the Society of Jesus could claim forty of the fifty-one (or more) parochial congregations in Maryland and the District, it never effectively exercised control over such churches as St. Partick's in Washington or St. Mary's in Hagerstown and would in a few years surrender most of the missions of Georgetown and Frederick Town as well as St. Ignatius in Harford County. In time the chapels maintained by wealthy families would also be closed, and three or four of the small congregations in the southern counties would disappear as populations shifted or shrunk. What remained, however, was still an impressive list. The nearly sixty congregations in Maryland, Pennsylvania, Virginia, and the District of Columbia, not to mention Georgetown College, placed a tremendous burden on twenty-four Jesuit priests and the half dozen secular priests they employed. At least six of the twenty-four were engaged full time as teachers or scholastic or novice masters. The reasons for the Society's willingness, even eagerness, to assume such a burden are not easy to fathom.

While accommodating so magnanimously the Society to which he had belonged, Neale had, in contrast to Carroll, little to do with their internal affairs. Though president of Georgetown College for seven years, he left the direction of that institution entirely to the Jesuits. In 1815 the college was incorporated by an act of Congress, and in 1817 the annual commencements began. The control of Bohemia Neale returned to the Society and settled for an annuity of $1,000.[28]

Bad News and Good

In granting control of so many congregations to the Jesuits, Neale doubtless assumed that they would be better, or at least more dependably, served than by secular priests. Unable to make diocesan visitations, he had to depend on the reports of his priests. These were infrequent and not always encouraging. Money was a recurrent problem. A recently ordained priest assigned to St. Ignatius in Harford County complained that the congregation was too poor to support a resident pastor, but he had spoken about money only once "lest if I should touch them on that point, it might prevent the good I might do among them."[29]

Francis Malevé, the Belgian Jesuit Carroll had sent to Frederick Town when Dubois moved to Emmittsburg, had taken to the rugged slopes like a duck to water. There were, he told his Jesuit superior, "9 or 10 other congregations, 30, 50, 100 miles from Frederick, where I may go and run as much as I please through woods and mountains, at my own expences [*sic*], I may say, because very little come through these affar [*sic*] congr[egations]." Malevé complained that the pastor of Taneytown had married two wealthy residents of Liberty, one of his missions, and had received as stipends more than he himself received from the whole congregation of Frederick.[30] James Redmond, a former Jesuit, reported to Neale that the four congregations of Montgomery County—Rock Creek, Rockville, Waring's Chapel, and Barnesville—had engaged to pay the priest who would settle in the central part of the county $100 a year each. The congregation at Rockville had incorporated in 1816 in order to build a church, and one was completed in 1817.[31]

There were encouraging developments. The sisterhoods grew under Neale. As archbishop he was more than ever determined to end a process he had begun more than fifteen years before. In his first letter to Rome as archbishop, Neale asked that the religious community in Georgetown be officially recognized as a house of the Visitation order founded by St. Francis de Sales. On December 28, 1816, soon after the indult from Rome arrived, he received the solemn vows of Mother Theresa (Alice) Lalor, her assistant, and the novice mistress. The next month the remaining thirty-two sisters were professed. Only then did Neale write to the motherhouse in France seeking affiliation. He asked also that experienced sisters be sent over to help form the American branch in the true spirit of the order. The house in Paris sent books about the order, forty silver crosses, and a doll wearing an exact replica of the Visitation habit. It would be a decade and more before the experienced sisters arrived.[32]

The direction of the Carmelites he left entirely to his brother Charles and that of the Sisters of Charity to John Dubois. The latter body had in 1815 been incorporated, its ends defined as "works of piety, charity, and usefulness, especially for the care of the sick, the succor of the aged, infirm, and necessitous persons, and the education of young females." As a further commitment to the works of charity the Sisters opened an orphanage at the motherhouse in 1816 and sent a colony to staff an orphanage in New York in 1817, their second mission outside Maryland.[33]

The Brief but Calamitous Rule

On May 31, 1817, Archbishop Neale ordained two Jesuits, one of them John McElroy, and two diocesan priests at Holy Trinity Church. It was his last public act. On June 16 he finished mass in the Visitation chapel and told the mother superior that he thought his end was near. That day he lapsed into a coma and died quietly in the early hours of June 18. He was buried the next day after a simple requiem in the tiny convent cemetery.[34]

Except among the sisters, his passing caused no outpouring of grief. Neale was not a popular bishop. The Jesuit Brother Joseph Mobberly said of him: "In his transactions with the foolish world, he was too candid to be agreeable. He never courted the applause of men, and never had much esteem for those who did. In his manners he was plain and simple, not elegant. He was polite without ceremony. He was a great enemy to insincerity and was extremely rough toward those who, he believed, intended to practice fraud. . . . He always supported his authority with vigor, and enforced regularity of life in very strong terms." Yet Mobberly found much to admire in Neale—his sermons, for example. "He wrote nothing and prepared nothing, for it seems he was always prepared." And perhaps his greatest compliment: "I never saw him embarrassed."[35] Not even his enemies denied that he was a pious and conscientious prelate.

In terms of the long-range consequences of his policies, however, Leonard Neale's brief rule must be judged calamitous. In the first place, he set in motion currents of ethnic discord, albeit inadvertently, that would not be stilled for almost a century. Secondly, and perhaps more important, his course of action made it virtually impossible for the trustee system to continue to operate in the American Catholic Church with any degree of effectiveness. While it may be argued that ethnic discord and "trustee-mania" were already on the scene and would have reached crisis proportions without Neale, his inflexible policy toward "that pernicious system" and its practitioners forestalled any possibility in the future of assuaging the discord or saving the system. So restricted were the options he bequeathed his successors that the process was irreversible.

Until the worth and potential of the laity was rediscovered in the post-Vatican II years, the passing of trusteeism was judged a blessing by American Catholic historians. John Gilmary Shea, a dutiful son of the church, was the principal creator of the myth of a malevolent system. Peter Guilday would impose his own elaboration of "lay interference": that of the paramount role of "national preference."[36] These historians, however, wrote in an age when a larger-than-life portrayal of American bishops was needed to sustain an embattled church. The troublesome trustees of the port cities were limned in darkest colors to render the victors even more heroic. Rarely was there an acknowledgment that these noisy vestrymen were the exception and that the majority of trustees, as was certainly the case in Maryland, performed their duties conscientiously and well.

The quarrelsome trustees were not evil men bent on the destruction of the church but Catholics with genuine concerns about its role in the new republic. Though few, if any, were as radical in their views as Dr. Oliveira Fernandez, the greatest number, perhaps, were convinced of the need for the church to adopt American models.[37] True, many were not models themselves of sobriety and good sense, but their intemperate language at least was as much a convention of the age as a display of bad temper. As often as not, moreover, the crisis was provoked by a problem priest who encouraged rebellion as a shield for his own aberrant behavior. It had been Carroll's policy to remove or reform the problem priest and trust to time, as at St. John's in Baltimore, to dissipate the ill will he had generated among the trustees. In New York, Philadelphia, and Charleston also Carroll had weathered crises. Despite the claim of the third archbishop and later historians, he had never come to regret his promotion of the trustee arrangement.[38] Time and patience were his solution to the excesses of the system.

The views of Edward Lynah, Carroll's confidant and former critic of Gallagher in Charleston, are instructive. In 1816 he wrote Neale that the conduct of Gallagher and Browne had been misrepresented to him. Lynah offered his own help, an offer ignored, to restore "that love and harmony that ought to reign amongst all good Christians."[39] After Neale's death he would write to Rome and compare Neale's handling of the Charleston controversy unfavorably with that of Carroll. The "Christian and benign spirit" of the latter, Lynah claimed, "tried always to heal," while Neale made small allowance for weakness and frailty.[40]

It was not inevitable that French pastors and Irish congregations clash, as the peaceful tenure of Moranvillé at St. Patrick's in Baltimore demonstrated. Given the autocratic temper of Clorivière and Lucas, however, one is almost tempted to conclude that it was Neale's design in appointing them to provoke rebellion and thereby discredit the system. But Neale was not a devious person, and so far as is known, was devoid of national prejudices.

Temperamentally as unlike Carroll as he could be, Neale, had he lived longer, would probably have made further inroads into the Maryland tradition than undermining the place accorded the laity by Carroll. There is little evidence that he was overly patriotic, civic minded, or ecumenical. Only in his attitude toward the Holy See did he resemble his predecessor.

Aloof, single-minded, and inflexible Leonard Neale certainly was. At the same time, he was a man of courage, unintimidated by a formidable opposition, unafraid to speak his mind, even to the pope. He was also one of those rare individuals in positions of power in the church who lived in penury and was beyond caring about his image in the eyes of others.

Though Neale had entrusted four-fifths of the missions of Maryland and the District of Columbia to the Society of Jesus, his passing effectively ended Jesuit dominance in the affairs of the oldest see. He was succeeded by a Sulpician who would devote a large part of his waking hours to the reduction of the power and influence of the Society of Jesus. Neale's death coincided also with the passing of the Revolutionary generation and its preoccupation with constitutions, personal rights, and parties. The inauguration of James Monroe as president in 1817 marked the beginning of the Era of Good Feelings, whose interests lay more with commerce than politics. The nation stood at the threshold of ambitious enterprises, of which Maryland would be a principal beneficiary: internal improvements that would open up the riches of the West, a tariff that would stimulate the growth of industry, and a banking system that would encourage sizable investments. In 1816 Baltimore, the third city in the nation, had pushed its borders outward to treble its geographic size.[41]

The Catholic Church had never enjoyed a more secure and respected position on the American scene than it did at the beginning of the Era of Good Feelings. The church that Carroll built was as confident and as optimistic as the nation in its growth, and its nerve center remained the city of Baltimore.

4   *Chosen for Trials*

THE BULLS APPOINTING Ambrose Maréchal titular bishop of Stauropolis and coadjutor with right of succession to the archbishop of Baltimore, dated July 4, 1817, did not reach Baltimore until November 10. On December 14 he was raised to the episcopacy by Bishop Cheverus, assisted by Bishop Connolly of New York and Rev. Louis de Barth, administrator of Philadelphia. He became by right of succession third archbishop of Baltimore, the first of four of foreign birth to occupy the premier see.

Born December 4, 1768, at Ingre in the diocese of Orléans, Maréchal had been destined for the study of law but chose instead the priesthood. Surrounded by the fury of the Revolution, he was ordained March 25, 1792, in the library of the Irish College in Paris and the following day fled to America. His first mass was said in Baltimore.[1] Most of his first eleven years in America were spent in parochial work, but he was teaching theology at the seminary in Baltimore when recalled to France in 1803. Unhappy with the change, he kept in contact with friends in the States and was consulted by Richard Luke Concanen, who wanted him for his coadjutor in New York.[2] With the temporary suppression of the Sulpicians in France in 1811, he seized the opportunity to return to St. Mary's Seminary. At his own insistence, the bulls for his appointment to the see of Philadelphia were revoked. With reluctance he accepted those for Baltimore. At least he would be near his beloved seminary.

Taking Stock

One of Maréchal's initial acts as archbishop was to publish for the first time the decrees of the first synod and the bishops' regulations of 1810. To these he appended directives of his own touching adult baptism and mixed marriages and prohibiting attendance at Protestant services and the erection of churches without his consent.[3] In the spring of 1818 he began an extensive visitation of the archdiocese.

Among the records Maréchal kept faithfully were notebooks to which he entrusted all the significant data gleaned in his visitations.[4] At Lower

Zachia, for example, he noted that those confirmed were well instructed. "The church decent but the grave yard without fence. The house & about 40 acres of land annexed to it, have been rented by the trustees for the yearly rent of $60."⁵ At Frederick Town he "went to take tea at Mr. [Roger Brooke] Taney's; an excellent gentleman indeed," and at Emmitsburg recorded: "Mrs. Seton in consumption, but far better than I expected."⁶

By and large, he found the Catholics of the southern counties the best served and those of the Eastern Shore the worst. Earlier correspondence prepared him not only for the discouraging conditions on the Eastern Shore but likewise in western Maryland. Except for Emmitsburg, the entire sweep of Frederick, Washington, and Allegany counties, plus several congregations in Virginia, were still attended by a single Jesuit, Francis Malevé, pastor of Frederick Town. The farthest mission, Arnold's Settlement, or Turkey Foot, took him 110 miles from home. In another brave attempt at English, Malevé told the archbishop: "I shall not be able to attend all nor ever was; it is work enough for 3: all their cryes [sic] are after Priest: They built and repair Churches but no Priest come except seldom."⁷ In the see city the completion of the cathedral was Maréchal's most pressing requisite, and a church was still badly needed for the eastern half of the national capital. In the vast expanse of the archdiocese below the Potomac, the problems were staggering. Not only were the widely scattered congregations poorly served for want of priests but the crises in Norfolk and Charleston hung like angry clouds. Tempests brewed in other dioceses, to which, as metropolitan, Maréchal had clear responsibilities. As Neale had predicted, he was "chosen for trials."

The Propaganda had more than once requested a detailed report from Carroll in his last year. The task had fallen to Neale, who began one but never finished it. In October 1818 Maréchal completed a sixteen-page report.⁸

The greatest part of the hundred thousand Catholics in the United States, he began, resided in Maryland.⁹ There were in the archdiocese fifty-three priests, fourteen of them French, twelve Irish, eleven American, and the rest Belgian, English, German, and Italian.¹⁰ Each missionary had a church and often two or three missions. Scarcely any of the churches were large enough to accommodate the growing number of Catholics. In the coming year, Maréchal claimed, ten churches would be built in various parts of his diocese. The see city, which in 1792 had counted scarcely eight hundred Catholics but now ten thousand, was well served except for the unfinished cathedral, for which he hoped to find "munificent" donors abroad. There were two seminaries in the archdiocese, one major and one minor, and two colleges. There were three sisterhoods. In nearly all his churches, Maréchal claimed, there were pious confraternities.

Americans differed from Europeans in a number of ways, the writer observed. "Among the principal vices of the Americans are the desire for unlimited riches, which seems to have seized the minds of all, and the vice of drunkenness among laborers and the lower classes. . . . The men live chastely enough, especially after they are once married. Those living in the cities go to the sacraments quite frequently, much oftener in fact than those in rural areas. . . . Their clothes are so luxurious that it is difficult to distinguish the daughter of a cobbler from European ladies of rank. Those who are not dutiful eagerly read books of romance and frequent theaters and dances. However they never do so on Sundays. The civil law forbids it and it is considered the greatest of scandals." Maréchal maintained, again with obvious exaggeration, that there was scarcely anyone in America who could not read or write. There were unfortunately a great number of books harmful to faith and morals, for which the civil laws had no remedy. "Americans strenuously defend the freedom of the press."

Maréchal admitted his inability to build a native clergy equal to his needs. Of the foreign born, English priests were the most desirable. Also "highly recommended" were Belgian, French, and German priests, who preached in a manner that was not displeasing to Americans, the calumnies of "Dr. Gallagher and his impious faction" notwithstanding. The Irish priests were "prompt in their work, speakers of no mean ability, and outstanding in their zeal for souls." Unfortunately they were also "given over to drunkenness or ambition," the root of "all the dissensions that have occurred in the Church in North America."

"All religions," Maréchal instructed his Roman superiors, "are tolerated here, and the laws of the Republic protect them all and most severely punish those who attempt to disturb the divine worship of any sect. And since religious liberty is the fundamental principle of the American Republic, there is no magistrate from the President to the least official, who can with impunity molest Catholics even in the slightest way. The only danger that blocks the path of our most holy religion, consists in the internal dissensions which divide the faithful against each other. The magistrates do not care about these dissensions."

The most serious of many difficulties, he claimed, was the dearth of missionaries. While care had to be taken to prevent more young women from entering convents than could be supported, young men were deterred from the clerical state by celibacy, the labor involved in theological studies, and the poverty of country missions. Many, moreover, had not the means

John Carroll, the first archbishop of Baltimore, was the architect of the Maryland tradition in American Catholicism. This portrait by Gilbert Stuart hangs at Georgetown University. (Catholic Review)

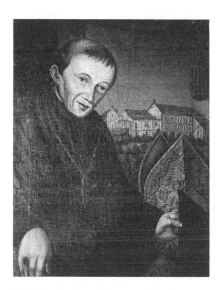

The brief rule of Leonard Neale, second archbishop of Baltimore, had far-reaching but regrettable consequences. In the background is the Visitation Convent and Academy he founded. (*Archives of the Archdiocese of Baltimore*)

Elizabeth Ann Bayley Seton founded the Sisters of Charity in the United States and was the first native-born American to be proclaimed a saint by Rome. This engraving from a 1796 miniature shows her nine years before her conversion to the Catholic faith.

St. Peter's Pro-Cathedral, built about 1770 and enlarged in 1784, appears on the right in this contemporary painting; its attached rectory is to the far right. A parking garage now claims the site of this first Catholic cathedral in the United States. To the left is the rectory of St. Paul's Episcopal Parish, still standing at the head of Liberty Street. (*Maryland Historical Society*)

The Cathedral of the Assumption took fifteen years to build (1806–21). A monument to Carroll's vision, it was one of the notable achievements of Benjamin Henry Latrobe, architect of the nation's Capitol. (Catholic Review)

The primitive chapel and priest's house built in 1794 at Hagerstown by Denis Cahill, the pioneer priest of Western Maryland and one of Carroll's problem priests, was typical of the early churches erected in rural areas.

Left, Ambrose Maréchal, third archbishop of Baltimore, was a French-born Sulpician who battled successfully the Holy See and the Society of Jesus but was intimidated by the bishop of Charleston. *Right,* the English-born James Whitfield, fourth archbishop of Baltimore, represented the last metropolitan of a church that was largely rural and southern. (*Archives of the Archdiocese of Baltimore*)

Top left, Samuel Eccleston, fifth archbishop of Baltimore, though Maryland born was the creator of the immigrant church in the oldest archdiocese, but he was also its most enigmatic archbishop. (Catholic Review) *Above,* Louis Regis Deluol, rector of St. Mary's Seminary for twenty years, was a friend and vicar general to Archbishop Eccleston. He helped to preserve the Maryland tradition in a time of change. (*Sulpician Archives*) *Bottom left,* Charles Ignatius White, a talented but eccentric pastor, was for many years the principal author and editor of the archdiocese. Until the day he died, he wore the clerical attire typical of the antebellum years. (*Archives of the Archdiocese of Baltimore*)

Archbishop Eccleston sits before the altar of the cathedral, with Father Deluol to his right, listening to the hour-and-twenty-five-minute sermon delivered by Bishop John B. Purcell at the opening of the Sixth Provincial Council of Baltimore. These councils addressed the disciplinary, administrative, and sacramental needs of the Catholic Church in America. (*Sulpician Archives*)

Between St. Mary's College, to the left in this etching of the 1840s, and St. Mary's Seminary, to the right, is St. Mary's Chapel, designed by Maximilien Godefroy and dedicated 1808. This first Gothic church in America still stands, but without its spire. (*Sulpician Archives*)

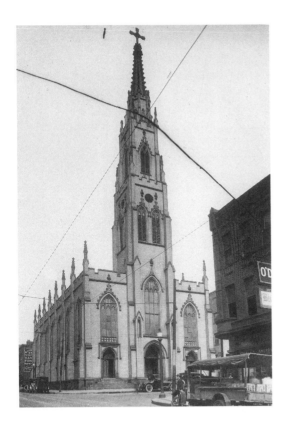

Left, St. Alphonsus Church, shown here in the 1920s, had changed little since its erection in 1842–45 for the Germans by Robert Cary Long, Jr. It is one of the earliest examples of the large Gothic churches favored by immigrant Catholics. (*Jacques Kelly*) *Below,* the church of St. Peter the Apostle was built by the same Robert Cary Long, Jr., in 1843–44. Its Doric style, a fine example of Greek Revival, offers a striking contrast to the Gothic St. Alphonsus. (Catholic Review)

Father James Dolan posed with his orphans about 1860. Pastor of St. Patrick's for twenty-nine years, he won the sobriquet "Apostle of the Point" as a result of his many charities. The orphanage was but one of a variety of institutions created to serve the needs of the immigrants.

The Daughters of Charity are pictured here at Lincoln Hospital in Washington, D.C., one of many they staffed during the Civil War. For ambulance corps and hospitals the Emmitsburg sisterhood supplied over 200 nurses. (Catholic Review)

Left, Francis Patrick Kenrick, the sixth archbishop of Baltimore, was its most scholarly one. An exacting administrator, he inaugurated the annual parish reports. (Catholic Review) *Below,* Martin John Spalding, seventh archbishop of Baltimore, persuaded four of the five other archbishops at the Second Plenary Council of Baltimore (1866) to pose at the rear entrance to the cathedral rectory: John McCloskey of New York, Francis Norbert Blanchet of Oregon City, John Baptist Purcell of Cincinnati, and John Odin of New Orleans. Spalding was one of the most active leaders and energetic builders of the immigrant church. (*University of Notre Dame*)

Bishops at the Second Plenary Council recess between sessions in front of the cathedral. Thomas Foley, first chancellor of the archdiocese of Baltimore and secretary of the council, stands at the far left. (*University of Notre Dame*)

The aristocratic James Roosevelt Bayley, eighth archbishop of Baltimore, was a nephew of Mother Seton's. Ill health limited his achievements in Baltimore (Catholic Review)

James Gibbons, ninth archbishop of Baltimore and created cardinal in 1886, is flanked by the two other cardinals created in 1911: John Farley of New York and William Henry O'Connell of Boston. A restorer of the Carroll church, Gibbons was the most honored American Catholic before John F. Kennedy. (*University of Notre Dame*)

The Blessed Gerard's Young Men's Literary Association of the Sacred Heart of Jesus Parish with its Redemptorist director was one of a host of young men's literary societies at the end of the nineteenth century that imparted a measure of culture to the sons of immigrants striving to enter the middle class.

A class at the Visitation Academy on Park Ave in Baltimore in 1884 exemplifies the quality education that was a hallmark of the archdiocese of Baltimore. At this time the Visitation nuns conducted five such academies in the archdiocese. (*Jacques Kelly*)

The faculty of St. Mary's Seminary pose on the occasion of its hundredth anniversary in 1891. At the center is seated Alphonse Magnien, the rector, who for almost twenty-five years was Cardinal Gibbons' most trusted adviser. (*Sulpician Archives*)

St. Charles College, the first minor seminary in the United States, is shown with some of its two hundred students about 1898. Next to Doughoregan Manor, it burned in 1911 and was rebuilt on Maiden Choice Lane, where the present Charlestown Retirement Community is now located. (*Sulpician Archives*)

A procession before the seminary building at Mount St. Mary's, Emmitsburg, celebrates its centenary in 1908. In front of the seminary is the overseer's cabin, since relocated, of John Hughes, an alumnus and later archbishop of New York. (*Rev. Michael J. Roach*)

The day nursery of St. Martin's in Baltimore in 1916, begun by the Bon Secours Sisters nine years earlier, was typical of the kind of social work coordinated by Catholic Charities in its formative years. (*Jacques Kelly*)

to pay for a seminary education, and the Sulpicians could receive only a limited number gratis.

Equally serious were the many schisms that plagued the church in America. The causes, Maréchal insisted in one of the longest parts of the report, were the democratic principles and practices of the nation, the example of Protestant bodies, cunning and impious priests, and title holding by lay trustees. Trusteeism he saw as the real root of the Norfolk and Charleston schisms.

The archbishop concluded his report with the recommendation that the two Carolinas, Georgia, and the territory called Mississippi be detached from the archdiocese of Baltimore and be made a diocese with the see city at Charleston. An Englishman, he insisted, should be chosen bishop, but he had no one to recommend.

The Trustee Battle Continues

Maréchal's approach to the trustee problems at Norfolk and Charleston was one of caution until the pope's letter upholding Neale's course of action arrived in September. Immediately, he demanded the submission of Gallagher and Browne. Both seemed disposed to obey, but most of the trustees absolutely refused to accept Clorivière as pastor. They took their case to the pope. "We assure your Holiness, that if the influence of the Jesuits and Sulpicians there [Maryland] receive not an immediate check, either a frightful schism will take place, or that the members of our church, will become protestants." They begged, as had the Norfolk trustees, that a diocese be created in the South with the Dominican Thomas Carbry as their bishop.[11] In the fall of 1818, Maréchal sent two young Jesuits to Charleston, Benedict Fenwick and James Wallace, to attempt a reconciliation. At Fenwick's suggestion Clorivière was removed, and in December Fenwick reported: "All difficulties settled." Unfortunately, the affairs of Norfolk intruded upon those of Charleston at this point, and matters took an ominous turn.[12]

Though the Propaganda had acknowledged a mistake in its support of the Charleston troublemakers, its response to the petition of the Norfolk vestry was calculated to fan the flames anew in that city. Addressed to Dr. Oliveira Fernandez, it seemed for the most part sympathetic to the trustees' wishes for a see with Carbry as its incumbent. If the privilege of patronage were granted, the cardinal advised, it could not extend to matters spiritual, but he was certain that such fervent men would not expect such. The doctor was granted a private chapel.[13] Bishop Connolly of New York, who sympathized with his compatriots in the South, recommended "warmly" to both the Propaganda and Maréchal the promotion of Carbry to a bishopric at Norfolk. With such support Oliveira Fernandez demanded of Maréchal the appointment of Carbry as pastor of that port city. In the spring of 1818 Maréchal visited Norfolk in an effort at peacemaking. Not only did this attempt fail, but it sent the doctor's pen flying in defense of the trustees' position.

A work of the doctor in all probability, a *Letter to Thomas Jefferson* was published by the Norfolk trustees in December 1818 and sent, according to Browne, to the governors and legislators of all the states. All but one of the American bishops, the *Letter* pointed out, were French, "Royalists by education, by religion, and by principle." The Jesuits in America, it claimed, were ambitious and covetous. The Irish, the overwhelming majority in the church, were denied their democratic rights. "For our own safety," it pleaded, "limit the power of foreign governments within our territory."[14] The *Letter* was apparently part and parcel of a conspiracy hatched by the disaffected of Norfolk and Charleston combined. In February Carbry in New York relayed a request, with the names of the petitioners carefully expunged, to a Franciscan in Ireland then in disfavor in Rome, Richard Hayes. Hayes was invited to go first to Utrecht to seek episcopal ordination from the schismatic archbishop there and then proceed to Charleston as head of an independent "Church of the Southland," where he would consecrate a bishop for Virginia.[15] Hayes sent the communication to Rome.

The turning point in the trustee controversies in America was Hayes's disclosure and not the pastoral Maréchal would issue soon after, as the principal historian of the controversy, Peter Guilday, would claim. Sentiment at the Propaganda shifted immediately from support of Carbry and the trustees to opposition. More important, perhaps, the officials of the Propaganda would begin to question their dependence upon the Irish Dominicans in Rome for advice and assistance on matters touching the church in America.

Sensing victory, Maréchal penned a lengthy pastoral in September to the Catholics of Norfolk exposing the conspiracy and attempting a refutation of all the arguments of the trustees from the learned disquisition of Dr. Oliveira Fernandez in 1816 to the *Letter to Thomas Jefferson*.[16] He sent a copy of the pastoral to Jefferson at Monticello, who acknowledged it politely and assured the writer: "My principles require me to take no part in the religious controversies of other sects."[17]

There were, nevertheless, developments that made a victory over the trustees less than certain. Browne was in Rome actively promoting a bishopric for Charleston. At the same time, the trustees of St. Mary's in Philadelphia petitioned the pope for the appointment of the Dominican William Vincent Harold as bishop of that long vacant see. They criticized the actions of Maréchal, alluded to the plight of the oppressed of St. Croix, Charleston, and Norfolk, and suggested a "convention of delegates" from all the suffering congregations "to devise a remedy."[18]

In 1820 the archbishop of Baltimore was dumbfounded and disheartened to learn that Rome had, without consulting a single American bishop, created sees at Charleston and Richmond and named secular priests in Ireland for the two new dioceses as well as for Philadelphia. Henry Conwell was ordained bishop of Philadelphia in England, and John England and Patrick Kelly were ordained bishops of Charleston and Richmond respectively in their native Ireland.[19]

Like his predecessor, Maréchal was not afraid to speak his mind. "I cannot convince myself," he wrote the new prefect of the Propaganda, Cardinal Francesco Fontana, "that you are the author of a document so full of inaccuracies throughout," or worse, have been taken in by "the intrigues of an evil Irish friar with five or six drunken fellow countrymen . . . thus degrading your high office."[20] Maréchal was particularly chagrined at the creation of the diocese of Richmond, having been assured that no diocese would be created for Virginia without his consent. When Bishop Kelly passed through Baltimore on his way to Richmond in early 1821, Maréchal read him a solemn protest that he intended sending to Rome and told him plainly that he could expect no help from his metropolitan in the troubles he was bound to encounter.[21]

On the advice of Archbishop Joseph Plessis of Quebec, Maréchal acquired an agent in Rome, Robert Gradwell, rector of the English College there. Gradwell convinced the Propaganda that its failure to consult the archbishop of Baltimore was the cause of many ills in America. "We now sail with another wind," Gradwell reported Fontana as saying.[22] The Propaganda, nevertheless, refused Maréchal's request that nominations to American sees be left exclusively to the archbishop of Baltimore in consultation with his suffragans and placed a negative also on his petition for a cathedral chapter.

Gradwell proposed that Maréchal himself come to Rome to press these and other matters at the Propaganda. Most of Maréchal's advisors agreed. One Sulpician, however, Simon Bruté, believed the visit would be interpreted as a "declaration of war against the Irish." Bruté thought that it was necessary to try to get along with the Irish, that to wish to establish the French system in America was ridiculous, and that French clergymen had given just as much scandal as Irish priests had.[23]

The Pension Controversy

Among the other matters that convinced the archbishop of the value of an *ad limina* visit to Rome was his battle with the Society of Jesus. He had not been in office long before he entered into a nine-year altercation with the Society. Often called the pension or stipend controversy, it was more than that. The pension controversy served merely as a test of strength. What was at issue was who, when push came to shove, would run the archdiocese of Baltimore, its ordinary or the order that controlled most of the missions and the bulk of its wealth, real or potential.

Maréchal raised the question of the annuity granted his predecessors two months after his consecration but did not make a formal request to the Corporation of the Roman Catholic Clergy for its continuation until June 1818. The board decided to give the archbishop $560 a year for three years as a "gratuitous grant." Principally on the basis of the Carroll-Molyneux agreement of 1805, Maréchal claimed that the archbishop of Baltimore was entitled to $1,200 a year in perpetuity. To this the board would not agree.[24]

The archbishop also objected to the practice of the superior, now Anthony Kohlmann, of removing Jesuits from the care of congregations without his consent. He cited what he called the "synodal statute" of the bishops in 1810, which had been occasioned in part by the like practice of Kohlmann's predecessors. Kohlmann denied that the bishops' ruling was a diocesan statute; in any case, he said, it could not be made to apply to exempt orders such as the Jesuits. "I do not hesitate to say," he wrote Maréchal in 1820, "with my very worthy predecessor, that the Society would sooner withdraw its subjects from America to be employed where Ecclesiastical authority puts no obstacle to the practice of its Institute than submit to such a pretention [*sic*]."[25]

On his part, Maréchal refused to recognize the Neale-Grassi agreement of 1816 assigning the bulk of the missions to the care of the Jesuits. "Divine Providence," he would later boast to the Propaganda, "happily destroyed the plan so vast, so inconceivable, and so obviously subversive to the see of Baltimore" by a falling out between the Jesuits and the pastor of St. Patrick's in Washington and by the death of Neale himself.[26] Increasingly Maréchal came to believe that some of the properties claimed by the Jesuits had been given to the church and not to the order as such. When the

Corporation decided in 1821 to sell a tract at Deer Creek acquired by donation, Maréchal denounced the sale as a "scandalous injustice," one that
would "enrich the Society by the breach of a religious trust."[27]

The archbishop complained about these differences with the Jesuits to
the Propaganda. The latter requested all pertinent documents. Maréchal
decided, therefore, to comb the archives and carry the documents with him
to Rome. He would not travel lightly.

As his negotiations with the Society worsened, however, Maréchal
made an effort to show that he harbored no animus toward the Jesuits as
such. He invited Kohlmann to bestow the pallium on him December 19,
1819, and in 1821 asked a young Jesuit, Roger Baxter, to deliver the sermon at
the dedication of the cathedral. In routine matters his dealings with the
Jesuits were cordial enough.

At Odds with Fellow Sulpicians

Another matter that Maréchal believed he could best handle personally in Rome was the establishment of new dioceses. Here Maréchal found
himself at odds with fellow Sulpicians: Bishops DuBourg and Flaget. Between 1816 and 1821 the states of Indiana, Mississippi, Illinois, Alabama, and
Missouri were admitted to the Union, and the territory of Florida was purchased from Spain in 1819. The creation of the diocese of Charleston in 1820
had isolated Mississippi and Alabama, still a part of the archdiocese of Baltimore. For all of these areas Bishops DuBourg and Flaget were busily
drawing plans that did not accord with the views of the archbishop of Baltimore. Among other things, they suggested to the Propaganda, without
consulting Maréchal, a province for the West. DuBourg proposed an archiepiscopal seat at St. Louis, which was not even a part of the province of
Baltimore.[28] Maréchal did not hold this fellow Sulpician in high esteem.
"*Badinage de Sa Grandeur*," he had scrawled on one of DuBourg's letters.[29]
The Propaganda, he believed, should be aware of his grandiose schemes.

Another problem Maréchal felt that he should take to Europe, but to
Paris, not to Rome, concerned the Sulpicians directly. It was a crisis that
resulted from the plans of another Sulpician who, like DuBourg, did not fit
the mold: John Dubois. At basis a conflict over the function of Mount St.
Mary's Seminary at Emmitsburg, it had important implications for the internal affairs of the American Sulpicians.

The ailing Nagot had been replaced by John Mary Tessier in 1810 as
rector of St. Mary's Seminary and superior of the American Sulpicians.
Tessier proved no match for the energetic and independent Dubois, nor, for

that matter, for several strong-willed members of the Baltimore community, notably Edward Damphoux, Louis Regis Deluol, and James Hector Joubert. In 1815 Emmitsburg was granted a certain autonomy by Antoine Duclaux, the superior general in Paris, who placed Dubois directly under himself but allowed Tessier a supervisory power and a degree of financial control. Mount St. Mary's was still burdened with debts. Though overworked, Dubois refused to surrender the parish at the Mount and his directorship of the Sisters of Charity. In this way he justified his demand for the return of Simon Bruté, who had been called to Baltimore in 1815 to head St. Mary's College. The latter's return to the Mount in 1818 without authorization precipitated the crisis. The Sulpician council in Baltimore, with the archbishop present, decided to suppress the Emmitsburg institution because the Society had not enough members in America to conduct two seminaries and two colleges. Dubois raised vehement objections. A flurry of correspondence ensued among Emmitsburg, Baltimore, and Paris. On Dubois's lengthy appeals and proposals Maréchal penned his usual cryptic notations: "Petitions, complaints as usual," "Evasive," "Plans, Schemes, etc.," "*ab irato*," and on one of Bruté's, "Wild."[30] As a temporary expedient Maréchal finally allowed the Mount to teach theology to seminarians too poor to pay at St. Mary's Seminary, who in turn could continue to teach the college students. But the final solution would await his return from Europe.

Finishing the Cathedral

The archbishop was determined to dedicate his cathedral before going abroad. In the fall of 1818 the architect, Latrobe, wrote his son: "Yesterday we closed with some ceremony & a great deal of punch the dome of the Cathedral [and] 3 cheers given, which resounded half over the city."[31] Another lottery was conducted in 1819. Individuals contributed munificently, Charles Carroll of Carrollton, David Williamson, Luke Tiernan, Thomas Courtney Jenkins, John Hillen, Basil Spalding Elder, and John Walsh $1,000 or more each. From abroad came the altar, paintings, candlesticks, and other adornments, all gifts. On November 23, 1820, the public sale of the pews took place, the better ones going for $400 or more. Though the portico and towers were still to be finished and a debt of $50,000 remained, the dedication of the Cathedral of the Assumption was performed by the archbishop on May 31, 1821, assisted by Bishops Cheverus and Conwell, in a ceremony designed to impress. There was reason for pride. "After thirty years of common effort, the Archdiocese of Baltimore had erected one of the finest churches in the nation."[32]

A Fruitful Roman Visit

Archbishop Maréchal sailed for Europe in October, visited all the right people in England, Belgium, and France and appeared in Rome sometime before Christmas. From early January he worked incessantly for six months, holding almost daily interviews, at least two of them with the pope, compiling reports, drafting proposals, and responding to questionnaires. The American archbishop was well received. The Holy See, in fact, went out of its way to make amends. The pope donated a chalice to the new cathedral and named Maréchal an assistant to the pontifical throne. He was also made a member of the Academy of Rome. At his request St. Mary's Seminary was raised to a pontifical university with the right to confer the degree of doctor of divinity.[33]

Maréchal began his *ad limina* visit with a report entitled "General Description of the Metropolitan Province of Baltimore in the United States of America."[34] In the province, he related, there were 8 dioceses and ordinary bishops, 88 secular priests, 34 religious priests, 100 churches, 15 ecclesiastical institutions, 423 male students, 208 sisters, and 163,500 Catholics. Half and more of these numbers were in the archdiocese itself, where there were 40 diocesan priests (including the Sulpicians), 18 religious ones, 52 churches, 155 sisters, about 400 students in two seminaries, three colleges, and the Jesuit novitiate, and 80,000 Catholics. The Catholic populations of the other dioceses were Philadelphia 30,000, New York 24,000, Bardstown 20,000, Charleston 3,600, Boston 3,500, and Richmond 2,400. Maréchal had no figures for the diocese of Cincinnati, created only the year before. The number of Catholics, he remarked, was limited to those counted in existing congregations. In a note he observed that there may have been as many as 60,000 Catholics in the diocese of Philadelphia and 50,000 in that of New York. He estimated, in fact, "without any danger of error," that there were "at least 1,000,000 Catholics in the United States"[35] On occasion the third archbishop was given to overstatement.

In a second report entitled "Notes on the Province of Baltimore" and subtitled "Calamities that have afflicted the Church in the United States and the means by which they can be averted," Maréchal focused on four problems. The first was the great number of unworthy priests allowed by Irish bishops to come to America. Rome should admonish these bishops and set down strict rules for their dismissal of priests. The second problem was the holding of church property by lay trustees and the evils it produced. Again Maréchal recommended an admonition from the Holy See. The third was the abuse of the right of appeal to Rome by priests and the readiness with which they were exonerated. The remedy was implied in the complaint. The fourth was the influence of Irish bishops in filling American sees. If the metropolitan and his suffragans were not granted the privilege of nominating candidates, Maréchal insisted, no nomination should be made without seeking their advice.[36]

In response to these and other problems raised in the course of the visit, Cardinal Ercole Consalvi, the papal secretary of state and now acting prefect of the Propaganda, presented Maréchal with a questionnaire. On June 4 he submitted his careful answers. His response concerning new sees and the problems in Philadelphia will be considered later. The trustee problem, Maréchal insisted, required special legislation. The best way the Holy See could aid the American Church would be to make wise selections for American bishops and regulate wandering priests. Most dioceses were too poor to support a seminary; his own would suffice until they were able to do so. On the advisability of holding a provincial council, Maréchal claimed that he would have held one if Rome had placed in new and vacant sees men proposed by himself and his suffragans, but as the province was now constituted, a council would do more harm than good. Diocesan synods were impractical because of the small number of priests and their dissimilar backgrounds; it was better presently for bishops to make their own rules after consulting their most learned and prudent priests. With regard to episcopal visitations, Maréchal believed himself and his suffragans conscientious enough.[37]

In general congregations of June 3 and July 8 the cardinals of the Propaganda responded as positively as Maréchal could wish to all but one of the recommendations and requests he had submitted.[38] He and his suffragans were not granted the exclusive privilege of nominating candidates for American sees, but they could submit three names to Rome when vacancies occurred. Maréchal's recommendations for new sees, however, were followed as well as his suggestions that the Holy See issue directives concerning trustees and Irish priests. The Propaganda instructed Irish bishops to grant dimissorial letters only to priests who had invitations from particular American bishops.[39]

On the matter of trustees, the Propaganda requested the pope to issue an apostolic brief to the American bishops, trustees, and faithful. In the brief *Non Sine Magno*, "the foundational papal response to trusteeism,"

Pius VII condemned first the actions of Rev. William Hogan and the trustees of Philadelphia and then those trustees in general whose immoderate claims were the cause of so much turmoil in the church. Properties acquired for church purposes, he declared, fell under the power of the church. Trustees who presumed to remove pastors at their pleasure and bestow revenues upon whom they pleased had subverted the laws of the church, making the pastor the subject of his flock. So that "peace and tranquility will again flourish in these regions," the pope declared, it was necessary to set down certain regulations.[40]

In a separate letter to the archbishop of Baltimore, the Propaganda had already laid out the regulations Maréchal himself had recommended. Only upright and honest men should be chosen as trustees. Their powers should be limited. They could employ no priest in bad standing. Priests should be independent of trustees in the exercise of their ministry. The title to churches in the future should be vested, whenever possible, in the bishop, and when not, civil contracts should be drawn with adequate safeguards before churches could be blessed. Consalvi instructed Maréchal to use these regulations at his discretion for the American church as a whole.[41]

Maréchal was equally successful in his suit with the Jesuits, but only after six months of claims and counterclaims, proofs and rebuttals. His principal antagonist in Rome was no less than the father general of the Society of Jesus, Aloysius Fortis.[42] In the initial interviews Fortis pronounced the Carroll-Molyneux agreement of 1805 an invalid concession and Maréchal's other arguments—that the properties had been given for the good of the church as a whole, for example—of no merit. Maréchal therefore submitted his suit to the Propaganda.

In May the case was sent to a committee of three cardinals, one of whom was Joseph Fesch, protector of the French Sulpicians during the reign of his nephew, the Emperor Napoleon. Rejecting a compromise proposed by Fortis, Maréchal told the committee he would resign his see if its rights were not upheld. In June the Propaganda ruled in Maréchal's favor in both the jurisdictional dispute and the pension controversy. In the first it decreed that the Jesuit superior in America could not move a subject without the archbishop's consent and his approval of the replacement. Though less publicized, this decree proved of greater consequence in the long run than the papal brief dated July 23, 1822, ordering the Maryland Jesuits to surrender the 2,000-acre core of the White Marsh plantation to the archbishop within a month of the reception of the order.

The archbishop left Rome at the end of July with his victories packed tightly in his bags. He spent the next two months in France and England

and sailed for Maryland October 1. Soon after his arrival in November, he handed the papal order to the Jesuit superior, now Father Charles Neale, the same who had initiated the jurisdictional dispute with Carroll.

The Jesuit Battle Continues

The American Jesuit refused to obey.[43] Neale sent an impassioned forty-four-page protest to Fortis with a litany of reasons for denying the papal brief. Four days before the expiration of the month allowed, he wrote the archbishop that he had no intention of surrendering the Society's most productive estate. The case had been prejudiced, the American Jesuits given no opportunity to present their side, and the verdict based on false premises. The litany to Fortis was repeated.[44] In the spring Gradwell informed Maréchal that the contempt shown by Neale for the archbishop, the general, and the pope had occasioned "great surprise and universal disgust in Rome." Neale died about the time Gradwell wrote and was succeeded by Francis Dzierozynski as superior. Voices lowered, but the battle continued.

In August Cardinal Fesch informed Maréchal of an ominous turn in the dispute: a Jesuit claim that the United States government would not permit the alienation of any American property ordered by Rome.[45] The Holy See hesitated. Maréchal made inquiries at the State Department. Daniel Brent, first clerk of the department, admitted that Secretary of State John Quincy Adams had indeed been asked to send a letter of protest to the Holy See. He was not sure that Adams would do so, but he was convinced that the government would "never view with indifference any further appeal to such foreign states." Maréchal sought the opinion of Roger Brooke Taney, which proved favorable to Maréchal, and sent it to Brent. Brent returned a guarded opinion that no protest would be made.[46]

Though Fortis was eager to make concessions, the controversy dragged on for another two years. The principal sticking point was the inability of the American mission of the Society to pay, strapped as it was with debts mounting to $35,000. When Fortis finally offered to send the archbishop $800 a year from Jesuit funds in Rome, Maréchal accepted with the understanding that the annuity be extended to his successors.

After his return from Rome, Maréchal pursued a firm policy with the Jesuits in the matter of removals, the granting of faculties, and landholding. For example, because they held title to the land, he refused to let them open a church they had built in Upper Marlboro.[47] In 1827 Dzierozynski offered "heartiest thanks" to the archbishop for the kindness he had shown the five Jesuits he had just ordained.[48] Yet Maréchal granted faculties to only the three of them assigned to congregations in the archdiocese. Eager to please, Dzierozynski sent, as the archbishop wished, six native-born scholastics to Rome to be educated in the spirit of the Society, a move originally suggested to Maréchal by Nicholas Sewall, the Maryland-born provincial of the English Jesuits.[49]

It was Dzierozynski's task to settle as best he could not only jurisdictional differences with the archbishop but also a jurisdictional conflict between the Society of Jesus and the Corporation of the Roman Catholic Clergy. The argument of Charles Neale that White Marsh did not belong to the Society but to the Corporation was not altogether a legal fiction. The management of the Jesuit properties remained with the board. Attempts to make the superior the agent of the Corporation and its board members his councilors proved unsatisfactory. There was tension between the native-born and alien Jesuits. Until naturalized, the latter could not be members of the Corporation. Dzierozynski was named superior in 1823 with instructions from Fortis to have the Corporation deed the Society all its properties. It was not until May 1825 that the Americans were persuaded to sign a statement of renunciation. By this act the Corporation as a viable body ceased to exist, and Carroll's experiment in clerical democracy came to an end.[50]

Taming the Trustees

As with the Jesuits, the other victories won at Rome carried no guarantee of instant compliance. Though the brief *Non Sine Magno* spelled the eventual doom of trusteeism as an effective mode of lay involvement, abuses continued in spasmodic but ever-diminishing outbursts. There was little danger of such eruptions in the archdiocese of Baltimore, but Maréchal moved quietly to carry out the regulations he had persuaded Rome to promote.

On his part, these regulations were the product of experience. In 1818 Maréchal had allowed the congregation of St. Ignatius, Hickory, surrendered by the Jesuits, to incorporate. The articles of incorporation stipulated that the trustees should be "elected" by the bishop and that they were, among other things, never to expel a pastor nor to accept one without the authorization of the bishop.[51] A week before the dedication of the cathedral in 1821, Maréchal had persuaded the trustees to disclaim by civil contract any right to interfere in the spiritual governance of the church.[52]

Soon after his return from Rome, Maréchal tried to induce the trustees of incorporated congregations, at least in Baltimore, to subscribe to the regulations he had carried back with him. When he approached those of St. John's, they refused to sign, fearing that the archbishop might deprive them of the privilege of having a German pastor.[53] The trustees of St. Patrick's, on the other hand, readily complied, explaining their action by a reference to the schisms "excited by the intrigues of disobedient clergymen and by impious and turbulent laymen."[54] When in 1825, however, an attempt was made to deed the ground on which St. Patrick's stood to the archbishop in trust, Maréchal's legal counsel advised that this could not be done in perpetuity. William Matthews, the Washington pastor, took "the liberty to suggest [that] you have yourself made an incorporation sole."[55] This would be done under Maréchal's successor.

Apparently, it was never Maréchal's goal to eliminate trustees but only to tame them. Despite the discomfort caused by rebels in those parts of the archdiocese now detached, the example of the vestries in Maryland could only have convinced him of their utility. As the pastor of Rockville reminded him: "The gentlemen trustees have done well their duty with regard to me" in providing regularly an adequate salary.[56]

Though active in enforcing the regulations in his own diocese, Maréchal gave only moral support to the suffragan bishops battling trustees and problem priests elsewhere. This was not the result of timidity but a refusal to intervene in the affairs of other dioceses. He entertained no appeals from trouble-ridden sees even though as metropolitan he had a right, and even a duty, to do so.

The bishop of Philadelphia desperately needed help. Though annoyed at the appointment of Henry Conwell, Maréchal soon came to sympathize with the seventy-four-year-old bishop in his struggle with the upstart priest, William Hogan, and the trustees who sided with him.[57] In Rome Maréchal had briefed the Propaganda on Conwell's plight and urged the condemnation that was voiced in *Non Sine Magno*. The situation worsened, nevertheless, after his return, despite Hogan's disappearance from the scene. In 1826 Conwell gave the schismatic trustees a virtual veto over the appointment of pastors. Maréchal suggested that Rome transfer Conwell to a tranquil Irish see. At the same time, he ignored an appeal from the Dominican William Vincent Harold, who with his friend John Ryan had returned to Philadelphia in search of a miter only to have his faculties revoked by Conwell. Maréchal refused to touch the case. In the summer of 1827, the Propaganda summoned Conwell to Rome and named Maréchal administrator of the diocese of Philadelphia. By then the archbishop was too ill to assume the burden, and it was placed upon the shoulders of William Matthews, the Washington pastor.

In New York the story was the same: an aged bishop had lost control of a faction-ridden see. Connolly, however, wished no help from Maréchal. When one of his priests asked Maréchal to hold an investigation shortly before his trip to Rome, Connolly fumed that no French bishop was qualified to conduct such an inquiry. Appeals multiplied after Maréchal's return as the mental and physical condition of Bishop Connolly deteriorated rapidly. They ceased with his death in 1825.[58]

Even before he had reached Rome, the Holy See had acceded to Maréchal's request to send Bishop Kelly of Richmond back to Ireland as soon as a see was vacant. Kelly, as it turned out, was only too happy to return, having failed dismally in his efforts to win over the Norfolk trustees. In 1822 the administration of the vacant see was entrusted to the archbishop of Baltimore, one burden he had no reluctance to assume.

By contrast, the efforts of Bishop John England of Charleston to bring his unruly trustees to heel was remarkably successful. From the start he showed himself an able and imaginative leader. In little more than a year, he had opened his own seminary and launched the first true Catholic newspaper in the country, the *United States Catholic Miscellany*. Even more important, he drew up in 1823 a constitution for his diocese modeled on that of the United States, providing for a two-house legislature, one for the clergy and one for the laity.[59]

Maréchal versus England

Though at first favorably impressed by the thirty-five-year-old bishop, Maréchal soon developed an antipathy toward England beyond telling. England's early attempts at peacemaking in Philadelphia and New York seemed to Maréchal unwarranted intrusions and a reflection on his own policy of nonintervention. Many of England's innovations he deemed as ill advised as his "democratic constitution." (He always used this adjective in a pejorative sense.) And he was increasingly discomfited by the contents of the *Miscellany*. "Altogether this journal is a very bad one," he told Gradwell.[60]

"Do not deem it arrogance in me," England wrote two months after his arrival, "the youngest in every way amongst the Bishops of this Union, that I suggest to your Grace the propriety of assembling us at some early period for the purpose of having established some uniform system of Discipline for the Churches, and of having common counsel and advice upon a variety of important topics regarding the causes and remedies of those disastrous contests which have torn and do still agitate this afflicted Church. I am certain your Grace must feel convinced of its necessity."[61] In almost every letter thereafter England pressed his metropolitan to convoke a provincial council. Those he wrote in the last year of Maréchal's life were the strongest of all; more than requests, they were rebukes for his failure to observe the Tridentine legislation requiring triennial provincial councils.[62]

While Maréchal was in Rome, England expressed the fear to Archbishop Troy that his own actions were being misrepresented to the Propaganda. "Yet I do not hesitate to say that I have travelled through much more of the country, know much more of the institutions, political and religious, and am better acquainted with the state of the churches, and of the wants and wishes and dispositions of the people than the Archbishop."[63] There was obvious resentment on England's part that to a man he deemed inferior to himself was entrusted the awesome responsibility of accommodating an old church to a new nation, while he, the youngest bishop, carried the blueprint for success in his pocket.

Fear of being overshadowed by the dynamic bishop of Charleston was undoubtedly one of the principal reasons for Maréchal's refusal to call a council. Soon after his return from Rome, he actually put on paper the tentative agenda for such a gathering.[64] The harder England pressed, however, the more determined he became not to call a council.

Choosing Bishops

A temperamental incompatibility also precluded any reasonable settlement of differences between Maréchal and DuBourg. The archbishop was angered when DuBourg upset the plans he had made in Rome to be relieved of Alabama and Mississippi. In 1825 Alabama and Florida were finally made a vicariate and Mississipi placed under the administration of DuBourg.[65] When DuBourg sailed for Rome in 1826, Maréchal, fearing another attempt to create a province in the West, warned the Propaganda once more not to be "deceived by the *romantic* colorings with which that prelate adorns his schemes."[66] DuBourg, it turned out, had gone to Rome to resign the diocese of Louisiana. He was named bishop of Montauban in France.

There Dubourg succeeded John Cheverus, who in 1823 had been recalled to his native France.[67] Though the transfer of Cheverus was a grievous loss for Maréchal, it provided him one of a number of new or vacant sees in the province of Baltimore by which to test Rome on the matter of nominations. Bishop Edward Fenwick of Cincinnati wanted a see at Detroit. New York, after the death of Connolly, and the vicariate of Alabama-Florida also needed bishops. Maréchal was careful to put no Frenchmen at the head of his recommendations for the two eastern sees where the Irish predominated, even though John Dubois was first choice of most of the other suffragans for New York. As it turned out, Dubois was named bishop of New York, Benedict Fenwick, Maréchal's choice for New York, bishop of Boston, and Michael Portier vicar apostolic for Alabama-Florida, while the matter of diocesan status for Detroit was postponed. On November 1, 1825, Maréchal raised Fenwick to the episcopacy in Baltimore's new cathedral, and on October 29, 1826, he elevated Dubois. For the most part, Maréchal was pleased with the new suffragans and satisfied that Rome had listened to the American bishops in the matter of episcopal candidates.

The Sulpician Solution

The removal of Dubois made easier the solution of the last of the problems he had carried to Europe. From Paris he had brought the decision that Mount St. Mary's at Emmitsburg could serve the Society of St. Sulpice only as a minor seminary. Impossible, said Dubois; without the tuition of the college students it could not be supported, and without the major seminarians as teachers the college could not be maintained. Rebuilding after a fire in 1824, Dubois had used the support of benefactors as another reason for keeping the college open. In 1825 Bruté himself had gone to Paris to plead the cause of the Mount, but in vain. In January 1826 Mount St. Mary's Seminary and College were stricken from the list of Sulpician institutions, and Dubois and Bruté ceased to be members of the Society.[68]

It was now up to the archbishop to decide whether to allow two major seminaries in the archdiocese. Maréchal was reluctant to suppress at once an institution that was producing almost as many priests as the Baltimore seminary and in the process also, perhaps, a flourishing college. When Dubois left for New York as bishop, Maréchal made an arrangement with the two young clergymen who had agreed to act as administrators, Michael Egan and John McGerry. The theology courses taught by Bruté could continue for only five years, during which time the administrators would have to find other teachers to replace the seminarians.

There were, after the separation of 1826, thirteen Sulpicians in their two institutions in Baltimore. Seven of these were Maryland born and another, from Saint-Domingue, had entered the Society in Baltimore. Maréchal's episcopacy was one of the most productive in native vocations, the

Society of St. Sulpice attracting such talented men as Michael Wheeler, Samuel Eccleston, and John Joseph Chanche.[69] Yet the seminary itself was not prospering. In Maréchal's ten and a half years as archbishop, only thirty-one students entered, at least eight of these from Emmitsburg. Eleven were natives of Maryland and eleven Irish born. At least twenty-two of the thirty-one who entered were ordained, thirteen of them for the archdiocese of Baltimore.[70]

Maréchal remained close to his confreres. A room was kept at the seminary for his frequent visits. Rarely did he make an important decision without consulting the council of the seminary. Yet there were strains. In 1823, after a visit to Deluol's room, the latter recorded in his diary: "He talked much of our taking all the priests of his diocese, and that he must have Mr. Eccleston. He wept often: the thought of those things often keeps him awake at night, and many times he has thought of asking Rome to let him resign as Archbishop of Baltimore. I tried to make him understand that, as far as we are concerned, he has no reason to fear, and that in letting his imagination create monsters without substance, he was making himself and us miserable."[71] Maréchal also believed his confreres prejudiced against his cathedral.[72]

The Colleges and Academies

While concerned about the seminary, Maréchal had reason to be encouraged by the second Sulpician institution. St. Mary's College was thriving as never before, despite the behavior of its talented but erratic president. Edward Damphoux had twice resigned and twice insisted on reinstatement. The college had no serious rival in the city and drew from other parts of the country and Latin America.

Georgetown College, on the other hand, went into another slump after the departure of Grassi. Under a succession of presidents, its student population slipped to thirty in 1825.[73] The Jesuits, however, had erected a house next to St. Patrick's in Washington as a scholasticate for the education of their members, but almost from the start day students were taken in. Opened in 1821, the Washington Seminary, as it was called, drew more students than Georgetown. "The Seminary goes on swimmingly," Benedict Fenwick wrote a fellow Jesuit in 1823. "I think Father General, knowing the circumstances of the country and the unfinished state of the Society here, will have no difficulty in sanctioning the payments of day scholars, when the same is necessary for the support of the scholastics employed."[74] On the latter point he was mistaken. The general did not sanction this departure from Jesuit practice. In 1827 he ordered the school with its 150 students closed. One of its Jesuit teachers left the Society and continued a school on Capitol Hill, initially with some success.[75]

The academies for young ladies were doing well. Though St. Joseph's Academy at Emmitsburg continued to attract the daughters of the best families, the Visitation Academy in Georgetown threatened to surpass it in popularity. This was due, in large measure, to Joseph Clorivière, to whom Maréchal had entrusted the direction of the sisters when he was recalled from Charleston in 1819. Overcrowding—forty-five sisters in 1823—contributed to an economic crisis, however, beyond Clorivière's power to resolve. When he died in 1826, a Sulpician, Michael Wheeler, was named spiritual director of the Visitandines.

Though the Sulpicians also directed the Sisters of Charity, Maréchal admired most the cloistered Carmelites of Port Tobacco. He was not as impressed as his former associates by the little mother at Emmitsburg. "Pious chat," he scribbled impatiently on a letter she sent him two years before her death in 1821.[76] Elizabeth Seton was succeeded by the able Rose White, under whom the Sisters of Charity expanded rapidly. In 1821 they took charge of the St. Mary's Orphaline Female School, which the cathedral trustees had incorporated in 1818. In 1823, eager to get into hospital work, they agreed to staff the Baltimore Infirmary (later the University Hospital). In 1824 they opened an academy and free school in Frederick and in 1825 a free school and orphanage near St. Patrick's in Washington.[77]

More Parishes

Churches and congregations also increased under the third archbishop. In January 1818 Father Malevé sent a report and map that showed that there were now churches at Turkey Foot (Arnold's Settlement) and Carroll Manor and a church under construction at Fifteen Mile Creek (Little Orleans) with churches planned at Maryland Tract (Petersville) and Liberty Town.[78] The one at Maryland Tract was not started until 1826 and finished only after Maréchal's death.[79]

St. Ignatius, Hickory, established two daughter parishes. In 1819 a small stone church was built in Cecil County just across the Susquehanna River at Conowingo (Pilot Station) for the mostly Irish laborers who had dug the Susquehanna and Tidewater Canal. Another church was built for the Catholics of Long Green Valley and blessed by Tessier May 18, 1822.[80]

At Annapolis a church was built by Charles Carroll of Carrollton about 1821. On the Eastern Shore a church was finished for the Catholics of Denton by 1825.

In the national capital the church envisioned by the Carrolls, Brents, and Barrys in the eastern part of the city became a reality. A plain brick church on the corner of Second and C Streets Southeast was dedicated by Tessier November 4, 1821, while the archbishop was on his way to Rome. James Lucas had been brought from Norfolk to take charge. At St. Peter's, which was owned by the archbishop, Lucas did not have to worry about trustees.[81]

Though the Catholic populations of Baltimore and Washington were growing rapidly and the national turnpike was drawing Catholics into the western counties of Maryland, the bulk of Maréchal's spiritual children could still be found in the southern counties of the state. While there were hardly more than three hundred communicants in all of Allegany County, almost ten times that number could be found in Charles County and double that, or nearly six thousand, in St. Mary's.[82] On the whole of the Eastern Shore, the number of communicants did not greatly exceed that of Allegany County.

The congregations of the southern counties continued the even tenor of their ways, a bit lethargic but observant enough to satisfy the archbishop. From Newtown Father Leonard Edelen wrote that the people were slowly overcoming their reluctance to contribute to the support of pastors and repair of churches, but he suggested that levies be fixed by the archbishop rather than the pastors.[83]

Father Malevé struggled valiantly to serve all the western missions until 1818, when he wrote: "I hope your Most Reverence [sic] Sir will provide more efectualy [sic] to these Peoples than by myself." If a priest were stationed at Hagerstown, he predicted, the people would contribute more.[84] The archbishop took up the suggestion and sent James Redmond, the former Jesuit, to Hagerstown to serve all the missions of Washington and Allegany Counties as well as those of Berkeley County, Virginia. Redmond was impressed with these hardy westerners, who thought nothing of riding twenty miles to mass on Sunday.[85]

The greatest impediment to growth, Redmond complained, was the want of time to instruct the younger generation in the faith. "There are Swarms of false teachers all thro the Country—at every Cross road, in every School house, in every private house—you'll hear nothing but night meetings, Quarterly meetings, Camp meetings, Class meetings, love feasts &c &c. . . . I declare most Rev. Father it is the ruin of Religion to suffer any priest to attend more than three or four congregations."[86] Redmond warned that travel over such rugged terrain could break any missioner's constitution within a few years. "Pray God to give me strength until aid comes."[87] Aid came too late. Redmond had to be replaced in 1822. Reentering the Society of Jesus, he died the following year of consumption. Malevé died the year before, and to his demanding station was sent a fellow Jesuit, John McElroy, a man in whom the mountains met their match, a priest known in time to Catholics well beyond the archdiocese.

Redmond's concern about backcountry revivalism approximated that of Father Leonard Edelen about the distribution of Protestant Bibles in St. Mary's County. An exchange between the Jesuit and the Episcopal minister who accused him of Bible burning was published in 1819.[88] Though it served as a stimulus to Catholic generosity in southern Maryland, it disturbed the peaceful relations between Catholics and Protestants. The Catholic Church, the archbishop claimed in his 1818 report to Rome with but slight exaggeration, was "venerated" in America. "The prejudices, with which formerly the young were imbued, have disappeared to such an extent that pseudoministers no longer dare to suggest them in their preaching; and if one of them does do so he is branded a calumniator by his hearers."[89]

At Home in America

It was, in part, Maréchal's fear of a revival of ill will between Catholic and Protestant that caused him to put a damper on the enthusiasm of those Jesuits who wanted to publicize the cure of Mrs. Ann Mattingly, sister of the mayor of Washington, in 1824 as a bona fide miracle.[90] As did most of the French bishops in America, Maréchal enjoyed a good rapport with Protestants. The presence of French prelates and priests, in fact, served to perpetuate the somnolent state into which antipopery had fallen in the Revolutionary era.

The third archbishop, as a matter of fact, moved with ease in most circles. On intimate terms with the Carrolls, he spent a great deal of time at Doughoregan Manor. He evidently enjoyed the company of young people. Deluol recorded an interesting scene: "A party at the Archbishop's: Ann Nelson fainted; her sister Mary took part in a duet; Dr. Sinnot got drunk; Jules Ducatel flirted with Miss Barry."[91] Carroll perhaps and Neale certainly would not have been comfortable in such a situation. Maréchal enjoyed also the company of farmers, tradesmen, and tavern keepers. On one of his visitations he went fishing. He was unpretentious and unprepossessing. The short, bespectacled prelate could easily be mistaken, as he once was, for a schoolmaster. He did not, however, involve himself in civic affairs to the degree that Carroll had. On the eve of his departure for Rome, he resigned as president of the Library Company of Baltimore.

Though personally unassuming, Maréchal was, as were most of the emigré bishops, authoritarian. Unable to suffer the discomfort of sharing power, he held the reins tightly at all times. Maréchal did not seek power, nor did he enjoy it particularly. But when it was thrust upon him, he guarded it jealously. He suspected, perhaps, that many of his contemporaries—DuBourg, England, and Flaget certainly—deemed him a man of mediocre ability, unsuited for his archiepiscopal role.

Ambrose Maréchal was, indeed, a man of middling talents, with, perhaps, an inferiority complex to match. The latter trait would explain his tendency to exaggerate as well as his habit of threatening to resign at each contretemps. Yet he used the talents he had conscientiously and was, in many ways, an excellent administrator. He kept a better set of records and knew his diocese more intimately, perhaps, after its reduction to Maryland and the District of Columbia, than any of the nineteenth-century archbishops of Baltimore. He made extensive visitations of Maryland, Virginia, and the District both before and after his visit to Rome, traveling in 1824 all the way to Wheeling.[92]

At Emmitsburg, in the course of a visitation in December 1826, the archbishop contracted a chest infection from which he never really recovered. He spent much of the summer and early fall of 1827 at Doughoregan hoping to recoup his health. When he returned to Baltimore at the end of September, however, it was to put his house in order and request a coadjutor, the man he had carefully groomed to succeed him: James Whitfield. To fill out the terna he sent to Rome, he added the names of two young Sulpicians of native birth: Samuel Eccleston and Michael Wheeler.

In his last days, a petition circulated among the Catholics of Baltimore addressed to Bishop England of Charleston expressing their preference for him as Archbishop Maréchal's successor. "In town," Deluol recorded, "they are saying that the people are getting worked up and that the intrigue in favor of Dr. England is gaining strength."[93] Maréchal died on January 29, 1828, uncertain as to who would succeed him.

The Legacy

The most important legacy that Ambrose Maréchal bequeathed the premier see was an altered relationship with Rome. Carroll and Neale had distanced themselves from the Holy See, making little effort to keep the

Congregation of the Propaganda informed on the true state of affairs in the new republic, a puzzle at best to the Roman authorities. Maréchal came to appreciate the fact that this did not serve well the interests of the archdiocese or of the American church. He labored diligently his six months in Rome, and of that effort was born a fresh awareness there of the importance of the archbishop of Baltimore. Thereafter he would be consulted on almost all American affairs, and rarely was action taken on those affecting the American church as a whole except through his agency. His immediate successors would not be happy in this unaccustomed role, but it was now inescapable.

Maréchal's victories over the trustees and the Jesuits also marked important milestones in the ever-widening road of episcopal power in the United States. That the American bishops would become almost absolute in their rule was due in no small measure to the pertinacity of the third archbishop in asserting episcopal rights at home and at Rome at a crucial stage in the development of the American hierarchy. That the American bishops would continue to maintain a measure of autonomy in their relationship with the Holy See was to no small degree the gift of an archbishop unafraid to speak his mind. It was a fearlessness that derived largely from a Gallican heritage. Though he doubtless harbored a nostalgia for the Ancien Régime, the same heritage rendered Maréchal responsive to the needs of the local church, bringing him also to an easy acceptance of religious freedom and the pluralism it presupposed. In this he was squarely within the Maryland tradition.

5 No Noisy Stirring Course

THE *UNITED STATES CATHOLIC MISCELLANY* of May 3, 1828, announced the appointment of James Whitfield as fourth archbishop of Baltimore. "In ecclesiastical rank," wrote the editor, who was doubtless Bishop England himself, "Baltimore is the first amongst our churches, and if circumstances permitted the Bishops of the Province to cooperate and to act as a body, having one object in view, the relations of the Archbishop would indeed be more extensive and important than they have been since the days of Archbishop Carroll." The bishop of Charleston was relentless. Neither England nor the two bishops who had seconded his appeal for a national synod, Edward and Benedict Fenwick, were invited to the consecration. The bishop of Charleston was hurt and told the new archbishop so. At the same time he expressed the hope that the consecrator, Bishop Flaget, with whom he had held extensive correspondence on the need for a council, had apprised Whitfield of the writer's views.[1] Whitfield had asked the bishop oldest in service, Benedict Flaget, to perform the consecration and Bishops Conwell of Philadelphia and Dubois of New York to act as his assistants. Prominent in the crowd that had filled the cathedral on May 25 were some thirty priests and a host of congressmen.[2] The vice president of St. Mary's College, Samuel Eccleston, delivered the sermon.

Whitfield was the only native of England to govern America's oldest see. Born in Liverpool in 1770 into an affluent merchant family, he had gone abroad at the death of his father in 1787. He had spent fifteen years in Leghorn, Italy, learning to be a merchant and, as a result of his meeting with Maréchal, eight years in Lyons, France, learning to be a priest.[3] From 1811 until 1817, when Maréchal persuaded him to come to Baltimore, he had served a small mission near his native city. Though he had entered the Jesuit novitiate upon his return to England, his stay was short. Whitfield remained a secular priest but at heart was a Sulpician. As archbishop he deviated little from the policies of his mentor, Ambrose Maréchal.

The First Provincial Council

Though he shared the misgivings of his predecessor about the ebullient bishop of Charleston, Whitfield bowed to the wishes of Flaget and Fenwick of Boston and announced to his suffragans in December 1828 the convocation of a provincial council on October 1 of the following year.[4] He also invited Bishops Rosati of St. Louis and Portier of Mobile even though their sees were not in the province of Baltimore, thus assuring that this and future councils would be truly national synods.[5] England was overjoyed at this "prospect of the dawn of our prosperity" and rich in proposals for discussion: a possible national seminary, means of counteracting the church's adversaries, education for the young, religious societies, Catholic publications, and uniformity of discipline.[6]

As it turned out, two bishops, Portier and Dubois, were abroad when the First Provincial Council convened on October 3, and Conwell was in forced retirement. Sitting with the archbishop and five bishops—Flaget, England, the two Fenwicks, and Rosati—were two priests—Matthews of Washington, administrator of Philadelphia, and John Powers of New York, Dubois's representative. Whitfield picked Fenwick of Boston as promoter and Father Damphoux as secretary. Seven of the remaining thirteen participants were also Sulpicians. Roger Brooke Taney and two other Catholic attorneys were brought in to advise on the incorporation of church property and ecclesiastical censures. On the second day of the council Whitfield received the pallium from the hands of Benedict Fenwick.

After two weeks of deliberations, thirty-eight decrees were sent to Rome for approval. Seventeen of these were aimed at uniformity in the administration of the sacraments. Ten dealt with priestly conduct, two with trusteeism, and three with Catholic publications. The thirty-fourth decree judged it "absolutely necessary" that schools for the young be established. The thirty-seventh called for diocesan synods to enforce the decrees and the thirty-eighth for another provincial council in three years, "unless for a grave reason the archbishop should postpone the same."[7]

The cardinal prefect of the Propaganda congratulated Whitfield on the masterly way in which the council had resolved those problems that threatened the peace of the church in the United States.[8] Whitfield reported to the Society for the Propagation of the Faith in Lyons that the bishops were "delighted" with all that had transpired. They had "opened their hearts" and had left "full of esteem and friendship for one another."[9] In his role as metropolitan James Whitfield, it seemed, was off to a good start.

The Rome of America

Whitfield's reports to the Lyons society reflected the optimism of the age. Baltimore, he boasted in the summer of 1829, was a "superb" city of eighty thousand, a fifth of whom were Catholic. The rest belonged to a multitude of sects, many of them torn by dissension and schism. There were in the city five Catholic churches: the ancient St. Peter's reopened for weekday services, St. John's for the Germans, St. Patrick's, St. Mary's at the seminary, and, of course, the cathedral. The last was "the most beautiful religious monument in the United States" with an organ that equaled that of Notre Dame of Paris and a choir whose renditions rivaled those of the best in France and Italy. In the see city were societies devoted to a variety of good works similar to those of the most pious cities of France.

Outside of Baltimore, he continued, churches with resident pastors could be found in Washington, Georgetown, Alexandria, Frederick Town, Taneytown, Emmitsburg, and Hagerstown. The Jesuits maintained a "magnificent" college in Georgetown. The Sulpicians had founded two seminaries, the one in Baltimore having been granted the privileges of a university by the Holy See in 1822. The Visitandines and Sisters of Charity were "singularly blessed enterprises," the latter with branch houses in distant parts of the country.[10] In a second report to the Lyons society in 1830 Whitfield bragged that Maryland was "of all the United States the one in which religion flourished the most and is propagated most rapidly."[11]

A note of "peace, unanimity, and prosperity" also pervaded the archbishop's reports to the Propaganda. "Our holy Religion in this City," he told the cardinal prefect in the spring of 1829, "& throughout the Diocess becomes always more & more respectable in the eyes of Protestants." The previous year a larger school for poor boys had been built, for which he hoped to procure religious brothers. A larger building for the orphan asylum, girls' school, and convent, which would cost $10,000, was also under construction.[12]

The *Metropolitan,* a monthly magazine begun in Baltimore in 1830, was even louder in its praise of the premier see and its outstanding institutions. "Baltimore," it claimed, "has, not improperly, been styled the Rome of the United States."[13] A young seminarian from Kentucky named Martin John Spalding on his way to the Urban College in Rome was mildly annoyed by these incessant allusions to the "Modern Rome" and its many advantages.[14]

Whitfield's two reports to the Society for the Propagation of the Faith won only 5,570 francs, among the lowest amounts awarded American bishops. He was told that, like his episcopal colleagues, he would have to speak with a poor mouth. An appeal dated February 16, 1832, was appropriately supplicant. Though unequaled in America, his cathedral was far from finished, needing towers, a portico, and vestibule. A minor seminary was under construction. For his projects he had incurred a debt of $50,000, three-fifths still to be paid at 5 or 6 percent interest. From his trustees he received only $400 a year, but since he had private means of support he spent not a cent of the society's subsidies on himself. Parts of his diocese were truly destitute. St. Mary's County, which was half Catholic, counted eight "miserable wooden churches little different from your sheds." Those of Charles County were even worse. Priests on the Eastern Shore had scarcely any means of subsistence. In the three towns of the District of Columbia—Washington, Georgetown, and Alexandria—there were nearly 10,000 Catholics in a population of 35,500 who attended four churches, but the most centrally located (St. Patrick's) was unworthy of the national capital.[15] The same report was sent to the Leopoldine Society founded in Vienna in 1829 to aid the American missions. This appeal elicited 20,000 florins (about $9,500), almost twice the total allocations of the Propagation of the Faith in the Whitfield years.[16]

The boasting letters were closer to the truth. The archdiocese of Baltimore was the most prosperous and least troubled of the American dioceses. The long parade of problem priests had all but ended. Though Whitfield complained of a shortage of priests, he could count seventy-two by the end of 1831, nearly a third of the entire American Catholic clergy. Of these, however, thirty-five were attached to seminaries, colleges, and convents, and four were inactive, leaving only twenty-nine for the missions.[17] The religious congregations, both men and women, took quantum leaps in the Whitfield years.

The New Jesuits

In the Jesuit community a new generation replaced the old. In 1828 and 1829 the young members sent to Rome to be educated returned. Among the native born were William McSherry, Thomas Mulledy, and Aloysius Young. They proved a talented and energetic lot. Georgetown College under Mulledy was reinvigorated, reaching 183 students in 1833. In response to a request sent to the Jesuit general in 1832, the American Province was erected February 2, 1833, and William McSherry installed as first provincial on July 8. The new province counted thirty-four priests, seventeen scholastics, and twenty-seven brothers.[18]

The pension question, however, was still a source of annoyance for the

Society and the archbishop alike. With the death of Maréchal the Jesuits proved reluctant to continue the subsidy, reminding Whitfield that he enjoyed a considerable fortune while the Maryland mission was in real need. Whitfield nevertheless won compliance through his Roman agent, Nicholas Wiseman, Gradwell's successor as rector of the English College.[19] In small ways relations between the Society and the archbishop continued to be strained, but good will would be restored under Whitfield's successor, who agreed to end the controversy once and for all upon the Society's payment of a lump sum of $8,000.[20]

The Sulpician "Revolution"

In February 1828 there occurred at St. Mary's Seminary what the Sulpician superior in Paris called "a second revolution." It was occasioned by Edward Damphoux's determination to be restored to the presidency of St. Mary's College, Louis Deluol's opposition to the change, and Tessier's indecision in this as in other matters. At basis it was a struggle for dominance in the community between two strong-willed men, Damphoux and Deluol. Though Joubert and Wheeler generally sided with Damphoux, Deluol had the unwavering support of Samuel Eccleston and John Joseph Chanche. All complained to Antoine Garnier, who had become superior general in 1826. Unable to come to America himself, Garnier sent Joseph Carrière as visitor in 1829. On the eve of the First Provincial Council Carrière conducted an investigation that ended in Tessier's being replaced by Deluol as superior of the community and rector of the seminary.[21] After "having turned everything upside down," the visitor left abruptly. Damphoux not only resigned the presidency of the college but withdrew from the Sulpicians.[22] Eccleston was named president. Damphoux moved to the cathedral to become the archbishop's secretary.

Deluol brought to the superiorship not only a needed decisiveness and efficiency but also a clearer vision of the place of the Sulpicians on the American scene. By 1829 he had become thoroughly Americanized and was even more disposed than his French confreres to make accommodations to the American character and to the needs of the American church. It was a vision and an approach shared by Eccleston and Chanche. Deluol also replaced Tessier as vicar general of the archdiocese. There can be little doubt that hereafter his opinions weighed heaviest in the counsels of the archbishop.

The future of Mount St. Mary's seminary and college remained in doubt. The plan to phase out the seminary over a five-year period was not

working. As Eccleston informed Garnier in 1828, the seminary at Emmitsburg was full while St. Mary's in Baltimore had only four theologians.
Eccleston looked forward to the "junction" of the two seminaries when the
five-year compromise would end in 1831.[23] Like his predecessor, Whitfield
was reluctant to suppress a flourishing institution. He therefore granted
the Emmitsburg seminary a year's reprieve in 1831 and at the end of that year
a two-year stay.[24] The problem was complicated further by the appointment of John Baptist Purcell, president of Mount St. Mary's College, as
successor to Bishop Edward Fenwick in Cincinnati in 1833 and of Simon
Bruté, mainstay of the seminary, as first bishop of Vincennes in 1834. Death
would overtake the fourth archbishop before he could render a final decision on the status of Mount St. Mary's Seminary.

The future of the seminary in Baltimore was itself uncertain. The
question of a national seminary was raised at the First Provincial Council.
Though Whitfield would like to have seen St. Mary's Seminary chosen for
that role, Bishop England, who strongly favored a national seminary, had
little use for the Sulpicians. Before Whitfield's death, moreover, the bishops
of Philadelphia, Boston, and New York would begin seminaries of their
own. This was not an auspicious development for St. Mary's.

The spadework was done at this time, however, for another important
contribution of the oldest diocese: the first minor seminary in the United
States. The school at Pigeon Hill, opened with such an institution in mind,
had moved to Mount St. Mary's to be absorbed by the college that developed there. A disappointing number of graduates from the three colleges in the archdiocese entered the Baltimore seminary. Suggestions
planted by Maréchal bore fruit in 1830 when the aged Charles Carroll donated 254 acres near his home at Doughoregan Manor and fifty shares of
bank stock for the founding of a college to educate exclusively "pious
young men . . . for the ministry of the gospel," as the charter stipulated.
The cornerstone was blessed by the archbishop on July 11, 1831. By 1833 the
building was two-thirds completed. The death of its benefactor and a shortage of funds brought a halt to the construction—a sixteen-year suspension
as it turned out.[25]

The Fourth Sisterhood

Spectacular was the expansion of the Sisters of Charity of Emmitsburg, who by 1830 numbered 126. Of these, 56 were on missions.[26] In
the nineteen years of existence before Whitfield's episcopacy they had established only three branch houses outside of Maryland. In his seven years

they averaged almost three a year in other states. Most were orphan asylums and poor schools. Some were hospitals. In 1833, ten years after the sisters had agreed to staff the Baltimore Infirmary, they moved also into the Maryland Hospital on Broadway.[27] Clearly in their choice of work they were moving closer to the Daughters of Charity in France.

The Visitation Sisters at Georgetown, some of whom desired affiliation with the Ursulines, committed themselves irrevocably to the Visitation rule when their Sulpician director, Michael Wheeler, returned from France in 1829 with three French Visitandines. One of them, Sister Madeleine Augustine, was elected superior in 1831. By 1829 there were some fifty nuns at the Georgetown convent, considerably more than the thirty-three allowed by rule. In 1832 Sister Madeleine Augustine herself led a colony of five sisters to Mobile to found the first daughter house. In 1833 Sister Mary Agnes Brent took nine others to Kaskaskia in Illinois at the invitation of Bishop Rosati to found a third convent school.[28]

In 1831 the Carmelites of Port Tobacco moved to Baltimore, a development to be treated in another connection.

To these three sisterhoods a fourth was added in 1829. Its founder was James Hector Joubert, a one-time tax agent in France but a man of property in Saint-Domingue at the time of the slave revolt. In Baltimore he entered the seminary, was ordained in 1810, and immediately joined the Sulpicians. In 1827 Tessier surrendered catechetical direction of the black community of the *chapelle basse* to Joubert. The latter wanted to start a school but was told by both Tessier and Maréchal that there was no money. Yet Whitfield gave him an unhesitating yes soon after the death of Maréchal. He also said yes when Joubert proposed that the young ladies of mixed blood conducting the school form a religious community.[29]

In June 1828 Elizabeth Lange, Marie Madeleine Balas, and Rosine Boegue began to live together in a rented house near the seminary, which sheltered also nine boarders and three orphans. The next May they moved to a larger home on Richmond Street purchased from Dr. Pierre Chatard, whose family proved warm friends of the new sisterhood. On June 5, 1829, the archbishop approved the rules of the Oblate Sisters of Providence drawn up by Joubert and based upon those of the Oblates of St. Frances of Rome. On July 2 Sister Mary (Lange), Sister Mary Frances (Balas), and Sister Mary Rose (Boegue) made their profession, the first having been elected superior for three years.[30]

It was a bold undertaking for this decidedly southern city. Some Catholics did not disguise their distaste for this "profanation of the habit."[31] Deluol observed in his diary (June 20, 1829) that Joubert was "amazed and mortified" that a fellow Sulpician, Chanche, had refused his request "to translate the prospectus of the Mulatto Ladies." For most, however, the project was palatable because the sisters were cultured, French-speaking Caribbeans. Whitfield's unflagging support, Joubert's enthusiasm, and the quiet courage of the sisters themselves carried the foundation through the first critical years. By 1830 there were eleven Oblates. A large number entered in 1833.[32]

Still More Parishes

The growth of parishes—and the word "parish" came increasingly to replace "mission" or "congregation"—was not as spectacular as that of religious orders but was steady. This was particularly true of western Maryland and Virginia, where the "transportation revolution" swelled the population.[33]

In 1829 Whitfield sent the first resident pastors: to Allegany County, Francis X. Marshall, and to western Virginia, the newly ordained John Baptist Gildea. In 1833 Wheeling was also assigned a resident pastor. Marshall built a church at Blooming Rose in 1831 and chose to live there.[34] At the western edge of the state, Blooming Rose was no byproduct of the transportation revolution but a throwback to a simpler age, a holdout of the mountain people, like Meshack Browning, the famous hunter and Catholic convert, against encroaching civilization.[35] For the more populous parish at Arnold's Settlement Marshall built a second and larger church, which the archbishop dedicated as St. Ignatius December 29, 1833. Two other churches begun in western Maryland under Maréchal were completed: Hagerstown's second church in 1828 and the church at Maryland Tract (Petersville) in 1829. Gildea resided at Martinsburg, (West) Virginia, where he completed a church in 1831. At Harper's Ferry, where the B&O Railroad crossed the Potomac into Virginia, he built another in 1833. In Frederick Town, later called simply Frederick, the cornerstone was laid for a large Jesuit church to replace the old one in 1833.[36]

Elsewhere in Maryland Whitfield allowed the Jesuits, finally, to open the church they had built at Upper Marlboro. The first mass was said April 8, 1829.[37] On the Eastern Shore at Denton services were commenced probably in 1831 in a church also begun under Maréchal. But the church on which Whitfield lavished most attention was that built for the only parish created in Baltimore during his episcopacy, appropriately named St. James. Planned for the growing number of Catholics in Old Town, that part of the city east of Jones Falls, its cornerstone was laid May 1, 1833, and its consecration conducted exactly a year later. Its cost was defrayed largely from Whitfield's private fortune, upon which he drew also for the completion of the cathedral rectory in 1830 and the south tower of the cathedral, where in 1831 was lodged a bell cast in Lyons, France.[38]

More churches were begun under Whitfield in Virginia than in Maryland. In addition to the two raised by Gildea, a brick church was opened in Norfolk in 1831 and a plainer one in Portsmouth in 1832. In Richmond the old church was replaced by a larger one, the future St. Peter's Cathedral, which was dedicated by Whitfield on May 25, 1834.[39]

Transformations

SOCIAL AND POLITICAL

Historically more important than the steady growth of the archdiocese and its appendage across the Potomac were the social, political, and economic changes that overtook the archdiocese in the seven Whitfield years. Indicative of the character of that transformation were the contrasting careers of Charles Carroll of Carrollton and Roger Brooke Taney.

Though Carroll moved from Annapolis to Baltimore in 1824 and busied himself with banking and transportation, he remained a planter at heart, more at home on his country estate, Doughoregan Manor, and more in sympathy with the slaveholding aristocracy of the Tidewater. His attempt to sustain this aristocracy by keeping intact his large estates was, as Alexis de Tocqueville observed in his visit to Baltimore, doomed to failure.[40] Carroll's death on November 14, 1832, at age ninety-five, the last surviving signer of the Declaration of Independence, put a period to an age. He was buried from the Cathedral of the Assumption. Samuel Eccleston preached the eulogy.

Taney, on the other hand, had moved from southern Maryland to Frederick Town in 1801 at age twenty-four and then to Baltimore in 1823, identifying completely with the rising western and urban parts of the state. Never a wealthy man, he contributed to the church in ways different from Carroll, giving generously of his legal and managerial talents.[41] Even as Attorney General of the United States (1831–33), Secretary of the Treasury (1833–34), and Chief Justice of the United States (1836–64) Taney remained a more consistently devout and practical Catholic than Carroll.

Few Catholics were active in the development of the second two-party system in Maryland. The exceptions were Taney, who in 1827 became chairman of the state committee for the election of Andrew Jackson, and Luke Tiernan, an almost equally active supporter of John Quincy Adams. Many

Catholics, however, considered Adams a bigot. "An Address to the Catholic Voters of Baltimore" signed by several prominent Catholic laymen
warned their coreligionists not to be taken in by the allurements of the
Adams camp.[42] As the Whig and Democratic parties developed, Maryland
Catholics gave allegiance along geographic and social lines. In the southern
counties they voted Whig, the party of property, in the western counties,
Democrat, the party of the common man. In the city of Baltimore most of
the merchant Catholics voted Whig while working-class Catholics, largely
newcomers, voted Democrat. Immigrants would constitute the most pre-
dictable segment of the Democratic party in Maryland.[43]

SHIFTING POPULATIONS

The future of the Catholic Church in the archdiocese of Baltimore lay
with the cities of Baltimore and Washington and the western part of the
state rather than with the counties that gave it birth. While in the 1830s the
southern counties and the Eastern Shore would lose population, Baltimore
would grow from 80,000 to over 100,000 and western Maryland from
128,000 to 147,000.[44] Though the cities and western counties drew Catholics from southern Maryland, Catholic growth was due as much to immigration. In Maryland, as in the rest of the nation, immigration rose from a
trickle in the 1820s to a stream in the 1830s to a torrent in the 1840s. Some
50,000 people disembarked at Baltimore in the 1830s. Most moved on, but
many remained to fill its workshops.

Baltimore expanded as business accelerated, old wealth giving way to
new. Astride the southeastern boundary the Canton Company was created
in 1830 on the old O'Donnell estate, "probably the nation's earliest, largest,
and most successful industrial park."[45] In the western part of the city the
nation's oldest railroad yards were constructed at Mount Clare, the estate of
Charles Carroll the Barrister. The area just north of St. Mary's Seminary
filled rapidly, the seminary itself selling a substantial piece of property for
urban development.[46] Old Town was pushing out Harford Road.

Immigrants were also drawn to the western part of the state by the
canal and railroad projects and the mining operations these projects made
possible. On July 4, 1828, Charles Carroll laid the cornerstone for the Baltimore and Ohio Railroad while at Georgetown President Adams turned
the first spadeful of dirt for the Chesapeake and Ohio Canal. Both were
intended, as their names indicate, to link the seaboard with the Mississippi
basin and accomplish for their termini what the Erie Canal had done for
New York City.[47] Also in 1828 the Maryland Mining Company was chartered by the Maryland Assembly, the first of some thirty coal or coal and

iron companies incorporated between 1828 and 1850.[48] The B&O Railroad and C&O Canal were constructed largely by immigrant Irish labor.

The advance of the immigrants was not always peaceful. In 1831 two outbreaks of violence alarmed the towns along the B&O. Outside Baltimore Irish laborers, defrauded of their wages, tore up their own work and were "reduced to order only by the military and Revd. Mr. [Charles] Pise."[49] Near New Market a fight broke out between Irish and black workers. When twenty or so of their ringleaders were arrested, some four hundred angry Irishmen marched to the jail to force their release. They were, however, pacified by Father John McElroy, who "placed himself at the head of the whole body and marched them off to their shanties."[50] Many of the Catholic construction workers remained to farm or to work the mines of western Maryland, where they were easily tamed by their pastors.[51]

URBANIZATION

Urbanization would dislodge the American Catholic Church in the 1830s from its largely southern and rural moorings. Catholic planters and farmers diminished in importance as a Catholic proletariat emerged. New York, Philadelphia, and Boston would in short order outstrip Baltimore, St. Louis, and New Orleans as the most active centers of Catholic strength. The move from a rural to an urban orientation was made evident in the archdiocese of Baltimore in the Whitfield years not only in the population shift already mentioned but also in the work of the clergy and religious congregations. By the end of Whitfield's episcopacy the majority of priests in the archdiocese could be found in Baltimore, Washington, and Frederick. At the same time religious orders were looking more to urban than rural settings as their field of labor.

In 1831 the Carmelites of Port Tobacco sold their deteriorating farm in Charles County and moved to Baltimore. Long desirous for a girls' academy in his see city, Whitfield convinced them to take up this work initially proposed by Carroll. The school they opened on Aisquith Street was successful enough to support the community.[52] Of the twenty-one branch houses opened by the Sisters of Charity in the Whitfield years, over half were above the Mason-Dixon line and in such urban centers as New York, Philadelphia, Boston, and Brooklyn. By contrast the Visitation nuns, with their more aristocratic clientele, moved to the dioceses of Mobile and St. Louis.

The most striking shift from rural to urban occurred among the Jesuits. Until the establishment of the province in 1833, the primary concern of the Maryland Jesuits was the plantations for which they had fought so hard in the Maréchal years. The 12,000 acres and some three hundred slaves who worked them were deemed indispensable for the well-being of the Society. Some of the younger members, however, considered the estates more of an encumbrance than a benefit. Thomas Mulledy and William McSherry, both from western Virginia, evidenced no strong loyalty to the "Maryland Way." After the establishment of the American Province the decisions were made to reduce the number of rural missions, to sell the Jesuit slaves, to sell some of the land and lease the rest, and to concentrate on the colleges and a mission band to preach in cities.[53]

The sale of the slaves would prove an unhappy sequel to the story of the urbanization of the Maryland Jesuits. Permission to sell was finally granted by the Jesuit general in 1836, but the negotiations were delayed by the Panic of 1837. The following year, 272 slaves were sold to a Louisiana planter for $115,000. Of this sum $8,000 ended the pension controversy with the archbishop of Baltimore, $17,000 liquidated the debt of Georgetown College, and the remaining $90,000 was invested for the training of young Jesuits. Reaction to the sale was decidedly negative. Some of the Jesuits themselves warned the slaves to hide. The odium fell upon Mulledy, who had succeeded McSherry as provincial. Mulledy was advised to submit his resignation in Rome and to remain there for a time.[54] Blacks in southern Maryland told an agent of the Maryland State Colonization Society that they now put no more trust in priests than in kidnappers.[55]

Another drastic change in the Whitfield years occurred in Maryland's attitude toward its residents of African descent. Fully a third of the 155,000 blacks in the state were free. A number of Maryland Catholics were enrolled in the American Colonization Society founded to send free blacks back to Africa, Charles Carroll of Carrollton becoming its second president in 1830. In February 1831 the Maryland State Colonization Society was organized but attracted small attention until the Nat Turner Rebellion in August in neighboring Virginia. "One must not hide it," an aroused alumnus of St. Mary's College told Alexis de Tocqueville in November. "The white population and the black population are at war."[56] In December Dr. Octavius Taney, a state senator and brother of Roger B. Taney, introduced a resolution at Annapolis calculated to remove free persons of color from the state.[57]

Some Catholics were active in the Maryland State Colonization Society. William George Read, a member of the board, tried to interest McSherry, the Jesuit provincial, in a strictly Catholic colony in Africa. Nothing came of the project until the American bishops some ten years later cooperated with the Maryland society in sponsoring such a colony.

Whitfield's successor would urge his priests in southern Maryland to cooperate in raising recruits. Despite the zeal of the pastors, an agent of the society would report, there was not a single volunteer.[58]

A Revival of Antipopery

A still more drastic change in attitude at this time was occasioned by the revival of antipopery, that peculiar brand of nativism that would have far-reaching consequences for the Catholic Church in the United States. In 1830 Whitfield reported to the Propaganda that there were many conversions in Baltimore, where the Church was so respected that "not one of the many public papers, though edited by Protestants, would consent to publish the prospectus of a most violent and anti-Catholic paper edited at New York called the *Protestant*." Its editor, Whitfield reported, "complains that Baltimore is lost to them being completely under the sway of popery."[59]

The *Protestant*, launched in January 1830, had as its avowed purpose to warn the nation of the growth of popery and the dangers it posed.[60] In March the editors declared: "We ourselves are enjoined to 'be quiet, and let the Marylanders alone!' We will not be silent. Their own Press dare not expose their iniquities: *ours shall*. Their own preachers are not at liberty to call things by their right names; we will."[61] When Taney was named Attorney General of the United States in 1831, the *Protestant* pronounced him a "thorough going Papist, possibly a concealed lay member of the order of the Jesuits." It also avowed that "every sincere Papist is disqualified de facto from holding office under a Protestant government," a sentiment heatedly condemned by the *Baltimore Republican*.[62]

Until Whitfield's last year, Maryland Catholics remained unruffled. In the summer and fall of 1832, in fact, the good will of non-Catholics in Baltimore was bolstered by the services of both the Sisters of Charity and the Oblates of Providence during the most devastating epidemic of the cholera to date. The plague claimed two Sisters of Charity and an Oblate, Sister Anthony Duchemin, who nursed the archbishop himself through an attack in September.[63] "It has become fashionable of late to applaud popery," the *Presbyterian* editorialized in 1833. "No ministers possess so much learning or display so much disinterested zeal, as those of the Church of Rome, and no females can fearlessly nurse in the cholera but the Sisters of Charity."[64]

On August 11, 1834, a mob burned the convent and school of the Ursulines of Charlestown, Massachusetts, the first of a long and painful series of attacks upon the Church of Rome.[65] In October rumors began to circulate in Baltimore that the Carmelite and Oblate convent schools were marked for a similar fate. Joubert sought the mayor's protection and with two younger priests slept in the convent parlor until the danger had passed.[66] The following May guards were posted at the Carmelite convent when a crowd gathered to taunt the nuns.[67] Whitfield had died before the frightening truth had penetrated Catholic consciousness: the premier see was no longer impervious to the nativist assault.

The Academic Flowering

It was inconceivable to Maryland Catholics that their schools and the religious who conducted them should come under attack. The colleges and academies were the crowning glory of the archdiocese. Under Whitfield they achieved a classic form that would not be altered until the end of the century. In 1830 there were only sixty colleges in the entire nation with hardly more than five thousand students.[68] In the same year the oldest archdiocese had four Catholic colleges for men, half the Catholic colleges in the United States, and three Catholic academies for young women. In 1831 the Carmelites added another academy. Under the presidencies of Mulledy, Eccleston, and John Baptist Purcell, Georgetown College, St. Mary's College, and Mount St. Mary's College reached the peak of their development. In 1829 Father John McElroy opened St. John's Literary Institute in Frederick, hardly more than a preparatory school at the start but in time a rival to Georgetown College.[69]

By 1830 both Georgetown and St. Mary's College had developed the full seven-year program, which required importing the apparatus needed for "natural philosophy" or science. The curriculum at Georgetown would serve as a model for other Jesuit colleges, that of St. Mary's for colleges founded by Sulpicians or their students. These Catholic colleges, like most non-Catholic ones, dispensed heavy doses of the Latin and Greek classics. The casual display of Latin quotes and classical allusions was a hallmark of the gentleman. The Catholic colleges of the oldest archdiocese played a crucial role in perpetuating the aristocratic values as well as the ecumenical bent that were part and parcel of the Maryland tradition. Friendships that developed between Catholic and non-Catholic students in these colleges were enduring.

Georgetown Visitation was the pacesetter for the girls' academies. Painting, music, needlework, and "domestic economy" held as important a place in the curriculum as grammar, mathematics, and science. St. Joseph's Academy at Emmitsburg upgraded its offerings in 1828 to approximate those of the Visitation and to a lesser extent St. John's Academy in Frederick, did, too. Other pay schools opened by the Sisters of Charity in Washington in 1831 and Alexandria in 1832 were short-lived. The curriculum of the pay school of the Oblates was modest.[70] The convent schools were held in high esteem, especially in the South, and were as important as the colleges in promoting aristocratic values and interfaith friendships. At these Catholic finishing schools the young ladies were carefully prepared for their roles as pious mothers, docile wives, and ornaments of the society in which they moved.

The Tocqueville Questions

In his November 1831 visit to Baltimore, the insatiably curious Alexis de Tocqueville recorded a conversation with the Sulpician president of St. Mary's College, John Joseph Chanche. Tocqueville asked if the Catholic atmosphere at the college produced converts. It was strong enough to remove prejudice, Chanche believed, but not strong enough to make converts. "What is more sure of effect," he added, "is the marriage of a Protestant with a Catholic girl. Such marriages are forbidden in Europe; we favor them here." This led the French visitor to probe: "What is the opinion of Catholics in America about the power of the Pope?" The Sulpician replied hesitantly, "It would be very difficult to say," but added, "In America as in Europe there are 'Gallicans' and 'ultramontanes.' The latter have the Jesuits as leaders. But up till now these questions are only asked within the circle of those who study theology. The masses have never come into it." To the question, "Are American Catholics zealous?" Chanche responded without hesitation: "Yes, I think America is called to become the hearth of Catholicism. It is spreading freely without the help of the civil power, without rousing hatred, simply by the strength of its doctrine and in perfect independence of the State."[71] It was one of the last expressions of Catholic optimism in the antebellum years.

Corporation Sole

Two important developments in the Whitfield years were the result of the First Provincial Council. Its fifth decree had required the title of all churches, whenever possible, to be vested in the bishop. Whitfield had told the prefect of the Propaganda shortly before the Council that though the cathedral and two other churches in Baltimore were under trustees, "we live in peace with them and they are perfectly submissive."[72] Nevertheless, a bill was introduced in 1832 at the December session of the Maryland Assembly to become law in March (Chapter 308) whereby property could be transferred from trustees to the archbishop of Baltimore in his capacity of corporation sole. It was the first such arrangement for a Catholic diocese in the United States and in time become the model for the majority of them.[73] Whitfield, however, left to his successor the implementation of the act.

Writers and Publishers

The First Provincial Council had also decreed the establishment of a Catholic book society under the archbishop of Baltimore. Whitfield had actually had a plan drawn up for such a society on the eve of the Council.[74] Many of the bishops, therefore, were surprised when the archbishop took no steps to carry out the decree. The action of the bishops, nevertheless, encouraged Catholic publishers in Baltimore to divert their principal energies to the publication of Catholic books, a decision that would make Baltimore the Catholic publishing center of the country.

It was a logical development because the oldest archdiocese could claim the greatest concentration of literary talent, not only among the Jesuits, Sulpicians, and secular priests, but also among the educated laity. The first important figure in American Catholic literature, in fact, was Charles Constantine Pise, a native of Annapolis, Roman educated and ordained in 1825. In 1827–30 he wrote and published a five-volume *History of the Catholic Church* and in 1829 *Father Rowland: A North American Tale*, the first Catholic novel published in the United States.[75] In 1830 he took upon himself the editorship of the *Metropolitan*, the first Catholic monthly. It lasted, however, only a year.

Both the *History* and the *Metropolitan* were published by Peter Blenkinsop. More important as a publisher was Fielding Lucas, Jr., who had moved from Philadelphia to Baltimore in the early 1800s. Though his press brought out an occasional Catholic book, including texts for St. Mary's College, it was not until 1829 that he became an exclusively Catholic publisher and for a decade and more thereafter the most prolific in the United States.[76] Another Baltimore bookman was James Myres, who from 1833 to 1837 published the *Catholic Almanac and Laity's Directory*. The *Directory* would be continued under the name, *Metropolitan Catholic Almanac*, by Lucas after the death of Myres in 1837.[77] An Irish-born apprentice named John Murphy would open a shop in Baltimore in 1835 and publish his first Catholic book in 1836. In time he would overtake Lucas as the leading Catholic publisher in the country.

Compelled to Lead

Whitfield's failure to follow through on the decree concerning a Catholic book society reflected his reluctance to assume a leadership role in the American church. Unlike Bishop England, he felt no obligation to intervene in the affairs of other sees. In his nearly seven years as administrator and archbishop, he never traveled beyond the borders of the archdiocese and the diocese of Richmond. Even when one of his own priests, William Matthews, was chosen administrator of the diocese of Philadelphia in 1828, he remained aloof from the affairs of that unhappy see, where Bishop Conwell had incurred Roman censure by conceding too much to the trustees and where William Vincent Harold and John Ryan had appealed to Secretary of State Henry Clay against their Dominican superiors and Rome, citing as a precedent the Jesuits' appeal to the government against Maréchal.[78] At the First Provincial Council the bishops had petitioned Rome to allow Conwell to remain in Philadelphia as its bishop but to place actual power in the hands of a coadjutor. The Dublin-born and Roman-educated Francis Patrick Kenrick, a priest of the diocese of Bardstown, was consecrated coadjutor bishop of Philadelphia June 6, 1830. With patience and determination he brought the most troublesome see of the United States under control.[79] In Kenrick, England found an ally.

Even more did Whitfield remain aloof from the affairs of the diocese of New York, where Dubois's tactless rule goaded trustees to new heights of insubordination, and from those of the diocese of Bardstown, where Flaget's badly managed effort to replace his failing coadjutor with a younger favorite occasioned a near revolt. Though he dutifully responded to the Propaganda's request to consult his suffragans on diocesan boundaries, Whitfield evidenced little enthusiasm for serving as a conduit for the Holy See in American affairs. He played little part in choosing a replacement for Bishop Fenwick in Cincinnati, who died in 1832, or filling the new sees of Detroit in 1833 and Vincennes in 1834, even though two of his own priests were nominated.[80]

In 1831 England reminded Whitfield of the decree of the First Provincial Council to convoke a second one in three years. "With regard to another Provincial Council," Whitfield told the bishop of Charleston flatly, "it is certain I shall not convoke it the coming year." The good effects of the first, he explained, were yet to be seen, and he had good reasons to apprehend "injurious effects from such a convocation." Bishops were better employed in their own extensive dioceses. "For my part," he concluded, "I am quite averse to unnecessary agitation and excitement; experience seems to prove, that walking silently in the steps of my predecessors, doing what good Providence may put in our way, & publishing it as little as possible has with God's blessing promoted Religion more & made it more respectable in the eyes of Protestants than if a noisy stirring course had been pursued."[81]

Though apparently pleased with the results of the First Provincial Council, the distrust of Irish bishops he shared with his predecessor was intensified with the elevation of Kenrick. To his Roman agent, Nicholas Wiseman, Whitfield confided that England and Kenrick had "strong Irish predilections in favor of Irish Bishops & Irish discipline." And if Purcell were named to Cincinnati, he predicted, he would be led by England, as was Kenrick.[82]

Whitfield may also have come to resent other bishops legislating for his own see. As required, he called a synod, the Second Diocesan Synod of Baltimore, on November 8, 1831, to put in force the decrees of the First Provincial Council. Where a contrary custom prevailed, however, it was decided to put the council's decree in force only gradually.[83] Kenrick suggested to England, then in Rome, that he might call the Propaganda's attention to the liberty taken by the Baltimore synod with several decrees, particularly the ones dealing with the use of English in services and placement of confessionals. "Does not the good of religion," he suggested, "demand perhaps that the archbishop and his clergy receive a lesson in Canon Law from the Sacred Congregation?"[84] In Rome England convinced the Propaganda that the archbishop was derelict in his duty by not calling a council. Whitfield was instructed that the Holy Father himself desired that a council be convoked.

The Second Provincial Council of Baltimore was held October 20–27, 1833. In attendance were the archbishop, nine bishops, and twenty priests. Eleven decrees were enacted, three of which concerned the boundaries of dioceses and one the method of nominating bishops for American sees.[85] On only one point did Whitfield have reason to be dissatisfied with the results. Rome did not accede to the council's request that the diocese of Richmond be suppressed and reunited to the archdiocese of Baltimore. By an unaccustomed exercise of power, and in an obvious attempt to put the bishop of Charleston in his place, Whitfield successfully countered every one of England's proposals. In the minority were England, Kenrick, and Frederick Rese, bishop of Detroit. Surprising was the lack of support of Bishop Purcell of Cincinnati for the minority.[86]

Both England and Kenrick confided their disappointment to their friend Paul Cullen, rector of the Irish College in Rome, Kenrick speaking of the "suspicion with which every measure emanating from Bishop England was received." England complained bitterly that the archbishop was "completely the tool of the Sulpicians, who have for a number of years created a government of intrigue and faction, instead of an honest, open, strong, administration, based upon their convictions and sustained by the affections of the Catholic body."[87] Deluol observed in his diary that England seemed to be "suffering cruelly," and added: "If it is true that he had his eyes on the see of Baltimore, his hopes are now dashed, by the nomination of Mr. Eccleston."[88] One of Whitfield's most notable successes at the Council was the support he had won for his choice of Samuel Eccleston as his coadjutor with right of succession.

The Passing of a Merchant

Now that he had weathered the storm, Whitfield awaited only the consecration of his successor before deciding it was time to die. Though not in poor health, he had never become accustomed to the torrid Maryland summers, which had taken their toll. The last was the worst. Yet he showed few signs of a rapidly deteriorating condition until after the ordination of Eccleston as bishop on September 14, 1834. A month later he took to bed. Immediately his mind began to wander. In lucid moments he spoke of bank stocks. On the 19th he died.[89]

The years James Whitfield had spent learning to be a priest never erased the years he had spent learning to be a merchant. In many ways he remained a merchant even as archbishop of Baltimore, going about his business quietly, cautiously, attentive to detail, careful in his relationship with others, confiding in few. Confident in his wealth, he shunned display and ostentation. Yet he was a "booster" who took pride in his achievements. He turned a profit and left all accounts balanced.

Posterity would dismiss the fourth archbishop as one of Baltimore's least consequential, deploring his unwillingness to assert a more active leadership in the American church. Yet it was precisely this refusal to divert his energies that rendered him one of the more competent of the archbishops of Baltimore. It was a competence, nevertheless, that was the result of a gift none of his successors would enjoy: the leisure to govern without providing the host of services demanded by an ever-growing number of immigrants. Whitfield could, therefore, claim the distinction of being the last archbishop of the Carroll church.

II

The Immigrant Church

Archbishop Samuel Eccleston 1834–1851

Archbishop Francis Patrick Kenrick 1851–1863

Archbishop Martin John Spalding 1864–1872

Archbishop James Roosevelt Bayley 1872–1877

"Charles Carroll the Signer is dead, & Archbishop Carroll is dead, and there is no vision in the land," Ralph Waldo Emerson would write sadly after a visit to the Baltimore cathedral in 1843.[1] It was in part a Protestant perception of the decline of Roman Catholicism in America in the Age of Jackson. The decline was a consequence, as many perceived it, of the failure of the church to produce leaders, lay or cleric, of the caliber of the Revolutionary gentlemen. To a greater extent it was the result of a dramatic transformation produced by immigration.

The effects of a progressive rise in the alien influx could be felt as early as the 1830s, but the transformation of the Catholic minority into an immigrant church of impressive proportions was not so rapid in the oldest archdiocese as it was in some of the newer ones. The change would come nevertheless, despite a reluctance on the part of the old families to acknowledge it before the onslaught of the Know Nothings in the 1850s. Well before the Know Nothings, however, the Carroll church would begin to give way to the immigrant church, whose attitudes and goals would often be in conflict with the Maryland tradition.

First would come the immigrant church, and the reaction to it would produce the ghetto church. Soon the adjectives could be used coincidentally, "immigrant" to describe the church's constituency, "ghetto" to explain its strategy. The fretfulness that the immigrant presence, especially that of the Catholic immigrant, awakened in the native born would produce an antagonism that sporadically turned violent. "Unwittingly the nativistic and anti-Catholic reaction of the forties and fifties furnished the hammer and the anvil by which this distinctly Catholic cultural unity was created," claims Thomas T. McAvoy, the principal authority on the transformation of the Catholic minority.[2] "The ghetto culture was not deliberately planned," John Cogley agrees. "It developed as an early defense measure, and as the years went on it matured into a whole set of institutions paralleling some of the basic structures of American life. In time it became the best organized of the nation's subcultures—a source of both alienation and enrichment of those born within it and an object of bafflement or un-easiness for others."[3]

The ghetto, however, was not a Catholic phenomenon. Not until the twentieth century, in fact, would a self-consciously Catholic ghetto de-velop fully. Many groups in the nineteenth century would attempt to "mark out sharp and clear boundaries" between themselves and a larger, hostile world. "It was the age of self-built ghettos—Catholic, Protestant, liberal, socialist."[4] To insulate themselves against a hostile environment, immigrants built walls. For the Catholic immigrant these walls took the form of Catholic or ethnic institutions and organizations that provided es-sential needs, material and psychic. More specifically Catholic immigrants established self-identifying congregations, or national parishes; schools, orphanages, and hospitals; insurance, home-building, social, literary, and devotional organizations. They also developed a demarcating piety and es-tablished a militant press.

Almost all of these developments would have their inception under Samuel Eccleston, the archbishop who would have to deal with the sudden inrush of ragged Irish fleeing starvation or clannish Germans seeking a bet-ter life. Paradoxically, it would be the Maryland-born Eccleston and a man of Maryland ancestry, Martin John Spalding, who would prove the most responsive of the archbishops of Baltimore before Michael Joseph Curley to the needs of immigrants. The Irish-born Francis Patrick Kenrick be-tween Eccleston and Spalding and the well-born James Roosevelt Bayley after Spalding would have been more at home in the Carroll church (though in Newark Bayley would be as attentive to the immigrant as any of his successors).

The three archbishops who would follow Eccleston would come to Baltimore unschooled in the manners and mores of Maryland Catholics. Able administrators in their former sees, they would bring to an arch-diocese beset with a laissez-faire mentality fresh ideas and new procedures. Though they would achieve a tighter control at the top and accountability at the bottom, tactics that worked elsewhere would somehow go awry in the oldest see. Kenrick would turn few pastors into first-rate bookkeepers, Spalding would bend the social habits of the Maryland elite hardly a bit, and Bayley would loosen pursestrings infinitesimally.

Piece by piece the immigrant church would be put in place by the legis-lation that came out of Baltimore. Five provincial councils and two plenary ones would continue to call all the bishops of the nation to the oldest see for this collective task. In the Second Plenary Council Spalding would produce in 1866 the *corpus juris* of the ghetto church. Spalding would also, more than any other, advance the interests of the Holy See, whose influence would grow in proportion to the expansion of the immigrant church. Bayley would represent, after Kenrick and Spalding, both Roman students, a return to the moderate Gallicanism of his Sulpician predecessors in Baltimore. And this despite the apparent death blow dealt Gallicanism at Vatican Council I, to which Spalding would lend his hand as avidly as any. Yet in their promotion of American ideals Spalding and Bayley would share that missionary fervor displayed by Carroll before them and Gibbons after.

6 Native Born and Newcomers

BISHOP KENRICK, FOR ONE, marveled that "a young man having no experience in the ministry, save that which he could have within College walls" should be raised to the archbishopric of Baltimore.[1] At thirty-three Samuel Eccleston would be the youngest by far of any man chosen to govern the premier see. He was also the first convert in the American hierarchy, a Catholic for hardly more than sixteen years when thrust into a demanding role at a bewildering time in the development of the Catholic Church in the United States. Throughout his episcopacy this tall and imposing prelate hid his insecurity behind a charming exterior.

Samuel Eccleston was the only child of the second marriage of Samuel Sr. and the first marriage of Martha Hynson, both Episcopalians. The father died shortly after Samuel Jr.'s birth on June 27, 1801, near Charlestown on the Eastern Shore. The mother moved to Baltimore, married an irascible Irish Catholic named William Stenson, adopted his faith, and had by him four children.[2] From the diary of Father Deluol, we know that Samuel was close to these half sisters and brothers, one of whom was mentally unstable and another incorrigible. At age twelve Samuel was enrolled in St. Mary's College, from which he graduated at age eighteen. "Mr. Damphoux came to tell me," Deluol recorded six months before, "that Mr. Sam Eccleston, who, after a rather wild life, had become a convert last year, had recently become worse than ever; he had just come to him (Mr. D) to tell him of his sincere desire to come back to God and courageously fight the human respect which had been his down-fall, last spring."[3] Two days after graduation Eccleston entered the seminary. Several times in the first month he thought of leaving. "I offered my Mass for Mr. Eccleston," Deluol wrote on one such occasion.[4]

Not long after ordination on April 24, 1825, Eccleston became the second American to enter "The Solitude" at Issy near Paris, the Sulpician novitiate. From there he informed Archbishop Maréchal of his attraction first to the study of canon law and then to the contemplative life. Maréchal refused permission for both, deeming canon law in America "only secondary and ornamental." Maréchal had plans for the young Suplician to teach

Sacred Eloquence in the seminary and adorn the pulpit himself.[5] Though as a speaker he did not disappoint his superior, Eccleston had no liking for the task, a fact that may explain a chronic throat condition that worsened in his episcopal years.

At St. Mary's College Eccleston proved himself, first as vice president from 1827 to 1829 and then as president from 1829 to 1834, when he was ordained titular bishop of Thermae.[6] His first episcopal task six days later was the ordination of a young priest named Henry Coskery on September 20. A month after that he was archbishop in his own right.

The Diffident Leader

Eccleston, Deluol, and Chanche, in that order, had been proposed to Rome as Whitfield's successor. They constituted the triumvirate that would rule the archdiocese until Chanche's elevation to the see of Natchez in 1840. To more than anyone Eccleston looked to Deluol, his vicar general, for guidance and support. Since his seminary days he had been to Deluol "Brother Sam." It was never really clear which of the two was running the archdiocese, at least in the earlier years. In 1838 Eccleston complained to Deluol that the latter's role as protector of the Sisters of Charity excluded him from any effective control of their affairs. Deluol told his friend plainly that if he wished to exercise his "Summum Jus" he knew "better than I in which manner he wishes to rule without me" and four months later offered his resignation as protector of the sisters.[7] It was not accepted.

The fifth archbishop depended also upon the advice and encouragement of his fellow bishops, especially Fenwick of Boston until the latter's death in 1846 and thereafter Purcell of Cincinnati. From the start he valued the opinions of Kenrick of Philadelphia on the fine points of canon law and theology and came in time to appreciate his unfailing kindness in times of stress.

Eccleston was no more enthusiastic than his predecessor in playing the national role thrust upon him by the Holy See and his fellow bishops. As metropolitan he had to organize and preside over the triennial provincial councils, now held as a matter of course, as well as expedite the nomination of American bishops. Having no representative of its own in the United States, the Holy See continued to channel matters of national import through the archbishop of Baltimore as well as request his services in the solution of special problems that arose. Neither were the bishops in council loath to saddle him with time-consuming responsibilities, such as the establishment of a metropolitan press, which he entrusted to the Sulpicians, and the preparation of the catechism.[8]

During his sixteen and a half years as metropolitan, Eccleston presided over five provincial councils. These meetings were, in effect, national synods. Conscientiously Eccleston prepared the agenda and performed his role as president with ease. By the end of the Fifth Provincial Council in 1843 the *Catholic Miscellany* judged him "well skilled in the dispatch of business" and worth the esteem accorded him by the bishops and theologians alike "for the impartial, courteous and dignified manner in which he discharged his duty even under those occasional circumstances that he might himself be inclined to designate as exceedingly delicate."[9]

If the approach was piecemeal, it was as much the fault of the suffragans as the metropolitan. Eccleston presented the proposals as the bishops and the Holy See had presented them to him with little attempt to sort major and minor. The Third (1837), Fourth (1840), and Fifth (1843) Provincial Councils, like the Second, produced eleven decrees each, the Sixth (1846) only five, and the Seventh (1849) seven. However uneven the results, they reflected in aggregate the overriding problems and concerns of the American church as the midcentury approached. Among them were the status and conduct of the clergy, trusteeism and the manner of securing church property, the perils of secret societies, the dangers of public schools and benefits of Catholic ones, the need for Catholic publications, the evils of mixed marriage and divorce, and the necessity of creating new sees and finding worthy bishops to fill them. In decrees touching the administration of sacraments there was a trend toward conformity with universal norms, in those touching feasts and fasts, allowance for divergence.[10]

Thirteen new dioceses were created by the five councils, and the diocese of Richmond was removed (by the Third) from the administration of the archbishop, no matter of regret for Eccleston. The archdiocese remained relatively unscathed in the selection of bishops. Richard Whelan, another mainstay of Mount St. Mary's, was consecrated bishop of Richmond and Chanche, president of St. Mary's College, bishop of Natchez, both in 1841.

Though Samuel Eccleston presided over more provincial councils than any other metropolitan in the history of the church in America, he apparently had no strong conviction of the need for the legislation they produced. He held only one diocesan synod at the end of his first year as archbishop, October 29–November 1, 1835, to put in force the decrees of the Second Provincial Council.[11] Its proceedings were never published. Ignored were injunctions attached to a number of decrees at later provincial councils that they be effectively enforced by diocesan synods.

Eccleston was compelled by a process worked out at the Second Provincial Council to take the lead in proposing candidates for vacant sees to Rome between councils. He shared little of the enthusiasm most of his episcopal colleagues brought to the task of picking bishops. It required him to send reports damaging to some. It involved him in the protracted maneuverings of Bishops Kenrick and England and Rev. John Hughes over the creation of a see at Pittsburgh and who should fill it.[12]

Unsettling were the roles assigned him by the Propaganda dealing with crises in other sees. In New York Dubois welcomed the coadjutor chosen for him in 1837, John Hughes, a former student at Mount St. Mary's. In Hughes the troublemakers met their match, but Hughes was incapable of playing second fiddle and Dubois unwilling to surrender power. The Propaganda ordered Eccleston to tell Dubois that he must retire but at a time and in the manner of Eccleston's choosing. The archbishop traveled to New York in the summer of 1839 and with the aid of Bishops Flaget and Purcell performed the thankless task.[13] A more complex case was that of Bishop Rese of Detroit, whose resignation was effected at the council of 1837 on evidence of public intoxication supplied by Eccleston himself. After initially exonerating Rese, the Propaganda pursued him for political indiscretions for two years over two continents. Eccleston was compelled not only to be its agent in the pursuit but also to play the disagreeable role of caretaker of a diocese in the process of administrative and financial collapse.[14]

Eccleston, however, was less inclined than his predecessors to shrink from involvement in the affairs of other dioceses when they seemed to warrant his intervention. With no prompting from the Propaganda, he concerned himself with Bishop Anthony Blanc's efforts to end the trustee problems that had long plagued the see of New Orleans, which included soliciting the advice of Chief Justice Taney.[15] He also demonstrated a special concern for the ecclesiastical affairs of distant California after its acquisition from Mexico in 1848. This involvement entailed several visits with the secretary of state and other officials, primarily for the purposes of safeguarding church property there.[16]

The Unassailable Aristocracy

The involvement of the fifth archbishop of Baltimore in national affairs, however, was hardly more than a footnote to the most important development of his career. It fell to Eccleston's lot to preside over the transition of the Catholic Church in the oldest archdiocese from a small, respected, and integrated minority into an immigrant church counting a variety of institutions. The archdiocese of Baltimore, however, differed from most dioceses in that the old continued for a time strong and healthy, hardly aware of the new order that was taking shape about it. The aristocratic ways and values seemed little affected by the immigrant influx before the rise of Know Nothings at midcentury. At the upper levels of society Catholics and Protestants associated as easily as in the days of Carroll, treating with disdain the absurdities of the nativist press.

The Catholic aristocracy in Maryland, in fact, deplored any action on the part of Catholic zealots in other parts that tended to disturb the accustomed cordiality between Catholics and Protestants in Maryland. Chief Justice Taney confided to Deluol and Chanche in the fall of 1841 that he thought Bishop Hughes' speech threatening a Catholic party in New York if public funds were not forthcoming for his schools calculated to do more harm than good.[17] Deluol and Chanche continued to frequent the prestigious clubs of Baltimore, the Monday Club founded by Robert Gilmor, for example, and the literary club founded by John Pendleton Kennedy, both Presbyterians.[18] The Sulpicians were totally at home in the cultural milieu of Baltimore and continued to promote the values of its Catholic elite.

The Catholic colleges and academies of Maryland and the District, in fact, which attracted almost as many Protestants as Catholics, were the principal perpetuators of the social perceptions and standards that had marked the Catholic gentry from the start. Under Eccleston the older ones flourished, and new ones were founded. Eccleston gave his assent to the continuation of both the college and seminary at Mount St. Mary's, Emmitsburg. In 1838 he himself selected the newly ordained John McCaffery to head both operations, a wise choice as it turned out.[19] In 1850 a fifth Catholic college would be opened by Andrew Baker at New Windsor named Calvert College, the first Catholic college in the country run by laymen.[20] A surprising number of secondary schools operated by laypersons were opened in the Eccleston years, most of them small and short-lived. In Baltimore there were three for girls and one for boys, including that of the Misses McNally, who boasted a Parisian background. A girls' academy was opened in St. Mary's County, but the most successful of all was the boarding school for young ladies begun at Bryantown in Charles County in 1849 by Misses Winifred and Mary Martin.[21]

At the same time, the Visitation Sisters from their base in Georgetown increased the number of their fashionable academies in the archdiocese by four. In 1837 a colony was sent to Baltimore and a school was built on Park Avenue and Centre Street. In 1846 they took over the combination asylum, day schools, and boarding school in Frederick from the Sisters of Charity and expanded the last into a finishing school. When the Sisters of Charity closed their pay school in Washington in 1850, the Visitation Sisters purchased a home built for the French ambassador and opened a convent school in the heart of the capital. That same year they decided to discontinue the boarding operation at their Baltimore academy and purchase a seventy-acre tract near Catonsville for a boarding school in the country to be named Mount de Sales Academy.[22] In the meantime the Jesuits reopened the Washington Seminary they had been forced to close in 1827 because of the tuition question. It was an instantaneous success. At the time of its first commencement in 1849 it counted 250 students, the largest college or academy for boys in the country. The commencement at Carusi's Saloon was "crowded to overflowing with the elite of Washington, the President of the United States amongst their number."[23]

An urban Catholic elite continued to grow in both Baltimore and Washington as the rural aristocracy of Maryland declined. The percentage of Catholics among the decisional elite of Baltimore, the movers and shakers, grew from 2 percent in the 1800s to 7 percent in the 1830s.[24] But Catholic wealth in the see city would produce no Enoch Pratt, Johns Hopkins, or George Peabody. The increasing immigrant presence would exert socially a downward tug.

The Immigrant Influx

The character of the Catholic body, both local and national, was changed dramatically by immigration. The ten years 1845–55 witnessed the greatest influx of foreigners in proportion to the population in the history of the nation, three million in a country of twenty million.[25] By 1850 there were some 19,000 Irish born living in Maryland and 26,000 German born. With over 19,000 of the latter residing in the city itself, Baltimore boasted the fifth largest number of German born, after New York, Cincinnati, Philadelphia, and St. Louis.[26] Baltimore clippers carried tobacco to Bremen, Germany's largest port of debarkation, and brought immigrants back. Most of them moved on to the farmlands and cities in the West, but at least a quarter stayed in Maryland.[27]

Though 30 percent of German immigrants were Catholic nationwide, the percentage was probably higher in Baltimore as a result of the publicity given the city by German mission-aid societies. A smaller number of Irish chose Baltimore, but the number of Catholics they added was probably not far behind that of the Germans since 80 percent of the Irish were Catholic.[28] In the city of Washington the number of foreign born was not so large— some 15 percent in the 1850s as compared to about 25 percent in Baltimore, but the Irish outnumbered the Germans in the national capital two to one.[29] The number of Catholics in the archdiocese in the Eccleston years (1834–51) grew from 80,000 to perhaps 120,000, a 50 percent increase, whereas the total population of Maryland and the District of Columbia grew only 30 percent.[30] The census of 1850 disclosed that the Catholic Church constituted the third largest denomination in Maryland with sixty-five churches that seated 31,000 and property valued at $1.1 million, the highest of any denomination.[31]

In Maryland, as elsewhere, immigrant growth brought problems. Though the foreign born in Baltimore would constitute only a quarter of the population, they would account for 40 percent of the jailed.[32] Labor violence continued to mark the progress of the B&O Railroad and the C&O Canal, one Irish faction often battling another and the Irish battling the Germans.[33] In the minds of most Marylanders the growth of violence, pauperism, crime, and disease was associated with the rise of immigration.

Nativists versus Newcomers

Whatever the roots of nativism, there can be little doubt that the leaders of the "Protestant Crusade" in antebellum America found a receptive audience in the lower-class laborers whose jobs were threatened by the immigrant influx. They were the basic constituency of the nativist mobs. The crusade was cloaked with a degree of respectability by reason of the prominent ministers who promoted it, such as Lyman Beecher, and the famous laymen who supported them, such as Samuel F. B. Morse.[34]

Nativism finally broke into the archdiocese of Baltimore in 1835 when a number of Protestant ministers met to form a Protestant Association. Its purpose was to defend the principles of the Reformation against the inroads of popery. Its organizing genius was Rev. Robert J. Breckinridge of the Second Presbyterian Church of Baltimore. Its organ, the *Baltimore Literary and Religious Magazine*, edited by Breckinridge and Rev. Andrew B. Cross, was a compendium of popish crimes and plots.[35] "We have had for some weeks past," Eccleston informed Kenrick, "choice specimens of Presbyterian zeal and eloquence. Calumny has been heaped upon calumny and abuse on abuse, until the more respectable protestants have felt themselves degraded by the unprincipled course pursued by a few of their apostles. The Catholic clergy have taken no public notice of declamations which best refute themselves. Their forebearance has made the happiest impression on the reflecting portion of the community and has contributed to make a number of converts. However the demon of fanaticism & sectarian jealousy is at work and preparing mischief in this hitherto peaceful metropolis."[36]

On a Sunday morning in August 1839, Sister Isabella (Olivia Neale) rushed from the Carmelite convent on Asquith Street and begged shelter in neighboring homes. Breckinridge left his pulpit to go to the aid of the "escaped" nun, who was immediately placed in a hospital.[37] Three nights of rioting ensued in front of the convent. Decisive action on the part of the mayor, the City Guards under Columbus O'Donnell, and a round of judges who tried offenders on the spot prevented a repetition in Maryland of the convent burning in Massachusetts. The frenzy subsided when a team of physicians pronounced the poor nun "a perfect maniac."[38] The *Awful Disclosures* of Maria Monk, nevertheless, and other "escaped nun" stories had made their impression even in Baltimore.

In thanking the mayor and others who had aided in protecting the convent, Eccleston observed: "It is with the deepest regret that I have witnessed those scenes of violence, which you were called upon to repel— scenes but little in accordance with the spirit of the Catholic Pilgrims who first landed on our shores, and offered the open hand of fellowship to the persecuted of every creed and clime. In Baltimore especially, I was not prepared to expect them, where the very name of the city reminds us of the Catholic founder of Maryland, one of the earliest and truest friends of civil and religious liberty."[39]

When Breckinridge vehemently denied the Catholic origin of religious liberty, Maryland Catholics became even more determined to publicize their claim. At the invitation of the Philodemic Society of Georgetown College, delegations from all parts of Maryland and the District converged upon St. Clement's Island in surprising numbers on May 10, 1842. The archbishop celebrated mass, and William George Read delivered an impassioned address.[40] The Maryland Pilgrims Association was born, and the pilgrimage to St. Clement's Island became an annual event.

Though the anti-Catholic animus that surfaced in the nunnery riot of 1839 waned thereafter in Baltimore, it waxed elsewhere. In Philadelphia in 1844 nativist riots resulted in the burning of churches and the loss of lives, forcing Bishop Kenrick to flee to Baltimore in disguise.[41] Despite the anti-papist fervor of Breckinridge and associates, nativism was xenophobic rather than anti-Catholic. Old-stock Catholics, in fact, could be found in nativist clubs. Among the founders and followers of the Native American Association in Washington were "many highly respectable members of the Catholic Church."[42]

The first effort at political nativism in Maryland, in fact, failed because it refused to exploit the religious issue. The American Republican Party was organized in Baltimore in 1844, but the city's representatives at the national convention in Philadelphia proclaimed that under no circumstances would they mix religion and politics or attack the religious beliefs of others.[43] The party had almost no support in other parts of Maryland and quickly died as the Mexican War and other issues moved to the forefront of political concern.

The slaveholding Catholic Whigs of southern Maryland had themselves strong nativistic tendencies. As late as 1850 a delegate to the state constitutional convention from St. Mary's County proposed that immigrants be denied the vote their first ten years in Maryland.[44] Later the same year Enoch Louis Lowe of Frederick, a friend of the immigrant, was swept into office by his Democratic supporters, the first Catholic elected governor by popular vote. The *Catholic Mirror* of Baltimore, begun that year and decidedly Whig under its editor Father Charles White, was quick to observe that Lowe had far from unanimous support among Catholics. St. Mary's County, it noted, gave the Whig candidate his greatest majority.[45] The Catholic flirtation with nativism would end when religion and politics would be successfully joined in the Know Nothing movement of the following decade.

The immigrant presence in Catholic churches often upset the native born. A pewholder at the cathedral complained that seldom did the hundreds who crowded the aisles, the vestibule, and the steps contribute a far thing to its upkeep. These "counterfeits of humanity" ought, he insisted, "to be required to bear their share of the burden."[46] A standee complained to the trustees that those "who had the largest purs [sic] and the finest garment may sit next to God" while the poor were considered fit only for the aisle or the door.[47] The pewholders surrendered none of their seats. The newcomers would have to build their own churches.

The Walls

Though the protective walls of the ghetto went up more slowly in the oldest archdiocese, they took the same shape as in the rest of Catholic America. Ethnic congregations became national parishes. Schools and other institutions were designed to keep the immigrant out of their public or Protestant counterparts. Associations were devised to serve social, economic, and cultural as well as religious needs. Religious exercises and devotions were multiplied to generate a distinctly Catholic piety and build religious strength. And a press was established to provide a psychological need for reassurance and stimulus for combat.

THE NATIONAL PARISH

Unlike Carroll, Eccleston encouraged the development of national parishes. The German parishes were the first to be identified as such and would be accorded a special status with the arrival of the Redemptorists. Irish parishes developed at the same time but remained territorial, or regular, parishes because the parochial idiom was English. By the 1840s, however, they were clearly identified as Irish, catering to the needs of arrivals from the Emerald Isle. This development coincided with the rise of neighborhood loyalties in Baltimore as the city grew beyond the ability of its citizenry to identify with the urban whole as well as it once had. Church and school became the foci, whether Catholic or Protestant, public or private.[48]

The first church dedicated by Eccleston was not an immigrant church, but it suggested features of future churches in its dimensions and in the showmanship that accompanied its dedication. In size second only to the cathedral, the second St. John's Church in Frederick was accorded an opening that a later age would call a media event. On May 13, 1837, the eight bishops at the Third Provincial Council were transported the 45 miles from Baltimore to lend as much solemnity to the occasion as possible.[49]

A third parish, long overdue, was heralded in Washington in 1838 with similar show. For the laying of the cornerstone of St. Matthew's Church a parade from St. Patrick's was led by the Marine band, the archbishop marching through the street "in full pontificals."[50] Though a large percentage of the parishioners were Irish born and the parish entrusted to a popular young Irish priest, John P. Donelan, this church two blocks from the White House would increasingly become the parish of the well-to-do and diplomats.[51]

The next urban parish, St. Joseph's in Baltimore, had a quiet beginning. Though peopled largely by Irish, it would not be thought of as an Irish parish for some time because of the nationality of its founder and pastor for ten years. As much a misfit in the cathedral household as at the seminary, Damphoux was allowed to establish a parish of his own for the growing population of South Baltimore. Eccleston laid the cornerstone on May 16, 1839, while Deluol blessed the church and Chanche delivered the dedicatory sermon on December 14 of the same year, all peace offerings of sorts.[52]

Identified as Irish from the start was St. Vincent de Paul Parish on Front Street. Planned for the English-speaking Catholics of Old Town displaced by the Germans at St. James, it was built large enough by its pastor, John Baptist Gildea, to accommodate the growing number of Irish immigrants. The cornerstone laying on May 22, 1840, was made to coincide with the Fourth Provincial Council. Twelve bishops "enriched" an audience of "little under 10,000," the *Catholic Miscellany* reported, to hear what proved a three-hour sermon delivered in two installments by Bishop England.[53]

At the council was Joseph Prost, superior of the Redemptorists in the United States. Founded by St. Alphonsus Liguori in Naples in 1732, the Congregation of the Most Holy Redeemer had sunk deep roots in German-speaking countries before sending its pioneers to America in 1832. Propelled by the heart to the Indians, they were brought back by the head to the Germans of the eastern cities. In Baltimore Prost was approached by Benedict Bayer, now pastor of the German congregation of St. John, who begged him to take charge of the still troublesome parish. Prost perceived at once the advantage of Baltimore as headquarters for the Redemptorists in America. He remained at St. John's while Bayer traveled to Vienna to inform the superiors of Prost's plan and beg funds from the Leopoldine and other mission-aid societies.[54] With him Bayer carried a letter "to each and all" from the archbishop of Baltimore that called attention to the misery of the German Catholics in America for want of priests who spoke their own language. Eccleston promised to build not only a new church for the Germans of his see city but also a college to prepare priests to serve Germans throughout the nation.[55]

While a national seminary for German-speaking priests got no farther than the planning stages, it proved an inducement not only to the Leopoldine Society and the Propagation of the Faith at Lyons but also to the Ludwig-Missionverein founded in Munich in 1838 to aid the American missions. From the three came some $17,000 in 1841 for the work of the Redemptorists, over half of it from Lyons.[56] Their generosity enabled the Germans to raise a magnificent church in Baltimore. St. James had also been given to the Germans. There the Redemptorists would live while the old church of St. John was being torn down and a new one built on the spot. On May 1, 1842, German societies with bands and banners paraded from St. James to Saratoga Street for the laying of the cornerstone of what would come to be called St. Alphonsus. It was the first public display in which the German Catholics of Baltimore could take pride. Canon Josef Salzbacher of the Leopoldine Society laid the cornerstone; the archbishop said the mass.

Measuring 150 feet by 68 feet with a spire that would reach 220 feet, St. Alphonsus was designed by Robert Cary Long, Jr., one of Baltimore's most famous architects.[57] It took almost three years to complete. The archbishop performed the dedication March 14, 1845, again amid much spectacle.

The Redemptorist presence effected a remarkable change in the German Catholic community. As Father John Nepomucene Neumann reported to the Leopoldine Society in 1843, scarcely half the congregation had gone to mass on Sunday at old St. John's Church in 1840; now one to two hundred could be counted on each weekday.[58] The German Catholics of Baltimore grew from four thousand in 1840 to some six thousand by 1846. A third church would soon be needed.

Eccleston wished the Redemptorists to take charge of all the Germans of the archdiocese.[59] They needed little prompting, pushing as they did as far north as York, Pennsylvania, as far south as Richmond, and as far west as Cumberland from their central house in Baltimore. At Eccleston's request they also began a parish in Washington. In 1846 Father Matthias Alig built a church at 5th and G Streets Northwest on land donated by General Peter Van Ness for the score of German Catholic families who did not feel at home in the basement of the "Irish" church. A need to retrench, however, caused the Redemptorists to surrender the church, called St. Mary Mother of God, in 1849, but Alig withdrew from the order and stayed on as pastor until his death in 1882.[60]

Whenever a Redemptorist appeared in Cumberland some 140 miles away, Neumann reported in 1843, 150 to 200 German Catholics would appear, some walking the thirty to eighty miles from Virginia and Pennsylvania.[61] By 1847 they had grown enough to petition the archbishop for a resident pastor. The Redemptorists agreed to establish a parish in Cumberland. On ground chosen by Neumann at the site of the old fort, the cornerstone for SS. Peter and Paul was laid July 4, 1848. A "free church" party wanted no pew rents, only voluntary contributions. In a one-sentence reply Eccleston told the Redemptorist superior no.[62] The church was completed by September 23, 1849, when it was dedicated by the Redemptorist vice provincial.

The growing number of Germans in Fells Point served from St. James needed their own church. A grammar school was built for them at Regester and Pratt in 1845. Next to it the cornerstone for the Church of St. Michael the Archangel was laid on October 30, 1850, by the archbishop, who would not live to see its completion.[63] In 1850 the Redemptorists at St. Alphonsus began also to serve a colony of farmers from Hesse Darmstadt who had settled near Fullerton, a few miles northeast of the city.[64]

In 1848 the Redemptorist mission in America was raised to a vice province under John Neumann. By 1849 there were forty-seven Redemptorist priests in the United States, ten of them in Maryland. In 1850 they were constituted a province under the able Bernard Hafkenscheid with headquarters at St. Alphonsus. In 1851 Hafkenscheid established a seminary for the training of the Redemptorists at Cumberland. The following year he would start a novitiate at Annapolis.[65]

Parishes for the Irish kept pace with those for the Germans. Baltimore was fortunate in the young and energetic pastors who placed these parishes on firm foundations and bequeathed to them fine traditions. In December 1840 the newly ordained James Dolan, age twenty-six, was sent to help the ailing pastor of St. Patrick's. The latter's death two months later opened the way for a pastorate that became a legend. Appropriately, St. Patrick's under Father Dolan became the most active of the Irish parishes of the city. At St. Vincent de Paul, John Baptist Gildea died rich in plans in 1845, at age forty-one. The equally active John P. Donelan, age thirty-four, would be transferred from St. Matthew's in Washington in 1847 to take his place. The priest called from Piscataway in 1842 to organize the parish of St. Peter the Apostle for the Irish of West Baltimore, Edward McColgan, age thirty, lived to be eighty-five. The parishioners themselves, largely employees of the B&O in the Mount Clare shops, dug the foundations of the church at Poppleton and Hollins. The bishops were in town again for another council; Bishop Hughes of New York laid the cornerstone May 22, 1843, and Bishop Peter Richard Kenrick of St. Louis gave the sermon. Hughes returned to give the sermon at the dedication September 22, 1844. The strikingly classic church was another of Robert Cary Long's masterpieces, but an interesting contrast to the Gothic St. Alphonsus.[66]

In 1847 the famine-Irish began to arrive in frightening numbers. In his diary Father Dolan wrote of a ship that had just arrived "freighted with human misery and death."[67] Only he and a Dr. Donovan attempted to find shelter for the dying passengers hastily discharged by ship captains at Fells Point. Without hesitation he assumed responsibility for the forty orphans assigned the Hibernian Society by the city. On land purchased with borrowed money at Govanstown four miles north of the city he built a home for orphan boys old enough to be taught a trade or farming. He placed in charge of the home the Brothers of St. Patrick whom he had brought from Ireland earlier to staff a new boys' school.[68]

Another parish came out of the "farm school" at Govanstown when a church was built in 1849 for those who crowded the school's chapel on Sundays. The dedication of St. Mary's Church on September 23, 1850, was rendered memorable by the ten societies, Irish and German, that trailed out from the center of the city with resounding bands and floating banners.[69]

In western Maryland the residual Irish from turnpike, canal, and railroad construction accounted for a large part of the population gain. In 1845 the B&O crossed back into Maryland at Cumberland, where Catholics had grown to almost half the population.[70] Two priests of German extraction did well by their Irish flock. Henry Myers, the first to establish residency in Cumberland, replaced the old log church with a brick one in 1838. His successor, Leonard Obermeyer, added 40 feet to the building in 1843. Eight years later he built an impressive Ionic style church, 152 feet by 61 feet, and changed the name when it was dedicated November 14, 1851, from St. Mary's to St. Patrick's to reflect the ethnic shift that had occurred.[71]

The church at Arnold's Settlement, or Mount Savage, would also be renamed St. Patrick's. Mount Savage stood at the head of a basin that ran north and south between the Dan and Savage Mountains and was drained by George's Creek. The basin contained one of the richest deposits of coal in the Appalachians.[72] Mining towns sprang up at Frostburg, Midland, Lonaconing, Barton, and Westernport, all of which would in time raise Catholic churches. The Redemptorists in search of German Catholics were the first to serve these largely Irish settlements; John Neumann was the pioneer.[73] In 1845 a resident pastor, Charles Brennan, was sent to Mount Savage. St. Peter's, Hancock was opened in 1834.

Immigration was partly responsible for four parishes that were definitely the result of the expansion of transportation and industry. At Ellicott City some ten miles west of Baltimore, the first terminus of the B&O, St. Paul's Church was built on a hill in 1837–38 on land donated by the Ellicott brothers near their mill.[74] At Laurel halfway between Baltimore and Washington was a factory town large enough to support the church named St. Mary's built in 1843–44 and served by the Jesuits of Georgetown.[75] At Havre de Grace, a railroad depot at the mouth of the Susquehanna, a first church built in 1844 had to be replaced by a second named for St. Patrick in 1848.[76] At Elkridge Landing, the last stop for the Patapsco River traffic and terminus of the Baltimore-Washington turnpike, a church named St. Augustine was raised 1844–45. Since a large number of Germans resided there, it was served from St. Alphonsus.[77]

OTHER PARISHES

Urban growth sent wealthy Catholics to country estates. They demanded churches. At Pikesville the fourth of four new parishes (with those at Ellicott City, Govanstown, and Fullerton) to ring the city of Baltimore,

St. Charles Borromeo, was built 1848–49 by Father Charles White.[78] Parishes were created for the largely well-to-do in such scattered places as Piscataway (1838) and Oxon Hill (1849) in Prince George's County, Seneca (1846) in Montgomery County, and Elkton (1849) in Cecil County.

At least twenty new parishes with churches were created in the Eccleston years.[79] In places besides Frederick and Cumberland, a number of larger churches replaced older ones—for example, St. Joseph in Emmitsburg (1842), St. Aloysius in Leonardtown (1849), Holy Trinity in Georgetown (1850), and St. John of Forest Glen (1851). Several churches were enlarged or improved, including the cathedral itself, where the second tower was finally added and a heating system installed.

An important development in the administration of parishes that coincided with the rise of the immigrant church was the transfer of power from the trustees to the ordinary of the diocese, a modification rising largely from the growing conviction that the trustee arrangement was inherently flawed. The editor of the *Religious Cabinet* of Baltimore, Charles White, who happened also to be rector of the cathedral in 1842, saw in the deterioration of the building "a remarkable instance of the inefficiency of lay government for the successful management of church temporalities." While the trustees themselves were men of "very high character," the fault lay in the "evil of the system."[80]

Under Eccleston, and probably at his insistence, many boards of trustees relinquished title and control of parishes, all in compliance with the act of 1833 granting the power of corporation sole to the archbishop. Among such parishes whose records survive are St. Mary's of Rockville in 1841, St. Patrick's of Fells Point in 1844, and St. Mary's of Bryantown in 1848.[81] In the last, and perhaps elsewhere, "the gentlemen whom long custom has styled trustees," as the minutes read, continued to hold regular meetings "pursuant to a request from the altar" to examine financial accounts. At the cathedral the trustees remained confidently entrenched. And elsewhere they continued to operate quietly, as at St. Ignatius, Hickory, for another hundred years.[82]

THE PAROCHIAL SCHOOL

The parochial school system, that most vital and visible product of the immigrant, or ghetto, church, took shape in the archdiocese of Baltimore in the Eccleston years. Of the nine schools for the poor at the end of 1834 six were either orphan or "benevolent" schools and only three built and supported by a parish: the separate boys' and girls' schools of St. Patrick's in Baltimore and the boys' school of Holy Trinity in Georgetown. Together they counted no more than eight or nine hundred pupils. By 1851 there were nineteen parish schools with perhaps thirty-five hundred pupils.[83] All but one of the eight parishes in Baltimore maintained free schools for both boys and girls, and the one, St. Joseph's, opened a school for boys in 1849. In the District there were schools for boys at Holy Trinity and St. Matthew's and a school for girls at St. Patrick's. In 1851 a boys' school would also be opened at St. Patrick's, Cumberland. By 1851 the concept of parish school as distinct from charity school had developed, and no stigma was attached to attendance at the former.[84]

Three religious congregations came to be identified in these years as teachers in the parish schools: the Sisters of Charity of Emmitsburg, the School Sisters of Notre Dame, and the Christian Brothers. A fourth group, the Brothers of St. Patrick, would be introduced in 1846 and even open a novitiate but would withdraw in 1852.

The Sisters of Charity decided in 1846 to give up most of their pay schools and devote themselves to orphan asylums, schools for the poor, and hospitals. Though in the beginning most of their free schools were run in conjunction with orphanages, they would increasingly staff parish schools in response to pressing invitations. By 1851 they had charge of the girls' schools at the cathedral, St. Vincent's and St. Peter's in Baltimore, and St. Patrick's in Washington, the first and last, however, still connected with orphanages.

The Redemptorists opened schools immediately for their parishes in Baltimore, erecting imposing buildings for that purpose in 1845 at St. Alphonsus and St. Michael's. In 1847 they brought the School Sisters of Notre Dame from Bavaria to staff the schools at St. James, St. Alphonsus, and St. Michael's, giving them their former rectory at St. James as a convent. Mother Theresa Gerhardinger, the foundress, and Sister Caroline Friess, destined to be the driving spirit of the School Sisters in America, were both a part of this pioneering effort.[85]

The School Sisters opened a pay school at St. James. The archbishop objected to the location and the Redemptorists to the semicloistered life the sisters led.[86] These objections may have played a part in the decision of the European superiors to establish the American headquarters of the School Sisters in Milwaukee, where a German bishop ruled, rather than in Baltimore.

Knowing through the Sulpicians of the success of the Frères des Ecoles Chrétiennes in Canada, Eccleston wrote the brothers in 1841 asking them to assume direction of a school he intended to build for the cathedral parish. The next spring the pastors of the cathedral and St. Vincent's, White and

Gildea, the latter desiring brothers for his orphanage, personally escorted five candidates to the Christian Brothers novitiate in Montreal. At the same time the old cathedral of St. Peter was torn down and on the site a two-story building with basement erected called Calvert Hall. Classes began there in September 1843 with lay teachers under Henry B. Coskery, who replaced White as rector of the cathedral. In the fall of 1845, two brothers arrived, one the sole survivor of the five candidates.[87]

In December Eccleston wrote to the superior general in Paris assuring him of the need for brothers in his see. Poor children, he explained, had heretofore been neglected and "greatly exposed in the Protestant public schools." For them it was not necessary to have learned brothers, but it was important to have as superior "an experienced Brother formed in the schools of France so that the same methods and spirit may be continued here."[88] In the fall of 1846 the archbishop announced joyfully that a brother had been sent from France and that a novitiate had been opened at Calvert Hall, the first for the Christian Brothers in the United States.[89]

OTHER IMMIGRANT INSTITUTIONS

The Sisters of Charity and the Christian Brothers also staffed most of the orphan asylums of the archdiocese. St. Mary's and St. Vincent's orphanages for girls in Baltimore and Washington respectively were founded under earlier archbishops primarily as works of charity. St. Vincent's Orphan Asylum for boys next to St. Vincent's church in Baltimore and an asylum for boys at St. Matthew's in Washington were entrusted to the Christian Brothers. From the 1840s on, Catholic orphanages were designed primarily to prevent the children of immigrants from being placed in public or Protestant asylums, where they were rarely reared in the faith of their parents. There was also Father Dolan's school for orphan boys and the orphanage in Frederick taken over by the Visitation Sisters.

Among the institutions produced by the ghetto church in part to safeguard the faith of the immigrants were also hospitals. Those run by the Sisters of Charity in the archdiocese will be considered in another context.

IMMIGRANT SOCIETIES

The variety of societies organized in the Eccleston years was impressive, for the immigrants had many needs. Surprisingly, the cathedral parish was the most productive. There was founded the Female Mutual Relief Society in 1834, the Calvert Beneficial Society in 1835, the Cathedral Fund Association in 1839, the Catholic Tract Society in 1839, the Catholic Library Association in 1840, the Young Catholic's Friend Society in 1842, the Metropolitan Temperance Society in 1845, and the Dorcas Society in 1850.[90] Though the cathedral parish led the way, other parishes, especially Irish and German ones, were quick to follow.

The Young Catholic's Friend Society and Dorcas Society were similar to older associations that directed their efforts toward the relief of the helpless poor. The indigent and sick societies of St. Vincent's and other parishes fell into the same category. More common in these years were the mutual aid societies that enabled those of slender means to assist one another and maintain a spirit of independence. Most often they were called beneficial societies. The ten societies that marched proudly to Govanstown in 1850 were of this type; among them was the Maryland Pilgrims Association, which also had insurance features.[91] Black Catholics of Baltimore had the St. John's Colored Beneficial Society. Usually the beneficial societies were parish based, and two or more of them might be found in a single German parish.

The German Catholics of Baltimore led the way not only among Catholics but among immigrant groups in general in the establishment of the mutual aid variety of savings and loan association for the purpose of acquiring homes. The first of several chartered by the Maryland Assembly in 1850–51 was the St. James Building Association sponsored by St. James Parish.[92] Germans were joiners, Neumann told the Leopoldine Society in 1843, and priests would have to work zealously to keep German Catholics from affiliating with Protestant and secret societies.[93]

The Germans, however, felt little attraction to the temperance societies so popular among the Irish. St. Patrick's Total Abstinence, often accounted the first Catholic temperance society in the United States, was established at St. Patrick's in Washington on July 4, 1840, by George Savage and other Sunday school teachers. St. Patrick's Temperance Beneficial Society was established by Father Dolan, a friend of Father Theobald Mathew, the Apostle of Temperance, at St. Patrick's in Baltimore in 1843.[94] Three years after he had organized a temperance society for the Irish of Cumberland in 1841, Obermeyer boasted that "the social, moral, and religious condition of immense numbers has been vastly improved beyond all expectations."[95]

The temperance movement was a matter of concern for the archbishop because the evangelical ministers who were its principal promoters were often antagonistic to the Catholic Church. The American bishops in general, though enthusiastic about temperance in their pastoral letter following the Fourth Provincial Council, modified their position in the one following the Fifth, declaring the teetotaler's pledge not binding in conscience.[96] When a Redemptorist, however, expressed delight at the pronouncement in a letter to the Baltimore *Sun* and condemned the temperance "mania" as a product of "the pestilential swamps of Puritan heresy," Eccleston suspended his faculties.[97]

Many of the associations that appeared at this time had an intellectual or cultural purpose, such as the library societies. Most of these were parish based. St. Peter's Institute organized at St. Peter's in Baltimore not only maintained a library but offered a series of lectures. The Young Catholic's Friend Society, though founded to distribute clothes to needy schoolchildren, also engaged speakers and planned such cultural offerings as musical oratorios.

Whatever the primary goals of these societies, they also played a social role, bringing members of the parish together for a common purpose often punctuated by parades or processions. Many provided amusement and recreation for the scant hours of leisure working families could claim. Fairs, picnics, and excursions at small cost to the participants began in the 1840s. Through these societies the lives of the immigrants were increasingly centered in the parish. Some were ephemeral, appearing in the records only once or twice; some, such as the Young Catholic's Friend Society and Maryland Pilgrims Association, showed a remarkable staying power, passing strong and healthy into the next century.

THE NEW DEVOTIONS

"Numerous pious sodalities of the Rosary, Bona Mors, &c. for persons of both sexes, are established in the diocese," the Baltimore contributor to the *Catholic Almanac* observed almost as an afterthought in 1850.[98] Not even mentioned was the most popular of the devotional organizations, the Sodality of the Blessed Virgin Mary, found in almost every English-speaking parish in Baltimore and Washington. Separate sodalities for men, women, boys, and girls, were installed with appropriate solemnity usually by the archbishop. In the German parishes the most popular devotional organization was the Archconfraternity of the Holy Family, introduced by the Redemptorists.

The devotions to the Blessed Sacrament, Sacred Heart, Mary, and the saints that proliferated in this period were calculated to distinguish Catholics from Bible-centered Christians.[99] To judge from the sudden increase in the number of prayer books and devotional guides published in the 1840s, Baltimore was the radial point for such growth.[100] The "new devotions" were also designed to render piety more emotive than rational, more communal than personal, more church than home centered, and more dependent on the mediating role of the clergy.[101] The principal promoters of the pious societies were the order priests who conducted parish missions. The missions often ended with the creation of new sodalities and confraternities.

Parish missions or retreats spread with amazing success in the 1840s. The Jesuits and Redemptorists from their base in the archdiocese were the principal promoters of this form of Catholic revivalism.[102] John McElroy and James Ryder were the Jesuit preachers of a particularly fruitful series of Lenten retreats in the English-speaking parishes of Baltimore in 1842. At the cathedral, pews, aisles, and galleries were thronged and the number of confessors increased from seven to twelve.[103] The retreats soon spread to the outlying parishes. In 1844 McElroy preached a retreat at St. Ignatius, Hickory, aided by the pastor and a Redemptorist.[104] In 1848 the pastor of St. Paul's, Ellicott City, sought the archbishop's approval for another retreat in the fall. "Nothing like it to shake Protestantism," was his justification.[105]

What the Jesuits accomplished for the English-speaking parishes, the Redemptorists did for the German ones. The Jesuits were prevented by their college work from forming a permanent mission band. This, however, was the dream of the Redemptorist provincial, Bernard Hafkenscheid, a band to preach English missions composed of talented young converts, Isaac Hecker among them. The group preached its first mission two weeks before the death of Archbishop Eccleston.[106]

A MILITANT PRESS

The Catholic press had sprung to life in the early 1830s in response to the nativist assault. In Baltimore its history differed from that of the other dioceses. The *Metropolitan*, a literary monthly, as noted, lasted only a year. Nine years later, in 1839, a month after the nunnery riot, Fathers White and Gildea called a meeting to organize the Catholic Tract Society. These tracts appeared with some regularity for five years.[107] By 1842 the authors of the tracts had found a more exciting medium, another literary monthly magazine. Called the *Religious Cabinet* the first year, its name was changed to *United States Catholic Magazine* in 1842. White was the editor, Dolan the manager, and John Murphy the publisher.[108]

Charles Ignatius White became the principal "pen" of the archdiocese after the transfer of Charles Pise to New York in 1834.[109] In the literary magazine he found a more congenial vehicle for his talent than the controversial Catholic weeklies published elsewhere. So too did a young priest in Kentucky named Martin Spalding, who became co-editor of the *Catholic*

Magazine, and a number of talented laymen in Baltimore, Bernard U. Campbell, William George Read, and William A. Stokes among them. Though Baltimore lagged behind the larger sees in bringing out an English-language newspaper, it could claim the second German Catholic weekly in the country. The *Katholische Kirchenzeitung* (Catholic Church News) was begun in May 1846 by Maximilian Oertel, a former Lutheran minister. A battler, sometimes coarse but never dull, Oertel won a national audience.[110] Though he had the support of the Redemptorists and the archbishop, his subscribers were so often in arrears that in 1851 he moved his paper to New York in search of a more secure financial base.

In 1849 White transformed his monthly into a weekly magazine. It was not a success. At the beginning of 1850 he began a weekly newspaper, the *Catholic Mirror*, resembling both in format and content its Catholic counterparts elsewhere.[111] In the fall of its first year it began a running battle with the *Methodist Protestant*, which had dared to characterize the band-and-banner dedication of the church at Govanstown as a "shameful desecration of the Sabbath." The *Mirror* blasted the "pharisaical cant" of the promoters of rowdy camp meetings.[112] No longer would such attacks be studiously ignored. White discovered that he liked a good fight.

The Archbishop's "Condition"

Archbishop Eccleston was not a fighter. Tending the needs of the immigrants eventually took its toll. The evidence suggests that he was neither physically nor mentally ever a well man. In his first year as archbishop, Eccleston began his frequent trips to Georgetown, where he would remain in seclusion for periods ranging from a few days to a month in the room once occupied by Archbishop Neale. They became a matter of concern and speculation. Apparently the archbishop offered no satisfactory explanation, even to Deluol.[113] Bishop Fenwick, his closest friend in the hierarchy, was the first to express concern to the archbishop himself after Eccleston had written him of "strange things" going on since the last provincial council.[114] "You are getting feeble," Fenwick wrote at the end of 1841, "(so at least they tell me) and I am getting both old & feeble too." He suggested that the both of them might well seek a coadjutor.[115]

At the provincial council in May 1843 Eccleston was too weak to say the opening mass. In the summer he and Deluol set out for a tour of the West, the purpose of which was not revealed, accompanied part of the way by Fenwick. At Uniontown, Pennsylvania, he took the innkeeper for a man long dead and complained of intruders into his bath. "Your archbishop is completely crazy," the innkeeper observed, to which Deluol was forced to admit, "Bishop Fenwick and all who saw him thought the same."[116] The hallucinations lasted only two days, and the journey to St. Louis and back was completed with no recurrence. The day after their return, however, Deluol "settled accounts" with the archbishop, telling him "as a friend and clearly" that he should abstain from strong wines.[117]

Word of the archbishop's strange behavior at Uniontown spread quickly among the American bishops. Purcell and Hughes, passing through Paris in September, informed the nuncio, Archbishop Raffaele Fornari, of the "complete breakdown" of the archbishop's mental powers and urged the nuncio to recommend to Rome a successor. In order to avert Gallicanism, Fornari added gratuitously in his report to Cardinal Giacomo Filippo Fransoni, prefect of the Propaganda, no Sulpician nor their students, and especially Chanche, should be chosen.[118] Possibly as a result of a report that Kenrick sent the Propaganda expressing his belief that the archbishop was physically, mentally, and morally sound, the Holy See took no action at this time.[119]

In the spring of 1845, Eccleston suffered a serious head injury when he leaped from a runaway carriage hurtling down a hill. In the fall he suffered hallucinations again in Wheeling on the way to Cincinnati. There were at this time also rumors of intemperance.[120] After the singularly unproductive council of 1846, the bishops presented the archbishop, through Kenrick some months later, the gift of a crozier and episcopal ornaments as a token of veneration for the "courtesy, dignity, and kindness" with which he had conducted the proceedings.[121] That December Kenrick traveled to Baltimore at the behest of Cardinal Fransoni to discuss with the archbishop the rumors concerning his aberrant behavior and to urge him to choose a coadjutor.[122] Eccleston had an assistant at the cathedral write in his behalf, then himself begged the cardinal prefect that the choice of a coadjutor be postponed a few years so as not to give rise to gossip and speculation within the archdiocese itself.[123] The Holy See complied.

Sulpician Retrenchment and the Sisters

As Eccleston's mental and physical faculties declined, the Sulpicians began to contract their sphere of influence and activity within the archdiocese. In 1845 Garnier died and was succeeded by Louis de Courson as superior general of the Sulpicians. The latter, who had no first-hand acquaintance with America, was determined that his subjects there adhere to Sulpician traditions and abandon all but seminary work.[124] The first move was to surrender the spiritual direction of the three sisterhoods they controlled.

The death of Joubert, founder of the Oblates, on November 5, 1843, precipitated a crisis in that community, which was already demoralized by the growing antipathy toward free blacks. Subsequent depletion of their ranks by death and withdrawals, a decline in the school, and the departure of Sister Mary Theresa Duchemin, the superior from 1841 to 1844, and another member for Monroe, Michigan, in 1847 to found a new religious community (Sisters of the Immaculate Heart of Mary) brought the Oblates of Providence to the verge of extinction.[125]

Deluol did what he could for them until another director could be found. Without a chaplain, the sisters were going to nearby St. Alphonsus for services. In the fall of 1847 Deluol conferred with the Redemptorist superior about the future of the Oblates. Both agreed the community had failed "and we cannot hope to preserve it."[126] A Redemptorist recently ordained offered to assume the direction, however, and the archbishop, with no great enthusiasm, gave his consent. After presiding over the election of a new superior on October 8, 1848, Deluol gave over the direction of the Oblates entirely to Thaddeus Anwander. Under the young Redemptorist the Oblates entered into a period of gratifying prosperity. New members appeared almost at once. School enrollment rose. The convent and chapel were enlarged.[127]

The Sisters of Charity were another matter. Well before 1845 overtures had been made to the Vincentian Fathers in France and America to assume the same control over the Sisters of Charity in the United States that they had over the Daughters of Charity in France, but without success.[128] Under Deluol's direction they had modified their activities and style of life so as to bring themselves more into conformity with their French counterparts. They had, for example, continued to expand their hospital work.

In October 1840 the Sisters of Charity severed their connection with the Maryland Hospital and began one of their own, which they named Mount St. Vincent. A large number of the patients were transferred from the mental ward from the old hospital, their families having asked the sisters to continue to care for them. In May 1844 Deluol purchased Mount Hope College, then a mile outside the city (at North and Park Avenues), and moved the hospital there.[129] In a short time Mount Hope Hospital was famous for its care and cure of mental illness, attracting patients from all parts of the country.[130]

Also like the Daughters of Charity, the American sisters began to restrict their efforts to the poor, the decision to give up pay schools in 1846 being one of the chief consequences. Another decision the same year, however, to discontinue the care of older orphan boys, gave rise to a crisis in New York. Bishop Hughes proved unwilling to accept the change. A long and spirited correspondence between Hughes and Deluol ended with the dispensation of thirty-one sisters, who chose to stay in New York under the control of the bishop.[131] Thus originated the second of the congregations of Sisters of Charity who trace their origins to Mother Seton.[132]

This painful rupture, plus de Courson's order to surrender direction, hastened Deluol's efforts to bring about an affiliation of the Sisters of Charity and the Daughters of Charity. Requests again were refused until Bishop Chanche in 1848 carried a petition signed by Mother Etienne Hall, Eccleston, Deluol, and himself to the Vincentian superior in Paris. The latter instructed Father Mariano Maller, the Vincentian visitor general in America, to proceed to Baltimore and Emmitsburg to examine the feasibility of such an affiliation. Many meetings and much correspondence concluded with the transfer of direction from the Sulpicians to the Vincentians on November 15, 1850, and permission for the Vincentians to found a parish, the Immaculate Conception, in Baltimore. Six sisters who had gone to France for a period of assimilation returned to Emmitsburg in the summer of 1851 and introduced the blue habit and the distinctive white cornette of the Daughters of Charity to the sisters in the United States.[133] Seven sisters in Cincinnati could not bring themselves to accept the change, and Purcell, now an archbishop, agreed to sponsor their separate foundation.[134] At the same time they surrendered control of the Sisters of Charity, the Sulpicians also relinquished direction of the Visitation Sisters.

The Resignation of Deluol

Louis Regis Deluol was not around to witness the change he had inaugurated, having returned to France the year before. On November 1, 1849, he wrote in his diary: "I told the gentlemen [of the seminary] I was leaving the fourth." There was little in his diary to prepare the reader for such an abrupt statement. The reasons for his recall can be reduced to two: his disagreement with the archbishop over St. Mary's and St. Charles Colleges and the opposition to him that had developed in his own household.

From its inception St. Mary's College had been deemed a temporary expedient, an initial feeder for the seminary until a minor seminary was opened. Obliged to remain in operation for thirty years by the lottery of 1806, its demise seemed certain with the launching of St. Charles College in 1830. In 1836, however, the latter was still a shell while the former, despite administrative and disciplinary problems since the departure of Chanche, enjoyed as much patronage and prestige as ever. Though the succession of de Courson in 1845 would seem to have signaled St. Mary's imminent closing, it had its defenders in its president, Rev. Gilbert Raymond, and surprisingly in Deluol, who apparently had come to see the college as the Sulpicians' link to the outside world, or more particularly the business and cultural elite of Baltimore.

In 1848 the Jesuits, eager to realize a long-cherished hope of the Society of a college in Baltimore, proposed the purchase of St. Mary's College and as much land as was needed for a day school. Eccleston favored the move; Deluol opposed.[135] At the same time, the archbishop was determined that the time had come to open St. Charles despite funding and personnel problems that to Deluol seemed insurmountable. I don't believe it will succeed," he confided to his diary, "but since the Archbishop wants it, it will be done."[136] While Deluol was seconded by Raymond, Eccleston found an ally in Francis Lhomme, the Sulpician he had persuaded to return to America with him in 1827. The latter was "totally convinced that the college must close."[137]

On October 31, 1848, Oliver Jenkins, Edward Caton, then a deacon, and four students began classes at St. Charles at Eccleston's insistence, with Jenkins as president, treasurer, and principal teacher.[138] The following year the Jesuits were given charge of St. Joseph's Parish in Baltimore in anticipation of a college foundation. At the same time Etienne-Michel Faillon and Constant Guitter arrived in Baltimore as official visitors to investigate the conditions at the seminary and colleges. The task took over a year.

The presence of the visitors fanned to flame a smoldering discontent on the part of Lhomme, Augustin Verot, and Pierre Fredet. Laying charges that ranged from petty to substantial, the most substantial being Deluol's preoccupation with exterior ministries, the trio called for his removal. Startled, angered, and embittered by turn, Deluol denied vehemently in a letter to de Courson that he had ever been unfaithful to the spirit of St. Sulpice.[139] In the fall of 1849, nevertheless, he was recalled to France, where he would later be given the direction of the Seminary of St. Sulpice in Paris. Lhomme was first named temporary superior and a year later permanent superior with instructions to close St. Mary's College.

Though Eccleston disagreed with Deluol on the matter of the colleges, he was in total accord with his policy of serving where the service was most needed. In vain he protested the withdrawal of the Sulpicians from the direction of the sisters and parochial work.[140] Chanche sent a letter of sympathy on the "great void" Eccleston must feel at the loss of Deluol. The latter, he admitted, had "singular ways but his advice was always wise and good."[141] The archbishop appointed Lhomme vicar general, as all previous Sulpician superiors had been, but it was clear that the Sulpician ascendancy had ended.

The Question of Primacy

Before the last provincial council over which Eccleston would preside, important changes had occurred in the American church. Manifest Destiny had placed an archiepiscopal seat at distant Oregon City in 1846 and another at St. Louis in 1847, shattering the unity of Eccleston's metropolitan jurisdiction. Since the new provincial boundaries had not yet been determined, Archbishop Peter Richard Kenrick of St. Louis, a brother of Francis Patrick Kenrick of Philadelphia, sat with the suffragan bishops of Baltimore at the Seventh Provincial Council in May of 1849. The time had come, the bishops decided, to raise also New York, Cincinnati, and New Orleans to metropolitan status. The province of Baltimore was left with six suffragan sees: Philadelphia, Pittsburgh, Richmond, Charleston, and the newly created dioceses of Wheeling and Savannah.[142]

The bishops also requested that the archbishop of Baltimore be honored with the title of primate. When approval of the council decrees arrived toward the end of 1850, it was found that the question of primacy had been deferred. Chanche, for one, expressed surprise to Eccleston. "It was the wish of the Pope," he insisted, "and Cardinal Fornari then at Paris pressed me to urge it." The New York papers, he also reported, claimed that Archbishop Hughes had gone to Rome for a cardinal's hat.[143] From the Eternal City itself, however, Purcell informed Archbishop Blanc of New Orleans that "Rome makes no secret of its dislike for primacies." And if any thought of making Hughes a cardinal were seriously entertained, he added, "it is now exploded."[144]

Succession

Eccleston was beyond caring. In the spring of 1851, he went to Georgetown to die. The cause of death on April 22, Chanche told Blanc, was bronchitis, ulcerated throat, and dropsy.[145] In the procession from Georgetown to the railroad station in Washington marched President Millard Fillmore, his cabinet, and members of Congress and the diplomatic corps. In Baltimore the funeral mass was said by Bishop Kenrick, the senior suffragan.

In the same capacity, Kenrick informed the new archbishops that Lhomme, the vicar general, had told him there were no priests in the arch-

diocese suitable as successor to Eccleston, whose preference was Bishop
John Timon of Buffalo. Accordingly, Kenrick and the three other bishops
present at the funeral, Michael O'Connor of Pittsburgh, Richard Whelan,
now bishop of Wheeling, and John McGill, his successor at Richmond, had
agreed to send only Timon's name to the other suffragans for their recommendations to Rome.[146] On their own, however, O'Connor and McGill
added Kenrick's name. The question of a successor was further complicated
by the discovery of a document in Eccleston's effects naming Henry Coskery administrator at his death and recommending as successor Chanche,
Whelan, Coskery, and Gilbert Raymond, the Sulpician, in that order.[147]
Chanche, who had preferred Timon to Kenrick, was "sickened" by the
whole procedure, complaining to Blanc that "straws show which way the
winds blow."[148] Kenrick was chosen sixth archbishop of Baltimore on August 3, 1851. Chanche died a year later.

Samuel Eccleston was the most enigmatic of the incumbents of the
premier see. For this he himself was largely to blame. He left fewer records a
year than any other archbishop of Baltimore, and these in an almost inde-
cipherable scrawl. He was like Carroll a private person, keeping his deepest
thoughts and feelings to himself. The roots of his aberrant behavior must
remain a matter of conjecture. His only reputable biographer suggests that
he was temperamentally inclined toward the contemplative life, the reasons
for his visits to Georgetown, but propelled always toward public service,
producing a psychic tension that at times became unendurable.[149] Perhaps.
In his last years Eccleston did spend long periods at the Dominican Priory
in Somerset, Ohio.

Despite his disabilities, Eccleston negotiated the difficult passage of
the oldest archdiocese from one era to another with outward dignity and
calm. Though identified by most with the gentry from which he had
sprung, he was, perhaps, more attuned to the needs of the nineteenth-
century immigrant than any archbishop of Baltimore except Martin Spalding. He marched in their processions, installed their sodalities, and
preached at their retreats. He created national parishes. He encouraged the
building of institutions and the organization of societies that the newcomers needed to survive in an unfriendly environment. An archbishop
who had been nurtured in the Maryland tradition and who should have
been expected to perpetuate the Carroll church had instead become the
builder of the immigrant church in the oldest see.

"Good and virtuous," read his memorial card, "modest in his looks,
gentle in his manner, graceful in his speech." This is how native born and
newcomer alike chose to remember him.

7 *Prerogative of Place*

FRANCIS PATRICK KENRICK RECEIVED the brief of his elevation to Baltimore on October 9, 1851. That same night he slipped quietly out of Philadelphia and was discovered next morning by the sexton of the Cathedral of the Assumption waiting to say mass. By midafternoon a number of priests had gathered hastily at the seminary for a reception. At least one was not impressed by their new leader. "Persons may prate about not wishing for honor and dignity," James Dolan, pastor of St. Patrick's, wrote in his diary, "but the gladness of his heart from the dignity conferred plays in his eyes. He is not however a Samuel although he may be a Solomon."[1]

Dolan was quicker than most in sizing up people. For the majority of his priests the tall, soft-spoken prelate would remain a mystery. Dublin born, in 1797, the son of a scrivener, as reflected in his meticulous hand, alumnus of the Urban College of the Propaganda, a plus in his relations with the Holy See, one-time missionary priest and seminary teacher in Kentucky, trouble-shooting bishop in Philadelphia, apologist, theologian, scripture scholar and published author fluent in four modern languages and three ancient ones, Kenrick carried to Baltimore a range of talents and depth of experience that gave promise of an outstanding episcopacy.[2] In many ways it was.

The First Plenary Council

The sixth archbishop rode to Cumberland almost two months after his arrival to confirm and inspect the two new churches there. With that exception and confirmations in his see city and the national capital, he remained sequestered in the cathedral rectory for seven months preparing for the First Plenary Council. Along with his appointment to Baltimore had come the brief naming him apostolic delegate to preside at this first plenary meeting of the hierarchy of the United States. On November 16 he received the pallium at the hands of Bishop Timon and five days later sent out letters of convocation.

On May 9 six archbishops, twenty-four bishops, a Trappist abbot, the major superiors of seven religious orders and the Sulpicians, forty-one theologians, and a host of minor officials and acolytes processed from the rectory to the cathedral in a "show of pomp," the New York *Observer* remarked, "such as Republicans are not wont to look upon."[3] The council lasted two weeks.

Its proceedings afforded the American prelates the opportunity to take the measure of their premier metropolitan. His performance did not please all. "My position in the council," Kenrick himself explained to Tobias Kirby, rector of the Irish College, "led me to great reserve in expressing my views, and the extreme sensitiveness of the Arch[bish]op of New York made me extremely cautious."[4] To his friend Bishop Michael O'Connor of Pittsburgh Kenrick confided that Bishop Ignatius Reynolds of Charleston had reproached him with "a weak dereliction of duty" in allowing Archbishop Purcell to "bully the council" but had not complained to Rome "through unwillingness to injure me."[5] At the conclusion of the deliberations, nevertheless, Archbishop Hughes thanked Kenrick in the name of all the bishops for his "meek and learned guidance."[6]

Thirty decrees were sent to Rome in the care of Bishop James O. Van de Velde of Chicago. Five would be rejected and a large number significantly altered. The first of those approved acknowledged the primacy of the pope and the second made binding upon the entire Church in the United States the legislation of the first seven provincial councils of Baltimore. Three decrees required the creation of councils of consultors, chancellors, and other diocesan officials. The delimitation of territorial parishes was also required. The establishment of free schools in each parish was urged and catechetical classes demanded. Three decrees called for a close financial accounting of church property and severe restrictions on the powers of lay trustees. Two encouraged the establishment of the Society for the Propagation of the Faith and a society for the conversion of non-Catholics in each diocese. The rest touched the use of the Roman ritual, bishops' residency, wandering priests, irregular marriages, marriage bans, benediction, baptism, and religious services for the military.[7]

In Rome exception was taken to a reference to the pope as "head of the episcopal college," which was changed to read "head of the entire episcopate." Among the decrees rejected were two that modified feasts and fasts in America, concerning which Kenrick was cautioned to avoid the introduction of practices that suggested a national church. Also rejected was a decree that claimed primatial status for the see of Baltimore.[8]

New Sees and Bishops

The Roman authorities also disapproved several new sees proposed by the bishops. Confusing and conflicting correspondence regarding new sees, plus Kenrick's surprising failure to forward the *acta* of the council, delayed final action for over a year. Two bishoprics for the province of Baltimore proposed by the suffragans but afterwards opposed by Kenrick through Bishop O'Connor, his intermediary, were rejected: the diocese of Wilmington, North Carolina, and the vicariate apostolic of Florida. The diocese of Erie at the other end of the province was approved.[9]

The most puzzling jurisdiction proposed was that for Washington, D.C. It had its inception in an interview Kenrick had granted the Jesuit provincial a few days after his arrival in Baltimore. The provincial laid claim to St. Patrick's parish and its properties on the basis of the 1817 Neale-Grassi agreement. Kenrick approved of the parish's transfer to the Society after the death of Matthews, the pastor. He soon learned, however, that Matthews had given Archbishop Eccleston title to the properties to prevent such a move. Kenrick conceived the idea of a bishop for Washington as a way of resolving the dilemma in which he had been placed by the Jesuit "pretensions."[10] He proposed the step to Rome, however, only after the conciliar documents had been delivered there.

To his surprise, Kenrick learned that Bishop Van de Velde, a former Jesuit, had proposed in Rome that Washington be made a vicariate and that he be allowed to resign as bishop of Chicago and be appointed vicar apostolic. "I cannot bear the idea of a Vicariate in Georgetown," Kenrick wrote O'Connor. It would complicate the appointment of future bishops "since all things would be absorbed by the Society." The matter, he suggested to Kirby at the Irish College, could be taken up again at a provincial council three years hence.[11] The cardinal who prepared the *ponenza*, for reasons that are not clear, proposed that Washington be made an archdiocese. "Negative" was the response of the cardinals of the Propaganda.[12]

Three years later, with Van de Velde safely in another see, the suffragan bishops of Baltimore again debated in council the possibility of a bishopric for Washington. Four voted in favor and three against, the archbishop of Baltimore abstaining. The Propaganda placed its second negative on a see at Washington. It also rejected once more diocesan status for Wilmington, North Carolina, but approved the vicariate apostolic of Florida.[13]

Creating sees was troublesome enough. Placing bishops in the province of Baltimore proved even more so. In Pennsylvania Kenrick tried unsuccessfully to get a bishop out of one see and keep a bishop in another.

Though he had favored the humble and ascetic Neumann as his successor in Philadelphia, Neumann proved a poor administrator. Attempts to create new and less demanding sees for him in 1855 and in 1858 proved unsuccessful, but a coadjutor was consecrated in 1857 in the person of James Frederick Wood three years before Neumann fell dead on the streets of Philadelphia.[14] O'Connor's attempt to transfer to a less demanding see in 1852 resulted in the appointment of Josue M. Young to Erie and O'Connor's eventual resignation in 1859 to enter the Society of Jesus.[15] To replace him in Pittsburgh went Michael Domenec, a Vincentian. To find bishops for the southern sees proved next to impossible. In 1855 Kenrick told Purcell that he had received a "scolding letter" from Cardinal Fransoni regarding Savannah and Charleston.[16] John McCaffrey, president of Mount St. Mary's, refused even a papal order to go to Charleston. Patrick N. Lynch, administrator there for three years, ultimately assumed the burden in 1858. In 1858 Augustin Verot, a Baltimore Sulpician, finally accepted the vicariate of Florida created in 1856 and was persuaded in 1861 to take also the bishopric of Savannah after several nominees had refused the see of short-lived bishops.[17]

Mother of All Churches

It was under Kenrick that the question of primatial status for Baltimore was resolved, though not in the way many of its proponents would have wished. When the decrees of the First Plenary Council were taken up in a general congregation of the Propaganda in August, two of the cardinals gave assent to the decree conferring primacy, but five either disapproved or voted that the matter be deferred.[18] Cardinal Fransoni promised some honorific title in the future.[19] Kenrick did not forget.

In 1857, when presented with the problem of finding worthy candidates for American sees, the cardinals proposed the appointment of an apostolic delegate without diplomatic status. He would serve, they said, as a unifying force, a symbol of authority, and a source of reliable information. Kenrick, "an alumnus of the Propaganda with proven attachment to the Apostolic See," was their choice. The pope, however, wished the matter reconsidered in a particular congregation. The naming of a delegate, he explained, "in the person of the archbishop of Baltimore might rekindle a desire for the appointment of a primate, a matter already aired." It might also pose a problem in the future if there were a question of naming an apostolic delegate who was not an American.[20] No action was taken, but the possibility of an apostolic delegate was not forgotten.

At the beginning of 1858, the *Catholic Almanac* began publication in New York City when John Murphy surrendered control. It placed the archdiocese of New York before that of Baltimore in its compilations. To Cardinal Alessandro Barnabò, prefect of the Propaganda since 1856, Kenrick objected vehemently, reminding him that the bull raising Baltimore to metropolitan rank had declared it the "head and mother of all churches" in the United States.[21] That May the bishops of the Ninth Provincial Council of Baltimore petitioned the pope to grant Baltimore "preeminence of place."[22] In a general congregation of July 19 the Propaganda approved this lesser dignity, and Pope Pius IX gave assent July 25. The decree, dated August 15, 1858, granted the archdiocese of Baltimore "prerogative of place" and its archbishop precedence "in councils, meetings and assemblies of whatever kind" over the other American archbishops.[23] It was hardly primatial status, but it confirmed what had long been implicit. Rome expected leadership to be exercised in the premier see.

Increasing concern in Rome about the behavior of the American bishops raised again the specter of a primacy in Baltimore. In January 1861 the cardinals of the Propaganda were asked to address a number of questions, among them the method for choosing bishops, the appointment of an apostolic delegate, and the propensity of the American bishops toward independence from the Holy See. This last, one of several shortcomings enumerated, the cardinals perceived in the bishops' desire to make themselves "a national Hierarchy with a Primate at its head" and in their coolness toward an American College in Rome designed to "strengthen the ties to the center of unity." The cardinals recommended papal encyclicals (never written) on the method of choosing bishops and the law of residency and the referral of all other matters to the next plenary council of Baltimore, which they presumed imminent.[24]

Kenrick and Hughes

The possibility of an American College was suggested as early as 1854 to the American bishops who had gone to Rome for the promulgation of the doctrine of the Immaculate Conception.[25] Apathy and administrative snarls slowed the pace of foundation. Two archbishops nevertheless tried to outdo one another in a show of loyalty to Rome by promoting the enterprise: Kenrick and Hughes. Kenrick, in fact, opposed the plan of his friend Bishop Martin Spalding of Louisville for an American College at Louvain for fear of endangering the Roman foundation.[26]

In 1855 the Eighth Provincial Council of Baltimore proposed for the consideration of other provincial councils a plan for funding the college in Rome. Cincinnati turned it down. St. Louis and New Orleans gave guarded approval. Hughes found the "Baltimore plan" inadequate and drew up his own, telling Kenrick pointedly that he was not "aware that any prelate in this country has been officially designated in behalf of the others."[27] The Propaganda, nevertheless, approved the Baltimore plan and did, in fact, designate Kenrick coordinator of the fund-raising efforts. In 1858 Kenrick proposed a national collection. Despite his zealous promotion, Baltimore raised only $2,660, New York over $6,000. Though disappointed with the response, the Propaganda opened the American College in Rome on December 8, 1859, with a priest from Mount St. Mary's Seminary, William G. McCloskey, as its first rector. Not until 1861 did Kenrick send his first two students.[28]

The rivalry between Kenrick and Hughes had deep roots. A coolness had developed during their early years together in Philadelphia. Hughes had attempted a thaw on more than one occasion. In 1852 he invited Kenrick to preach at the laying of the cornerstone of his new cathedral.[29] But Kenrick kept his distance. Temperamentally they were opposites; they spoke to different worlds. Kenrick had fled the Philadelphia riots in 1844, while Hughes had warned that his see city would become a "second Moscow" if one of his churches was touched. "Rather let every church burn," Kenrick explained, "than shed one drop of blood."[30] Kenrick was consistently cautious. Hughes was ever the battler and always in the headlines.

The status of Baltimore, as well as the relationship of the two men, was affected by the periodic attempts of Hughes' friends to place a red hat on his head.[31] When the possibility was first rumored in 1851, Kenrick wrote Kirby that he was not at all pleased with the prospect of a cardinal in the United States, "Please whisper this to his Eminence."[32] Some ten years later when the rumor surfaced again, Kenrick felt compelled, he told Cardinal Barnabò, to reveal that Hughes had scandalized his clergy by excessive drinking, a problem that Bishop Timon, Kenrick's source, now believed he had overcome.[33]

Though Hughes was the more outspoken of the two, he was no match for Kenrick at episcopal gatherings, where the latter was highly esteemed for his knowledge of theology and canon law. Such was especially the case when several American bishops traveled to Rome in 1854 for the proclamation of the doctrine of the Immaculate Conception. In the bishops' review of the commission's formula, Hughes sat mute while Kenrick proved a prime example of the "audacity of foreign bishops claiming to teach Roman theologians."[34]

On a practical or personal level, Kenrick came off worse. He had supported the Redemptorist Isaac Hecker in his trip to Rome to win permission for an English-speaking house for his order in America.[35] Hecker was dismissed from the Redemptorists, however, and returned to New York, where under the auspices of Hughes he proceeded to found his own religious congregation, the Paulists. With Hughes Kenrick argued the irregularity of the project and insisted that Francis A. Baker, a noted convert from his see city who had followed Hecker to New York, return to Baltimore. Thomas Foley, Kenrick's chancellor, informed Hecker confidentially that the archbishop's feelings were hurt; if Baker applied to Kenrick directly for an exeat, all would be well. Baker applied, the exeat was granted, and no more was said of the New York foundation.[36]

The Civil War provided a final opportunity for the archbishop of Baltimore to complain of the archbishop of New York. Kenrick remonstrated against the blessing of a cannon by the chaplain of the New York 69th, an indiscretion Hughes readily admitted while reminding Kenrick of similar lapses in the South.[37] When Hughes visited France as a representative of the Federal government, Kenrick urged Barnabò to bring an end to the mission as soon as possible.[38] Kenrick refused to reprimand the editor, M. Courtney Jenkins, of his offical organ, the *Catholic Mirror*, when it denounced Hughes as a "champion of desolation, blood and fratricide," claiming that he never interfered with its editorial policy.[39]

Baltimore and New York

The relationship between the two archbishops mirrored a barely concealed rivalry between their respective sees. The Catholic population of New York was double that of Baltimore. After 1857 neither see supplied population data for the *Catholic Almanac*. Baltimore by 1860 could still boast a slight edge in the number of churches and priests and a commanding lead in the number and variety of its institutions and religious orders.[40] But it seemed only a matter of time before the largest would surpass the oldest even in these categories.

In one endeavor the rivalry was overt, that of Catholic publishing. Dunigan, Sadlier, and O'Shea in New York were pushing for larger markets at the expense of John Murphy, Fielding Lucas, Jr., and Kelly, Hedian, and Piet of Baltimore. In 1853 Murphy revived the literary monthly under the title of the *Metropolitan* with Charles White, Jedediah V. Huntington, and Martin J. Kerney the editors in succession. With Huntington's departure in 1855, the New York *Freeman's Journal* sniffed that the *Metropolitan* had "ceased to be worth looking at."[41] It ceased publication in 1859, the victim, it would seem, of the fading literary interests of the immigrant church. Kerney, however, had begun in 1857 the *Catholic Youth's Magazine*, a monthly designed as an "antidote" to "seductive publications." It was well received nationally, even in New York, but it died with Kerney in 1861.[42] Though Murphy surrendered publication of the *Catholic Almanac* to Dunigan of New York in 1858, the consequences already described persuaded Kenrick, it would seem, to induce Murphy to begin publishing the *Almanac* again in 1859. Back in Baltimore it did not survive the Civil War. In the late 1850s Murphy was still the largest Catholic publisher in America, but New York edged past Baltimore in the number of Catholic books published.[43]

As the English-speaking market shrank for Baltimore's Catholic publishers, the German-speaking market expanded. A group of Catholic Germans in Baltimore brought out in 1852 the *Religionsfreund* to fill the void left by the removal of Oertel's *Kirchenzeitung* to New York. Initially it claimed two thousand subscribers, five hundred more than the *Catholic Mirror*, but it ceased publication shortly before the appearance of another and more successful German Catholic newspaper. In 1858 Joseph Kreuzer came from Buffalo to Baltimore and was soon joined by his brother Christopher. Together they began in 1860 the *Katholische Volkszietung*, which in time became the leading German Catholic paper in the United States.[44]

Even in journalism the rivalry between Baltimore and New York was never blatant, and the divergent interests and pursuits of the two metropolitans precluded more frequent clashes between them. Except in their duties as ordinaries, they traveled different roads. Hughes absorbed himself in politics and polemics, Kenrick in scholarship and ecumenical endeavors. For both of the latter Kenrick was well known. At both, however, he ultimately failed.

The Oxford Movement in America

Kenrick's ecumenism differed from that of Carroll or Maréchal. It was, for the most part, a product of the intellectual currents set in motion by the Oxford movement in England. In America it took the form of high church or "Catholic" tendencies within American Protestantism.[45] So optimistic had Kenrick been of its impact that in 1841 he had addressed a *Letter on Christian Union* to the Episcopal bishops in the United States inviting them to follow to its "legitimate consequences" the movement begun in England.[46] The movement touched even Evangelicals like Rev. John W.

Nevin, whom Kenrick in 1852 felt was "fast approaching us."[47]

In Philadelphia Kenrick had brought into the Catholic fold a number of cultured Protestants, and he was unfailing in his encouragement of such prominent converts as Orestes Brownson.[48] His contacts included most of the converts who would win miters in the Catholic Church—Josue M. Young, James Frederick Wood, James Roosevelt Bayley, Richard Gilmour, Sylvester H. Rosecrans, Edgar P. Wadhams, and Thomas A. Becker. In Baltimore he continued to cultivate the friendship of cultured Protestants. In 1853 the conversion of the popular pastor of St. Luke's Episcopal Church, Francis A. Baker, and his friend Dwight E. Lyman, also an Episcopal clergyman, had an electrifying effect on the city.[49] Baker immediately entered the Redemptorist novitiate and Lyman St. Mary's Seminary. "These remarkable conversions," Kenrick wrote Kirby, "with many others elsewhere, lead us to hope that our holy religion will spread rapidly."[50]

Elsewhere Levi Silliman Ives, Episcopal bishop of North Carolina, converted in 1852. Kenrick sought the assistance of Bishops Spalding and O'Connor to obtain Roman approval for minor orders for married convert ministers such as Ives.[51] Rome was as cool to the proposal as were some of Kenrick's fellow bishops. "Surely," Archbishop Purcell wrote Kenrick, "we are not going to admit Dr. Ives, or any of the married convert Parsons, into our sanctuaries, into our councils, or into such relations with us as w[oul]d give them the opp[ortuni]ty of being too well acquainted with the frailties of any portion of our clergy—which their wives would soon know."[52]

Concerned that fears of economic insecurity might impede conversions, Kenrick established in 1853 a convert Relief Fund, to which he induced most of the bishops to contribute.[53] He also tried to find suitable employment for famous converts. The Sulpicians, he told Spalding, would not accept Ives as a professor, "being unwilling that externs should meddle with their institution."[54] To Baltimore he brought Jedidiah V. Huntington to edit the *Metropolitan* and to help him with his own literary works. But the convert who gave greatest concern to Kenrick was the erratic genius Orestes Brownson, without doubt the greatest "catch" for the church in the antebellum years.[55] Kenrick attempted to shield him from the cumulative wrath of his fellow bishops, who by 1855 demanded that their endorsement in *Brownson's Quarterly Review* be dropped. "If he had been our greatest enemy," Spalding fumed after one offensive article, "he could not have worked us greater mischief."[56] Kenrick encouraged subscriptions to the failing *Review* and contributed articles himself.

In his ecumenical outreach Kenrick was overly optimistic. Ultimately the time and effort he expended in the pursuit and care of converts counted for very little. Even if a revival of nativism in the 1850s had not brought an abrupt halt to the high church movement, it is doubtful that the mass conversions he so confidently anticipated would have ever taken place.

The Scholarly Archbishop

Not unrelated to his ecumenical activities were Kenrick's literary efforts. It was, in fact, his acquaintance with the literature of the Oxford movement that prompted his *Letter on Christian Union* as well as an exchange of letters with an Episcopal bishop that was eventually published as *The Primacy of the Apostolic See Vindicated*.[57] The last became a part of the polemical literature that Kenrick disliked. When it was republished in Baltimore, he wrote a convert friend: "Controversial writing seldom convinces the adverse party. Prayer is more effectual."[58]

Even in his most important effort, an English translation of the Bible, Kenrick gave evidence of his ecumenical bent. Bishops Timon and Spalding both deplored his concessions to Protestant readings and phraseology.[59] In Baltimore he began the Old Testament in 1857 and finished it in 1862. An invitation to collaborate with John Henry Newman on an official English version of the Scriptures was thwarted by Newman's own reluctance to proceed.[60] Attempts after Kenrick's death to have his translation adopted as the official version in the United States would also come to naught.[61] The Kenrick Bible would remain an academic curiosity.

Not only in the failure of the latter to win acceptance did time and effort devoted to scholarly pursuits prove so much wasted effort but also in the failure of his works on dogmatic and moral theology to be widely adopted as texts in American seminaries, for which he had intended them. The *Theologia Dogmatica* and *Theologia Moralis* were published in his Philadelphia years but revised and republished in Baltimore. Though used at the seminary in Philadelphia and at Mount St. Mary's and adopted also, surprisingly, by Bishop Hughes for his seminary in New York, the works were not employed by the Sulpicians in Baltimore nor apparently by the professors of other seminaries except as reference works.[62]

Putting the House in Order

While he gave more time to literary pursuits than any other of the scholarly archbishops of Baltimore, Kenrick was also one of the most scrupulous in the performance of his roles as ordinary and metropolitan. This is best seen in the regularity with which he held provincial councils and diocesan synods. Triennial councils were held in 1855 and 1858 despite the lack of urgent business to engage the bishops. No decrees, in fact, were passed at the Ninth Provincial Council.[63] A triennial council was not held, of course, during the war years, but a synod was. No other archbishop of Baltimore held as many synods—three in his twelve years.

Kenrick's first synod, held on June 5, 1853, was the most important. Its thirty statutes were devoted primarily to enforcing the decrees of the First Plenary Council. Territorial parishes were delimited in the cities and "quasi-parochial rights" granted their pastors. Catholics living within their boundaries could avail themselves of the services of no other pastor unless they rented pews in his church. Germans were to be served only by the priests of the German parishes. The salaries of parish priests were to be determined in consultation with the archbishop and a report filed with the chancellor each year on all income over this amount. A delay of two months incurred suspension. Banns had to be proclaimed at stated times. Catholics married by other than Catholic priests incurred excommunication. Burial rites could be performed only in Catholic cemeteries and only in Latin. The sacraments were to be denied Odd Fellows, Sons of Temperance, and members of other secret societies of this kind.[64]

Kenrick was the first archbishop of Baltimore to create a diocesan curia. The archbishop's council of consultors, according to the decrees, was to consist of the vicars general (Coskery and Lhomme), the chancellor, and the Redemptorist and Jesuit superiors in Baltimore. It was to meet monthly. The rectors of St. Mary's Seminary and Loyola College were named censors of books. Baltimore's first chancellor, Thomas Foley, was presumably appointed soon after Kenrick's arrival in the city.

The ten statutes each of the synods of 1857 and 1863 were mostly restatements or modifications of those of the first. To attend services outside one's parish, for example, a whole pew and not just a seat had to be rented. The ecclesiastical superior of the Sisters of Charity in Emmitsburg and the rector of Mount St. Mary's were added to the archbishop's council. There were, however, some fresh decrees. The Forty Hours Devotion was introduced by the second synod as well as a procedure for priests' trials copied from that of St. Louis. The third synod provided for quarterly conferences of the clergy in Baltimore to discuss moral and disciplinary problems.[65]

Kenrick's synodal legislation allowed him to address certain problems within his jurisdiction with greater authority, particularly the abuses or laxity that had crept in during the last years of his predecessor. Inebriate priests had become a problem again, but Kenrick reformed or dismissed the worst during his first years in Baltimore. A more persistent problem was the lackadaisical way in which parish finances were handled. After several years of infrequent and unsatisfactory reports, Kenrick forced the popular pastor of St. Patrick's in Washington, Timothy O'Toole, to transfer to New York by threatening a trial for the mismanagement of funds.[66] Dolan of St. Patrick's in Baltimore refused to itemize his receipts. Others sent vague and confusing reports.

As poor as they were, the annual reports required by the first synod provided Kenrick with a grasp of the finances of the archdiocese enjoyed, perhaps, by none of his predecessors.[67] None of his priests subsisted as formerly on salaries supplied by lay trustees. The principal source of income was pew rents. In his first and only full report, Dolan revealed that he had received the previous year $879.43 from pew rents, $444.00 from cemetery receipts, and $208.00 from Sunday collections. The pastor of Mount Savage, on the other hand, declared in 1854 that he ran a "free church" with no pew rents. Since the "penny collection" did not even pay for candles, he had to appropriate cemetery revenues for his salary. Counting stole fees, however, he collected about $550 a year. Most did not report stole fees.[68] The greatest income, as might be expected, was reported by the cathedral parish, which in 1856 realized $6,242.79 from pew rents, $2,400.22 from cemetery sales, and $1,741.36 from Sunday collections. There was still a debt of $23,689.16 for the cathedral, however, and $5,365.30 for Calvert Hall.[69] Most of the parishes were poor. Though the Catholic population was growing, per capita wealth was not

Parishes East and West

The Catholic population of the archdiocese of Baltimore in the 1850s grew to about 140,000.[70] A report drawn by Kenrick in 1862 gave Baltimore 60,000 Catholics, Washington 20,000, Frederick and Cumberland about 1,000 each.[71] The Catholic population was, therefore, almost 60 percent urban. Eleven percent of the state's, but 24 percent of Baltimore's, population in 1860 was foreign born. The German born in Baltimore had grown from 19,274 to 32,613, double the 15,536 Irish born. The foreign born in the national capital had increased 60.5 percent, while the total population had grown only 31 percent.[72]

Of the twenty-nine new parishes created under Kenrick only eight were erected in Baltimore and Washington, but urban parishes were from five to ten times larger than rural ones. Second churches were built in

1854–57 and 1857–59 for the congregations of the Immaculate Conception and St. Michael's in Baltimore only a few years after their first churches had been opened. St. Patrick's was also enlarged.

Three new parishes or missions were established for the Irish of Baltimore and one for the Germans. St. John the Evangelist in that part of Old Town called Gallows Hill would in time surpass St. Vincent's and St. Patrick's as the largest and most active Irish parish in the archdiocese. In 1853 Kenrick assigned the young Bernard J. McManus to complete a temporary chapel begun by others. McManus, who would rule St. John's for thirty-five years, built a permanent church in 1855–56.[73] For St. Patrick's Father Dolan founded two out-missions. St. Brigid's Church, named for Dolan's mother, was built 1854–55 for the Irish moving into Canton. In 1859 he opened St. Lawrence O'Toole for their compatriots across the water in Locust Point. In 1861 the two missions were entrusted to the newly ordained James Gibbons.[74] For the Germans of South Baltimore St. Alphonsus established a mission called Holy Cross. Like St. Michael's it started with a schoolhouse in 1855. A church was built in 1858–60.[75]

Two parishes were founded in the see city for "old" families at both ends of the social spectrum—St. Ignatius for the whites and St. Francis Xavier for the blacks—both by the Jesuits. As one of his first acts, Kenrick gave the Jesuit provincial permission to open not only a college in Baltimore but also a parish to be called St. Ignatius Loyola. While the church was building in 1853–56 at Calvert and Madison, not many blocks from the cathedral, the congregation worshiped at Crey's Chapel.[76] On September 20, 1857, the basement of St. Ignatius was dedicated to St. Peter Claver as a chapel for the black Catholics of Baltimore. For eight years they had been faithfully served by Father Anwander from St. Alphonsus at the Oblates' St. Frances Chapel. When Anwander was transferred in 1855, Father Peter Miller, SJ, became not only their pastor but also chaplain of the sisters. In 1857 the congregation moved to the new basement chapel. With the outbreak of the Civil War, however, the resentment felt by some of the whites in the upper church caused the Jesuits to purchase in 1863 a Universalist church at Calvert and Pleasant. On February 21, 1864, St. Francis Xavier was dedicated, the first parish church in the United States "for the exclusive use of the colored people."[77]

The Jesuits also achieved what had long been one of their goals—a parish in the national capital. An elderly Irishman, Ambrose Lynch, gave them land in a northeastern section of the city called "Swampoodle" to build an orphanage.[78] Instead the Jesuits decided to build a church. The archbishop gave his consent for a new parish. St. Aloysius was dedicated by the Jesuit provincial on October 16, 1859. Archbishop Hughes delivered the sermon. The president, his cabinet, and members of the diplomatic corps were in attendance, but the archbishop of Baltimore was not.[79]

The national capital also acquired a Dominican parish. In his first year Kenrick invited the Dominicans, whom he had known in Kentucky, to open a parish in a part of the city called "The Island" between a canal, where the Mall is now located, and the Potomac. The first St. Dominic's Church was built 1853–54. In 1856 the Dominicans agreed to take charge also of the congregation at Boone's Chapel. This was replaced in 1859 with a new church called Holy Rosary.[80] The Redemptorists sank even deeper roots in Maryland when in 1853 they accepted the offer of Mrs. Emily McTavish and her titled sisters in England of the old Carroll mansion in Annapolis. Lady Marianne Wellesley wrote a friend in that city: "I have no doubt in a few years they will build a handsome Church; the Redemptorists do everything so well."[81] The sons of St. Alphonsus did indeed build a handsome church, St. Mary's, in 1858–60, destined to be the mother of many churches in Anne Arundel County and beyond. Their chief activity in the state capital, however, centered on the novitiate they established there.[82]

Near Baltimore three other parishes were founded. Some ten miles north St. Joseph's Church was opened in 1852 for the Irish working the limestone and marble quarries around the village of Texas.[83] West of the city, near the developing village of Catonsville, land was given for a church called St. Agnes, built in 1852–53 and served by Edward Caton, chaplain of nearby Mount de Sales Academy.[84] A little farther west land was also donated near Clarksville for St. Louis Church, built in 1855–56 and served by the Sulpicians of St. Charles College.

Immigration mostly accounted for a multiplication of churches in the west. To Allegany and what would become Garrett Counties, Irish and Germans were still being drawn by the construction of the B&O and the opening of new mines. The new church builder of the west was Rev. Michael Slattery, who was sent to Frostburg at the head of George's Creek in 1852 to establish a new parish. St. Michael's began in an old hotel, one wing the church and the other the rectory. From Frostburg Slattery served the Catholic settlements along George's Creek—Midland, Lonaconing, Barton, and Westernport—while the Cumberland Redemptorists continued to meet the needs of the Germans of that region. Slattery also followed the B&O westward to Bloomington and Oakland, and from the latter town made occasional visits to the isolated settlements of Cross Roads (Hoyes) and Blooming Rose. Besides St. Michael's in 1852, Slattery built St. Peter's in Oakland in 1852–53 and St. Peter's in Westernport in 1854–57 and began churches in Bloomington, Lonaconing, and Barton.[85] The rugged mountains took their toll, however, and Slattery was recalled to Baltimore in 1860 to take charge of St. Joseph's Church, which the Jesuits had surrendered.

The churches opened for new parishes in other parts of the archdiocese were largely the result of native growth—St. Thomas at Mooresville and St. Augustine at Williamsport both in Washington County in 1854, St. Mary's at Pylesville in Harford County in 1855, Our Lady of Mount Carmel at Mechanicstown (Thurmont) in Frederick County in 1856, St. Thomas at New Windsor in Carroll County in 1861, St. Ignatius at Hill Top and St. Peter's at Beantown, both in Charles County in 1860, and St. Denis at Cross Roads (Galena) in Kent County on the Eastern Shore in 1856.[86] At Port Deposit in Cecil County a chapel was opened in the residence of the priest sent to seat a parish there in 1859.[87]

New churches replaced older ones. Fire destroyed the ones at Long Green and Govans. Others simply collapsed. In 1860 the *Catholic Mirror* announced that a new church would be raised at Little Orleans on land donated by Lady Elizabeth Stafford, one of the Caton sisters.[88] In Washington laymen laid plans for a church to replace the "antediluvian" St. Patrick's, but the archbishop quashed their grandiose scheme for a "magnificent cathedral."[89] In 1862–63, however, he added a portico to his own cathedral.

Sisters and Brothers

Other institutions kept pace with the churches. Schools, orphanages, and hospitals, in fact, placed demands on the religious communities already in the archdiocese that they were unable to meet. New religious orders had to be imported—the Sisters of Mercy and the Sisters and Brothers of the Holy Cross.

In 1852 the Sisters of Mercy accepted an invitation to staff the Washington Infirmary in the capital. In 1855 at the invitation of Father McColgan Sisters of Mercy came from Pittsburgh to staff the girls' school at St. Peter's in Baltimore. In a residence purchased for them by the perennial benefactress Emily McTavish, they opened a novitiate and an academy. In accord with their accustomed work, they also opened a home for poor girls and began to visit the abodes of the sick and the needy. In 1863 they took charge of the girls' school of St. Aloysius in Washington.[90]

The Sisters of the Holy Cross came from Indiana in 1855 at the invitation of Father O'Toole to open St. Joseph's Orphanage for boys in Washington. In 1859 Father Dolan procured the services of both the Brothers and

Sisters of the Holy Cross, the brothers to take charge of the older boys at the orphanage abandoned by the Brothers of St. Patrick and the sisters to take care of the younger boys and to staff the parish school. The orphanage and trade school for older boys were moved to a farm on Harford Road but did not succeed. The brothers withdrew in 1863. The sisters not only remained but opened an academy, or pay school, at St. Patrick's.[91]

In the meantime the older religious orders expanded their activities in the archdiocese. The Daughters of Charity, still commonly called the Sisters of Charity, continued their remarkable growth. In the Kenrick years they took charge of the girls' schools of St. Joseph's, St. John's, and the Immaculate Conception in Baltimore and St. Matthew's in Washington. More important was their establishment of St. Vincent's Infant Asylum in Baltimore in 1856 and St. Ann's Infant Asylum in Washington in 1860 to take in the growing number of abandoned babies of the urban poor. In 1860 they moved to a larger Mount Hope on Reisterstown Road. In 1862 they accepted the gift of Charles M. Dougherty of a mansion on Lanvale Lane in Baltimore for a free hospital for the sick poor with a certain number of private rooms for paying patients. They named it St. Agnes Hospital after the donor's wife.[92]

The Christian Brothers and School Sisters of Notre Dame concentrated their principal energies in other dioceses in these years, the former withdrawing from Cumberland and Washington. They moved, however, the boarders at Calvert Hall to a school they had purchased at Ellicott City in 1857 and named it Rock Hill College. The School Sisters of Notre Dame agreed in 1857 to staff St. Anthony's Orphan Asylum begun by the Redemptorists in 1854 for German orphans.

The Oblate Sisters of Providence opened a pay school for black boys in 1852 and in 1857 accepted an invitation of the Redemptorists and the Jesuits to teach the black children in St. Michael's and St. Joseph's parishes. They also opened a home for widows in 1860. That same year, however, the boys school closed and, toward the end of the Civil War, the two parish schools.[93]

Kenrick persuaded the Carmelites in 1851 to close their academy and return to a purely contemplative life. With the academies begun by the Sisters of Mercy and Sisters of Holy Cross, however, and the academy of the School Sisters of Notre Dame in Baltimore, plus the Visitation academies in Baltimore, Catonsville, Georgetown, Washington, and Frederick and that of the Sisters of Charity in Emmitsburg, middle-class families of the oldest archdiocese had an ample choice of finishing schools for their daughters.

Higher education for young men suffered no setback with the closing of St. Mary's College in Baltimore in 1851. In the fall the Jesuits opened Loyola College in temporary quarters on Holliday Street and moved to their new building next to St. Ignatius Church in 1855.[94] The old Washington Seminary was renamed Gonzaga College and chartered in 1858 but not moved next to St. Aloysius in Washington until 1871. Rock Hill College opened in Ellicott City in 1857 and Borromeo College in Pikesville in 1860.[95] Calvert College continued until the Civil War, but St. John's Institute in Frederick suffered a setback even before the war from which it never recovered. Few of these institutions had as fully developed college curricula as Georgetown and Mount St. Mary's College. But as with the girls' academies, middle-class families could pick and choose in quality and cost.

Immigrant Societies Slacken

The growth of fraternal, charitable, and devotional organizations was not as spectacular under Kenrick as under Eccleston. Beneficial and temperance societies, in fact, waned. With but one exception, Kenrick took little interest in such organizations. The exception was the Catholic Institute, over whose founding he presided in 1853. The Catholic Institute furnished a library and reading room and brought guest lecturers from distant parts. Among the many distinguished donors to the library was Chief Justice Taney, who contributed a set of Bishop England's works.[96] The Catholic Institute was a social as well as literary club for the well-to-do. For the less favored, St. Peter's Parish had its Young Men's Catholic Lyceum and St. John's its Eccleston's Literary Institute.

Of the charitable organizations, one, at least, doubled its membership in Baltimore—the Young Catholic's Friend Society. Branches were also established in Washington, Alexandria, and Ellicott City. The Washington unit was especially active in promoting the establishment of Catholic schools. From it also was recruited the first branch of the St. Vincent de Paul Society in the archdiocese, at St. Matthew's in Washington in 1857 by Father Charles White, the new pastor. St. Patrick's and St. Aloysius followed suit, and in March 1861 the Particular Council of the District of Columbia was founded.[97] At the same time the *Catholic Mirror* complained that, in striking contrast to the Protestants and their flourishing associations, the Catholics of Baltimore had difficulty sustaining the few they had.[98]

Nor was there an increase in pious societies, sodalities, and confraternities similar to that of the Eccleston years. Kenrick, in fact, waged a quiet war on devotions he deemed extravagant, such as a volume of litanies published in New York and approved by Archbishop Hughes.[99] "How much devotional trash," he complained to Bishop Spalding, "disfigures our books!"[100]

Kenrick shared Carroll's distaste for public display. There is no record of his ever having paraded through the streets as had Eccleston. As often as not, he gave over the task of laying cornerstones and blessing churches to major superiors or to his vicars general. Except for the Germans, who refused to forego their bands and banners, there was little noise and color in the Kenrick years. It was only after his death, but soon after, that the Jesuits in Washington organized a parade down Pennsylvania Avenue for the opening of the parochial schools at St. Aloysius. Led by the Marine band, it was "one of the grandest demonstrations," a viewer reported, "that has taken place in this city for a long time."[101]

The Reappearance of Antipopery

Kenrick's promotion to Baltimore did not signify the coming to power of the Irish in the American church. He was, in fact, representative of that class of Irishmen who had enjoyed a remarkable degree of economic success and social acceptance in the era of the emigré bishops—the Walshes, Tiernans, and Barrys in Baltimore and Washington, the Careys in Philadelphia, the Mullanphys in St. Louis. In the antebellum years, theirs was not a story of upward mobility but of the downward tug of kinship with the contemned minority that inundated America. The Irish-born Kenrick had, in fact, smaller appreciation of the sensitivities and needs of his immigrant charges than the native-born, Anglo-Saxon archbishops who preceded and followed him. Intellectually he was more attuned to Maryland's Catholic elite. Yet it was during his episcopacy that a bond was forged between rich and poor in the Catholic community. This was due to the most violent outbreak of nativism in the history of Maryland.

In the 1850s politics and religion were successfully joined, and the comfortable Catholics of Maryland could no longer smile condescendingly at the rantings of nativist preachers. Chief Justice Taney, formerly more tolerant than most, now deplored the change that had taken place. There was no state, he wrote a friend in 1856, "in which the clerical influence has been so strenuously exerted to form the Protestant mind against those who belong to the Catholic Church as in Maryland. I am Mordecai the Jew sitting at the King's gate, and their zeal will hardly flag while I remain there."[102]

Antipopery had barely touched upper-class Protestants in Maryland before the 1850s, but a change was signaled as early as 1851, when the cornerstone for the House of Refuge for delinquent boys was laid. George Brown, its principal founder and one of the city's first millionaires, blamed foreigners in his address for the "horrible multiplications of robberies, and drunkenness and murders." As if to bear him out, the House of Refuge soon sheltered 350 inmates, 60 percent of them of foreign-born parentage.[103]

In April 1852, Martin Kerney, the Catholic editor, now chairman of the House Committee on Education in Annapolis, introduced a bill that, among other things, allowed public funding for parochial schools. When it was attacked in the press, Kerney withdrew the bill.[104] In the fall, however, four prominent lay Catholics—Basil R. Spalding, Dr. Francis Neale, M. Courtney Jenkins, and T. Parkin Scott—invited the two contenders in the Baltimore mayoral race to state their views on funds for private schools. Both were evasive.[105] The next March Kerney pushed a similar bill. A number of Protestant ministers "met in council," the *Catholic Mirror* reported, to prevent its passage, and the Friends of the Public Schools was organized.[106] Dr. Neale, Scott, and Captain William Kennedy then organized the Friends of Free Education and published a resolution insisting that Catholic schools had a constitutional right to a portion of the general tax. A similar statement signed by the archbishop and a number of leading Catholics was presented to the city council. The response of the council, prepared at its request by a Protestant minister, remarked that the "silly document" was obviously from "the head and heart of a foreigner . . . incompetent both by birth and education to understand the genius of our institutions."[107] In an indignant reply to this apparent attack on the archbishop, T. Parkin Scott declared himself, a native of Baltimore and the third generation of Maryland born, the author of the statement.[108] Ultimately the bill was buried in committee.

The following month Archbishop Gaetano Bedini visited Baltimore. Styled nuncio to Brazil, he was in reality charged with a mission to examine conditions in the church in the United States.[109] A step ahead of Bedini's visits to other American cities, an apostate priest, Alessandro Gavazzi, inflamed receptive audiences against the nuncio. His tour became a nightmare of insults and mob violence. Cutting short his mission, Bedini returned to Washington, where it was apparently his intention to win acceptance for an official representative of the Papal States to the American government. Kenrick reminded Secretary of State William Marcy that the possibility had been entertained under his predecessor.[110] A second visit to

Baltimore was canceled when, on the night of January 16, 1854, mobs burned an effigy of Bedini a few blocks from the cathedral and "saluted with firing of pistols and hellish yells" the archbishop's residence, the seminary, the orphan asylum, and the Visitation convent.[111] Later in his report to the Roman officials, Bedini would praise the archbishop of Baltimore for his "vast doctrinal knowledge and modest manner" but would express the wish that he show more initiative and less timidity.[112]

The Know Nothings

The Bedini tour served to accelerate the pace of reawakened nativism. By the time of his departure, it had gone political. Out of a host of secret societies with patriotic names—the largest being the Noble Order of the Star Spangled Banner—a political party was born. Called Know Nothings because of the oath of secrecy they took, its members grew as rapidly in Maryland as anywhere. In the spring elections of 1854, the Know Nothings captured Hagerstown and Cumberland and in the fall the city of Baltimore itself.[113]

In 1855 the American party, as they chose to call themselves, organized nationally, their secrecy abandoned. Standing for the Bible, the public schools, and stricter immigration and naturalization laws, the party also called for resistance to the "aggressive policies and corrupting tendencies of the Roman Catholic Church." Its anti Catholic impulse was even more apparent in the pages of the *Know Nothing Almanac*, which boasted the party's "Anti-Romanism, Anti-Bedinism, Anti-Pope's Toeism, Anti-Nunnerism, Anti-Winking Virginism, Anti-Jesuitism, and Anti-the-Whole-Sacerdotal-Hierarchism with all its humbugging mummeries."[114] Its stock in trade were the banners and transparencies emblazoned with political symbols and slogans and its demonology the drunken Irish, radical Germans, and scheming Jesuits. Though the Know Nothings in Maryland made an initial effort to distinguish between native and foreign-born Catholics, this distinction was lost in the flush of victory and power. A surprising number of prominent citizens, among them Johns Hopkins and Enoch Pratt, flirted with Know Nothingism when they did not give actual support.[115]

Nativist literature reached new heights of salacity. Though Breckinridge had moved on, his associate, Rev. Andrew B. Cross, addressed a series of letters to T. Parkin Scott which were published in 1854 as *Priests' Prisons for Women*. Toward the end of the year Miss Josephine Bunkley, a novice at Emmitsburg, left the novitiate and lent her name to a ghostwritten account originally published as *My Book, or the Veil Uplifted; A Tale of Popish Intrigue and Policy.*[116] Cross in 1856 laid a petition before the state legislature that called for the regulation of convents. After some debate, it was laid upon the table. Subsequent petitions of similar tenor were dismissed with dispatch.[117]

The Know Nothings captured the state Assembly in 1855 and the governor's chair in 1857 as the Whigs declined. They ran the city of Baltimore fairly well, except at election time, and at Annapolis put into law hardly any of the nativist goals of their party. For the most part, they were discomfited by the tirades of preachers and press and embarrassed by the excesses of the gangs that ran riot in their name. Loosely affiliated with the American and Democratic parties were clubs of workmen, for the Know Nothings the Rip Raps, Plug Uglies, Black Snakes, Blood Tubs, and others with equally fearsome names, and for the Democrats the Bloody Eights, Eighth Ward Black Guards, and Butt Enders. Mayhem and murder, unchecked by the police, came to be expected each election day. Only the Eighth Ward, or "Old Limerick," with St. John's at its center, remained loyal to the Democratic party in Baltimore.

Nationally the issue of slavery tore the American party apart. In 1856 it nominated former President Millard Fillmore as its presidential candidate. He carried only the state of Maryland! There the party survived for three more years. In 1859 the Democrats recaptured the Assembly and in 1860 wrested control of the police in Baltimore from its Know Nothing mayor. In the fall a Reform slate, on which Catholics were conspicuous, consigned the Know Nothings to oblivion.[118]

In Maryland the Know Nothing movement had as unsettling an effect as anywhere, but there the American Party was not a sponge for homeless Whigs. The southern counties that were the stronghold of Whiggery and Catholicism alike moved into the Democratic Party, while the Know Nothings gathered their greatest strength from Democrats in Baltimore, Catholics excepted.[119] No longer would Catholic Maryland divide between wealthy Whigs and working-class Democrats. A sense of solidarity anchored both in the Democratic party.

The Know Nothing assault also stirred new heights of Catholic patriotism, as reflected in the bishops' pastoral following the Eighth Provincial Council in 1855. The bishops had told the Holy Father himself, they insisted, that they had "rejected as calumny that we were in civil matters subject to his authority."[120] After the Ninth they urged the clergy and laity "to support the General and State government at every sacrifice, to prove yourselves worthy of the rights of free citizenship."[121] In its editorial support of separation of church and state, the *Catholic Mirror* even suggested that payment of chaplains in Congress and the military was "opposed to the spirit and letter of our Constitution."[122]

Sectional Discord

With the collapse of the Know Nothing movement, Maryland Catholics moved from one dilemma to another. Sectional discord touched them in an almost equally painful way. While opposed to disunion, they viewed the abolitionists as subversives. In the pastoral following the Ninth Provincial Council the bishops, reflecting Kenrick's own opinion, declared that, while the church had striven always to mitigate the condition of slavery, "she has never disturbed established order, or endangered the peace of society, by following theories of philanthropy."[123] In a review of *Uncle Tom's Cabin*, the *Metropolitan* dismissed as "fanatical and extreme" the "false philanthrophy, which springs from false religion," and the *Catholic Mirror* lumped the abolitionist movement with the Know Nothings and "such vagaries as Spiritualism, Fourierism, Women's Rightism, *et omni genus*, evidences of a corrupt and vitiated state of society."[124] At the same time, the *Mirror* opposed the filibustering expeditions into Central America designed to open new slave territories, and Archbishop Kenrick himself refused faculties to a priest sent by the American-controlled government of Nicaragua as emissary to Washington.[125]

"What true American," the *Mirror* asked on the eve of the election of 1860, "could be insane and vicious enough to arrest this country's march to greatness by destroying her unity, its very first element?"[126] Soon after the election of Abraham Lincoln, however, it editorialized that it would rather have the Union broken up than see the new president and his party "destroy what we believe to be southern State Rights."[127] The *Mirror* became increasingly sympathetic to the newly formed Confederacy, engaging in spirited exchanges with the pro-Union Pittsburgh *Catholic* and Cincinnati *Catholic Telegraph*.[128] Its publishers, Michael J. Kelly and John B. Piet, would be twice arrested for printing works of a "treasonable character" and on the second occasion confined in Fort McHenry.[129]

A week after the firing on Fort Sumter, the passage of Union troops through Baltimore occasioned a riot that claimed several lives. A Catholic graduate of Georgetown living in New Orleans, James Ryder Randall, was moved to write a poem, "Maryland, My Maryland," which would become the state anthem. "Avenge the patriotic gore," it ran, "That flecked the streets of Baltimore." In September the archbishop ordered Carroll's prayer for civil authorities read in all churches just as several pro-southern legislators, including T. Parkin Scott, were arrested by the Union general. When Kenrick the following Sunday began reading the prayer, which contained a plea for the preservation of the Union, a number of people left the cathedral, as James Gibbons remembered, while others expressed disapproval by "a great rustling of papers and silks."[130] Kenrick later informed the Propaganda that he had ordered the reading of the prayer discontinued at once so as "to avoid suspicion of our loyalty to the present government."[131]

The sentiment of the great majority of his flock, however, now lay unmistakably with the South. Many of the sons of Baltimore's Catholic elite enlisted in the Confederate Army. Ex-Governor Enoch Lowe fled to Virginia to command a Confederate brigade. Nevertheless, a few, like Captain William Kennedy, were outspoken in their support of the Union, and the Catholics of western Maryland, in all probability, shared the pro-Union sentiment of their neighbors. Kenrick's suffragans likewise shared the loyalties of their respective regions. To Kenrick, Bishop Young of Erie denounced secession as a "most criminal & treasonable outrage."[132] To the president himself Kenrick appealed to avert the arrest of Bishop Whelan of Wheeling and obtain the release of Father Thomas Becker of Martinsburg, both accused of disloyal prayers or sermons, and he brought Becker to Baltimore for the duration of the war.[133]

The war proved disruptive in a number of ways. A Catholic officer circulated a petition to exempt Catholic churches and other institutions from military seizure, an appeal prompted by the appropriation of Georgetown College, the Visitation convent, Trinity Church, and St. Aloysius Church, as well as the Jesuit novitiate in Frederick, for use as hospitals. The congregation of St. Aloysius, in fact, put up a building to keep their church from being commandeered.[134] Expressing disapproval to the Visitation Sisters for keeping a door open to receive the news, Kenrick added: "Be cautious not to take sides in the politics which divide the country, but pray for peace and respect the constituted authorities."[135] It was doubtless the same advice he gave to all the priests and religious of his diocese.

Sisters served the war's victims unstintingly and without distinction. At Emmitsburg, despite a strong sentiment in favor of the South, they housed and fed the Union Army on its way to Gettysburg. The day after the battle, a wagonload of sisters proceeded to the battlefield, about which Sister Matilda Coskery was moved to write: "O! this picture of human beings slaughtered down by their fellow men in a cruel war was perfectly awful."[136] For the ambulance corps and hospitals the Sisters of Charity of Emmitsburg supplied 232 nurses, more than all the other sisterhoods combined. The Sisters of Mercy staffed three military hospitals in Washington and the Sisters of the Holy Cross the hospital near St. Aloysius.[137]

Four days after the battle of Gettysburg, on July 8, 1863, Archbishop Kenrick was found dead in his bed, the apparent victim of a heart attack. Archbishop Hughes came down for the funeral but was too weak to finish the private mass he had started. Six months later he was also dead. Baltimore had to wait ten months to learn the name of Archbishop Kenrick's successor. Some blamed the delay on the Federal government, but they were mistaken. For the second time Henry Coskery filled the role of administrator in a quietly effective way.

A Sulpician Assessment

Kenrick's death prompted Joseph Paul Dubreul, the Sulpician superior, to confide in Archbishop John Odin of New Orleans: "It has often been noted, and it has struck me in the same way, that life, stimulus, and organization have been wanting in the [arch]diocese of Baltimore for a long time. The elements for good are more numerous here than elsewhere and yet the works do not exist or are languishing. Baltimore should be the model diocese, the Rome of the United States, but it is outstripped by others. The clergy ought to be, comparatively speaking, the most numerous and remarkable but they are not at all. It would be difficult to find one man of truly distinguished merit in the secular clergy." Dubreul blamed this deficiency largely on a lack of vocations.

"What is the cause of all this?" he asked. Episcopal leadership, he believed. "Our archbishops for 30 or 40 years have all been eminent prelates from several points of view. The last one especially, whom we mourn, was the glory of the church for his knowledge, holiness, prudence, and modesty. But their spirit does not seem to have been actively directed to the creation and organization of works." Though things had not gone badly, the archdiocese was where it was twenty-five or thirty years earlier. It needed now an active prelate, one like Bishop Timon, Dubreul suggested.[138]

It was an accurate assessment. Kenrick was not a builder, but his spiritual children were proud of his learning and of the unruffled dignity with which he graced his office. Kenrick was the most cerebral of the archbishops of Baltimore. The multiplication of edifices and organizations he left to others. He was, perhaps, the most systematic of the archbishops of

Baltimore, bringing order to the administration of the archdiocese at a time when it was badly needed, regularizing procedures and clarifying relationships.

Unfortunately, Kenrick lacked warmth. He was comfortable with the gentry but ill at ease with his immigrant charges. His modesty and prudence were, perhaps, a mask for timidity and his diffidence a shield from criticism. Though he appeared to be above the petty bickerings of ordinary men, he could occasionally be less than magnanimous, as John Hughes could well testify. Yet he was an outstanding example of the gentle Irish as Hughes was of the battling ones. The cathedral rectory of Baltimore would house more of the former.

Temperamentally the Irish-born Kenrick was much more in the Maryland tradition than such militant bishops as Hughes were. Deploring conflict, he wished Catholics to be as American as they could be and to extend the hand of friendship to non-Catholics. Unlike Carroll and the Sulpicians who followed him, however, this alumnus of the Urban College was thoroughly Roman, ultramontane in his basic theology and undeviating in his application of the discipline promoted by the Holy See. In this he would resemble his successor.

8   *The Lion of Baltimore*

ARCHBISHOP KENRICK HAD PICKED three priests as possible successors: Henry Coskery, his vicar general, Thomas Foley, his chancellor, and Oliver Jenkins, president of St. Charles College—all natives of Maryland. The American bishops found none of them possessed of the qualifications needed. But there agreement ended.[1] The cardinals of the Propaganda, however, had no difficulty in accepting the obvious preference of the member who prepared the *ponenza*, Cardinal Karl von Reisach. His choice was a former subject at the Urban College, Martin John Spalding, Bishop of Louisville, who was "pious, zealous, learned, eloquent, amiable, highly regarded in Baltimore, and of Maryland origin."[2] The pope approved the choice on April 3, 1864, and the bulls were inscribed May 6.

Spalding was installed on July 31, feast of St. Ignatius Loyola, patron of the Maryland missions. "A profound scholar," the New York *World* was moved to remark, reflecting the opinion of other journals, "a gentleman of refined and cultivated manners, a man of rare and unaffected piety, and a person of untiring diligence in his profession, he unites in his character the very qualities that are needed here, as head of the most important province."[3] That the American bishops could not have agreed on one who came to the premier see with such universal approbation is a matter of wonder.

Maryland Catholics welcomed him as one of their own. His ancestors had lived four generations in Maryland before joining the wave of Catholic yeomen who crossed the mountains at the end of the eighteenth century seeking a new and better life. Born in 1810 on a Kentucky farm, Spalding proved something of a prodigy and was sent to the Urban College of the Propaganda to complete his studies for the priesthood. In 1848 he was named coadjutor bishop of Louisville with right of succession.[4] Though as bishop of Louisville he had shown himself a gifted administrator, his reputation at large was based upon his apologetical writings and his oratory.[5] At episcopal gatherings he demonstrated legislative skills beyond the ordinary.

Initial Undertakings

Spalding's initial undertakings in Baltimore were directed toward the disadvantaged. Before leaving Louisville, he had arranged with the Sisters of the Good Shepherd to found a penitent asylum for wayward girls in Baltimore. Four days after his installation, a group arrived from Kentucky to take possession of their new home, another gift of Mrs. Emily McTavish.[6] In September he issued a circular encouraging greater support for the orphans, "God's own favorite children," and called a special meeting to establish branches of the St. Vincent de Paul Society, perhaps his favorite organization, in the parishes of his see city. The society would not only provide material relief and medical aid for the needy but also, at the archbishop's suggestion, find jobs for the unemployed.[7]

The war had brought a halt to church building at a time when new churches were badly needed. Spalding recommended the process in those places whose needs and resources he was able to study. Two weeks after his arrival, he gave permission to the pastor at Texas to build a stone church at Monkton. He required the pastor to make application again when the walls were up as a check on expenditures.[8] His healthy fear of inordinate debts prompted a plan for the development of city parishes. A temporary chapel would be built by the pastor whose parish was being divided, then a permanent church when the new congregation was ready to fund it. The temporary chapel would be converted into a school.[9] The pastors of St. Patrick's and St. Matthew's in Washington were told to put the plan into operation at once.

The Wages of War

Archbishop Spalding was eager to make a visitation of the entire archdiocese to acquaint himself with its people and their needs, but Confederate raids continued into Western Maryland. During his first year, in fact, the new archbishop was constantly bedeviled by problems arising from the war, some addressed to him as metropolitan, others his because the national capital was a part of his diocese. To effect the release of Bishop Elder of Natchez, who had been arrested for refusing to read a prayer for the president, Spalding worked quietly through Michael O'Connor, the bishop turned Jesuit and a personal friend of Secretary of War Edwin Stanton. Bishop Lynch of Charleston was abroad and unable to return because of services rendered to the Confederacy, and Bishop Verot of Savannah was fighting the Union commanders at every turn.[10]

On April 15, less than two weeks after the surrender at Appomattox, Baltimore's bells tolled to announce the president's assassination. "Words fail us," the archbishop wrote in a circular, "for expressing detestation for a deed so atrocious, hitherto happily unparalleled in our history. Silence is, perhaps, the most appropriate expression for a sorrow too great for utterance."[11] But General James A. Hardie, Inspector General of the Army, a convert and Spalding's most trusted adviser in Washington, thought more was needed. Unless crepe were hung on all Catholic edifices, he insisted, "we are in danger of disorder, destruction of property, riot and perhaps bloodshed." Father White particularly would need such an order.[12] Spalding saw to it that when Lincoln's body passed through Baltimore on April 21 some 150 priests and seminarians joined the procession. He, however, would visit a remote part of the archdiocese.

That several Catholics figured prominently in the assassination plot did not go unremarked. Fearing a fresh outburst of nativism, Spalding agreed with Bishop Timon on the inexpediency of agitating Mrs. Surratt's innocence. He had, he told the bishop of Buffalo, written Father Jacob A. Walter "strongly urging him to adopt the course of silence."[13] The pastor of St. Patrick's in Washington had attended the unfortunate Mary Surratt at her execution for complicity in the assassination plot.[14] A dispute between Father Walter and General Hardie about her treatment had broken into print. Spalding enjoined a twenty-five-year silence on the outspoken pastor concerning the Surratt affair.[15]

Spalding did not wish the controversy to complicate his efforts to have Bishop Lynch return to his war-torn diocese. The archbishop wrote Attorney General James Speed, a friend from his Louisville years, and Secretary of State William H. Seward to see if Lynch might come back without incurring penalties. Speed through Walter advised that for the present Lynch would not be allowed to return. But when Lynch himself appealed to Seward, Spalding wrote directly to the president and obtained a pardon.[16]

Spalding disliked the necessity to deal with the Federal authorities in behalf of his church. He made no effort to win friends in the White House or on Capitol Hill. "I have made it an invariable rule," he wrote an office seeker, "not to interfere in politics & political appointments. Besides I really have no personal acquaintance with the President, & but slight influence with the government."[17]

From his war-time involvement in the affairs of his suffragan sees, Spalding had obtained a bleak picture of the distress of the "conquered provinces." In late summer he ordered a collection to help stave off starvation in the South during the winter and urged bishops in the North to do the same. What he collected he sent to bishops and priests in the South to be distributed "irrespective of creed" and doled out himself smaller amounts to destitute supplicants. "Many thanks," wrote Bishop Lynch, decrying the failure of northern bishops to follow Spalding's lead, "for your (I am sorry to say *unexampled*) kindness for our poor."[18]

Visitation and Synod

Even before Appomattox, the seventh archbishop began a visitation of the entire archdiocese. In the spring he covered the western counties, in July Montgomery County, and in October the southern counties. In November he moved to the head of the Bay, down the Eastern Shore, across to Anne Arundel County and was back in Baltimore December 7. The last and longest circuit, more than five hundred miles, was, in some ways, the most satisfying. Though the congregations of the Eastern Shore were the smallest, their faith was strong. The eagerness of non-Catholic neighbors to aid in the erection of the five or six churches projected by the archbishop was due largely to their desire for immigrant labor "now that the Negro was his own master." But Spalding saw it as a fertile field for conversions and preached or lectured there as often as three times a day.[19]

In the course of his visitation the archbishop laid plans for the construction or completion of some twenty churches and the enlargement and improvement of many others. With a number of congregations he had to insist upon the decent maintenance of the church and support of the pastor. Though impressed by the new church of St. Joseph in St. Mary's County, he told the congregation of nearby Sacred Heart bluntly that he had never seen "a more miserable apology for a church" and threatened that of St. Mary's, Bryantown, with the loss of their pastor if he were not better supported. In some places he himself chose parishioners to assist the pastor in planning improvements or in teaching Sunday school. By the end of 1865 he had visited 106 congregations and had confirmed 7,279 people, of whom 871 were converts.[20]

During his first year, Spalding held a synod, May 24, after a retreat for his priests that he himself conducted. In a pastoral letter the archbishop touched on eleven of the nineteen decrees enacted. The dearth of vocations in a state so Catholic in its traditions, he explained, prompted the first statute requiring each pastor to send at least two candidates to the minor seminary. He also explained the reasons for the decrees calling for the instruction of children on the sacraments four times a year, the solemn celebration of the patronal feast of each church, a yearly instruction on matrimony wherein the pastor should call attention to the earlier decree on excommunication for any Catholic who contracted marriage before a Protestant minister, an annual collection for the Holy Father, the publication of marriage banns, sponsors at confirmation, and burial in consecrated cemeteries. He alluded likewise to the decrees urging frequent benediction, support of the societies for the Propagation of the Faith and Holy Childhood, and the establishments of associations of pious ladies in each parish similar to the one recently founded in the cathedral parish for the instruction of poor girls.[21]

The rest of the decrees concerned only the clergy. Some modified matters already legislated, such as clerical conferences (now also in rural areas), mass stipends, and priests' salaries. The written permission of the archbishop was required not only for an initial indebtedness but for any improvement involving more than $200. A cathedraticum, or voluntary "gift" of the pastors for the maintenance of the ordinary, was set at 5 percent of the annual income of congregations whose pew rents exceeded $1,000 and 3 percent for those whose pew rents were less.[22]

The decree concerning candidates for the minor seminary stemmed from Spalding's need for priests to fill places he had promised. Two urgent appeals to the Society for the Propagation of the Faith won the 5,000 francs needed to enroll the archdiocese as a patron of the American College of Louvain, of which he was the principal founder. Mindful of this role, the rector promised one or more priests immediately. Informed also by the rector of the missionary college of Genoa that two priests were available, Spalding asked Cardinal Barnabò to have them assigned to Baltimore. He could, he explained, put twenty priests to work at once. Protestants were ripe for conversion. The freed blacks had innumerable needs. And an upswing in immigrant labor was expected now that the war was over.[23] All Hallows College in Ireland also promised three priests. In June 1865 the archbishop ordained three of his seminarians. Once the initial pinch was alleviated, personnel would constitute one of the least of Spalding's concerns.

A Burst of Construction

The burst of construction, enlargements, and improvements in his first four years in Baltimore was unmatched by any of his predecessors. "I am trying," he told Bishop Wood in early 1865, "to stir up my people to a greater energy & spirit of improvement." He himself was about to renovate the cathedral "in the best style" and complete the exterior by the addition of a clock and carillon ordered from Paris. Two wings and a third story would also be added to his "palace."[24] The last-named improvement was made possible by a gift of $15,000 from Captain William Kennedy, who would prove to be one of Spalding's most generous and consistent benefactors.

In Washington the pastor of St. Patrick's, Father Walter, built the temporary church for the new parish, the Immaculate Conception, as he had been told, but the pastor of St. Matthew's, Father White, loath to see his fashionable parish broken up, found excuses for delay. The two pastors, moreover, were not on the best of terms, White complaining of Walter's "meddlesome disposition" and "palpable selfishness and ambition."[25] White, however, was quite willing to build a church for the black Catholics who had flocked to Washington from southern Maryland after emancipation. The chapel of Blessed Martin de Porres was finished in 1865. Only after the Immaculate Conception was made a separate parish in 1866, however, did White begin a church called St. Stephen's. It became a parish in 1867. White saw to it that it had a permanent church from the start. Immaculate Conception did not begin a permanent church until 1870. Martin de Porres was also made a parish in 1867 and placed under Felix Barotti, one of the two priests obtained from the missionary college in Genoa.[26]

For the first parish he created in Baltimore, Archbishop Spalding waived his own requirement for erecting a temporary chapel first. The parish he created for the Catholics moving into West Baltimore he named for his patron saint. The laying of the cornerstone for St. Martin's Church on July 9, 1865, was a spectacular event, some twenty thousand people viewing a colorful parade nearly two miles in length.[27] When dedicated in 1867, St. Martin's was placed under John Foley, brother of the chancellor and future bishop of Detroit.

In 1864–65 St. Bartholomew's Church was built in Manchester largely for the Germans, many of whom, the *Catholic Mirror* explained, had gone over to the Lutherans.[28] In 1865–66 St. Lawrence was built at Jessup's Cut and Our Lady of Sorrows at West River (Owensville), both for new parishes in Anne Arundel County. In 1866 SS. Peter and Paul was begun at Easton on the Eastern Shore, St. Francis de Sales at Abingdon in Harford County, St. Philip Neri at Sunnybrook in Baltimore County, and St. Michael's at Clear Spring in Washington County. In 1867 six churches were begun or bought for new parishes: St. Mary Star of the Sea in South Baltimore, St. Thomas Aquinas between Hampden and Woodberry and St. Bernard's on Hillen Road, both just north of Baltimore, St. Joseph's at Sykesville in Carroll County, St. Ann's at Tennallytown in Washington, and the Church of the Immaculate Conception in Calvert County.[29]

As important as the churches for new parishes were the new churches that replaced old ones in existing parishes. Both Baltimore and Washington were growing at such a rapid rate that for the foreseeable future an edifice of impressive proportions and design would in most parishes supplant its modest predecessor within a few years. These second-growth churches were created as perpetual monuments to enterprising pastors and as temples that filled an apparent need of the immigrant Catholic to be overpowered by ambience. Almost as many second churches were built in the Spalding years as original ones. The two most ambitious were both begun in 1865, St. James in Baltimore by the Redemptorists and St. Dominic's in Washington by the Dominicans. St. James was finished in 1867, St. Dominic's not until 1875. Not all replacements were the result of second growth, however. At Mount Savage the church of St. Patrick superseded that of St. Ignatius in 1865 because of the need to relocate on land donated by the Mount Savage Iron Works.[30] Deterioration likewise demanded replacements, especially for the dilapidated churches of southern and western Maryland that made the new archbishop anxious.

Institutions for the Needy

Some of the archdiocese's most famous institutions were founded in the Spalding years. A long-standing preoccupation of the seventh archbishop was the fate of wayward children. For this reason he had induced the Sisters of the Good Shepherd to come with him to Baltimore, on whose streets roamed some three thousand vagrant children the last year of the war.[31] In 1866 he started St. Mary's Industrial School. It was a type of Catholic institution still in its experimental stage, a combination orphanage, reformatory, and trade school. With the Catholic Protectory of New York, it would serve as a model for later institutions of like purpose.[32]

Mrs. McTavish, benefactress of the House of the Good Shepherd, offered also a hundred acres outside the city. To her sister, the Duchess of Leeds, Spalding explained the need for help "in saving the poor Catholic boys of our City & vicinity from going astray & losing their faith & souls—as hundreds of them are now doing by being sent to the House of Refuge & other institutions, where they are either proselytized or reared up without faith."[33] He induced the Xaverian Brothers, whom he had introduced into the United States in 1854, to take charge of the school. From two gatherings of Baltimore's wealthiest Catholics came pledges totaling $32,000. Though short of the sum needed to build on the scale he envisioned, Spalding made a start, partly to encourage additional contributions, partly to impress the bishops who would come to Baltimore in October for the Second Plenary Council with the importance of the work.[34] When contributions still lagged, Spalding reached beyond the affluent and launched a dollar campaign in every parish. He also enlarged the board to include not only the chief pastors and prominent laymen but also the mayor and members of the city council. In 1867 he began a five-story stone building. Still in desperate need of funds at the beginning of 1868, he applied for both city and state aid. From the city came $5,000, and after intensive lobbying in the Assembly, $20,000 came from the state. By the end of the year, with some $80,000 already expended, Spalding believed the future of the industrial school assured.[35]

An infirmary opened by the Sisters of Charity in the national capital during the war was expanded after the conflict, with grants from a grateful Congress, and named Providence Hospital. One of Spalding's first acts was to give the Redemptorists permission to bring in Franciscan Sisters from Philadelphia to serve the Germans. In 1867 they opened a hospital in the northeastern part of Baltimore. It would be called St. Joseph's.

The Religious Orders

Besides the Sisters of Good Shepherd and the Xaverian Brothers, Spalding invited the Passionist Fathers to come to Baltimore and open a monastery. Impressed by the papal jubilee they had preached in 1865, he offered them also St. Agnes Parish. The cornerstone for St. Joseph's Monastery on Frederick Road was laid in 1867 and the building dedicated a year later.[36] In 1867 the Calced Carmelites were invited into the archdiocese to take over the Redemptorist monastery and missions in and about Cumberland. Spalding's invitation to the Religious of the Sacred Heart to open a finishing school for girls in southern Maryland would be answered after six years of persuasion.[37]

Though they surrendered their missions in Allegany County, the Redemptorists enlarged their activities elsewhere in Maryland. They took charge not only of the new parishes of St. Bartholomew in Manchester, St. Bernard's just outside Baltimore, and Our Lady of Sorrow at West River but also the new parishes on the Eastern Shore. As it turned out, only two of the latter materialized in Spalding's lifetime, the churches at Easton and Salisbury.[38] The Redemptorist scholasticate was moved from Cumberland to a spacious edifice built in 1867–68 at Ilchester outside Baltimore.

The Jesuits decided to separate their scholasticate from Georgetown and build one near Baltimore. The huge granite structure at Woodstock was begun also in 1867 but not finished until 1869.[39] The Sisters of Mercy shifted their center of activities from St. Peter's Parish to a spot just outside the city. Through their friend Charles Dougherty, the same whose benefaction had made possible St. Agnes Hospital, they acquired a former girls' school run by the German Reformed Church at Mount Washington. The new academy and boarding school they opened there in 1867 was named Mount St. Agnes, also for Mrs. Dougherty. The motherhouse and novitiate would be transferred to this site the following year.[40]

Almost as many new religious congregations came into the archdiocese under Spalding as under all his predecessors put together. His relationship with the religious, old and new, were cordial. Except for a brief misunderstanding with the Carmelites of Cumberland, he suffered a serious disagreement only with the Sulpicians. Even in this he was at pains to note that his dispute was with Father Debreul, the superior, and not with the "gentlemen of the seminary."[41]

The Sulpician Disagreement

In the Kenrick years both the major and minor seminary in and near Baltimore had experienced a remarkable growth, attracting a growing number of students yearly from other American dioceses.[42] By 1865 the archdiocese of Baltimore itself had eighteen at St. Mary's and forty-five at St. Charles. But Spalding was unhappy with the policies and pedagogy that had been in force at St. Mary's since the resignation of Deluol. From Louisville he had brought a bias against the "old fogies" from Europe who were unable to bend to American ways. When Dubreul failed to respond to his recommendations for changes, Spalding wrote directly to the superior general in Paris, Michel Caval, in 1866. "To work well and prominently in this vast country," he insisted, "your Society, ought, it seems to me, to adapt itself to the circumstances and the nationalities of those with whom it finds itself engaged. The Fathers, especially the superiors, ought to remember that they are no longer in France."[43] Spalding wanted Caval to replace Dubreul, to supply professors whose native tongue was English and who better understood contemporary problems, and to modify the teaching, discipline, and administration at St. Mary's. A series of lectures on contemporary problems was introduced, but Caval was unable to supply professors of Spalding's description and said nothing of Dubreul's removal.[44]

When Spalding requested a financial statement from Dubreul on the use of the annual collection for the seminary, Dubreul sent with the statement a demand that the archdiocese pay tuition for its students as did other dioceses. Spalding replied heatedly that Dubreul was asking of him something the seminary had not required of his predecessors. Avowing "filial affection," Debreul lowered his demand by half, but renewed it in Spalding's absence at the beginning of the next school year. Upon his return, Spalding reported the "unanimous opinion" of his council that the archdiocese could accept no permanent arrangement beyond the annual collection. In May 1868 Debreul finally stipulated that the major seminary would accept as many students as the annual collection warranted. Spalding agreed. "I will only add, in conclusion to this very disagreeable discussion, that this matter having been thus *finally settled, the subject must not be reopened.*"[45] Though some changes were made, Dubreul remained, and the archdiocese was now obliged to continue the annual collections for both seminaries. But it was probably in response to Spalding's complaints that the talented Alphonse Magnien was sent to Baltimore in 1869. As Dubreul's successor he would effect the reformation Spalding had wished.

Priests and People

Spalding had a much easier rapport with his priests than had Kenrick and developed a pleasant intimacy with his episcopal household. Business was relieved by banter. Nicknames were appropriated from the sons of Jacob: Coskery, the vicar general and rector of the cathedral, was Ruben; Foley, the chancellor, was Joseph; and James Gibbons, brought in as Spalding's secretary in 1865, was Benjamin. Until his return to Virginia, Thomas Becker was also a member of this convivial group. Spalding was also well liked by rank-and-file Catholics of the archdiocese. Initially delighted at his coming, the Catholic elite was soon discomfited by his disarming familiarity and democratic ways as well as his efforts to bend their social habits. When he banned certain types of dances, some of the younger socialites proved rebellious.[46]

Planning the Council

Spalding was, perhaps, the hardest working of the archbishops of Baltimore. While he pushed the many improvements of his first four years, he also took upon himself the burden of an ambitious plenary council. He was the only archbishop of Baltimore actively to promote a national council. It was he who suggested to the Propaganda that one be held immediately after the war as a proof of unity of the Catholic Church and to address the many problems arising from the altered condition of the country and the growth of the church since the First Plenary Council.[47]

Though second to last in seniority among the seven metropolitans, "prerogative of place" justified the initiative he seized in this and other matters touching the American church as a whole. Yet he was aware of the need for tact. Though he had established a comfortable relationship with the quiet and judicious John McCloskey, Hughes' successor as archbishop of New York, his friendship with his former metropolitan, Archbishop Purcell of Cincinnati, was a brittle one and his efforts to cultivate a closer acquaintance with the taciturn archbishop of St. Louis, Peter Richard Kenrick, younger brother of his friend and predecessor, were but partially successful. Yet he was determined to involve the four closest metropolitans, including Odin of New Orleans in the preparation of the council. Kenrick, though initially cool to the project, proved to be the most active collaborator.

To the archbishops Spalding wrote: "As to sending a President from Rome, I would regard it as implying distrust of the American Episcopate, and I would moreover apprehend another Bedini affair."[48] As he doubtless anticipated, he was named apostolic delegate to preside over the council. The instructions sent by Barnabò, however, touched none of the problems that had worried the Propaganda in the Kenrick years.[49]

Spalding envisioned nothing less than a comprehensive code of law for the church in America, coordinating all previous legislation and supplying whatever else was needed. The needs of the American church, as he saw them, were embodied in the *schema quaestionum* he sent the bishops. Should the council provide an official English version of the Bible and a uniform English and German catechism? Should it emphasize the danger of attending the public schools? Should there not be an industrial school in every diocese? Was it not a time to establish a Catholic University in the United States? Should married convert ministers be admitted to minor orders? How should the salvation of the blacks be promoted? Should there not be Catholic tract societies and libraries like those of the Protestants? Should labor unions be condemned as secret societies? Should cathedral chapters be introduced? A number of questions touched the stabilization of structure, discipline, and worship in the American church and the promotion of societies that filled many needs.[50]

The needs of the emancipated blacks were foremost in Spalding's mind. "I think it is precisely the most *urgent* duty of all," he had written to McCloskey, "to discuss the future status of the *negro*. Four million of these unfortunates are thrown upon our Charity, & they silently but eloquently appeal to us for help. It is a golden opportunity for reaping a harvest of souls, which neglected may not return."[51]

From the metropolitans' uneven contributions and other responses Spalding fashioned a tentative code—a formidable document of 566 decrees—with the aid of a committee of theologians he had brought to Baltimore. The latter included Thomas Becker and the priest whose talents Spalding came to value most, James A. Corcoran of Charleston. At a preliminary session of the council each bishop was handed a copy of the tentative code, or "libellus," as Spalding called it.[52]

The Second Plenary Council

On October 7, 1866, 47 prelates, 120 other council participants, and a host of attendants processed from the rectory to the cathedral, Spalding bestowing his blessings on the curious and the devout who packed sidewalks, windows, and rooftops. As the august column entered the cathedral, the orchestra struck up "with thrilling effect" the grand march from Tannhaüser. "The scene was one which Raphael would have delighted to transfer to the glowing canvas," the *Catholic Mirror* rhapsodized.[53]

The impressive beginning did not portend a smooth proceeding. The council moved, as Archbishop Purcell later reported, "under a higher pressure than the boilers c[oul]d well bear."[54] On the fifth day Archbishop Kenrick proposed, in effect, that the *libellus* be discarded and the council start afresh. When the motion was defeated 32 to 12, he entered a formal protest against the procedure and abstained from further debate on the decrees. Spalding was shaken but maintained his equanimity.

At the beginning of the second and final week, he appointed two other bishops to help him select only the more important decrees for discussion. Even then it was necessary to call an extraordinary session after the solemn closing to dispose of important business. On the matter of a special ministry for the blacks, Kenrick declared that it was the duty of bishops to rule, not carry out the instructions of the Propaganda, and threatened to walk out if the discussion was not closed.[55] The subsequent discussion of metropolitan jurisdictions was even more turbulent, Kenrick, according to Bishop Verot, appearing "out of his mind." In Spalding's absence the bishops voted that Philadelphia and Milwaukee be archdioceses, Philadelphia by a vote of 21 to 20.[56]

Fearing that Kenrick might cause the emended *libellus* to be rejected in Rome, Spalding wrote to, among others, his friend from his days at the Urban College, Cardinal Paul Cullen. "You may safely say to [Barnabò]," he concluded, "that with perhaps one exception, there is not in the entire American Episcopate, a single element or vestige of *Gallicanism*—Thank God! We are Roman to the heart."[57] Though recovering from a nearly fatal illness, Spalding went to Rome for the eighteenth centenary of the martyrdom of SS. Peter and Paul in the spring of 1867 to convince the Propaganda to accept not only the work of the council but his own recommendations on its decrees. When the Propaganda's decisions arrived the following February, he wrote triumphantly to McCloskey and Purcell: "Our Brother of St. Louis was not sustained in hardly a single particular, & the Bishops of Milwaukee & Philadelphia owe it chiefly to him that their cause is delayed."[58]

Though the cardinals of the Propaganda made few changes in the *libellus*, it had been emasculated in Baltimore itself. Some of the decrees Spalding wanted most were expunged by the council fathers, such as acceptance of the Kenrick translation of the Bible as the official English version, a uniform cathechism, and the establishment of cathedral chapters. When not eliminated, some were reduced to a pious wish, such as the establishment of a Catholic university. The question of a special ministry for the blacks was relegated to provincial councils.[59]

Though the Second Plenary Council produced few innovations of moment, it gave greater organization, strength, and specificity to existing legislation and tightened structures, discipline, and worship in a church heretofore run by rules and procedures that were ambiguous or flaccid. It emphasized the indispensability of parochial schools and other Catholic institutions, the importance of pious associations and other organizations, and the value of a Catholic press. It encouraged parish missions and those devotions and practices that had come to characterize the ghetto church, such as the Scapular, May devotions, Stations of the Cross, Apostolate of Prayer, and Forty Hours. In short, it represented the "apex" of the legislation that had over the past thirty-five years served to refashion the Catholic Church to meet the needs of the immigrants.[60]

In the matter of episcopal jurisdictions and their incumbents, Spalding's recommendations were followed in every particular. Ten new dioceses and five vicariates apostolic were created but no new archdioceses despite the votes on Philadelphia and Milwaukee. To the province of Baltimore were added the dioceses of Wilmington, Scranton, and Harrisburg and the vicariate of North Carolina.[61]

None of the other provincial and plenary councils of Baltimore was so much the work of one man. No other archbishop possessed the imagination, boldness, and energy to break the pattern of piecemeal legislation that had characterized previous councils. If the Second Plenary Council failed to do all that Spalding had wished it to, it did provide a model for the next one, when the bishops would be ready to move on such matters as a uniform catechism, a Catholic university, and aid to the blacks. If Spalding can be faulted in his planning and direction of the council, it is for his apparent expectation of a perfunctory approval for the predigested legislation.

The School Question

Spalding never allowed his preoccupation with the council to interfere with his duties in the care of the archdiocese. During his seven months abroad in 1867, Foley and Gibbons reported frequently. "All our operations here," the former wrote in July, "at Good Shepherd—Industrial School &c—are stopped by the foolish action of the Carpenters who are on strike for eight hours work on Saturdays. The times and Country seem out of joint. Congress has passed new reconstruction [acts] more diabolical than the former." Foley included scraps of information for "Old Ruben" and told the archbishop that he expected a "hornet's nest" about his head when he pried the dependent churches from Father White. He would handle the "tea-pot tempest with becoming severity."[62]

Though Maryland escaped the "carpetbag" government imposed upon former states of the Confederacy, it suffered Republican control until 1866. Conservative Democrats, many Catholics among them—most conspicuously Aloysius Leo Knott—recaptured the state government and revamped the constitution.[63] Plans were laid for the reorganization of the public school system. Spalding summoned the pastors of Baltimore to consider the advisability of now applying to the General Assembly for public funds for the Catholic schools. Though the German pastors favored the move, most of the others feared an anti-Catholic outburst similar to that of 1852–53. Spalding himself was reluctant to see the expected appropriation for St. Mary's Industrial School endangered.

He nevertheless instructed Gibbons to draft a report on parish schools and send it to Annapolis. The parochial schools of greater Baltimore had accommodated 7,089 pupils the past year, it revealed, the average annual attendance over the past decade being 5,744 with a cost of about $5.00 per pupil, which did not include expenditures exceeding $300,000 for lots and buildings. "In submitting this report," Gibbons concluded, "the Archbishop directs me to add that it is not his intention to offer any advice. . . . He is aware that the subject is one of great delicacy and difficulty, and which required for its solution calm and dispassionate examination. He is willing to leave it to the prudent counsels and wise conclusions of your honorable body."[64] The funding was not forthcoming. "Perhaps we shall fare better another year," Spalding confided to his journal. "We shall make a better fight in our attempts at equality and justice—if it seems prudent under the circumstances to do so."[65]

Many of his pastors were in favor of using the sacraments to coerce attendance at the parish schools. "We have not been in the habit of denying absolution to those who send their children to the public schools," Spalding wrote to one, "but our priests have relied more on moral means & strong suasion. The confessional is odious enough, & should not be made more so—at least not more than is absolutely necessary. However, you may announce from the pulpit that Catholic children are not permitted to join in prayers and worship with others in the public schools; & unless this can be prevented parents are strictly bound to withdraw their children."[66]

The Archdiocesan Code

When in 1868 the official documents concerning the plenary council finally arrived from Rome, Spalding moved at once on the items that called for action. On August 16 in the cathedral he raised to the episcopacy two of his proteges: Thomas Becker as bishop of Wilmington, Delaware, and James Gibbons as vicar apostolic of North Carolina. On September 3 he held his second synod in Baltimore. In it he fashioned a *corpus juris* for the archdiocese as he had done for the American church, organizing all former synodal legislation under six titles and incorporating fresh enactments required by the council or by needs newly perceived. In all there were sixty-six statutes.[67]

An assortment of diocesan officials were created, many of them new to the archdiocese: archpriest (Coskery) and archdean (Foley), rural deans, synodal examiners, and judges of cases. To the four rural deans was entrusted the superintendence of personnel and properties in their respective areas: Edward Brennan in Washington and Allegany Counties, John McCaffrey in Frederick and Carroll Counties, Dwight E. Lyman in Baltimore County, and Joseph Enders, SJ, in St. Mary's and Charles Counties. The number of consultors was fixed at twelve.

Many of the decrees the archbishop underscored in a pastoral letter. Picnics and excursions under parish auspices were prohibited. Waltzes, German, and round dances were banned in Catholic colleges and academies. The annual collections were fixed. A schedule for the Forty Hours Devotion was set for the entire archdiocese. All pastors were enjoined to assist those specially assigned to the blacks. The archbishop also explained the decrees on mixed marriages and instruction of Catholic children in public schools, warned against spiritism, and exhorted the Irish to follow the example of the Germans in founding immigrant-aid societies.[68]

One of the means Spalding employed to assure that the decrees did not become dead letters was the clergy conference, which was held four times a year in the cities and twice a year elsewhere. All priests, secular and religious, involved in parish work were obliged to attend. Dubreul, rector of the seminary, was asked to make annual evaluations. The first conference he judged a success but discerned an "air of incorrectness" in some of its conclusions. Appropriate responses, he declared, were as much the result of common sense as of the application of theological principles.[69]

Planning and Building: Part Two

Soon after the synod, Spalding began his second systematic visitation. Though satisfied with the physical signs of progress, he was saddened by what seemed to him a deteriorating morality, even in his flock. In a much publicized Lenten sermon in 1869, he came out forcefully against extravagance and immodesty in dress, sensational theatrical performances, and the most abominable act of all—abortion.[70] On the score of dress, dancing, and the theater, age had doubtless heightened a Jansenism he had imbibed on the Kentucky frontier. But his was not the only voice to deplore the corruption and excesses of the Grant era.

Institution building slackened not a bit in Spalding's later years. Several new parishes were created. A German Reformed church on the property acquired by the Sisters of Mercy in Mount Washington was given over to the archdiocese in 1868 and rechristened the Shrine of the Sacred Heart. That year the president of Gonzaga College, Bernardine Wiget, SJ, obtained Spalding's permission to begin a church near the Capitol, which he envisioned as a national shrine for the Germans, a duplication of the Cologne cathedral. The walls were hardly above ground, however, when Wiget fell ill and funds ran out. In 1870 a modest frame structure was placed on a massive base, the dream of national shrine forgotten. Spalding probably regretted in this instance he had not exercised his usual caution.[71]

In 1870 the Redemptorists began a church not far from St. Martin's to serve the Germans of West Baltimore and called the parish Fourteen Holy Martyrs. When the Redemptorists informed Spalding the same year that some of the leaders of the Bohemians in Baltimore were trying to obtain the services of a schismatic clergyman, the archbishop applied to the rector of the American College of Louvain for a priest who could speak their language. Rev. Wendelin Vacula came in 1871 to attend the four hundred or more Bohemian families of the city in the parish hall of St. Michael's until Spalding purchased a Lutheran church for them in November. It would be called St. Wenceslaus.[72] Elsewhere St. Francis de Sales was begun at Salisbury on the Eastern Shore just before the separation in 1868, St. James at Boonsboro in Washington County also in 1868, and St. Michael's at Ridge in St. Mary's County in 1870.

Parochial schools were opened in all new urban parishes, now a set policy in the archdiocese, and new religious orders imported to teach them. The Redemptorists brought in the Brothers of Mary to staff their boys' schools, the Dominicans the Dominican Sisters to take charge of St. Dominic's parochial school, and the Carmelites the Ursuline Sisters for the girls' school in Cumberland. Three new girls' academies were added to the nine existing ones. The Sisters of the Holy Cross opened St. Cecilia's Academy in Washington in 1868. In 1871 the Religious of the Sacred Heart finally acceded to Spalding's request and opened an academy at Rosecroft, the ancestral home of their own Mother Aloysia Hardey, in St. Mary's County.[73] The same year the School Sisters of Notre Dame obtained Spalding's permission to purchase land out Charles Street and the next spring began construction of what would become the College of Notre Dame of Maryland.

In addition to St. Mary's Industrial School for boys, Spalding wanted also homes where orphan girls who had reached fourteen could be taught marketable skills. The Sisters of Charity opened St. Joseph's House of Industry on a modest scale in Baltimore in 1865 and moved to larger quarters in 1867. The school they opened in Washington in 1868, however, St. Rose Technical School, became even more a model for this type of institution.[74]

Never satisfied that he had filled all the needs of his see, especially for those unable to help themselves, Spalding was ever alert to new opportunities. When he heard that the Little Sisters of the Poor were opening homes for the destitute elderly in the United States, he invited them to Baltimore. The Little Sisters arrived in April 1869 to occupy temporary quarters while a spacious home for the aged was being built.[75]

The English-speaking beneficial societies of Baltimore formed a union in 1865. When the board amended its constitution in 1869, Spalding readily approved it, recommending "two objects of special charity, besides those referred to in the Constitution: namely, attention to poor Irish Catholic emigrants arriving in Baltimore, and to the education in Catholic Parochial Schools, of the children of Irish parentage who go to the Public Schools, or are in danger of going astray."[76]

A Special Concern

The people for whom he evidenced the most concern, however, were the blacks. While he failed to move the American bishops as a whole in their behalf, he did better in his own province. At the Tenth Provincial Council in May 1869, the suffragans agreed, in effect, to follow his example in the matter of spiritual missions for the blacks, separate churches and schools, and special collections "as far as circumstances will permit."[77] Father Francis Boyle reported to Spalding on one of the missions he preached: "Eight lectures and three sermons aroused an enthusiastic spirit, spinning new sentiments of gratitude and devotion in that poor Colored race, who are at once, the most forgiving of past injuries & the most responsive to present kindness."[78]

Spalding encouraged the Oblates of Providence to extend their usefulness to other dioceses, to seek incorporation, and to rebuild. In November 1870 he invited all the societies in the city to attend the laying of the cornerstone for a combination motherhouse, academy, poor school, and orphanage. "I rejoice to see Germans, Irish, and Americans here today, carrying out the true spirit of the Church," he told the assembly. One of his closest friends at the Urban College, he revealed, was an Abyssinian. "There are no parties in heaven. I want all my children—Irish, German, American, African—I want them all to go to heaven."[79]

His crowning achievement in behalf of the blacks was the introduction of the St. Joseph's Society of the Sacred Heart for Foreign Missions, popularly called Mill Hill Fathers in England, where it was founded in 1866 by the future cardinal, Herbert Vaughan. In America it would be known as the Josephites.[80] "As Baltimore is the natural & most appropriate point for the mother house of any institution for the benefit of the colored people," Spalding wrote Vaughan in 1871, "whence it may form branches for the entire South, you should, I think, begin here."[81] When Vaughan and the four pioneers arrived in December, Spalding persuaded the Jesuits to surrender St. Francis Xavier, the "colored" parish, to this latest of several religious orders to make Baltimore their home.

The Syllabus of Errors

As archbishop of the premier see, Martin Spalding took seriously his role of promoting the interests of the American church as a whole. For this reason he continued to write and to speak in spite of the added burdens. At the behest of Isaac Hecker and Edward Sourin, he wrote tracts for the

Catholic Publication Society and articles for the *Ave Maria*. The most significant essay of his early years in Baltimore, however, was a defense of the *Syllabus of Errors* issued by Pope Pius IX at the end of 1864.

Reprobating as it did pantheism, rationalism, socialism, liberalism, freedom of speech and of worship, separation of church and state, progress and modern civilization indiscriminately, the *Syllabus* placed American Catholics in an uncomfortable if not untenable position. "To stretch the words of the Pontiff," Spalding explained in a pastoral designed to reach beyond the borders of the archdiocese, "evidently intended for the standpoint of European radicals and infidels, so as to make them include the state of things established in this country, by our noble Constitution . . . were manifestly unfair and unjust." The founding fathers, "neither Latitudinarians nor infidels," had acted "wisely and prudently" in providing for separation of church and state and free exercise of religion.[82]

Despite the assurance with which he clothed his arguments, Spalding was not altogether certain they would win the endorsement of the Roman authorities. To Cardinals Barnabò, Reisach, and Giacomo Antonelli, the papal secretary of state, he wrote requesting a statement to the effect that the *Syllabus* was not meant to reprobate "the order of things existing here." To the last he added a note on the First Amendment: "For us, this is a beneficial provision which I would not want to see disturbed; otherwise great harm would come to our Holy Religion."[83] His requests for Roman endorsement of American principles, however, were pointedly ignored.

The response in America, however, was enthusiastic. In a second edition of the pastoral, Spalding noted that his interpretations were "identical" to those of the more famous defense of the *Syllabus* by Bishop Félix Dupanloup of Orléans. This was not altogether true, for Spalding had posited no distinction between "thesis" and "hypothesis," the ideal and the practical. For him the American experience was hardly an *hypothèse*.

A Friend of Labor

The Roman authorities, nevertheless, valued Spalding's opinions, perhaps more than those of any of his predecessors, and sought them often. Spalding gave them gladly. On most problems, spiritism in America, for example, his episcopal colleagues were quite willing for him to answer for them all.[84] A subject on which his advice was judicious and ultimately beneficial was that of secret societies. On the Fenian Brotherhood, an association of Irish nationalists, he urged inaction rather than condemnation. As he had guessed, this quixotic body evaporated almost as rapidly as it had grown in the United States. His opinion of the brotherhood was influenced to no small extent by his fear of a growing sentiment in favor of a general proscription of secret societies that would include even labor unions.[85]

In the postwar years the labor movement had suddenly mushroomed and in few places more than in Baltimore, where the National Labor Union was founded in 1866. "Secret political, oath bound societies and trade unions are becoming fearfully multiplied," Archbishop Purcell wrote Spalding soon after his transfer to Baltimore. "We shall have a herculean task to encounter in the endeavor to keep Catholics from combining with them."[86] Spalding had not the same apprehension with regard to labor unions. At the Second Plenary Council a majority of the bishops were won to the decree he had inserted exempting labor unions from the blanket condemnation of secret societies.[87]

Three months after the council, he advised the archbishop of Quebec against a condemnation of associations of "the laboring poor, whose special friend the Church has always been."[88] The Canadian bishops, however, continued to voice concern about the labor unions spilling into their country from the United States. In 1869 they asked the Holy See's guidance on the Knights of St. Crispin, a shoemakers' union that had established a lodge in Baltimore only a year before. Cardinal Barnabò sought Spalding's opinion. In a statement intended for the Holy Office, he advised that it was almost impossible to dissuade Catholics from joining such societies because they would otherwise have great difficulty finding employment. "Here, especially," he added "whoever has money believes he can freely oppress the poor, and he does it whenever he can. In all commercial countries, especially Protestant ones, *capital* (money) is the *despotic ruler*, and the worker is its slave. This being the case, I say, leave the poor workers alone— there being little danger that they can do injustice to the tyrannical employer." This was the reasoning, he insisted behind the decree (No. 519) of the late plenary council concerning labor unions.[89] When the Propaganda finally answered the Canadian bishops in 1870, it referred them to this decree.[90] In staying the hands of the critics and counseling the wavering, Spalding rendered a service to the labor movement at a critical juncture of its development more important, perhaps, than the more publicized one of Cardinal James Gibbons to be considered later.

Other Responses to Rome

Spalding's relationship with the Holy See did not go smoothly at all times. He was not anxious to help an agent selling papal bonds in America. Nor was he eager to encourage young Catholics to go and fight for the Holy Father, as some militant Catholic papers were doing. An occasional correspondent of the New York *Freeman's Journal*, Miss Ella Edes, then at the beginning of her long career as self-appointed adviser to the Propaganda on American affairs, reported Cardinal Barnabò as expressing surprise that Spalding had not informed him of the desire in the States to send a unit of volunteers. Devoted to New York, she urged her inquirer to contact Archbishop McCloskey, because Spalding "has no influence here."[91] A soldier of fortune of Maryland antecedents, Charles Carroll Tevis, was also at work in Rome persuading the pope and his military commander to issue a call for an American battalion. When the call came, Spalding, McCloskey, and Purcell met at Emmitsburg, McCloskey acting also for Kenrick, and composed a letter to Barnabò to convince him that the promotion of such a project was ill advised. The same sentiment was expressed in a statement to the public.[92] The Holy Father, Barnabò replied, was satisfied with the archbishops' explanation and had ordered the project abandoned.[93] The Roman authorities had obviously blundered in not consulting the American bishops while claiming that the call had been made at their behest. Spalding was prudent enough not to say so.

His response to the Propaganda's appeal to save the American College in Rome from financial ruin, though belated, was all the distressed officials could hope. One of his own priests, Silas Chatard, was now rector. As chairman of the committee on affairs of the college, Spalding worked out a plan for endowing the institution with burses for individual students donated by wealthy Catholics. The campaign was launched in Baltimore, which set an example by pledging nearly $22,000, including gifts of three full burses at $5,000 each.[94] Though the campaign fell short of its goal, the continuation of the college was assured and the archbishop of Baltimore found himself head of a permanent committee on the American College.[95]

Priests' Rights

A stumbling block to full cooperation on the part of the bishops was the role of some of the alumni of the American College in the antagonism that developed at this time between bishops and priests. Partial to Roman students and at ease with his own clergy, Spalding was slow to appreciate the smoldering discontent of secular priests that threatened to erupt into open rebellion.[96] Initially he encouraged Roman students in Chicago to report irregularities on the part of their bishop, James Duggan, to Rome. An article, however, appeared in the New York *Tribune* in the midst of the campaign for the American College that angered Archbishop McCloskey and, more important, Archbishop Spalding. It represented the Chicago controversy as a conflict between conservatives and progressives. The latter, it claimed, had the support of Archbishops Spalding and Purcell, members of the "anti-absolutist" party, Spalding especially having endeavored to impart "an American character" to Catholicism.[97] McCloskey mistakenly believed the author to be one of his own priests, Edward McGlynn, a member of the first class of the American College. McGlynn was one of the leaders of a clerical coterie that shocked the sensibilities of many Catholics by voting Republican, espousing the cause of blacks, supporting the public schools, promoting cooperation with non-Catholics, and questioning devotional and disciplinary practices of the church.[98]

When ordered by the Propaganda the following year to investigate conditions in the diocese of Chicago, whose bishop, it turned out, was insane, Spalding reported that cupidity was the chief cause of the "scandalous tumults" there and left little doubt as to the chief culprits. To bring peace to that unhappy see, Spalding was willing to sacrifice his righthand man, Thomas Foley, as a replacement for the ailing bishop. Foley would not disappoint the expectations of his friend and mentor.[99]

In the meantime, James McMaster, publisher of the *Freeman's Journal*, smarting over a perceived rebuke on the part of the archbishops for his promotion of the American battalion, launched a crusade in his weekly for priests' rights that featured a series of articles by one of the aggrieved who styled himself "Jus." The latter flayed the American bishops unmercifully for their tyranny.[100] Three of the eight decrees of the Tenth Provincial Council of Baltimore in 1869 were designed to assuage the discontent of the clergy. One called for the appointment of consultors and judges in every diocese, a second urged that priests have a say in the preparation of the data for prospective bishops, and a third provided for the support of priests under suspension.[101]

While Spalding was trading guesses with McCloskey on the identity of Jus, he refused to intervene in a struggle between Bishop Amadeus Rappe of Cleveland and a group of his priests seeking his ouster. As it turned out, the leader of the disaffected priests, Eugene O'Callaghan, was also the author of the antiepiscopal essays. Had he known it was in his power to crush the infamous Jus, Spalding might have been less reluctant to intervene in this second quarrel between bishop and priests.[102]

He was not so reluctant to intervene in a third quarrel, where he had a decided interest at stake. His brother Benedict, who had administered the diocese of Louisville since the death of Spalding's successor in 1867, himself died in a tragic accident in 1868. Spalding retained a proprietary attitude toward his former see that ran counter to the independent spirit of the new bishop, William McCloskey, former rector of the American College, who arrived soon after the death of Spalding's brother and proceeded to antagonize a large portion of his clergy.[103] Spalding, as administrator of his brother's estate, wished to use his legacy to endow Louisville with an industrial school, a wish McCloskey refused to honor. Less than a year before his death, Spalding, as a result of almost daily complaints from his former priests requested an investigation of Bishop McCloskey's administration. Barnabò assigned the task to the metropolitan, Archbishop Purcell, a friend of McCloskey since their days at Mount St. Mary's. He exonerated the bishop of Louisville on every count. A year after Spalding's death, McCloskey would boast to Purcell that "having fought the great old lion of Baltimore, I am not now going to be afraid of his whelps."[104]

Purcell's "whitewashing" of McCloskey, as one of the "whelps" termed it, occurred after Spalding had antagonized Purcell—and other American bishops—in Rome during the First Vatican Council. At this momentous gathering Spalding played a significant but ultimately frustrating role.

The First Vatican Council

Fifteen months after the preparatory commissions had begun their work for Vatican Council I, Cardinal Barnabò asked Spalding to select an American theologian to join them. His choice of the man whose contribution to the Second Plenary Council had impressed all, James Corcoran, met with a nearly unanimous approval. "They apparently need some one [in Rome]," Bishop Bayley of Newark added wryly, "to inform them that this country was discovered some years ago, and is now settled and partially civilized."[105] From Rome Corcoran sent alarming news to Spalding. The dogmatic commission to which he was assigned was using the *Syllabus of Errors* as a basis for its work. A definition of papal infallibility, moreover, was a "foregone conclusion" unless opposed by a significant number of bishops on the ground of expediency.[106]

Four months before the opening of the council, Spalding sent to Barnabò for the consideration of the commissions a list of propositions that he claimed represented the views of at least a third of the Catholic bishops of the world! Since the intent of the *Syllabus* was not always obvious, he declared in the "Memoranda," clear and affirmative decrees should be formulated. On the matter of church and state, care should be taken not to reprobate the arrangements that prevailed in the United States, Britain, and Prussia but to commend them as models for Catholic countries where the church enjoyed small liberty. Indifferentism should not be extended to that civil indifferentism that precluded state action in religious affairs. The punishment of heretics and resort to the secular arm were anachronisms that were better ignored. Distinctions should be made between the false progress of materialism and the human betterment that popes in past ages had promoted by their endowment of the arts, letters, and sciences.

Foremost among his concerns, Spalding continued, was papal infallibility. Though he himself had not the slightest doubt about it, he questioned the advisability of an explicit definition and suggested instead an implicit one. Should the bishops, however, deem it expedient to frame an explicit definition, he advised, the limits of its exercise should be accurately marked.[107]

The forty-six American bishops who were on hand for the opening of the council on December 8, 1869, were dismayed by the intense campaigning of the "infallibilists" and "inopportunists," as the proponents and opponents of a definition were called. More Americans than not declared themselves inopportunists.[108] Though he sympathized with the inopportunists, Spalding remained neutral, in part because of his appointment to the congregation on proposals and his election to the deputation on faith, the two most powerful bodies at the council, and in part because of his desire to promote a compromise. When it appeared that the council fathers were hopelessly divided, he offered a compromise in the form of the implicit definition he had suggested the previous summer. His formula avoided the use of the word "infallibility" but restated former condemnations of antipapal teachings.[109] The moment for compromise, however, had passed.

At that point, the part of the preparatory commission's *schema* on the church with the propositions that Spalding had sought to eliminate or modify by his "Memoranda" was distributed for discussion. There can be little doubt that the American bishops would have rallied behind the leadership of the archbishop of Baltimore to play an important role at Vatican Council I had the debates proceeded as scheduled.[110] Instead it was decided to advance the discussion of papal infallibility, which by the spring colored, absorbed, or excluded all else.

In March a *guerre des brochures* had broken out, which Spalding entered on April 4 with a letter to Bishop Dupanloup of Orléans, leader of the anti-infallibilists. Spalding protested Dupanloup's use of his compromise definition to make it appear that he supported the position of Dupanloup and his followers. Now that "inopportunity" was no longer the issue, he declared, the bishops could side only with the pope or his enemies. He himself would "never stray from the glorious paths in which our young church in America has followed up to this hour with unshaken fidelity."[111]

In his reply Dupanloup included a letter of "several archbishops and bishops of North America" who denied that Spalding spoke for all the American bishops and complained that in pretending to do so without consulting them he had acted contrary to custom. They also contended that he had been an inopportunist before his elevation to the two commissions. The letter found its way into several newspapers over the signatures of Archbishops Kenrick and Purcell. Spalding guessed correctly that the "several" were no more than a half dozen, but among them were two of his suffragans: Bishops Verot of St. Augustine and Domenec of Pittsburgh. Spalding penned a long reply to Dupanloup but never published it, being unwilling to enter into a controversy with his American confreres. Stung by the charge of inconsistency, however, he released to the press the text of his summer proposal for an implicit definition, noting that it did not preclude the possibility of an explicit one.[112]

It was ironical that, while under attack by the opponents of papal infallibility, Spalding was working with moderates in the deputation on the faith to soften the excesses of the *zelanti* and conciliate the opposition. He was not, as some suggested, under the spell of Archbishop Henry Edward Manning of Westminster. His views were closer to those of Archbishop Victor Dechamps, primate of Belgium, who, like Spalding, was liberal in matters of church and state but undeviating in his devotion to the Holy See.[113]

On May 23 Spalding celebrated his sixtieth birthday at the American College. All of the American bishops in Rome were there, and the rest of the sixty guests covered a spectrum of nationalities and attitudes. "It was a pleasant sight," wrote young Bishop Gibbons as correspondent of the *Catholic Mirror*, "to witness so many Prelates of different nations fresh from the arena of discussion, lay aside their heavy Theological armor and entertain each other for a while with the lighter weapons of harmless mirth and humor."[114] Spalding was at his best at such gatherings, but the wounds were too deep to be healed by an evening of conviviality.

Echoes of the American quarrel were to be heard on the council floor and in published statements almost till the end of the council. In a lengthy defense of his own position, which raised objections that went beyond expediency, Kenrick quoted a work of Spalding to the effect that papal infallibility was only an opinion and that no Catholic would fault the Gallican Bossuet for want of orthodoxy.[115] Spalding had, in fact, changed his views on papal infallibility. In his earlier writings he had insisted that it could be exercised only in conjunction with the bishops either dispersed or in council.[116] He now came to agree with those who would have the pope exercise infallibility of himself "and not from the consent of the Church," as it was defined by the final vote taken July 18, 1870.

The reason for the change he explained in a pastoral issued the day after as "Gallicanism revived." The heated controversies surrounding the council, he insisted, had brought him to realize that opposition to papal infallibility was rooted in Gallican principles, not inexpediency. From his Roman studies and subsequent readings Spalding had carried a conviction that Gallicanism was an unmitigated evil. Now he was as strongly convinced that it must be destroyed.[117]

Spalding was still in Europe when Rome fell to the Italian army on September 20. With the concurrence of Archbishops Dechamps and Manning, he asked Barnabò to approach the pope on the possibility of shifting the council to Malines. Some months later Pius IX informed Spalding through the Propaganda that under the present circumstances the resumption of the council was impossible.[118]

The Last Year

Archbishop Spalding's return was made the occasion of public protests of the "sacrilegious" invasion of Rome. The protests, he reported to Manning, had drawn more than fifty thousand people in Baltimore and at least thirty thousand in Washington, where President Grant had joined the procession. "It was glorious! Not for me, but for the Holy Pontiff."[119] Almost every letter to Rome in 1871 alluded to past, present, and future efforts in behalf of the pope. On the twenty-fifth anniversary of the coronation of Pius IX, Spalding cablegrammed the celebrant: "Grand Jubilee Demonstration in Baltimore—General Communion—Illumination and Torchlight Procession—Hundred Guns—Hundred Thousand People." For three days the city was treated to a panorama of sight and sound unsurpassed in its history.[120] Spalding would soon erect a church to be called St. Pius V as a memorial of the event, he informed Barnabò, and he could assure the Holy Father that "his most devoted children will contribute with alacrity to such a *Pious* object."[121]

St. Pius was not the only church Spalding planned for Baltimore in his last year. In addition to the Bohemians, the Germans moving into Canton needed one, as well as the growing number of Catholics around Bolton Depot in the northwestern part of the city.[122] The two achievements that afforded the ailing archbishop special satisfaction in his last months were the coming of the Mill Hill Fathers to serve the blacks, already noted, and the establishment of large parochial schools for boys and girls in the cathedral parish.

Chronic ill health intensified in his last year. The accustomed congeniality of the episcopal household had vanished with the departure of its earlier members. The estrangement that had developed between Spalding and Kenrick, Purcell, and Verot continued to the end. Yet the imagination and interests of the seventh archbishop suffered no diminution. When he was "last dying," he wrote Isaac Hecker, whom he had named his literary executor, he was taken by the beauty of the Psalms in the breviary and was tempted to turn them into prayers for the laity. "Our present prayers in English are more or less dull & prosaic," he admitted.[123] His last trip was to New York to confer with Archbishop McCloskey and three other bishops on the possibility of the American hierarchy's organizing its own insurance company, a scheme suggested by the disastrous Chicago fire. He returned with a cold that developed into bronchitis.

With difficulty Spalding said his last mass on Christmas and became progressively worse. The week before he died, his episcopal friends and protégés—McCloskey, Foley, Gibbons, and Becker—and some of his relatives from Kentucky came to see him for the last time. The day before his death, he joked: "If I get well, I intend to write a treatise on the art of choking to death."[124] He died February 7, 1872.

A Range of Achievements

The eulogies and obituaries were uncommonly lavish in their praise. Brownson, with whom he had disagreed on more than one occasion, knew no member of the hierarchy who excelled him "in singleness of purpose, in devotion to Catholic interest, and in intense zeal and activity in the cause to which his life was consecrated and devoted without reserve."[125] It was the one point no contemporary assessment failed to mention. Few American prelates drove themselves so relentlessly and with less heed for the consequences. That his chronic ill health—five times he had skirted death—escaped remark was indicative of Spalding's habit of making light of his maladies. He literally worked himself to death three years before he could claim the prize he so obviously coveted. Had he lived until 1875, there can be little doubt that Spalding and not his friend John McCloskey would have been the first American cardinal.

Few, if any, American prelates surpassed Martin Spalding in his range of interests, activities, and achievements, whether as organizer, administrator, legislator, apologist, author, orator, or scholar. With the possible exception of John Hughes, no prelate at midcentury was more influential in shaping the attitudes and promoting the institutions of the immigrant church. What gave particular character to Spalding's episcopacy was the concern and compassion he evidenced for the Negro, the orphan, the destitute, the delinquent, the day laborer, the ignorant, and the aged. He spoke to children as to equals. Spalding possessed a touch of vanity. He was not always candid and open with his episcopal brethren and was sometimes less than generous in his treatment of those who opposed or offended him. But these defects were outweighed by his industry, devotion to duty, amiability, accessibility, unpretentiousness, simple piety, sense of humor, and quiet forbearance in the face of suffering and death.

A wall builder, Spalding evidenced little of the ecumenical spirit and sense of civic concern characteristic of the Maryland tradition. He was quite comfortable within the confines of Catholicism. At the same time, he outdid even Carroll in his missionary fervor, advancing the merits of American principles to the church universal as he argued the superiority of his church to Protestant Americans. Of all the archbishops, he achieved best that amalgam of ardent love of native land and intense devotion to the Roman pontiff that would distinguish American Catholics generally.

Without doubt, Spalding was the most forceful, effective, and popular incumbent of the premier see between Carroll at the beginning of the century and Gibbons at the end. Carroll had been compelled by the very nature of the infant church to break new ground. Gibbons would be, in many ways, the spokesman for more imaginative and dynamic churchmen. Spalding was the most remarkable in his unblushing exercise of leadership. None was as eager to seize the reins of power and put his talents at the disposal of the church.

Not only to Bishop McCloskey of Louisville was Spalding "the lion of Baltimore," though others may have used the term more admiringly. In appearance he possessed a certain majesty, plain but commanding. He possessed also, what many may have sensed, the arrogance and quiet ferocity of one who knew he was born to rule.

9   *No Lasting City*

"COME ON DOWN HERE," Archbishop Spalding wrote Bishop Bayley of Newark in 1868, "to stay a week or two—drop everything if you can. I want to talk to you about matters & things."[1] By this time the seventh archbishop of Baltimore had made up his mind that Bayley should be the eighth, and Rome rarely refused him anything. For form's sake Spalding added the names of Bishops Lynch of Charleston and Elder of Natchez to the *terna* he prepared for Rome. At the Vatican Council Bayley tried to dissuade Spalding from thrusting the burden upon him. "Do you remember," he asked Bishop Gibbons, "when the good Archbishop called you to witness, that he crossed my name off the list? We were riding in the Borghese Villa—I wish he had persevered in his good resolution."[2] It was not the conventional demur. Bayley was happy at Newark and wanted to die there.

When the bulls, dated July 30, 1872, arrived, the archbishop-elect began a letter to Cardinal Barnabò: "As I am convinced that I am altogether unworthy of so exalted a position I must beg leave to return them to the hands of your Eminence, and request of you in the most correct manner to ask our Holy Father the Pope to appoint another to the place." He had had only one year of theology, he explained. He was imperfect in Latin. He had made decisions injurious to religion. His health was not good; hereditary gout pained him more each year.[3] He stopped in the middle of the sentence and never sent the letter. Instead he adopted as the motto of his archiepiscopal arms: *Non habemus hic manentem civitatem*—"We have not here a lasting city."

The Convert Bishop

James Roosevelt Bayley had one important tie to the oldest archdiocese: his aunt. He was the son of Guy Carleton Bayley and Grace Roosevelt. Guy was the half brother of Elizabeth Ann Bayley Seton. (Grace was sister of Isaac Roosevelt, great-grandfather of Franklin Delano Roosevelt.) To his cousin Catherine Seton, Bayley wrote soon after his conversion: "I often think, I know not why, that it has been the prayers of your sainted Mother, that has obtained for me this blessing."[4]

Born and baptized in the Protestant Episcopal Church in 1814, Bayley had been ordained an Episcopal priest in 1840. A descendant of colonial English, Dutch, and Huguenot families, he had played as a child with the De Lancy, Jay, and Munro children. His life was everything his aristocratic family and friends had thought it should be until soon after his ordination he began to discuss his attraction to the Church of Rome with a priest destined to be a cardinal, John McCloskey. In Rome itself he was received into the Catholic Church in 1842.[5]

Bayley entered the Seminary of St. Sulpice in Paris to study for the Catholic priesthood. He returned to New York in 1844 to be ordained by Bishop Hughes, whose secretary he became in 1846. In 1853 he was ordained first bishop of Newark by Archbishop Bedini on the eve of the latter's ill-starred tour of the United States. He proved an excellent administrator. While the Catholic population of the new diocese doubled in his nineteen years there, its institutions and personnel tripled.[6] Everyone expected great things of him in Baltimore. "Bishop Bayley," the *Catholic Mirror* informed its readers, "is a convert and a progressive American in the true Christian sense of the much maligned term. By nature bold and energetic, his conduct is as decided as are his convictions."[7]

The Unapplauded Sentiment

The eighth archbishop was installed October 13. At the same time, he received the pallium. In his address he praised the "eminently conservative" character of the Catholic Church. "Whoever heard of a good Catholic joining the International?" he asked. "Whoever heard of even a bad Catholic joining the Mormons, or making speeches in Women's Rights Associations or any similar gathering?"[8] At the banquet that followed, however, he praised the heroic spirit of Lord Baltimore and, at least according to the New York *Herald*, said that he "never did believe in opposing liberty of conscience and was an earnest advocate of its fullest exercise." At this point, the *Herald* observed, "Archbishop Bayley looked toward Archbishop McCloskey, who was sitting on his right, and paused as if awaiting his approving smile. Every eye was fixed upon him and many of the clergy, with uplifted hands, stood ready to applaud the sentiment, but the Archbishop of New York, with rigid face, sat unmoved and gave no manifestation of approval. Archbishop Bayley, however, reiterated the sentiment."[9]

Three months later Bayley wrote Michael A. Corrigan, his former vicar general who was soon to be his successor as bishop of Newark: "I have received another letter from Rome in regard to the after dinner speech—from Miss [Ella] Edes who is a sort of Ass[istant] Sec[retar]y to Card. Barnabò. She says that the Card. told her, that I would be called upon to write a refutation or denial. Pleasant state of things when Bishops are called upon to answer every lie that any miserable penny a liner may choose to write."[10] Corrigan had already taken it upon himself "to contradict the foolish rumor." Writing to Chatard at the American College, he insisted that the archbishop had offered no toast to religious liberty, nor had McCloskey turned "black in the face," nor was there "any particular applause" from the attending bishops (none of which the *Herald* had claimed).[11] In any event, Rome thought better about demanding a refutation.

A Coolness in Baltimore

Aunt Mary Roosevelt was pleased that the new archbishop would "be placed where you will enjoy *refinement & culture*."[12] Bayley did, in fact, enjoy the social life of the Tidewater, but he was more attracted to the wealthy Catholic families of Washington than those of Baltimore—to the Ewings, Sands, Riggs, Merricks, and especially Mrs. Madeleine Vinton Dahlgren, the "self-appointed doyenne of Washington society," and Mrs. Ellen Ewing Sherman, wife of General William Tecumseh Sherman.[13] In Baltimore he seemed more at home in cultured Protestant circles than in Catholic ones. After a reception at the Walters Art Gallery, he wrote in his memorandum book that he had had "little time to look at the pictures," so engaged was he in conversation with "Mr. Garrett & Mr. King, Pres. & V. Pres. of the Balt. & Ohio R.R.. Genl. McClellan who is spending the winter in Balt. & whom I had met before: Genl. Donaldson—Pres. Gilman of the new [Johns Hopkins] University here."[14]

In his visitations elsewhere he met those whom he charmed and who in turn charmed him. Of the Shrivers of Union Mills he wrote: "One of the nicest Catholic families I ever met with."[15] In St. Mary's County he found Mr. Mattingly "a very worthy man & good Catholic of the old school" and his son Ignatius "as fine a specimen of a noble young country gentleman as one could wish to see."[16] After his return from southern Maryland, the *Catholic Mirror* commented: "Your old Marylanders have an invincible prejudice in favor of gentlemen. In Archbishop Bayley they found one."[17]

And yet, the eighth archbishop was not embraced warmly by the Catholic aristocrats of his see city. The coolness was due in part to Bayley's dislike of Baltimore itself, whose "odoriferous Basin" at the mouth of Jones

Falls was a constant irritant to him. It was due even more to Bayley's efforts to bestir the wealthy from a lethargy that stood in striking contrast, as he was not reticent to observe, to the zeal and generosity of the poorest Catholics of Newark. "They are very stingy here," he complained to his memorandum book before the first year in Baltimore was out.[18] "We are jogging along here as usual," he wrote Corrigan in 1876, "—in the old ruts—my scoldings are like water on a duck's back."[19] Yet he was prepared to admit that there were individuals whose benefactions were princely—Captain Kennedy still, C. Oliver O'Donnell, and several of the Jenkinses. Bayley himself set an example. Dispensing lavishly from investments of his own, he was the most generous of Baltimore's archbishops.[20]

Setting Things Aright

There were many things that disturbed the new archbishop that he was determined to set aright. One was the cathedral debt. Maintained like a badge of distinction by the trustees for more than fifty years, it had prevented for the same time the consecration of the cathedral. At the end of his first year, Bayley established a Cathedral Debt Association. To his cousin, Monsignor Robert Seton, he complained, as the latter recalled, of the "difficulty he had among the Baltimore Catholics to pay off a miserably small debt on the Cathedral which he could have raised in his Newark diocese in a week."[21] On May 25, 1876, the Cathedral of the Assumption was finally consecrated with appropriate ceremonies. It was a "great triumph," Bishop Corrigan noted, to have thus "overcome the *vis inertiae* of Baltimore."[22]

Bayley was also disturbed by the lackadaisical record keeping of his predecessors, especially with regard to mass foundations, whose neglect Seton found unconscionable.[23] With the help of Bishop Corrigan and the Jesuit provincial, Bayley organized and classified the records in the archdiocesan archives.[24] In his first year he brought a semblance of order to the annual reports begun by Kenrick by sending out standardized forms for the pastors to use. The returns, called *Notitiae*, were carefully preserved.

On August 27, 1875, after a close scrutiny of the needs of the archdiocese, Bayley conducted a synod. He amplified the sixty-six statutes of the last one and added forty-one of his own. Among the latter were the requirements: that priests wear the Roman collar; that parochial schools be established wherever possible, and when not possible, that a Society of Christian Doctrine be introduced; that church services start on time; that no pastor accept money for mutual funds or other deposits; and that pastors receive an annual salary of $1,000 and assistants $600.[25]

One of the decrees (No. 81) reflected Bayley's distress over the state of church music in Baltimore. It forbade profane, theatrical, or worldly renditions in church, especially the solos women were accustomed to sing. It was a decree calculated to alienate even more the socially prominent of his see city. At his installation solos had been sung by Mrs. Robert Jenkins, Mrs. Emma Shriver, Mrs. C. Oliver O'Donnell, and Mrs. William George Read. Bayley encouraged the formation of St. Cecilia Societies in every parish. He himself was enamored of the Gregorian chant that they promoted and had it sung in the cathedral. The *Catholic Mirror* was convinced that a trial of six months would correct the false tastes begotten by years of listening to "florid operatic airs."[26] Bayley's success in reforming church music in the oldest see was partial at best.

A Literary Bent

Archbishop Bayley's efforts to organize the archives reflected the literary interests he shared with many of his predecessors. As a priest he had written a modest history of the Catholic Church in New York and a slim biography of Bishop Bruté. More important was his encouragement of others to compose histories and compile bibliographies.[27] In Baltimore he not only emboldened John Gilmary Shea to embark upon his monumental history of the Catholic Church in the United States but gave him free access to the archdiocesan archives and wrote in his behalf to the custodians of similar repositories.[28]

His own literary efforts in Baltimore were limited to his pastorals— the Lenten pastoral of 1876 was one of the best ever written by an archbishop of Baltimore— and letters to journals that never failed to elicit the attention of the reading public. Among the latter was a "racy" letter to the New York *Herald*, disguised as a private communication to someone else, accusing the famous British statesman, William Gladstone, of anti-Catholicism.[29] Another was a letter to the Cincinnati *American Israelite* disassociating himself from anti-Semitic sentiments found in the Baltimore *Katholische Volkszeitung* and expressing regret for them. At the same time he reminded the *Israelite* of anti-Catholic utterances on the part of Jewish supporters of Bismarck in Germany, for which he would not think to hold the Jewish people responsible.[30]

Poor Health

Bayley's exertions in behalf of the church in Baltimore were performed at great cost to his health. A physical deterioration so gradual that few were aware of its seriousness began soon after his installation. In January 1873, when he went to Florida to recuperate from the first serious bout of illness, the *Catholic Mirror* denied vehemently a report of the well-informed New York *Herald* that the archbishop had Bright's disease and that he would never recover.[31] It was the disease, it turned out, that limited Bayley's tenure in Baltimore to ten days less than five years.

His frequent trips for health's sake were seldom understood in Baltimore, especially as most of them were to the cathedral rectory in Newark, St. Elizabeth's Convent, where his cousin Robert Seton lived, or Seton Hall College, all in New Jersey. From St. Elizabeth's he wrote to Dubreul, his vicar general, in 1875: "My old Doctor at Newark says that I *must* stop working. The prescription is very simple, but how am I to take it?" He would return to Baltimore but only for a few days, "for it seems to me that if I were to remain there in my present state, and the 'Basin' continued to perfume my room as it did the day before I left, that my career would be a short one."[32] From western Maryland he reported some three months later: "I am nearly dead. I am not fit for this sort of work any more."[33] The next year Bishop Bernard J. McQuaid of Rochester, another of Bayley's protégés in Newark, scolded him for crowding the upcoming month of June with enough work to kill a young man. "When you go out of your way and put your life in peril there is scarcely a kind word in return. . . . Baltimore will have to be allowed to drop into its old ruts and stay in them."[34] As early as the summer of 1874 Bayley began to think seriously of a coadjutor.

A Cautious Growth

In Baltimore Bayley was not an institution builder despite his work in Newark. Ill health was partly to blame. An unaccustomed caution also overtook him. The memorial church of St. Pius that Spalding had planned was not erected in Bayley's five years. A problem of location was the excuse. Three months before he died Bayley advised the man he had picked for his coadjutor to tell no one, not even the pastor appointed by Spalding, of $40,000 donated by C. Oliver O'Donnell for the church. He gave the coadjutor, nevertheless, permission to proceed.[35]

Bayley continued with some of the other churches planned by Spalding. On November 3, 1872, despite objections from some of the parishioners, he laid his first cornerstone as archbishop. St. Patrick's second church in Washington was to cost some $200,000 but would be built on a pay-as-you-go basis. A serious depression intervened. It would not be finished until 1884.[36] On September 7, 1873, Bayley laid the cornerstone of the church planned for the Germans of Canton, or Highlandtown as the area came to be called. Sacred Heart Church, under the Redemptorists, was dedicated the following May.[37]

Only four other parishes or missions were created in Bayley's five years. In 1873, Captain Kennedy, some nine months before his death, began a church at his own expense ($55,000) on his summer estate on York Road, then just outside the city. St. Ann's was blessed by the archbishop on January 31, 1874, and made a parish church at once.[38] Sacred Heart Church near Reisterstown (Glyndon) was begun by the pastor of St. Charles, Pikesville, in 1873 as a mission but not completed until 1877.[39] St. John's was established at Clinton below Washington in 1875 and Holy Family at Randallstown west of Baltimore in 1876.

The second churches built for the Immaculate Conception and St. Dominic's in Washington were finally completed in 1875, the latter being the most imposing Catholic church in the capital. Historically, however, the most important church erected in the District in the Bayley years was the one that replaced the chapel of Blessed Martin de Porres, which had served the blacks of Washington for a decade and more. A mile-long parade preceded Bayley's laying of the cornerstone of the church now called St. Augustine on July 14, 1874. The black Catholics were proud of the large Gothic church 140 feet by 64 feet, dedicated June 11, 1876, whose cost their esteemed pastor, Felix Barotti, had kept to about $75,000.[40]

For years the most impressive Catholic church for blacks in the country, St. Augustine's proved a mixed blessing. Bayley's synod of 1875 imposed upon blacks the same restrictions placed upon Germans: their spiritual needs could be served only in parishes created for them. For many this worked a real hardship, especially the large black community that had been accommodated at St. Peter's Parish some four miles from St. Augustine's.[41]

The black Catholics of Baltimore had a different kind of problem, a dispute between the Josephites, who ran the parish of St. Francis Xavier, and the Jesuits who refused to surrender title to the property. The Josephites appealed to Bayley, who in turn appealed to both the Propaganda and the Jesuit general. By the time the Jesuits gave over the property to the Josephites, Bayley was dead. In the process they acknowledged the virtual monopoly of the Josephites of the ministry to the blacks of the see city.[42] The Josephites agreed also to take charge of the parish at Upper Marlboro and four dependent missions, where a large number of blacks were to be found.

At Upper Marlboro they took the place of the Carmelites, who in the summer of 1875 withdrew from the archdiocese altogether. In Cumberland the Carmelites were replaced by German Capuchins who had fled Bismarck's Kulturkampf.[43] In the fall Bayley reported to Dubreul that the "Capuchins had already gained the heart of all."[44]

A small number of institutions appeared, expanded, or relocated in the Bayley period, but the impetus for all was provided by others. In Washington, for example, Ellen Ewing Sherman and other "charitable ladies" opened a home for "poor but deserving women" seeking employment and persuaded Sisters of Notre Dame de Namur to come from Cincinnati to take charge.[45] For only one project did Bayley take the initiative, a home for "Street Arabs," but for want of financial support—"the great trouble about everything in Baltimore," Bayley grumbled—the project languished.[46] He did, however, induce the Sisters of St. Joseph of Chestnut Hill, Pennsylvania, to enter the archdiocese and staff several schools.[47]

A new St. Joseph's Hospital was built in Baltimore in 1871–72. St. Agnes Hospital had acquired from Lady Stafford a site next to St. Mary's Industrial School and there in 1875–76 built a large hospital. At the same time, the Sisters of Charity withdrew from the Baltimore Infirmary, or Infirmary of the University of Maryland as it was now called, where they had been since 1823, because of differences with the authorities and opened St. Vincent's Hospital at the old Mount Hope.[48] In 1874 the Sisters of Mercy took charge of the Baltimore City Hospital begun a few years before by the faculty of the Washington University School of Medicine, the forerunner of Mercy Hospital.[49]

To their home for the aged in Baltimore, the Little Sisters of the Poor added another in the national capital. They had occupied temporary quarters provided by Father Walter in 1871 until a home was completed in 1873. In 1875 Father White of St. Matthew's purchased a house at 19th and R Streets for a home for elderly black people and to it bequeathed $3,000.[50]

An institution in which Bayley took a decided interest was St. Catherine's Normal School, built by the Holy Cross Sisters to train poor girls to teach in parish schools. After the dedication on March 11, 1875, Bayley complained to his diary that only one of the priests of the city was there to assist him, "showing how much interest [his priests] take in the cause of Christian education."[51] To the school he contributed a third of $15,000 that C. Oliver O'Donnell had given him to distribute as he liked.

Bayley was not as taken with the fashionable academy the School Sisters of Notre Dame had opened out Charles Street in 1873 called the Collegiate Institute of Notre Dame. Though he disliked commencements, Bayley attended the one held there in 1876, dining with President Grant, whose niece was a student.[52] Mother Caroline Friess, who came from Milwaukee in 1876 to establish a second province for the School Sisters of Notre Dame at Baltimore, was also discomfited by the "grandeur and style" she perceived at Notre Dame, which, at least according to Father Dwight Lyman, she found out of keeping with the School Sisters' spirit and constitutions.[53]

Another religious order made Baltimore the center of a province in 1876. The Xaverian Brothers had run St. Mary's Industrial School since 1866 and St. Patrick's boys' school since 1872. In 1876 they opened a novitiate and the third Catholic college of the greater Baltimore area, which they called Mount St. Joseph.[54]

Unlike his predecessor, Bayley was devoted unreservedly to the Society of St. Sulpice. In 1873 he named Joseph Dubreul his vicar general and leaned heavily upon him in times of illness. He also encouraged the Sulpicians to raise a new seminary building on Paca Street and to enlarge St. Charles College. Three archbishops and nine bishops were in attendance when he laid the cornerstone for the former on May 31, 1876.[55]

The Parish Society Explosion

The most noteworthy development, perhaps, of Bayley's short span in Baltimore was the virtual explosion into existence of parish societies and other lay organizations. The development that had begun under Eccleston had waned under Kenrick and had come to an almost complete halt during the Civil War. A revival, however, began after the war and climaxed in the middle to late 1870s. Both Spalding and Bayley encouraged this proliferation but not always for the same reasons.

THE BENEFICIAL SOCIETIES

Twelve mutual-aid societies had met in Baltimore in 1865 to form the Board of the Consolidated Catholic Beneficial Societies.[56] The large and active beneficial societies at St. Patrick's and St. Vincent's, however, did not join until after the death of Father Dolan in 1870 and Father Myers in 1873.[57] In Washington the Hibernian Benevolent Society, the oldest Catholic one in the country, was revived in 1865. By 1871 it had 94 members and a year later claimed 332.[58] It served as a model for four others of the same name founded in Washington in 1871–72. Among several other beneficial societies established in the capital about the same time was the Colored Catholic Beneficial Society. Toward the end of 1872 a District Catholic Benevolent Union of both beneficial and temperance societies was formed.[59]

These regional unions were a part of the trend toward consolidation of Catholic societies throughout the country in the postwar years. To the third annual convention of the Irish Catholic Benevolent Union (ICBU), organized in Ohio in 1869, the beneficial societies of Baltimore and Washington sent their first delegates in 1871. In October 1874, 143 delegates representing 25,685 members of the ICBU met in Baltimore for its sixth annual convention.[60] In his address Archbishop Bayley offered several caveats, among them meddling in ecclesiastical and political matters, and several expectations, the most important being the diversion of Catholics from secret societies, particularly those "miserable associations" called labor unions. "Their idea is so Communistic," he warned the delegates, "and no Catholic with any idea of the spirit of his religion will encourage them."[61]

The financial benefit offered by the fraternal insurance organizations was monetary relief in time of sickness and support for widows and orphans. There was an entrance fee that varied with age, an assessment of 25 to 50 cents at each monthly meeting, and the collection of usually $1.00 per member for the widow of a deceased associate. The monthly meeting, however, served a more important function than collecting money. It provided an opportunity for a camaraderie that the immigrant Catholic would with difficulty find anywhere else than the neighborhood saloon. Most of the beneficial societies were parish based and closely monitored by the pastor, who was often "elected" president. When Father Myers of St. Vincent's forbade any debates at the meetings, a few of his parishioners withdrew, but most remained.[62] Father McManus of St. John the Evangelist allowed no balls.[63]

The Irish beneficial societies were not without their critics. One, echoing a frequent lament, complained in 1875 that the ICBU was good only for parades and conventions and did little for Irish immigrants.[64] A defender quickly retorted that an agency for Irish immigrants had been established in Baltimore the previous year. True, it had not yet an employment bureau, but Archbishop Bayley, he reminded the critic, had advised them "not to attempt too much at once."[65]

Beneficial societies were not, of course, confined to the Irish. Four of the sixteen societies that had met in Baltimore in 1855 to form the German Catholic Central Verein were from Baltimore parishes, but they had disappeared from its rolls before the Civil War.[66] In 1873 St. Michael's Parish took the first steps to establish a union of German beneficial societies in Baltimore. By 1876 there were five divisions with more than six hundred members.[67]

The beneficial societies of Maryland and the District of Columbia followed the trend of the ICBU, which in 1876 peaked with thirty thousand members nationally and declined until it reached a plateau of about sixteen thousand five years later.[68] Under Bayley's successor, the indigenous societies would in large measure be replaced by fraternal insurance organizations introduced from without.

THE TEMPERANCE SOCIETIES

Almost as spectacular as the resurgence of beneficial societies in the postwar years was that of temperance or total abstinence societies. They had also formed regional unions, the first in Connecticut in 1869, the fourth in New Jersey in 1871. In November 1871 Bayley as Bishop of Newark addressed the latter in a speech that, as another bishop observed, "stamped a character and dated a movement."[69] The New Jersey union invited all temperance societies to meet in Baltimore to form a national organization. The union of the District of Columbia, the sixth in the country, joined that of New Jersey in issuing the call.[70]

The first convention of the Catholic Total Abstinence Union of America (CTAU) met in Baltimore February 22–23, 1872. Father Edward McColgan, pastor of St. Peter's, famous as a champion of temperance, was chosen temporary chairman and Major Benedict J. O'Driscoll of Washington secretary, a post he would continue to hold for many years. Prominent in the deliberations were the assistant pastors of St. Patrick's and St. Matthew's in Washington, John J. Keane and James McDevitt. Keane led in the balloting for president but deferred to McDevitt, who was elected the first president of the CTAU. The delegates were disappointed that Bishop Bayley, now considered the leading advocate of temperance in the American hierarchy, was unable to address them.[71]

When the CTAU met again in October in Cleveland they sent a telegram to Bayley that hailed his "elevation to the Primatial See of Baltimore with unbounded joy," regarding it "a signal manifestation of Divine interposition in our favor."[72] In a one-sentence reply through his vicar general, Bayley wished the union well. His apparent coolness toward the national organization was the result, as the delegates probably guessed, of his attitude toward its president, who had left the archdiocese of Baltimore in a vain attempt to find a bishop more to his liking. In 1873 they elected another president.[73]

McDevitt's leave-taking had a demoralizing effect on the temperance

movement in Washington. The Father Mathew Total Abstinence and Benevolent Society he had founded in 1871 disbanded.[74] Even Baltimore
ceased to play a significant role at the national conventions. Every year,
however, the Maryland affiliates of the CTAU—six in greater Baltimore
and four in western Maryland, but probably fewer than half of all such societies in the archdiocese—would meet at St. Peter's under McColgan's
presidency to elect delegates to the national convention and transact other
business. The strength of the movement in western Maryland was due
largely to the pastor at Westernport, Jeremiah O'Sullivan.[75]

The temperance movement was almost exclusively a "Hibernian Crusade." None of the German parishes of the archdiocese would seem to have
had a temperance society. Nor, for that matter, had any of the black parishes. Though the Blessed Martin de Porres congregation in Washington
had a beneficial society, it had not a temperance one, "for the very satisfactory and gratifying reason," it was explained, "that there is not a person of
intemperate habits in the congregation."[76]

THE KNIGHTHOODS

While the beneficial and temperance societies had their roots in the
prewar years, a phenomenon almost entirely a product of the Bayley years
was Catholic knighthood. The knights grew out of the beneficial societies,
and almost all had insurance features. But for the immigrant they served a
need beyond that of economic security and socializing, namely, a craving
for greater visibility. The initial investment in hats, belts, badges, sashes,
and swords was considerable but gladly borne.

The Knights of St. Patrick could be found in Washington as early as
1871 and was possibly an offshoot of the Hibernian Benevolent Society. The
Knights of St. Patrick of Baltimore was created in 1872 by a Patrick Reilly,
who had been inspired by a visit to the knights of Washington. Its stated
aims were to honor St. Patrick, to keep alive both faith and Irish nationalism, and to maintain a library. The dues would also be used to build a hall
and support widows. With the approval of the pastor of St. Patrick's, they
began their monthly marching drills.[77] Between 1872 and 1875 knightly societies were established in at least five parishes in the District and four in
Baltimore, including one for blacks in each city. In 1875 the Knights of St.
Michael for Germans was organized at St. Michael's parish in Baltimore
and the Knights of St. Joseph at Mother of God's German parish in Washington was incorporated. By 1877 almost every parish in Baltimore and
Washington had a commandery.[78]

The knights, of course, were enthusiastic marchers, and parades became longer, noisier, and more colorful in the Bayley years. Bayley himself deplored this development. Only a few months before his appointment to Baltimore, he had told Bishop Gibbons that he would like to see the St. Patrick's Day parades abolished, for "they block up the streets for hours, and they do no possible good."[79] To the great disappointment of many societies, he ruled out a parade at his installation in Baltimore. At the laying of the cornerstone of the second St. Patrick's in Washington less than a month later, he allowed a parade but no music. "The display was very fine," the *Catholic Mirror* noted, "but it lacked the enthusiasm which drum and fife would have imparted."[80] At the St. Patrick's Day parade in Washington only four months later, the bands of the Marine Corps, the United States Naval Academy, and the Fifth Maryland Regiment marched with the Catholic societies past the White House, where the parade was reviewed by President Grant. It was the "largest and finest procession of Irish-American societies ever witnessed in this city," a correspondent of the *Mirror* exulted. "Not an intoxicated person was seen in the line or on the streets during the march."[81] The new archbishop knew when he was beaten.

YOUNG MEN'S LITERARY SOCIETIES

Young men's literary societies also experienced a remarkable revival in the Bayley years. The Catholic Institute that Kenrick had encouraged was a casualty of the war, but on September 11, 1872, the Young Men's Catholic Association was founded in Baltimore "to promote frequent social intercourse among young Catholic gentlemen, and so provide intelligent recreation . . . and aid toward employment when necessary."[82] Bayley praised the association for its "diffusion among all of a better knowledge of the truths of religion and the refutation of errors," gave his first lecture in Baltimore at the end of 1873 for its benefit, and donated $2,000 from his own pocket for a headquarters.[83] By 1875 it had 500 members and 980 volumes in its library, but attendance at the weekly meetings was falling off.[84] In 1877 its name was changed to the Catholic Library Association. More successful and enduring was the Carroll Institute, established September 7, 1873, by the president of the Young Catholic's Friend Society of Washington, Edmund Mallett. In additon to the usual lectures and library rooms it provided its members, it also conducted night classes and sent reading material to Catholic soldiers.[85]

It soon became the goal of each parish to have its own literary society. The Hibernian Literary Association was founded at St. Patrick's in Baltimore in 1870. In 1872 the Literary Association of the Immaculate Conception Parish, the St. Brigid's Library Society, and the Young Men's Catholic

Lyceum of St. Peter's, all in Baltimore, held excursions or picnics. The St. John's Literary and Dramatic Association offered both plays and musicales. In the rooms of the St. John's Institute on Aisquith Street reading and "quiet games"—dominoes, checkers, and chess—were allowed but no cardplaying.[86] Some parishes, such as St. John's and St. Peter's, had two or more such societies for young adults, the result of different tastes. The *Catholic Mirror* warned in an editorial against "cliques and bickerings."[87]

As with the other forms of association, these literary societies soon established a national organization: the Catholic Young Men's National Union. At its first convention in 1875, there would seem to have been no delegates from the archdiocese of Baltimore. In 1876 the Carroll Institute affiliated with it, and Father John J. Keane, so prominent in the temperance movement, became even more active in advancing this form of association.[88] For many years, however, it was the only archdiocesan society in the national union.

CHARITABLE ASSOCIATIONS

Charitable associations also registered a decided increase under Archbishop Bayley and often as a result of his prompting. The St. Vincent de Paul Society spread to more parishes. In May 1875, St. Michael's became the first German parish to establish a conference.[89] The Young Catholic's Friend Society continued to clothe poor children in parochial schools. But the most notable development was the increase in women's organizations involved in charitable work. For many years the Dorcas Society, founded at the cathedral in 1850, was the only such group in the archdiocese. On January 18, 1875, however, the Ladies of Charity were organized in Washington to assist the St. Vincent de Paul Society by collecting and mending clothes and visiting the poor.[90] On March 8 at St. Vincent's in Baltimore the Ladies Relief Society was organized for the same purpose at the prompting of the archbishop, who wanted such societies in all city parishes.[91] About the same time, the Ladies' Charitable Association was formed by Father McColgan at St. Peter's. And there were others.

DEVOTIONAL SOCIETIES

The activities of devotional or pious societies were less publicized than other organizations, but they too would seem to have spread in the postwar period. On May 12, 1872, Father McColgan founded the Confraternity of the Holy Thirst and Agony of Jesus as part of his crusade against intemperance.[92] It would soon spread to other parts of the country and abroad. Most of the sodalities did more than pray. The Young Men's Sodality of St.

Ignatius, for example, held singing and elocution classes at their weekly meetings.[93] Closely related to the pious associations were the sanctuary societies formed in many parishes in this period. In 1876 Father Keane organized the Tabernacle Society in Washington for wealthy ladies to make altar linens for poor parishes.[94]

Catholic Social Life

As important as the avowed goals of this array of organizations were the social activities that served as their cement. These activities themselves took many shapes: picnics, excursions, fairs, festivals, tournaments, balls, and entertainments of several sorts. Archbishop Spalding's synodal prohibition against picnics and excursions was a dead letter, it would seem, the moment it was promulgated. The decree of the synod of 1875 touching such activities was more realistic. They could be held so long as the pastor took part and excluded intoxicating beverages and immodest dances.[95] Almost all of the societies sponsored one or more social events.

Picnics and excursions, the latter by boat or train to amusement parks or points of interest, were usually scheduled for July Fourth or Lady's Day (August 15), but some were held in the spring. Fairs, sometimes called bazaars, were customarily winter events, but some were conducted in the spring or summer. Raffles were the main attraction of the fairs, and tables vied with one another to realize the largest revenue. Among the prizes at the St. Patrick's Fair held in the Masonic Temple in Washington in April 1875 were a basket of champagne, a bust of William Shakespeare, a china tea set, a silver service, a gold watch, a portrait of Archbishop Bayley, and biographies of St. Patrick and Daniel O'Connell.[96] Balls were winter events. Festivals, it would seem, fell between fairs and picnics and were held in warm weather. Strawberry festivals were popular in the spring. Concerts were also money-raising events. The wealthy matrons of Washington held promenade concerts for the Little Sisters of the Poor. Amateur plays and musical soirees drew enthusiastic audiences.

Even rural parishes had societies entrusted with the organization of the country picnics and tournaments for which Maryland was famous. At the picnics ham, cold mutton, tongue, veal cutlets, fried chicken, pone cake, gingerbread, homemade pickles, cole slaw, cider, cherry bounce, birch beer, lemonade, and mead were served at three or four sittings on long wooden tables under the trees. Banter, pranks, hoedowns, and Virginia reels filled the time before pies and cakes were served in the evenings. Surreptitious flasks of apple jack or Hunter's Rye often made the rounds. There would be more dancing before the horses were hitched to wagons well into the night.[97] The tournaments, peculiar to Maryland, were conducted mostly in the southern counties and on the Eastern Shore but some in the rural parishes outside Baltimore and Washington. "Knights" at full gallop aimed their lances at small rings. The champions chose the queen and her maids in succession with appropriate ritual. Prominent politicians usually delivered the "charge" to the knights or the coronation speech.[98]

The abuses that Spalding had deplored were never totally eliminated. Beer costing $35 and a keg of ale were part of the expenses of a fair at St. Ignatius, Hickory, in 1872.[99] Periodically the *Catholic Mirror* was compelled to remind pastors and faithful alike of the prohibition of liquor and of round dances at such events. At one of the balls in Baltimore, a Catholic councilman was fatally shot, prompting the pastor of St. John's to denounce "in plain and forcible language" public balls given under the guise of charity.[100]

The increasing number of societies and their activities, of course, brought Catholics, particularly immigrant Catholics, into greater contact with their parishes and their church. St. Vincent's in Baltimore could by the mid-1870s, perhaps, boast the greatest variety of organizations, with its Father Myers Beneficial Society, St. Vincent's Beneficial Society, St. Vincent's Temperance Society, Cadets of Temperance, St. Vincent's Literary and Dramatic Society, St. Vincent de Paul Conference, Young Catholic's Friend Society, Female Benevolent Society, Ladies Relief Society, and several sodalities.[101] In time almost all urban parishes would be so endowed.

Yet in 1877 the *Catholic Mirror* would complain that Baltimore was far from the leading Catholic city that it should be. It had sent no pilgrims to Rome for the Jubilee and no delegates to the national convention of the St. Cecilia Society. It had no Catholic colonization society and no Catholic Indian Missionary Association. Its young men had not affiliated with the Catholic Young Men's National Union. The majority of its temperance and beneficial societies had not joined the archdiocesan union. It had not as many sodalities, societies, libraries, and the like, as it should have, and those it had were not patronized as they should be. "When will there come a change?" the editorial concluded, as another on the same page began: "Wake Up, Catholic Societies!"[102]

Immigration and Labor Unrest

The growth of societies was not unrelated to another surge in immigration now that the war was over. By 1874 Baltimore had filled the borders drawn in 1816. (In 1851 it had divorced itself from Baltimore County.) Horsecars were creating or enlarging centers beyond, such as at Highland-town, Waverly, Hampden, Pimlico, Pikesville, and Catonsville.[103] Their residents had left those parts of the city being filled by a new wave of immigrants. The German influx regained its former volume, which counted now a large number of Bavarian Catholics fleeing the Kulturkampf. At its convention of 1872 the German Catholic Central Verein gave Baltimore the nod over New York as a port of entry because of an arrangement that existed between the North German Line and the B&O.[104] The Bohemians, as well as the Poles and Russian Jews who were now beginning to come in, were, for the time being, considered peripheral to the German core.[105]

The seven fat years that followed the war gave way to seven lean years of a bleak depression that began in 1873. The emerging labor movement was one of its principal casualties. The Shoe and Leather Board of Trade had organized in Baltimore to fight the leatherworkers' Knights of St. Crispin, one of the most successful of the new labor unions. After 1873 the Knights lost every battle. Prominent in the Board of Trade were members of the Jenkins family. William Jenkins and Captain William Kennedy were two of the three principal organizers of the Merchants and Miners Steamship Company, whose main cargo was boots and shoes. Kennedy was likewise president of the Mount Vernon Cotton Mills near Hampden, one of the few such mills that emerged from the depression stronger than before. The cotton mills had the lowest paid women and children in the work force of greater Baltimore.[106]

Catholic merchants, manufacturers, and bankers stood on the launching pad of the industrial revolution in Maryland in the postwar years. A group that included Francis Neale, Charles M. Dougherty, C. Oliver O'Donnell, John Murphy, Alfred and John W. Jenkins, Daniel J. Foley (the bishop's brother), Matthias Benzinger, and Columbus C. Shriver were among the founders of a Beneficial Savings Fund Society in 1867, which was exclusively Catholic and which in 1876 became the Metropolitan Savings Bank.[107] Its shareholders were among the principal beneficiaries of the immigrant influx as the Metropolitan provided the capital for new Catholic institutions. From their education or associations, these Catholic entrepreneurs had little reason to think of themselves as "exploiters of the working class" and probably agreed with their archbishop as to the "Communist and International character" of labor unions.

Labor discontent as a result of the depression reached a critical point in 1877, when B&O workers outside Baltimore launched a strike that raced along the rails of the nation. In response to riots in Baltimore and Cumberland, Governor John Lee Carroll, great-grandson of the Signer, appealed to the president for federal troops to quell the rioters.[108] Archbishop Bayley was in Europe, a dying man. Bishop Gibbons, returning from Canada, reached Baltimore at the height of the riots and hastily left for Richmond.[109] Governor Carroll warned the workers: "No political platforms can be of use to the working man or furnish him with work. In a free country like ours, the relations of capital and labor must always adjust themselves, and are regulated by conditions which politicians cannot control."[110] Working Catholics may have seriously questioned the laissez-faire philosophy of their Catholic leaders.

Catholics versus Reformers

The lord of Doughoregan Manor had been elected governor November 2, 1875, "despite all that the Radical and Reform parties could devise," the *Catholic Mirror* boasted, and despite the Know Nothing cries raised against him.[111] Carroll had actually been picked by the new boss of the Maryland Democratic machine, Arthur Pue Gorman, who with the political boss of Baltimore, Isaac Freeman Rasin, would control the politics of Maryland for the next quarter century.[112] Carroll's election sealed an uneasy alliance between the Catholic Church and the conservative Democratic machine in Maryland.

The Maryland reformers in 1875–77 moved to tax church property, a movement that coincided with President Grant's call for the same as well as for a constitutional prohibition of public funds for sectarian schools.[113] The reformers obtained an injunction to halt the Baltimore city council's appropriations to private charitable institutions, about a third of which were Catholic. The institutions appealed. In 1877 the case was decided in favor of the plantiffs, but upon the advice of the judge the state passed a law enabling the city council to appropriate sums up to $25,000 to St. Mary's Industrial School and the House of Refuge.[114] This advice was induced in part by an "exciting debate" in the city council in which the "hydra-headed monster of Know-Nothingism" had again been injected. A councilman had proposed that St. Mary's share be increased from $10,000 to $16,000 because it housed forty more boys than the House of Refuge, for which $20,000 was targeted. St. Mary's was finally awarded the $16,000 by a vote of 10 to 9.[115]

In 1877 the Sisters of Charity of Emmitsburg also appealed an attempt to tax their land, livestock, and furnishings, and several Baltimore institutions contested similar taxes.[116] Ultimately the decisions went in favor of the appellants, except for certain stocks owned by St. Mary's Seminary, and a Maryland law was passed remitting "to a great extent" the tax on church property.[117]

With a few exceptions, Maryland Catholics, rich and poor, remained steadfastly Democratic. When it appeared that Samuel J. Tilden, the Democratic contender, had won the presidential election in 1876, they saw it as a triumph over "low, selfish, thieving demagogues who have sought to ruin the land."[118] When a special commission decided in favor of the Republican candidate, Rutherford B. Hayes, they perceived it as a "premeditated insult" to the Catholics of the country.[119]

The Church at Large

Though hardly devoid of political interests, Archbishop Bayley's principal concerns were ecclesial. Though his greatest preoccupations were local, his energies were diverted to Catholic affairs of national import as often as those of his predecessors had been. To a second inquiry regarding possible archiepiscopal status of Milwaukee, Bayley finally responded to Barnabò in the summer of 1873 that he had consulted the archbishops of New York, Cincinnati, and St. Louis, and a change should be deferred "until a more opportune time." He would give the reasons in his next letter.[120] Barnabò insisted, however, that he take up the question of metropolitan sees in a meeting of American prelates "as soon as possible" and send the minutes of the meeting to him.[121] "This," Bayley complained to Purcell, "would be almost impossible, and certainly is not necessary." To this plaint he added another: "I am constantly receiving letters from Rome and any corner of the earth I may say, as if I had supreme jurisdiction over everything in this country, so I hardly get time to say my prayers."[122]

Nevertheless, Bayley invited the archbishops of New York, Cincinnati, and St. Louis and several bishops to meet in Cincinnati to discuss the creation of new archdioceses. The prelates held their meeting May 4–5 and decided, among other things, that Philadelphia, Boston, Milwaukee, and Santa Fe should be accorded metropolitan status. This they communicated to Cardinal Alessandro Franchi, Barnabò's successor as prefect of the Congregation of the Propaganda.[123] On June 17, 1875, as a result, Bayley would bestow the pallium on Archbishop Wood and thus sever the state of Pennsylvania with Philadelphia and its five suffragan sees from the province of Baltimore.

In Cincinnati the archbishops had to address another question proposed by Cardinal Franchi for their consideration: the advisability of a policy of withholding absolution from Catholic parents who sent their children to the public schools. James McMaster, the irrepressible editor of the *Freeman's Journal*, had declared war on the "godless" public schools and had pressed the Roman authorities with requests that they make explicit certain injunctions of the *Syllabus of Errors* by ordering all Catholic children removed from them.[124] As devoted as he was to parochial schools, Bayley was annoyed by the Roman questionnaire. Such a general ruling, he confided to Bishop McQuaid, was "neither good theology, nor good sense. McMaster is growing more & more dogmatic about this as well as other matters."[125]

The archbishops advised against a ruling on Rome's part. They saw little danger of perversion in the public schools in areas where Catholics and non-Catholics mingled well. There were places where there were no Catholic schools and places where the public schools were far superior to the Catholic ones. Individual cases should be weighed as to special circumstances.[126] In 1875, nevertheless, the Holy Office ruled that Catholic children could be sent to public schools only when the occasion of sin was rendered remote. Bayley filed the document away.

Though not revealed in their minutes, the archbishops may also have discussed the Indian problem. In 1870 Grant, in what he called his "Peace Policy, had left the supervision of the Indian tribes to the religious denominations who worked with them."[127] The Catholic Church, however, had no representative among the Indian Commissioners, and Catholic missions received little recognition and even less money. The Paulist George Deshon, a roommate of Grant at West Point, conferred with the president, won from the secretary of the interior the promise of a "general overhauling," and recommended General Charles Ewing as the Catholic agent for Indian affairs in Washington. Acting for the bishops concerned, Bayley informed the secretary that he had appointed Ewing Catholic Commissioner for Indian Missions in January 1874.

When virtually nothing came of the new arrangement, the *Catholic Mirror* did its best to induce action. The "infamous peace policy" it saw as the culmination of a "long series of outrages, of promises made and broken, of treaties signed and violated while the ink was still fresh on the parchment."[128] In Washington Mrs. Sherman, Mrs. Ewing, Mrs. Dahlgren, and "other noble hearted ladies" formed the Catholic Indian Missionary Association to solicit contributions. In almost no time the association had spread to twelve dioceses. Archbishop Bayley himself pledged $200 annually. An Indian Mission Fund was chartered; Bayley was empowered to fill the board. He made several trips to the capital to pave the way for the creation of the Bureau of Catholic Indian Missions, which occurred two years after his death.[129]

By the end of 1875 the financial situation at the American College in Rome was again precarious. When the businesslike remedies he recommended were ignored, Bayley threatened to resign from the executive committee. In December, however, he asked the bishops of wealthier dioceses for additional annual sums. Most complied.[130]

A Disappointment in Baltimore

In March 1875 Bayley learned that Archbishop John McCloskey of New York had been created a cardinal and that he himself had been named to confer the biretta. He wrote to congratulate his friend. "Your Eminence is the right man in the right place," he insisted. "Some have no doubt felt that the honour belonged to Baltimore as being the oldest See, and because of peculiar associations which cling about it, but they should remember that the Cardinalate is a personal dignity and does not belong to places—and this consideration settles the question—I do not think I am playing traitor to Baltimore, when I say that I am glad for more reasons than one that the honour has been given to New York."[131] Bayley's Protestant cousin in New York thought otherwise. Robert Roosevelt was "extremely disappointed" with the choice. "I felt & I think the community felt that it would be conferred upon the See that was not only the oldest but the most generally respected for talent & success."[132]

Archbishop Bayley conferred the red biretta in New York on April 27. The reporter of the New York *Herald* surmised that he "labored under a strong emotion, for the sheets trembled in his hand."[133]

The Catholics of Baltimore remained discreetly mute. Some two years after the event, however, the *Catholic Mirror* carried without comment an article on "Former Catholic Councils" from the Baltimore *Sunday Telegram*. Had Archbishop Spalding lived, it claimed, there would have been a provincial council in 1872. "Indeed, his death was a calamity not alone to Baltimore but to the entire province. Had he survived, the See of New York would not possess a Cardinal today, and enjoy greater privileges than its mother—Baltimore; nor is it likely that the Episcopal meeting held in Cincinnati two years ago . . . would have occurred there contrary to every precedent in ecclesiastical records. Had he survived, these Archbishops and Bishops beyond a doubt, would have met where their predecessors gathered so often before—the cathedral of Baltimore."[134]

There were perhaps as many opinions as there were those disposed to give them as to why McCloskey and not Bayley was chosen to be the first American cardinal. Health was probably not an issue. Despite his serious bout at the end of 1873, few in 1875 thought Bayley gravely ill. Some undoubtedly remembered McCloskey's stony reaction to remarks, whatever the exact wording, in Bayley's inaugural address concerning liberty of conscience. Many were aware of Bayley's lack of enthusiasm in responding to directives from Rome, and many doubtless thought him indiscreet in voicing his low opinion of the way matters were conducted there. When Corrigan, for example, mentioned rumors of a nuncio's being sent to Washington, Bayley replied that he had heard no such rumor, though the move would not surprise him. "They do not think it necessary to consult any of us, about the state of things here—they could not choose a worse time."[135] Though uttered a year after the arrival of the red hat in New York, it was typical of earlier criticisms. Those aware of attitudes in Rome, moreover, knew that Bayley's Sulpician training would not weigh favorably in the balance. McCloskey was the prudent choice, a man of mediocre talents, perhaps, but safe.[136]

The choice of McCloskey over Bayley may be read as a triumph of the immigrant church over the Carroll church. In the distance he placed between himself and Rome Bayley, perhaps, resembled Carroll most. In his espousal of religious liberty, his patriotism, his friendliness toward non-Catholics, and even his aristocratic mien he helped perpetuate the Maryland tradition. In Baltimore Bayley proved less a bishop of the immigrant then he had been in Newark.

Too Late a Coadjutor

Bayley had mentioned the need for a coadjutor as early as 1874. In 1876 he became more insistent. To one of his requests for support, Purcell replied: "May God enable you to preside over our Church 'ad multos annos,' and do not let your 'non habemus hic' [suggest that] you trade Baltimore for yr. beloved and loving Newark."[137] Purcell may have guessed right. In any event, the Propaganda did not respond at once to Bayley's request for a coadjutor. He had told the other bishops that there was only one man right for the job, James Gibbons, and there was no use putting other names on the list. Official procedures, however, could not with impunity be ignored; Cardinal Franchi ordered the usual *terna* to be sent. Gibbons was finally chosen on May 27, 1877.[138]

Even before he learned of the appointment, Bayley went to Europe to seek a reversal of his rapidly deteriorating health. It was a false hope. He returned in August and died October 3, 1877, in his old bedroom in New-ark. At his own request he was buried beside his aunt at Emmitsburg. Bishop McQuaid would later insist that he did not want to be buried in the cathedral of Baltimore "because he never felt that he was *persona grata* to most of the priests of the diocese and to many of the rich laity of the Cathe-dral. . . . Archbp. Bayley was very sensitive and felt keenly the coldness of the social atmosphere of Catholic Baltimore."[139] Though written some thirty years later, when McQuaid would have even less reason to look kindly upon the premier see, the explanation cannot be totally dismissed.

"Though some of you," Bishop Foley told his fellow Baltimoreans in the eulogy at Bayley's requiem, "may have been unable to understand his deep and strong attachment to his old diocese, you should all feel most grateful for his eminent services."[140] James Roosevelt Bayley was, in truth, a conscientious prelate, whose death was doubtless hastened by the ener-gies expended in behalf of the oldest archdiocese. His greatest contribution was perhaps in the area of organization, where even Kenrick could claim but partial success in a see long accustomed to casual arrangements. In the businesslike approach he carried from the north to ecclesiastical procedures in the south, he presaged the ethos of the industrial revolution that would soon overtake the city on the Patapsco. But Maryland Catholics were not ready for the rapid transformation he had demanded of them. So they wel-comed now a man who knew them, a man who would not push. James Gibbons did not come to Baltimore under the onus of the lavish expecta-tions laid upon his predecessor.

III

The Gibbons Church

Archbishop James Gibbons 1877–1886

Cardinal James Gibbons 1886–1921

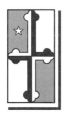 "Bishop Carroll did not wish to see the Church vegetate as a delicate exotic plant," Cardinal Gibbons would write a century later. "He wished it to become a sturdy tree, deep rooted in the soil, to grow with the growth and bloom with the development of the country. . . . His aim was that the clergy and people should be thoroughly identified with the land in which their lot is cast; that they should study its laws and political constitution, and be in harmony with its spirit."[1] This excursion into American Catholic history was primarily for the benefit of the first- and second-generation Catholics whose needs had altered the Carroll church in so many ways. It was Gibbons' aim to restore it, to revivify the Maryland tradition as he perceived it.

In his devotion to American principles, his deep-felt patriotism, his civic sense, his all-embracing ecumenism, and the esteem in which he would be held by his fellow citizens, James Gibbons could be taken as a reincarnation of John Carroll. He was also, like Carroll, uncomfortable with the immigrant presence but totally at ease with men of wealth and power. During his long reign of forty-three years and almost six months, he seldom lost sight of the goal of reviving the Carroll church in his archdiocese and in the American church at large.

For most of the forty-three years the Catholics of the oldest archdiocese would revel in a golden age. From the Third Plenary Council of 1884 until his death in 1921 Gibbons would be the unchallenged spokesman of the Catholic Church in the United States. For twenty-five of those forty-three years he would be the only cardinal in the United States. For the thirty-five years he was a cardinal he was rarely without a reporter at his heels. He was a friend of presidents. He was a friend of everyone.

Until chosen as apostolic delegate to preside at a council for which he saw little need, his achievements in Baltimore would be unremarkable. In his role as ordinary, in fact, the accomplishments of all forty-three years would need hardly a sheaf of paper for their telling. He was not an institution builder. He was, in fact, discomfited by the walls that separated Catholics from their fellow citizens.

Neither had he any compulsion to be a national leader in his early years in Baltimore. He would be maneuvered into the role by friends who had the good sense to see that he could do more with a smile than they with stirring rhetoric. Once recognized as spokesman, however, he would come to enjoy the preeminence he seemed to win effortlessly. He would survive unscathed the debacle of "Americanism" that would send his friends—John Ireland, John Keane, and Denis O'Connell—into the shadows.

His career was an anomaly. As the Catholic Church in America moved into the most heroic years of its heroic age—years of battle, years of building the most plentifully endowed church, the most observant, devout, generous, and loyal body of Catholics in the Catholic World, drawing in the process the lines of demarcation more sharply—Gibbons would be increasingly honored for his irenicism and Americanism. As his church became more and more the object of suspicion, abhorrence, or even assault, he would become the object of greater respect, veneration, and acclaim. His career was an anomaly in another respect. As his Americanism became more pronounced, his church would become more alien, a result of the mounting waves of "new" immigrants at the end of the century that transformed Baltimore as much as other metropolitan areas.

"Gibbons was an authentic product of nineteenth-century Americanism—more than a little jingoistic, utterly sold on the notion of the nation's 'manifest destiny,' and imbued with the idea that in the United States the *novus ordo seclorum* that the Pilgrims established was truly opening up a new page in the history of mankind. He was convinced that even the Church had a great deal to learn from the experiment with political freedom being made in the New World."

To his evaluation John Cogley adds: "He might have been overly cautious about taking a stand at times but he always acted in the belief that nothing essential in Catholicism would be lost if the Church put less trust in *Romanita* and adapted its ancient ways to the new order."[2] In Gibbons Gallicanism would be Americanized even as "Americanism" would suffer the fate of Gallicanism.

In 1933 Frederick V. Murphy, head of the school of architecture at the Catholic University of America, envisioned this Gothic superstructure for the new cathedral to be funded by the multimillion-dollar bequest made by Thomas O'Neill at his death in 1919. (*Jacques Kelly*)

Dedicated in 1959, some forty years after its benefactor's death, the Cathedral of Mary Our Queen sought to modernize traditional elements on a grand scale. One of the largest churches in the United States, it seats 1,900. (*Joseph F. Siwak*)

Left, the dedication of the $200,000 Holy Rosary School on Eastern Avenue in 1922 was attended by the governor, mayor, and other notables. It served as a model for the many schools that followed during the administration of Archbishop Michael J. Curley, tenth archbishop of Baltimore. (*Jacques Kelly*) *Below,* a rally of the Holy Name Society before the Washington Monument in 1924 after what the *Baltimore Catholic Review* characterized as "the longest parade in the history of Washington." At the center is President Calvin Coolidge and to his left is Cardinal O'Connell and Archbishop Curley. (*Archives of the Archdiocese of Baltimore*)

First Holy Communion at St. Jerome's Church in Baltimore in 1924 offered the typical bower of flowers where well-coached children kneeled to receive communion during one of the most elaborately staged events of the church year. (*St. Jerome's Parish*)

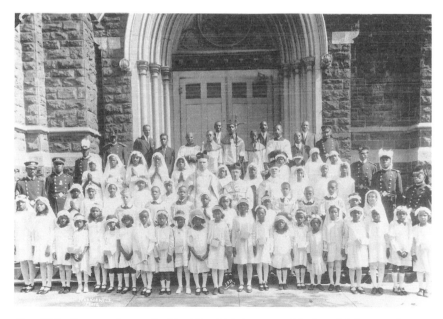

First Holy Communion at St. Pius V, which became a black parish in 1931, the year this picture was taken, was as elaborate an event as that of white parishes. The Knights of St. John act as an honor guard. (*Josephite Archives*)

Archbishop Curley and the Oblate Sisters of Providence gathered at the cathedral for their hundredth anniversary in 1929. Mother Consuela Clifford, the superior general, is to the archbishop's right. (*Archives of the Archdiocese of Baltimore*)

Choir Sisters of the Good Shepherd pray before the grille that separated them from the altar in their former Mount Street chapel. This sisterhood, like many others, divided the members' time between contemplation and an active ministry, in their case the reclamation of delinquent girls. (*Jacques Kelly*)

Above, Holy Cross Sisters join students at play in the 1950s in the schoolyard of St. Patrick's, the parish that boasted the oldest parochial school in the archdiocese until it was closed in 1987. (*Fred G. Kraft*) *Right,* Daughters of Charity prepare for an in-service workshop for high school science teachers at St. Joseph College in 1958, a legacy of the Curley years, when the professional competence of religious sisters and brothers was greatly advanced. (Catholic Review)

The annual outdoor May procession at St. Martin's, like this one organized in 1932, was a major event in West Baltimore. (*Jacques Kelly*)

The annual firemen's mass was inaugurated at St. Ignatius Church in 1931 and it continued for three decades. Annual masses, banquets, and retreats brought Catholic workingmen and professionals as groups closer to their church. (*Jacques Kelly*)

A larger St. Joseph's Monastery Church was built in a typical rowhouse neighborhood at a cost of $425,000 during the Great Depression and dedicated in 1932. (*Jacques Kelly*)

In 1939, when the District of Columbia was constituted the archdiocese of Washington, Curley became archbishop of both the oldest and newest arch diocese. Here he distributes cigars at the home of the Little Sisters of the Poor in Washington to celebrate his installation on March 25, 1940. (*Archives of the Archdiocese of Baltimore*)

Left, the contest of the Newman Club's girls' basketball team of St. Peter Claver's Parish, coached by Rev. John McShane, SSJ, with the St. Brigid Golds in 1942 represented a breakthrough in interracial relations in the archdiocese (*Josephite Archives*) *Right,* Monsignor Stanislaus A. Wachowiak, for fifty years the "pope" of Baltimore's Polonia, is shown surrounded by the Polish American War Mothers of Holy Rosary Parish, one of the many organizations he created.

Archbishop Francis Patrick Keough is installed as eleventh archbishop of Baltimore in 1947 by the apostolic delegate, Archbishop Amleto Cicognani. Seated at Keough's right is Monsignor Louis C. Vaeth, a master impresario. (*Archives of the Archdiocese of Baltimore*)

Friday night meetings of the Catholic Youth Organization, here with a moderator, Rev. Martin Flahavan, were well attended during the 1950s, when the CYO
was one of the most effective bodies for focusing the interest of teenagers on
their church. (*Jacques Kelly*)

The annual summer carnival, often of two weeks' duration, as was this one at
Holy Rosary in 1958, survived in southeast Baltimore as an important source of
parish revenue. (Catholic Review)

Left, the repository altar of Holy Thursday at St. Alphonsus bespeaks a traditional piety that persists in the post-Vatican II church of Baltimore. (Catholic Review) *Right,* President Dwight D. Eisenhower is awarded an honorary degree by Archbishop Keough at the commencement of Mount St. Mary's College on the occasion of its 150th anniversary in 1958. Between them is Monsignor John L. Sheridan, president of the college. (*Archives of the Archdiocese of Baltimore*)

Archbishop Lawrence Joseph Shehan reviews the St. Patrick's Day parade in 1962 sponsored by the Ancient Order of Hibernians, of which he was the national chaplain. With him, from left to right, are Thomas D'Alesandro III, city council president, Monsignor George Hopkins, chancellor, Thomas B. Finan, state attorney general, Mayor J. Harold Grady, grand marshal, John J. Sweeney, chairman of the parade, and Francis Burch, city solicitor. (*Joseph F. Siwak*)

With Cardinal Shehan at the translation of Mother Seton's body to the new chapel in 1968 are the major superiors of Mother Seton's Daughters, the six sisterhoods (from New Jersey, Pennsylvania, Ohio, Maryland, Nova Scotia, and New York) that claim her as their founder. To the cardinal's left is Sister Eleanor McNabb, provincial superior of the Daughters of Charity of Emmitsburg. (*Archives of the Archdiocese of Baltimore*)

The criticism provoked by Our Lady of Hope Church in Dundalk, dedicated in 1970, was largely put to rest when it won for its architect, William Gaudreau, a national award. (Catholic Review)

St. Alphonsus School was one of the inner-city parish schools that managed to survive, but with a more heterogeneous student body than this Sister of St. Casimir would have taught some thirty years before. (Catholic Review)

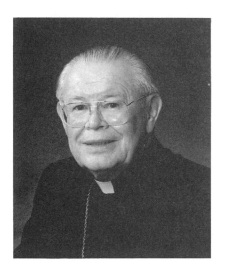

Left, Archbishop William Donald Borders headed the archdiocese between 1974 and 1989. (*Denise Walker*, Catholic Review) *Right*, William Cardinal Keeler was named the fourteenth archbishop of Baltimore in 1989 and in 1994 was elevated to cardinal by Pope John Paul II. (*Archives of the Archdiocese of Baltimore*)

10 *A Masterly Inactivity*

JAMES GIBBONS WAS THE first of two archbishops of the premier see to be able to call Baltimore his native city. The oldest son of Thomas Gibbons and Bridget Walsh was born July 23, 1834, in a house, no longer standing, on the west side of Gay Street just north of Fayette. Twelve days later he was baptized by Father Charles White in the cathedral from which he would be buried.[1]

His father had come from Ireland to Baltimore by way of Canada only a few years before and would move several times more before returning with his family to Ireland in 1837. In Ballinrobe, in county Mayo, Thomas Gibbons ran a grocery store. In 1853 his widow and her five surviving children emigrated to New Orleans. James worked in a grocery store until he decided to enter St. Charles College in Baltimore in 1855. In 1857 he transferred to St. Mary's Seminary, where for all the qualities valued in a priest he rated a nine out of ten. On June 30, 1861, he was ordained for the archdiocese of Baltimore.[2]

His pastorate at St. Brigid's ended abruptly in 1865 when Archbishop Spalding called him to be his secretary. From then on his rise was rapid. Named vicar apostolic of North Carolina on March 3, 1868, he became on August 16, at age thirty-four, the youngest bishop in the Catholic world. At Spalding's recommendation he succeeded John McGill as bishop of Richmond in 1872 while retaining his charge of North Carolina. Bayley also perceived in Gibbons qualities above the ordinary and procured him as coadjutor with right of succession.[3]

A Flourishing Domain

Without ceremony Gibbons slipped behind his desk on October 19, 1877, and wrote in his diary: "I arrived here, in Baltimore, my future home, from Richmond, & immediately entered on my new duties."[4] The rector of the cathedral, he noted, was Thomas Sim Lee, the chancellor William E. Starr, and his secretary Alfred A. Curtis, all Bayley appointees. The latter two were, like Bayley, converts to the faith.

Having been a frequent visitor to his native city, Gibbons needed little time to assess the resources of the archdiocese at the beginning of what would prove by far the longest tenure of any archbishop of Baltimore. Though the informant of the *Catholic Directory* of 1878 (representing data for things as they stood about the time of Gibbons' arrival) claimed 126 churches and 35 chapels and stations in Maryland (exclusive of the Eastern Shore) and the District of Columbia, only 120 churches could be counted in the actual listing and only 19 chapels.[5] There is no way of determining the number of stations, mostly private homes where mass was said for Catholics of the neighborhood, because 35 was the number given without fail for "chapels and stations" from 1869 to 1889. It was not an era when precision in record keeping held the highest priority.

Of the 120 churches, 21 could be found in Baltimore, 11 in the District, 27 in the northern counties, 29 in the southern, and 32 in the western.[6] Of the 120 churches, 69 had resident priests and 51 were missions. Many, perhaps most, of the missions were visited but once or twice a month and some as infrequently as every fifth Sunday or, as in the case of the mountain church at Blooming Rose, every three months. Religious priests controlled 22 of the resident parishes and 25 missions, or nearly 40 percent of the 120 churches. Of these the Jesuits could claim 35, but only nine of them had resident priests.

Six of the twenty-one churches in Baltimore were for German-speaking Catholics, one for the Bohemians, and one for the blacks. Four of the six German churches were under the Redemptorists—St. Alphonsus, St. James, St. Michael's, and Sacred Heart in Highlandtown. Holy Cross had been given over to a secular priest in 1869 and Fourteen Holy Martyrs to another in 1872. In 1874, however, the latter was replaced by German Benedictines. Two of the eleven churches of the District were for the Germans—St. Mary Mother of God and St. Joseph—and one for blacks. Eight of the nineteen chapels could be found in Baltimore and three in the District. Most were chapels connected with convent schools or hospitals in which neighboring Catholics were allowed to worship.

Though the "recapitulation" of the *Catholic Directory* of 1878 gave 234 for the number of priests of the archdiocese, 252 were actually named in the parishes and other institutions. Of these 78 were secular priests, all but 9 of them in parochial work, and 174 religious priests. Of the latter little more than a third were involved with parishes, the rest with schools, seminaries, and novitiates. The nine different religious orders or societies of priests in the archdiocese were represented by seventy Jesuits, fifty-three Redemptorists, sixteen Sulpicians, eight Vincentians, eight Passionists, seven Capuchins, six Dominicans, five Josephites, and one Benedictine.[7]

There were thirteen orders or congregations of sisters and three of brothers (apart from the coadjutor brothers belonging to orders of priests). Most of these taught in the parochial schools: the School Sisters of Notre Dame in six, the Sisters of Charity, Holy Cross Sisters, and Christian Brothers in five, the Visitandines, the Sisters of Mercy, the Sisters of St. Joseph, and the Brothers of Mary in two; and the Dominican Sisters, Franciscan Sisters, Ursulines, Sisters of Notre Dame de Namur, and Xaverian Brothers in one each. The Sisters of the Good Shepherd conducted a penitent asylum in Baltimore, the Little Sisters of the Poor homes for the aged in Baltimore and Washington, and the Oblate Sisters of Providence an academy and orphanage in Baltimore.[8]

Most of the sisters and brothers also maintained pay schools or academies, the meager stipends offered for their services in the parish schools being inadequate for their needs. Visitation academies could be found in Georgetown, Baltimore, Frederick, Catonsville, and Washington. The School Sisters of Notre Dame ran Notre Dame Collegiate Institute of Maryland and the Institute of Notre Dame, the Sisters of Mercy Mount St. Agnes and their academy on Poppleton Street, and the Holy Cross Sisters an academy and St. Catherine's Normal School, all in or near Baltimore. In addition the Holy Cross Sisters operated St. Cecilia's and St. Matthew's Academies and the Dominican Sisters Sacred Heart Academy in Washington. St. Joseph's Academy of the Sisters of Charity at Emmitsburg was still flourishing. The Sisters of Mercy also maintained St. Edward's Academy in Cumberland and the Sisters of St. Joseph St. Joseph's Academy at Hagerstown. The Christian Brothers conducted Rock Hill College at Ellicott City, Calvert Hall in Baltimore, and St. Matthew's Institute in Washington, the Xaverian Brothers Mount St. Joseph College near Baltimore. Carroll Hall, a small academy for boys in Cumberland, was run by a layman.

Counting Georgetown, Loyola, and Gonzaga Colleges, operated by the Jesuits, and Mount St. Mary's College, still run by secular priests, there were in the archdiocese of Baltimore nine colleges or academies for boys and young men. For girls and young ladies there were seventeen academies and a normal school. Though surpassed by the archdioceses of Philadelphia and New York in the number of academies for young ladies, Baltimore could still claim a lead in most other categories. It had six hospitals: Mount Hope Retreat for the insane, St. Vincent's, St. Agnes, St. Joseph's, and Baltimore City hospital staffed by the Sisters of Mercy, all in or near Baltimore, and Providence Hospital in Washington. It could claim nine orphan asylums: St. Mary's, St. Vincent's, St. Patrick's, St. Anthony's, and St. Frances of the Oblates in Baltimore and St. Vincent's and St. Joseph's in Washington plus the two infant asylums, St. Vincent's in Baltimore and St. Anne's in Washington. There were three industrial schools: St. Mary's for boys in Baltimore, St. Joseph's for girls in Baltimore, and St. Rose for girls in Washington. The Good Shepherd penitent asylum in Baltimore and Little Sisters' homes for the aged in Baltimore and Washington have already been mentioned. There was also a home for aged blacks in Washington.

The oldest archdiocese could not have maintained this number and variety of institutions without the religious sisters and brothers to staff them. They constituted not only a cheap but a dependable and, for the most part, pliant labor force. In 1877 only the School Sisters of Notre Dame and the Dominican Sisters supplied numbers for the *Catholic Directory*. At the motherhouse near Govans the School Sisters counted fifty-four sisters and thirty postulants and at the Institute of Notre Dame twenty sisters and thirty-eight novices. In their other convents they totaled forty-two. The Dominicans in Washington had seven sisters and five novices. With all the different religious communities working in the archdiocese, however, it was still necessary to employ lay teachers for about a fifth of the parochial schools. The goal, nevertheless, was to have religious teachers in all of them.

The *Catholic Directory* in these years failed to give summary totals not only for sisters and brothers but also for the pupils and inmates of schools, orphanages, and other institutions. A report of the Young Catholic's Friend Society in 1882, however, indicated that there were 19,141 students in all types of schools in the archdiocese. Of these 3,345 were found in twenty-nine seminaries, colleges and academies, leaving 15,796 for parochial schools, orphanages, and industrial schools.[9] The parochial schools accounted for at least 14,000 of this number. The report also indicated that there were thirty-two parochial schools in Baltimore, fifteen in the District, and twenty-nine elsewhere—seventy-six in all. Over half the parishes of the two major cities, however, maintained two schools, one for boys and one for girls. Where there was only one, boys and girls were, for the most part, taught in separate classrooms.

A Few Difficulties

Adequate institutions and personnel—aside from the perennial shortage of priests for country missions—would never constitute a major problem for Gibbons throughout his long reign. Within his circle of concern as ordinary, however, he was never without problems. His first three or four years conditioned him to difficulties of many sorts. In Washington the Dominican priests and sisters were at odds over the latter's attempt to create a public cult for a deceased member. After Father White's death in 1878, no one wished to assume responsibility for the home for aged blacks, and there were strong objections to the man Gibbons sent to replace the "eccentric but good and earnest Dr. White" at St. Matthew's.[10] Another chaplain had to be found for the Tabernacle Society when Father Walter charged its genteel members with being "unladylike, unchristian, and certainly *un-Catholic*."[11] And in 1881 the pastor of St. Augustine's, Felix Barotti, died, leaving debts beyond the ability of the black parishioners to pay. In western Maryland Catholics were joining the Knights of Labor and trouble was brewing in the mines. From Barton came pleas to replace a pastor who was seeing too much of the organist. And Mount St. Mary's Seminary and College was forced to declare bankruptcy.

The New Immigrants

The most vexing problems were those of the see city that were the result of a new phenomenon. Gibbons was the first archbishop of Baltimore who had to provide in a systematic way for the immigrants from eastern and southern Europe, who were very unlike the older ones from Germany and Ireland. The new immigrants did not come in overwhelming numbers until the end of the century, but their presence was felt in Baltimore as early as the 1870s. For the Catholic Church there it meant the Bohemians, Poles, Italians, and Lithuanians. The eastern Europeans, though often fused in the public mind, sought their separate identities and separate churches. As the Bohemians had split from the Germans in Spalding's time, so would the Poles from the Bohemians in Gibbons' early years and the Lithuanians from the Poles in his later ones. The Italians, dispersed and speaking several dialects, presented a different problem.

THE BOHEMIANS

The first pastor of the Bohemians, or Czechs, Wendelin Vacula, had resigned under Bayley but had remained in the city to drive his successor out. Gibbons persuaded Peter Koncz, a priest who spoke both Czech and Polish, to come from Milwaukee and take charge of St. Wenceslaus in 1878. The next year, however, Koncz told Gibbons he was unable to work with the Bohemians and left them, taking the Poles with him to establish another parish. After several tries Gibbons found a Bohemian priest named

John Hojda, who was in Baltimore less than a year when he apostasized.[12] In the fall of 1880 Gibbons persuaded Rev. John Videnka to come from Wisconsin.[13] Videnka proved not only financially irresponsible and intemperate but also involved himself in an attempt to oust Koncz as pastor of the Polish church.[14] Gibbons finally induced the Redemptorists, who had served St. Wenceslaus intermittently, to take permanent charge of the Bohemians of Baltimore.[15] A Unitarian church on East Baltimore Street was acquired and enlarged in 1886 for the growing Czech colony.

THE POLES

The Polish immigrants came from three different nations of Europe, but as in the Old World they strove for ethnic unity. The earliest in Baltimore, fleeing economic oppression and the Kulturkampf, came from Prussia.[16] Though they originally attended the Czech church, they formed their own association, the St. Stanislaus Kostka Beneficial Society, as early as 1875. In 1879 Gibbons gave Koncz permission to found a separate parish for the more than five hundred Polish Catholics of Baltimore. They worshiped in a house Koncz rented on Bond Street until the church of St. Stanislaus Kostka was built in 1880–81 on lots acquired by the archbishop on South Ann Street.[17]

Gibbons' troubles with Baltimore's Polonia were far from over. In 1881 a second Polish Catholic association was created, the St. Joseph Beneficial Society, apparently by Koncz to counter the St. Stanislaus Kostka Society. The latter wanted a Polish-speaking pastor from Prussia. Koncz, they declared in a petition to the archbishop in 1882, being a Lithuanian, spoke Polish imperfectly. Also they claimed, among a litany of charges, that he insulted the Poles in his sermons, declared the members of the St. Stanislaus Society damned but those of the St. Joseph Society saved, and refused to rent pews to the former.[18] After hearing the arguments of representatives from both sides, Gibbons decided in favor of Koncz.

The next year the St. Stanislaus Society made an even more strenuous effort to effect Koncz's removal by a charge of immorality. When the priest was tried, the president of the society told Gibbons that if their testimony was not strong enough, they would come five hundred strong with a band and present themselves "before your Highness' large mansion." If Koncz was not removed, he said, they would publish the scandal and appeal to Rome.[19] Refusing to be intimidated, Gibbons decided a second time for Koncz. The next year a new president tried again and with the same charge. Koncz reminded the archbishop of upheavals in four Polish communities throughout the nation, where they had either burnt the church, attempted to kill the priest, or gone into schism. At St. Stanislaus, he claimed, with its now 1,500 devout members and well-attended school, trouble was fomented by only a few malcontents who spent their Sundays in taverns rather than in church.[20] When Gibbons stood by Koncz for the third time, the members of the St. Stanislaus Society went back to St. Wenceslaus Church.

Still peace did not come to St. Stanislaus parish. Now the members of the St. Joseph Society itself wished Koncz replaced by Rev. Peter Chowaniec, whose preaching had greatly impressed them. In 1885 Gibbons upheld Koncz for a fourth time. He was spared still another when on February 8, 1886, Koncz died, age forty-seven, at St. Joseph Hospital. The certificate gave scurvy as the cause of death. Inevitably there were rumors of an assassination.[21] In Koncz's place Gibbons appointed his assistant, Rev. John Radowicz. At the same time, however, he gave Chowaniec permission to found a second Polish parish. Holy Rosary began in a church purchased from the Methodists in 1887.

THE ITALIANS

Italians had been in Baltimore for a long time. One Italian had sculpted the human body that topped its Washington Monument and another the figure of Victory that crowned the Battle Monument.[22] Only New York drew more vessels from Italy than did Baltimore. Many who settled in were from Genoa, but they came from many parts of Italy.[23] In 1873 Rev. Joseph Andreis, originally from Turin, was sent to St. Vincent's to attend the needs of the Italians of that area. In 1879 Gibbons asked him to report on the number of his countrymen in the city. Because many had returned to Italy, he explained, there were only about five hundred, but more were expected. Most of them lived between St. Joseph's and St. Patrick's. There were always many seamen. Andreis believed the time had come to build a church for the Italians.[24] Gibbons agreed.

On September 11, 1880, he laid the cornerstone for a church at Exeter and Stiles not far from St. Vincent's. It was named St. Leo in honor of the new pope, Leo XIII.[25] Even before its completion, the pastor of St. Vincent's, Edmund Didier, complained to Gibbons that Andreis was trying to lure his best parishioners to the new parish. When he learned that Andreis was preaching in both English and Italian, Didier reminded the archbishop of his promise that St. Leo's would not be a mixed congregation.[26] At Gibbons' insistence, Andreis promised to preach only in Italian. Didier reported soon after that he was still reading the gospel and making announcements in English and was still enticing prominent parishioners of

St. Vincent's to St. Leo's. The only remedy, the disgruntled pastor insisted, was to place a "real Italian" there who would "hunt up" and attend the Italians who were sadly neglected.[27]

Less than a year later Andreis told Gibbons that St. Leo's had not the resources to sustain itself. English-speaking Catholics were "debarred from giving me the needed help by causes, which are too unpleasant to mention." He must fail, Andreis insisted, unless the archbishop came to his assistance.[28] A month later the Catholics of Baltimore were told that St. Leo's was a mixed congregation composed of predominantly English-speaking parishioners.[29] For the latter Andreis proved a zealous and creative pastor. But as long as he lived, the Italians of Baltimore played second fiddle to the largely Irish-American members of St. Leo's parish.

New Churches for the Old Immigrants

The largest number of immigrants entering Maryland were still German. An unofficial estimate in 1887 maintained that 100,000 of the 425,000 inhabitants of Baltimore were German-Americans. Well over a third of these were Catholic. That same year the readership of the *Katholische Volkszeitung* peaked at 25,600.[30] The older German parishes were still growing. St. Michael's would soon be the largest parish in the archdiocese. Holy Cross Church was enlarged in 1885. A new church called St. Anthony of Padua was built by the pastor of St. Joseph's Fullerton for the largely German Catholic population of Gardenville just north of the city in 1884–85.[31] In Washington, however, the number of German Catholics was shrinking.[32] When the Jesuits surrendered St. Joseph's on Capitol Hill to a secular priest in 1886, it ceased to be an exclusively German parish. That left only St. Mary Mother of God. Cumberland could still claim a large German community served by the Capuchins at SS. Peter and Paul.

Immigration reinforced the Irish only in Baltimore, and even here there would be no additional parishes that were distinctly Irish. As the newcomers found homes in the older Irish parishes, second-generation Irish moved to one of the new churches that ringed the city's core. There they mingled with old-stock families whose roots were in southern Maryland and occasionally with second- or third-generation Germans.

Six of these encircling parishes were built in Gibbons' first ten years, fanning from the northeast to the southwest: St. Andrew's in 1878, St. Pius V in 1878–79, St. Edward's in 1879–80, Corpus Christi in 1881, St. Gregory the Great in 1884, and St. Jerome in 1887–89. St. Pius, of course, was the result of the promise made by Archbishop Spalding in 1871. St. Andrew's, near the site of the future Johns Hopkins Hospital, was a small parish entrusted to a priest whose "habitual insanity," Gibbons was told, had worsened as younger priests were allowed to build churches.[33] It was a gamble, but it paid off.

It was Gibbons' intention to perpetuate the policy begun by Spalding: to build a combination church and school first and make this the school when the parish was able to fund a permanent church. This happened quite soon in two cases as a result of munificent benefactions. Soon after the church-school of Corpus Christi at Bolton Depot or Mount Royal was completed, the children of Thomas Courtney Jenkins, who had just died, offered to build the permanent church as a memorial to their parents. Begun in 1886, it would take five years and about $100,000 to complete.[34] Patrick McKanna, a rags-to-riches merchant, left $38,000 to erect a church for St. Gregory the Great on Baker and Gilmor. Built 1885–86 at a cost of $50,000, it included a tower whose cross was said to be then the highest point in the city.[35]

North of Baltimore the people of Towsontown finally agreed to fund a modest church, which was built in 1883–84 and called originally St. Francis of Assisi.[36] West of the city the Sunday school activities of the Jesuits of Woodstock produced four mission churches: St. Stanislaus Kostka at Elysville (Daniels) in 1879, Holy Family at Harrisonville in 1880, St. Michael's at Poplar Springs in 1882, and St. Alphonsus Rodriquez at the village of Woodstock in 1885.[37]

Washington could boast only one new church and a new church-school in the same period: St. Teresa in Anacostia in 1879 and St. Paul's in the northwestern part of the city in 1886–87. Some thirteen miles north of the city at Ammendale, St. Joseph's Church and a novitiate for the Christian Brothers were built in 1879–80 on land donated by Admiral Daniel Ammen. Just over the city's border St. Jerome's was built in 1886–88 for the Catholics of Hyattsville.

Outside the two major cities and their peripheries, the few new churches that were established in this period were less the result of growth, perhaps, than of a growing reluctance to travel great distances to church. In Prince George's County a small house of worship was erected at Woodville (Aquasco) in 1879 and another at Wilson's Station (Mitchellville) in 1885. In St. Mary's County churches were erected at Mechanicsville in 1879–81 and at Great Mills in 1887.[38] In Frederick County St. Ignatius was built at Urbana in 1878 and St. James at Point of Rocks in 1881.[39] And at Cresaptown in Allegany County St. Ambrose was raised in 1886 for the Catholics of the villages along the B&O southwest of Cumberland.[40]

The Blacks' Appeal

The needs of black Catholics in this period were only partially met. With the death of Felix Barotti in 1881, Gibbons asked the Mill Hill Fathers, or Josephites, to assume charge of St. Augustine's in Washington with a promise to help them with the huge debt. The Josephites also purchased a Methodist church in South Baltimore occupied by the Salvation Army and on January 21, 1883, dedicated St. Monica's Church for the second black parish of the see city.[41] A second church was badly needed for the black Catholics of the eastern part of the national capital, a number of whom appealed to the new archbishop in 1878 to revoke Archbishop Bayley's ruling that they could be served only by the pastor of St. Augustine's.[42] In 1886 the pastor of St. Peter's finally purchased land near Lincoln Park for a church for them but then decided to use it for a parish for the whites who complained of the distance to St. Peter's.[43] The blacks would have to wait a few more years.

Two new institutions, however, would be established and a religious order imported to serve the blacks. Mary Herbert, abandoned by her husband and with a deformed child, began a nursery in a Baltimore alley. In 1878 John Slattery, the Josephite, began a subscription to help defray expenses, and Mrs. Austin Jenkins bought a house on St. Paul Street for a permanent asylum. In 1882 Franciscan Sisters of Mill Hill, originally an aristocratic Anglican order, arrived to take over what would be called St. Elizabeth's Home and to devote themselves to the other needs of American blacks.[44] In Washington wealthy Catholics, including E. Francis Riggs and Thomas E. Waggaman, incorporated St. Monica's Asylum and Industrial Home for blacks in 1886.[45]

Other Needs

Two homes for young working Catholics were opened in Gibbons' first decade. The first permission he granted, in fact, was to the trustees of St. Mary's Industrial School to start a home for working boys from St. Mary's and elsewhere. "Many arabs it is hoped will thus be reclaimed," he wrote in his diary.[46] Black Horse Tavern at the corner of High and Low Streets was purchased and rechristened St. James Home in honor of the new archbishop and entrusted to the Xaverian Brothers. Didier, the pastor of St. Vincent's, opened St. Vincent's Home for Working Girls near his church in 1885.

More important was one of the few works initiated by Gibbons himself. In 1870 a newly wed woman from Baltimore had been taken ill in Paris and was attended by one of the Sisters of the Bon Secours, a nursing order founded in Paris in 1822. Their members went directly to the homes of the sick. Such was the newlyweds' impression of the sisters' work that they and a number of physicians persuaded Gibbons to invite them to Baltimore. In the course of his first *ad limina* visit to Rome in 1880, Gibbons called at the motherhouse in Paris and won acceptance. In 1881 the first group arrived, and the next year they secured a permanent home on West Baltimore Street. The Bon Secours Sister with her black bag and fluted cap became a familiar figure not only on the streets of Baltimore but as far away as Pennsylvania and Delaware.[47]

In the meantime the Sisters of Mercy had expanded their work by staffing in 1880 the Lombard Street Infirmary, from which the Sisters of Charity had withdrawn. In 1887 they purchased land near the Baltimore City Hospital to build a hospital of their own. The Sisters of the Good Shepherd established their second asylum for penitent girls in the archdiocese in Washington in 1883. New wings were built for St. Mary's and St. Rose Industrial Schools and for Providence Hospital. The driving engines of institutional growth in the Gibbons years were the major superiors of religious orders, and more often women than men.

Still More Societies

Though temperance societies declined in the 1880s, other fraternal, charitable, and devotional organizations, most of them parish based, continued to thrive in the oldest archdiocese. Among the last named, the Sodality of the Blessed Virgin Mary and the League of the Sacred Heart spread fastest. The Archconfraternity of Our Lady of Perpetual Help was introduced into the United States by the Redemptorists at St. James in 1878.[48] The Confraternity of Perpetual Adoration had its beginning at St. Ann's in 1883 and from there would spread to other Baltimore parishes.

As with the temperance and beneficial societies earlier, the knighthoods moved toward national unification. The starting point was Baltimore. In December 1877 at the invitation of the Knights of St. Patrick, a Grand Union of Catholic Knights of Baltimore was formed. Gibbons approved the constitution two months later and became its chaplain. By the end of 1878 it included ten commanderies with an average of sixty uniformed knights each.[49] In the summer of 1879 the Baltimore Union sent out an invitation to all uniformed knighthoods in the country to meet in Baltimore October 15 to form a national union. Though it was attended only by units from Baltimore, Washington, and Cincinnati, this first convention created what came to be called the Roman Catholic Union of the Knights of St. John, with James Donnelly, the superintendent of Baltimore's City Hall, its first grand commander.[50]

The Knights of St. John came close to an early demise at their second annual convention in Cincinnati in June 1880. Exhilarated by a large attendance, the delegates ignored the warning of Bishop William Elder, now coadjutor of Archbishop Purcell and administrator of the archdiocese, and carried their festivities well into the night.[51] Elder informed Gibbons that a missionary priest had urged him to write to the archbishop of Baltimore, whom the knights had elected their chaplain, and have him "rebuke their folly." Elder was also fearful that a national combination of the knights might give the appearance of a Catholic army. It were better, Gibbons counseled the uneasy prelate, for Catholics to belong to authorized societies than dangerous and condemned ones.[52] At a later date Gibbons would again counsel the apprehensive Elder in regard to secret societies: "I believe that more good will result from a vigilant, masterly inactivity than by any hasty legislation."[53]

Only a few of the knightly societies of the archdiocese of Baltimore attended the next annual convention of the Knights of St. John in Buffalo, but Gibbons as chaplain let it be known that he was proud of the union's success.[54] When the Knights of St. John would meet in Washington in 1889, it would boast some 150 commanderies, as opposed to the fifteen that met in Baltimore in 1879, and Gibbons, now a cardinal, would still be their spiritual director.[55]

The Cincinnati affair, and Gibbons' admonitions perhaps, induced a certain caution in the Baltimore units. When the Knights of St. Andrew was organized in 1882, it wrote into its constitution that there would be no hops or soirees, no intoxicating beverages at picnics and excursions, no round dances, and no activity that went beyond 10:00 P.M.[56] Despite the inaugural role it had played, however, Baltimore would not in the future be conspicuous in the counsels of the Knights of St. John. Other national fraternal and insurance organizations would prove more attractive to people in the premier see.

Enter the National Societies

In the 1880s the local, independent beneficial societies of the archdiocese, whether knightly or not, rapidly lost ground to well-organized national Catholic bodies as the former's insurance benefits proved unsatisfactory and law suits multiplied.[57] The national Catholic bodies with more attractive benefits, the result of better actuarial policies, were needed as rivals of such life insurance companies as Prudential and John Hancock and of employees benevolent associations such as the one adopted by the B&O in 1880.[58] In the 1880s the most successful of the national Catholic bodies in attracting members in the archdiocese of Baltimore were the Emerald Beneficial Association, the Catholic Knights of America, and the Catholic Benevolent Legion.

The Emerald Beneficial Association (EBA) was founded in Reading, Pennsylvania, in 1869. Besides insurance benefits it offered the features of a literary society. When a local literary society folded in Emmitsburg in 1879, the St. Joseph Branch No. 1 of the EBA in Maryland was organized.[59] In 1883 the Immaculate Conception Branch No. 1 of the EBA in the District of Columbia was established. In 1884 Star of the Sea Branch No. 2 of Maryland, the most active and enduring in Baltimore, was organized. When five more branches were founded in the city in 1887, a state union claiming about a thousand members was organized at St. Mary Star of the Sea.[60]

The Catholic Knights of America (CKA) was founded in Nashville, Tennessee, in 1877. Its members were eligible for $2,000 in benefits but were assessed according to their age. In 1881 two branches were organized in the District of Columbia, No. 170 at St. Aloysius and No. 199 at St. Peter's.[61] Like the branches of the EBA, most were named for the parishes in which they were established. Three more were founded in Washington before 1887 and perhaps one in Cumberland. No branches of the CKA were established in Baltimore, however. No more were founded in the state and only one more, it appears, in the District after 1887, perhaps because the national treasurer absconded with the funds entrusted to him.[62]

The greatest success story before the coming of the Knights of Columbus to Baltimore at the end of the century, and in some ways even more spectacular, was that of the Catholic Benevolent Legion (CBL). The legion was founded in Brooklyn, New York, in 1881. It offered several policies, the largest for $5,000. The first branch established in Maryland in July 1882 and based at St. Joseph's was appropriately called the Maryland No. 12 (the twelfth branch in the country). Father Myers No. 15 at St. Vincent's soon followed. Over the next two years the majority of new branches established by the CBL were in Baltimore. Attractive policies were undoubtedly a strong inducement, but most of the credit seems due to the salesmanship of one F. A. Lucchesi, who was elected president of the state council when it was organized in 1883.[63] By early 1886 the council had 22 branches and some sixteen hundred members, Maryland ranking only behind New York and

New Jersey in membership.[64] By 1887 there were twenty-nine branches in Maryland and the District of Columbia, two of them in Washington, one each in Frederick, Cumberland, and Annapolis, the rest in Baltimore. Even the German parishes joined the CBL, the Father Alexander Branch No. 41 at St. Alphonsus being the first in 1883.

In these years another fraternal organization was quietly organizing in Maryland: the Ancient Order of Hibernians (AOH). Discredited by its associations with the Molly Maguires in the Pennsylvania coalfields in the late 1870s, the AOH aroused the distrust and even hostility of many bishops, including Archbishop Bayley. Gibbons himself was lenient with the organization and believed its efforts to establish a good reputation sincere, as he told Archbishop Elder.[65] Under Gibbons' policy of masterly inactivity, the Hibernians grew in Maryland but without the publicity accorded other fraternal societies. Largely through Gibbons' efforts, the committee of the American archbishops called upon to determine its status refused in 1886 to condemn the AOH.[66] The first notice taken of it by the *Catholic Mirror* was in 1887, when its delegation was noted among others at the dedication of St. Ambrose in Cresaptown.[67]

The Lyceum Movement

The literary societies, on the other hand, received a great deal of attention in the pages of the *Mirror*. The number of young men's literary societies not only multiplied during Gibbons' first decade in Baltimore but took on even more the coloration of the lyceum movement, with its message of self-improvement and enrichment.[68] Increasingly the Catholic literary societies of Maryland called themselves lyceums, beginning with St. Vincent's Lyceum of St. Vincent's Parish in 1879. In 1879 several of the literary societies of Baltimore formed a union. It was sometimes called the Young Men's Catholic Union, reflecting their affiliation with the Catholic Young Men's National Union, and sometimes the Union of Catholic Literary Associations. For most of the 1880s, however, the majority of such societies remained unaffiliated. In 1887 only four from Baltimore and three from Washington, perhaps a third of all the literary societies, attended the annual convention of the archdiocesan union.[69]

The lecture and the library remained important features of these societies. In 1884 the Carroll Institute of Washington boasted not only the largest membership, 235, but the largest library, 2,500 volumes. Next was St. Vincent's Lyceum in Baltimore with 140 members and 540 volumes.[70] Musical and dramatic entertainments became more popular as vehicles for the display of hidden talents. In the 1880s sports also became an important part of lyceum activities. By 1882 the Carroll Institute had a rowing club, and in 1883 St. John's Institute played St. Vincent's Lyceum in baseball, while the Immaculate Conception Lyceum challenged the Pius Memorial Institute. It was, perhaps, the athletic activities of the literary societies that encouraged organized sports in the Catholic colleges of the archdiocese. In 1883 Rock Hill College proudly announced a "fully equipped gymnasium."[71]

For all their myriad activities, it was undoubtedly the social life that appealed most to members, the weekly meetings "enlivened by racy debates or literary and musical exercises," balls, hops, picnics, excursions, and conventions. When the archdiocesan union, however, voted $1,000 to entertain the delegates of the Catholic Young Men's National Union, which had chosen Baltimore as the site of its convention for 1884, the editor of the *Catholic Mirror* pronounced it "a lavish, wasteful, and sinful generosity" that could have been put to better use by the St. Vincent de Paul Society and labeled the young members of literary societies in general "utopian."[72] Yet the editor uttered not a word of criticism when his paper detailed the menu of a sumptuous breakfast complete with orchestral entertainment offered the older and presumably more mature delegates at the fourth general assembly of the St. Vincent de Paul Society three years later.[73]

Undoubtedly the young men who joined these societies were the targets of caution from press and pulpit alike against "demoralizing dramatic and operatic performances" and especially "those hot-houses of debauchery known as low variety theatres."[74] The caveats against the latter were often coupled with a reminder of the prohibition against waltzes, polkas, germans, and other round dances, those "fashionable dances . . . revolting to every feeling of delicacy and propriety."[75] Gibbons, however, was not as disturbed as his predecessors about the demoralizing effect of round dances, and cautions against them gradually disappeared from both press and pulpit during his episcopacy.

Despite the excesses that gave occasional concern, the social events of parish and society slackened in no way. Fairs, in fact, became colossal undertakings. For special causes Catholics and non-Catholics alike responded generously. A twelve-day bazaar to enable the Bon Secours Sisters to liquidate the debt on their convent netted $10,000.[76] More than $20,000 was raised in 1887 at a fair for St. Dominic's in Washington, which had been gutted by a fire in 1885.[77]

Archbishop Gibbons himself gave only occasional encouragement to such undertakings. Some aspects of them he liked; others he did not. He was not happy with the foreign character of some of the societies and their activities. "I wish something could be done," he confided to an episcopal friend, "to make them more American in name and spirit."[78] Yet he put no brakes on the proliferation of societies that occurred in the first decade of his episcopacy.

The Third Plenary Council

Increasingly his principal focus of concern was directed to places and events beyond the boundaries of the archdiocese. The Propaganda continued to employ the archbishop of Baltimore as its principal agent, requesting him in 1884 and 1885 to conduct investigations into the affairs of other dioceses.[79] The most time-consuming task of the first ten years, however, was the Third Plenary Council of Baltimore.

The poor health of Cardinal McCloskey precluded any strenuous exercise of leadership, to which, in any case, he had never been disposed. Many continued to look to Baltimore as the pivotal see in America. When a campaign was launched in 1881 to save the bankrupt Mount St. Mary's, John McCaffrey, the president-emeritus, told Gibbons that McCloskey, its most famous alumnus, had written that "the intiative should be made in Baltimore."[80] Reluctantly Gibbons agreed to serve as treasurer of the fund. At suggestions for another plenary council he showed a similar lack of enthusiasm.

All through his life, as his most able biographer has noted, "he showed a marked disinclination to launch ambitious projects."[81] When thrust upon him, however, he played his role conscientiously and often with remarkable zeal. Though Gibbons' coolness toward a national synod was shared by most of the eastern bishops, the Propaganda agreed with the western prelates who pressed for such a gathering and in 1883 summoned to Rome several archbishops to help prepare the agenda. The *Catholic Mirror* never told its readers why their archbishop had gone to the Eternal City.

When word was returned that an Italian prelate would be chosen to preside at the council, however, the *Mirror* was irate. The "separated brethren," it declared, would never countenance such "foreign interference." Such an appointment would also cast "a slur upon the ability of Archbishop Gibbons, whose natural right it is to preside over American councils." It was a right based upon the primacy of Baltimore. To the New York *Freeman's Journal*'s protest at the latter claim, the *Mirror* quoted the decree of 1858 granting prerogative of place.[82] In any event, the plan for an Italian president was dropped, and James Gibbons was named apostolic delegate to preside at the Third Plenary Council.

With the *schemata* prepared in Rome as a guide, Gibbons parceled the chapters to the archbishops and called theologians to Baltimore to coordinate their work in the manner devised by his mentor, Archbishop Spalding. Remembering complaints at the time of the Second Plenary Council, however, he sent the tentative decrees to the bishops three weeks in advance, and the time of the council was extended from two to four weeks, from November 9 to December 7. Once it was under way, Gibbons touched the helm as lightly as possible, cautioning prudence or moderation in such matters as irremovable rectors and secret societies. Despite an anxious moment or two, Rome approved the work of the council fathers in September 1885.[83]

Under Gibbons the Third Plenary Council provided what Spalding had sought in vain to extract from the second, most notably a Catholic University, a uniform catechism, and aid for the blacks. The third also hardened into precept the exhortations of the second, its decree demanding the erection of parochial schools being the prime example.[84]

The Last Synod

On September 24, 1886, Gibbons held a diocesan synod to incorporate the decrees of the Third Plenary Council into the legislation of the archdiocese.[85] It would be the last synod held in Baltimore just as the third plenary was the last of the national councils. Much of Bayley's synod was left intact, the decrees on the sacraments totally. It was in the area of government and administration that the most significant changes were effected. The number of consultors was set at six and they were to meet at least four times a year as the conciliar legislation required (No. 7), but nothing was said about half of them being elected by the clergy, as decreed by the council. Other officials, including synodal examiners and judges for the matrimonial court and court for disciplinary causes, were provided and the procedures laid down as the Third Plenary directed (Nos. 8 and 11). Irremovable rectors would also be chosen within the prescribed three years (No. 18), but nothing was said of the percentage required by the Third Plenary.

Some important changes Gibbons had already effected in his curia. Dubreul had died in 1878 and the Sulpician general had asked that the superiors at St. Mary's Seminary no longer serve as vicars general. Gibbons named Edward McColgan, pastor of St. Peter's, to this post. In 1885 McColgan became the first monsignor in the archdiocese since Edward Damphoux had been named a prothonotary apostolic in 1852.[86] In 1887 Gibbons named three irremovable rectors: William T. Gaitley and Edmund Didier, the pastors of St. Patrick's and St. Vincent's in Baltimore, and Jacob Walter, pastor of St. Patrick's in Washington.[87]

Baltimore's tenth synod also stipulated that only the catechism published by order of the council could be used (No. 33). There was, however, no response to the council's decree that societies be established in all port cities to assist the immigrants, and its only allusion to aid for blacks was the fifth annual archdiocesan collection for Negroes and Indians added to four prescribed by earlier synods (for the major and minor seminaries, for St. Mary's Industrial School, and for the pope). Gibbons was head of the board of directors of the Commission for Negroes and Indians created by the council to oversee the collection and allocation of contributions to these two races. The synod's decree on parochial schools was not as strong as that of the council. It called for a school in every parish "unless the Archbishop judges it be deferred because of serious obstacles" (No. 34). A pastoral on "Christian Education" the previous year would suggest a strong commitment. The fate of Catholicism in the United States, Gibbons had said, would be determined by the success or failure of its day schools; as Archbishop Bayley had well remarked, "a parish without a school scarcely deserves the name."[88] Yet Gibbons' advocacy of parochial schools was not as remarkable after 1884. While most pastors of new city parishes would start with a building that would house both church and school, rural parishes were often hard pressed to finance the latter, and the ninth archbishop did not push.

The Catholic University

Initially, Gibbons evidenced no great enthusiasm for the Catholic university that the Council had decreed. This decree was the result of an offer of $300,000 by Mary Gwendoline Caldwell, a young heiress and friend of Bishop John Lancaster Spalding of Peoria, and of the latter's forceful sermon in favor of such an institution. Gibbons was not happy at the prospect of having this university in his archdiocese, but Miss Caldwell would have it in no place else than the national capital.[89]

Three people, besides Spalding, proved strong advocates for a Catholic university. All three were destined to play important roles as friends and prompters of Gibbons in the battles that lay ahead. One was John J. Keane, one-time assistant at St. Patrick's in Washington and Gibbons' successor as bishop of Richmond. The second was the dynamic bishop of St. Paul, John Ireland. The third was Denis J. O'Connell, a priest whose talents

Gibbons had recognized in Richmond. In Baltimore Gibbons had brought about his appointment to the rectorship of the American College in Rome, where he would be the archbishop's man on the spot.[90] The three pressed Gibbons to a more active advocacy of the Catholic University of America.

When Spalding declined the rectorship of the future university, Gibbons won the appointment for Keane. In the fall of 1886, Keane and Ireland went to Rome to win papal approval for the institution. An unexpected difficulty arose when its champions learned of the opposition of Michael Corrigan, archbishop of New York since the death of Cardinal McCloskey in October 1885, and of his friend Bernard McQuaid, bishop of Rochester. Up to this point Gibbons had counted Corrigan as one of his closest friends in the hierarchy.[91]

The Knights of Labor

Following a mandate of the Third Plenary Council, the American archbishops had met as a committee in Baltimore in October 1886 to decide the fate of secret societies considered dangerous. The three in question were the Grand Army of the Republic, the Ancient Order of Hibernians, and the Knights of Labor. The first two were judged unobjectionable. Two of the archbishops, however, disapproved the Knights of Labor, whose counterparts in Canada had been condemned by the Holy See in 1884 at the request of the archbishop of Quebec. Since the American archbishops could not achieve unanimity, the question, as the council decree directed, was submitted to Rome for a decision, and this at a time when approval of the Catholic University was pending.[92]

The Knights of Labor had been founded in 1871. In 1878 the first assemblies were organized in Baltimore and in the coalfields of western Maryland. In 1879 Terence V. Powderly, a Catholic, was elected grand master workman and proceeded to eliminate features objectionable to the Catholic Church. Gibbons studied the new constitution and found nothing objectionable.[93] Again he urged upon Archbishop Elder a "masterly inactivity & a vigilant eye."[94]

In the aftermath of the B&O riots of 1877, Gibbons had shared the anxiety of other Marylanders about industrial workers. In an address on "The Dignity and Necessity of Labor" in January 1878, he had condemned the evils of idleness—as if the condition were a matter of choice in these depression years—and derided the tramp and the fop alike.[95] His sympathy for the workingman developed to a great extent from his acquaintance with the struggle of the miners of western Maryland to better their condition.

Most of the Catholic miners had joined the Knights of Labor, only the more religious holding back because of the uncertainty of their church's stand on the union.[96] The pastors at Frostburg and Lonaconing had in 1879 counseled their parishioners not to join.[97] In 1882, however, the miners went on strike and won the sympathy of at least the pastor at Frostburg, Valentine F. Schmitt, and apparently of Gibbons himself.

The president of the largest mining company, Charles F. Mayer, brought in foreign strikebreakers, many of them Catholic, and requested through Daniel Foley (brother of Bishops Thomas and John Foley) that Gibbons send another priest to the area because Schmitt was a "strong sympathizer and encourager" of the Knights of Labor.[98] Schmitt admitted his sympathy for the poor miners. "Our Catholics are the first to suffer," he explained to Gibbons. "They are the most honest and outspoken of the miners, and at the same time the most improvident among them for most of them live in Company houses." He advised Gibbons to tell Mayer he had no Polish priest because most of the strikebreakers were Poles.[99] The miners lost the strike of 1882, and the number of Knights in Allegany County declined rapidly thereafter. The Catholic centers of Frostburg, Lonaconing, and Westernport were hardest hit. Many moved away.[100]

The *Catholic Mirror*, reflecting perhaps Gibbons' known sentiments, grew increasingly pro-labor. In 1885 it described a strike in Chicago as a revolt against "the grinding oppression of capitalistic sharks."[101] The following spring it praised Powderly as "a man of brains and heart" while declaring that the "blood and tears" of the victims of the Goulds, Vanderbilts, and other railroad magnates drenched their "ill-gotten gold."[102] About the same time, Gibbons played a significant role in effecting favorable legislation at the end of a strike of streetcar conductors in Baltimore by a public statement that "the amelioration of the condition of the working class deserves every encouragement."[103] The rededication of Holy Cross Church in May he used to deflect the anger directed at workingmen because of the Haymarket Square violence in Chicago by calling it the work of a "small but turbulent element . . . [who] preached the gospel of anarchy, socialism, and nihilism." Socialism he denounced as a "noxious exotic" but warned his audience against dangerous secret societies and demagogues.[104]

By the time it became necessary to appeal to Rome for a decision on the Knights of Labor, Gibbons was convinced that a condemnation, as in Canada, would be disastrous for the church and the Catholic worker alike. Yet there were other American bishops besides the two archbishops who voted against the Knights who would have welcomed a Roman condemnation. One was Archbishop Corrigan of New York, who was at the time battling a rebellious priest considered a friend of the workingman: Edward McGlynn. Much against his will, Gibbons was drawn into this controversy.

McGlynn was the New York pastor who had given Archbishops Spalding and McCloskey some grief. Now he had become a chief supporter of Henry George, author of the scathing critique on industrial America, *Progress and Poverty*, and the founder of the single-tax movement. George was much admired among the members of the Irish Land League in America, which had many adherents in Baltimore itself. Corrigan suspended McGlynn when he refused to break with George and wrote a pastoral in defense of private property. He also petitioned Rome to have George's works placed on the Index. Gibbons believed that such a condemnation would, as with the Knights of Labor, be injurious to both church and worker. He would later grant an interview to Richard Burtsell, McGlynn's closest friend, which Corrigan would take as an unfriendly gesture.[105]

A Red Hat for Baltimore

In February 1886, however, what everyone was sure would happen seemed to have happened. Archbishop Corrigan relayed the news to Gibbons that he had been named a cardinal. The news was published and congratulations came from every quarter. It was a mistake. Corrigan had misread a cablegram from Rome. Those who were privy to the fact were greatly embarrassed. Corrigan explained his blunder to the Propaganda and begged that a red hat be given to Baltimore. On May 4 Gibbons received a cablegram from the papal secretary of state. The Holy Father would place him in the College of Cardinals at the coming consistory. The Roman officials chose Archbishop Kenrick of St. Louis to bestow the biretta, and Gibbons chose June 30, the twenty-fifth anniversary of his ordination, as the date. Ten archbishops and twenty-four bishops assembled for the event.[106]

The new honor, of course, heightened every comment from the archiepiscopal residence in Baltimore and strengthened Gibbons' hand in the several controversies in which he was engaged. Besides the Catholic University, the Knights of Labor, and the case of Henry George and Edward McGlynn, another problem arose in the period between June 30 and his arrival in Rome on February 13, 1887, to receive the red hat from the pope himself: the Abbelen petition.

The German Problem

German Catholic complaints against the dominant and overbearing Irish were often loud and bitter. In the fall of 1886 the Rev. Peter Abbelen, spiritual director of the School Sisters of Notre Dame in Milwaukee, called at the cathedral rectory and persuaded Gibbons to pen a letter of introduction to the Roman authorities. Gibbons obliged, apparently unaware of the full extent of the complaints of discrimination and demands for redress that Abbelen was carrying at the behest of prominent German priests of Milwaukee, St. Louis, and Cincinnati.[107] In the bill of particulars was an accusation that the recent synod of Baltimore had deprived the Germans of their parochial rights. When he learned of the charge, Gibbons was shocked. His relationships with the Germans of Baltimore were as harmonious as he could wish, for which he could in large measure thank the Redemptorists. It was Keane who informed Gibbons of this "villanous tissue of misstatements."[108]

Gibbons' failure to respond to the Abbelen petition, as well as his indecisiveness on the Catholic University and even the McGlynn affair, Keane wrote him some three weeks later, had led some to suggest that he was "uncertain and vacillating," eager "to please this one or that one." Keane found "a growing inclination to look elsewhere than to your Eminence for reliable information & judgements—a tendency, not only here but among the bishops of the United States, to look to New York rather than to Baltimore for the representative & leader of our Hierarchy." The injustice of such views galled him, Keane insisted, and he hoped that Gibbons would not take offense when he urged him to "regain the lost ground, by showing such singleness, such consistency, such firmness, such nobleness, in every word and act, as to fully realize the grand ideal of your position in the fore-front of the foremost Hierarchy in the world."[109] It may have been one of the strongest, but it would not be the only, prod that Keane, Ireland, and O'Connell would apply to induce the response they deemed appropriate on the part of the cardinal archbishop of Baltimore.

Even before his departure for Rome, Gibbons, at the suggestion of Corrigan himself, assembled the archbishops of Boston, New York, and Philadelphia to draft a letter to Rome denouncing the Abbelen petition. Gibbons arrived at the center of the Catholic world on February 13 ready to play the role that Keane, Ireland, and O'Connell had drawn for him. Immediately he closeted himself with his friends to plan strategies and draft memorials.

The Roman Actions

Gibbons alone signed the letters and statements that issued from the combined efforts in Rome, though the documents were composed in French, a language with which both Ireland and Keane had a greater familiarity than did Gibbons. A lengthy letter to the pope rehearsed the efforts to establish a Catholic university in America and rebutted the arguments that Corrigan had sent to Rome. Leo XIII issued a brief of approbation that was all its champions could wish.[110] To the Abbelen petition Keane and Ireland had already submitted a strong remonstrance. Gibbons presented the case personally before the cardinals of the Propaganda. Minor concessions were granted the Germans but not the major ones they demanded.[111] Gibbons relayed to McGlynn the pope's request that he obey the summons to Rome through both Corrigan and Burtsell. Then he signed a memorial on the inadvisability of placing the works of Henry George on the Index. As it turned out, McGlynn did not obey and was excommunicated. The decision on George's works was long in coming. When it did in 1889, it condemned the writings but refrained from publishing the condemnation.[112]

The most important pronouncement that came out of the combined efforts of Gibbons, Ireland, and Keane was a memorial on the Knights of Labor. The principal argument it advanced against a condemnation of the Knights was the danger of alienating the working class in America. "To lose the heart of the people," it warned, "would be a misfortune for which the friendship of the few rich and powerful would be no compensation." There was the danger, moreover, that Catholic workers might not obey it, since "in our age and in our country, obedience cannot be blind."[113] In a somewhat abbreviated form the memorial was leaked to the New York *Herald*, which editorialized that American Catholics had "a representative of whom they may well be proud." The conservative *New York Times*, on the other hand, saw Gibbons as a "man of weak judgement" and hoped the Catholic Church in America would not make the "terrible blunder" of following his lead in this matter. The memorial received international attention. Cardinal Manning stated publicly: "The Cardinal's argument is irresistible."[114] The Roman authorities agreed to the extent of granting the Knights of Labor a conditioned toleration.

Hard on the heels of the publicity given the memorial was that accorded Gibbons' sermon at Santa Maria in Trastevere, the Roman church of which as cardinal priest he was now theoretically pastor. O'Connell had persuaded him to use the occasion of taking possession to deliver a major address. The sermon was a paean of praise for his native land, whose prosperity he saw as a result of the "civil liberty we enjoy in our enlightened republic." The new American cardinal expressed his "deep sense of pride and gratitude, and in this great capital of Christendom, that I belong to a country where the civil government holds over us the aegis of its protection without interfering in the legitimate exercise of our sublime mission as ministers of the Gospel of Jesus Christ."[115] The *Catholic Mirror* glowed: "No such words have ever been uttered to the world by an American bishop since Archbishop Carroll founded our See of Baltimore, nor ones to make every true American citizen thank God he has such a representative at the Eternal City."[116] The utterances that issued from this Roman visit did, in fact, win for Gibbons a prominence enjoyed by no previous American Catholic prelate with the possible exception of John Carroll.

A Popular Apologist

Still another factor that contributed to his increasing fame was a facile pen that allowed Gibbons to reach an audience well beyond the borders of his archdiocese. In this he perpetuated a tradition of literary archbishops. But his works, though slightly fewer in number than those of Kenrick or Spalding, would surpass them all in popularity. *The Faith of Our Fathers*, published his last year in Richmond, had enjoyed a phenomenal success.[117] Its never-slackening sale encouraged him to do more. From 1883 to 1888 he wrote, among other things, a series of scholarly articles for the *American Catholic Quarterly Review* that would become in 1889 the concluding chapters for the second of his five books, *Our Christian Heritage*.

The Americanizers

In truth, however, Gibbons did not in his first ten years in Baltimore aspire to leadership in the American church. A "masterly inactivity" informed his approach to both national and diocesan affairs. His elevation to the College of Cardinals, however, itself in large part the result of the presidency of a national synod to which he brought initially little enthusiasm, suggested to others the role he might play. There would seem to be little doubt that Keane, Ireland, and O'Connell conspired to thrust him into the part of spokesman for a vision they shared. Though Keane and Ireland may have been the principal authors of the memorial on the Knights of Labor and O'Connell that of the sermon at Santa Maria in Trastevere, these statements represented also Gibbons' views and attitudes. It was not a matter of converting him to a vision but of convincing him of the need to abandon the more congenial role of conciliator. In the tradition of the gentle Irish, Gibbons was not a battler. Yet under the tutelage of this trio and another whose opinion he valued, the Sulpician Alphonse Magnien, a battler he would become. The vision that all shared was a Catholic Church in the United States not unlike that of the days of John Carroll—respected, republican, involved, but larger and even more active in the promotion of American principles and ideals. "In Abp. Carroll's time," Ireland would tell Gibbons in 1889, "the Church was truly American. Later the flood of Catholic foreign immigration overpowered us, and made the Church foreign in heart & in act. Thank God we are recovering from this misfortune."[118] Gibbons, Ireland, Keane, and O'Connell were ashamed of the alien character of their church. They were eager to assimilate the foreign born, to propel them into the mainstream of American life.

When the second church of St. Wenceslaus was dedicated in December 1886, Gibbons spoke to the foreign born of his flock through the Bohemians. "You have not only a duty of religion to discharge to your God," he told them, "but also of loyalty to your adopted country and to this city in which you have cast your lot. Strive to be law-abiding citizens; study and obey the laws of the country; be always in harmony with the spirit of its Institutions; set your face against those pernicious schools of anarchy, nihilism and socialism and other dangerous organizations whose apostles are striving to destroy but make no effort to build up and strengthen the glorious edifice of constitutional freedom, in which all alike, both native and foreign, find a home and a shelter." Gibbons praised his hearers for "gracefully submitting" to the ordinance forbidding band music on the streets on Sunday. "We are justly proud of our quiet and peaceful Christian Sabbath."

"Cultivate a spirit of industry," the cardinal also told his audience. Who were the real princes in America? "They are men who have risen to independence and affluence by patient industry and persevering toil . . . [men] not only blessed with this world's goods, but what is more, [who] have won the confidence and esteem of their fellow citizens. The same field is open to you."[119] His Eminence was also an effective preacher of the Gospel of Wealth.

Gibbons and Ireland were overly optimistic in their expectation of transforming the foreign-born Catholic into a middle-class American who shared the values, the manners and mores of the core culture. Neither of them had, in fact, a feel for the deepest needs and aspirations of the immigrant. The ardent Americanism of Gibbons, Ireland, Keane, and O'Connell was doomed to founder on the rock of immigrant fears and insecurities well before it raised a hue and cry among the conservative churchmen at home and abroad.

11 Prince of the Church

UPON HIS RETURN FROM Rome in 1880 and again in 1884, Gibbons had ruled out the elaborate receptions being prepared for him. In 1887 he was not so reticent. A parade of sixty-three societies counting eight thousand marchers bedazzled one hundred thousand onlookers.[1] Before the year was out, he had traveled to Philadelphia for the centennial celebration of the Constitution, where the president, a host of other government officials, justices of the Supreme Court, and seventeen governors had paid their respects to him, and he had completed a "march of triumph through the West" to confer the pallium on Archbishop William Gross of Oregon City, a native of Baltimore, stopping frequently en route for the warm receptions accorded him.[2] "This everlasting talk about the *head* of the *American Church* annoys me," Bishop McQuaid grumbled to the archbishop of New York.[3]

For the rest of his life James Gibbons was seldom out of the limelight. President Grover Cleveland and members of the Cabinet joined him on May 24, 1888, when he laid the cornerstone for the Catholic University of America, and again on November 13, 1889, when he opened the same institution. The latter event was held in conjunction with the centennial of the diocese of Baltimore and of the American hierarchy, a three-day spectacular in which Baltimore's ninth archbishop was always center stage. In 1892–93 he was conspicuous at the several celebrations commemorating the four hundredth anniversary of the discovery of America. In October 1893 he accepted the homage of the most publicized silver jubilee of an American bishop to date. Gibbons came not only to tolerate but to enjoy these events staged to do honor to the republic's second and most popular prince of the church. At almost all of them he wore his red robes.

The Providential Role

In addition to the attention paid his every utterance, the increasing reliance of the Roman authorities on Gibbons' leadership in America made it all the more desirable for Ireland, now an archbishop, Keane, and O'Connell to have him as spokesman and defender. Ireland and Keane returned to America to present their blueprint for the church of the future. Keane called upon "the young giant Church of the Western World" to "gird herself with the majesty befitting her providential vocation," while Ireland at every turn alerted American Catholics to their "glorious mission."[4] Theirs was no less a "responsibility" than that of reconciling the universal church to the new age. O'Connell, of course, remained at the American College to advance the trio's views in Rome and make converts throughout Europe. They were convinced they had a mandate from the pope himself. "He [Leo XIII] recognizes in our country," Keane wrote in 1888, "the furthest advance yet attained by the true spirit of our era; the most symmetrical and orderly development of democracy which the world has yet beheld."[5]

Though Gibbons may have smiled at the overblown rhetoric of his friends, he shared their ardent patriotism, their belief in the providential role of their country, and their missionary fervor. This he made clear by his endorsement of the sermon of Archbishop Ireland at the centennial of the hierarchy, wherein the latter outdid himself in praise of his adopted land. A "party of advanced views," Archbishop Corrigan warned Cardinal Camillo Mazzella in Rome, was "now seeking to rule the church in this country." Corrigan supplied several names, Ireland and Keane included, "acting with and under His Eminence of Baltimore."[6]

The press did, in fact, begin to speak of the "liberals" at this time.[7] Despite the role in which he was cast, however, Gibbons was not their true leader. For the most part Ireland provided the rhetoric and the drive, Keane the rationale, and O'Connell the strategy. Gibbons was at best an uncertain ally and never quite privy to the master plan. A person who was, and the man the three depended upon to keep the cardinal in line, was Alphonse Magnien, the Sulpician superior in Baltimore, whose admiration for Ireland often exceeded his loyalty to Gibbons. "He is the head and heart of the whole movement in America," O'Connell would later tell a European partisan with perhaps slight exaggeration.[8]

Cahenslyism and the School Question

In the spring of 1891 a German named Peter Paul Cahensly presented the pope with a memorial that had come from a meeting of the St. Raphaelsverein at Lucerne, Switzerland. It claimed a loss of ten million immigrants in America as a result of neglect and, like the Abbelen petition, called for German parishes and German bishops. Ireland denounced the memorial as an attempt to Germanize America. The heated debate that followed was fueled in part by the appointment of the Austrian-born Frederick X. Katzer as archbishop of Milwaukee against the recommendations of the American archbishops. Katzer invited Gibbons, nevertheless, to bestow the pallium. In Milwaukee's cathedral in August 1891 the cardinal delivered a resounding sermon. "Woe to him who would sow tares of discord in the fair fields of the Church in America!" he warned. "Loyalty to God's Church and to our Country!—this our religious and political faith." He would have the foreign-born declare in the spirit of Ruth: "Thy people shall be my people and thy God my God." The sermon was, he later claimed, one of the most audacious things he had ever done.[9]

His belief in rapid assimilation made it relatively easy in this instance for Gibbons to take up the cudgels the archbishop of St. Paul had laid down for him. It took a greater effort to enter the hornet's nest that Ireland stirred over Catholic education. Gibbons was still a firm believer in the value of Catholic schools and on more than one occasion had listed among the three great evils of the nation "an imperfect and vicious system of education, which undermines the religion of our youth."[10] Through Keane he had sought to justify the Catholic school at the National Education Association in 1889. In 1890, however, addressing the same body, Ireland proposed a compromise whereby the parochial school could be incorporated into the public school system and ended with a defense of the public school: "Withered be the hand raised in sign of its destruction."[11] Even the *Catholic Mirror*, normally receptive to Ireland's views, was startled by his promotion of the "transcendent glories" of the public school system.[12]

Cardinal Mariano Rampolla, the papal secretary of state, wrote Gibbons that the Holy Father wanted his opinion on Ireland's speech. O'Connell reminded Gibbons that in matters touching the American Church "yr. opinion carries the greatest weight," and Ireland told him that any rebuke he might receive for his address would be taken as "a censure of my 'Americanism,' & as a proof of the hopeless foreignism of the church."[13] With Magnien's help Gibbons composed a lengthy defense of his friend. Ireland's principal intent, he told the pope, was to assuage the ill will that sprang from Catholic opposition to the public schools and to effect changes that would make them less objectionable for Catholics to attend.[14] Magnien encouraged Thomas Bouquillon, professor of moral theology at Catholic University, to do a piece in defense of the state's right to educate, but a rebuttal by a New York Jesuit kept the water boiling. In the meantime Ireland had arranged for two of his parochial schools, at Faribault and Stillwater, to be taken over by the local school boards with allowance for religious instruction outside school hours.[15]

The controversy spread. Corrigan and McQuaid sided with the Germans and the Jesuits. Catholic and secular press alike had a field day. The rumor that Rome would summon Archbishops Ireland and Katzer to explain the two sides of the controversy prompted Ireland to exclaim to Gibbons: "Imagine the insult to myself and to the Republic, to be brought to argue with Katzer, a man who knows as little of America as a Huron."[16] To Rome, nevertheless, Ireland went at the beginning of 1892 to explain his position. Gibbons sent a second lengthy defense to the pope. In April the Propaganda decided that Ireland's Faribault plan "could be tolerated."

The extent to which the school controversy modified Gibbons' views is not altogether clear. To Cardinal Vaughan in England he explained that it had produced "a great deal of unnecessary heat." Some of the prelates who opposed Ireland's plan, he explained, sanctioned it in particular cases in their own sees. There were fourteen dioceses with similar arrangements. In any case, Gibbons predicted, it seemed unlikely that American states would make the concessions Ireland wished. But how to provide for the one to two million Catholic children not attending Catholic schools? If all applied, said Gibbons, "we could not find room nor bear the expense."[17] He did not mention that there were at least two public-parish schools in his own diocese, at St. Joseph's, Texas, and St. Thomas, Hampden.[18]

In July 1892 Gibbons also gave permission to the priest in charge of the mission at Curtis Bay to negotiate with the county commissioners. He stipulated the conditions under which they could assume charge of the school being planned, conditions that resembled those of Ireland's Faribault plan.[19] Apparently nothing came of it. At the end of the year the Baltimore *Sun* printed a circular drawn up by a group of priests and laymen of the city in support of an arrangement like that of the Faribault plan for the archdiocese of Baltimore. The *Catholic Mirror* revealed, however, that His Eminence was "too deeply impressed with the necessity of Christian education to assent to any arrangement which would hamper or interfere in the slightest degree with the religious education which Catholic children should every day receive in the schools which they attend."[20] And that seemed to settle the matter.

The Apostolic Delegation

In Rome the archbishop of St. Paul apparently traded favors. In return for Roman approval of his school plan he would support the pope's desire to have a representative in the United States. O'Connell (and probably Keane) joined in the plan that was carefully laid, but Gibbons was, for the most part, kept in the dark.[21] The cardinal archbishop of Baltimore was not likely to show great enthusiasm for a move that would diminish his own role or the preeminent position of his see. Nor was the appointment of the apostolic delegate likely to bring joy to the American bishops in general, but Ireland and O'Connell believed it would favor the liberal cause.

Without consulting the Propaganda, Pope Leo and Cardinal Rampolla worked out with Ireland and O'Connell a plan to place an apostolic delegate in Washington with as little fuss as possible. The man was Archbishop Francesco Satolli, a philosophy teacher turned diplomat. The pretext was a valuable set of maps from the Vatican Library that Satolli would escort to Chicago for the opening of the Columbian Exposition in October 1892. O'Connell rushed Satolli past Corrigan in New York and delivered him to Ireland, who rarely let the Italian prelate out of sight. At the meeting of the archbishops in November, Satolli presented fourteen points that favored Ireland's position in the school controversy and then proposed a permanent apostolic delegation in the United States. On both questions Ireland was the only archbishop to express approval.[22]

Archbishop Corrigan was deputed to draft a letter to the pope on the inadvisability of an apostolic delegation, but it went out over Gibbons' signature. While it was in transit, Gibbons received a cablegram from O'Connell dated January 14, 1893, that the pope had appointed Satolli permanent delegate. Quickly, Gibbons sent a second letter to thank the pope, claiming that "the entire nation" had indicated its "highest appreciation."[23] Satolli's first significant act, the result of special faculties granted him to hear priests' appeals against their bishops, was to lift the excommunication of Edward McGlynn.

Ireland had little trouble convincing Satolli that Corrigan was his chief opponent in the American hierarchy and the source of critical articles in several papers. Rampolla asked Gibbons in the summer of 1893 to act as peacemaker between Corrigan and Satolli. Well aware of Gibbons' tendency to play the conciliator and of his former friendship with the New York metropolitan, Ireland and his friends endeavored to prevent a rapprochement. At the beginning of 1894, Ireland confided to Gibbons that Corrigan had gotten the idea that Gibbons wanted him deposed so that he could take his place in New York. "The man is crazy," Ireland insisted. He was also "a liar and a hypocrite."[24] A year later Keane sent Gibbons a lengthy account of two interviews with the pope, whom he reported as saying: "But the Cardinal goes so much with *that Corrigan!*" He had "clearly intimated that he wished you had been less conciliatory with N.Y."

In the same letter Keane also claimed that Leo was displeased at the

Propaganda's disparagement of the apostolic delegation, which was an element of his policy of countering the Triple Alliance of "monarchism, militarism, & the oppression of the papacy" by enhancing the influence of democratic France and America. He had seen in the enthusiastic reception of Satolli (as reported by Gibbons) a "rallying of all democracies around the Pope." The Holy Father, Keane reported, was preparing an encyclical that would clearly express his views.[25]

Longinqua Oceani, which finally appeared in January 1895, was far from what the liberals had hoped. It did, in fact, praise the young nation, reminding American Catholics that "when popular suffrage placed the great Washington at the helm of the Republic, the first bishop was set by apostolic authority over the American Church [*Americanae Ecclesiae*]." Leo praised especially the impressive achievements of nation and of church and the freedom of action the former afforded the latter. "Yet," he added pointedly, "it would be erroneous to draw the conclusion that in America is to be sought the type of the most desirable status of the Church, or that it would be universally lawful or expedient for State and Church to be, as in America, dissevered and divorced." The Church would, the pope insisted, "bring forth more abundant fruits if, in addition to liberty, she enjoyed the favor of the laws and the patronage of public authorities."[26] From the Holy See had finally come an answer to the question posed by Archbishop Spalding some thirty years before. The encyclical, however, was intended primarily as a defense of the apostolic delegation.

The Conservatives Triumphant

The worst was yet to come. In 1895 it became painfully clear that the apostolic delegate had gone over to the camp of the conservatives. As early as the fall of 1893 Satolli had shown discomfort at the Catholic participation in the Parliament of Religions held in conjunction with the Columbian Exposition. In 1895 participation in such gatherings was banned by the pope. Also in 1893, on Thanksgiving Day, Satolli had spoken (in Latin) at Gonzaga College in Washington on the value of Catholic schools, branding as "absurd" reports that he was opposed to them.[27] In April 1895 at the dedication of a school in Pottsville, Pennsylvania, he not only made clear his support of the parochial school but also his warm regard for the Germans.[28] And as early as 1893 Satolli had expressed surprise at the leniency shown secret societies at the archbishops' meetings. In 1894 the Odd Fellows, Knights of Pythias, and Sons of Temperance were condemned by the Propaganda. Gibbons refused to promulgate the decision until he knew better the mind of Rome. Satolli complained to Rampolla that Gibbons seemed not to have "the correct idea of what a cardinal ought to be in his own province and nation."[29] Gibbons went to Rome in the spring of 1895 to seek a reversal of the condemnation. Not only did he fail, but he suffered the shock of seeing Denis O'Connell dismissed as rector of the American College.

In asking for O'Connell's resignation, the Pope had acted largely on evidence supplied by Corrigan. O'Connell was accused of absenteeism, of alienating the majority of American bishops, and of unbecoming familiarity with Miss Virginia McTavish of Baltimore. The sticking point in the last complaint, however, would seem to have been the indiscretion of the young lady in visiting the queen of Italy after visiting the pope, for which she was duly snubbed by the black aristocracy of Rome.[30] Gibbons kept O'Connell in the ancient city by naming him vicar of his titular church.

Satolli's final contribution to the American church—he had been named a cardinal and Gibbons had bestowed the biretta in the cathedral of Baltimore—was the dismissal of John Keane as president of the Catholic University. Gibbons himself handed Keane the letter from the pope dated September 15, 1896, and wept when Keane said good-bye to faculty and students. Keane accepted the compensatory offer of a sinecure in Rome.[31] There were rumors that Gibbons and Ireland were next on the list.

"Americanism"

By early 1897, however, the liberals were back in stride. O'Connell suggested to Ireland that he tar their enemies as *refractaires*, the term the pope had used to describe the opponents of his French policy.[32] This Ireland did in another of his sensational sermons, which he entitled "The New Age" and delivered at St. Patrick's in Washington. In Rome Keane and O'Connell created a network of like-minded intellectuals throughout Europe. In his apartment O'Connell held weekly meetings of "the Club" to promote American solutions to the problems of the church.

The message, however, suffered a sea change, especially in France, where allies, emphasizing American freedom, energy, and individuality, often came close to being antiauthoritarian, even anarchic, and their foes, perceiving an "invasion of barbarism," smelled Masonry, Protestantism, Judaism, and even Satanism.[33] A simple biography of Isaac Hecker gave focus to the vague notions already being called "Americanism."

The providential role that the founder of the Paulists had assigned the "Saxons" in general and the United States in particular was a source of inspiration for many American liberals, especially Ireland and Keane. Ireland wrote an introduction to the biography authored by the Paulist Walter Elliott. In it he emphasized Hecker's devotion to America and the stress he had placed upon the natural and social virtues and individual initiative. Corrigan gave his imprimatur to the book, which was published in 1891, three years after Hecker's death. It was little read until the Abbé Félix Klein of the Institut Catholique in Paris wrote in 1897 a second introduction for a French translation that put even greater emphasis on the personal freedom that came from the inner working of the Spirit. It provoked a wordy war indeed.[34]

In August O'Connell took his turn putting words into Hecker's mouth at a meeting of the International Catholic Scientific Congress at Fribourg. Ignoring the warning of *Longinqua Oceani*, he called upon the church to accept the American concepts of religious freedom, the superiority of Common Law over Roman Law, and the separation of church and state. This, he claimed, was the true Americanism.[35]

The conservative reaction was frenetic. A work entitled *Le Père Hecker, est-il un saint?* accused the Paulist founder and his ideological followers of heresy. Gibbons sent one of his strongest protests to Rome when the work was granted an imprimatur there. French monarchists and other conservatives were determined to have "Americanism" condemned as a means of silencing their antagonists. In Rome they found powerful friends, including Cardinals Satolli and Mazzella, the latter an authority on American affairs by reason of his many years at Woodstock. The American liberals, nevertheless, were convinced that the tide was with them. "Let us be prudent and active," Alphonse Magnien wrote O'Connell from Baltimore in March 1898 "and the future is ours."[36] Despite the failure of Ireland to persuade his government to avoid war with Spain, a task assigned him by the Vatican, O'Connell told the archbishop of St. Paul that he had reached "the providential period" of his life, "where all your dreams are to be realized and all your poetic visions are to be turned into prophecies."[37]

Testem Benevolentiae, the condemnation of "Americanism," came in the form of an apostolic letter addressed to Gibbons and dated January 22, 1899. In general Leo XIII condemned the notion that the church should adapt itself to the age and adopt modern theories and methods. In particular he condemned reliance on the inner working of the Spirit at the expense of external guidance, the promotion of the natural and social virtues over the passive and supernatural ones, and the depreciation of religious vows. He was certain, however, the American bishops would repudiate such ideas, which implied that American Catholics wished a church different from that in the rest of the world.[38] Gibbons told the pope a bit more bluntly than was his wont that he was certain no American entertained the "extravagant and absurd" notions the pope described.[39] Of all the archbishops, only Corrigan and Katzer thanked the pope for checking the growth of heresy in the United States. At the archbishops' meeting in the fall, Ireland proposed, in effect, a joint denial of the existence of heresy. But, as he told O'Connell, "Baltimore cried 'peace, peace, death even for the sake of peace.' "[40] And so the controversy ended in a crushing defeat for the liberals.

A refusal to read the danger signals, an inability to negotiate the tangled thicket of Catholic politics abroad, and an amazing capacity for self-deception made the defeat of these American innocents inevitable. Gibbons' eclipse was only temporary. Ireland, Keane, and O'Connell would never fully recover, however, the appointment of Keane as archbishop of Dubuque in 1900 and of O'Connell as rector of the Catholic University in 1903 notwithstanding.

True Americanism

Keane had tried to explain to Rampolla some months before the condemnation was published that "Americanism" was no more than the satisfaction, gratitude, and devotion that American Catholics felt toward their country, "to which Archbishop Carroll first gave expression."[41] Gibbons attempted no definition and refrained from public comment on *Testem Benevolentiae*, but many must have felt that an address entitled "True Americanism" delivered by the distinguished Charles J. Bonaparte on Maryland Pilgrims Day (March 25) reflected his sentiments.

The "reverent acceptance of our Holy Father's decision," Bonaparte observed, had been "accompanied by general surprise that a name so peculiarly inappropriate" had been given the aggregate of doctrines. True Americanism, he insisted, was devotion to but one nation that spoke but one language. He denounced the "crude and outlandish" proposal that would have balkanized the American hierarchy on the basis of language. The grandsons of the Irish and German victims of the Plug Uglies of the 1850s had become as thoroughly American as if their ancestors had arrived on the *Ark* and the *Dove*, and now recent immigrants, "Poles and Italians, Hungarian peasantry and Russian Jews," were being ground into shape like the proverbial paving stone by "the wheels and burrs of our orderly freedom." And so might it be with Cubans and Puerto Ricans, even Hawaiians and Filipinos. Picking a quote from *Testem Benevolentiae* on "free will and choice," Bonaparte declared that in granting religious liberty but, at the same time, producing a religious people, the United States had "given a new hope to the world."[42]

This native of Baltimore, a grandson of Jerome Bonaparte and Betsy Patterson and a future Attorney General of the United States, was for his generation what Charles Carroll and Roger Brooke Taney had been for theirs: the lay spokesman for the local Catholic community and to a degree for the Catholic Church in America. Reflecting the attitudes of the Maryland Catholic elite, and certainly those of James Gibbons, he could not claim, any more than Gibbons could, to speak for the inarticulate immigrant Catholics of the see city and the national capital. Only a little less biased than Ireland in his attitude toward foreigners, Gibbons shared the Americanists' embarrassment at the alien character of his church. Like them he wished the process of assimilation to proceed as rapidly as possible.[43]

Immigrants Demur

If the German Catholic people of Baltimore may be taken as representative, at least the Germans of the archdiocese did not share their cardinal's views. The *Katholische Volkszeitung* and the *Catholic Mirror* exchanged angry words over the Lucerne memorial.[44] Gibbons was perturbed that Archbishop Patrick J. Ryan of Philadelphia, an ally of Corrigan, was supplying the *Volkszeitung* with articles against him.[45]

The Redemptorists may have stifled criticism in their parishes, but the pastor of St. Mary Mother of God in Washington was outspoken. At the opening of the Forty Hours Devotion in 1896, with Satolli pontificating, Father George Glaab predicted that any attempt to hasten the amalgamation of national groups would "unquestionably be productive of most disastrous consequences."[46] Father Valentine Schmitt at the former German parish of St. Joseph, however, believed like Gibbons that the sooner the Germans adopted American customs and language the better. He considered Glaab a "German of the Germans," always stirring up national feeling. Those who cried loudest for a German church, Schmitt insisted to Gibbons, frequented their parishes only on those occasions when the air was "impregnated with beer."[47]

Immigrant and Middle-Class Economy

The archdiocese of Baltimore in the middle years of Gibbons' episcopacy was becoming more rather than less foreign in character and so less inclined to be receptive to the message of the Americanizers. Immigration from Europe accounted for only 5 percent of the 240,000 increase in Baltimore between 1870 and 1900.[48] But of the Catholic increase for the same period, roughly 45,000, perhaps, as many, came from abroad as from the hinterlands or from natural increase. The parish populations of the southern and western counties remained about the same for these thirty years. The increase was mostly in the two major cities.

Catholic newcomers from eastern Europe settled where factories followed the waterfront and the tracks of the B&O and Pennsylvania Railroads into Canton, Highlandtown, Locust Point, and Curtis Bay. Italians tended to cluster around the markets; they were yet to create their Little Italy. Bohemians, Poles, Germans, and Italians could all be found in the canneries that in 1890 claimed Baltimore's largest work force. It was largely family labor, children snapping beans beside their mothers. After the Civil War immigrant women and children largely replaced the blacks shucking oysters. Bohemians shoveled coal on the wharves and Irishmen and Germans worked with Negro trimmers before the Poles moved in. Bohemian and Lithuanian girls could be found among the Russian Jewish girls in the sweatshops of Old Town. The Irish still monopolized the occupations involving horses, and many could still be counted in the B&O workshops and the foundries. Italians could be found on construction gangs and in the men's clothing factories on Baltimore Street as well as at the fruit markets.[49]

But the second- and third-generation Irish, German, and even Bohemian families were climbing the socioeconomic ladder with alacrity. A large number of Germans were respectable furniture-, piano-, and cigar-makers, or bakers, butchers, and brewers. Many of the Irish were white-collar clerks and bookkeepers, and some—like Thomas Shehan of St. Ann's Parish, father of a future archbishop—drummers for Baltimore's largest industry: men's clothing. As these immigrant descendants moved upward socially, they continued to move outward geographically, following new carlines to the edges of residential development. Baltimore had a larger percentage of families that owned their own homes than did most large cities. Most of the rowhouse residents at the end of the century were of Irish, German, or Bohemian descent, skilled workmen or shopkeepers for the most part. In home owning the Bohemians outpaced even the Germans.[50]

The average earnings of a Baltimore family were little more than $600 a year.[51] The newcomers, of course, earned considerably less, while Catholic families who had climbed into the middle class earned slightly more. The enhanced standard of living for middle-class Catholics of Baltimore at the end of the century could easily be gauged from advertisements in the *Catholic Mirror* featuring such artifacts of the comfortable as pianos and organs, stained-glass windows, steam heating, gas fixtures, tiles, wall decorations, picture frames, sewing machines, paperhangers, carpet cleaners, liquors, and cigars.

The clergy in general lived better than their parishioners. The $1,000 a year granted pastors and $600 their assistants were over and above room and board and other benefits provided by the parish. The *Catholic Mirror*, without embarrassment, described an eleven-room rectory being built in a small country parish with "all the modern conveniences," including speaking tubes and an "elegant" bathroom.[52] The pastor of Corpus Christi in the fashionable Bolton Hill area complained to the cardinal of the unsuitability of the rectory for himself and his assistant but added that it "would be all that could be desired for years for a small community of four or five religious."[53] A sister received about $200 a year and few of the parochial benefits accorded the residents of the rectory next door.

Acting as the "mouthpiece" of the hardworking laity, the *Catholic Mirror* in 1882 had been so bold as to suggest that parishioners' consent be sought on impending obligations. It questioned whether they should be saddled with huge mortgages on "palatial" churches while there were so many and more urgent needs to be met.[54] The article was a plea for relief, however, from the middle class, who more often complained to the cardinal of such burdens. From the dollar-a-day laborers who bore the bulk of the cost of Catholic expansion came not even muted signals of protest.

Old Immigrants Assimilate

It is probable that for Catholics of foreign-born parents in the oldest archdiocese the process of Americanization proceeded at a faster pace than in the dioceses where there were not already well-assimilated old-stock families. The latter in Catholic Maryland had been, of course, on the scene longer and in greater numbers than in any other state. For a century they had been moving up from southern Maryland and into Baltimore and Washington from surrounding counties. These were families who had never penetrated the patrician circle but who had retained much of the Maryland tradition bequeathed by John Carroll. In the city's new neighborhoods they settled beside and joined the same parish societies as the Irish and Germans who had moved from downtown.

Only two parishes in the core suffered appreciably from migration to the fringes, the mostly Irish St. Vincent's and St. Leo's. As the Irish (and others) moved out of St. Leo's, the Italians moved in. St. Patrick's, St. Peter's, St. Martin's, St. John's, St. Brigid's, and Star of the Sea retained their largely Irish character. Even more did the German parishes maintain their German stamp. There would be no new Irish, German, or Bohemian parishes, but St. Wenceslaus would build a larger church in 1902–3, the third of four times it would outgrow its home, and the German parish of the Sacred Heart in Highlandtown was the fastest growing parish in the archdiocese. The new parishes in the city's industrial areas would, with the exception of St. Luke's at Sparrows Point, be peopled mostly by Poles, Lithuanians, and blacks.

A Polish Revolt

A church built for the factory town at Curtis Bay, not yet a part of the city, was originally not intended for a Polish parish. When completed in 1890, St. Athanasius was entrusted to Father James R. Matthews, but in 1894 he was replaced by Father Andrew A. Duszynski, so rapidly had the Poles moved in. With them came small numbers of Lithuanians, Bohemians, Slovaks, Slovenes, and Ukrainians. Including older Germans and native Americans, it represented the richest ethnic mix in the archdiocese. 1907 the adjoining factory towns of Wagner's Point and Fairfield were detached from St. Athanasius when the family of Martin Wagner, the Catholic founder of the large packing firm at Wagner's Point, offered land and $10,000 for a church.[55] When built in 1907, St. Adalbert's was entrusted to Father Charles Kotlarz, a product of Louvain. Over two-thirds of his flock were Polish.[56]

The already existing Polish parishes, St. Stanislaus and Holy Rosary, would continue to be a matter of concern to Cardinal Gibbons. While the Germans may have grumbled, the Poles presented the greatest challenge to his policy of assimilation. Baltimore's Polonia was not unaffected when compatriots in other parts of the country "mounted the most aggressive and significant campaign against Americanization."[57] The Poles of Baltimore were also divided by the contest between the nationalist and clericalist factions that split Polish communities elsewhere. Nationalists represented by the Polish National Alliance, vied increasingly with the clericalists, who maintained the Polish Roman Catholic Union. The PNA had founded its first lodge in Baltimore as early as 1886.

The St. Stanislaus Benevolent Society that had created both St. Stanislaus and Holy Rosary Parish remained the most aggressive as well as most nationalist Polish body in Baltimore. In appropriating the dominant role the nobility had played with regard to the church in their homeland, these former peasants came closest to reviving trusteeism in the oldest archdiocese.[58] Peter Chowaniec, the first pastor of Holy Rosary and a nationalist, encouraged lay trusteeship. Limiting his own role largely to the spiritual, especially in his ministrations to the newly arrived on the docks of Baltimore, he left the control of temporals to a committee drawn from the St. Stanislaus Society. In 1892, however, the zealous Chowaniec died suddenly, and matters took a drastic turn at Holy Rosary.

Gibbons obtained the services of a newly ordained priest from SS. Cyril and Methodius Seminary in Detroit, who was accompanied by the vice rector, Miecislaus Barabasz, to help him get a start. Barabasz liked Baltimore so well that he decided he would make a better pastor than his young protégé. Gibbons approved. In 1893 Barabasz rescinded the powers of the committee, but the committee refused to surrender the accounts of pew rents, school and cemetery fees, and other revenues. Gibbons was persuaded to take legal action against the committee.[59] The court case, as well as the struggle between pastor and committee, dragged on for four years and more. Barabasz established a Polish Catholic newspaper, *Przygaciel Domu* (Friend of the Hearth), to further his cause.[60]

In the course of the struggle the leading trustees made contact with Polish independent movements in the country, their first being with that of Cleveland in 1894. Two days before the case went against the committee in March 1898, an independent Polish parish was incorporated in Baltimore with the promise of a priest from the Polish Catholic Independent Church of Buffalo.[61] To avert schism, Gibbons issued a letter to be read in all the Polish churches. "While loving America," he said, "love your own nation also [and] do not stain by apostasy your national traditions and dignity." He urged his Polish charges to be true to their heritage and its strong union with the chair of Peter.[62] It was a far different message from that delivered in 1891 in the cathedral of Milwaukee, but it did not deflect the dissident Poles of Baltimore from forming their independent parish. Its name, Holy Mother of Unceasing Help, would be changed to Holy Cross Parish when it later affiliated with the Polish National Catholic Church. In 1905 Gibbons named Barabasz dean of the Polish Catholic clergy of the archdiocese, "the first office of the kind."[63]

St. Stanislaus Kostka Parish also remained troublesome, largely by reason of the poor judgment of pastors and assistants. In 1904 the pastor, Thomas Morys, had one assistant arrested and was accused by another of financial irregularities. Gibbons sent Morys packing. When he next visited St. Stanislaus, he had to be rescued by the police from a mob demanding

Morys' reinstatement.[64] Gibbons wrote his brother that his "nervous system" had been greatly upset by the incident. "They are full of faith," he explained, "but are very violent and quarrelsome."[65] In 1905 Gibbons prevailed upon the Franciscan Conventuals, who had just established a Polish province in America, to take over St. Stanislaus. The next year he induced the same order to assume control also of St. Casimir's, a mission Morys had founded in 1902 for the Polish Catholics moving into Canton.

A Lithuanian Parish

The cardinal also had reason to be apprehensive about the Lithuanians of Baltimore. The Lithuanian Society of St. John the Baptist organized a parish of about five hundred people on February 8, 1888. Services were conducted by a Passionist in the basement of St. Peter's on Poppleton Street until the next year, when a Jewish synagogue at Lloyd and Watson was purchased and christened St. John the Baptist. The first pastor was Rev. Casimir Polujanskas. Neither he nor his three successors lasted long, but the third managed to persuade the society to surrender the deed of the church to the cardinal in 1892. Joseph Lietuvnikas of the Polish Seminary in Detroit was ordained December 23, 1893, and immediately installed as pastor.[66] In time he curbed the separatist tendencies in his flock, most of whom remained faithful even when an ex-seminarian who called himself a priest set up a rival but short-lived schismatic church soon after the Poles had created theirs in 1898.[67] In 1904 Lietuvnikas purchased a larger church at Saratoga and Paca for the growing Lithuanian community.

Slovaks, Slovenes, and Hungarians could also be found in Baltimore but never in sufficient numbers to warrant a separate parish. Some eastern Europeans went to the mining areas of western Maryland. Father Kotlarz served the Slavs of Allegany County briefly before his transfer to St. Adalbert. By 1906 a priest was coming from Pennsylvania to hear the confessions of Hungarians living near Midland.[68] Almost all moved on eventually, probably because they had no parish of their own.

Italian Parishes

While the Poles and Lithuanians were deeply devout, the Italians wore their religion lightly. Father Andreis cited this indifference as the reason for his failure to build a true Italian parish at St. Leo's but complained to Gibbons in 1901 when fifteen hundred Italians, mostly from Cefalù in Sicily, petitioned for a priest from that region. A Sicilian priest would split Balti-

more's Italian colony, Andreis insisted, and he begged Gibbons to try instead to obtain one from his native town near Turin.[69] Andreis died in 1903
and his successor, Thomas Monteverde, in 1905. The priest who had come
in answer to the petition, Pasquale di Paolo, was then placed in charge of St.
Leo's. Italians moved into the changing neighborhood in great enough
numbers that Baltimore soon needed a second Italian parish.

Washington needed a first. In 1904 the apostolic delegate, Diomede
Falconio, sent Gibbons a clipping that described the work of Protestant
groups among the Italians who had come to the capital to help build Union
Station. He regretted that the Catholic church was doing nothing for them
and suggested that the cardinal contact the Jesuits at St. Aloysius.[70] Gibbons explained that the situation had only recently been brought to his
attention and that he would ask the Jesuits to do what they could.[71] Some
fifteen years before, however, the *Catholic Mirror* had described a colony
of Italians on Capitol Hill, mostly fruit peddlers and organ grinders, it
claimed, and about two years later pronounced such colonies "a shame and
a scandal." In their irreligion they had no one but themselves to blame, the
Mirror insisted, for churches were open to all.[72] Two months later, in an
apologetic tone, it declared that only a hundred or so of the fifteen hundred
Italians in Washington were of the sort described. "It is safe to say there are
no Mafia here."[73]

A number of Italians had gone to western Maryland to work for the
Union Mining Company. A mission was established for them at Moran-
town about 1903, and a church called Our Lady of Mount Carmel was built
in 1908 to be served by Father Anthony Scarpati from Midland. After its
erection, however, most of the Italians moved away, and the mission was
abandoned.[74]

Black Parishes

Black Catholics of the archdiocese of Baltimore were better served
than the Italians. Through the efforts of Father Slattery, the Josephite, a
third parish was opened for them in the see city in 1893 in the original
chapel of St. Gregory the Great. It was called St. Peter Claver.[75] The
Josephites also opened a fourth parish in 1907, when they bought an Episcopal church at Biddle and Argyle named St. Barnabas and kept the name.
In 1893 the black Catholics of the eastern part of Washington finally got a
parish when Gibbons sent the priest they themselves requested as pastor,
Father James Matthews, to supervise the building of a substantial church.
On May 27, 1894, the cardinal dedicated St. Cyprian's. In 1891 it had been

estimated that there were ten thousand black Catholics in the national capital, slightly more than in Baltimore itself.[76] In 1902 the Jesuits established the first separate parish for the blacks of St. Mary's County, which they called St. Peter Claver.[77]

A Multiplication of Parishes

The greatest number of churches erected in the twenty years between 1888 and 1908 were, as already suggested, for the Catholics who moved to the new neighborhoods of Baltimore and Washington or the villages just beyond. It was largely a middle-class growth. Compared to the six new churches built for immigrants and blacks, the see city could count thirteen others nearer or just outside its boundaries. In the order of construction they were: St. Paul's at Caroline and Eager built in 1888–89, St. Mark's in Catonsville in 1888–89, St. Luke's in Sparrows Point in 1888–89, St. Clement's in Lansdowne in 1890, St. Benedict's out Wilkens Avenue in 1893, St. Mary's in Ilchester in 1893, Our Lady of Mount Carmel in Middle River in 1893, St. Elizabeth's on East Baltimore Street facing Patterson Park in 1895, SS. Philip and James out Charles Street in 1897–98, St. Cecilia's in Walbrook in 1902–4, St. Ambrose on Park Heights Avenue in 1907, St. Katharine of Sienna on East Preston Street in 1902–3, and St. Dominic's in Hamilton in 1906–7.[78] Not all were middle class; St. Luke's was built for the workers of the company town of the Maryland Steel Company. Though raised by the Benedictines of Fourteen Holy Martyrs and thought by many to be German, St. Benedict's was from the start a mixed congregation.

During the years 1888–1908 new parishes or missions appeared with such tedious regularity—on the average of two or three a year—that their dedications were, for the most part, allowed to pass without the accustomed bands and banners. In Washington and its suburbs churches or chapels were opened for eleven new parishes or missions besides St. Cyprian's: St. Gabriel's at Great Falls in 1890, Holy Name at 11th Street Northeast in 1891, St. Anthony of Padua in Brookland in 1892, the Shrine of the Sacred Heart on 13th Street Northwest in 1901, Nativity in Brightwood in 1901, St. Martin's on North Capitol in 1902, St. Vincent de Paul on South Capitol in 1903, Holy Comforter on East Capitol in 1906, St. Francis de Sales at Langdon (the site of the old Queen's Chapel) in 1908, and by 1908 Little Flower in Bethesda and St. Margaret's at Seat Pleasant.[79]

Churches were provided for Cumberland and for at least nineteen new parishes or missions outside of urban areas. New churches were, in many instances, the result of shifting populations or local demand rather than real growth. In St. Mary's County the Jesuits opened St. Francis Xavier at St. George's Island in 1893 and Holy Angels at Avenue in 1904. In Charles County they opened Sacred Heart at La Plata in 1905 and in Prince George's County Holy Family in Woodmore in 1890 and Ascension in Bowie in 1894. In 1903 they would move their residence from White Marsh to the latter. In Calvert County missions were created at Solomons (Our Lady Star of the Sea) in 1888, at Benedict (St. Francis de Sales) in 1893, and North Beach (St. Anthony) in 1903.

In Anne Arundel County two pious sisters built a church at Dodon in 1890 called Holy Family on condition that it be entrusted to a religious order. Gibbons induced the Marists to take it. In the same county the Redemptorists at Annapolis built mission churches at Millersville and Robinson. In Montgomery County St. Peter's at Olney was opened in 1898 as a mission of Rockville. Three more mission churches were opened in Harford County: St. Mark's at Fallston in 1889, St. Paul's at Cardiff in 1905, and St. Margaret's at Bel Air in 1905.[80]

In 1900–1901 in Cumberland, a third church was built for the southern part of the city, and named St. Mary's. Also in Allegany County St. Joseph's was opened at Midland in 1892, just three miles from Lonaconing, and St. Stephen's at Grantsville in Garrett County in 1895.[81] St. Francis at Brunswick in Frederick County was completed in 1907.

Almost as many churches replaced older, smaller ones in established parishes, some long overdue. The most notable of these were St. Peter's (1889) and St Mary Mother of God (1890) in Washington and St. Patrick's (1898) in Baltimore. Particularly ambitious was the new church of St. Matthew in Washington begun in 1893 by Monsignor Thomas Sim Lee and not completed until 1913.[82] Some parishes grew so fast that the second church followed hard upon the first, as was the case with St. Paul's in Washington (1894) and St. Paul's in Baltimore (1904). Each cost about $100,000. Some second-growth churches also involved name changes. The one that replaced St. Lawrence O'Toole in Locust Point in 1890 was named Our Lady of Good Counsel. The one that replaced the mountain church near Emmitsburg in 1897 was called St. Anthony's Shrine.

Not all the first churches for new parishes in the cities were of the church-school type. A number, in fact, especially in Washington, had no schools at all. It would seem that Gibbons now left it up to the pastor of a new parish whether to build a school or not. The expense was no greater, for in the 1890s most parishes, for want of teaching brothers, merged the boys' and girls' schools. By 1908 only five parishes in Baltimore and one in Washington still had boys' schools taught by brothers. The Poles, however, proved as devoted to the parochial school as did the Germans. All Polish parishes had them. St. Stanislaus, Holy Rosary, and St. Casimir brought in the Polish Felician Sisters.[83]

A Slowdown in Institution Building

Remarkably few new institutions, other than churches and schools, appeared in these twenty years. The Sisters of Mercy built a new City Hospital in 1888–89 on the land they had purchased in 1887.[84] Georgetown University opened Georgetown University Hospital in 1898. The Good Shepherd Sisters provided an asylum for black penitents in Baltimore in 1892. To his other undertakings Father Didier added a home for newsboys in 1889 and a home for aged ladies in 1899. Father Slattery purchased an old hotel near St. Mary's Seminary and opened in 1888 St. Joseph Seminary to train Josephites, white and black. In 1890 he purchased another hotel in Walbrook for a preparatory seminary he called Epiphany Apostolic College. In 1891 he began an industrial school for black boys but moved it to Wilmington the next year. Two years later he negotiated the separation of the Josephites in America from Mill Hill in England.[85] The initiative in institution building in the archdiocese of Baltimore was still in the hands of the religious orders.

Catholic Higher Education

There was only one new academy, the Immaculata Seminary begun by the Sisters of Providence of Indiana in Washington in 1904. But more significant changes were taking place in higher education in the archdiocese of Baltimore than in any other diocese. With its schools of law and medicine Georgetown was developing into a true university. In 1893 Satolli suggested to the Jesuit general that Georgetown transfer these schools to the Catholic University, but Georgetown's president resisted the move.[86] In 1895, however, graduate schools of philosophy and social science were inaugurated at the Catholic University and opened to lay students. This move suggested to some that the time had come to provide higher education for women. On April 2, 1896, Notre Dame of Maryland was chartered as a four-year women's college, the first Catholic one in the country. Six bachelor degrees were granted in 1899.[87] In 1900 the Sisters of Notre Dame de Namur opened Trinity College near the Catholic University, the first women's college devoted totally to "post-graduate" work, by which was meant that it had no preparatory department.[88] Loyola College in Baltimore was taking more seriously its collegiate status. Several secondary schools for boys that called themselves colleges claimed to have primary, intermediate, and college departments, but the last was poorly developed in most, and hard decisions would have to be made.

Catholic Clubs

CLUBS FOR YOUNG MEN

While the growth of Catholic institutions in Gibbons' middle period was hardly impressive, lay societies, especially for young men, continued to multiply and develop in surprisingly different ways. Ireland and Keane's frequent forays into Gibbons' domain preaching temperance induced a revival of total-abstinence societies. These lent strong support in the late 1880s to a drive for high license fees in Baltimore, where 2,100 saloons could be counted.[89] Local beneficial and knightly societies continued to multiply in at least the national parishes, but the most notable developments were seen in the young men's literary associations and the national fraternal organizations.

The centennial of the archdiocese of Baltimore and the American hierarchy reinvigorated all societies but particularly the literary associations. Preparations for a torchlight parade were begun months ahead. Anticipation was heightened the evening before by a gas and electric illumination that featured an enormous gilt eagle perched above the cardinal's residence with an American flag in his beak. Then on the evening of November 12 the parade described in the headlines of the *Catholic Mirror* as "Thirty Thousand Strong—A River of Fire—The Grandest Pageant in Baltimore's History" took two and a half hours to pass the smiling cardinal.[90] Almost every society in the archdiocese could be counted in the eleven divisions.

In the course of preparation, members of the literary associations, or lyceums, discussed the possibility of a union. In February 1890 the United Catholic Literary Associations was launched.[91] At its height the UCLA counted no more than twenty affiliations, perhaps a little more than half of all such groups in Baltimore. The Germans had one or more literary societies in every parish, but only three joined the union originally and then withdrew. The Poles and Italians apparently had none. Of the eighteen societies in the directory of the UCLA of 1893, nine were still called lyceums, four literary associations, two institutes, two clubs, and one a circle. Their activities were as varied as their names.

A pastor who styled himself "Parochus" grumbled in print in 1893 that with but "a few honorable exceptions" there never existed a "more arrant humbug" than the societies that masqueraded as "literary." Billiards, "hops (saltatorial)," smokers, receptions, and picnics, were, he insisted, their principal fare, and once in a while a play.[92] In most of the calendars, in fact, the social outweighed the literary events. For many, sports became the principal activity. St. Leo's in 1890 was the first to build a parish gymnasium and call its society the St. Leo's Gymnasium and Literary Association. It became a model for others. By 1900 St. Martin's, St. John's, St. Elizabeth's, and possibly others had well-equipped gyms. Some still had libraries.

In 1899 another critic observed that pastors often judged the young men's society "an unmitigated nuisance." It starts well, he said. Interest wanes. Routine work falls on a few. The worst element often gets the upper hand. Members wander out of monthly meetings to find amusement elsewhere—the theater, the saloon. Denunciation from the pulpit brings the "end of the organization and the bright dreams of its founders." The demands of business and married life, the critic admitted, also take their toll.[93] A defender, admitting his "wicked lack of years," insisted that Catholics should enjoy the same benefits as members of the Young Men's Christian Association. The church might not need such societies, but its young men did.[94]

That fall the UCLA affiliated with the Young Men's Institute, a national Catholic organization modeled on the YMCA. It failed to infuse the new vigor its promoters had hoped for. In 1901 a supporter of the young men's associations lamented that the lyceum was now out of vogue. The allurements of dance halls and saloons, "gilded palaces, often of perdition," were unfortunately too great. Young men wanted to be "fast." While admitting the ephemeral character of such institutes, the supporter noted, with some truth, that there were in Baltimore men without any special advantages of education except those derived from membership in the literary societies who were now successful citizens and a credit to their church.[95]

A CLUB FOR THE RICH

The centennial of the archdiocese spurred the organization of a more exclusive society. The *Catholic Mirror* had complained in 1883 that wealthy Catholics reacted to invitations to join fraternal and literary societies "as if the committee had small pox."[96] It was a matter of social standing. Wealthy Catholics wanted a society similar to the prestigious Maryland Club. In 1889 the Catholic Club was organized. Among those who sought incorporation in 1891 in order to secure better lodgings were James R. Wheeler, president of the Catholic Club as well as of the Commonwealth Bank and usually grand marshall for Catholic parades, Charles J. Bonaparte, J. Thomas Scharf, the historian, Michael Jenkins, Richard McSherry, and Mark O. Shriver.[97]

Members of the Catholic Club were not only richer but older than those of the parish literary societies. Yet the club's headquarters opposite the cathedral rectory boasted a gymnasium, bowling alley, and billiards room, in addition to a library, reading room, music room, smoking room, hall for entertainments and lectures, parlors, and, in warm weather, a garden. By contrast Foley Hall of St. Martin's Parish, which housed the St. Martin's Union and the St. Martin's Literary and Dramatic Association, had a better equipped gymnasium and several bowling alleys on the first floor, smoking, reading, and meeting rooms, plus a billiards room, on the second, and a concert hall seating five hundred on the third, but apparently no library.[98] Despite its pretense to exclusivity, the Catholic Club counted four hundred members by 1893 and was willing to accommodate seven hundred.[99] Parish literary societies rarely counted more than a hundred.

CLUBS FOR THE MIDDLE CLASS

While such national fraternal and insurance organizations as the Catholic Knights of America and Emerald Beneficial Association barely held their own in the 1890s in the oldest archdiocese, the Catholic Benevolent Legion continued its remarkable growth. By 1891 it had thirty-seven councils in Maryland and more than three thousand members (thirty thousand nationally). In 1899 it counted forty-two councils and nearly seven thousand members (fifty-two thousand nationally). Though in 1902 Richard Tippett, a Baltimore attorney born in St. Mary's County, was elected the first national president from outside New York state and though the number of local councils would continue to grow, the CBL had peaked in numbers and enthusiasm in 1899. The Catholic laymen of Maryland and the District of Columbia were looking for a new type of organization.

This interest was signaled in December 1895, when the Catholic League was founded in Baltimore "to foster a spirit of patriotism among its members."[100] In 1897 recruiters for the Knights of Columbus appeared in Baltimore and Washington. The K of C, founded in New Haven, Connecticut, in 1882, differed from the CBL in significant ways. It was not parish based, though its councils were often identified with particular parishes. It accepted associate as well as insurance members. It offered degrees of membership. And most important, its goals and its principles were closely attuned to the fervent patriotism that touched most Americans at the end of the century.[101] On February 21, 1897, Baltimore Council 205, the 205th in the nation, was instituted.[102] On April 25 Washington Council 224 had its official beginning.

The order spread rapidly in Maryland and the District. By 1899 there were enough local councils in Baltimore to form a state council. In 1901 a council was formed in Cumberland and by 1908 councils existed in Westernport, Mount Savage, and Hagerstown, as well as others in Baltimore.[103] By 1899 there were five councils in the District of Columbia. Keane Council 353, which counted many of the faculty of the Catholic University, was particularly active. The national body was persuaded to endow a chair in American history at the University.[104]

The Ancient Order of Hibernians also experienced a phenomenal growth in the archdiocese in the 1890s. By 1900 there were twenty-one divisions in the state, eleven of them in Baltimore, with 1,652 members.[105] Most of the others were in Allegany County. There were also nine divisions or more in the District. While the K of C aligned itself with the Maryland Pilgrims Association to celebrate Maryland Pilgrims Day, the AOH stole the commemoration of the Battle of North Point (September 12) from the Junior Order of United American Mechanics, a nativistic society.[106]

Still another organization that took root at this time, and in terms of future developments the most important, was the Holy Name Society. The branch established at St. Dominic's in Washington in 1878 by the founder in America, Father Charles H. McKenna, OP, was the second in the country. A Roman prohibition of more than one branch in a city except by special dispensation was not rescinded until 1895.[107] Seven or eight, notwithstanding, had by then been established in Baltimore itself, the first by Father Starr at Corpus Christi in January 1891.[108] By 1908 Baltimore counted no fewer than twenty branches, and the society had spread to other parts of Maryland and the District.

The Holy Name Society was a devotional organization whose principal goal was to combat swearing and promote frequent communion among men. By 1908, however, it had assumed many of the social features of the beneficial and literary societies. But because it had none of their impedimenta, because it was more easily controlled by the pastor, and because it proved more congenial to men than the Sodality of the Blessed Virgin Mary, it soon provided the readiest vehicle for organizing large numbers of males at the parish level.

Many who joined one of the above-mentioned organizations joined all, or nearly all. A good example was Patrick J. Haltigan, chief clerk of the House of Representatives, whose stentorian voice would become a trademark of national Democratic conventions. Haltigan was an active member of the AOH, K of C, Third Order of St. Dominic, St. Vincent de Paul Society, and Holy Name Society, besides the Elks and the Washington Chamber of Commerce.[109]

The CBL and K of C, and to a slightly less extent the AOH and Holy Name Society, were essentially middle-class organizations and, as such, effective agencies for assimilation. That was the principal reason Gibbons encouraged them, especially the K of C. Before World War I, and well beyond in some instances, the Bohemians, Poles, Lithuanians, and Italians would have little to do with them.

CLUBS FOR THE IMMIGRANTS

The new immigrants stayed with their own societies, whether religious or secular. On the Fourth of July in 1892 the St. Wenceslaus Society and St. George Sharpshooters of St. Wenceslaus Parish marched with the Bohemian Pleasure Club and the Sixth Ward Bohemian Democratic Club to Standard Park for a picnic, while the Unione Fratellanza, the Society of Christopher Columbus, and the Society of Francesco Crispi (an anticlerical but popular statesman of Italy) marched to Darley Park.[110]

The Italians became increasingly attached to their parish societies. That of St. Anthony of Padua was formed after the Baltimore fire of 1904, the result of a vow to the saint in the event St. Leo's Church was spared.[111] The Blessed Sacrament Society was equally popular. Baltimore's Italians moved easily between religious and secular societies. Michele Vicari, president of the Vicari Fruit Company, belonged to the Unione Fratellanza and the Christopher Columbus, Francesco Crispi, and the Blessed Sacrament Societies. All had large delegations at St. Leo's for his funeral.[112]

CLUBS FOR WOMEN

There were before the 1890s a few women's beneficial societies, like that of St. Barbara at Fourteen Holy Martyrs, but they received little attention in the press or pulpit. In the 1890s Catholic women began to promote national organizations in the archdiocese of Baltimore. The most popular was the Catholic Women's Benevolent Legion, like but distinct from the CBL. Maryland Council No. 12 was organized in 1895. By the end of 1901 there were twelve councils of the CWBL in Baltimore with some eight hundred members.[113] The Father Walter Council No. 120 was in 1898 the first in Washington. That same year the Carroll Institute organized a ladies auxiliary. In 1899 the state council of the Catholic Knights of America for the District of Columbia voted to admit women and persuaded the parent body at its national convention to follow suit.[114] The AOH and Knights of St. John also created ladies auxiliaries. The former were well represented in Baltimore.

Nativism and Progressivism

It was no coincidence that the creation of Catholic societies accelerated as nativism reared and roared again. The American Protective Association, founded in 1887 to oppose anew the growing power of the Church of Rome, did not greatly trouble Maryland Catholics until it circulated in Baltimore in 1894 the bogus Jesuit oath to destroy all Protestants. When the Republicans swept both city and state elections in 1895 for the first time since Reconstruction, Maryland Catholics generally blamed the APA, which had, among other things, publicized the Catholic connections of the Democratic candidates.[115] The following year the *Catholic Mirror* ran an exposé of the APA in Maryland, to which it later credited the organization's precipitous decline.[116]

The APA assault had obscured for many Catholics the true character of the elections of 1895, which marked in reality the stirrings of reform, the beginnings of the Progressive Movement in Maryland. Even Catholics had complained of the mismanagement and corruption of the Gorman-Rasin machine that had come to power in the 1870s, and this despite the fact that Rasin, the city boss, was married to a Catholic and had chosen as his chief lieutenant John J. "Sonny" Mahon, the son of immigrant parents and an active member of St. Vincent's Parish.[117] James Ryder Randall, whose conservative column enlivened the *Catholic Mirror* for many years, guessed correctly that in "punishing Gorman some of our Catholic brethren carried the revolt farther than they intended."[118]

Among the "Catholic brethren" could certainly be counted Charles J. Bonaparte, who would become the acknowledged leader of Maryland Progressivism. Randall probably also had in mind the cardinal archbishop and the devoutly Catholic sons of Arunah S. Abell, founder of the Baltimore *Sun*, whose editorial views usually reflected Gibbons'. Increasingly Baltimore's cardinal would speak in support of reform goals and be credited in great measure with their success. He was particularly outspoken in his promotion of city planning, public health, consumer protection, the regulation of sweat shops, and the prevention of the disfranchisement of Maryland blacks.[119] On the last-named issue he broke with the *Sun*, which judged disfranchisement a reform measure that would eliminate fraud and corruption in politics. "If he [the black] is indeed ignorant," Gibbons was quoted, "educate him; if he be corrupt and venal, punish him . . . , but above all things, let us not condemn the righteous for the sins of the unrighteous."[120] Gibbons also spoke out in favor of local option with regard to the sale of spirits when liquor dealers made it appear that he was opposed to such an enactment.[121]

Baltimore Catholics were prominent in the Progressive Movement, though not in the same proportion to their numbers as were Episcopalians and Jews. Besides Gibbons and Bonaparte, the Catholics whose names appeared most frequently among the reformers were attorney Robert W. Biggs, architect William M. Ellicott, attorney Thomas Foley Hiskey, Judge Charles W. Heuisler, Dr. Charles O'Donovan, and banker James R. Wheeler.[122] The Catholic wards were surprisingly warm in their support of Progressive candidates. Only Sonny Mahon's Ninth consistently supported the machine's choices.

Unlike Ireland and Keane, who proudly acknowledged their Republican allegiance, Gibbons kept his party preference to himself. In national elections he tended to vote Republican but in local ones Democratic.[123] The friendships he cultivated in Republican circles nationally could not have been easily missed. At the same time, his closest friends in Baltimore, with the exception of Bonaparte, were Democrats, as were most of the Catholic elite. Gibbons' political principles were, like those of Ireland, Keane, and Bonaparte, of the Mugwump variety, evidencing a reform mentality that disliked messy politics as well as power based on mass appeal. Such an attitude would not have been shared by Sydney E. Mudd, a Catholic and a force in the Republican Party by reason of the black Catholic vote he commanded in the southern counties.[124] Gibbons was undoubtedly closer in his political philosophy to Catholic aristocrats than to Catholic workingmen of Maryland. The former were as devoted to property and power, neither of which they had any intention of surrendering, as to democratic principles. While Gibbons was more concerned with power than property, his basic conservatism can be best appreciated in his treatment of those for whom the acquisition of property was, ultimately, of greater concern than that of power: the Catholic laity, organized labor, women, and blacks.

Conservatism of the Cardinal

None would have expected Gibbons to question the hierarchical character of his church. Many, however, would have expected greater enthusiasm about the plans of the laity for a gathering similar to the Catholic congresses of Europe to be held in conjunction with the celebration of the centennial of the American hierarchy. Henry Brownson, son of the indomitable Orestes, and Peter Foy especially were upset by his delaying tactics, his demand for an episcopal committee to review all papers, and his attempt to have a priest deliver the paper on the independence of the Holy See. Gibbons finally allowed Bonaparte to make the latter presentation.[125] When the request was made again in 1893 for a lay congress to be held in conjunction with the Columbian Exposition, Gibbons wanted to postpone a response until the meeting of the archbishops when, as he told Ireland, the latter could "try to kill it, or that failing, to determine that this should be the last Congress."[126] It would, in fact, be the last lay Catholic congress.

The reputation he had acquired as a friend of the workingman Gibbons sought to sustain in the interviews he often granted concerning labor problems. While he would support any reasonable demand short of attacking property legally acquired, he told a reporter of the London *Chronicle* in 1894, he opposed strikes and boycotts except for "desperate" causes.[127] The same views reached a larger audience in an article entitled "Organized Labor" published in *Putnam's Monthly* in 1907.[128]

In practice Gibbons often disappointed his admirers in the unions. In 1908 the newly organized Employers' Association declared a lockout against the Building Trades of Washington. In October the latter's grievance committee asked Gibbons through his chancellor that nonunion men imported by the association not be employed in the construction of a proposed parish school.[129] The union sent at once the full statement Gibbons requested and waited three months before writing again. The chancellor replied that it was too late; the contract was now signed. If the cardinal had been notified earlier, the chancellor quoted Gibbons as saying, he would have conferred with the pastor in question.[130]

Some ten years later the United Building Trades of Baltimore would appeal to Gibbons as a "friend of labor" to support their strike against Frainie Brothers, who were renovating the cathedral rectory. On the request Gibbons wrote simply: "Ack[nowledged] July 28 & shown to Frainie."[131] The year before, he would write to Charles A. Schwab, the Catholic president of Bethlehem Steel, which had acquired the factory at Sparrows Point, to ask that he make the gift of land and fund a church at a new location under consideration. "I do not have to urge that a Catholic church, especially in places made up of workingmen, is a tremendous power for conservatism, virtue, and industry."[132] The implication could hardly have been missed.

While Gibbons complimented women also for their virtue and industry, he and his diocesan organ made no attempt to hide their disdain for feminists. In 1892 the cardinal told the St. Agnes Reading Circle that there were certain things that women could not do, like preach in church, and that he was unalterably opposed to the franchise for women, for with it the woman "would unsex herself."[133] Women's rights socialites Gibbons branded in a 1900 address entitled "The Christian Woman" as "the worst enemies of the female sex."[134] As agitation for the women's suffrage amendment gathered momentum, Gibbons' list of appeals to the fair sex to remain upon her pedestal became embarrassingly long.

Catholic blacks of the archdiocese of Baltimore, who included a greater number of professionals than those in other parts of the country, were increasingly restive at restraints encountered at every turn. Washington blacks were particularly prominent at the five Afro-American Catholic Congresses held between 1889 and 1894.[135] At the first, held in Washington some nine months before the larger Catholic congress, Gibbons counseled moderation and harmony.[136] Before the last, a report was issued citing instances of discrimination against blacks throughout the country, including Washington and Baltimore. When questioned about their being relegated to backless benches in the cathedral, Gibbons blamed the trustees.[137] At the last congress, held in Baltimore, Gibbons again counseled "wisdom, forbearance, prudence, and discretion."[138] In 1898 one of the leaders of the black congress movement wrote a letter to the *Washington Star* insisting that Gibbons was, as the pastor of St. Augustine's paraphrased it, "a southern sympathizer [who] never cared for the colored people."[139]

A heated debate was provoked in the oldest archdiocese by a sensational sermon delivered by Archbishop Ireland at St. Augustine's in 1890 calling for the abolition of the color line.[140] Gibbons felt obliged to issue a letter in which he suggested that the two great needs for the blacks were religious education and instruction in those trades "best suited to their inclination." Until they had achieved greater progress through these, he declared, it was "useless to deal in speculations as to their true rights."[141] That Gibbons' pronouncements against the disfranchisement of Maryland blacks in 1904 and 1909 represented no real change in these beliefs would be made apparent in 1918 when a "Committee of Fifteen" seeking to end discrimination would call upon him to favor the admittance of blacks into the K of C and other Catholic societies. On this request would be placed the gist of his reply: "Card[inal] of opinion after years of experience that interests of Colored Man served best by forming societies of his own."[142]

A Veneration Notwithstanding

A remarkable facet of the life of Cardinal Gibbons was the esteem and even affection he continued to command from those whose expectations he had disappointed most. This was due partly to an exceptional ability to coat unpalatable judgments with soothing words and to couch harsh dicta in disarming rhetoric. If he was, moreover, aristocratic in his views, he could be, when occasion demanded, democratic in his manner. He could spend a Fourth of July, for example, with the miners of Mount Savage and the next day leave in a private railroad car with a Republican governor of Maryland to visit another Republican high in the national organization. One of Gibbons' admirers claimed: "No American leader has so few [enemies]."[143]

But this admirer was also a critic. Rev. John Talbot Smith of New York, an astute observer of the Catholic scene, gave other reasons for Gibbons' unparalleled success as a leader as early as 1895. "Ruling a diocese where public opinion is of the quiescent sort," he contended, "where agitation is unknown, where popular feeling has never burst into tumult since the war, he has enjoyed a leisure and routine which enables leaders to think out social problems without anxiety, and to present the solution to society at the right moment and in the most taking fashion. The Cardinal has, in consequence, fewer mistakes to his credit than most churchmen." But to have made no enemies and no egregious blunders, Smith also maintained, was to pursue an overly cautious course. "It is safe to say that the Cardinal will pass to his reward with the same honor that has attended him in the episcopate. He is not personally ambitious, but he will not allow the brilliancy of the past to be tarnished by taking risks in the future." Having said all that, Smith was willing to concede that the red hat had "found a perfect fit in Baltimore."[144]

12   A Twilight Aura

AN AGE ENDED ALMOST without notice. On June 29, 1908, Pope Pius X issued the constitution *Sapienti Consilio* for the purpose of restructuring his curia. Among other changes, he removed American Catholics from the jurisdiction of the Congregation of the Propaganda Fide and placed them under the Consistorial Congregation. The lifting of missionary status after so many years made little difference in day-to-day affairs. More demanding would be the application of the new code of canon law of 1918. The cardinal archbishop of Baltimore would have to reorganize his board of consultors and make it keep minutes.[1]

The observance of the hundredth year of archiepiscopal status in Baltimore in 1908 was overshadowed by the celebration of the centennial of the creation of the diocese of New York. Gibbons readily accepted the invitation of Archbishop John M. Farley to speak on the occasion. His friendship with Farley precluded any discomfort in 1911, when the latter also received a red hat.[2] But when he heard that Archbishop William Henry O'Connell of Boston, an enemy of the Sulpicians, was named to the college of cardinals at the same time, Gibbons is said to have wept.[3]

Modernism

The Catholic Church in the United States entered the new age with a sense of unease occasioned by the papal condemnation of modernism the year before. *Longinqua Oceani* and *Testem Benevolentiae* had, of course, warned the American church against divergent tendencies. *Pascendi Dominici Gregis* renewed the warning when it saw a causal relationship between Americanism and modernism, especially in the promotion of the active or social virtues. With more truth it might have pointed to the demand of both ideologies that the church assimilate new ideas and try new methods.[4] Only a few teachers in a few American seminaries and universities, however, were even conversant with the biblical and historical controversies in Europe that occasioned the condemnation.

In March 1908 Gibbons presided over a quarterly conference of the clergy at which the presenter theorized that modernism did not encompass the idea of doctrinal development as taught by Vincent of Lerins in the fifth century and Cardinal Newman in the nineteenth.[5] But allusions to modernism thereafter were more cautious. Baltimore had already produced one of the only three authenticated modernists in the United States, and antimodernists were pointing fingers at the American Sulpicians and professors at the Catholic University.[6]

Baltimore's modernist was John Slattery, the Josephite provincial. Discouraged in his work among the blacks and upset over the direction the church was taking, Slattery sought respite in Europe in 1902. There he studied under Adolph Harnack and was befriended by Albert Houtin. In 1906 he returned to America, announced that his priesthood had "dropped" from him, and began to promote the teachings of the modernists.[7] But none of his modernist views, so far as the cardinal could tell, rubbed off on his former subjects in Baltimore.

With the Sulpicians it was the superiors who were uneasy about some of their subjects. The Society had experienced a remarkable growth in the United States at the end of the century, assuming control of the seminaries of Boston (1884), New York (1896), and San Francisco (1906). Under Alphonse Magnien the American Sulpicians had imbibed an even greater openness to new ideas and fresh approaches. When Magnien, the last of the French superiors in American, died in 1902, he was replaced by the scion of an old Maryland family, Edward R. Dyer.[8] At Dunwoodie, the New York seminary, six talented members of the Society began a journal, the *New York Review*, which seemed a harbinger of a new age of Catholic theological inquiry in America.[9] In 1906 five of the six, disillusioned by the failure of the Paris superiors to support their work and to create an American province, became priests of the archdiocese of New York. With the condemnation of modernism the *Review*, with its decidedly modernist slant, was forced to cease publication.

The sixth, Joseph Bruneau, who remained a Sulpician, eventually returned to Baltimore. In 1910 Gibbons was directed by Cardinal Raffaele Merry del Val, papal secretary of state, to inquire into Bruneau's writings. Gibbons defended the orthodoxy of Bruneau in particular and of the Sulpicians in general. At the same time, however, he supported those who wished to rid the Catholic University of a teacher of scripture, Rev. Henry A. Poels, who was under suspicion in Rome. Poels left the university to engage in social work in his native Holland but he resented the role played in his dismissal by Gibbons.[10]

A Remarkable Recovery

Despite the shadows modernism momentarily cast on St. Mary's Seminary and the Catholic University, both experienced a new growth in the second decade of the century. The university recovered remarkably from a decade and more of misfortunes and poor administration. Thomas J. Conaty, Keane's successor, unable to restore harmony and health to the institution, was eased out by Gibbons and others to make room for Denis O'Connell.[11] However republican and liberal O'Connell may have been before *Testem Benevolentiae*, as rector he proved an autocrat and something of an integrist.[12] In 1904 Thomas E. Waggaman, treasurer of the university, head of the St. Vincent de Paul Society for the District, and manager of Peter's Pence for America, went into bankruptcy and nearly carried the university with him. Gibbons, with remarkable energy, rallied the bishops and others to its support and saved the institution he had come to love.[13] Financial necessity induced it to open its doors to undergraduates in 1905. A growing number of religious orders ringed the Catholic University with houses of studies. Bishops sent priests they had earmarked as chancellors, superintendents of education, and heads of charities to study there. When the National Catholic Welfare Conference would be organized in 1919–21, it would draw heavily upon the Catholic University for its personnel and paperwork. Much of this could be credited to Monsignor (later Bishop) Thomas J. Shahan, who succeeded O'Connell as rector in 1909.[14]

The Sulpicians also played a role in the development of the Catholic University. When the decision was made in 1905 to open an undergraduate seminary there, the Society considered the possibility of transferring the overcrowded St. Mary's Seminary to its campus. Complications developed in 1911 when St. Charles College, next to Doughoregan Manor, was totally destroyed by fire. It was decided to rebuild near Catonsville on land acquired earlier for a house of philosophy. Ultimately St. Mary's Seminary under John F. Fenlon, Dyer's successor, sent its more promising upperclassmen to the seminary the Sulpicians themselves built at the Catholic University in 1918–19.[15]

Demise of the Catholic Mirror

In 1908 the *Catholic Mirror* ceased publication. Though moderate to progressive in its views, it was a victim of modernism only in the sense that it was part of a pattern of lay surrender to diocesan control of the Catholic press in America about the time of the condemnation. Under the editorship of William J. O'Brien, politican and litterateur, from 1884 to 1892, the *Mirror* had known its best days.[16] Thereafter its progress was erratic. Under a priest editor, Matthew O'Keefe, 1898–1901, it called itself the official organ but wasn't really. Only on rare occasions did Gibbons intrude himself upon its operation and editorial policies. When in 1889, for example, it declared the temporal power of the pope "neither essential nor indispensable," Gibbons ordered O'Brien never to publish on the subject again without consulting him.[17]

When it finally died of inanition in 1908, the *Mirror* announced that His Eminence had taken steps to put out another paper in which the clergy would play a more prominent role.[18] The first issue of the *Baltimore Catholic Review* did not appear until November 29, 1913, almost five and a half years later. The days of lively Catholic weeklies would now be reduced to a memory in Baltimore as in the rest of the country.[19]

Tributes Unparalleled

Baltimore was without a Catholic weekly at the time of the greatest acclamation paid its cardinal archbishop. Cumulatively the tributes showered on James Gibbons had few parallels even in the secular history of the nation. Each return from abroad—in 1901, 1903, 1908, 1911, and 1914—was made a civic event. In 1901 the *Baltimore American* claimed that never had any citizen received such a welcome home.[20] The most remarkable outpouring was the occasion of his fiftieth year as a priest. In the national capital business virtually came to a standstill on June 6, 1911, as almost every important official made the trip to Baltimore to honor the cardinal. Among the speakers were the president and a former president. "Probably the world never witnessed," said the *Washington Post*, "a more generous outburst of enthusiasm for one with whose theological principles many of the participants are at variance."[21] At the time of his fiftieth year as a bishop in 1918, messages came from all parts of the world, but the celebration had to be postponed till early 1919 because of an epidemic of influenza. The mass in Washington was attended by two cardinals, twelve archbishops, fifty-eight bishops, and the leading Catholic laymen.[22]

Gibbons was on intimate terms with every president from Grover Cleveland to William Howard Taft, but especially with Theodore Roosevelt. Though his relationship with Woodrow Wilson was not so cordial, all sought his advice on matters touching the Catholic Church. His public utterances always claimed close attention. As he grew older, they became more frequent and more arresting. His New Year sermons came to be awaited eagerly.

The Cardinal Speaks

On matters of war and peace Gibbons was particularly eloquent. In 1896 he joined the other two English-speaking cardinals, Herbert Vaughan of Westminster and Michael Logue of Armagh, in a call for a permanent tribunal of arbitration to settle disputes between the United States and Great Britain.[23] In 1906 he participated at the Twelfth International Conference for International Arbitration.[24] At a requiem for the casualties on the battleship *Maine* in the Baltimore cathedral, he denounced the war-mongering of the yellow journals. "The nation is too brave, too strong, too powerful, and too just to engage in an unrighteous and precipitate war," he insisted. More credit would be won "by calm deliberation and masterly inactivity than by recourse to war."[25] Gibbons' support of the Spanish-American War was lukewarm at best. In his New Year sermon of 1901, he deplored the arms race in Europe and denounced war and militarism as unchristian.[26]

With World War I, however, it was different. The cardinal aligned himself with the proponents of preparedness rather than the pacifists, supporting military conscription as a deterrent.[27] "The primary duty of a citizen is loyalty to country," he declared. "It is exhibited by an absolute and unreserved obedience to his country's call."[28] When war came, Gibbons accepted the honorary chairmanship of the League of National Unity, whose purpose was a more vigorous prosecution of the war. At Camp Meade he told the soldiers they would be proud of the wounds they carried back. "Go forth to battle and victory, and God be with you!"[29]

In the matter of American imperialism Gibbons likewise began well but ended badly. In 1904 he signed a petition in favor of independence for the Philippines. For this he was taken to task by Roosevelt. Thereafter he opposed resolutely any attempt to lift colonial status from those distant, restless islands. His letter to the American bishops at the request of President Taft in 1912 was in part responsible for the original defeat of the Jones Act with its promise of early independence.[30]

Though many of Gibbons' pronouncements mirrored public opinion, his statements in 1904–8 to defend the King of Belgium against charges of exploitation of the natives of the Congo proved ill advised.[31] Small success also attended his defense of the peace note of Pope Benedict XV in 1917, which seemed to many to favor the Central Powers.[32] Not a few Catholics remained cool to Gibbons' initial defense of the president's conduct of Mexican affairs. When Wilson failed to protest the anticlerical constitution of Mexico in 1917, however, Gibbons' surprising criticism of the government proved unpopular among Protestants.[33]

On domestic matters Gibbons opposed the Seventeenth, Eighteenth, and Nineteenth Amendments and such Progressive measures as the initiative, referendum, and recall. While he declared that Prohibition would be a "national disaster," he favored high license fees for Baltimore and local option for the rest of the state, especially the Catholic counties in the south. On occasion he spoke louder by silence. To a delegation of prominent Catholic suffragettes from several eastern cities, headed by Mrs. Edwin F. Abell of Baltimore, he listened politely and responded: "I will reflect upon these matters."[34] When the Nineteenth Amendment was passed, however, he urged women to vote. "How are we to know which side is right," a woman wrote from Bardstown, Kentucky, "unless we are convinced by some able & well instructed man like you?" On the letter Gibbons wrote simply: "Declined."[35]

Yet he supported many of the national Progressive goals. To an early environmentalist he wished every success in the promotion of Roosevelt's program of conservation. In a hundred years, he observed, the United States had squandered more of its natural resources than had the nations of Europe in their centuries of growth. "Mother Earth is not only a fruitful mother, she is also a grateful mother and repays her children for every kindness and tenderness."[36]

Many of the public statements of Baltimore's cardinal were designed to soften the wrath of fellow Catholics who felt themselves the victims of bigotry or discrimination. He was discomfited by the "petulant complaints, and sweeping and uncharitable denunciations" against which Charles Bonaparte had warned his coreligionists in 1889.[37] At Madison Square Garden in 1916, however, Gibbons found himself powerless to quiet an audience aroused by Cardinal O'Connell's ringing denunications of a recrudescent nativism.[38] Gibbons' initial coolness toward the American Federation of Catholic Societies, organized in 1901 with the strong support of several bishops as well as the *Catholic Mirror*, was due in large part to a belief shared by other bishops that its promoters had in mind a militant Catholic party. To Ireland, Gibbons confided his fear that such a coalition would "unite the neutral population . . . against us."[39]

No Melting Pot

National and international concerns pressed upon Gibbons at a time when his see city also craved attention. Not only was Baltimore being industrialized but its industries were being absorbed by giant national trusts. It was fast becoming a city of branch offices tributary to New York and Chicago, where concern for its social health was as remote as the distance between the cities. In Baltimore itself the gap between the unwashed and the well scrubbed was widening. The new immigrants now outnumbered the old and were arriving in unprecedented numbers.[40] To his dying day Gibbons believed in the efficacy of the melting pot, but with *Testem Benevolentiae* he had lowered the flame.[41]

In response to a request from the Holy See for information on Catholic immigrants, Gibbons reported in 1913 that there were in Baltimore twenty thousand Poles, eight thousand Bohemians, and twenty-five hundred Lithuanians, all in compact communities with their own churches, priests, and schools. The numbers may have been a little low. The two thousand Italians in Baltimore, mostly from Cefalù in Sicily, he reported, were scattered over the city and more difficult to attend. The same was true of the two thousand Italians in Washington. The Germans and Irish he did not enumerate because he considered them already assimilated.[42]

The cardinal did not tell Rome that the Italians in particular were the targets of proselytizing. In 1904 Francesco Guglielmi, a Catholic priest turned Protestant minister, began a Methodist church in Little Italy.[43] When the pastor of St. Leo's, Pasquale di Paolo, received an anonymous death threat in 1906, Guglielmi was naturally blamed.[44] In 1909 Gibbons persuaded German Pallotine Fathers from Italy to take charge of St. Leo's. In 1915 they brought in Pallotine Sisters to staff an Italian orphanage they opened. In 1917 the Pallotine Fathers also assumed control of St. John the Baptist on Paca Street, which Gibbons had obtained from the Lithuanians for the Italians living in the area of the Lexington Market.[45]

In 1913, not long after his report to Rome, he appointed Father Nicholas De Carlo to found a church for the Italians of Washington. De Carlo immediately ran into difficulties. None of the pastors, because of a general anti-Italian bias, particularly among the Irish, wanted an Italian church within the borders of his parish. For fear the Italians would be won over by the Methodists, the pastor of St. Patrick's, William T. Russell, finally agreed to the erection of a church in the northeastern corner of his parish provided it were succursal.[46] The cornerstone for Holy Rosary at 3rd and F Streets

Northwest was finally laid in 1919. It would be dedicated as a national church in 1923.

A problem peculiar to the Italians, as Russell pointed out, was that secular priests who came from Italy to serve their compatriots were soon attending more affluent English-speaking Catholics. Data concerning Italian priests requested by the Consistorial Congregation in 1919 revealed that only three of the seven in the archdiocese were serving their countrymen.[47] Two of the three soon moved on, leaving only De Carlo.

The three Polish churches in southeast Baltimore and two in the Curtis Bay area were able to absorb the growing number of Polish immigrants. On at least two occasions, one in 1913 and one in 1915, the Independent Polish Catholic Church of Holy Cross took halting steps toward reconciliation. On the first occasion, however, the board of directors informed the cardinal that two hundred members opposed such a move, and "*vox populi, vox dei.*"[48] All overtures were ultimately rejected because Gibbons did not wish to assume the enormous debt of the church and the closest Polish pastors did not want a rival parish.

Though the nationalist/clericalist split within the Polish communities became more pronounced throughout the country, under Father Barabasz and the Franciscan Conventuals the clericalists easily gained the ascendancy in Baltimore. Barabasz died in 1914. In 1916 Gibbons finally found an able successor in the thirty-year-old Stanislaus A. Wachowiak, whom he named pastor of Holy Rosary. For the next fifty years and more Wachowiak's presence would dominate Baltimore's Polonia.

The Poles were also well served by Rev. Paul J. Sandalgi, a native of Odessa in Russia and the son of a Syro-Armenian father and a French and Polish noblewoman. Coming to Baltimore by way of Louvain and Fribourg, he was ordained in 1909 and assigned to the polyglot parish of St. Athanasius. There he served not only the Slavic groups of the Roman rite in Curtis Bay but also the oriental-rite Catholics who settled there and in other parts of Baltimore. For the Ukrainians he helped establish SS. Peter and Paul in Curtis Bay in 1910 and St. Michael's in southeast Baltimore in 1913.[49] Gibbons was as upset as any of the American bishops by the coming of oriental-rite Uniate Catholics with their married clergy and variant liturgy. By 1894 the archbishops had persuaded Rome to allow none of their married priests to live in America. Despite the reaction of Gibbons, Ireland, and others to the Germans' demand for special status, they raised no objection whatsoever in 1907 to the appointment of a bishop for all Ruthenians and Ukrainians living in the United States.[50] In 1913 they were removed from Gibbons' jurisdiction and placed under Bishop Soter Ortynski in Philadelphia. Sandalgi continued to serve the oriental-rite Catholics when the need arose.[51]

The new immigrants recreated the farming villages of Europe on cobblestones and concrete. An unsuccessful attempt was made by the National Slavonic Society to settle Slavs, mostly Czechs and Slovaks, in St. Mary's County in 1911–14 to grow produce for a prospective home for the elderly and orphan asylum there.[52] Many of Baltimore's Slavs and Italians moved to the countryside in the planting and harvest seasons. But few, if any, stayed. A symbol of the new immigrant's ascendancy over the old was the Redemptorists' agreement in 1917 to sell St. Alphonsus to the growing Lithuanian congregation. The Lithuanians, as already noted, surrendered St. John the Baptist to the Italians.

The eastern Europeans and Italians of Baltimore proved unusual in their ability to acquire their own homes. Following the example first set by the Germans under Redemptorist direction in the 1830s, they formed building and loan associations. The Poles could claim twenty such by 1914.[53] One of the most successful was the St. Casimir's Savings and Loan Association founded in 1911. The Polish pastors often acted as bankers but were required after the commotions of 1904 to send the chancellor lists of depositors with their annual reports.[54] Unique, perhaps, to Baltimore's Italian community was the absence of the padrone banker. In 1914 the Colombo Savings and Loan Association opened in Little Italy as the first for Italians. Others soon followed. Thomas D'Alesandro, Jr., was a charter member of the President Street Savings and Loan.[55]

In 1910 the Immigrants and Sailors Protective Association of the Archdiocese of Baltimore was finally organized to help the newly arrived. Father Francis Pyznar, pastor of St. Stanislaus, was president. It opened a home at Locust Point, where newcomers were offered temporary shelter, help in finding relatives, and legal aid. Many were saved from deportation.[56]

Catholic Social Service

Living and working conditions for the Slavs and Italians (and Russian Jews) of Baltimore were considerably worse, as a result of industrialization, than for the earlier immigrants and urban poor. "Filth is most marked among the Italians, Poles, and negros," the Health Department reported at the end of the first decade of the century.[57] In education (except vocational) and the care of its delinquents and dependent minors, the Catholic Church in Baltimore had an excellent record, but in matters of health and hygiene it was laggard. Only City (Mercy) Hospital had a ward for immigrants, "absolutely unventilated." Health inspection in Catholic schools led to mass vaccinations, and vermin slips were handed out in several languages.[58] Infant mortality was high among the new immigrants, especially the Poles. In 1920 Father Wachowiak reported burials of 96 adults and 172 children—a not atypical year. The other Polish parishes reported like proportions.

To Rev. William J. Kerby of the Catholic University Gibbons boasted in 1903: "In my own diocese we are happily blessed by Catholic organizations with ends so varied as to leave no human wants unsatisfied, no human ills unalleviated."[59] There were, as a matter of fact, even more human wants unsatisfied than those reported by the Health Department. The Italian and Slavic immigrants were the principal beneficiaries of the program of social service developed by Maryland Catholics in the first two decades of the century, a wide ranging program that incorporated many features of the social gospel and settlement house movements launched a decade or two earlier under Protestant or secular auspices. Though several sisterhoods had pioneered in such activities, lay organizations became increasingly involved about 1910, the inspiration and energy often supplied by individual members.

THE LAITY IN SOCIAL SERVICE

In Maryland the St. Vincent de Paul Society was, without doubt, the most effective organizer, and its driving spirit in Baltimore was its president Robert Biggs, an attorney and sometime politician. For a quarter century its members had visited needy Catholic families as well as jails, almshouses, and hospitals. In 1901 Gibbons requested the society to collaborate with the local Charitable Organization Society. At the same time it worked with city welfare agencies to promote the passage of a juvenile court bill. One of its members, Charles H. Heuisler, drafted the bill and was named judge of the juvenile court in 1902. In 1906 the Baltimore Council began a summer camp for poor children at Cloud Cap, which had to move when the Sulpicians repossessed the property for a new St. Charles. Members of the St. Camillus Society, made up of seminarians from St. Mary's, cooperated with the St. Vincent de Paul Society in its visitation program.[60]

Contact with other organizations convinced Biggs of the need for greater cooperation and coordination and a trained and salaried staff. In 1907 a central office opened under the management of a woman social worker, the first such Catholic office for family social work in the country. Its principal activities were family relief, child placement, visitations, summer work, and legal aid.[61]

Beginning in 1911 the Particular Council of Baltimore met annually to hear the reports of the parish conferences and other Catholic agencies and organizations under the central office. By December 1917 there were thirty conferences with more than three hundred members, eight women's auxiliaries, and fourteen other bodies, such as the Young Catholic's Friend Society, Dolan Children's Aid Society, and Cathedral Charitable Relief Society. Included also were three settlement houses and three day nurseries.[62]

Almost equal in energy were the Washington conferences of the society. The Particular Council of the District, for example, sponsored the Good Samaritan League and its home for discharged prisoners and derelicts founded in 1894 by William F. Downey, probably the first halfway house in the archdiocese.[63] In 1909 the society in Washington established a Catholic Home Bureau and in 1919 created also a central office.

About 1910 lay groups in Baltimore began to organize settlement houses and day nurseries. Copying non-Catholic models, the settlement houses provided both instruction and recreation primarily for immigrants, and the day nurseries relief for working mothers. The Gibbons Guild settlement house was begun in 1911 by the Ladies of Charity of SS. Philip and James Parish, who were first organized in 1907. In 1916 it added a day nursery. In 1914 the pastor of SS. Philip and James founded the Catholic Settlement Association.[64] By then there were also the Ozanam, St. Jerome, and Curtis Bay settlement houses in Baltimore. A pioneer in the settlement house movement in Washington was a crippled member of an old Maryland family, Mary Virginia Merrick. In 1886 she had founded the Christ Child Society to provide gifts for poor children at Christmas. Gradually the work of the society expanded to include fresh air activities and wholesome food for children and in the winter convalescent care. Miss Merrick also opened a settlement house for the Italians of Washington. Branches of the Christ Child Society were planted in several cities outside of Maryland.[65]

World War I provided further impetus for settlement houses in the archdiocese. Catholic women who came together to operate a center for soldiers in Washington continued the center as a community house after the war. More ambitious was the Catholic Community House established in southeast Baltimore by the National Catholic War Council and entrusted in 1920 to the Sodality Union. It proved the most professional and successful of all the settlement houses in the archdiocese.[66]

The Sodality Union of Baltimore in 1918 also opened a home for working women called Casa Regina, despite the advice of Gibbons and others to wait until they had sufficient funds to assure success. A group of Catholic women in Washington, with Miss Nannie Riggs as chairman of the board, opened a similar house in Washington called the Martha Home.[67]

THE SISTERS IN SOCIAL SERVICE

All of these activities had been carried on before with Gibbons' blessing by three orders of sisters founded in the oldest archdiocese to serve the unaddressed needs of the poor. The oldest and most enduring was that of the Mission Helpers, Servants of the Sacred Heart.

The Mission Helpers were founded by Father Slattery, the Josephite, when Mrs. Anna Hartwell, a widow, came from New York in 1886 to serve the blacks of Baltimore. Beginning with sewing and catechetical classes, the sisters were soon visiting the blacks in jails, almshouses, and hospitals and in 1893 opened St. Peter Claver's Industrial School for girls. In 1894 Gibbons gave his permission to extend their work to whites reached by no other Catholic agencies. In 1897 they opened St. Francis Xavier's School for the Deaf. In other sees they conducted day nurseries that served as catechetical centers. Despite internal difficulties about 1906, in which Mother Hartwell was replaced by Mother Demetrias Cunningham, the Mission Helpers continued to expand.[68]

The Salesian Sisters of the Holy Eucharist were founded in 1904 by a small group of Baltimore women. St. Raphael's Institute on Hanover Street was incorporated in 1907. They had also a motherhouse in Forest Park. By 1921 there were twenty-four sisters operating a day nursery and school, an industrial school, an orphanage, and a home for working girls, for mothers and children, and for elderly women, all at St. Raphael's. By this time, however, trouble had developed with a branch house in Pittsburgh that would bring about a dissolution of the order.[69]

In 1909 Gibbons gave his permission to Katherine Dietz to found a religious community to serve the poor. The Daughters of the Eucharist wore no religious garb and were not obliged to live in community, though most did. They engaged in various types of settlement work—instruction in sewing and typing, for example. The work, however, was limited by reason of the few members they attracted.[70]

To a lesser extent older sisterhoods were drawn to these new forms of social service. The Sisters of Bon Secours began St. Martin's Day Nursery in 1907. The Holy Family Day Nursery was begun in Washington in 1916 by diocesan Ursulines, who made increasing use of the personnel of Catholic Charities of the capital.[71]

Catholic Charities

In 1910 Washington became the headquarters of the National Conference of Catholic Charities. At the prompting of Rev. William J. Kerby and Charles P. Neill, teachers of sociology and economics at the Catholic University of America, the rector, Thomas Shahan, sent out invitations to the twenty-six men most active in Catholic charities. (No women were included despite their prominence in social work.) Of the twenty-six—eight priests, one brother, and seventeen laymen—nine were from the archdiocese of Baltimore, Robert Biggs being one of the most articulate. Shahan was elected president, Kerby secretary, and William DeLacy, judge of the juvenile court of the District of Columbia, treasurer.[72] In 1920 Kerby would be succeeded by a former student, Rev. John O'Grady, who soon after would be named head of Catholic Charities in the District.

Much of the work of Catholic Charities, particularly the settlement house, was prompted by what was seen as the proselytizing efforts of Protestant counterparts. The founders of the Catholic Community House in Baltimore made no bones of the fact that "influences are at work to draw away souls from the true faith and it is to counteract these forces that the Sodality Union is entering this new field."[73] The Mission Helpers were praised for their work of protecting children from the "pernicious influence of Protestant missionaries."[74] At the same time, the clerical editor of the *Baltimore Catholic Review* believed that too much attention was being given "to what is called social service . . . putting spiritual services in the background." The task of the minister, he insisted, was salvation. One could find little in the gospel about social services "except the injunction to look after the poor."[75]

The Business Benefactors

Baltimore could claim the distinction of being "the birthplace of Catholic Charities in the United States" for more reasons than those given.[76] Among them would be the tradition of princely benefactions to the destitute. A tradition begun by Richard Bennett III, sustained by the Carrolls, and perpetuated by the Captain Kennedys and C. Oliver O'Donnells, had outstanding exemplars in Gibbons' time. One would be a close friend, Michael Jenkins, whom Gibbons would eulogize as an "uncrowned emperor among God's noblemen" at his funeral in 1915.[77] One of the children of Thomas Courtney Jenkins who had built Corpus Christi Church, he continued giving throughout his life, quietly, never in astounding amounts or for spectacular projects. To a greater extent perhaps than any of the great givers of Baltimore, he regarded wealth as a trust to be put at the disposal of the poor.[78]

The Catholic elite of Baltimore remained conspicuous in its business growth. Michael Jenkins was president of both the Merchants and Miners Transportation Company and the Safe Deposit and Trust Company. The latter became the archdiocese's bank. Catholics represented about 9 percent of the city's corporate executives, somewhat above the national average.[79] They were, perhaps, even better represented in the professions, especially law and medicine, in real estate and homebuilding, and in the military, especially the Navy. They were probably better represented in the social register than Catholics in other cities.[80] Catholic patricians joined all the right clubs. Michael Jenkins was a member of the Maryland Merchants, Elk Ridge Hunt, Green Spring Valley Hunt, University, Baltimore Country, and Bachelors Cotillion.

The two most magnanimous benefactors of the Catholic Church in Maryland in the early twentieth century, however, were men of immigrant background who had lifted themselves from penury: Frank A. Furst and Thomas J. O'Neill. As benefactors, however, they differed significantly.

Furst's family had come from Baden in Germany in 1848 when Frank was only three. After a brief exposure to the brothers at St. Michael's school, he had begun his economic career as a tobacco stripper. His first known benefaction was the only five dollars he had, which on his wedding day he gave for a home for the same brothers. His fortune in dredging, sand and gravel, and real estate came late. About 1910 he merged them all into the Arundel Corporation. From this economic base he also became a power in the Democratic party. Like Michael Jenkins, he gave away most of his money without publicity. At death, he could claim little more than a million dollars. He served as chairman of numberless financial committees for Catholic and other enterprises. Furst stood at the center of a network of Catholic businesses that hired in Catholic neighborhoods and recruited their managers from Loyola College. He would be buried from St. Cecilia's in 1934, where he had for many years passed the collection box on Sunday.[81]

Thomas O'Neill was born in County Cavan in Ireland in 1849. He came to Baltimore at age sixteen and began to work as an apprentice in a linen shop. From this modest start he built one of the most fashionable department stores in the city. Most of O'Neill's wealth, however, came from real estate. O'Neill attended mass daily and was a member of the Knights of Columbus, the Holy Name Society, and the Hibernian Society. When the great fire of 1904 threatened his store, he is said to have rushed to the Carmelite convent to beg their prayers. The fire stopped at the walls of his emporium. In his lifetime he was not the consistently generous benefactor that Frank Furst was, but the $5 million he left in 1918, aside from modest bequests to his wife, siblings, and employees, was earmarked for three Catholic enterprises. To Loyola College went $300,000 for a church. "Knowing of so many so-called charitable hospitals where God's poor receive scant treatment," he designated a third of the remainder for a free hospital. The balance was to be set aside for annuities for a cathedral church in the city of Baltimore.[82] There is no evidence that he consulted the cardinal before drawing his will. The O'Neill legacy would prove a mixed blessing for the premier see.

Funding New Churches

In the final analysis the greatest benefactors of the church were the dollar-a-day laborers who gave proportionately more on a year-to-year basis than did the wealthy. Next would come the members of the lower middle class. From these two groups came the bulk of the funding for the second-growth churches that cost $100,000 and more per church as well as for the original structures of the many new parishes in the two major cities. In 1918 Baltimore would triple its size by pushing its borders out again. Most of the new territory was empty and green, but some Catholic churches were already there and more would come.

From 1908 through 1921 eight churches would be completed for new parishes or missions in or just outside Baltimore, not including the two Ukrainian churches already mentioned. The eight were Blessed Sacrament on Old York Road in 1911, All Saints out Liberty Heights Avenue in 1912, St. Lawrence in Woodlawn in 1912, Ascension in Halethorpe in 1913, St. Rose of Lima in Brooklyn in 1914, St. Michael's in Overlea in 1914, and St. William of York in Ten Hills in 1914. Some would have humble beginnings, St. Lawrence, for example, in a barn; some more impressive, like St. William of York, a memorial church for William Lanahan, a wealthy distiller of Maryland rye. St. Rose of Lima would soon suffer the first of several calamities in its history. The first church consumed by fire, a second would replace it in 1916. Originally a mission of St. Athanasius, St. Rose would plant two missions of its own in 1919: Holy Trinity in Glen Burnie and St. Jane Frances de Chantal in Riviera Beach.[83]

In or near Washington places of worship would be provided for eight new white parishes or missions, not including the Italian church of Holy Rosary. These were St. Margaret's in Seat Pleasant in 1908, Our Lady of

Victory on Conduit Road in 1909, St. Matthias in Capitol Heights in 1911, Holy Redeemer in Kensington in 1911, Holy Redeemer in Berwyn in 1912, St. Thomas the Apostle on Woodley Road off Connecticut Avenue in 1913, Assumption at 7th and Alabama Southeast in 1916, and St. Gabriel in Petworth in 1920. The last would have a modest beginning in a K of C hut hauled from Camp Meade. Two new churches would also be opened for blacks, Incarnation in Deanwood in 1914 and Our Lady of Perpetual Help in Anacostia in 1921, and a third begun, Holy Redeemer on New York Avenue in 1920.[84]

Parish Revenue

By the end of 1920, according to the Notitiae, or annual reports, Holy Rosary in Baltimore with 10,000 Poles was the largest parish in the archdiocese. Second was Sacred Heart of Highlandtown, which with 8,269 was now the largest German parish. The third was St. Martin's, with 7,302 the largest Irish parish. St. Wenceslaus with 7,000 was the fourth. The largest parish in Washington was St. Aloysius with 5,500, mostly Irish. Close behind were Sacred Heart and St. Martin's with 5,000 each. Downtown it was a different story. Immaculate Conception had been in 1910 one of the largest parishes in the capital with 3,000 members who were 40 percent Irish, 29 percent old Maryland stock, and 20 percent German. By 1920 it had experienced an influx of former black sharecroppers. Other Washington churches viewed with alarm a changing population.[85]

With receipts totaling $95,700 St. Martin's was in 1920 the most prosperous parish in Baltimore.[86] With incomes of over $50,000 each, the Polish parishes of Holy Rosary and St. Stanislaus were doing surprisingly well. St. Leo's, by contrast, reported an income of $14,000.

By 1920 offertory collections in most parishes were bringing in almost three times as much as pew rents. At St. Martin's, for example, pew rents totalled $5,600, and offertory collections $17,400. Some $32,000, however, came from its schools and $12,600 from its June carnival. Holy Rosary derived almost $5,000 from pew rents, $12,000 in offertory collections, $2,700 in "entertainments," $9,200 from "seat offerings," $6,900 from its cemetery, and $3,600 from its schools. The Lithuanians of St. Alphonsus, on the other hand, contributed $5,000 in pew rents, less than $4,000 to the offertory collections, and $7,000 to "Shrines," but schooling was free. At St. Leo's pew rents brought only $32! The Notitiae suggest little uniformity in the sources of income. Pastors could apparently tap whatever wellsprings they chose.

There was no space on the Notitiae forms for stipends and stole fees, a considerable source of income. In 1920 the honoraria for low masses was set at $5.00 and for high masses at $25.00.[87] There were few complaints in the archdiocese of Baltimore that finances figured prominently in sermons. Over half the parishes of the see city, however, carried debts that totaled some $950,000 in 1920. At the same time, the total debts of Washington parishes came to about $580,000 and those of the country parishes to something near $100,000.

Outside the Cities

Outside the two major cities parish populations and parish revenues were, with a few exceptions, in the hundreds rather than the thousands. Excepting St. Mary's and Charles Counties, only two new parishes were created in 1908–21: St. Joan of Arc at Aberdeen, a product of the war, and St. Martin's in Gaithersburg, both in 1920. In Charles County, where the number of churches under diocesan priests was growing, St. Francis de Sales was opened for a new parish at Rock Point in 1908, St. Catherine of Alexandria for another at McConchie in 1911, and St. Mary Star of the Sea for a third at Indian Head in 1918.

St. Mary's County was surprisingly productive. Besides the new churches of St. Mary's at California in 1912 and St. James at Ridge in 1916, four parochial schools appeared where before there were none. St. James opened schools for blacks and whites, St. Peter Claver a school for blacks, and St. Michael's a school for whites, all in 1916–18. In 1909 the Jesuits opened an agricultural high school called Leonard Hall, which they gave over the following year to the Xaverian Brothers.[88] As early as 1916 plans were being laid for an industrial school for blacks in the county.

Despite these rare accomplishments, Catholic life in St. Mary's County continued much as it had for three hundred years. A study in contrast with urban Catholicism was limned by the gifted John LaFarge, SJ, who between 1911 and 1926 labored in St. Mary's County to give birth to several of the institutions mentioned above. The piety of its Catholics, he observed, "was traditional; they were steadfast, family-minded, highly devotional with a strong moral sense, a strict observance of the proprieties of life and of decency in their language and conduct. On the other hand, they lacked the vigor and aggressiveness of a typical Northern Catholic parish."[89] Their churches were as plain as the ancient chapels in which their forebears had worshiped. Parish life was sustained by a minimum of parochial societies.

Like most young Jesuits, LaFarge was bemused with such customs as "eating the priest" on Sundays and such characters as Aunt Pigeon, a black woman of a hundred years and more who walked almost a mile to mass every day. Her prescription for longevity was "love God and dance." He was startled to hear the bells of St. Aloysius peal in celebration of the dry victory of local option in the "land of the flask and the fiddle." It was a happy time for the aristocratic Jesuit despite the unbending but benevolent racial prejudice that would drive him to the most important crusade of his life.[90]

The Most Unproductive Period

The parochial schools of St. Mary's County were exceptional. To an even lesser extent than in the previous twenty years did pastors of new parishes build schools. The period 1908–21 was, in fact, remarkably unproductive of new institutions of any description, the most unproductive, in fact, in the long history of the oldest see. A noteworthy achievement was Baltimore's Bon Secours Hospital blessed by Gibbons in 1918, the gift of George C. Jenkins, a brother of Michael, and his wife.[91] In 1911 Sacred Heart Hospital was opened in Cumberland and a home for genteel aged ladies was opened in Washington. And that was it.

But Societies Almost Numberless

Parish societies, by contrast, multiplied as never before. In 1915 the diocesan paper exclaimed that they were "numerous and almost numberless"! The present trend, it observed correctly, was toward the Knights of Columbus, young men's clubs, and the Holy Name Society. Some grew at the expense of others, the Catholic Benevolent Legion, it claimed, having been dislodged by the K of C.[92] The CBL, however, took its time being "dislodged." Twenty councils gathered in 1919 for one of its largest reunions in years. The K of C nevertheless experienced a phenomenal growth. Seventeen councils were founded between 1908 and 1921 in Maryland. Baltimore Council 205 with 1,100 members in 1915 was the largest in the south.[93]

More significant was the formation of the Holy Name and Sodality unions. In 1909 Gibbons appointed his newly consecrated auxiliary, Bishop Owen Corrigan, director of the Holy Name Society. In 1911 Corrigan effected a union of the Baltimore, Washington, and western Maryland sections, which, however, retained their separate identities.[94] Every year, except during the war, the Baltimore and Washington sections of the HNS would march in the national capital, some seventeen thousand strong in

1915. Baltimore had by then thirty-nine adult branches and twenty Junior Holy Name branches. By 1921 there were some twenty-one thousand adult members almost equally divided between Baltimore and Washington, the latter counting thirty-one branches.[95] In May 1916 a union of the Sodality of the Blessed Virgin Mary was effected in Baltimore and affiliated with the parent body in St. Louis. In Washington the Sodality Union was established in 1918. The stated goals of the Baltimore Union were to achieve personal holiness, help one's neighbor, and defend the church.[96] Though by 1921 the Sodality was still not as impressive in numbers as the Holy Name Society, it was considered by many a sort of feminine counterpart.

Until a legal dispute between the two feminine counterparts of the K of C was settled in 1921, the Catholic Daughters of America in Baltimore and the District called themselves the Daughters of Isabella.[97] The CDA established its first court in the archdiocese, Court District of Columbia 212, in 1913. In 1915 Court Baltimore 254 was founded in the see city. By 1921 there were courts in Frederick, Hagerstown, Havre de Grace, and Upper Marlboro, as well as two more in Baltimore.

A woman's organization founded in Maryland that soon spread far and wide was the International Federation of Catholic Alumnae. The IFCA was in 1914 the brainchild of two graduates of St. Joseph's College in Emmitsburg, Clara Douglas Sheeran and Clara I. Cogan, who sensed the growing power of educated Catholic women. Its goals were the promotion of Catholic education and the ideals of Catholic womanhood. In time it would set a number of concrete objectives.[98]

A development peculiar to the oldest archdiocese was the founding and growth of the Catholic League and the Catholic Fraternity. So similar were the two in organization and activity that it is difficult to account for their separate existences. There was never any hint of rivalry. Both were insurance and social societies. Both had separate assemblies for men and women equal in privileges and power. Both were parish based and met weekly to plan joint socials and outings. The Catholic League's Marquette Assembly No. 1 for men and Mother Seton Assembly No. 2 for women were founded in 1896. The league put greater emphasis, perhaps, on patriotism. One of its founders, Philip C. Mueller, was also prominent in the K of C. By 1921 the league claimed ten assemblies in Baltimore and one in Bradshaw. The Catholic Fraternity was founded in 1906 and incorporated in 1910 with the Lafayette Assembly No. 1 for men and the Lord Baltimore Assembly No. 2 for women its first foundations. Its motto was "Love, Liberty, and Loyalty." By 1921 the Fraternity counted seven assemblies in Baltimore and two in Washington. Though the activities of league and fraternity were amply covered in the pages of the *Baltimore Catholic Review*, enrollment figures were never given.

Young men's clubs continued to appear, disappear, and reappear, but hardly any called themselves lyceums any more. Particularly active were the St. Jerome's Pleasure and Dramatic Circle, the St. James Juvenile Beneficial Association, and the Springfield Athletic Club of Blessed Sacrament Parish. Except for dramatics, literary interests had lost out almost entirely to athletics. Beginning in 1914 at St. Ann's, Catholic Clubs were founded in several parishes. The reason seems to have been to create an Independent Catholic League as an alternative to the Catholic Baseball League, which had been on the scene for a number of years.

Except for the Holy Name Society, which could be found in Italian parishes, the bodies above mentioned continued to be spurned by Slavs and Italians in favor of their own. Beneficial and devotional societies continued to multiply in the Bohemian, Lithuanian, and Polish parishes. The pastor of St. Wenceslaus reported "over 30" of the former in 1920 with 50 to 250 members each. The Italian societies created in these years, however, reflected regional loyalties, such as the Abruzzi-Molisi and Cefalùdese societies, or occupational ties, such as the Fruitti Vendoli di Mutuo Soccorso, rather than religious ones. The pastor of St. Leo's listed in his annual report for 1920 the sodalities for men, mothers, and young men, the Children of Mary, and the St. Rita's, St. Anthony's, and Sacred Heart societies.

While sodalities and other devotional organizations were mostly the creations of the clergy, the beneficial, fraternal, and probably young men's societies were, as before, more often initiated by laypeople and based upon needs they felt. The faithful were generally left to pick and choose. Gibbons' attitude toward societies, institutions, and personnel was remarkably laissez-faire. This was due in part to interests outside the archdiocese but in part also to an assumption, conveniently ignoring important lacunae, that the oldest archdiocese was well endowed and well served.

Vicars and Auxiliaries

Baltimore's cardinal was, in fact, well served by the men upon whom he leaned. As much as any of his predecessors, he looked to the superior of St. Mary's seminary for advice and support. Though he had ten chancellors in his forty-three years, he had only three vicars general: Edward McColgan, Alfred Curtis, and Owen Corrigan. The three were quietly judicious and willing to serve as lightning rods in the deflection of temperamental displays, particularly on the part of the clergy. When Curtis returned to Baltimore in 1897 after his resignation as bishop of Wilmington, he became, in effect, an auxiliary bishop. When he died, Owen B. Corrigan was appointed, on September 29, 1908, the first official auxiliary bishop of Baltimore. When needed, the bishop rectors of the Catholic University also performed ordinations and confirmations.

In 1912 his auxiliary and nine consultors and irremovable rectors presented Gibbons with a formal request that he seek a coadjutor in order to assure a successor of his own choosing.[99] Unknown to the petitioners, he had written Denis O'Connell only four months before: "I have made up my mind for a considerable time to be contented with my auxiliary and to have no coadjutor. Things move peacefully and satisfactorily, and my few remaining years I place in the hands of Providence."[100]

The Washington Protest

Gibbons did not readily surrender power. In 1914 rumors were strong enough to convince him that Washington would soon be severed from the archdiocese and made a separate see. With the help of John Fenlon, superior of St. Mary's Seminary, he composed lengthy protests to the pope and Cardinal Gaetano De Lai, secretary of the Consistorial Congregation, and set out for Rome to argue in person the inadvisability of such a move.

He could not believe, Gibbons told De Lai in the longer and stronger statement, that any person in authority in Rome would entertain such an idea, particularly in his lifetime. Baltimore, though not a large archdiocese, was important, not only because it enjoyed the "primacy of honor" but also because it included the national capital and the Catholic University. The loss of Washington would inflict a "grave injury and injustice" on the oldest archdiocese. Though Washington had sixty thousand Catholics, it had not the resources to maintain a bishop. He had had to contribute personally to two churches, St. Augustine's and St. Matthew's, to save them from bankruptcy. Though Washington would never be as important as such capitals as London, Paris, or Berlin, Gibbons predicted, he was prepared to admit that it deserved some special honor. This, however, could be conferred, as the apostolic delegate himself had suggested, by linking the two names in the title of the archdiocese.

Half of the lengthy protests addressed a second but related rumor, namely, that the apostolic delegate would be named archbishop of Washington. Such a move, Gibbons stated boldly, would be a "crime against religion." It would mean "death to the most cherished principle of American government, which is separation of Church and State." Already American Catholics were suspected of desiring diplomatic relations between the Vatican and the White House "to attain our ends secretly through politicians rather than openly through the people." Anti-Catholicism was again gathering strength. If a foreigner were sent from Rome, he would be the target of abuse and calumny. When the government was obliged to consult on important matters, Gibbons reminded De Lai, it chose him rather than the apostolic delegate. Bishops should be natives, especially the archbishop of Baltimore, who "must be as truly American as he is Catholic."[101]

Gibbons' reluctance to see any diminution of the prestige of the archdiocese and of the power of its ordinary was demonstrated also in the action he took to preserve the important centers of religious orders in the archdiocese. He coaxed, for example, the Sisters of the Good Shepherd to return their provincial headquarters to Baltimore and pleaded in 1905 with the Jesuits, who had moved their novitiate from Frederick to the archdiocese of New York in 1902, to leave Woodstock College where it was.[102]

Carroll Redivivus

The jealous stewardship Gibbons exercised in Baltimore derived largely from his recognition of the need to revivify the Carroll church. Of all the successors of the first archbishop, Gibbons sensed best what it was Carroll had tried to accomplish and saw himself as bringing his goals to fruition.[103] One of Gibbons' practices that signified his affinity to Carroll was the frequent use of his prayer for civil authorities, the same that had caused such turmoil at the outbreak of the Civil War. When he became archbishop, Gibbons ordered the prayer said in all churches despite the open opposition of some of his priests.[104] When asked to give the benediction for the important civic commemorations in Philadelphia, Chicago, and elsewhere, as well as the 1920 Republican convention, he used the Carroll prayer or a variation of it.[105]

Gibbons resembled Carroll most, perhaps, in his unfailing support of American principles. Though hardly democratic in practice, he was unfailingly so in his public utterances. His praise of American institutions seldom admitted of qualifications.

Gibbons also approximated Carroll's ecumenism more closely than did any of his predecessors. Like Carroll he cultivated friends among the clergy of other faiths. He was particularly close to Bishops William Paret and John Gardner Murray of the Protestant Episcopal Church, Rev. Lincoln A. Ferris of the Mount Vernon Place Methodist Church, and Rabbis William Rosenau of Eutaw Place Temple and Charles A. Rubenstein of Har

Sinai Temple.[106] Gibbons endeared himself to Jewish Americans by his frequent condemnation of the persecution of Jews in Russia and elsewhere and his support of a homeland in Palestine.[107] Gibbons also regarded as close friends President Daniel Coit Gilman and Professor Basil L. Gildersleeve of Johns Hopkins University, an institution not held in highest esteem in some Catholic circles.[108]

The terms "Christian" or "Catholic Christian" Gibbons used as often as "Catholic" in referring to those of his own faith. In spite of his cordiality, however, he refused to compromise on what he considered fundamental points of discipline or dogma. When the Episcopal rectors of Washington wrote him in 1896 that young ladies of their faith who wed Catholics should be allowed to marry in their own churches, Gibbons replied: "I should be sorry to think that a difference of religious faith and practice could be the rock set for the ruin of the good will that subsists between us. . . . [But] I could not hold out to you any hope of [the regulation's] being modified by higher authority."[109] On another occasion he declared that the reunion of the scattered branches of Christianity was a "consummation devoutly to be wished." But the "first essential requirement," he insisted, was the recognition of the Sovereign Pontiff as "the divinely appointed head of Christendom."[110] A spokesman for the Salvation Army nevertheless reflected an almost universal sentiment when he thanked Gibbons for an endorsement that breathed "that spirit of broad tolerance and democracy which has made you beloved and venerated by all Americans."[111]

Like Carroll, Gibbons was a joiner, a compulsion derived from his civic sense. The organizations he joined ranged from the Charles Street Association to the Anti-Vivisection Society to the National Child Labor Committee. Though not as actively involved as Carroll in the direction of such organizations, Gibbons joined many more. As his secretary explained to a fellow priest, the cardinal was "always ready to lend the use of his name to an organization which makes for constructive Americanism."[112] Despite a certain caution exercised, the practice led to embarrassment on occasion. In 1919, for example, he was informed that the Educational Aid Society had been using his name as a member of its advisory council to induce several teaching sisterhoods in Chicago to make use of its services often to their detriment. Gibbons immediately asked that he be dropped from the council.[113]

Also like Carroll, Gibbons interpreted Roman directives rather broadly. A notable example was the reception accorded the *motu proprio* of Pius X on church music in 1903, with its insistence on Gregorian chant. In 1907 Gibbons created a commission on church music, but placed in charge a priest,

William T. Russell, who enjoyed singing solos during church services. Masses by Haydn, Mozart, and Gounod, and solos with organ, harp, or orchestra continued as in the days of Archbishop Bayley. In 1908, when St. Aloysius in Washington replaced its outstanding choral group with a chancel choir of men and boys, the pastor remarked sadly: "I suppose the pope when he issued his encyclical [*sic*] little realized what difficulties he was raising for the churches in America." The *Catholic Mirror* added that country churches would probably have to continue using women.[114] As late as 1919 the *Mirror*'s successor complained that the papal directive on church music was being perverted in many urban churches.[115] It probably had in mind, among other perversions, the magnificent Easter mass rendered by the orchestra of St. Michael's Parish under Professor Martin Zech.[116] The cardinal archbishop had not a word to say about any of this.

Gibbons was never asked to explain why the decree of 1894 against secret societies was not enforced in Baltimore, but he was often called upon to explain in general the failure in America to conform to church canons and practices. In 1909 he had to persuade one of the curial cardinals that in the United States it was a necessity for nursing sisters to attend men. "I can assure Your Eminence that the hospitals directed by the Sisters are a true blessing for religion."[117]

In 1913 the apostolic delegate sent to Gibbons for his comment the copy of a letter from an unnamed bishop explaining why the latter permitted the euchre parties and dances condemned by the Second Plenary Council. Young people persisted in attending such dances, the bishop had explained. Prohibition would be a source of harm rather than good.[118] In all probability Gibbons agreed. In 1903 he had refused to allow one of his priests, Luigi Sartori, to publish a "little treatise" condemning round dances. Sartori sent him a letter of endorsement from a neighboring Methodist minister who said that he admired the cardinal but not gambling fairs, dancing, and euchre parties. "I am sorry to say," the minister explained to Sartori, "your church seems to lead in this matter."[119] Sartori asked Gibbons for permission to return to his native land, "where I will not be surrounded by drunkards, blasphemers, and priests, who are not [*sic*] hirelings leading their flock to destruction."[120] The permission was readily granted.

Problem Priests

In his gentle approach to problem priests, Gibbons also resembled Baltimore's first bishop. Admittedly he had none so notorious as Denis Cahill, John Ashton, or Simon Gallagher, but the behavior of some was exasperating enough. One was John Baptist Manley, who was like Gallagher a sporadic alcoholic but a zealous priest who would raise several churches in a long career. His carping criticisms were a source of pain to the cardinal. In 1913 he wrote Gibbons protesting a "pompous nuptial affair" at the cathedral and the part Gibbons had played. "The rich can obtain anything," he quoted a layman as saying.[121]

Even more vexing were the actions of Father Valentine Schmitt, former champion of the Knights of Labor in western Maryland, but as a Washington pastor an unbearable misanthrope. For a number of years he carried on a vendetta against the Jesuits. By 1913 he had developed an intense dislike for his young assistant and his work among the "worthless Italians."[122] Complaints from his parishioners had become so voluminous and insistent that Gibbons decided to seek his removal on the canonical charge of his having incurred the odium of the faithful. Schmitt tried to prevent the action by threats. Among other things, he reminded Gibbons that Archbishop Spalding had ordered pastors to build schools under pain of removal. "How is it today?" he asked.[123] When the request for his resignation came, Schmitt wrote Gibbons that he was sorry to spoil his visit to New Orleans but that he was going to appeal to Rome against his "star chamber trial."[124] Gibbons finally agreed to reinstate the troublesome pastor if he expressed regret publicly for his transgressions and promised to resign should he repeat them.[125] There were, of course, more complaints, but Gibbons chose not to make a case of them.

And then there was Father Caspar Elbert, an excellent example of the danger of allowing loose rein to pastors in financial matters. In 1909 Elbert incurred a parish debt of $130,000 at St. Katharine of Sienna by investing in harebrained schemes. Gibbons assumed the debt personally and appealed to his pastors to help bail out the bankrupt parish. Bishop Corrigan, to whom the case was entrusted, told reporters that the sad affair had "put us all in our mettle, and I believe a more strict scrutiny of accounts will be made in all the parishes hereafter."[126] The unfortunate Elbert was sent to Mount Hope Retreat for the insane.

The majority of pastors, however, were dependable, hardworking, and respected by their flocks. Some were outstanding, like Monsignor George W. Devine, pastor of St. John's Parish in Baltimore. Out of gratitude to Gibbons for honoring a request that he not be considered for episcopal rank, Devine was the largest contributor to the Elbert fund.[127] The tall, shy priest ruled "Little Limerick" in the manner of the classic Irish pastor.

An Energizing War

Despite his worries and responsibilities, Gibbons aged remarkably well. His good health he attributed to a spartan diet and frequent walks. The years following his eightieth birthday, which corresponded to World War I and its aftermath, were the busiest in his life. As it did for most Americans, the war energized the old cardinal, who visited camps, opened K of C war huts, and spoke at Liberty Loan drives. He also gave his blessing to the founding of the National Catholic War Council in August of 1917 at the Catholic University, a body first envisioned by the Paulist John J. Burke. Gibbons played the leading role in the bishops' assumption of control of this new amalgamation of Catholic organizations designed to arouse maximum Catholic support for the war effort.[128]

A diocesan war council was organized in Baltimore with Robert Sargent Shriver as president. One of its first acts was to open a Catholic service club at the home of the Catholic Club opposite the cathedral rectory. At Gibbons' invitation the delegates of fifty societies of Catholic women met at the K of C hall to form the Catholic Women's War Relief. More than two thousand women were soon assembling mass kits for chaplains, knitting sweaters, gathering literature, and preparing entertainments for Camp Meade.[129] A profound sense of patriotism and involvement touched every parish and institution. At St. John's, Baltimore, eight hundred men of the Holy Name Society went to communion to demonstrate "their manhood, their Americanism, their Catholicism."[130] St. John's headed the honor roll of servicemen from Catholic parishes. At St. Mary's Industrial School a cadet corps began to drill even before American entrance into the war. "Brother Paul, the director, is intensely patriotic," the *Sun* of March 26, 1917, observed. "He is constantly impressing upon the minds and hearts of the boys that religion and patriotism are inseparable." Two alumni of St. Mary's, gunners on a merchantman, were Baltimore's first casualties.[131]

The celebration of Gibbons' fifty years as a bishop in February 1919 was made the occasion of transforming the National Catholic War Council into the National Catholic Welfare Council, a permanent body under the American bishops for the purpose of coordinating Catholic activities.[132] Though John Burke, the Paulist, was named executive secretary, John Fenlon, president of St. Mary's Seminary, and several members of the faculty of Catholic University helped to shape the structure and even fill some of its important offices. One was Monsignor John A. Ryan, professor of moral theology and head of the NCWC's Social Action Department. Ryan composed what an episcopal committee would call the "Bishops' Program for Social Reconstruction."[133] Some of the bishops, when they got around to reading it, were less than enthusiastic about its broad proposals for social reform, including social security, a minimum wage, and public housing. Nevertheless, at the first annual meeting of the entire hierarchy on September 24–25, 1919, the structure and membership of the NCWC were approved and, tacitly, the "Bishops' Program for Social Reconstruction." Gibbons, of course, presided and gave his hearty concurrence to all.

The Passing of an Era

The year before, Ireland, Keane, and Farley had all died. The only friend left from the days of battle was Denis O'Connell, now too old to hope to succeed Gibbons in Baltimore. In December 1920 Gibbons himself had a serious sinking spell at the Shrivers' home in Carroll County after ten games of euchre. He rallied and continued routine business until March 20, when his condition began to deteriorate rapidly. He died four days later and was buried seven days after that. Maryland observed a minute of silence as the requiem mass began.

Gibbons' death was more than a milestone in the history of the premier see. It marked the end of Baltimore's preeminence in affairs of the Catholic Church in the United States. His eighty-seven years and eight months carried this status well into the twentieth century, for there was never any doubt of the locus of power as long as Gibbons lived. Baltimore Catholics basked in the aura cast by the aging cardinal, who well before his death had become a living legend.

As the oldest archdiocese grew in prestige under Gibbons, however, it declined proportionately in the indices by which great sees in America were usually measured. Its quarter million Catholics in 1921 could hardly compare with the 1.5 million in New York or the 1.1 million in Chicago. As sees in the northeast and midwest grew prodigiously, Baltimore crept forward slowly, its population expanding by little more than 75,000 in Gibbons' forty-three years. Churches in Baltimore grew from twenty-one to fifty-five and in Washington from eleven to twenty-eight, while those in the counties fell from eighty-eight to sixty-five. Parochial schools grew by only a score. The increase in priests from 252 to 608 was due partly to the growth of the Catholic University. The number of colleges and academies for young men changed from nine to eleven, colleges and academies for young women from eighteen to nineteen, industrial schools from four to six, hospitals from five to eight. In all it was not an impressive growth.

"With regard to the present state of the archdiocese," wrote Giovanni Bonzano, the apostolic delegate, in a report to Cardinal De Lai two months after Gibbons' death, "it cannot be said unfortunately that it is flourishing." Gibbons had done little for it. While dutifully attending all public functions, he had shunned acts of administration that involved responsibility and odium. His curia was one of the worst organized, and "most ironically he who had presided over the Third Plenary Council as apostolic delegate paid little attention to its dicta and decrees. In parochial matters [he] acted like a Pope, granting in good faith faculties and dispensations he had no power to grant."

Another thing that reflected ill on his administration, Bonzano claimed, was the great influence the superior of the Sulpicians had exercised over him in such matters as the choice of pastors and assignment of curates. This the apostolic delegate knew from members of the episcopal household and curia. In his early years, Bonzano readily admitted, Gibbons had rendered great service to the church, especially in assuaging the bigotry and intolerance of Protestants. With consummate tact he had become the friend of men of every condition, race, and faith, so that at his death he was exalted in the press as a patriot, a citizen, a statesman, a man of great vision whose words on national questions were always peaceful and just. In church matters, he had succeeded, as some journals expressed it, "in adapting Roman dogma to American ideas." Having become an idol of the people, however, he was not disposed to sacrifice his popularity. His fear of offending non-Catholics could be seen in the growing number of mixed marriages. The cardinal had continued to preside at such weddings, especially those of the socially prominent, even when told that it was against the rulings of the Holy See. His example was unfortunately followed by the majority of clergy and bishops.[134]

One had to comb the literature of the church's enemies or the correspondence of a handful of critics within, such as Bernard McQuaid, to find anything resembling these strictures of the apostolic delegate. To a disenchanted few Gibbons was, indeed, vain or devious or lacking in courage. To his many admirers he was assured, prudent, and gentle, the same attributes turned inside out.

Many facets of Gibbons' character might explain his great appeal. He was simple, outgoing, and seldom without a smile. "[H]e had a way of saying the right thing at the right time and saying it tactfully but plainly."[135] Many attributed his alertness and vitality to his custom of keeping in contact with the young. He visited St. Charles College frequently.[136] On his daily walks he often invited a seminarian to accompany him. In the spring of 1920 the twenty-one-year-old Lawrence Shehan was so honored. They talked about the cardinal's books.[137] But in the final analysis, Gibbons' tremendous popularity remains a mystery.

More than any Catholic before him, not even excepting John Carroll, James Gibbons was embraced by his country. "There are other Catholics in this continent," the *Sun* had editorialized some five years before his death, "but there is only one Cardinal Gibbons. The Catholic Church has given many distinguished prelates and priests to its work in this country, but none who has inspired the same general confidence and the same earnest esteem." The *Sun* attempted its own explanation: "To all he seems to speak in their own tongues by some Pentecostal power, or by some subtle affinity that makes nothing human foreign to him."[138]

IV

The Curley Church

Archbishop Michael Joseph Curley 1921–1947

Archbishop Francis Patrick Keough 1947–1961

 In an editorial entitled "Keeping Up with the Times," the *Baltimore Catholic Review* told its readers in the summer of 1921 that the Church "sees beyond the present and prepares for other times when jazz and noise and vulgarity shall have sickened their votaries." Her attitude toward the big questions "is the same today as yesterday."[1] As non-Catholic America entered a period of doubt and disillusionment following World War I, "Catholics set out as 'providential hosts' to defend the values and promises of American idealism which seemed threatened by various forms of irrationalism."[2] In their keeping innocence would survive.

With a self-assurance that brooked no questioning, American Catholics would convince themselves that they were in the forefront of every important social, cultural, and intellectual movement in the country. The proof would all be there in a multivolume *Catholic Builders of the Nation* published in 1923.[3] That few of the builders found prominent places in secular biographical dictionaries did not matter. Over the next three decades Catholic "intellectuals" would speak with an even greater degree of sophistication and authority, but the basic assumptions would remain. Catholics would be daily reassured in the Catholic classroom, Catholic press, and Catholic pulpit that their church had the answer to every question worth asking. Never would they think to look beyond these sources for confirmation.

"We were, thus, a chosen people—though chosen, it seemed, to be second-rate," recalled Garry Wills, a beneficiary of these assurances and for several years a resident of Baltimore.[4] The in-built inferiority of the ghetto church was carefully hidden by an apologetics ultimately rooted in neo-Thomism that would allow even literate Catholics to assume a God-given superiority. Upon this apologetical undergirding the Catholic ghetto of the twentieth century would be confidently constructed.

The Catholic ghetto was an extension of, but not the same as, the ghetto church. In the period following World War I Catholics would increasingly distinguish themselves by their religious affiliation and with a growing militancy and self-assurance. The ghetto walls would expand to encompass more than the institutions and organizations of survival—the schools, orphanages, and hospitals, the fraternal, insurance, and devotional societies. It would now include also the organizations designed to establish the distinctly "Catholic" professional—the doctor, lawyer, writer, artist, and scientist—and even the "Catholic" workingman—the policeman, fire-fighter, and postal employee. Moving from what was largely a defensive posture, Catholics under their clerical standard-bearers would take the offensive. The Catholic ghetto would leave no challenge unaddressed, no injury unavenged, no insult unreproved. Catholic organizations, most notably the Holy Name Society and the K of C, would be used effectively as pressure groups. The recognition that was won before by bands and banners on narrow streets would now be achieved by numbers and staging in the largest stadia. A climactic moment of the Catholic ghetto was the International Eucharistic Congress played out in Chicago in 1926, when Baltimore's archbishop would address a crowd of two hundred thousand, including twelve cardinals, in Soldier Field.

Baltimore's tenth archbishop, Michael Curley, with a boldness and vigor unequalled by any American bishop in the interwar years, would place the oldest archdiocese squarely in the Catholic ghetto. All of the successes of his predecessor in restoring the Carroll church would be quickly undone. The Curley church would stand at the opposite pole of American Catholicism. The careers of Gibbons and Curley would, in fact, offer one of the most striking contrasts in styles of leadership. Curley was a battler and a builder. He had little use for the values of mainstream America. He would also be an organizer, centralizing education, Catholic Charities, and missionary activities.

While the Depression would bring a temporary halt to institution building, it would deepen Catholic attachment to the institutional church and generate a more intense piety. World War II and postwar prosperity would allow American Catholics to launch their greatest building spree. In the 1950s the church of ghetto Catholicism would come to full flower, a process hastened by an intensification of the hostile milieu as Protestants and Other Americans United for the Separation of Church and State (POAU) trumpeted again the threat of Catholic power. Catholic interests would enlarge as Catholics entered the middle class en masse. Eisenhower affluence would allow them to fund bigger and more magnificent churches, colleges, headquarters, and motherhouses as well as an astounding variety of societies, clubs, and guilds, the counterparts of secular organizations for almost every conceivable activity.[5]

As an old church reached full flower, however, a new church would be germinating. In the oldest archdiocese this would occur under Francis Patrick Keough, the eleventh archbishop, but with little encouragement from the transplanted New Englander. The task of planting seeds would fall to a restless few for whom the old reassurance of the ghetto church, the myth of majestic changelessness, rang hollow.

13   *Who Is Like God*

EVERY SUMMER THE ARCHBISHOP from America could be seen wandering alone amid the ruins of the ancient monastery of Clonmacnois. According to Irish legend, the monastery and its school were founded in 544 by St. Kieran, who had been moved by the dream of a tree planted by a stream in the middle of Ireland, whose fruit went forth over the seas. There the last king of Ireland was buried. The ruins overlooked the River Shannon a few miles south of the Curley farm at the edge of the town of Athlone. As a boy Michael Joseph Curley amid the ruins daydreamed of the life of a missionary priest in the Fiji Islands. Shortly before his sixteenth birthday—he was born in 1879 on the anniversary of Columbus's discovery of America—he went to Mungret College to study for the priesthood.[1]

The visit to Mungret of a bishop from Florida induced Michael Curley to volunteer for missionary service in that underdeveloped part of the Catholic world. In 1900 he went to Rome to finish his studies in the College of the Propaganda. The rector in his last days was Monsignor Giovanni Bonzano. No one doubted that as apostolic delegate to the United States Bonzano was responsible for Curley's being named bishop of St. Augustine, Florida, in 1914 at the age of thirty-four as well as archbishop of Baltimore seven years later.[2]

Ordained in 1904, Curley went to Florida that year to take up his duties at DeLand, the center of a parish of 7,200 square miles, a thousand more than his future archdiocese. His first rectory was a rented room over a store near a diner, where a $5.00 ticket entitled him to twenty-one meals. As bishop of St. Augustine he attracted national attention by battling a convent inspection bill and a law forbidding sisters to teach black children.[3] Still his name was unknown to most Maryland Catholics when the news of his elevation to Baltimore came four months after the death of Gibbons. The *Evening Sun* was sure that Rome had tried to secure a successor as much like Gibbons as possible. Both, it observed, had been made bishops of southern sees in their midthirties and sent to Baltimore in their early forties. The tenth archbishop, like Gibbons, was "tolerant, simple, and very democratic . . . an eloquent speaker." The *Baltimore American* was certain that Archbishop Curley would soon be a cardinal and that Baltimore would continue as "the true capital of American Catholicism."[4] Time would prove both wide of the mark.

The Day of Organization

On November 21, 1921, Baltimore staged a reception in no way inferior to those accorded Gibbons. At the installation Bishop Corrigan welcomed the new archbishop in the name of the clergy, and Robert Biggs, standing at the sanctuary gate, welcomed him in the name of the laity. In his address Curley paid due honor to his predecessor before declaring in the sonorous tones that would become familiar in Baltimore: "The battles of the future will be fought on the fields of education." Then he voiced what would become his most frequently delivered dictum: "Where there is doubt as to which we shall erect—a stately church or a capacious school—let us have no hesitation in making our choice: the school." With hardly less emphasis Curley proclaimed that it was "the day of the layman" but added: "It is the day of organization. You must be organized so that from unity you can gather strength."[5]

Through organizations Curley began his tenure by scattering responsibilities. In December he told the St. Vincent de Paul Society that he wanted a conference in every parish and in January that he expected a dramatic increase in the orphans collections in the future as well as a poor box in every parish. To a gathering of the International Federation of Catholic Alumnae he asserted the need for free high schools for Catholic boys and girls so that Catholics might cease to be hewers of wood and drawers of water. Until they were erected, he wanted scholarships to the private Catholic secondary schools. These should be provided by the academies themselves and by pastors, societies, and individual donors. In February he enjoined the Holy Name Society of Washington to take a stand against bigotry and the next month the Holy Name Society of Baltimore to organize the Big Brothers Association. The same month he told the Catholic Daughters of America to help Father LaFarge establish in St. Mary's County a vocational school for blacks that had been planned under Gibbons. In March he urged the National Conference of Catholic Women to oppose birth control propaganda.

At the end of March the first annual Teachers' Institute was held at Calvert Hall. Curley told the sisters and brothers assembled of his plans to standardize the parochial schools of the archdiocese and to appoint a diocesan superintendent of education. At the same time he denounced the

Sterling-Towner bill and its efforts to federalize education.[6] In April he promised his full support to the pastor of St. Louis, Clarksville, Rev. W. Howard Bishop, who wished to promote Catholic schools in rural parishes.[7]

Though schools were his primary interest, Curley moved vigorously on several fronts. In June he appointed the largest number of pastors ever named at one time, taking young assistants from city parishes and placing them over rural ones.[8] He reorganized his board of consultors and Tribunal, dropping octogenarians and naming younger priests. In June he also appointed committees to survey parochial limits and determine the need for new parishes and held a meeting to map plans for an archdiocesan bureau of Catholic Charities. In October he named pastors and lay experts to a building committee that would approve all designs for future structures. He also announced plans for a diocesan synod (which was never held).

No Weak-Kneed Laity

To Constantine E. McGuire, editor of the *Catholic Builders of the Nation*, he would write in 1925 that he had come to Baltimore to find "a Clergy run riot in individualism and a Laity that had absorbed large doses of American Liberalism." Not only did he have to take on the work of fundamental organization that should have been done twenty-five or thirty years before, but he had to confront a "peculiar psychology" that "permeated the whole atmosphere." He had had to "educate the archdiocesan mind," he claimed, as well as build buildings.[9]

In November 1922 Curley made a public pronouncement that startled many, particularly the Catholic elite, by its bluntness and belligerency. He berated the Scottish Rite Masons as well as the Ku Klux Klan, the former as the authors of the Oregon bill that would force all children to attend public schools. Robert Biggs, among others, told the archbishop he thought the condemnation ill advised. Curley retorted: "One thing is certain, the time has come when the Catholic laity of the Archdiocese of Baltimore must be neither squeamish nor weak-kneed in the matter of stating their Faith, its principles, its stand, clearly, distinctly and forcefully. . . . We never gain anything by being apologetic and we have no reason to be."[10] For a few years, nevertheless, he would moderate a tendency to loose thunderbolts.

Searching for a Leader

Whether as archbishop of Baltimore Michael Curley contemplated an exercise of leadership comparable to that of Gibbons is difficult to say. From the start events conspired against this youngest archbishop. Gibbons, it is true, had also begun in Baltimore with a cardinal in America, but McCloskey, largely because of ill health, had been quite willing to defer to the youngest archbishop of his day. Cardinal O'Connell of Boston, however, as ranking prelate was eager to step into Gibbons' shoes. A number of bishops were anxious that he not do so. One was Bishop Louis S. Walsh of Portland, Maine.

Soon after the conclave that placed Pius XI on the papal throne in February 1922, the National Catholic Welfare Council was suppressed by a decree of the Consistorial Congregation. An emergency session of the administrative committee of the NCWC was held on April 6 in Cleveland, and three days later Bishop Walsh, a member of the committee, wrote Archbishops Curley and Patrick Hayes of New York almost identical letters. Declaring the American hierarchy "openly humiliated," he perceived the decree as an "underhanded blow from Boston, aided by Philadelphia," both of whom realized at the last meeting that they could not control the bishops as a body. If Curley and Hayes would take a "firm and clear stand," the bishops would rally behind them and deliver a "really needed object lesson" to the cardinal archbishop of Boston. Curley had a "golden opportunity," he suggested, to render a great service to the hierarchy by securing a repeal of the decree.[11] What Curley told Walsh in Washington two weeks later is not known.

Bishop Joseph Schrembs of Cleveland was sent to Rome by the administrative committee to plead for the continuance of the NCWC. Already in the ancient city was Bishop William Turner of Buffalo, like Curley a product of Mungret College. On May 29 Turner wrote Curley that in a long audience the pope had assured him that it was never the intention of the Holy See to hamper the works of the NCWC and that the annual meeting would probably be restored. "Meanwhile," Turner added, "Cleveland is muddling things and indulging in 'multiloquia'." On June 6 Turner wrote again that on the "very best of authority" he could say that a decree was being prepared that would "exceed our greatest expectations." Bonzano should have the good news from Curley because the former's "praise of the general attitude of the Hierarchy toward the Holy See has had much to do with the solution."[12] Curley himself would find, when he came to Rome that summer, that "many high up" had been prepared by Turner's "few words" to listen to the archbishop of Baltimore on this and other matters.[13] The "NCWC decree" was second on the list of things to talk about in Curley's audience with the pope of July 28, but what he said he did not record.[14]

On September 28 the American bishops met. Bishop Walsh complained to Curley of the dictatorial methods of the "eminent Chairman" [O'Connell] and suggested that Curley organize a "round table conference" of bishops to deal with the problem.[15] Curley responded that he was well aware of the "twistings and turnings" of the chairman, knowing beforehand of his opposition to the meeting as well as the contempt in which he held the administrative committee. The problem, however, should not be solved by a round table conference but a "figurative bomb shell thrown into the heart of the Eternal City." There Walsh should carry his differences with Boston and not to Bonzano, whose low opinion of O'Connell was well known. Curley also told Walsh that the Holy See made a clear distinction between the American hierarchy and the NCWC.[16]

The distinction was one Curley himself would make increasingly as he detected a "liberal" slant in the leadership of the NCWC. He would, in fact, in his early years in Baltimore be elected to the administrative committee but would resign immediately so that he might be free to criticize it.[17] After five years in the oldest see Curley complained to the Rev. Peter Guilday, the historian, that few bishops knew of the prerogative of place of which Baltimore was entitled. Gibbons, he explained, "as senior Cardinal and senior Archbishop and senior everything," had no reason to invoke it. Curley wanted Guilday to do an article on the prerogative. "I do not care whether I am first, last or in the middle, but I feel that I have a duty to the See of which I am the incumbent."[18]

The School Builder

THE PAROCHIAL SCHOOL SYSTEM

In his first few years in Baltimore, Curley took little notice, aside from his slap at the Masons, of national and international affairs. He devoted his principal energies to the organization, consolidation, and institutional expansion of the archdiocese. His most impressive achievements, as he predicted, were in education.

In October 1922 he created a diocesan school office. Over it he placed Rev. John I. Barrett, who was still at work on a Ph.D. in education at the Catholic University. Barrett in turn appointed a committee of supervisors from the sisterhoods most engaged in parochial school work. One of the school office's most notable achievements was the standardization of curricula, texts, and tests. It also planned the annual Teachers' Institute. That of 1925 involved a ten-weeks course in educational philosophy and psychology. Beginning in 1924 Barrett issued annual reports on achievements and goals. Many dioceses copied his policies and procedures. In 1926 Curley could boast: "I defy any system of grammar school education in the United States to prove itself superior to the system that is being maintained in the Archdiocese of Baltimore."[19]

The $200,000 school opened in the fall of 1922 in Holy Rosary Parish provided a model for others. Within ten years well over $10 million was expended on the construction of parochial schools where none existed or where existing ones were cramped. By 1931 the number of parochial schools had grown by 47—12 in Baltimore, 11 in Washington, and 24 in the counties—giving the archdiocese 141 parish schools in all. Their enrollment had swelled from 30,000 to 50,000.[20] St. Elizabeth's with nearly 1,500 pupils had the largest enrollment, Sacred Heart with over 1,400 the second largest, and Holy Rosary with 1,300 the third. Four others in Baltimore claimed 1,000 or more. With 715 pupils Holy Comforter was the largest in Washington.[21]

Curley's proudest boast in 1931 was the large percentage of schools in rural areas—in large measure the fruit of the one-man crusade of Father Howard Bishop. When members of the Catholic Daughters of America from Baltimore and Washington went to Clarksville to present the proceeds of their rummage sales for the building of a school, Father Bishop organized what would come to be called the League of the Little Flower. Its purpose was to raise money to help rural pastors erect and maintain parochial schools or conduct vacation schools where parishes were unable to support grammar schools. Curley approved an annual collection for the league in all parishes.

Several sisterhoods entered enthusiastically into the work of rural schools. The School Sisters of Notre Dame developed at Bryantown an excellent grammar and high school. The Sisters of Mercy went to distant Oakland in Garrett County to staff a parish school in 1924 and soon after took charge also of schools at Texas and Woodstock. Their initial attempt at a vacation school at Solomon's Island in Calvert County in 1926 was unsuccessful, but the vacation school they began in 1927 at Glymont in Charles County for both whites and blacks, where two buses provided by Father Bishop rounded up the pupils daily, succeeded beyond all expectations.[22] Most of the vacation schools, however, were conducted by the Mission

Helpers of the Sacred Heart. In 1923 the archbishop persuaded the Sodality Union of Washington to support the rural schools of southern Maryland.

HIGH SCHOOLS AND COLLEGES

Under Curley there were also significant advances in Catholic secondary education. In the 1920s several of the so-called colleges for boys—most notably Gonzaga and St. John's in Washington and Mount St. Joseph in Baltimore—dropped the pretense of a collegiate section and developed a curriculum similar to that of the public high schools. When Rock Hill College burned in 1922, it was not rebuilt. Georgetown and Loyola continued their preparatory departments but moved them to separate campuses. Mount St. Mary's College dropped its preparatory school in 1936. The dozen or so Catholic academies for girls also came to resemble their public school counterparts, closing the era of the "finishing school." In 1934 Trinity Prep was opened at Ilchester by the Sisters of Notre Dame de Namur, while in 1937 Dunbarton Academy in Washington would become a four-year college.

The scholarship fund that Curley had created his first year was not a great success. It could by 1924 provide a free secondary education to about sixty of the six hundred or more who would yearly take the competitive exam. The first of the "free" high schools, or diocesan schools, that Curley envisioned was Seton High. This opened in 1926, when the Sisters of Charity transformed St. Joseph's Industrial School into a high school. Though they staffed Seton, they offered it to the archdiocese, which assumed the cost of operation except for income from a minimal tuition of $25 a year.[23] The next diocesan high school, however, would be long in coming.

Until diocesan high schools were built, the need for a free secondary education was filled by parish high schools, one or two of which had appeared before Curley's advent. St. John's in Baltimore, Immaculate Conception in Towson, and St. Peter's in Westernport opened high schools his first year. Many of these parish high schools, however, were little more than one- or two-year extensions of the grammar schools, and many were short-lived. Several limited their offerings to business subjects and called themselves commercial schools. By 1939 there would be one parish high school in Baltimore (St. Martin's), eight in Washington, and sixteen in the counties, but eleven commercial schools in Baltimore, two in Washington, and only one in the counties (at Cumberland). These could claim enrollments ranging from 4 (in St. Peter Claver's High School at Ridge) to 305 (St. Patrick's

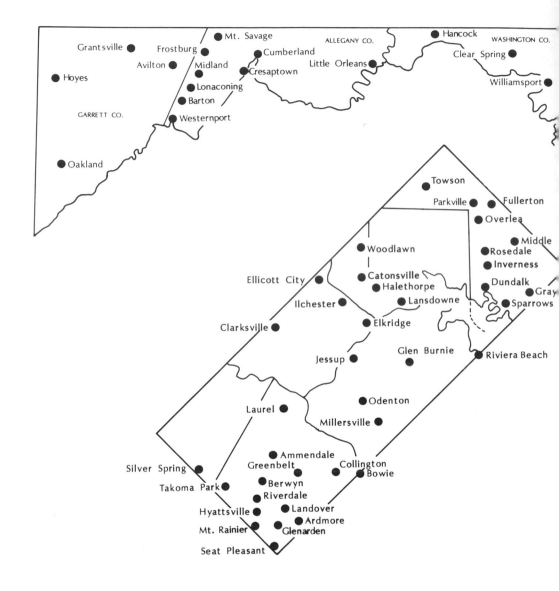

Map 2. Locations of Parishes and Missions of the Archdiocese of Baltimore at the Beginning of 1947

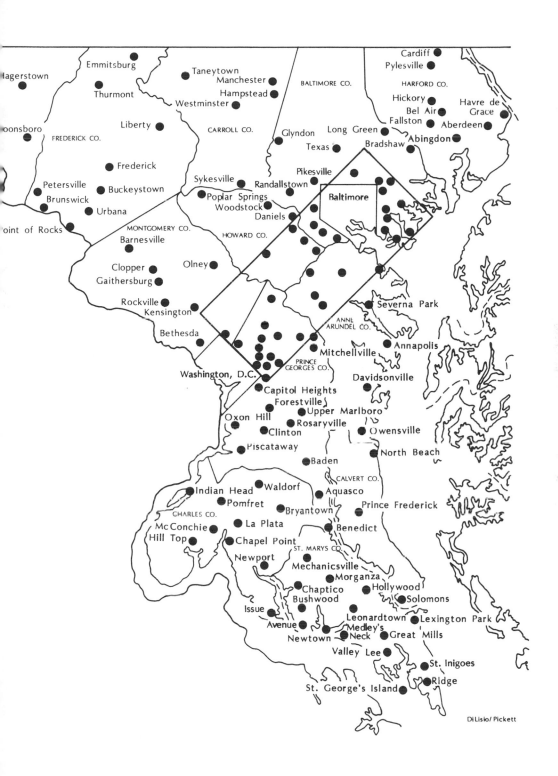

Hagerstown

Emmitsburg

Taneytown
Manchester
Hampstead
Westminster

Thurmont

BALTIMORE CO.

Cardiff
Pylesville

HARFORD CO.

Hickory
Bel Air
Fallston

Havre de
Grace
Aberdeen

oonsboro

Liberty

FREDERICK CO.

CARROLL CO.

Glyndon

Long Green

Texas

Bradshaw

Abingdon

Frederick

Petersville
Brunswick
Urbana

Buckeystown

oint of Rocks

MONTGOMERY CO.

Barnesville

Sykesville
Randallstown
Poplar Springs
Woodstock
Daniels

Pikesville

Baltimore

HOWARD CO.

Clopper
Gaithersburg

Olney

Rockville
Kensington

Bethesda

Severna Park

ANNE
ARUNDEL CO.

Mitchellville

Annapolis

Washington, D.C.

PRINCE
GEORGES CO.

Davidsonville

Capitol Heights
Forestville
Upper Marlboro
Oxon Hill
Rosaryville
Clinton

Owensville

Piscataway

North Beach

Baden

CALVERT CO.

Indian Head
Pomfret

Waldorf

Aquasco

Bryantown

Prince Frederick

CHARLES CO.

McConchie
Hill Top

La Plata

Chapel Point

Benedict

Newport

ST. MARYS CO.

Mechanicsville
Morganza
Hollywood

Chaptico
Bushwood

Issue

Solomons

Avenue

Leonardtown
Medley's
Neck
Newtown

Lexington Park
Great Mills

Valley Lee

St. Inigoes

St. George's Island

Ridge

DiLisio/Pickett

High School in Washington), but most were under 100.[24]

In his first year he organized a board of prominent Catholic laymen, including Admiral William S. Benson and Senator David I. Walsh of Massachusetts, and appealed to several American bishops and national organizations for contributions to establish the "Catholic Tuskegee" in St. Mary's County envisioned by Father LaFarge. Called Cardinal Gibbons Institute, it opened in October 1924 with Victor and Constance Daniel, a talented black couple, in charge.[25] In his first year Curley also pushed for the completion of a new and larger St. Mary's Industrial School, now famous as the institution that had trained Babe Ruth. The original buildings had been destroyed by fire in 1919, and a debt of over $400,000 remained from the $1 million needed to rebuild. Among other things, Curley persuaded a friend from his school days at Athlone, John McCormack, the famous tenor, to give a benefit performance.[26]

THE SEMINARY AND THE UNIVERSITY

The energy Curley expended in pushing a languishing project was even more evident in his efforts to build a new St. Mary's Seminary. Though the buildings on Paca Street had been overcrowded for decades and were in a badly deteriorated neighborhood, neither Gibbons nor the Sulpician superior had the courage to tackle a project of such magnitude. Soon after his arrival, Curley discussed the possibility with the superior, Father Edward Dyer. When plans were completed, he notified all pastors that within three years they would be expected to pay the quotas determined by himself. The delinquents he hounded until all had paid. The sum was set initially at $1 million. On November 18, 1928, the cornerstone was laid on an eighty-acre tract on Roland and Belvedere Avenues. The coming of the Sulpicians to Baltimore, Curley claimed in his address, was the most important event in the history of the Catholic Church in America next to the appointment of Carroll as first bishop.[27] Before an array of civic and episcopal dignitaries, the new St. Mary's was dedicated a year later and received most of the theologians. The philosophers remained at Paca Street. On the occasion of the silver jubilee of his ordination in 1929, Curley passed on to St. Charles College most of the $200,000 gift he had received so that its administration building could be finished. In 1932 when the Holy See, in effect, deprived St. Mary's of pontifical status, Curley fought successfully to have it restored.[28] Though uneasy at the appointment of Curley in 1921, the Sulpicians came to look upon him as "unequivocally their greatest benefactor" since their arrival in Baltimore.[29]

Of even greater concern to Curley was the Catholic University of

America, which he felt should be the "apex of the Catholic Educational system in the United States."[30] As its chancellor, he was unhappy with the efforts of the rector, Bishop Shahan, to build a $1 million shrine when, as he told Cardinal O'Connell, "we would seem to be facing intellectual bankruptcy in the real work of the University."[31] A Roman decree touching universities in 1922 provided Curley the excuse he needed to conduct a survey and effect reforms. With much labor a new constitution was drawn and finally approved by Rome in 1926. Faced with the awesome task of restructuring the university, Shahan asked that his name not be considered for a third term. Rome in 1928 finally chose from the *terna* sent by the board Rev. James H. Ryan, a philosophy teacher at the university.

Though Curley had remained neutral in the selection, he came to appreciate the talents and vision of the fifth rector. He supported Ryan's wish to have two prominent members in the School of Theology removed when they fought his efforts to reform the school and in 1933 won episcopal rank for him. If the University was "on the verge of a great development," Ryan said on this latter occasion, it was all due to its chancellor.[32]

Ryan's efforts to make the institution a true university aroused deep misgivings on the part of the Dominican archbishop of Cincinnati, John T. McNicholas, and others who believed Ryan was trying to "make a little Harvard, Yale or Princeton" of it instead of restoring "that pontifical character it once had."[33] As head of a visiting committee empowered by Rome, McNicholas recommended that Ryan be replaced. When the fifth rector was named bishop of Omaha in August 1935, Curley was irate. He wrote to a former auditor of the apostolic delegation, placing the entire blame for the "calamity" that had befallen the university on the "juvenile Savonarola of Cincinnati." The latter was also conniving, he claimed, to place in Ryan's stead the inept rector of the Philadelphia Seminary, Joseph M. Corrigan, a man who could "talk, smoke and sleep at the same time."[34] When Corrigan was chosen rector, however, Curley gave him all the support his dedication to Catholic education compelled.

The Bureau of Catholic Charities

In addition to being dedicated to Catholic education, Curley was convinced of the need to advance the cause of Catholic charities in the archdiocese. In December 1921 he placed Rev. Edwin L. Leonard in charge of an organizational effort. With the help of Father John O'Grady, the man who would help set up most of the bureaus of Catholic Charities in the nation, Curley organized that of the District of Columbia first, placing O'Grady himself in charge. Because of the latter's many responsibilities, however, Curley would in 1929 give him as assistant director the young curate at St. Patrick's, Lawrence Shehan.

In Baltimore itself an organizational meeting was held in June 1922, but the bureau, under Father Leonard, did not take final form until April 1923, when it replaced entirely the Central Bureau of the St. Vincent de Paul Society. As Curley probably anticipated, Robert Biggs, who had headed this office for fourteen years, objected vehemently. Six of the eighteen conferences voting also opposed the move.[35] But under Leonard the archdiocesan bureau of Catholic Charities operated smoothly and efficiently. The success of Catholic Charities in Baltimore and Washington was due not only to the determination of the archbishop but also to the presence in the archdiocese of such men as O'Grady and William Kerby and the School of Social Work at the Catholic University, which supplied professional case workers.

After the forced retirement of Biggs, however, the direction of Catholic Charities fell entirely to the clergy. The St. Vincent de Paul Society became little more than a volunteer force for the implementation of decisions made in the bureau's office. O'Grady complained in 1925 that parish involvement had actually slackened with the creation of the Washington bureau. When Curley allowed the bureau to join the Community Chest in 1928, it diminished even more.[36] Curley declined to let the bureau in Baltimore join the Community Chest there, fearing the "cold lifeless thing" efficiency would bring.[37] Relief of the poor at the parish level was, nevertheless, as O'Grady had feared, "swept away in the wave of centralization . . . divorcing the laity from active participation in charities."[38]

Curley was displeased at the slow growth of the St. Vincent de Paul Society, which by 1930 could claim conferences in only twenty-five of Baltimore's fifty-seven parishes. The Ladies of Charity could be found in only eight. The number of active units of the Young Catholic's Friend Society, now the oldest organization in the archdiocese, was down to fifteen. The Great Depression would place enormous burdens on the bureaus of Catholic Charities of both Baltimore and Washington, but it would spur a remarkable expansion of the charitable societies. By 1934 there would be more than forty conferences of the St. Vincent de Paul Society in Baltimore alone, and the Ladies of Charity would be able to count thirty-three branches in Baltimore, twenty-six in Washington, and twenty-six in the counties.[39]

Until the Depression Curley held a banquet every year to publicize Catholic Charities, at which Catholic businessmen pledged generous sums. In 1929 he was happy to report that nearly $1 million had been paid out the previous year by the Baltimore bureau and the institutions under it: $239,096 for 836 dependent children, $284,856 for 996 delinquent children. $32,449 for children in boarding homes, $44,376 by the St. Vincent de Paul Society, $3,000 by Big Brothers, $6,000 for the Catholic Community House in southeast Baltimore, $110,656 for the home for the aged, $45,000 for the home for incurables, and $135,000 for the works of the bureau itself, mostly in the form of groceries, rent, clothing, and funerals for "the friendless dead."[40] No mention was made of salaries for the increasing number of caseworkers nor the percentage of revenues that came from city and state appropriations, considerable in the case of orphans and delinquents. There developed in Baltimore a good working relationship among Catholic Charities, Big Brothers and Sisters, and the courts.

Propagation of the Faith

In 1925 Curley named Rev. Thomas J. Toolen to organize the archdiocesan office of the Home and Foreign Mission Society for the Propagation of the Faith. In the first full year of operation it collected $147,000, an amazing sum for the oldest archdiocese. Toolen was named bishop of Mobile in 1927 and was replaced by Rev. Louis C. Vaeth, an indefatigable booster.[41] In 1928 and again in 1929 the society collected over $210,000. Vaeth was also made moderator of the Catholic Students' Mission Crusade, which had recently been established in the archdiocese. In no time the CSMC was solidly planted in every parish. Vaeth became famous for the mammoth CSMC rallies he staged. In 1930 fifty thousand students attended mass at the stadium to hear cannons boom and bugles blare at the consecration.[42]

Churches New and Old

Among other needs of the archdiocese Curley was anxious to fill were new parishes with new churches and new churches to replace old ones. Twenty-seven new parishes or missions were created in the years 1922–39. In South Baltimore Our Lady of Sorrows in 1924 became as the third Italian parish. Also in Baltimore, to the southeast, Our Lady of Pompei was erected 1923–25 for the city's fourth Italian parish and entrusted to the Italian Vincentians, and Sacred Heart of Mary was raised in 1925–26 for the sixth Polish parish. Out Liberty Heights in the northwest, where Catholics were in short supply, the American Vincentians built their second parish church in the city, Our Lady of Lourdes, in 1925–26. For second- and third-generation Germans and Irish moving out the northeastern corridors the Shrine of the Little Flower was erected in 1926–27 and St. Francis of Assisi in 1927–28. To the west, out Edmondson Avenue, James Keelty, Jr., bore the expense of St. Bernardine's in 1928–29 to serve the buyers of the rowhouses he was building in the neighborhood. Just outside the city the parish of St. Rita was created in 1922 for the industrial community of Dundalk. In 1924 Curley persuaded the Redemptorists to begin the parish of St. Clement Mary Hofbauer in Rosedale. In 1933 a chapel was built for a new mission called St. Ursula in Parkville, and in 1936 the mission of Our Lady of Perpetual Help was created for the Catholics of Woodlawn.[43]

In Washington the Josephite parish of Holy Redeemer and a mission, Epiphany, were opened for black Catholics in 1922 and 1925. Also in the capital St. Francis Xavier was dedicated in 1924 in the southeast. In the communities circling the city the growth was more impressive. In 1923 a mission was opened at Ardmore for whites and one at Glen Arden for blacks by a priest at the Catholic University. In 1926 Our Lady of Lourdes was created in Bethesda, in 1930 St. Michael's in Silver Spring, in 1932 Our Lady of Sorrows in Takoma Park, and in 1937 St. Joseph's in Beltsville.

In Anne Arundel County missions were established at Odenton in 1924 and Davidsonville in 1929 and the parish of St. John the Evangelist, Severna Park, in 1927. In Prince George's County a mission called St. Michael's was created at Baden in 1922. In Garrett County the mission of the Immaculate Conception was completed at Kitzmiller in 1928. In St. Mary's County Our Lady of the Wayside was opened at Chaptico in 1938, and at Prince Frederick in Calvert County St. John Vianney in 1939.

More than thirty churches replaced older and smaller ones in established parishes. Among the most impressive were those constructed for the Polish parishes of St. Casimir in 1926–27 and Holy Rosary in 1927–28, both of which cost about half a million dollars. A larger building was acquired in 1933 for the black parish of St. Francis Xavier. In Washington St. Augustine's built its second church for blacks at a new location. The Shrine of the Sacred Heart out 16th Street would cost over a million dollars.

With a church, of course, went a rectory and with a school a convent. By the end of Curley's first ten years one or more of these four kinds of buildings (usually more) had been erected in forty-five parishes in Baltimore, twenty-one parishes in Washington, and forty parishes in the counties.[44] Except for projects already on the drawing board, the Depression would bring a virtual halt to this unprecedented building boom.

Other Institutions

In addition to schools and churches an assortment of other institutions was provided before 1939, most before the Great Depression. A day nursery for blacks was opened by the Mission Helpers in 1925; the Keating Memorial Day Nursery was dedicated in Cumberland in 1928; and a nursery and Polish center was begun by the Servants of Mary Immaculate in 1936 at the edge of Patterson Park. Several homes for the middle-class aged were opened: the St. Margaret Mary House in Washington in 1922; the Sacred Heart Home in Hyattsville by the Servants of the Holy Ghost in 1926; Kirkleigh Villa, another Jenkins family benefaction, on Roland Avenue in Baltimore in 1927. The Jenkins Memorial Hospital for Incurables, a legacy of Elizabeth Jenkins, was also opened near St. Agnes Hospital in 1927. In 1926 the Benedictine Thomas Verner Moore of the Catholic University began St. Gertrude's School for retarded children. In 1927 the Mission Helpers opened St. Francis Xavier School for the Deaf in the Irvington section of Baltimore. In 1932 the St. Vincent de Paul Society of Washington organized Christopher Inn for homeless unemployed and ex-convicts. When the government assumed this responsibility in 1936, the home was reopened for working women as the Brent House.[45]

The Favored Lay Organizations

Of much greater interest to Curley than to Gibbons were Catholic lay organizations. He had no desire, however, to see the species multiply. He refused, for example, to allow the Daughters of Isabella into the archdiocese because the Catholic Daughters of America were already well entrenched. Those who proposed new organizations he propelled toward existing ones, especially the Holy Name Society. It was his wish to see the HNS in every parish and every man in the parish enrolled. By 1936 there were 48,000 members scattered throughout the archdiocese. There were also Junior Holy Name Societies. Holy Name men received communion once a month and almost as often, it seemed, marched en masse to places designated by the archbishop. With impressive results the HNS also operated the Big Brothers Association in Baltimore.

Next on the list of male societies favored by the archbishop was perhaps the St. Vincent de Paul Society. Then came the Knights of Columbus. By 1926 the Maryland State Council of the K of C numbered more than eight thousand members and that of the District of Columbia perhaps a third as many, but thereafter membership declined because of restrictions placed by the national body on associate members. In Washington the K of C opened a law school and offered evening classes to veterans as early as 1922. In Baltimore it built in 1924–26 a $1.2 million headquarters on Cathedral Street called the Alcazar. In 1927 the Knights organized the Columbia Squires—a Junior K of C—and in 1932 established the Catholic Action Guild to study Catholic teachings and to work as lay apostles.[46] Energetic and well organized, the Maryland K of C responded eagerly to tasks assigned by both the national headquarters and the archbishop, tasks that were seldom in conflict.

The three women's organizations that Curley favored were the Sodality of the Blessed Virgin Mary, the Catholic Daughters of America (CDA), and the International Federation of Catholic Alumnae (IFCA). As with the HNS Curley wanted the Sodality in all parishes and all the women enrolled. The Sodality Union of Washington under Miss Mary Mattingly was particularly active. In Baltimore the principal undertaking of the CDA was the old Casa Regina transformed into a Catholic YWCA called the Cadoa. The Daughters took up tasks assigned by the archbishop even more quickly than did the Knights. The IFCA Curley used mainly to broadcast his views on Catholic education. The willingness of local chapters to follow his lead, however, often placed them in conflict with their national leaders in matters other than education.

The CSMC proved an excellent vehicle for marshaling the children of the archdiocese as well as promoting vocations. In October 1936, however, Curley sent a letter to all pastors urging them to establish Boy Scout troops. The Scouts he also assigned to Father Vaeth, thus assuring a rapid growth of Catholic Boy Scouts and later Girl Scouts throughout the archdiocese.

In his first year or two Curley made an honest effort to see the National Council of Catholic Men and the National Council of Catholic Women, bodies created by the NCWC, spread throughout the archdiocese. Finding them without purpose or drive, however, he gave up the attempt and in time became openly critical of both, especially the NCCM. When in 1926 hearings were conducted in Congress on the Mexican question and the "voice of American Catholic manhood" was needed, Curley complained, the NCCM was as "silent as a sphinx." The HNS, on the other hand, responded within forty-eight hours.[47]

Unprecedented growth in membership of Catholic organizations, therefore, occurred in only the favored few. Other groups resented the indifference of their ordinary and his official organ. In 1930, in fact, the *Baltimore Catholic Review* in praising the Holy Name Society belittled members of the Catholic Benevolent Legion, the AOH, and other bodies for being found at banquet tables but not the communion rail. The state secretary of the CBL, which still counted some twelve hundred members in twenty-two councils, denied the charge emphatically and complained of the *Review*'s reluctance to cover its activities.[48] Except in the national parishes, the variety of parochial organizations diminished in the Curley years. The decline was most noticeable in those in which a measure of lay initiative was exercised, especially the young men's literary societies and even athletic associations.

Though the retreat movement was the result of lay initiative, it became one of the most effective vehicles for the transmission of attitudes the archbishop wished to promote. The League of Laymen's Retreats had been founded in 1914 by Mark O. Shriver, Jr., and others. Until 1921 its retreats were conducted at Georgetown and then at Mount St. Mary's. In 1926 the Jesuits built a center for the league on the Severn River and called it Manresa. Patrick J. Haltigan, long-time leader of the HNS, was elected president in 1928. The Manresans, as the members came to be called, held annual banquets, more than a thousand attending that of 1935.[49] J. Edgar Hoover was one of the speakers engaged for both banquets and retreats. The retreat center for women opened by the Sisters of the Atonement near the Catholic University in 1923 received but a fraction of the attention accorded Manresa by the *Catholic Review*.

An organization the archbishop seized upon with enthusiasm but one in which laymen assumed, with striking success, the clerical role of preaching (they called it teaching) was the Catholic Evidence Guild. Training courses were begun in Washington in 1931, and before the end of the following year "pitches" had been located at Mount Vernon Place, Hollins Market, and Patterson Park in Baltimore and Franklin Park in Washington. Frank J. and Maisie Ward Sheed came down to help. The archbishop waxed enthusiastic over the guild's success.[50] But then he was never stinting in his praise of any organization that stood up boldly for the church.

Romanization

The advent of Michael Curley signified for the oldest archdiocese what the elevation of Roman-trained prelates in the early twentieth century meant in other metropolitan sees: the "Romanization" of the Catholic Church in the United States.[51] Curley boasted in 1934 to the rector of the North American College in Rome that he had maintained ten to twelve seminarians there yearly since his coming to Baltimore.[52] Scrupulously he enforced all directives of the Roman congregations, some of which Gibbons would have filed away with bemusement. In 1927 the Consistorial Congregation complained that, contrary to a Roman decree of 1916, the St. Patrick's Players in Washington were conducting dances under the direction of a priest. This violation in a city where resided the pontifical representative, the order ran, should cease immediately.[53] Curley disbanded the Players at once and commanded a general cessation of the practice, but he complained to Moses E. Kiley in Rome that the decree was being "violated all over the country." He had been given no liberty in carrying it out, and its enforcement caused "a great deal of bitterness and comment" on the part of the clergy.[54] Despite the discomfort enforcement sometimes occasioned, in only one instance, which will be considered later, did Curley fail to act immediately on the directives, even suggestions, of those representing the Holy See.

A Marked Dissimilarity

In more than his strict adherence to Roman policy and procedures, his energetic promotion of centralization and consolidation, and his ambitious program of institution building did Curley's actions provide a striking contrast to those of Gibbons. In his relationships with his priests, with the Catholic elite, and with his immigrant charges the tenth archbishop also displayed a marked dissimilarity.

PROBLEM PRIESTS

Curley had small patience with not only problem priests but also incompetent, lax, and irresponsible ones. Failure to pay bills, he told one pastor, was "common highway robbery minus the revolver."[55] The same priest he told some years later: "You may rob a bank, you may become a public hold-up man, but neither you nor your Assistants . . . may be late with your Masses."[56] A young priest professor at the Catholic University, Fulton J. Sheen, he admonished: "I have nothing but professional contempt for the priest who takes off his Roman collar and clerical garb to pose before the public as a layman." On this matter and irregularities in his household he enjoined him to exercise "a little priestly prudence and good sense."[57]

To the rural deans and his auxiliary bishop he assigned the task of investigating problem priests. He told one culprit: "I think that instead of appointing you to a parish I should have consigned you for the rest of your life to Mount Hope [for mental cases]. I wonder if you realize what an impossible man you are." If he incurred another debt over $20, the offender was told, he would be suspended ipso facto.[58] A week later the hapless pastor was suspended and removed from his parish.

The priest against whom Curley moved with greatest severity was one whose offensive behavior Gibbons had endured. John B. Manley was an able administrator and builder of several churches in greater Baltimore: St. Dominic's, St. Francis of Assisi, and St. Ursula. Following one of a series of admonitions for lapses past and present, however, Manley sent the archbishop a veiled threat of "digging up Florida" and "other matters since your coming to Baltimore."[59] Curley suspended the priest immediately and ordered him to make a ten-day retreat, after which he had full permission to investigate all charges he might wish to make. Then he should "put up or shut up."[60] At the end of the retreat Manley apologized.

Curley did not hold grudges. Three years later he told Manley that he was in no hurry to find pastors for St. Francis and St. Ursula because "they are in good hands when in your hands."[61] Curley was as kind as he was stern. To pastors struggling to make ends meet he sent letters of encouragement usually with a check enclosed. To timid ones he might suggest: "Don't you think it's time you took a vacation?" Some years he would send lengthy comments to every pastor in the archdiocese after carefully scrutinizing their annual reports. Some he praised, others he pilloried. He did not have to worry about losing priests. He had more than he could use, especially during the Depression years.

THE RICH

Unlike Gibbons, Curley kept "a respectable distance" from the rich. He made it his policy never to officiate at their weddings. Nor did he allow them to have private chapels, as Gibbons had done, a privilege, Curley claimed, Gibbons had no right to bestow.[62] He made little effort to hide his disdain for the first families. Descent from the good people who came in the *Ark* and the *Dove*, he told the historian Guilday, "seems to be a guarantee of ignorance about everything but snobbishness."[63]

THE IMMIGRANT POOR

By contrast, he had a genuine sympathy for the immigrant poor of the archdiocese. And he was not eager, as was Gibbons, to see them move into the mainstream. He encouraged them, in fact, to hold on to their language and traditions. When made a monsignor in 1929, Stanislaus Wachowiak, pastor of Holy Rosary, bespoke his gratitude for the archbishop's message to the Poles to maintain their Polish characteristics in the face of a "forceful, improper Americanization."[64]

Curley readily accepted Wachowiak's role as dean of Baltimore's Polonia. While he centralized the work of Catholic Charities, Curley allowed the Poles to deal with their poor in their own way and instructed Wachowiak to organize such an effort.[65] In a rivalry that developed between Wachowiak and Stanislaus Wikarski, pastor of the new parish of the Sacred Heart of Mary and a spokesman for the Polish National Alliance, Curley came out squarely on the side of Wachowiak.[66]

Curley had also a great respect for Father Sandalgi, who shepherded not only the Poles of Curtis Bay but other Slavic groups in the city. These included the Uniates, whom Curley had no desire to Latinize. When a married priest arrived to serve the Ukrainians, Curley readily followed Sandalgi's advice, requesting Rome not to enforce the ban against such priests in the United States.[67]

Curley's contact with some of the other pastors of national parishes was not so harmonious. Father Lietuvnikas of St. Alphonsus was a case in point. While most of the forty to fifty thousand Poles in Baltimore were devout churchgoers, hardly a sixth of the six thousand Lithuanians were, and 70 percent of their children were in the public schools.[68] Lietuvnikas blamed other pastors for taking his parishioners away from him. A "back to the faith" movement, however, was already underway among the Lithuanians. The young assistant, Louis J. Mendelis, who would succeed Lietuvnikas in 1943, was one of its promoters. For the Bohemians of Baltimore, Catholic sokols were founded to counteract, successfully for the most part, the nationalist and anticlerical ones.

Curley had his problems with the two secular priests who served the Italians: Nicholas De Carlo, pastor of Holy Rosary in Washington, and Luigi Arena, pastor of Our Lady of Sorrows in Baltimore. The latter parish was created in 1924 to quiet the shrill complaints of the non-Italian people and pastor of St. Joseph's, which had until then served the Italians of South Baltimore. Arena was given the church vacated by the blacks of St. Monica's. The parish was small, but Arena was popular with those Italians of Baltimore, a minority, who admired Mussolini. Curley could hardly have been flattered by Arena's assurance that his letter to one of the Italian societies, "in the fascist spirit and the style of Mussolini," had had "a marvelous effect."[69] When Arena visited Italy in 1934, Curley gave the church building back to St. Monica's and advised Arena not to return. In 1927 he reluctantly had the Pallotines of the German province replaced by those of the Italian one, giving "wretched nationalism" as the excuse.[70] Despite the exasperation they frequently provoked, Curley had a deep regard for the Italians. When he was made a Grand Officer of the Crown of Italy in 1927 for his services to them, he told the Italian ambassador that he was proud to have been able to win their affection.[71]

Responding to the Blacks

Curley's genuine sympathy for the blacks was even more severely tested. From the start he was caught in a tangle of conflicting expectations. The militant and highly sensitized blacks of Washington under Thomas Wyatt Turner, president of the Committee for the Advancement of Colored Catholics, complained of the Josephites' refusal to advance black candidates to the priesthood. Despite his admiration for the Josephites and his wish to have them eventually take charge of all the black parishes of the archdiocese, Curley agreed to be spiritual director of the Federated Colored Catholics, which in 1924 succeeded the committee. In 1925 he addressed its first annual convention in Washington and listened patiently to all the speeches.[72]

Among the delegates from twenty states who gathered in Baltimore for the fifth annual convention in 1929 was a Jesuit from St. Louis, William Markoe, whose goal, it soon became clear, was to transform the federation into an interracial body with broader goals than agitation for equal rights for blacks. In this he found an ally in Father LaFarge, who had moved to New York in 1926. When Turner resisted the change, they sought to have him ousted from the presidency. It was Turner's aim, as he himself told a colleague in Washington, to keep the federation strictly in the hands of laymen. "I thought Markoe and LaFarge understood this, but evidently they decided they could grab the land, put up their flag and claim the country as their own. This is what the white has done throughout the ages," Turner concluded sadly.[73] The result was a split in 1932, the western and New York delegates supporting the presidency of a pliant black, George Conrad. Both sides appealed to Curley, who refused to have the "bawling baby" dumped in his lap.[74] He resigned as spiritual director and tried to remain neutral. This proved difficult because the fate of Cardinal Gibbons Institute was at stake.

Though Curley was still chairman of the board, the direction of the institute remained in the hands of LaFarge even after his transfer to New York. To keep the school going, Curley was compelled to support LaFarge in a power struggle first with the executive secretary of the board, who wanted the dismissal of the Daniels as managers, and then with the Daniels themselves when they proved ardent supporters of Thomas Turner in his struggle to keep control of the Federated Colored Catholics. To Turner, Curley wrote in frustration that he was "disgusted" with the "whole nonsensical debacle." He was particularly annoyed at a series of articles in the Baltimore *Afro-American* by "Cora Grace Inman," whom Curley believed to be Constance Daniel of Cardinal Gibbons Institute.[75] In the end the $30,000 that Curley diverted from mission and archdiocesan funds to keep the school from bankruptcy proved unavailing. As a result of the Depression and the dismissal of the Daniels, the Institute closed in December 1933. It would, however, in 1938, at Curley's prompting, be reopened by the Jesuits on a much reduced scale. In the meantime the group LaFarge had organized in New York to help the institute evolved into the Catholic Interracial Council.

Curley quietly pushed pastors to allow blacks in their churches. Pay no heed, he told one pastor, to the "calamity howl" that would inevitably follow a black man's receiving communion in his church.[76] Pastors and ushers alike he enjoined to treat the blacks who entered their churches not in a "Hitleristic way" but with the "kindness and gentleness of Christ."[77] It was true, nevertheless, that in his approach to the racial question Curley exercised a caution that was rarely in evidence in his handling of other issues of the day.

The Militant Editor

Historically the most significant difference between the episcopacy of Michael Curley and that of James Gibbons was the dramatic change in temper that characterized the oldest archdiocese as it came to exemplify the self-conscious Catholic ghetto. Curley was, without doubt, the most vociferous of the archbishops of Baltimore, the only one who spoke without heed for the consequences and with a brashness and belligerency that, suprisingly, came to be admired by perhaps a majority of his Catholic subjects. His reputation as a warrior prelate, however, was won with the help of a layman hardly less bellicose or less devoted to his church: Vincent de Paul Fitzpatrick, managing editor of the *Baltimore Catholic Review*. In many ways he was Curley's alter ego.

Fitzpatrick had come from the *Sun* in Gibbons' last year to assist the *Review*'s editor-in-chief, a priest. In no time, partly because of Curley's unqualified support, he was running the *Review*. His style was unmistakable.

Fitzpatrick was master of the gratuitous headline, triumphal and hortatory by turn. "The Catholic Church Always Wins; Christ Has Granted Her Victory." "Catholics Will Stop Building Schools on the Morrow of Doomsday." "Play Hard, Boys and Girls; A Sturdy Body Makes a Strong Mind." His readers were well aware that the Catholic to be pitied was "spineless," "wishy-washy," "wobbly-kneed," a "jellyfish," or, his favorite, a "pussyfooter." The real Catholic was, of course, candid, manly, courageous, and loyal.

Fitzpatrick was tireless in prodding his readers to action. When drugstores near the cathedral, for example, had the temerity to display birth control literature, the *Review* demanded: "What are you going to do about it, Holy Name men, Knights of Columbus, Catholic Daughters of America, Hibernians, members of the Central Verein and representatives of other societies?" The CDA responded immediately, but before the others could swing into action the offensive literature had disappeared. The *Review* observed, however, that "filthy newspapers" could still be found in the same stores."[78]

Few editors could strike such terror in the hearts of publishers and radio sponsors. As president of the Catholic Press Association in the late 1930s, Fitzpatrick's power was enhanced. When the *Washington Post* praised Spanish Loyalists (Leftists) as neither cowards nor weaklings, the *Review* thundered: "You Catholic men and women, you various Catholic organizations in Washington, if you have any backbone, if you have any spunk, you will ask the Washington *Post* to tell you what it means. . . . If you let the Washington *Post* get away with such insults, God pity you. The Catholics of the country will be ashamed of you."[79] Two weeks later Fitzpatrick congratulated the priests and laymen of the capital who had written to the errant paper, so many that the *Post* had "crawled."[80] On rare occasions the *Review* overreached itself. When in 1929 the Washington Public Library excluded Father Finn's boys' books as not up to its literary standards, the *Review* accused it of being anti-Catholic. Several priests, including Joseph Nelligan and Paul Hanley Furfey, rushed to the defense of the library. The *Review* offered an apology of sorts.[81]

Battling the Sun

The archbishop was as quick to note slurs upon his church, whether inadvertent or not, and even more effective in holding the culprit to account. The Red Cross magazine made such a slip. Curley informed its officials that they had "driven a sword through the hearts of twenty million people." Two of them had come "in fear and trembling," he later reported, and were "tearfully apologetic."[82]

Curley's fiercest effort to wring an apology from a newspaper became a legend in Baltimore—and elsewhere. The much respected *Sun* was his target.[83] Gibbons, Curley informed Bishop Francis C. Kelley of Oklahoma City, had "read his Breviary and the *Sun* with equal devotion." Since his death, however, the *Sun* had "never missed an opportunity to give me a dig. . . . I am not at all bashful about admitting that I was looking for an opportunity [to retaliate]."[84] It came in June 1934, when a correspondent expelled from Nazi Germany compared Hitler to Ignatius Loyola. Curley demanded an apology. When the *Sun* demurred, as he doubtless anticipated it would, Curley took his battle to press and pulpit. The 300,000 Catholics of the archdiocese, he claimed, repudiated this "brazen mendacity." He was not saying that they should not buy the *Sun* nor deal with its advertisers, but they had no obligation to do so.[85] Enough took their cue from their archbishop that the *Sun* was compelled to make a qualified apology. This the archbishop pronounced unsatisfactory as he embarked for Ireland for the summer. John M. McNamara, his auxiliary bishop since 1928, and other archdiocesan officials met with representatives of the *Sun*, including H. L. Mencken, and worked out another statement that the *Review* judged an appropriate apology.[86]

The Curley Crusades

In his first busy years Archbishop Curley was frugal with his bombshells. One such followed his efforts to eliminate discrimination against Catholics in Washington agencies, especially the Treasury Department. At the laying of the cornerstone of the Alcazar in 1924, he went public with the evidence he had accumulated. He finally complained to the president himself in 1925. Coolidge responded that such cases were "distressing" but almost impossible to remedy. "It is one of the defects of our human nature and is not confined to any denomination, but breaks out in all of them." He appreciated, nevertheless, the "discreet way" in which the archbishop had proceeded.[87]

Curley waited until 1926 before he unleashed without restraint his store of indignation. On four different matters he dealt manifestos that drew national attention: the Curtis-Reed bill advocating federal control of education, the persecution of the Catholic Church in Mexico, the threat to Catholic education posed by the Catholic Foundation plan, and the failure of the National Council of Catholic Men and National Council of Catholic Women to organize the laity effectively. His attacks on Mexico and the Catholic Foundation plan were sustained and impassioned. These two plus the attack on Loyalist Spain constituted his three principal crusades.

THE CATHOLIC FOUNDATION

The Catholic Foundation was a center of studies and social life at the University of Illinois promoted by Rev. John A. O'Brien, a leader in the Newman movement, as a model for other such centers for Catholic students attending secular universities.[88] Curley feared that the plan would, as he told O'Brien himself, "pull the foundations from under the great edifice of Catholic education in America."[89]

When in 1927 the *Review* failed to dissuade the news service of the NCWC from releasing an item concerning a prayer on which O'Brien, a minister, and a rabbi had collaborated, Curley voiced his strongest condemnation of O'Brien in an address to the IFCA. The plan, "deceitfully labeled Catholic," by a man, Curley noted pointedly, who was a member of the advisory board of the Department of Education of the NCWC, would expose Catholic children to the "soul-searing influence of unbelief and secularism."[90]

In a letter to the apostolic delegate intended for the Holy Office and another to the Cardinal Secretary of State Merry del Val, he went even further. To Merry de Val he complained of the "atmosphere" promoted by O'Brien and condoned by the NCWC "redolent of unbelief and sheer materialism where people are exposed to the constant temptations of expressing themselves in a 'big, broad, liberal way'."[91] The apostolic delegate, Archbishop Pietro Fumasoni-Biondi, told Curley that the matter was already under investigation and that he should refrain from any further public statements concerning "this unfortunate affair."[92] There were no more public, or private, statements.

THE MEXICAN CRUSADE

Whereas Curley shared the stage with the Jesuit editors of *America* in his criticism of O'Brien, he surpassed even Bishop Francis Kelley as the most vocal critic of the persecution of the church in Mexico and the failure of the American government to intervene. The Paulist John J. Burke, executive secretary of the NCWC, who was working quietly to ease the situation in Mexico, noted in a memo: "To our utter amazement on February 22nd Archbishop Curley made a public address in Washington [before the K of C] in which he calls for a nationwide protest and meetings of protest against the present government of Mexico." He then attacked the United States government for its delinquency, Burke also noted, and nudged the "indifferent" K of C to take action.[93] The Maryland K of C, even before the national body, and other local organizations responded zestfully with rallies and resolutions.

President Coolidge and Secretary of State Frank B. Kellogg, through the president of Georgetown University, sought to silence the angry archbishop.[94] Instead, Curley closeted himself with Congressman John J. Boylan of New York and framed a resolution calling upon the secretary of state to open his files on the Mexican situation. "Working together," Curley told Boylan, "we have given the matter national, and almost international publicity."[95] Curley also wrote a series of articles for the *Review* published in the summer by the International Catholic Truth Society of Brooklyn as *Mexican Tyranny and the Catholic Church*, in which he continued to lambaste the administration in Washington. In April he sent a letter to President Coolidge urging a break with Mexico.[96]

Though Curley was not, as Burke wondered, an agent of the Vatican in a secret plan to topple the government of Mexico, his agitation was encouraged by Archbishop George Caruana, apostolic delegate to Mexico, as well as Archbishop Fumasoni-Biondi, apostolic delegate to the United States.[97] Curley, in turn, wondered about Burke. Suggesting to Fumasoni-Biondi in March that the NCWC take action, he added: "At times like this, one does not know just who or what the N.C.W.C. is. In its ultimate analysis, it seems to be Father John Burke and nobody else."[98] In 1927 Burke began to work quietly with the new ambassador to Mexico to effect an accommodation with the Mexican government. This he finally achieved in 1929. At the time, Curley, in Rome, was asked by the cardinal prefect of the Consistorial Congregation, Carlo Perosi, to report on the "alleged undue influence" of Burke over Fumasoni-Biondi. After his return and several inquiries, Curley wrote Perosi to defend the actions of both Burke and the delegate. "The N.C.W.C. is another matter," Curley concluded. "On that I will write Your Eminence later."[99] He never did.

After a brief respite, the persecution in Mexico was resumed. In 1934 Curley was roused to action again when the ambassador to Mexico, Josephus Daniels, injudiciously praised the remark of a Mexican leader to the effect that it was the aim of his government "to take possession of the mind of children." Curley had the *Catholic Review* address a letter to President Franklin D. Roosevelt calling for Daniels' resignation. The *Review* asked the president to read its "exposé of the bestial, pederastic and sodomistic campaign of socialistic education which has gone on in alliance with the other methods of warfare against God, Religion and Common Decency in Mexico."[100] The exposé was an essay, the first of a series, by a Jesuit named Michael Kenny, one of the most rabid but articulate critics of the Mexican government.[101] The issues with the Kenny essays were mailed to the White House and State Department and circulated widely in Mexico itself. Congressmen wrote for copies. In December Curley, at the request of Archbishop Leopoldo Ruiz y Flores, the apostolic delegate to Mexico in exile, organized the Baltimore Archdiocesan Confederation for the Defense of Religious Liberty in Mexico and put Father Vaeth in charge. Visited frequently by other exiles, it became a national clearing house for information on Mexico.

In early 1935 Senator David Walsh of Massachusetts informed Curley that the State Department had been told that a Senate resolution to investigate persecution in Mexico did not have the support of the NCWC.[102] When Archbishop Edward J. Hanna, chairman of the administrative committee, confirmed the report, Curley retorted angrily: "As you may know, the Administrative Committee has no right whatsoever to speak my mind nor the mind of any other Bishops on a matter on which we have not been consulted." He would say so publicly if the committee's decision was taken as that of the American hierarchy.[103] At the same time, Curley responded to a question posed by the new apostolic delegate, Archbishop Amleto Giovanni Cicognani, on the feasibility of holding another plenary council in America. Curley advised that the time was not ripe. In addition to the long preparation it would entail, it would "demand a harmony and a unity on the part of the hierarchy of this Country that at the present time can scarcely be said to exist, particularly amongst those occupying the highest places in that same Hierarchy."[104]

In a hard-hitting speech before the Washington Sodality, Curley blamed Roosevelt for the ultimate failure of the Senate resolution. The administration may think it can ignore twenty million Catholics, the K of C, the HNS, and the Sodality, he declared, "but they will have a chance to vote in 1936." The *Review* reported that the "applause was deafening" and that the *New York Times* had covered the speech on page 1.[105] To the Baltimore Sodalists Curley exclaimed: "Let our gentle, sacerdotal diplomats stay at home." The Good Neighbor Policy should not excuse the atrocities committed in Mexico.[106] Senator Walsh reported in a "personal" letter that he had had meetings with Burke and some bishops and that the NCWC now approved of mass meetings. "I am sure that they cannot help but feel that your leadership in this matter has not only been courageous but wise and that you have shown a vision which is only now beginning to dawn upon them."[107]

At their meeting in November the American bishops created a Committee for Mexican Relief composed of Curley, Bishop Francis Kelley, and Archbishop Arthur J. Drossaerts of San Antonio, with Curley as chairman. Before the year was out, the committee had invited three other bishops to join it, had incorporated, and had engaged a fund raiser. It had also written Cardinal Secretary of State Eugenio Pacelli seeking papal approval for its work. Pacelli immediately cabled approval and sent a sizable donation.[108] The apostolic delegate, Archbishop Cicognani, was uncharacteristically agitated by the steps taken by Curley and Kelley. "The former," he told Burke, "was not honest; the latter had no brains."[109] Apparently Cicognani in late January 1936, and then the administrative committee, apprised Curley of their displeasure. He and Kelley, they claimed, had exceeded the bishops' mandate. The corporation should be dissolved.[110] Curley's blood pressure soared.

After three weeks in bed, Curley resigned from the NCWC, claiming to act on doctor's orders. The apostolic delegate, the chairman of the administrative committee, now Archbishop Edward A. Mooney, bishop of Rochester, and Father Burke all begged the archbishop to reconsider. His resignation, said Mooney, "would be most unfortunate" and, added Burke, "a sad disappointment."[111] Burke also avowed: "Your work as a leader in the church in this country is beyond question." Deeply despondent, Curley answered: "I never was, and I am not now, of any importance whatsoever to the Church in America."[112] He refused to reconsider. The committee's work of creating a seminary in the United States for Mexican priests went on without him.[113]

HELL'S HATRED IN SPAIN

By then persecution in Mexico was on the wane. But events in Europe would reactivate the warrior prelate. By the summer of 1936 Spain had replaced Mexico on page 1 of the *Catholic Review*. Almost every issue carried vivid accounts of atrocities committed by the Loyalist government upon innocent bishops, priests, and religious. "Hell's Hatred Seen in Plans of God's Foes," ran one of Fitzpatrick's headlines. The *Review* also challenged the *Sun* to answer its charge that the *Sun* was "favorably inclined to communistically-governed countries."[114] Some analysts would later claim that the *Sun* had switched from pro-Loyalist to pro-rebel after warning shots from the Catholic pulpits and the *Review*, a claim the *Review* would emphatically deny.[115] Whereas the *Review* had urged intervention in the case of Mexico, it demanded a hands-off policy in the case of Spain, where the rebel forces under General Francisco Franco had the advantage.[116]

The Spanish Civil War induced the archbishop of Baltimore to launch a national crusade against communism, which will be considered in the following chapter. On January 3, 1939, he wrote a letter to be read in all churches urging the faithful to attend a mass meeting at Constitution Hall in favor of retaining an embargo of arms against Spain. When the Spanish ambassador invited Curley and others to go to Spain to see for themselves that there was no persecution, Curley shot back: "He is a common, ordinary liar."[117] The *Brooklyn Tablet*, among others, praised the "bold and fearless speech for which Baltimore's Archbishop is renowned."[118]

Rousing the Rank and File

Though his denunciations of the White House had small effect at the ballot box, where the economy carried more weight than foreign affairs, Curley had probably a greater ability to inflame and to energize rank-and-file Catholics than any of his predecessors. Laity and clergy alike, the director of the Manresa retreat center assured him, yearned for *"strong, red-blooded, fearless, episcopal leadership."*[119] Under Curley's prodding even members of Maryland's first families took fire. Mark O. Shriver, Jr., for example, complained in a letter to the *Review* of the Catholic Church's being slighted in a pictorial map at the Pratt Library.[120]

Curley's Jove-like pronouncements, nevertheless, caused some to interpret his episcopal motto, "Who is like God" (*Quis ut Deus*), in a way that Curley had never intended.[121] "Iron Mike" he was called by both admirers and critics. Some were appalled by his bullying. "Your intemperate utterances," said a defender of John O'Brien, "are the more painfully shocking because they are in such stark and violent contrast to the charity, prudence and discretion of your illustrious and saintly predecessor."[122]

In no period of the history of the archdiocese were Catholics more ready to march en masse at the beck of their spiritual commander. In his first year Curley himself led 35,000 Holy Name men, "rugged farmers, athletic young men, hardy veterans"—religion was "not effeminate," the *Review* noted parenthetically—down Pennsylvania Avenue to the foot of the Washington Monument, where 60,000 gathered.[123] From the early 1930s on Holy Name men in Baltimore would parade to St. Mary's Seminary or later the Fifth Regiment Armory, and in the national capital to the Washington Monument, for the feast of Corpus Christi. The greatest display of a

militant faith occurred in 1934, the tercentenary of the establishment of the
Catholic religion in Maryland, when 100,000 swung into the Baltimore
stadium, among them "retiring nuns . . . with the free step of Red Cross
nurses on parade."[124] In the 1930s Catholic policemen, firemen, postal employees, and others began as groups to attend special masses. Catholic identity was never more important.

Political Preferences

Despite the frequency with which he intruded himself into the political process, Archbishop Curley had no overriding interest in politics as
such. He had little acquaintance with the Irish bosses of Baltimore's Democratic machine, John "Sonny" Mahon or Frank S. Kelly, and had no interest
in their feuds. Even less, after the death of both in 1928, did he interest
himself in the career of William "Willie" Curran, a Catholic who would
rule the city until 1946.[125] On the other hand, he became a close friend of
Albert C. Ritchie, Democratic governor of Maryland from 1920 to 1935,
whose conservative philosophy—Ritchie opposed the growth of federal
power—he shared.[126] Frequently, Curley helped Ritchie with his speeches,
injecting a quote from Aquinas into the Chicago speech that made him
presidential timber.[127] Curley preferred native-born Protestants like
Ritchie to run for office. He supported one of them against Herbert R.
O'Conor of St. John's Parish when the latter captured the governor's seat in
1938. O'Conor he considered "wishy-washy."[128]

Maryland Catholics had voted for Warren G. Harding in 1920, only
the steadfast Irish tenth and the Polish second wards polling Democratic in
Baltimore. A fresh wave of nativism, however, sent them scurrying back to
the fold of their fathers. In 1921 a former Marist brother was pelted with
eggs in the middle of an anti-Catholic diatribe at Aberdeen.[129] In southern
Maryland the Ku Klux Klan was cowed by the K of C. The Klan's anti-
Ritchie campaign in 1923 attracted Catholic blacks to the Democratic party.
St. Mary's County, as a result, went Democratic in 1924 for only the second
time in a presidential election since Reconstruction and would continue to
do so.[130] The defeat of Al Smith in 1928 was traumatic. Catholic parents, the
Review bemoaned, could no longer tell their boys that they could be presi-
dent of the United States.[131] The climate, however, improved appreciably
in the New Deal years. In 1938 Maryland voters sent not only Herbert
O'Conor to Annapolis but Thomas D'Alesandro, Jr., of Little Italy to
Washington as one of its Congressmen.

The Jazz Age and "Dirty Movies"

Maryland Catholics reveled in the prosperity of the 1920s. For one thing, they discovered the car. Most priests got one. Curley never did. As early as 1922 the *Review* carried Sunday mass guides for motorists. Installment buying brought luxuries as well as conveniences, from victrolas to diamond rings. The Jazz Age provoked pulpit warnings, however, mostly against women's styles and "dirty" movies. At the same time, the clergy, taking their cue from their archbishop, railed against "shotgun morality" as exemplified by prohibition and antigambling laws. Catholics would rejoice at repeal in 1933 more than most. Bingo would begin to replace card parties in the late 1930s. Some pastors complained that the radio was keeping their parishioners from evening devotions.

While drinking and gambling were sources of small concern, indecency was another matter. In 1924 the International Federation of Catholic Alumnae, under the presidency of Mrs. Harry Benzinger of Baltimore, at its national convention declared war on indecency in dress, literature, the stage, and the movies.[132] On the matter of "rotten, immoral, dirty, and smutty" movies the archbishop was almost as outspoken as on persecution in Mexico.[133] By 1931, therefore, he was at war with the IFCA, or at least its president, Mrs. Rita McGoldrick, and her policy of "boosting the best and forgetting the rest." Curley, who believed that McGoldrick, the Hays Office, and the motion picture industry were in collusion, wrote in 1931 a series of articles denouncing McGoldrick and the "white list" approach to indecent movies. These, he believed, should be blacklisted.[134] Will Hays, he told Archbishop McNicholas, chairman of the bishops' committee on motion pictures, had sent his assistant "to beg me to let up."[135]

Even before the American bishops accepted the "black list" approach by creating the Legion of Decency in 1934, pledge cards were being distributed to Catholics in the archdiocese of Baltimore. Curley had also persuaded the Maryland chapter of the IFCA to defy its national president and her "white list" campaign. He cooperated actively with the Citizens League of Maryland for Better Motion Pictures and fought distributors over their blind and block booking practices. "The Review will tear them to pieces editorially if they try to oppose the Legion of Decency," Fitzpatrick assured the archbishop.[136] For the next thirty years the archdiocesan assault upon "dirty" movies was unrelenting.

Popular Piety

Popular expressions of piety increased in the same proportion as Catholic preoccupation with public indecency. The March Novena of Grace in honor of St. Francis Xavier begun at St. Ignatius Parish in 1857 had spread throughout the nation.[137] It was Baltimore's most popular devotion. For years trolley cars marked simply "Novena" had carried thousands downtown. Attendance peaked in the Curley years. The Novena of the Miraculous Medal commenced at St. Alphonsus in 1935 and the Perpetual Novena in honor of St. Jude began at St. John the Baptist by the Pallotines in 1941.[138] Almost every parish, however, had its particular devotion and its special shrine surrounded by votive lights.

The Great Depression

The growth of popular devotions was not unrelated to the painful bite of economic want, accelerating as both did in the Depression years. The Great Depression touched Baltimore and Washington later than other cities of comparable size, but as soon as he returned from Ireland in the fall of 1931, Archbishop Curley called all the priests of the city to discuss the crisis and announced a drive for the Archbishop's Relief Fund. By 1933 revenue in most urban parishes had fallen 25 to 30 percent and in the Polish ones almost 50 percent. In Baltimore's substantial St. Martin's, $5,750 was expended for the parish poor in 1931, $18,813, "largely government relief money," in 1932, and $36,000 in 1933, more than income from the offertory collection and pew rents combined.[139] By 1935 some 35 percent of the 110,000 people on relief in Baltimore, or half of the whites, were Catholic, who counted less than a quarter of the population.[140]

Catholic self-help alleviated much of the distress even before the emergency measures of the New Deal came into play. Baltimore Germans, Bohemians, and Poles, despite unemployment and hunger, held on to their residences. Their savings and loan associations "performed feats of solidarity, as parishes rallied to save their neighbors' homes."[141] Archdiocesan and parish charities outdid themselves even though the clothing and furniture collections of the St. Vincent de Paul Society fell off by half.

Before 1939 the archdiocese as such had little direct contact with the New Deal. Curley declined a seat on the state board of the National Recovery Administration. The archdiocesan representative most actively involved with public relief organizations, especially the Baltimore Emergency Relief Commission, was Father Leonard, director of Catholic

Charities, who insisted on Catholic workers for Catholic clients.[142] In 1938 he was replaced by Rev. Edward J. O'Brien. In Washington Lawrence Shehan made better use of the St. Vincent de Paul Society even before he became head of Catholic Charities there in name as well as in fact in 1938.[143]

A casualty of the Depression was the parochial school. From 1931 till Curley's death, the number of parish schools and pupils would remain about the same. Pastors still without schools used the Depression as an excuse not to build. Curley's plans for a diocesan high school for boys was likewise suspended. The Depression also brought an end to the era of magnificently proportioned churches. The last two, begun on the eve of the Depression and not totally finished till after, were those of St. Joseph's Monastery and SS. Philip and James.

A beneficial consequence of the Depression was the appearance in the archdiocese of Catholic Worker houses of hospitality and similar shelters for the down and out. The first Catholic Worker house, the Blessed Martin de Porres Hospice, was opened in Washington in 1935 by a devout black convert, Llewellyn J. Scott, who was inspired by a talk by Dorothy Day.[144] A second, St. Anthony's House of Hospitality, would be opened in Baltimore in 1940 by three college graduates. Inspired by the Catholic Worker movement, Rev. Paul Hanley Furfey, professor of sociology at the Catholic University, founded in 1935 the Campion and Il Poverello Houses, racially integrated enterprises staffed partly by university faculty and students. Out of the latter would come Fides House in 1940.[145]

Still another consequence of the Great Depression was the envelope collection at Sunday mass. To a pastor on the brink of bankruptcy, Curley urged its adoption as "in every well conducted parish. . . . The pew rent system is about as dead as a door nail."[146] One of the first to use envelopes was St. Martin's, Baltimore, at the end of 1925. As a consequence, its income from offertory collections jumped from $20,000 in 1925 to $35,000 in 1927. But by 1933 it had fallen back to $25,000, where it would remain until 1937.[147]

In 1937 the economy of Baltimore itself turned the corner with significant upswings in the steel, aircraft, and shipbuilding industries. Bethlehem Steel's biggest customer was the Emperor Hirohito.[148] Critical developments in different parts of the world would rapidly converge upon the port on the Patapsco.

14   The War Years

BY THE APOSTOLIC CONSTITUTION *Supremae Ecclesiasticae Potestatis*, dated July 22, 1939, the District of Columbia was constituted the archdiocese of Washington with Michael Joseph Curley its first archbishop. It was an unusual arrangement. Baltimore and Washington were now two distinct sees, but they claimed the same archbishop and shared the same curia. When told he would also be vicar general of the new archdiocese, Bishop McNamara expressed surprise. "I had taken it for granted that it would be an arrangement like Savannah-Atlanta."[1]

Such was, in fact, the proposal Curley had made to the apostolic delegate early in the year, "to have the See of Baltimore known hereafter as the Archdiocese of Baltimore-Washington." With a population of about half a million, the District of Columbia had some 75,000 Catholics, he recounted, 34 parishes, 111 priests, 26 parish schools, the Catholic University and Georgetown University, with 28 houses of study associated with the former, 2 colleges and 2 junior colleges for women, 7 high schools for boys and 2 for girls, 8 Catholic institutions devoted to social work, and 2 hospitals.[2] He had placed the matter before his consultors almost a year ago, Curley revealed, and they had gone on record "as being opposed to and afraid of any division such as mentioned years ago to His Eminence, the late Cardinal Gibbons."[3]

News of the change was not released until October 12, the archbishop's birthday. Congratulations poured in. Attorney General Frank Murphy hoped that Curley would "be with us as a good shepherd for many years to come."[4] Senator Millard Tydings of Maryland, on the other hand, expressed the "fervent wish" that he would be chosen to fill one of the two places recently vacated by death.[5] Cardinal Mundelein had died unexpectedly on October 2. New York was probably meant for the other, but Francis J. Spellman had been chosen successor to Cardinal Hayes the previous spring. Bishop Ireton wrote from Richmond: "Some of the old timers from Archbishop Carroll down are probably turning in their graves at the possible future division when the daughter mayhap will outgrow the mother in relative importance, if not size. But that will be after our time, so the future can take care of the future." Ireton added: "There has been enough red over the Capitol; I seem to see a new shade of Red."[6]

To one of those who expressed the belief that a red hat would soon follow, Curley confided that Baltimore would never see another cardinal. "There are excellent reasons why there should not be such an individual here and I thank God for these reasons because I can still hang on to a strap in the subway for a nickel and travel twenty miles."[7] Curley never divulged his reasons for thinking Baltimore would never see another cardinal.

Archbishop of Washington

In February 1940 Archbishop Cicognani warned Curley that the title would lapse if he did not take possession of the new see on or before March 25.[8] From the hospital Curley wrote that March 25 it would be, but he hoped the apostolic delegate would agree to a simple ceremony that would not include government officials or the diplomatic corps.[9] Five days before the event he informed Cicognani that there would be a small luncheon for the bishops of the province and the monsignori. That was all. He himself would celebrate by providing a dinner for the old folks at the Little Sisters of the Poor in Washington.[10] "This may seem a little radical," he explained to Bishop McNamara, but he had just heard of $125,000 being raised for "a coming great Pontifical function" and he thought it "about time for someone to start something simple and maybe something that may edify instead of giving cause of scandal."[11]

The archbishop of the oldest and newest archdioceses in the country was installed in St. Matthew's Cathedral by the apostolic delegate on Easter Monday. In a brief address he said he had no new plans but would continue the program announced in 1921 with a pledge to promote the growth of lay organizations. He and the apostolic delegate then proceeded to the Little Sisters of the Poor, where the archbishop of Baltimore at least thoroughly enjoyed himself.[12]

Curley was doubtless satisfied that the White House would have no opportunity now to promote a prelate more to its liking for a newly created archdiocese of Washington. Secretary of the Interior Harold L. Ickes would later tell Father Maurice Sheehy that he had "more than once" urged the president to "push the pope" to have Bishop Bernard J. Sheil, Mundelein's liberal auxiliary, made archbishop of Washington.[13] Apparently unaware of the creation of the archdiocese some months before, Roosevelt wrote the American ambassador to Italy on February 8, 1940: "Can you personally and discreetly get word to the Secretary of State of the Vatican that if it is planned to appoint a Bishop or Archbishop for Washington, I would like to emphasize the utmost importance of a close relationship with the Government at the seat of Government. . . . [W]ords spoken here are heard throughout the Nation." Myron C. Taylor would be glad, the president added, "to speak to the Holy Father if it is desired."[14] In a memorandum to Taylor, whom he had just named his personal representative to the pope, Roosevelt suggested that he pass the word that there was "a great deal of anti-Jewish feeling in the dioceses of Brooklyn, Baltimore, and Detroit and that this feeling is said to be encouraged by the Church."[15] In the case of Baltimore the president was badly misinformed.

The dual role into which Michael Curley was thrust made no difference in the day-to-day operation of the two jurisdictions he now controlled. It was a paper change whose only purpose was to open the door to a future split and perhaps compensate an archbishop who could never hope for a red hat but who had rendered signal service to the apostolic delegation. His most notable contribution was the time and energy expended in providing a new residence for the apostolic delegate. Though the site was picked by the delegate himself in 1931, it was Curley who over the next six years sent literally thousands of begging letters to bishops, religious superiors, monsignori, and Catholic organizations to raise the necessary sum.[16]

A Foe of Communism

For the new archbishop of Washington the war that erupted in Europe in September 1939 was a matter of utmost concern. His strong views on communism convinced him that his country must at all costs remain aloof from the conflict. By the outbreak of World War II Curley had become one of the most knowledgeable and certainly one of the most outspoken members of the hierarchy on the menace of communism. "Long before it became the fashion to indict Communism," Bishop McNamara would claim at his bier, "he did so." The protests that followed only encouraged him to speak louder.[17] Implanted by the Mexican question and nourished by the Spanish Civil War, this deep-seated aversion became increasingly the central concern from 1936 on. "Whilst a study of the life of St. Paul is always absorbing," he wrote a hopeful author in 1936, "the most practical question of the hour is Communism."[18]

Fittingly, the first blast to attract national attention was loosed before the Washington Monument following a Holy Name parade on the feast of Christ the King in 1936. There he told a crowd of twenty thousand that it was their duty to learn about communism in order to combat it.[19] To the

Convert League of the Catholic Daughters of America he announced his intention three months later of launching a crusade against "this most dangerous of all heresies."[20]

Because the American bishops seemed largely unaware of the rising threat of communism, Curley would later claim, he proposed at the bishops' meeting in November 1936 that a study of the problem be made during the year and a report given at the next meeting. Though the committee that was appointed to make the study through the Social Action Department of the NCWC was reluctant to have the report aired, the bishops voted for publication at their 1937 meeting.[21] A survey on the threat of communism based on data returned from fifty-three dioceses appeared in January with a recommendation that a committee be formed in each diocese to offer a program of Catholic social teachings as the most effective weapon against communism.[22]

The archbishop of Baltimore was quick to implement the recommendation. He sent eight priests to the National Catholic Social Action Congress in Milwaukee. Then he selected John F. Cronin, SS, professor of philosophy and economics at St. Mary's Seminary, to draw up a program for a School of Social Action to be conducted for the Baltimore clergy in October 1938 and the Washington clergy in January 1939. Associated with the Sulpician in this first course of studies were Monsignors Francis J. Haas and Fulton J. Sheen of the Catholic University and Dr. Elizabeth Morrissy of the College of Notre Dame. Other specialists and spokesmen for labor, industry, and government were brought in to speak on such varied topics as the Negro problem in Baltimore, child labor laws, the National Labor Relations Board, and farm labor in Maryland.[23] In the spring of 1939 a labor school for Catholic workers and other laypeople was begun at the Community House on Broadway, and labor schools were gradually established in key parishes and other centers in Baltimore and Washington. Before each spring and fall session the archbishop penned an official letter encouraging fullest participation. The labor schools continued through the war years and beyond.

In his determination to educate his flock on the dangers of communism, the archbishop expounded on the subject at confirmations, conventions, banquets, and similar gatherings and encouraged others to speak and write. "It is well and effectively organized," he told Rev. Edward L. Curran, president of the International Catholic Truth Society, "and has entered the ranks of the working man, of the CCC Camps, of Government Departments and only God knows where it has not gone with its deceptive programs and its promises of heaven on earth. It is a godless, soulless thing and why American workers are attracted by it I do not know."[24]

To George E. Sullivan, a prominent Washington attorney and active anticommunist, Curley wrote in early 1937: "Keep up the good work. You are about the only layman in Washington at the present time who is taking a real active part in the finest kind of Catholic Action."[25] Curley had just joined forces with Sullivan to prevent the repeal of the so-called Red Rider, a piece of legislation designed to avert communist propagandizing in the public schools of the District.[26] To Congressman John W. McCormack of Massachusetts, a leading foe of repeal, Curley revealed that the Cardinal Secretary of State Eugenio Pacelli, when in Baltimore the previous fall, had told him that communist propaganda was "the most brilliantly organized and the most effective for evil that the world has ever known."[27] In the fall Curley congratulated Sullivan on his pamphlet, "Wolves in Sheep's Clothing," published by the Washington Sodality Union, which the archbishop judged the best exposé of communism he had seen.[28]

The crusade gathered momentum as other organizations and individuals caught fire. Fitzpatrick of the *Review* was an ardent lieutenant from the first. The ranks of the K of C and Holy Name remained as solid in this as in the other causes. An intellectual tone was given the crusade by such priest-professors as Fulton J. Sheen and Joseph Thorning. The outbreak of war in Europe brought no abatement. At the 1941 commencement of Mount St. Mary's College, the archbishop berated the coddling of Reds in Washington and defended the Dies Committee in its search for subversives.[29] The message was ill timed. In less than two weeks Germany invaded the Soviet Union, and the status of American communists improved dramatically.

Even worse timed was the archbishop's loudest salvo against communism and the Soviet Union. On December 2, 1941, Curley granted the Baltimore *News-Post* an interview that was picked up by the leading papers in the country. He warned that Russia would yet bite the hand that fed it. Bitterly he denounced "these moronic Hollywood 'geniuses,' these scions of millionaire families, these jewel bedecked 'thinkers' in Washington, these university professors, these writers" who had "flopped from one side to another" at the behest of the "Browder boys." The United States, he declared, now found itself aligned with "the greatest murderers the world has ever known."[30] Among the many messages that came in the next few days was one from Archbishop Francis J. Beckman of Dubuque. "The Christ-haters of Moscow," he said, "and their international brethren . . . may well take note of the Church Militant when she becomes aroused."[31] Hardly had the archbishop filed the mass of clippings and messages away when the Japanese bombed Pearl Harbor.

A Friend of the Jews

In spite of his staunch anticommunist stance, the archbishop of Baltimore shared none of the covert regard for fascism that characterized many Red baiters nor the anti-Semitism that was its concomitant. His detestation of fascism, in fact, was hardly less intense than his aversion to communism, and his sympathy for the Jews was genuine. It probably came as something of a shock to discover that for many of his fellow warriors anticommunism was simply a sanctified form of anti-Semitism. Such a one was the author of "Wolves in Sheep's Clothing."

In March 1938 Sullivan submitted an article to the *Catholic Review* in which he attempted to demonstrate a Jewish plot at the bottom of world communism. It was rejected as being anti-Semitic. It was, Curley explained, "a dangerous matter to handle at this time when, throughout the world, there is growing a fierce hatred, expressing itself in violence against the Jewish people."[32] When Sullivan persisted in his efforts to expose a "Talmudic" conspiracy, the archbishop stopped answering his increasingly rabid letters, with one exception. Sullivan was outraged by a leaflet entitled "The Catholics and the Jews," which bore Curley's imprimatur. The author, Edwin Ryan of St. Mary's Seminary, suggested that Catholics say to themselves at the consecration of the Mass, "I am now worshiping a Jew."[33] The archbishop told the apoplectic attorney plainly: "I support it."[34]

Archbishop Curley's regard for the Jews extended back to his first years in Baltimore. In 1923 he had praised the Baltimore *Jewish Times* for improving understanding between Jew and gentile and had denounced the hatemongers who rent "the very fabric of civic government."[35] The archbishop developed a close and long-standing friendship with Rabbi William A. Rosenau of Oheb Shalom Congregation, Rabbi Edward L. Israel of the Har Sinai Congregation, and Rabbi Aaron Levin of the Adath Israel Congregation. In the spring of 1934 Curley invited Rosenau to address the clerical conference of Baltimore. The rabbi's discourse on the philosophy of Nazism was well received.[36]

It was its anti-Jewish aspect that disturbed Curley most about fascism. On November 13, 1938, at Holy Comforter Church in Washington he uttered what may have been his strongest words in a long history of hard statements. "I denounce the madness that has taken possession of the Nazis of Germany in these days of persecution of helpless, innocent Jews whose only offense is that they are members of the race of which Jesus . . . was a member." Centuries after Hitler the Jews would still be found in Germany. If that "madman" did not like what he had to say about him, the archbishop declared, let him take it up with the State Department as he had done when Cardinal Mundelein had criticized him.[37] Though the German government ignored the attack, the Berlin radio took notice of the archbishop of Baltimore on at least one occasion, branding him as anti-British. This would later be used by the archbishop's enemies.

A Champion of Isolationism

Despite his sympathy for the Jews and his awareness of the evils of fascism, Curley could not bring himself to support the interventionists in the prewar years. It was an attitude that sprang from his reluctance to give aid and comfort to the Soviet Union—and perhaps more. Curley carried on a long correspondence with Congressman Louis Ludlow of Indiana, author of the Ludlow Amendment, which would have required a referendum of the people for a declaration of war. In 1935 Curley wrote the congressman: "Nations have been lashed unwillingly into war by high powered propaganda carried on under the supervision of swivel chair gentlemen who keep far away from the danger point in all wars, and at the same time the people have been made the victims of the wretched individuals who have made countless millions of dollars out of, so to speak, the dead flesh of the youth of the world."[38] Curley declined to be a member of the board of a national committee on the war referendum organized by the congressman, but throughout the hard-fought campaign gave wholehearted support.[39] On January 10, 1938, the Ludlow Amendment was defeated in Congress by a vote of 209 to 188.[40]

At the same time, Curley was decidedly cold to the Catholic Association for International Peace (CAIP) founded by Monsignor John A. Ryan and others associated with the NCWC in 1927. In 1936 he gave Ryan permission to hold a convention of the CAIP in Washington but demanded there be no more attacks on himself in his absence.[41] The first Catholic peace organization in America was never large but counted among its members Haas, Sheehy, and John Tracy Ellis, all of the Catholic University. Its president for many years was Maryland-born Charles G. Fenwick, professor of international law at Byrn Mawr. Strong in support of the League of Nations, the World Court, and internationalist goals in general, the CAIP increasingly belabored isolationists while it emphasized the Catholic doctrine of a just war.[42] The only true Catholic pacifists in the archdiocese were the Catholic Workers in Baltimore and the disciples of Paul Hanley Furfey in Washington. Their numbers were small and their presence hardly noticed.

The *Catholic Review*, taking its cue from the archbishop, was aggressively isolationist. After the outbreak of World War II its isolationist editorials were almost weekly events. Soon after Germany invaded Russia, it carried an ad from the America First Committee rebutting an earlier one from an interventionist group. "Don't let anyone confuse you," it read. "We do not, we will not, we cannot grasp the crimson-stained hand of Josef Stalin." It was signed by nineteen pastors or religious superiors and six laypeople of the archdiocese of Baltimore and Washington.[43] John L. Bazinet, a Sulpician and leading spirit in the Maryland chapter of America First, had sent the statement to Curley to pass on to the *Review*, reminding him of his words on communism at Mount St. Mary's commencement.[44]

On September 8 and 9 Archbishop Curley spent eleven hours closeted with the leading isolationist in the American hierarchy, Archbishop Beckman of Dubuque. They agreed that General Robert E. Wood, national chairman of America First, should issue a statement, which Beckman and Bishop Gerald Shaughnessy of Seattle, another outspoken isolationist, would sign. At the same time Curley would contact senators favorable to the America First movement to see what could be done to halt the drift toward war.[45] Curley, Beckman, and Shaughnessy found themselves increasingly out of step with the rest of the hierarchy as the NCWC and Rome itself sought to rally support for Roosevelt. In October the apostolic delegate, Archbishop Mooney, chairman of the board of the NCWC, and Michael Ready, its general secretary, selected Archbishop McNicholas to modify the earlier papal condemnation of any form of cooperation with communism. Curley chose to ignore Cicognani's claim that the Holy Father had called for a moratorium on statements critical of the president.[46] In November General Wood asked Curley to pressure Senator Tydings on neutrality revision, then before the Senate, and told him that Beckman would come to the bishops' meeting fortified with confidential firsthand information. He hoped that Curley and Beckman would be able to rescue the Catholic Church from its "present dangerously compromised position."[47] Curley sent a night letter to the two Maryland senators: "For the love of God," he begged, "do not vote to send your Maryland constituents to death."[48] These appeals proved as ineffectual as his actions at the bishops' meeting.

Silencing the Archbishop

On December 7 the archbishop returned to the cathedral rectory from a confirmation late in the afternoon. A reporter for the *Sun* phoned to get a statement on "the attack in the Pacific." Thinking another American ship had been torpedoed, Curley remarked: "We're looking for war, so I see no reason why we should not have a war in the Pacific, on all the seven seas and everywhere." Asked if his comment was for publication, Curley said: "Yes, go ahead, but I'm afraid you won't be able to keep the humor of it in the writing."[49] Later that evening he heard the news of the bombing of Pearl Harbor and the next morning called in a *Sun* reporter to explain what had happened. On December 9 he issued a letter to priests and laity. "Today is no time," he declared, "for any word or deed that might even seem to weaken national harmony and unity so essential for the successful defense of these United States."[50]

But the damage had been done. The enemies of the outspoken archbishop had a handle to silence him. On January 9, 1942, Curley paid a visit to the apostolic delegate at the latter's request. Representations had been made to Rome, Cicognani explained, concerning Curley's statement on communism of December 2 as well as his remarks of December 7 and the impact they had had at this critical juncture.[51] The delegate alluded also, it would seem, to the Berlin broadcast concerning Curley. He apparently did not tell him, however, that the Holy See had instructed him to dissuade episcopal critics of the administration from further statements calculated to weaken Catholic support for the president.[52] With the archbishop of Baltimore he was circumspect.

Five days after the interview, Curley sent Cicognani copies of his statements of December 2, 7, and 9. In a covering letter he explained that he had spoken forcefully on any number of problems. "I know that I have said things that did not give pleasure to highly placed people in the Nation, but I certainly am not going to be silent when it is a matter of the Church's welfare or its teaching simply because I might displease someone." The Berlin broadcast, he added, that had twisted one of his statements into a condemnation of British policy toward the church did not mention what he had said about Germany's policy toward the church. "Frankly, Your Excellency, I have no apologies to make and I rely upon the fine sense of justice of the Holy See not to find myself condemned on what might have been said to the Holy See by some interested Agent of the Government."[53]

Archbishop Cicognani thanked the writer for his "kind letter" and assured him he would present the matter to the Holy See accurately, "seeking to illuminate other factors which perhaps were not included in the original source of information."[54] Despite the refusal of the archbishop of Baltimore to apologize for anything he had said and the reassurance of the apostolic delegate, Curley would, in fact, refrain the rest of his life from any public pronouncements on world affairs or domestic politics. His antagonists had, after all, accomplished their goal. Yet Curley felt he had been unfairly treated by the Roman authorities he had served so well. In a moment of exasperation he would tell the historian John Tracy Ellis: "Rome will use you, abuse you, then throw you away."[55]

Winning the War

Overnight the isolationist sentiment so pronounced in the oldest archdiocese evaporated. "To Our Posts!" commanded an editorial in the *Catholic Review*, which stressed America's duty to arm Britain, Russia, and China as well.[56] The archbishop's exhortation to the faithful to volunteer for defense work was hardly needed. A surge of righteous anger, a willingness to sacrifice, and even a sense of excitement set the Catholics of the oldest and newest archdioceses in motion.

Well before Pearl Harbor the war had boosted Maryland's economy, providing fifty thousand jobs in defense plants under government contract.[57] Farmers, miners, and workers with lesser paying jobs elsewhere flocked to Baltimore, filling trailers, cellars, and other habitable spaces. Baltimore's blue-collar invasion was matched by Washington's white-collar inundation, which rose to five thousand new residents a month.[58] Civilian employees clustered around Aberdeen, Edgewood Arsenal, Fort Meade, and other military installations. In the summer of 1941 Congress voted appropriations for churches, hospitals, and other institutions overtaxed by the influx of defense workers. Three Catholic hospitals of Baltimore and two of Washington made application for $500,000 or more each. Cadoa, St. Rita's in Dundalk, St. Rose of Lima in Brooklyn, St. Clement's in Rosedale, and Our Lady of Lourdes in Bethesda applied for amounts ranging from $2,800 to $100,000.[59]

Catholic organizations and individuals responded patriotically to wartime needs. Cadoa ran nursery classes, dances for servicemen, and blood-donor programs. The Ladies of Charity attended Red Cross classes, engaged in Civilian Defense work, and helped newcomers to settle in, but their greatest contribution to the war effort was to staff the USO centers sponsored by the National Catholic Community Services. The requisitions of the War Production Board ranged from beeswax to typewriters. Cuts in oil brought cuts in class hours in Catholic schools. In 1944 the state war manpower director asked the *Catholic Review* to inform its readers of the need for sixteen thousand workers in critical industries. Aircraft production was fifteen percent behind schedule, he warned.[60]

The two archdioceses had also to surrender a large number of priests to the armed forces as chaplains. Before the war was over, thirty-two secular priests, and perhaps as many members of religious orders laboring in the two archdioceses, had become service chaplains. A number of active clergy were called upon to serve as auxiliary chaplains for bases where there were no service chaplains or where the service chaplain was overworked.[61] The two archdioceses produced their war heroes. Major James P. Devereux of the U.S. Marines commanded the stubborn but futile defense of Wake Island in the first days of American fighting. A movie called "Bombardier" honored Colonel John P. Ryan, a Loyola graduate who helped develop the Army's secret bombsight. Rev. Eugene P. O'Grady of Baltimore, one of the five Catholic chaplains to wade ashore on Normandy Beach, was awarded a Bronze Star before he was killed in action in Germany on November 29, 1944.[62] The 29th Divison, to which O'Grady and a great number of Maryland Catholics belonged, was awarded several distinguished unit citations and the French Croix de Guerre with Palm. It claimed also one of the highest casualty rates, 19,814 men.[63]

A Casualty of the War

One of the earliest casualties of the war was the Catholic Worker movement of Baltimore and the pacificism it represented. In January 1940 Jim Rogan and two other recent college graduates opened St. Anthony's House of Hospitality on South Paca Street with the aid of the Josephite Pacifique Roy, an assistant at St. Peter Claver who had, in great part, lured them to Baltimore. Workers from New York and Philadelphia, including Dorothy Day, came to Baltimore for the days of recollection that Roy conducted. "We often listened to him," Miss Day remembered, "to the tune of snoring guests. . . . These were beautiful days. It was as though we were listening to the gospel for the first time."[64] The archbishop was curious enough to have the Workers investigated but otherwise left them alone.[65]

When St. Anthony's moved from South Paca to West Barre Street in December, a storm broke. The Workers were arrested for "running a disorderly house." In Baltimore, Jim Rogan explained ruefully to the *Catholic Worker*, a disorderly house was one in which blacks and whites slept in the same room and ate at the same table. The Baltimore Quakers offered legal

assistance. Father Roy went to the station to deliver a sermon on race prejudice to a constabulary that was largely Catholic. All attempts to placate the
neighbors failed.[66]

When St. Anthony's House of Hospitality closed in March, 1942, it
was not, Rogan was careful to explain in a letter to the *Catholic Review*, the
result of public pressure but of the draft.[67] Two of the Workers went to a
camp in New Hampshire run by the Association of Catholic Conscientious
Objectors (ACCO), an organization created by the Catholic Workers.
Some of the objectors who went to the camp relocated in 1943 in Maryland,
first at Oakland, then at Rosewood Training School for the mentally retarded in Owings Mills. One of them was Gordon Zahn.[68] In the last year
of the war Zahn wrote Archbishop Curley to win him to the cause of the
ACCO. "I see no purpose," Curley responded, "in trying to build up a
postwar organization of the A.C.C.O.s." It would be a very small group
because returning Catholic veterans "would not be in any humor to accept
the philosophy of the Conscientious Objectors."[69] On the last point the
archbishop was doubtless correct; yet remarkably, his letter contained not a
trace of the antiwar spirit he had shown in the days before Pearl Harbor.

Wartime Prosperity

Despite the sacrifice, sorrow, and suffering the war entailed, it proved
a boon in many ways to the archdioceses of Baltimore and Washington.
The Catholic population, which had stood at 362,211 in 1938, reached
426,782 by 1943. Baptisms increased from 10,961 to 16,727 in the same period and marriages from 4,770 to 9,303. Many harried but happy pastors
were hard pressed to provide the extra masses and extra classes required
for swelling parishes. Money was ready for expansion, but war needs
came first.

One of the most welcome results of the war was the return of prosperity. War wealth was apparent in the collection baskets. In 1939 Monsignor Vaeth reported that the collection for the Propagation of the Faith for
the past year was $139,350; in 1946 he reported $488,788.[70] Even the collection for the Negro and Indian Missions climbed from $5,000 in 1939 to
nearly $15,000 in 1945.

The war years witnessed the inauguration of the Archbishop's Confraternity Campaign. It was born of necessity rather than a desire simply to
tap the wealth that flowed from the war.[71] By 1939 the archdiocese of Baltimore, exclusive of the District, was expending about $800,000 a year on
the various charitable and social works that fell under the Bureau of Cath-

olic Charities. City and state supplied about $250,000. The rest came from the cathedraticum (parish taxes) and charitable contributions of several sorts. The days of the Jenkinses and Fursts were over, insisted Rev. Edward J. O'Brien, the new director of the bureau, in a report for the year ending August 1, 1938. An appeal should be made to the public at large similar to the New York Catholic Charities drive for some $200,000 a year, he advised.[72] In the summer of 1940 the chancellor instructed O'Brien that the bureau could no longer function at a deficit and that no new cases should be taken.[73] In the fall the O'Neill Fund lent the Bureau $48,000 to keep it solvent.

By now the archbishop was converted to the idea of a drive, not only to supply the needs of Catholic Charities but also to achieve his goal of Catholic high schools for boys. A plan was worked out in the fall with the McKeown System of New York. A confraternity would be created whose members, the financially able of the parishes involved, would pledge so much and receive in return certain spiritual benefits. A census would be taken of the seventy-eight parishes of greater Baltimore that would participate, and a goal of $750,000 in pledges would be set to be collected over a two-year period.[74]

Illness prevented the archbishop from launching the campaign until May 1941, when the *Catholic Review* announced a six-goal fund-raising effort: (1) child welfare, (2) a boys' high school, (3) education of the diocesan clergy, (4) care of incurably ill, (5) care of old and infirm priests, and (6) care of aged laity.[75] On May 20, at a testimonial dinner for the archbishop attended by the governor, the mayor, and a host of businessmen, the business community pledged $127,500. The campaign exceeded all expectations. An impressive $965,710 was pledged, $851,066 by the parishes.[76]

At the end of the two-year period the archbishop decided on another, more modest drive. A goal of $300,000 in one-year pledges was set. It was oversubscribed by some $75,000.[77] Thereafter the Archbishop's Confraternity Campaign, or Campaign for Charity and Education as it was also called, became an annual event. In 1944 the business community was again included and the goal was raised to $518,300. It was once again surpassed.[78] For the remaining Curley years the annual campaign realized a half million dollars or more each year.

War wealth and growing needs emboldened the archbishop to map out a $3 million building program for the postwar years. When it was announced in 1944 in the *Catholic Review*, however, the chancery and assorted rectories were so besieged by contractors that nothing more was said of the plans until the fall of 1946, when the *Review* revealed that some $10 million had actually been spent on churches, schools, and other projects since it had made that first exciting announcement.[79]

To the surprise of many a new cathedral was not a part of the archbishop's plans, the O'Neill legacy notwithstanding. "We have an old Cathedral that a hundred million dollars could not rebuild," he told a reader of the *Review* in 1944. "I [have often] stated that I would prefer to build a little four room school for Catholic Colored children."[80] When the question of using the O'Neill legacy to complete the National Shrine of the Immaculate Conception in Washington was raised by Bishop John F. Noll in 1942, Curley wrote the hopeful prelate: "The O'Neill Will is bomb-proof from any and every quarter. I shot at it the biggest shells I could procure in 1921–1922." Although he had made "embryonic plans," he did not expect to be around, he told the bishop, for either the laying of the cornerstone of a new cathedral or the completion of the National Shrine.[81] The "embryonic plans" included the purchase of a fifteen-acre lot on Charles Street for a new cathedral and permission granted to Frederick V. Murphy of the Catholic University to do a blueprint and architect's sketch.[82] When the death of Mrs. O'Neill in 1936 released the estate, nothing was said of a new cathedral.

Even before the death of the widow, the estate could be used for investment purposes. Under John J. Nelligan, father of the chancellor, the Safe Deposit and Trust Company, as executor, allowed the archbishop to lend substantial sums from the O'Neill fund to struggling parishes and other institutions during the Depression at far below the going interest rates.[83] This was probably the greatest service Thomas O'Neill rendered the archdiocese. By 1944, the O'Neill Fund had grown from almost $7 million at the time of the widow's death to about $12 million, while the amount invested for Good Samaritan Hospital provided by the same legacy had increased from $4 million to $7 million.[84]

With the Good Samaritan fund Curley seemed more inclined to act, telling a group of nurses in 1937 of his plan to make the Good Samaritan Hospital a center of Catholic medical research.[85] Not long after, a prospectus was sent by Dr. J. Albert Chatard to some fifty doctors all over the country seeking their opinions on the proposal outlined therein.[86] In March 1947, however, shortly before Curley's death, Monsignor Nelligan informed the board of Good Samaritan, Inc., that the archbishop thought the hospital should be of the "general type." All agreed and then discussed a site.[87] It would be another twenty years before the Good Samaritan would become a reality.

Wartime Expansion

The economic upswing of the war years allowed parishes to retire onerous debts and others to engage in extensive renovation. Before the War Production Board called a halt to church-building in June 1942, four large second-growth churches were completed, including St. Edward's in Baltimore and St. Mary's, Govans. For the next three years makeshift structures or rented halls had to serve the needs of new congregations. The Church of the Annunciation on Massachusetts Avenue in Washington, for example, dedicated in 1943, was the same frame structure that had served Our Lady of Lourdes in Bethesda so long.

Annunciation was but one of eight new missions or parishes created in or near the national capital as a result of wartime expansion. Many of these were black congregations. In 1944 St. Matthew's at Collington and Our Lady of the Angels at Crain's Highway were begun as missions of Holy Family for those blacks who could not get to church because of restrictions on transportation. St. Benedict the Moor was created as a parish for the blacks of the Lincoln Park area in 1946. Our Lady of Mercy, Kenilworth, was begun in 1943 as a mission of St. Margaret, Seat Pleasant, for whites but would soon become a black church. All of these Curley entrusted to the Josephites, as well as St. Cyprian and Our Lady of Perpetual Help, the latter as a result of the death of the dedicated Father Schneeweiss in 1942.[88] In southeast Washington Our Lady Queen of Peace began as a mission in 1943 and St. Bernadette's at Four Corners as a mission in 1944. St. Hugh's was created as a parish in 1947 at Greenbelt, a government project north of the capital.

In Baltimore and its environs six new missions were established: St. Adrian at Inverness and St. Mildred at Gray Manor in 1943 as missions of St. Rita's, Dundalk, the fastest growing industrial community. Also in the Dundalk area a mission was begun in 1945 by the Josephites for the blacks at Turner's Station which would eventually become Christ the King Parish, and a mission called St. Veronica was created for the blacks of Cherry Hill. The Redemptorists at Sacred Heart began the missions of Holy Redeemer and St. Gerard in 1944. Our Lady of Perpetual Help, Woodlawn, was raised to parochial status in 1943 as were the two missions of St. Rose of Lima in 1946, Holy Trinity of Glen Burnie and St. Jane Frances de Chantal of Riviera Beach. The fast-growing Holy Trinity was entrusted to Rev. Arthur E. Slade.

In 1946 St. Frances Cabrini was created in Carroll County and St. Augustine for the blacks of Annapolis. In St. Mary's County missions were established for military personnel at the Patuxent Naval Air Base and the Torpedo Training Station at Piney Point. For the former the Church of the Immaculate Heart of Mary in Lexington Park would be dedicated in 1947.[89]

New institutions were opened and old ones relocated or transformed in the war and postwar years. On November 11, 1941, Cardinal Dougherty, the ranking American prelate, laid the cornerstone for the chapel of St. Mary's Seminary as part of the sesquicentennial celebration of the Sulpicians in the United States. The next week Bishop McNamara dedicated a $400,000 library at Notre Dame of Maryland and two weeks after that the Salvatorian Seminary at Lanham. In 1945 the Sisters of Notre Dame de Namur acquired the Wickes estate outside Baltimore for Trinity College Preparatory School (Maryvale) and the Christian Brothers the Airlie estate on Rock Creek in order to relocate the St. John's College High School. The movement to the suburbs had begun. In June 1945 fire destroyed the novitiate of the Oblate Sisters of Providence, and appeals went out while the novices were lodged at the novitiate of the Sisters of Notre Dame de Namur.[90] Several institutions conducted six-figure drives. There seemed no question of the archdiocese's ability to sustain so many appeals at the same time. Pledges for new church and school buildings were as generous as they were frequent in these prosperous years.

Still, the archbishop had difficulty accumulating enough to build a boys' high school, more than ever a necessity. The New Deal had abolished child labor, and public high schools had to expand to absorb this new age group. The archbishop was more than ever determined to build a sizable diocesan high school for Catholic boys. A large part of the Confraternity Campaign was earmarked for this goal. By 1946 there was $700,000 on hand, an architect's sketch ready, land acquired, and a teaching brotherhood selected, but death came to the archbishop before the goal was realized. Land was also acquired for a boys' high school near the Catholic University in Washington.

Catholic girls were better served in the New Deal and war years. As the enrollment of Seton High School grew—eventually almost 1,300—the Glen Riddle Franciscans agreed also to build and maintain a large diocesan high school for girls. The $450,000 Catholic High School on Edison Highway was dedicated October 8, 1939. By 1947 it had more than a thousand students. Girls' private academies remained relatively small and fairly exclusive, but parochial high schools, usually coed, reached the zenith of their development in this period. They contained, however, hardly more than a fifth of all the students in Catholic secondary schools.

The need for a Catholic education for high-school boys was filled mostly by the older private "colleges," like Calvert Hall, Mount St. Joseph's, and Loyola in Baltimore or Gonzaga and St. John's in Washington, which expanded their facilities as their tuition rates came within the reach of a new industrial working class. Mount St. Joseph grew from 380 students in 1932 to 1,140 in 1947 to become the largest boys' high school in the two archdioceses. In the fall of 1943 the *Catholic Review* expressed surprise at the 10,173 in Catholic high schools in view of the fact that military service and defense work had taken so many of high-school age.[91]

The end of the war opened a new era for Catholic colleges and universities. The educational benefits of the GI Bill of Rights induced many returning veterans to look to the campus rather than the job market. Sixty percent of the six hundred who enrolled at Mount St. Mary's College at the opening of the school year in 1946 were ex-GIs, and Loyola's enrollment went from about three hundred in 1945 to more than a thousand by 1948.[92]

The two archdioceses developed a number of organizations to keep within the ambit of the church those Catholic boys and girls between the age of fourteen and marriage and not in Catholic high schools and colleges. Veteran units of the CSMC were promoted for young adults. Junior Newman Clubs were introduced into public high schools. One of their most successful activities was organizing the October retreats, an annual event from 1943 on. Eventually this activity was taken over by the Catholic Social Clubs. The latter became the Catholic Youth Organization or CYO.

The Catholic Social Clubs of Baltimore had developed independently of the CYO founded by Bishop Sheil of Chicago. A number of social clubs for the young sprang up in scattered Baltimore parishes before 1941, when Rev. Philip M. Hannan, assistant at St. Thomas Aquinas and future archbishop of New Orleans, brought them together under the title of the Council of Catholic Social Clubs. When Hannan entered the Army in 1942, Rev. William Kailer Dunn became moderator. By the spring of 1944 there were thirty-one affiliated clubs with almost three thousand members. In 1945 a full-time lay activities director was installed in a downtown office to coordinate the social, religious, and athletic events. At the fall clerical conferences the archbishop urged a club in every parish. In February 1946 Dunn and the priest moderator of the District, attended a national meeting of the CYO in Boston. When the council was reorganized as the CYO of Baltimore later that year, Rev. Thomas J. Mardaga replaced Dunn as director.[93] Dunn had created a senior branch of the council for Catholics between nineteen and thirty which was absorbed by the CYO.

Another organization aimed at the same age group for which Dunn had also helped lay the basis was the Catholic War Veterans. Founded in

New York in 1935, the CWV made little headway in Maryland until it launched a nationwide campaign to recruit returning veterans. Archbishop Curley was asked as early as 1941 to serve on an Episcopal Guidance Committee.[94] He refused with a smile, but five years later endorsed the national headquarter's efforts to organize "a post in every parish." The former chaplain of the 175th Infantry, John E. Albert, was assigned to help and then to serve as archdiocesan director. In 1947 the Department of Maryland held its first convention. The District also had a department. "Should the Chancery office," wrote its commander, "at any time deem it advisable to have a militant body of Holy Mother Church demonstrate in the cause of our faith, we stand ready to serve."[95]

In 1943 John Murray, an envoy of the Concilium (headquarters) of the Legion of Mary in Dublin arrived in Baltimore with the hope of organizing a curia there and in Washington. The archbishop gave a push at the clerical conferences. By the beginning of 1946 the Baltimore curia under John N. Paulus, president, could boast of praesidia in ten parishes and junior groups in two. The Washington curia counted praesidia in nine parishes, four of them black, and at Theological College conducted by the Sulpicians. There was also a praesidium at SS. Peter and Paul in Cumberland. The Baltimore curia also took upon itself the task of organizing and sustaining praesidia in Delaware, South Carolina, and Georgia.[96] The principal work of the active members of the Legion of Mary in the archdioceses of Baltimore and Washington was visiting Catholic families for the purpose of reclaiming fallen-away or lax members and of persuading parents to transfer children from public to parochial schools. The Baltimore curia by 1947 could claim but 115 active members in eleven parishes, but they were an exceptionally dedicated group.

While encouraging the development of new organizations to meet new needs, the archbishop continued to promote the growth of old ones. In 1941 he urged again the creation of a branch of the St. Vincent de Paul Society in every parish, and in 1945–46 he backed a campaign for the expansion of the Holy Name Society.

War-Begotten Attitudes

A CAUTIOUS ECUMENISM

The war years witnessed a cautious opening up on the part of the archbishop and some of the clergy and laity to non-Catholic organizations and movements. When the archdiocese was invited to participate in the Baltimore War and Community Fund campaign in the fall of 1943, Curley agreed to serve as one of three vice chairmen and to speak at the opening luncheon. This decision his chancellor interpreted as "quite a departure from his policy in the past."[97] There was a proviso: no funds would go to any group advocating birth control. On at least one occasion thereafter the archdiocese caused a cancellation of a meeting at which representatives of Planned Parenthood were scheduled to speak.[98]

Until the early 1940s the archbishop displayed an attitude toward the National Conference of Christians and Jews that his chancellor characterized on one occasion as "not particularly enthusiastic" and on another as "passive."[99] His sympathy for the Jews, however, drew him closer to the organization. When in 1944 the Baltimore Round Table of the NCCJ organized a drive to raise $25,000 for its activities, Curley urged the leading Catholic lay organizations to contribute and asked Joseph P. Healy to form a committee of Catholic businessmen to solicit donations.[100] His promotion of subsequent Round Table drives was no less energetic. Several Catholic laymen, among them Thomas Pangborn, and some of the clergy, Monsignor Nelligan in the forefront, played an increasingly active role in the NCCJ.

REVIVAL OF ANTICOMMUNISM

Curley's preoccupation with communism in no way abated. But as he explained to William Franklin Sands, who had just published a book on American diplomacy: "I had to place myself outside national and international politics and keep quiet since Pearl Harbor." Though he could not resist the temptation to deplore the "kowtowing to atheistic forces," which he felt were achieving exactly what they wanted, he caught himself and concluded: "Little said is easily mended."[101]

While obliged to stand on the sidelines, he encouraged others in their fight against communism, especially the Sulpician John Cronin, whose social action schools had made him a respected figure in Baltimore. In 1943 an FBI agent asked Cronin to help uncover information about Communist infiltration in the labor movement in Baltimore. Through the social action schools Cronin obtained access to several locals and was upset at what he discovered. The Communist party had moved into Maryland to seek control of the war industries. In the Baltimore area it was strong in the shipyards and drydocks and was pushing hard for control of Glenn L. Martin, which the CIO was attempting to unionize, of Bethlehem Steel, and of several electrical industries.[102]

At a clerical conference Cronin gave a confidential report on Communist activities in Baltimore and won a pledge of support.[103] He then set in motion plans to use parish facilities and lay organizations to activate Catholic and other workers in the struggle at the local level. All of this he outlined in an essay entitled "Second Front Menace," which he published in *Sign*.[104] The first great victory was won at Glenn L. Martin in the fall of 1943. "At long last," he told the archbishop the next spring, "we are beginning to see signs of substantial success in our labor work. Since I returned I have started to fight the Communists in Westinghouse and Maryland Drydock. That about completes the major plants where they have been strong. As a result they are being opposed on every side."[105] Only in Maryland, of all the industrialized regions of the country, did Communist party membership decline in 1944, Cronin would later claim. In 1945 the People's Institute of Applied Religion, a Communist front, chose Baltimore for a meeting to discuss "Religious Fifth Columns in the Trade Unions," which focused on a "fascist" priest (Cronin) who had written a book called *Economics and Society*.[106]

Because of the close acquaintance he had developed with Communist activities, Cronin was asked by the bishops at their November meeting of 1944 to take a year off to investigate and prepare a detailed report on Communist influence in the nation. From other labor priests and a number of contacts in the government, especially the FBI, Cronin amassed a body of far-ranging data. "The Problems of American Communism in 1945: Facts and Recommendations" was ready for the bishops' meeting of November 1945. A "confidential report" of 146 pages, it exposed Communist influence in government, labor, and elsewhere and spelled out its implications for the Catholic Church. Its principal recommendation to the bishops was that the church take care not to associate itself with the anti-Semitic, antiblack, and other conservative forces fighting social reform as Communist inspired but instead should organize programs of social action to educate both clergy and laity.[107]

The report was largely responsible for Cronin's becoming "a crucial figure in the genesis of the domestic Cold War crusade."[108] It was, of course, leaked by several bishops to important Catholic laymen in government and business. A congressman from Wisconsin put Cronin in touch with Richard M. Nixon, a new face in the House. The Sulpician became one of the future president's principal mentors on Communist activities. From Cronin's report Nixon knew well in advance about the House Un-American Activities Committee's investigation of Alger Hiss. When the Congressman from California would become vice president, he would select John Cronin as his speech writer.[109]

Cronin moved to Washington in early 1946 to be assistant director of the Social Action Department of the NCWC. There he parted company with ardent anticommunists in one respect. He deplored the repressive campaigns that were being conducted against domestic Reds and suggested instead a pitiless exposure of Communist ideas and tactics to the sunlight of public opinion.[110]

BLACK MILITANCY AND A BREAKTHROUGH

Cronin did not believe, as did the archbishop of Baltimore, that the Communist party was behind much of the black militancy that developed in the war years. To the editor of the *Catholic Missions* Curley sent in 1942 an essay he had written suggesting the possibility of missionary work among the 12.7 million non-Catholic Negroes in America and remarked privately: "The Colored people themselves were never more Race conscious than they are at this time. Communism is making inroads into the Race. You would be surprised to see the situation we have around us here."[111]

The new horizons for blacks and the accompanying discontent created by the war were nowhere more evident than in Baltimore, to which blacks were moving in unprecedented numbers. As early as February 1940 Father John T. Gillard, perhaps the most informed Josephite, warned Curley: "The mentality of the 'New Negro' is definitely anti-white." Gillard proposed an eleven-point program for expanding work among the blacks of the archdiocese as a means of softening frustrations.[112] The "New Negro," Curley found, was much more difficult to handle than the old Federated Colored Catholics. While he was willing, even eager, to do more for blacks, Curley became increasingly apprehensive about the possibility of violence.[113]

When Baltimore blacks threatened a March on Annapolis in 1942 to protest the killing of black men by the Baltimore police, Curley paid a visit to his old nemesis of the *Afro-American*, Carl Murphy, to see what could be done to quiet the "unruly element," as Monsignor Nelligan termed it.[114] At the end of 1943 he joined with a prominent rabbi and Protestant minister in an appeal to "all our fellow Citizens to use every influence to prevent and restrain any outbreak of racial prejudice" that might result from the "potentially serious and tragic situation" involving race relations in local industrial plants.[115]

Two weeks later Curley received a letter from Father LaFarge telling him that A. Philip Randolph, president of the Brotherhood of Sleeping Car Porters, wanted the archbishop of Baltimore to be a member of the National Council for a Permanent Fair Employment Practices Committee. A congressman from Baltimore would introduce a bill for a permanent

FEPC, LaFarge revealed, if Curley gave his approval.[116] John A. Ryan seconded LaFarge's request. Race riots over toilets had been narrowly averted in Baltimore, Curley told Ryan. What would be the effects of a "wide-open Bill?" he asked. "Are we going to have Race Riots all over the nation?"[117]

Despite his growing caution, Curley continued his efforts to educate the faithful on the question of race relations. At almost every confirmation, he told the dean of Howard University in 1943, he spoke of the need for understanding not only between Christians and Jews but also between the white and black races.[118] About the same time, he asked the black members of the CSMC to remain behind after mass at the cathedral, told them they had a right to sit anywhere in any church, then sent them across the street to the communion breakfast at Calvert Hall, much to the discomfort of the moderator, Monsignor Vaeth.[119] At the beginning of 1945, he told Anita Williams to add his name to the petition in favor of a repeal of Maryland's Jim Crow transportation law of forty years to be presented at a hearing at Annapolis and issued a statement calling for repeal that won a warm expression of gratitude from Murphy of the *Afro-American* and Lillie Jackson, head of the Baltimore branch of the NAACP.[120]

While the archbishop of the sees of Baltimore and Washington trod his cautious path, others took bolder steps in eliminating segregation from Catholic institutions. About the first of March 1942 St. Peter Claver's hitherto unbeatable Newman Club girls went down in defeat to the St. Brigid Golds 37 to 21 in St. Peter Claver Hall. Judge J. Abner Sayler of the Supreme Bench of Baltimore "hailed the game as the beginning of a new era in Maryland interracial relations."[121] A return engagement was played by both the girls' and boys' basketball teams, but that was the end of the first attempt at interracial sports. The archbishop advised a halt.

In February 1944 black and white members of the CSMC from St. Francis Xavier's Parish and Mount St. Joseph High School met to form an interracial study club under their moderators, Father Thomas Monahan, SSJ, and Brother Mario Perry, CFX. They met every two weeks for a year alternating between the church and the school. The next year they were joined by groups from other black churches and white high schools, boys and girls. When in 1946 units from three colleges also joined, they took as their official name the Baltimore Catholic Students Interracial Council. Among the many activities the council sponsored was a picnic in the country, interracial masses, and a speakers bureau. By the fall of 1946, it counted fifty members from the three colleges and eight high schools.[122] It was a small but significant beginning, significant because it was successful.

The eventual establishment of an adult Catholic Interracial Council in

Baltimore was the work of the leaders of the Students Interracial Council, particularly Brother Mario. With Leo V. Miller he organized a small group of former students, who were allowed to hold meetings in the conference room of the chancery. The archbishop gave his approval in November 1946. After his death the chancellor asked Miss Anita Williams to assume the presidency of the Catholic Interracial Council.[123]

The Catholic Interracial Council, founded by Father LaFarge in New York in 1934, was also established in Washington, largely by Father Wilfrid Parsons, SJ, now professor of political science at the Catholic University, in the fall of 1944. Monsignor Lawrence Shehan, "the priest of the helping hand," offered St. Patrick's Hall for its monthly meetings, which he himself attended.[124]

One of the last tasks Archbishop Curley performed was to instruct his chancellor to tell Miss Mary Mattingly, who had just received the *Pro Pontifice et Ecclesia* award for twenty-five years of outstanding service as president of the Sodality Union of Washington, that the union must admit black units. The archbishop, Nelligan wrote, considered any policy of exclusion in contradiction to the gospels and the teachings of the church. The matter should not be put to a vote; it was beyond debate. The archbishop would be sorry if she were hurt by the decision, but he was certain that the faith that had inspired so great achievements would lead her to realize its necessity.[125]

PROLABOR STILL

In spite of his refusal to accede to Monsignor Ryan's request to support a permanent FEPC, Archbishop Curley made a peace of sorts with the indefatigable champion of Catholic social thought in the war years. In 1941 he thanked Ryan for having given him credit for the "full measure of academic freedom" he had accorded him. "Anyway, I feel you have done a great piece of work for Labor, and because for Labor, you have done a great work for the Church. When we get away from the laboring men we stand to lose a great deal."[126]

An instinctive sympathy for the underdog informed Curley's attitude toward blacks and blue-collar workers alike and induced a healthy respect for the champions of the New Deal. When a Washington businessman complained to Curley of Ryan's attack on the free enterprise system, Curley wrote the monsignor: "I can see the young, successful capitalist objecting to the liberal tendency of today and any man, of course, who speaks for Labor is liberal."[127] To the young capitalist Curley insisted that if he went into "the whole question of Capital and Labor from the days of the so-called Reformation and the Manchester School down to sometime ago, the chances are that you would be terribly tempted to become a thousand times more radical than Monsignor Ryan." Moreover, it would be "a fatal mistake for any man, Catholic or otherwise, to think that the Priest or any Minister of the Gospel, should sit in the Sacristy or the Sanctuary, twisting his thumbs with his ears closed to the cries of either Capital or Labor in this Country of ours that has known Capital at its worst and is liable to know Labor at its worst."[128]

Curley's own dealings with organized labor were not consistent. In spite of earlier statements and correspondence that indicate a simple lowest-bid policy, he replied to a petition from parishioners of Our Lady of Lourdes in Bethesda, who wanted union labor to build the parish school: "Whenever it was possible in the past eighteen years in the spending of millions of dollars, I have stood by Union Labor."[129]

NCWC and the University

In his last years Archbishop Curley also made his peace with the NCWC. When Monsignor Michael J. Ready, the general secretary, was named bishop of Columbus in 1944, he wrote: "I am sorry you are leaving us. When I say that I am sorry, I mean just that."[130] He presided over the annual meeting of the hierarchy whenever the cardinals were absent, as in 1942, 1943, and 1944. He rarely missed this meeting and was not slow to speak his mind. When failing health prevented attendance in 1946, Cardinal Mooney, as presiding officer, sent an account of the proceedings as well as the "affectionate greetings" of all present. "We missed your own piquant and pertinent remarks on the Friday morning 'Varia,' " the cardinal added. "I always enjoyed them very much."[131]

As chancellor of the Catholic University and chairman of the executive committee of its board, Curley continued to play an important role nationally. It was still a demanding role. The rector, Monsignor and later Bishop Corrigan, was neither an administrator nor financier. Student enrollment dropped precipitously at the outbreak of the war.

"I am very, very tired of the whole business," he told Archbishop McNicholas in the spring of 1942, "and frankly I would like to be relieved of any official connection with the University."[132] McNicholas defended Corrigan and his "great gifts of mind and heart" and ability to cultivate good will and to secure the cooperation of the bishops. He hoped that for the sake of the university Curley and Corrigan could settle their differences and be friends again.[133] "I have no friends," Curley retorted, "and if I have enemies, I do not know them, but their existence is perfectly all right with me. . . . All I want is devotion to the great cause of Catholic education as exemplified in the University, and, if that be there, I will give my very life to help any man who advances that sacred cause."[134] The archbishop of Cincinnati had touched a sensitive nerve again.

After Corrigan's death three months later, the result of a heart attack, Curley hoped to relieve the financial distress of the university by raising the returns from the annual collection. The contributions of some dioceses, he confided to one bishop, were "small beyond telling." He would send out a special appeal to all the bishops in the fall and have the new rector speak to them at their annual meeting.[135] The response to the fall appeal was gratifying. For the first time the archdiocese of Baltimore exceeded $30,000, topping the list. Every year thereafter Archbishop Curley would issue a special appeal before the fall collection and publish the results.

The Last Battle

Despite a seemingly robust vitality, the tenth archbishop had a medical history unmatched in a long line of ailing archbishops. The history began when he was a Roman student with a setback diagnosed as "neurasthenia of the brain."[136] Thereafter he suffered severe bouts of influenza, pneumonia, and a streptococcal infection of the sinuses. Sinusitis would be a recurrent complaint. To these ailments could be added poor eyes, bad teeth, intestinal disorders, lumbago, and a cardiac condition. His most serious illnesses, however, were stress related. The summer of the battle with the *Sun* he developed shingles of the face. Each flare-up thereafter—and there were many over the thirteen years left to him—brought intense suffering. Bromides brought some relief, but improper dosages on more than one occasion made him dull and disoriented.[137]

The ailment that finally brought him down was high blood pressure. When Curley learned that the administrative board of the NCWC had pulled the rug from under the Mexican relief committee in 1936, his pressure soared to 210. In 1941 another confrontation boosted it to 250! It was a contest with Edward B. Bunn, SJ, president of Loyola College, over a legacy. Against the advice of the apostolic delegate, Curley took Bunn to court—and lost.[138]

Another siege of high blood pressure in the early months of 1943 produced a hemmorhage of the left eye and then a detached retina, which an operation failed to correct. In February 1945, when he tried to address a clerical conference, Curley found himself unable to speak. On May 5, 1945, he rose at five and switched on the light. There was no light. He was blind.

The archbishop carried on the business of the archdiocese with the competent assistance of the chancellor, Monsignor Nelligan, often from Bon Secours Hospital, which from the mid-1930s had become a second home.

There was need for a second auxiliary bishop. McNamara himself was not in good health and, in any case, unequal to heavy responsibilities. Curley chose Lawrence J. Shehan, pastor of St. Patrick's in Washington. Many were surprised, including the Washington pastor, thinking that Monsignor Nelligan would be the choice.[139] On December 12, 1945, the apostolic delegate raised the forty-seven-year-old pastor to the episcopacy in his own parish church. Soon after, Bishop Shehan was named pastor of SS. Philip and James in Baltimore.

On December 29 the archbishop suffered what he called a "quasi-paralysis" of the legs, the result of another stroke. He forbade any celebration of the twenty-fifth anniversary of his installation in Baltimore. Bishop McNamara, however, headed an effort to raise a testimonial of $100,000. Twice the amount was realized. Curley thanked his priests at a clerical conference on December 17. Within two days almost half the amount was expended on charities. It was one of the last real joys the ailing archbishop experienced.[140]

Passing of the Warrior Prelate

On February 21, 1947, Curley fell, and was anointed. Still he lived until mid-May. Before the chancellor left the evening of the 16th, he approved incardination for the historian John Tracy Ellis. It was his last official act. About nine o'clock he suffered a cerebral hemorrhage. Death came quickly.

Messages of condolence came from the mighty—the presidents of the United States and the Irish Free State—and the lowly, from many religious bodies, such as the Baltimore Jewish Council, the Greek Orthodox community, the Maryland Federation of Men's Bible Classes, and the Salvation Army. All gave evidence of an awareness that an exceptional person had passed from the scene. "In the death of Archbishop Curley," read the telegram of Archbishop McNicholas, "the Church loses a warrior prelate for its unchangeable teachings . . . , a champion of Christian education of our youth, a friend of the missions, an almoner of the poor."[141] The *Sunday Sun* pronounced the deceased prelate "one of the most forceful and effective citizens this community has seen." The source and basis of his power was "obvious enough" to the *Sun*. It was "his faith."

The apostolic delegate said the requiem mass. Bishop McNamara delivered an affective sermon. Cardinals Dougherty and Spellman were in attendance, but there was only half as much purple as at the requiem of Cardinal Gibbons. Some ten thousand people, however, stood in the rain outside the cathedral to listen to the mass over the loudspeaker.

Pulpit praise was perhaps closer to the truth in the case of Michael J. Curley than most because he lived with less regard for the opinions of men. He was without doubt the most open, honest, and outspoken member of the American hierarchy in the years between the wars. There was never any doubt where he stood. His public utterances were unabashed and unambiguous, his private conversation unguarded. Even his critics admired his directness and candor as they complained of his lack of tact. For some of his spiritual children the battling archbishop was a source of pride, for others an embarrassment.

Even more did friends and foes alike admire his simplicity of life and love for the poor. He had, in fact, almost a compulsion to be as poor as the poor he never patronized. In 1939 J. Edgar Hoover, a close friend, sent him through the Manresa director a gift for the silver jubilee of his episcopal ordination. The director thanked the bureau chief and added: "He is a poor man personally and I know for a fact that whatever he receives he gives to the poor."[142] To Monsignor Shehan the archbishop returned a check that had been offered for his having pontificated at a Pan American mass. It was too late in life, the archbishop explained, to violate a rule he had made at the time of his episcopal ordination to accept no gifts whatsoever for any of his "pontifications."[143]

The Internal Revenue Service, unable to believe his tax returns, sent an inspector in 1941 to make inquiries. The inspector discovered that the archbishop had no household expenses of his own, no servants, and no automobile and that he claimed a salary of only $1,200 a year. Most of his well-worn clothes were gifts. The inspector was impressed, the chancellor recorded.[144] In his last years he started giving away even his clothes and books. "There are no pockets in shrouds," he explained. Often he gave to the poor when he had nothing to give. To a religious sister seeking help, he revealed: "I keep a respectable distance from the rich, so I am never remembered in their wills. I have borrowed twenty thousand dollars to help our poor, and all that is gone. So yourself and myself are in the same boat, and it is a leaky one at that."[145]

For all his disesteem of wealth Archbishop Curley was an excellent administrator. He had a remarkable tolerance for the tedium of detail. He delighted, in fact, in pouring over the annual Notitiae, in sifting the data, and in sorting out significant problems. Nor could he tolerate procrastination. "I never kept a letter overnight," he boasted on one occasion.[146]

A managerial revolution of sorts occurred under the tenth archbishop. Compared to the loose and somewhat lax operation that ran largely by itself under his predecessor, the archdiocese under Curley was a beehive of productivity. His greatest organizational achievements were the Bureau of Catholic Charities and the Office of Education, which controlled in an orderly way the two areas of most significant growth from 1921 to 1947. The Home and Foreign Mission Society, League of the Little Flower, Catholic Evidence Guild, and Big Brothers Association were other examples of his ability to develop vehicles of healthy growth. Under Curley the dozen or more directorships of activities were more than honorary positions awarded worthy pastors. Curley picked skilled men to fill the posts and expected a high level of performance. Lay organizations under him became large and vibrant. The St. Vincent de Paul Society, Ladies of Charity, Holy Name Society, Sodality, Knights of Columbus, and Catholic Daughters of America of Baltimore and Washington had few rivals in other American sees.

In the twenty-five and a half years he governed the oldest archdiocese, its Catholic population increased from 276,000 to 429,517, the number of churches and chapels from 275 to 390, parish grammar schools from 97 holding 31,802 pupils to 143 holding 50,545 pupils, diocesan priests from 283 to 417, religious priests in diocesan work from 325 to 1,009, religious orders and congregations of men from 22 to 40.

In spite of his impressive accomplishments, there were those who felt that the premier see deserved better than this blunt and bluff Irishman, his commanding appearance and pulpit flare notwithstanding. Michael Curley, in fact, was never fully accepted by the Catholics of Maryland. To his dying day he lived in the shadow of his princely predecessor, a fact that colored his attitudes and his own style of leadership. He bequeathed to the archdiocese, nevertheless, perhaps because of his feelings of inferiority, a muscular Catholicism suited to an American subculture striving to breach the last barriers.

The Curley church would be perpetuated under his successor, but never would the Catholics of the oldest archdiocese be more a part of the immigrant church than under this builder and battler, whose passing for some who can remember is still a matter of regret.

15   *Breezes in the Storied Land*

AS HE PASSED THE GOVERNORS, senators, mayors, and other prominent officials from Maryland and Rhode Island after his installation as eleventh archbishop of Baltimore, Francis Patrick Keough stopped suddenly. Handing his crozier to an attendant, he walked over to an elderly man, put his hand on his arm, and said: "Hello, Sam. How are you?" Samuel Greenburg was an immigrant Jewish cobbler who had settled in New Britain, Connecticut, on the same street as the Keoughs. A kind and generous man, he had befriended the two fatherless Keough boys, particularly Francis, whom he encouraged during his years as grocery boy, newsboy, and clerk to get a good education and even to enter the seminary. The warm friendship that lasted for the rest of Sam's life allowed the eleventh archbishop to begin his stewardship in Baltimore with an ecumenical gesture.[1]

Born December 30, 1890, in New Britain, Francis Keough entered the preparatory seminary of the diocese of Hartford but was sent to the major seminary of Issy in France. There he developed a proficiency in French that would later stand him in good stead with the many French Canadians of Rhode Island. Recalled at the outbreak of World War I, he finished his studies at St. Bernard's Seminary in Rochester and was ordained in 1916. Three years a curate and then the move upward: director of the Society for the Propagation of the Faith, assistant chancellor, secretary to the bishop of Hartford, and in 1934 bishop of Providence, Rhode Island. At Providence he enjoyed many successes, especially in his charity drives and promotion of the CYO.

Bishop Keough's executive ability, graciousness, and contributions to the NCWC were doubtless factors in the choice of a successor for Archbishop Curley. When he learned of the appointment, dated November 28, 1947, however, Keough went to Washington to see the apostolic delegate. Archbishop Cicognani had ordained him bishop and had remained a close friend. Keough's plea to remain in Providence was met with the flat response: "One does not refuse the Holy Father."[2] The installation took place February 24, 1948.

In the coming of Archbishop Keough, the archdiocese suffered yet another diminution in its long history of geographical reductions. The Holy See had deemed it "contributory to the dignity" of the national capital to "perpetually disjoin" the archdiocese of Washington and the metropolitan see of Baltimore. At the same time, five counties—St. Mary's, Charles, Calvert, Prince George's, and Montgomery—were detached from the oldest and awarded the youngest archdiocese. Thus was the premier see severed from its roots, shriveling from 6,463 to 4,801 square miles. Its Catholic population also shrank by well over a third; its 265,000 Catholics hardly matched the 425,000 the new archbishop had left in Providence. Such offices, moreover, as chancellor of the Catholic University fell now to the first archbishop of Washington in his own right, Patrick A. O'Boyle, whose installation at St. Matthew's Cathedral had taken place a month before Keough's.

At the NCWC

In Keough, nonetheless, the archbishop of Baltimore continued to play an important role in national affairs by reason of the confidence he enjoyed among the American bishops. As bishop of Providence he had been appointed assistant bishop to the executive department of the NCWC and assistant episcopal chairman of the education department. With his elevation to Baltimore he was chosen assistant to the ailing chairman of the administrative board of the NCWC, Archbishop McNicholas, for the year 1948. At the annual meeting in November 1948 he was elected vice chairman of the board as well as chairman of the education department. In 1950 on the death of McNicholas he was elected chairman of the board and was reelected for 1951 and 1952. He was then voted chairman of the legal department for 1954 and chairman of the social action department for 1955, positions indicative of the skills and interests attributed to him by his fellow hierarchs. In November 1955 he was returned to the chairmanship of the Board, which office he retained by reelection through 1958.

Archbishop Keough worked well with prelates of like temperament, especially Cardinals Samuel A. Stritch of Chicago and Edward A. Mooney of Detroit, successively the ranking cardinals. Together they served as a counterweight to the growing influence and power of Cardinal Spellman of New York.[3] Keough was particularly close to the Maryland-born Mooney. Though the bishops respected his quiet efficiency and moderation, there would be those in his new see who puzzled at the source of his popularity in the NCWC.

Francis Keough was not a man given to publicizing his feats or to encouraging others to do it for him. When news of his appointment to Baltimore was released, the *Sun* described him as "modest almost to the point of shyness" and marveled that "one so lacking in assertiveness" could have accomplished so much in Providence.[4] No one was surprised when he named Bishop Shehan his vicar general, but many wondered when he replaced Monsignor Nelligan as chancellor and consigned him to the suburbs. When the archbishop told the children during his first confirmation tour, "There will be no questions," Maryland Catholics guessed that their New England-born ordinary was of a different stripe than his predecessor.

Another Builder

In his first spring in Baltimore, Keough conducted the Confraternity Campaign along the lines laid out by Curley but told an audience at the K of C's Alcazar that it would be different in the future.[5] The following spring Catholics were told that there would be no quotas, no kick-off dinners, no final celebrations. Cash gifts would eliminate the expensive bookkeeping required by pledges. The campaign would now be called the Catholic Charities Appeal. Schools would no longer be among the recipients. Besides the eight Catholic orphanages, the charities benefited would be the CYO, St. Vincent de Paul Society, Ladies of Charity, and foster-home program of the Associated Catholic Charities. In addition, there would be two long-range goals, a home for the aged and a consolidation of the small, scattered orphanages at a single center.[6]

A home for the aged was the archbishop's first major project. There was a need, he claimed, to provide such facilities for the substantial body of elderly Catholics who fell between the well-to-do, served by such institutions as Kirkleigh Villa, and the destitute, served by the Little Sisters of the Poor. Hardly less imperative was the need for a modern home to replace the antiquated and overtaxed orphanages of another era.

In proportion to the Catholic population, the number of Catholic waifs was dwindling. There were also fewer Catholic delinquents and fewer Catholic working teenagers. St. James Home for Boys shut down in 1949 after seventy-one years, and in June of the following year, when the state failed to vote its annual appropriation, the nationally known St. Mary's Industrial School closed its doors after eighty-four years. Associated Catholic Charities would not assume the burden, its new priorities reflecting changing needs.

In the fall of 1949 it was announced that the success of the charity appeal had enabled the archbishop to purchase a 180-acre estate called Long

Crandon on Dulaney Valley Road north of Towson. There would be located both the old folks home and a dependent children's village. Ground was broken the following May for Stella Maris Hospice, which would feature singles, doubles, and four-bed accommodations for 243 elderly. A year later, however, there was no sign of construction. The archbishop admitted to being "an ultra conservative New England Yankee." There was not enough money. His wish, he explained, was to own and not to "rent," the equivalent of a long indebtedness. "The Church always owns." He was emphatic, moreover, in his refusal to include schools in the annual appeal. He wished only Catholic contributions for this purpose. "We are careful about our schools," he declared. "We cannot risk outside pressure."[7]

The Catholic, non-Catholic, and business community's response to the annual charities appeal was generous, though not comparable to the success Keough had come to expect of the drives in Providence. The total contributions climbed gradually from $660,000 in 1949 to $1 million ten years later, where it remained for the rest of his administration.[8] At the same time, however, the cost of operating the dozen components of the Associated Catholic Charities rose steadily, from $185,000 in 1951, for example, to $300,000 in 1954. In 1953 the community was told that funds in hand were insufficient to complete the building program, now expanded, and that it would, after all, be necessary to borrow. By May 1955 $4.2 million had been expended on the program, the appeals fund covering $3.4 million of this amount, leaving an indebtedness of $800,000.[9]

By 1953 three other goals had been announced, the first as early as the fall of 1949: a new cathedral, the Good Samaritan Hospital, and a boys' high school. None of them would be covered by the charity appeals. The first two would, of course, be funded by the O'Neill legacy, but there was not enough on hand for the boys' high school planned by Archbishop Curley. The year 1958 had been set in 1951 as the target date for completion of the five major projects. It was overly optimistic. Stella Maris Hospice was dedicated September 12, 1953, in a simple ceremony before a few ecclesiastical guests, but ground would not be turned for what was first called Children's Village until October 1957. In the summer of 1960 some 120 orphans, boys and girls, were finally sent to their new home called Villa Maria from St. Mary's Villa and St. Vincent's, St. Leo's, St. Patrick's, and the Dolan Aid orphanages, which locked their doors without ceremony. The boys' high school would not open until September 1961. One of the factors that delayed the building of the Good Samaritan Hospital until well beyond the Keough episcopacy was the need to let the principal of the O'Neill bequest grow to cover the full cost of facilities planned. Another was the possibility of constructing a motherhouse for the Sisters of Bon Secours, for whom an American province was created in 1958, near the hospital they had been asked to staff in the O'Neill will.[10]

Without doubt the Cathedral of Mary Our Queen was the most noteworthy, and perhaps controversial, achievement of the eleventh archbishop of Baltimore. By the time plans had fully matured, that part of the O'Neill legacy designated for the new cathedral had grown to $20 million, considerably more than was needed. The most respected architects in Catholic circles, Maginnis, Walsh, and Kennedy of Boston, were engaged. From three sketches—traditional, modified, and modern—the archbishop and his auxiliary chose the modified Gothic.[11]

Designed to last a thousand years, it would be 270 feet long including the sanctuary, 46 feet wide, and 86 feet tall with stone towers rising 134 feet surmounted by 29-foot metal spires. The edifice would accommodate nineteen hundred people.[12]

Ground was broken October 10, 1954, on a twenty-five-acre tract, the greater part acquired by Archbishop Curley, on North Charles Street in what had become a fashionable neighborhood. While the cornerstone was laid in a simple ceremony on May 31 following, two cardinals, fifteen archbishops, and nearly a hundred bishops, including the Episcopal bishop of Maryland, gathered for the dedication on November 15, 1959. The apostolic delegate said the mass. Bishop Shehan, now bishop of Bridgeport, delivered the dedicatory sermon.

"Impressive" was the word most often chosen to describe the Cathedral of Mary Our Queen, but reservations were guardedly expressed by those attuned to liturgical reform, largely unincorporated in its architecture and art.[13] The cathedral, rectory, school, and convent would cost $12.5 million. Many wondered that no provision was made for the O'Neill bequest to cover maintenance, but Keough wished to establish the right of the archdiocese to use the remainder of the O'Neill fund for school construction.[14] The Consistorial Congregation had on September 21, 1959, designated the Basilica of the Assumption the co-cathedral. In practice the new cathedral came to be called simply "the cathedral" and the old one "the basilica."

One other goal would be set by Archbishop Keough before his death. A gift of $525,000 from clergy and laity on the occasion of his twenty-fifth year as a bishop in May 1959 prompted him to announce that the sum would be used in the construction of an archdiocesan office building, a task that he would leave to his successor.

To the Suburbs

Francis Keough's fourteen years in Baltimore coincided with a period of urban expansion that spilled the residents of Maryland's largest city into the suburbs in unprecedented numbers. They also witnessed an end to 228 years of steady growth. In 1957 the city's population peaked at approximately 985,000, never reaching the million so confidently predicted, and began an inexorable decline. Baltimore mirrored the history of other industrial centers in the postwar years. Blue-collar workers moved from the inner city to the suburbs as they moved from the lower class into the middle class.

The migratory patterns of Baltimore followed lines already developed in the prewar and war years. The greatest Catholic expansion occurred in the eastern and northeastern sectors of the metropolitan area. Polish and German families from southeast Baltimore pushed into Dundalk and Essex. German, Irish, and some Polish and Italian families from the north central and eastern parts of the city followed the Harford and Belair Road corridors to such northeastern communities as Overlea, Fullerton, and Parkville. Catholics of mixed origins took Charles Street and Loch Raven Boulevard out to Towson and Baynesville. At the western edge of the city Catonsville became a Catholic stronghold, largely German and Irish. To the south Glen Burnie attracted a large number of ethnic Catholics.

Parishes boasting the greatest increase in the fourteen Keough years, that is, from the beginning of 1948 to the end of 1961, were Holy Trinity, Glen Burnie, 1,100 to 12,500; St. Agnes, Catonsville, 1,300 to 7,800; Immaculate Conception, Towson, St. Michael's, Overlea, St. Ursula, Parkville, and St. Mark's, Catonsville, all from about 3,000 to 8,000; St. Anthony's, Gardenville, 3,100 to 12,200; and the Shrine of the Little Flower, Belair Road, 5,900 to 12,200. Two parishes created at the beginning of the Keough years registered equally remarkable increases: St. Matthew's on Loch Raven Boulevard grew to 14,000 and Immaculate Heart of Mary, Baynesville, to 10,000.

As the parishes on the periphery mushroomed, those of the inner city shrank. Professional and blue-collar whites moved out; nonwhite minorities and whites from depressed areas moved in to fill the vacuum. This in turn accelerated the outmigration, which even in the Keough years came to be called "white flight." Few of the new arrivals in Baltimore were Catholic. The greatest losses recorded in the Notitiae of the Keough years were St. Katharine of Sienna, 8,000 to 1,300; St. Paul's, 6,000 to almost 600; St. Ann's, 5,200 to 1,000; and St. John the Evangelist, 4,000 to fewer than 500.

St. Martin's, St. Edward's, and St. Cecelia also registered significant drops.

During Keough's fourteen years in Maryland, twelve new parishes were created and six missions raised to parish status, all but one in response to Baltimore's urban sprawl. The exception was the parish of St. Joseph at Halfway in 1951, and that was a suburb of Hagerstown. The last seven parishes in Baltimore, filling in the last empty spaces, were the Most Precious Blood established in 1948, St. Matthew's in 1949, Our Lady of Fatima in 1951, Our Lady of Victory in 1952, St. Pius X in 1957, the Cathedral of Mary Our Queen in 1959, and St. Thomas More in 1961. The houses of worship of Our Lady of Victory and St. Pius X were actually across the city line.

Caution was the keyword with respect to building under the eleventh archbishop. Our Lady of Victory used the abandoned St. Mary's Industrial School and then its parish hall for a church during the Keough years.[15] St. Pius X would have a church the year after it was established for the growing population of Rodgers Forge. Mass would be said in the school auditorium of St. Matthew's throughout Keough's episcopacy even though a $400,000 drive for a church on Loch Raven Boulevard was oversubscribed. Our Lady of Fatima, begun at the eastern edge of the city as the sixth mission of Sacred Heart, Highlandtown, would lay a cornerstone for a church in 1953 but not see a dedication by Keough.

The burgeoning suburbs demanded four new parishes. The Immaculate Heart of Mary, created in 1948 at the center of a development near Baynesville just north of the city on land donated by the developer, fashioned a church that could be expanded in stages.[16] Our Lady Queen of Peace in 1953 and St. Clare in 1956 were both started by the pastor of Our Lady of Mount Carmel, Middle River, whose parish had grown to more than twelve thousand. For some time a hall would serve as a church for one and the basement of a school for the other. Christ the King was unique. Created for the blacks of Turner's Station shortly before its church was dedicated in 1957, it would be surrendered by the Josephites when whites took over the neighborhood.[17]

Two of the Redemptorist missions of Annapolis would be among the six raised to parochial status: Our Lady of Sorrows, Owensville, in 1953 when a church built by Richard Bennet Darnall in memory of his parents was turned over to the archdiocese, and St. John the Evangelist, Severna Park, in 1959.

The slowness with which some new parishes built churches was more than compensated by sixteen houses of worship raised as second-growth churches or replacements for the makeshift arrangements of the war. In and around Baltimore they would include, in the order of completion, St. Rita's of Dundalk, St. Agnes out Route 40, the Shrine of the Little Flower on Belair Road, St. Anthony's of Gardenville, St. Rose of Lima of Brooklyn, St. Francis of Assisi on Harford Road, St. Ursula of Parkville, Sacred Heart of Mary of Graceland Park, and St. Dominic's of Hamilton. Catholicism was growing strongest in the northeastern reaches of the city.

The churches built in the Keough years were not the vaulted Gothic and Romanesque structures of earlier days. As Catholics rose socially, their need to be overpowered by ambience seemed to diminish. Financial caution, moreover, carried over from the Depression. St. Agnes on Route 40 just outside the city, opened in 1951, was typical of the churches built in the 1950s and early 1960s. Less imposing and more compact than earlier houses of worship, it featured an upper and lower church of almost equal capacity for simultaneous masses. The new church for the Shrine of the Little Flower, dedicated in 1952, was one of the last of impressive proportions but one of the first to be air-conditioned.

The Peak Years for Parish Schools

An adherence to Curley's policy of the school first continued to determine building priorities at the parish level. For every church that went up in the Keough period, at least two schools or school annexes were constructed. School buildings, wings, or extra stories appeared in well over a third of all the parishes of the archdiocese. The number of pupils in parish elementary schools jumped from 35,677 in 1948 to 61,063 by 1962, an increase of 71 percent in the fourteen Keough years (as compared to a 59 percent increase in the twenty-five Curley years).

Keough's would represent the peak years of the parochial schools, when a more accurate measurement of parish growth and vitality than a parish census would be school enrollment. St. Michael's, Overlea, for example, counted only 384 pupils in 1948 but 1,346 by 1962. A ten-room school, convent, and rectory were built in 1950. A third story was added to the school in 1953, and ground was broken in 1959 for another six-room school and school hall. Six more classrooms would be added under the next archbishop. In greater Baltimore the elementary school enrollment of St. Anthony of Padua, St. Mark's, St. Ursula, and St. Agnes tripled or quadrupled. With 1,958 pupils St. Matthew's was by 1962 the largest parochial school in the archdiocese. It employed nineteen School Sisters of Notre Dame and nineteen lay teachers. Immaculate Heart of Mary, Baynesville, with 1,835 pupils, was second. The number of teachers in the parish grammar schools rose from 860 to 1,269 in these fourteen years, but by 1962 35 percent of these were lay teachers as compared to fewer than 1 percent in 1948.

Shrinking enrollment characterized the parochial schools nearer the center of the city. St. Katharine of Sienna's parish school, for example, declined from 1,133 to 264 in the fourteen years and St. Martin's from 1,051 to 306. In the southeast St. Elizabeth, Sacred Heart, and Holy Rosary held steady. With 1,513 pupils in 1962 St. Elizabeth's was still the largest of the older parish schools.

High Schools and Colleges

In the two decades following World War II the products of parochial schools moved increasingly into Catholic high schools rather than the job market. Across the nation bishops, not pastors, assumed the responsibility for the development of this second level of the Catholic school system. The archdiocese of Baltimore was no exception, but it took longer than most to erect its diocesan high schools. The boys' high school that Archbishop Curley had wanted so badly did not materialize until Archbishop Keough's last year, a wait of more than thirty years!

By the beginning of 1960 work had begun on both a boys' high school on Erdman Avenue in the eastern part of the city and a girls' high school on Northern Parkway in the north. The girls' school was entrusted to the Sisters of Mercy, and Mercy High School opened its doors to 350 freshmen in September 1960. The Black Franciscans agreed to staff the boys' school. Fittingly called Archbishop Curley High School, the first diocesan high school for boys opened its doors to 420 freshmen in September 1961. By then work had begun on Cardinal Gibbons High School, utilizing parts of the old St. Mary's Industrial School, and plans had been carefully drawn for another girls' high school on land next to it.

In the meantime two more parishes had established high schools: Our Lady of Pompei in 1957 and Our Lady of Mount Carmel, Middle River, in 1959. Four parishes replaced older with newer and larger high schools, but the days of the parish high schools were numbered. Private high schools, on the other hand, continued to grow. Calvert Hall, where only one in three applicants could be accepted, acquired thirty-five acres in Towson, and the new $2.5 million Calvert Hall began operation in September 1960. The College of Notre Dame of Maryland decided to separate the secondary and college operations and relocate the former on sixty-six acres near Hampton. Notre Dame Preparatory School opened its doors also in September 1960. By contrast Mount St. Joseph High School announced in 1961 the beginning of a long and costly process of total reconstruction on the original site.

Students in the Catholic colleges of the archdiocese rose from 2,996 in 1948 to 4,582 by 1962. A junior college was added to the five existing four-year colleges when Villa Julie was opened by the Sisters of Notre Dame de Namur in September 1952. The five older colleges all crowded their campuses with new buildings. At Loyola, for example, a $2.5 million development program was launched in the fall of 1956 for an engineering and physics building and a student union center.

CYO and CCD

The Catholic Youth Organization (CYO) and Confraternity of Christian Doctrine (CCD) continued to expand their activities, largely to satisfy the needs of Catholic youth unable or unwilling to enroll in Catholic schools. The interest in the CYO that Archbishop Keough carried from Providence to Baltimore was reflected in the enlarged athletic, religious, social, and cultural activities of the organization and the publicity they received.[18] By 1955 the CYO could report 6,000 members in forty-eight parish clubs. Three years later there were 8,000 members. The Baltimore CYO was among the first to introduce adult supervision and youth leadership courses. In 1950 an annual lay leaders' dinner was inaugurated, in 1956 an annual Youth Crusade, and in 1957 an annual Mardi Gras with big name vocalists.

The impetus the new archbishop lent to the CCD was hardly less pronounced. Though introduced in 1936, it had not flourished under Curley, who was preoccupied with the parochial school. There was, however, by 1948 a growing conviction that a significant number of Catholic children would never see the inside of a Catholic school. At the clergy conference in the fall of 1949, the archbishop encouraged attendance at the fifth regional CCD conference in Baltimore. The number of archdiocesan CCD directors was increased and a three-phase plan launched to extend the program to all parishes. Not only did its work include the instruction of Catholic children in public grammar and high schools but also discussion clubs for teenagers, college students, and adults. The results were uneven until confraternities with proper certification were demanded and Rev. Thomas J. Mardaga was put in charge in 1955. From 4,400 in 1948 the number of public school pupils under instruction jumped to 22,000 in 1962, 15,000 of them from the public grade schools and 7,000 from the high schools.

Bigger and Better Buildings

In the Keough years larger and more up-to-date seminaries, novitiates, and motherhouses were built, usually in the suburbs, to accommodate the growing number of vocations. The Capuchins, Paulists, and Trinitarians established novitiates and houses of study in the archdiocese, and ground was broken in 1960 for an $800,000 dormitory and classroom building at St. Charles College. Three sisterhoods transferred their motherhouses to the suburbs. The plan of the Oblates of Providence to transplant their generalate, which included an academy, novitiate, and infirmary, to a large piece of land on Gun and Rolling Roads in Arbutus moved slowly. Our Lady of Mount Providence was not ready to receive its new residents until the end of 1961. The Mission Helpers began in 1954 to move their motherhouse, novitiate, and house of studies to Joppa Road. The Carmelites in 1961 left their cloistered quarters on Biddle Street for newer ones off Dulaney Valley Road. Often architecturally imposing, commodious, and pleasant, these structures of tile and glass contrasted strikingly with the dark and antiquated buildings on noisy streets their residents had outgrown.

Catholic hospitals expanded their facilities or were totally rebuilt in the Keough years to accommodate the increasing number of Catholics who could now afford hospital care—Blue Cross and other medical coverages were now available—and to incorporate advances in medical technology and services. A nurses' home was added to Bon Secours Hospital in 1954 for the lay students first admitted in 1952 and a five-story wing added to the hospital in 1958.[19] In 1956 the decision was made to rebuild Mercy Hospital on its downtown site. An $8 million drive was launched in 1957, and ground was broken in the fall of 1958. Groundbreaking for a totally new St. Agnes Hospital, also at its same location, occurred the following spring. Plans were afoot as early as 1958 to move St. Joseph's Hospital from Caroline Street to York Road in the county.

Catholic Income and Identity

Institution building at the diocesan level was accompanied by the growth of organizations at the parish level. St. Bernardine's Parish under Monsignor Vaeth set the pace, but few were far behind. At St. Bernardine's could be found a Holy Name Society, Sodality of the Blessed Virgin Mary, Holy Family Social Club, CYO, Youth Athletic League, Daylight Adoration Society for Women, Nocturnal Adoration Society for Men, Working

Girls Adoration Society, Youth Adoration Society, St. John Bosco Club for boys and Our Lady of Good Counsel Club for Girls (both vocation clubs), nine Cub Scout dens, one Boy Scout troop, three Brownie troops, four Girl Scout troops, one Senior Girl Scout troop, and the Pamphlet and Votive Guilds.[20] Parish fund-raising events also served to draw parishioners into closer contact.

There was never any doubt about a parish's ability to build a church or a school or to fund its diverse organizations. Besides the collection basket there were drives and subscriptions, week-long carnivals and weekly bingo, crab feasts and bull roasts, bake sales and flea markets. Parish revenues rarely fell below expectations. The free-will offerings of the faithful, in fact, scaled upward yearly. Maryland Catholics, it seemed, were loosening their purse strings.

This expansive generosity, however, was more apparent than real. While the response to the annual charity appeals climbed from $660,000 to $1 million, a 52 percent increase, from 1949 to 1959, and the contributions to the Propagation of the Faith from about $320,000 to $450,000, a 41 percent increase, the median family income in Maryland for the same decade rose from $3,308 to $6,309, a 91 percent increase.[21] And this at a time when the Catholic population grew by almost 50 percent. Catholics of the oldest archdiocese gave proportionately less of their income to the church as their economic condition improved. Life in the suburbs, "the storied land of power mower and charcoal cookout," as the Baltimore-born bishop of Richmond termed it in 1960, made its own demands on upwardly and outwardly mobile Catholics.[22] An altered economic status would in time produce an altered outlook.

Neither new wealth, however, nor higher education had an immediate impact on Catholic attitudes, which in the early Keough years evidenced an even more heightened sense of Catholic identity. The retreats for Catholic professionals and periodic masses for Catholic policemen, firefighters, and mailmen begun under Curley drew even larger numbers. Maryland Catholics were quick to single out the Catholics in the entertainment, sports, and political worlds. In 1956 the *Catholic Review* ran a series on the ten Catholic members of the Baltimore Colts, all, of course, exemplary Catholics. The Jubilee Year (1950) and Marian Year (1954) spawned Catholic travel bureaus, which arranged tours to Catholic shrines to which Catholics could travel in the comfortable fellowship of other Catholics shepherded by a Catholic priest.

Cold War Catholics

Catholic attitudes continued to be politically conservative in the early Keough years. This was most apparent in the Catholic community's increasingly anticommunist posture as well as in its opposition to pornography in all forms.

"The strongest organization to join the anti-communist crusade in Maryland was the Roman Catholic Church," an authority on the postwar years has claimed.[23] In the fall of 1946 the Maryland Council of the K of C anticipated the parent body's national campaign against communism by its protest of the "mock trial" of Archbishop Aloysius Stepinac of Yugoslavia.[24] Before the end of the year the Maryland chapters of the Ancient Order of Hibernians, the Catholic War Veterans, the Catholic Daughters of America, and the International Federation of Catholic Alumnae had all passed resolutions in favor of a stronger American stance against communism.[25] In January 1947 Auxiliary Bishop Lawrence Shehan warned the Holy Name Society that the Atlantic Charter had been scrapped, and in May Catholics gathered in designated places to pray to Our Lady of Fatima for the conversion of Russia.[26] The Polish and Lithuanian parishes held masses for their oppressed kindred behind the Iron Curtain, and the Maryland Board of Motion Picture Censors banned a documentary, "Our Polish Land," as propaganda because it showed priests and the religious freely entering churches.[27] Outrage followed the imprisonment of Cardinal Josef Mindszenty of Hungary. Archbishop Keough proclaimed the first Sunday of February 1949 Cardinal Mindszenty Day. At the same time, a small group of Catholic businessmen in Baltimore founded the Maryland Action Guild.

The twofold aim of the Maryland Action Guild was to promote the social goals of the papal encyclicals and to combat communism in every form.[28] The first was seen as the most effective way of achieving the second. The guild revived the labor schools operated under Archbishop Curley and basically for the same reason: to counteract communist influence in the unions. For four years the Institute of Industrial Relations offered an impressive course of studies in scattered parishes each fall and spring. In addition the guild invited well-known anticommunist speakers to Baltimore and addressed open letters to the president, congressmen, and other important officials urging a more militant course of action against world communism. In the summer of 1950, when it claimed a thousand members, the guild organized a "mass meeting" to hear Maryland Senator Herbert O'Conor call for an ouster of the Reds from the United Nations.[29]

The *Catholic Review* gave ample coverage to the work of the guild and other anticommunist activities and was a power in its own right in the battle against the Red menace. In November 1949 Martin J. ("Mike") Porter became managing editor. He brought a more cogent style than that of the somewhat pietistic Fitzpatrick and matched the conservative views of the editor-in-chief, Rev. John Sinnott Martin, issue for issue. The *Review*'s support of Senator Joseph McCarthy was muted but unmistakable. It served as a ready vehicle for disclosures on communist subversion supplied it by Senator Herbert O'Conor, information the latter obtained as chairman of an Internal Security subcommittee.[30]

No more ardent spokesman, however, for the anticommunist crusade could be found in Maryland than the ordinarily taciturn archbishop of Baltimore. Keough not only gave his blessing to the founding of the Maryland Action Guild but also kept it afloat financially and said the annual mass for Cardinal Mindszenty that it sponsored.[31] In June 1950 he warned the graduating class of the University of Notre Dame at South Bend that in Eastern Europe almost two thousand years of Christianity were "crumbling before the hideous juggernaut of Communism." The United States, he claimed, was the best hope for restoring spiritual nourishment to the world.[32] As chairman of the administrative board of the NCWC in 1950 and again in 1952, he delivered a similar message to the American bishops.[33]

The Antiobscenity Crusade

The "thaw" of the mid-'50s softened somewhat the shrill voices of anticommunism in Catholic Maryland, but by then another crusade was at full throttle. In no period did Maryland Catholics make a more determined effort to slay the dragon of obscenity, now rampant, as they perceived it, in magazines, the movies, and the media. The two crusades were not unrelated in the Catholic mind. "Filthy Literature Is a Top Communist Weapon," ran an editorial caption in the *Catholic Review* in 1953.[34]

As early as 1951 the Maryland Action Guild resolved to back the antiobscenity efforts of the K of C and the *Catholic Review*. The Knights assumed responsibility for policing the book racks of drugstores and the newsstands. The *Review* staunchly defended the Maryland State Board of Motion Picture Censors, now fighting for its life. When a Baltimore judge overruled the board's ban of *The Moon Is Blue* in August 1953, the *Review* blamed the pressure of "secularists and the ultra liberals" and fairly shouted, "Shall we let loose a deluge of filth?" when in the same month the courts cleared six pictures over the objections of the board.[35]

In September 1953 the K of C invited all Catholic societies to the Alcazar to plan an active campaign against indecent movies and to spearhead Catholic opposition to the growing assault on film censorship. Twenty-nine societies and some three hundred members of the laity responded and the Catholic Committee for Decency was born.[36] In January 1954 the *Review* gloated that no Baltimore theater had dared "brave the ire of the Decency Committee" by booking *The Moon Is Blue*.[37] In the Christmas season of 1956, Archbishop Keough forbade Catholics to attend the movie *Baby Doll*, as Cardinal Spellman had done the week before in New York. The *Catholic Review* ran contrasting photos of a deserted street before the theater showing *Baby Doll* and a crowded street before the one offering *The Ten Commandments*.[38]

Over the long haul, however, it was a losing battle. When a rash of condemned movies hit Baltimore in January 1958, a Catholic delegate introduced a bill in the state legislature restricting such movies to those sixteen and over. When the bill failed, the *Review* complained that, despite its prodding, not a single Catholic organization had aroused its membership to action and few of its readers had even bothered to write their delegates.[39] In the summer of 1959 it sadly reported that the Maryland Board of Censors had "caved in" and approved the movie *Lady Chatterly's Lover*.[40]

Moderating Breezes

By the end of the 1950s the majority of Maryland Catholics had either accepted the futility of fighting the liberal tide, the same that would carry John Kennedy into the White House, or had been swept into the current themselves. As early as 1953 the *Review* expressed surprise that "some few literate Catholics" had accused it of undermining constitutional safeguards by its call for censorship.[41]

Censorship was but one of the many issues that put Catholics increasingly on the defensive. By 1960 birth control, Sunday sales, tax exemption for churches, Bible reading in public schools, and busing for parochial school children were all questions working their way up to the highest court in the land. Archbishop Keough's statement opposing Sunday sales in 1959 was carried in every Sunday edition in the state.[42] The resolution of most of these cases would run counter to the public position of the Catholic Church, though not necessarily to the private convictions of a growing number of Catholics.

Moderating breezes could be felt in the archdiocese of Baltimore well before the winds of change of Vatican Council II. Almost imperceptibly attitudes were altered, values transformed, and priorities rearranged in the 1950s so that to the practiced eye the local church of the late '40s was a chasm away from the groping body of believers in the early '60s. The quiet change in the local church was part of a congeries of interrelated changes. The city of Baltimore itself showed two faces: blight and bloom. As the old city began its decline, having reached a population peak in 1957, an urban renaissance was being plotted.[43]

Changing Politics

The changing political climate mirrored even more accurately the attitudinal changes of the Catholic community, a shift well exemplified in the political careers of three Catholics: Herbert R. O'Conor, Thomas D'Alesandro, Jr., and Francis X. Gallagher.

O'Conor at age forty-two became in 1938 Maryland's youngest governor and its fourth Catholic one. This event marked, as his biographer read it, "the formal emergence (in Maryland) of the Catholic proletariat from the political ghetto wherein it took refuge in the nineteenth century."[44] Devoid of the "crude parochialism" of the Irish immigrant politician, O'Conor was still a conservative Democrat. His opposition to the encroachment of federal power and lack of enthusiasm for costly welfare measures was undisguised. In 1946 he was elected to the United States Senate, where he developed an overriding preoccupation with communist subversion. Finding himself increasingly out of touch with liberal Democrats, he declined to run again in 1952 so that he might be free to speak frankly on the "trend toward Socialism" that weakened the nation "in the great struggle against Communism."[45]

If the *Catholic Review* was an accurate gauge, Maryland Catholics applauded his duels with the Fair Deal almost as heartily as his assaults upon communism. Under John Sinnott Martin and Mike Porter the *Review* berated in like manner Truman liberals for trying to socialize America and undermine states' rights and the free enterprise system.[46]

Thomas D'Alesandro, Jr., a near contemporary of O'Conor, had no quarrel with the growing power of the federal government nor with the New Deal programs that cost millions but drew millions into the Democratic fold. An immigrant's son who found the Holy Name Society a useful conduit to political advancement, he was elected to the state legislature at age twenty-two, the first of twenty-three consecutive victories. He served nine years in the United States Congress before spending twelve unprecedented and productive years as mayor of Baltimore, 1947 to 1959.[47]

In a sense "Tommy" D'Alesandro was a transitional figure, a Roosevelt Democrat who weaned Maryland Catholics from O'Conor conservatism and provided the framework for the Kennedy followers of the next generation. Among the latter could be found his own son, Thomas D'Alesandro, III, and Francis X. Gallagher, classmates in law school. Though he held few prominent offices, Gallagher was well known for his contributions to civil rights and constitutional reform and was a power in the state Democratic party. A man of broad concern and sympathy, pragmatic, hard-working, and self-effacing, he embodied much of the best of the growing number of Catholic liberals of the Kennedy years and beyond. In 1958 he was chosen by Archbishop Keough as attorney for the archdiocese.[48]

A growing sophistication among Catholic voters was accompanied by an abatement of anticommunist zeal. In 1959 the Maryland Action Guild quietly dissolved itself. When Maryknoll Bishop James E. Walsh, of the Cumberland, Maryland, Walshes, was arrested by the Chinese Communists in 1958 and sentenced to twenty years in prison in 1960, there was hardly a ripple of protest. The archbishop's call for a "real crusade of prayer" during the visit of Nikita Khrushchev in 1959 elicited almost no response.

The New Journalism

Nowhere was the transmutation of Maryland Catholics in the Keough years more obvious than in the pages of the *Catholic Review*. In equal measure, perhaps, did the diocesan weekly both reflect and stimulate the change that occurred in the second half of the 1950s after the retirement of John Sinnott Martin in 1953 and the death of Mike Porter in 1954. In the spring of 1956 Gerard E. ("Gerry") Sherry, age thirty-four, came to the *Review* as managing editor. A native of England and a founder of the English Young Catholic Workers, Sherry had discovered in American Catholic journalism a proper scope for his views on the church and the world at large. In one of his early editorials in the *Review* he decried enforced segregation as "a thing that corrupts and enflames the soul of man."[49] Maryland Catholics were unaccustomed to such sentiments in their diocesan paper.

In the fall of 1956 Sherry observed editorially that Catholics were so obsessed with communism that they were blind to other evils. "When Communism is merely a notation in the history of the world, there will be poverty, hunger, and injustice; there will still be greed and exploitation."[50] In the fall of 1958 he ran under his own name a much-acclaimed series on urban renewal in Baltimore. In it he criticized the city for giving so much attention to its business district and so little to its blighted neighborhoods.

"Those of us who live outside this man-created slummery," he insisted, "are, in a sense, as guilty as those (mainly absentee) landlords who exploit not only the poor Negro, but also poor white families."[51]

Sherry was well aware that not all his readers embraced his views, not only those on communism, segregation, and urban renewal, but also his opinions on right-to-work laws, the Supreme Court, the UN, and international affairs, all of which contrasted with earlier positions taken by the *Review*. The *Catholic Review* nevertheless commanded a growing respect nationwide for its fresh and forthright views. The Catholic Press Association praised Sherry as a "provocative, crusading editor who combines both technical and writing skill to produce one of the finest weekly newspapers in the United States."[52]

It was not all Sherry's doing. He drew upon the talents of others, especially young priests alert to new ideas. Joseph Gallagher and Joseph Connolly were among those who took their turns as the thought-provoking "Justin Smith." In 1959 Gallagher, then assistant at the old cathedral, a gifted writer, and a brother of attorney Francis X. Gallagher, came to the *Review* as consulting editor.[53]

At the end of June 1960 Sherry resigned for family reasons but was succeeded by a man of his own choosing, Robert Osterman from New York. The new editor's stay was even shorter-lived, not quite a year. He did not enjoy the confidence the archbishop accorded Sherry. A blistering attack on the conservative *Brooklyn Tablet* and a slam at the American Legion caused one reader to yearn for the "old times" of Father Sinnott Martin and another to complain: "It will be a happy day for the Catholics of Baltimore when you pack your carpet bags and join the other carpetbagger who was the past editor."[54] In April 1961 David Maguire took over as managing editor. A native of Baltimore, he was more sensitive to the feelings of his readers but ready to promote the concerns of his predecessors. In the fall the *Review* gave editorial nods to the freedom rides on Route 40 and the sit-ins at the Baltimore lunch counters.[55]

A Church in Transition

When the new editor expressed a wish to become better acquainted with liturgical change, the consulting editor sent him to Father Joseph Connolly at St. Gregory the Great. The latter, who had worked wonders there with his liturgical experiments, was in turn one of the active young priests who in their seminary years had come under the spell of the Sulpician Eugene A. Walsh.

"Gene" Walsh began to teach educational psychology at the Paca Street Seminary in 1948. Through his teaching, counseling, and informal contacts he exercised increasing influence. The Walsh-directed seminarians were exceptional in their openness toward, and even eagerness for, new and challenging ideas.[56] They were also more responsive to the liturgy he fashioned at Paca Street and at the old cathedral when the seminarians went over to take part in the services. By the mid-'50s his influence in liturgical circles was national.[57]

One of his most receptive students was Joseph M. Connolly. A former Marine ordained in Rome in 1951, Connolly was assigned to the comfortable parish of St. Charles, Pikesville, but acquired there the jobs of Catholic chaplain at a black college and moderator of the Catholic Interracial Council of Baltimore. Under the presidency of the remarkable Anita Williams, the CIC continued in a variety of ways to pursue its principal goal of raising Catholic consciousness to the problem of racism. Among them was a letter to the archbishop requesting that he integrate the parochial schools; it was politely received but unproductive.[58]

In 1957 Connolly was sent as curate to the dying parish of St. Gregory the Great. There he fashioned a liturgy that incorporated as much participation, music, and English as the law allowed. Church attendance increased dramatically as whites came from many parts of the city to worship with the black parishioners. Many parishes copied all or parts of the services at St. Gregory, which drew national attention.[59]

The new liturgy stimulated change in other areas, providing as it did an altered perception of church and community. It was the door through which many priests and laypeople entered the arenas of community service, social action, and ecumenical dialogue. At St. Gregory Connolly launched a number of other projects: a catechumenate program modeled on that of the archdiocese of Paris; an outdoor mission, a form of outreach to the black community, conducted in the plaza of a nearby housing development; and the Young Catholic Workers modeled on the Jocists of Europe.[60] It was also one of his principal goals to bring the Church into more vital contact with the city, which by the mid-'50s was well over a third black. With the Josephite Henry J. Offer, who came to nearby St. Peter Claver in 1960, and the Sulpician William J. Lee, professor of sociology at Paca Street, he met frequently. "We saw a dying Church in a dying city," Offer later recalled.[61] The trio worked out a blueprint for future action which envisioned, among other things, an inner-city deanery.[62]

In 1959 Connolly was also named archdiocesan director of radio and television, which he seized as an opportunity to present the Church to non-

Catholics in a more favorable light. With its long history of interfaith harmony, the oldest see was more receptive than most to the ecumenical dialogue begun in the 1950s by such churchmen and pluralists as Robert
McAfee Brown, Will Herberg, and Gustave Weigel of Woodstock College
on the edge of the city. At the beginning of 1960 the *Catholic Review* ran an
editorial entitled "Preparing for Unity," in which it waxed enthusiastic at
the blossoming ecumenical spirit.[63]

A Caution at the Top

The changing temper of the Keough years was largely a middle-level
phenomenon. It sprang from a restlessness among the younger clergy and
educated laity. It developed in spite of the archbishop and, for the most
part, with little encouragement from the higher echelons of the archdiocese. By temperament Archbishop Keough was unreceptive to any change
but institutional growth. Soon after his advent in Baltimore, he moved to
Long Crandon in the country and commuted daily in the manner of other
professionals who had fled the city and its problems. If the plight of the
blacks was a matter of concern for him, he kept the fact as well hidden as
other facets of his life.[64] He took no pains, however, to conceal his distaste
for liturgical reform. "The liturgists," he told Father Connolly pointedly in
1960, are "the Communists in the church, trying to take the mass away from
the people."[65]

Despite his repugnance for change, however, Keough had not his predecessor's love for open-field battle. He was, except on rare occasions, a
gentle person considerate of the feelings of others. The reason he is said to
have suffered the presence of Eugene Walsh in his see city was that the Sulpician's mother lived there. The respect he had, moreover, for the persons,
if not always the opinions, of Gerry Sherry and Francis X. Gallagher had
also a moderating influence.

Archbishop Keough was a cautious man who measured carefully the
costs and pondered long the consequences. He was also a very private person who confided in others as little as need be, even his auxiliaries.[66] None
was privy to his master plan. At heart he never left Providence, a fact be-
trayed by the many times in Baltimore he let slip such an expression as "my
good people of Providence." In many ways he resembled James Roosevelt
Bayley, whose heart and mind remained in Newark, who disliked the city
of Baltimore, and who had come with a promise that was frustrated by ill
health.

Whatever his shortcomings, Keough had a genuine concern for the working class from which he sprang. One of his principal goals was to bring within the reach of Catholics climbing from the lower into the middle class a high school education and old-age health care. He never employed any but union labor. If the achievements of his fourteen years in Baltimore fell short of those of his thirteen and a half in Providence, ill health was largely to blame, a condition he sought to conceal.[67] There were mild heart attacks in the spring and fall of 1953 before the massive one of November 23 of the same year. To the amazement of his physicians, he was back at his desk by the end of February, but he moved from Long Crandon to Stella Maris Hospice, where he stayed the rest of his life.

The archbishop lost auxiliary bishops at critical junctures. Nine days after the massive attack, Bishop Lawrence Shehan was installed as first bishop of Bridgeport, Connecticut. To replace him as auxiliary, Jerome Daugherty Sebastian, the pastor of St. Elizabeth's in Baltimore, was named December 22, 1953. The choice surprised many. Sebastian had labored in no other parish than St. Elizabeth's nor held any position higher than archdiocesan director of the Sodality. The fourth auxiliary himself died of a cerebral hemorrhage on October 11, 1960, at a time when the archbishop's health was worsening alarmingly. On September 27, 1961, Bishop Shehan arrived in Baltimore as coadjutor archbishop with right of succession, "a priceless jewel returned to its proper setting," as Keough had expressed it when the appointment was announced the previous July.[68]

On November 30 Archbishop Keough suffered a stroke and was taken at his own request to Georgetown Hospital. There he died December 8, 1961, the third archbishop of Baltimore to enter eternity from Georgetown but the first to be buried at the new cathedral.

Francis Keough left an archdiocese economically sound and well endowed with the institutions needed for a Catholic population that had grown from 265,000 to 448,000 by the end of 1961. Many areas of concern were left unaddressed, however, by the aloof and chary archbishop, whose flock would remember him with neither the veneration awarded Gibbons nor the awe accorded Curley. This conservative New Englander was even less attuned than his predecessor to the Maryland tradition. His administration represented a continuation of the Catholic ghetto shaped by Curley. The small place the older tradition could find in Keough's worldview would make its restoration under his successor all the more striking.

V

 The Council and Beyond

Archbishop Lawrence Joseph Shehan 1961–1965

Cardinal Lawrence Joseph Shehan 1965–1974

"I find in most of the Catholic utterances on education," a representative of the public schools had said at the annual meeting of the National Education Association in 1889, "no sense of obligation to the whole, no civic breadth, no thought of any children but their own."[1] It was an irrefutable indictment of the immigrant church. Not only the parochial schools but the hospitals, orphanages, reformatories, homes for the aged, and other institutions built for the poor were for the Catholic poor alone. The church, of course, had enough to do to take care of its own, but there was little evidence of regret that it was not able to address the needs of the non-Catholic also.

Robert McAfee Brown, a Protestant commentator on Vatican Council II, would find the Pastoral Constitution on the Church (*Gaudium et Spes*) a "highly significant" document in that it "turned outward to examine the ways in which a Church subject to 'reform and renewal' should relate to those beyond its walls." He was delighted that the Council had "concluded on a note of concern for others."[2] Baltimore's second cardinal, Lawrence Joseph Shehan, would also judge the Council "especially noteworthy" for its emphasis on "the Christian's duty to help build a just and peaceful world, a duty which we must carry out in brotherly cooperation with all men of good will."[3] In this redirection of interests and energies the postconciliar church would reclaim that sense of public service that was a hallmark of the Carroll church.

Vatican Council II would in many ways represent a call to American Catholics in general and to Catholics of the oldest archdiocese in particular to return to their roots in the Maryland tradition. The Constitution on the Liturgy, for example, would speak to the need to adjust the spiritual life of a people to its particular culture and to "supplant certain popular devotions with authentically liturgical piety" that recognized the "centrality of Scripture," as Jaroslav Pelikan, another Protestant observer, read it, in effect something akin to the republican piety of the Carroll church.[4] In the "Introduction" to the *Documents of Vatican II* he was invited to write, Cardinal

Shehan would rank the Constitutions on the Church (with its emphasis on collegiality and the role of the laity), on Revelation, and on the Liturgy, as well as the Decree on Ecumenism, among the most significant achievements of the Council. "As an American," he would add, "I would also consider the Council's Declarations on Religious Freedom and the Church's Relationship with non-Christian Religions, including the statement against anti-Semitism, as among its most satisfying achievements."[5] The twelfth archbishop of Baltimore would, in fact, play an important role in the formulation of some of these documents that would accord so well with the convictions and objectives of the Maryland tradition. This was particularly true of the Declaration on Religious Freedom (*Dignitatis Humanae*), more than any other document the American contribution to the twenty-first ecumenical council of the church.

With vigor and determination would the twelfth archbishop of Baltimore lead the Catholics of the premier see back to their roots. In the process he would accomplish a more thoroughgoing reconstruction of the archdiocese than any of his predecessors except Carroll and thus exemplify the experimentalism that was another feature of the church that Carroll fashioned. The network of consultative bodies set up at all levels would prompt one commentator to observe of the postconciliar church what would certainly be true of the premier see: "Never before in the Church's history had so much paper work been moved around by so many people; never had there been so much conferring, talking, consulting, and reporting back."[6]

The emphasis for the second cardinal would be directed toward four principal areas: ecumenism, the liturgy, the laity, and racial justice. In each area, in its own way, directions taken would represent a reclamation of the Maryland tradition. Working toward racial justice would, for example, enkindle again the civic concern so prominent in the life of the first archbishop. At the same time, racial justice, not itself one of Carroll's primary concerns, and the resistance to war and violence that the twelfth archbishop would come to espouse would represent a broadening of the tradition. As the old enemies of the ghetto church, the Protestant and the secular liberal, were won over in the years following Pope John XXIII and President John Kennedy, a new enemy would appear to keep alive some of the militancy and cohesiveness characteristic of the immigrant church—the social devil. The new enemy would appear in several guises: poverty, discrimination, bigotry, racism, war. Not all Catholics would readily recognize the social devil, however, and a new tension would develop in the church reminiscent of the old one rooted in ethnic discord. Nor would all readily accept the passing of the ghetto church whose walls had meant safety and security. For many the challenges of the postconciliar church would prove not only unsettling but frightening.

In some ways, in fact, the twelfth archbishop would represent a continuation of the immigrant church. He was a builder and a fundraiser. He would raise the kind of buildings that had served the immigrant well: larger schools and churches, an old age home, a penitent asylum. Lawrence Shehan would never see himself as replacing an old church with a new one. He was simply carrying out the mandates of Vatican II as a dutiful son of the Holy Father. *Humanae Vitae* would represent a turning point in his career. He would become increasingly discomfited by the "runaway church." He would, perhaps, at no point of his stewardship in Baltimore have smiled if told he was the architect of a second revolution.

16   The Council

By the time Lawrence Joseph Shehan became archbishop of Baltimore in his own right, the archdiocese, with its 450,000 Catholics, had slipped to twenty-second place among the dioceses of the nation.[1] The prominence of the premier see was further diminished on February 21, 1962, when Atlanta was raised to an archdiocese, taking with it several of Baltimore's suffragan sees. The Province of Baltimore was now reduced to the archdiocese and the dioceses of Richmond, Wheeling, and Wilmington. Archbishop Paul J. Hallinan of Atlanta offered graciously to leave Baltimore in first place in the *Catholic Directory*, but Archbishop Shehan was less jealous of his prerogative than some of his predecessors had been.

After only a month in office, Baltimore's twelfth archbishop began, it seemed to many, to move mountains. On January 5, 1962, he created a Commission on Ecumenism. On February 16 he announced the future convocation of the Tenth Synod of Baltimore, which laypeople would play a part preparing and where the role of the laity would be a principal topic. On February 23 he established a Liturgical Commission. In the first week of March he issued an unequivocal statement in favor of an equal accommodations law. In these fresh areas of concern— ecumenism, the liturgy, the laity, and racial justice—he signaled the more pastoral role the archbishop of Baltimore would play in the future.

The Last Builder

A large part of his working day, however, was given to the brick-and-mortar projects that had occupied his predecessors for more than a century. As an institution builder, Shehan took second place to none of them. The apprenticeship at Bridgeport provided mastery. In his eight years there, he had produced seventeen new churches, fifteen new parochial schools, four regional high schools, a new chancery building, new wings for two Catholic hospitals, and a multi-million dollar home for the aged.[2] Like institutions would be raised on a grander scale in Baltimore. So ambitious were the plans laid in his first weeks in office that an auxiliary was urgently needed to serve as vicar and adviser and to share confirmations. On July 3, 1962, T. Austin Murphy, pastor of St. Rose of Lima, was ordained titular bishop of Appiaria by the apostolic delegate.

Several of the institutions raised by Archbishop Shehan were planned by his predecessor. Quite unexpectedly, John Eyring, the architect, informed him soon after Keough's death that designs for a central office building were nearly completed. The new archbishop had reservations about the location, the site of the old Calvert Hall, but approved an enterprise so far advanced. This and other projects he entrusted to Monsignor Joseph Leary while he was in Rome for the Council and placed Leary at the head of a new Archdiocesan Building Committee.[3]

The Catholic Center at 320 Cathedral Street, built at a cost of $3 million, was ready for occupancy in the fall of 1965 and was blessed by Bishop Murphy on November 7. To the seventh floor went the furniture and files of the archbishop, the Chancery, and the Archives from 408 North Charles, to the sixth floor the Tribunal from 7 West Mulberry, and to the fifth Education from 330 North Charles. To the third floor Associated Catholic Charities moved from 415 Cathedral, to the second the *Catholic Review* from 115 West Franklin, and to the first the Catholic Information Center from 125 West Saratoga. To the fourth floor a number of other offices were transferred from other addresses. Under the same roof each unit became aware of the existence of the others. The archdiocese of Baltimore, they discovered, was a big operation.

Keough had also failed to inform his coadjutor fully of plans for new high schools. Even before Cardinal Gibbons High School was opened in the fall of 1962, the architect dropped by to tell the new archbishop he was ready to start drawings for an adjoining girls' high school. Shehan summoned those closest to his predecessor. Plans for three high schools, he learned, were well advanced at the time of Keough's death. In addition to this girls' school on Caton Avenue, land had also been bought for high schools in Cumberland and Bel Air. The archbishop signed contracts for all three. Insistent pleas for diocesan high schools came from many parts, particularly from Pikesville, Dundalk, and Glen Burnie. The arguments of the last named, where the pastor of Holy Trinity needed the rooms of an already overcrowded parish high school for his grade school, seemed most convincing. In the spring of 1965 a site was chosen at nearby Severn for another girls' high school.[4]

John Carroll High School at Bel Air, built at a cost of $3.2 million, opened in September 1964. Archbishop Keough High School for girls on

Caton Avenue, contracted for $3.4 million, opened in September 1965. The opening of Bishop Walsh High School on Haystack Mountain in Cumberland, named for the imprisoned bishop, coincided with that of Martin Spalding High School at Severn in 1966. Keough and Spalding, like Curley and Gibbons, were designed for twelve hundred students, Carroll and Walsh for eight hundred with an expansion allowance of a thousand.[5] The latter two were coeducational. Opened as a girls' school, Spalding would in time also go coed. With the completion of Martin Spalding High School, the *Catholic Review* boasted, Catholic high schools of the archdiocese would be able to accommodate 80 percent of the girls coming out of Catholic grammar schools.[6]

Another Schoolman

Archbishop Shehan told the Advocate Club at the beginning of his administration: "My greatest efforts will be in the field of education."[7] At the same time, he denied that he had in a speech before the National Catholic Education Association in 1959 suggested abolishing Catholic primary education. He would later claim, nonetheless, that some people, presumably himself included, would favor the Catholic high school over the grade school if a choice had to be made.[8] While the number of parish grammar schools remained at 104 in the first six years of his administration, enrollment in these schools dropped from 61,000 to 55,000. In the same period, diocesan and parochial high schools increased from twelve to eighteen and their enrollment from 3,373 to 6,504.

The twelfth archbishop had, nonetheless, an abiding concern for Catholic education in general. In September 1962 he created a board of education that included several influential businessmen. As episcopal chairman of the NCWC's Department of Education from 1958 to 1963, he was considered an outstanding champion of the Catholic school. When Mary Perkins Ryan in *Are Parochial Schools the Answer?* in 1964 questioned the need for such schools in an ecumenical age, Archbishop Shehan wrote what many judged the most effective rebuttal, an article entitled simply "The Parochial School." The value of the Catholic school, he insisted, stemmed from the very nature of education itself. Religious truth must serve as an integrating force. The movement toward Christian unity could never be fostered at the expense of Christian [Catholic] truth. High costs and a shortage of personnel, he predicted in one of his less prescient moments, would be solved by state aid and an increase in vocations.[9] The ten thousand copies of the article printed by *America* and distributed by the NCEA convention in Atlantic City had, the *Catholic Review* reported, "a heartening impact on the delegates."[10]

The growth of diocesan high schools had a slightly negative impact on private high schools, which fell in number from sixteen to thirteen and from an enrollment of 9,857 to 7,823 during the six years in question. Growth in higher education was gratifying. The 4,582 students in six Catholic colleges at the beginning of 1962 increased to 6,479 in seven by 1968. Mount Providence Junior College was opened by the Oblate Sisters in 1962. Mount St. Agnes, Loyola, Mount St. Mary's, and Notre Dame of Maryland all added new buildings. In 1965 St. Joseph College launched a $12 million development drive.

Hospitals and Headquarters

The prosperity of the Keough years continued without faltering, providing limitless resources, it seemed, for all the needs of the archdiocese. There was an unparalleled expansion of hospital facilities. To the new St. Agnes Hospital and the wing of the Bon Secours Hospital built in the late Keough period was added on February 3, 1963, the $8 million twenty-one-story Mercy Hospital, "the very model of the modern high-rise hospital." Within a month a victory dinner was held for an over-the-top drive for a new Sacred Heart Hospital in Cumberland, plans for the Good Samaritan Hospital were announced with seeming finality, and ground was broken for the new St. Joseph Hospital in Towson.[11] The $12 million St. Joseph Hospital was dedicated on November 20, 1965. From a $5 million project the Sacred Heart Hospital grew to an $8.5 million undertaking with a psychiatric unit and other up-to-date facilities. It was dedicated June 11, 1967.

True to form, the Good Samaritan Hospital showed no compulsion to hurry to completion. The O'Neill bequest for the Good Samaritan corporation had grown to $15 million when it was announced that a hospital primarily for the treatment of chronic diseases with twenty free rooms on a forty-four-acre tract on Loch Raven Boulevard would be begun in late 1964 or early 1965. Groundbreaking did not occur until March 20, 1966. In the fall the archdiocese entered into an agreement with the Bon Secours Sisters and Johns Hopkins Hospital and University whereby the former would assume responsibility for the nursing services and the latter for physician and administrative services, the intern program, and research. The Good Samaritan Hospital would be dedicated September 29, 1968, a $15 million center for research and treatment of the chronically ill.[12] Bon Secours Hospital, like Mercy Hospital, would elect to remain in the inner city when it planned another expansion in 1968.

Motherhouses continued their search for more ample facilities in the suburbs. The Oblates and the Carmelites completed their moves. The $1.5 million motherhouse of the Mission Helpers built on Joppa Road was finally dedicated June 28, 1964. The Bon Secours Sisters chose Marriottsville to erect a capacious provincialate, novitiate, and infirmary complex whose cost was never disclosed. Two institutional landmarks, however, the Little Sisters of the Poor and the Good Shepherd, needed the help of the archdiocese to make similar moves to the suburbs. Their obvious needs prompted Archbishop Shehan to launch the most ambitious drive ever attempted in the city of Baltimore.

The Cardinal's Campaign

The "Cardinal's Campaign" had its inception in the first of the archbishop's annual St. Joseph's Day visits to the Little Sisters of the Poor and later to the House of the Good Shepherd. Both establishments were nearly a century old, parts of the Good Shepherd older. Both were tinderboxes. Both sisterhoods lacked the resources to rebuild. The Good Shepherd Sisters on Mount Street wished to merge this and the house on Calverton Road for black girls. The archbishop and his advisors decided that an appeal to the public would have to be made "such as had never been attempted before."[13]

In 1964 it was finally determined that a new plant for the Little Sisters on a thirteen-acre tract on Maiden Choice Lane purchased from St. Charles College would require some $3 million in aid and a combined Good Shepherd Center on land acquired in Halethorpe $2 million. The latter figure was made possible by the sale of the Mount Street land for a public school. To these amounts another half million was added for the St. Elizabeth School for Special Education planned by the Franciscan Sisters. It was decided, however, not to go public with the appeal until after the annual Charities drive of 1965. Before that event the rank of cardinal was bestowed on the archbishop of Baltimore, an honor that will be considered in a more appropriate context. The New York firm engaged to conduct the drive suggested that it be called "The Cardinal's Campaign." Shehan's reluctance to exploit his new honor was overcome by Henry J. Knott, who had agreed to act as general chairman of the campaign. Knott himself ran the dinner that launched the appeal even before an official announcement was made. He assured the businessmen invited to the mansion of Long Crandon on June 28, 1965, that it was a once-in-a-lifetime event for the cardinal and urged them to dig deep, setting an example himself by pledging $346,000. The final total for advance gifts was $1,959,671.[14]

By the time plans for the Cardinal's Campaign were unveiled in September, the goal had been raised to $11 million to include high school construction and the operating expenses for Catholic Charities that year. The campaign was formally opened on January 14, 1966. It represented a return to the pledge system of Archbishop Curley. By June pledges had edged past the $11 million goal. When the books were closed, $11,787,329 had been collected.[15]

As soon as it was evident the campaign would be a success, the three principal beneficiaries proceeded with their plans. The cardinal, in fact, signed the $628,000 contract for St. Elizabeth School for Special Education in December 1965, and the school was opened in the fall of 1966. The other two undertakings were more complex. The St. Martin Home for the Aged, built on Maiden Choice Lane at a cost of $4,764,500, would not move the 117 elderly from Valley Street until May 1969. The $4.8 million contract for the Good Shepherd Center on its seventy-acre site in Halethorpe was not signed until February 1968, and the dedication would not take place until September 10, 1970.

New Parishes and Old

The twelfth archbishop took pride also in new parishes.[16] In his first six years he founded five and raised five missions to parochial status. All but St. Ann's, a new parish created in Hagerstown in 1966, were the result of the exodus from Baltimore to suburbia and exurbia. It was a process facilitated by the Baltimore Beltway, completed in 1962, and the interstate highways that radiated from it.[17] Interstate 95 and the military expansion at Aberdeen and Edgewood as a result of the Vietnam War drew many into Harford County. In 1963 a new parish, Holy Spirit, was planted in the middle of a real estate development at Joppa, and St. Francis de Sales at Abingdon was made a parish in 1964.[18] Larger churches replaced older ones at Aberdeen and Bel Air. Out Interstate 70 the mission of St. Michael at Poplar Springs was also made a parish in 1964. Off Interstate 83 the church of St. Joseph, Texas, was enlarged.

South of Baltimore a new parish, St. Philip Neri, was created in 1964 in the fast-growing suburb of Linthicum Heights. It was a wealthy parish that had little trouble in funding a church, school, and rectory at the same time. A church for twelve hundred was opened in 1965.[19] Just over the western edge of the city, where the Social Service Administration had its "white-collar factory," St. Lawrence in 1962 became a parish with a new school-church-rectory complex. Just over the eastern edge St. Adrian's and St. Mildred's were fused into Our Lady of Hope parish in 1967.[20] The mission of Our Lady of the Fields, Millersville, was surrendered by the Redemptorists at Annapolis. No new parishes were created inside Baltimore, but four existing ones built new churches. Our Lady of Fatima and St. Matthew's built their first churches. At St. Brigid's a new church replaced the one erected in 1854. On February 9, 1967, the roof of St. Rose of Lima collapsed, seriously injuring 43 of the 120 worshipers.[21] The decision to rebuild was made at once.

The most significant parish established in the first six years was St. John the Evangelist in Columbia, a "new town." In March 1964 the National Council of Churches resolved to make Columbia a pilot site for an experiment in new forms of cooperative ministry. The religious needs of the community would be met in centrally located complexes that afforded maximum flexibility. Ownership of the centers would be vested in nonprofit corporations formed by the religious denominations that wished to participate. The archdiocese of Baltimore agreed to take part in this "unique opportunity to rethink church planning."[22] When the parish of St. John was established at the village of Wilde Lake in 1967, mass was said in a hall of the Interfaith Center shared by other denominations. The archdiocese agreed that there would be no parochial schools in Columbia.

The creation of ten new parishes in six years would be partially offset by the closing of four old ones, all the victims of outmigration. St. Joseph's on Lee Street, for many years the shell of a parish, was "temporarily closed" in 1962. A German parish, Fourteen Holy Martyrs, was absorbed by an Irish one, St. Martin's, in 1964, while an Irish parish, St. John the Evangelist, was absorbed by a German one, St. James, in 1966, which was renamed St. James and St. John. St. Adalbert became a part of St. Athanasius in 1967. All had, of course, lost their ethnic character. In Annapolis St. Augustine's, a mission of St. Mary's, Annapolis, for the blacks, was abandoned when the roof was irreparably damaged by a snowstorm in 1966. Few of the blacks returned to St. Mary's.

The Pastoral Goals

Brick for brick and dollar for dollar, Lawrence Shehan outdid all of his predecessors as builder and fundraiser, but it was as a pastoral leader that he was outstanding. His promotion of racial justice, one of the important goals of his episcopacy, was dictated in part by concern for the plight of his native city. In his civic sense, the second cardinal resembled both Carroll and Gibbons, placing his time and talents at the disposal of city and state alike. In the summer of 1965, for example, he accepted an invitation from representatives of the city's commercial banks, the Baltimore Human Relations Commission, and the Congress of Racial Equality to arbitrate a dispute over employment practices.[23]

As a pastoral leader the twelfth archbishop set himself four major goals: (1) the promotion of interfaith harmony, (2) the development of the worshiping community, (3) the empowerment of the laity, and (4) the elimination of racial prejudice and discrimination. Though not articulated at the same time and slighted, except for racial justice, in his own memoirs, the four objectives were set forth early in his administration and linked at the beginning of his fifth year in an expression of his priorities.[24] His pastoral activities can be organized around the four goals: ecumenism, liturgical reform, lay involvement, and racial justice.

Ecumenism and the Council

Ecumenism came easier to Baltimore, perhaps, than to other sees. It was a spirit as old as Carroll and as warm as Gibbons. Even under the more conservative archbishops it showed a remarkable vitality. Lawrence Shehan attributed his own outlook and approach to the example of the illustrious cardinal who in so many ways served as his model.[25]

As already noted, he announced on January 5, 1962, the establishment of a commission on ecumenism to advise on matters of church unity. Later called the Archdiocesan Commission for Christian Unity, it was chaired by Monsignor Joseph Nelligan, now restored to prominence, and consisted of such well-known scholars as Raymond Brown, SS, of St. Mary's Seminary and Walter Burghardt, SJ, of Woodstock. Consultors included Avery Dulles, SJ, Gustave Weigel, SJ, Professor Harry Kirwin of Loyola College, and David Maguire, managing editor of the *Catholic Review*. The first ecumenical commission of the Catholic Church in the United States, its creation attracted national attention. *America* observed that the oldest see still managed on occasion "to set the pace for its juniors."[26] The commission met monthly. It brought in speakers, consulted with Protestant ministers, prepared bibliographies, and in general did all it could to enlighten itself first and then the Catholic community at large.

Five months before the opening of Vatican Council II on October 11,

1962, the Baltimore commission was affiliated with the preparatory commission in Rome. Soon after the opening of the Council, Cardinal Augustin Bea inquired of Monsignor Porter White the names of the American bishops most likely to favor the work of the Secretariat for the Promotion of Christian Unity that he headed.[27] The archbishop of Baltimore was invited to become a member of the Secretariat and Monsignor White a consultant.

Archbishop Shehan had left for the Council thinking it would be fairly brief and largely a matter of approving the work of preparatory bodies. In its first two-month session, Baltimore's archbishop waited, watched, listened, and learned. The schema on divine revelation he found "totally lacking in the spirit of the ecumenism." The attack of Bishop Emile DeSmedt of Bruges on the schema on the church for its triumphalism, clericalism, and juridicism he judged the "most eloquent and memorable speech of the whole Council."[28] Before his death on June 3, 1963, Pope John XXIII, at the suggestion of the man soon to succeed him as Paul VI, instructed the Theological Commission to work closely with the Secretariat for Christian Unity in rewriting the schema on the church.[29]

It was, more than anything, his strong sense of ecumenism that prompted the several interventions (speeches) of the archbishop of Baltimore in the next three sessions of the Council. When he returned to Rome in the fall of 1963, he brought with him not only Monsignor White, who prepared the Latin texts for these interventions, but also a second peritus, the Sulpician James Laubacher, former rector of St. Mary's Seminary and Shehan's confessor when he was auxiliary bishop in Baltimore.

Archbishop Shehan's first appearance at the podium (October 10) was to address the question of papal infallibility, which he considered "the main source of difficulties with our separated brethren." An infallible pronouncement, he contended, should never be understood as apart from or opposed to the consent of the church.[30] Thus did the twelfth archbishop of Baltimore play a part in restoring the role of the bishops, a role the seventh archbishop at Vatican Council I had felt obliged to constrict in order to slay Gallicanism.

Two weeks later Shehan took the microphone to speak to the question of the separation of church and state. Disturbed by the use of the expression "deplorable separation" (*infausta separatio*), he had told the American bishops at their weekly meeting of his intention to voice his disapproval. The bishops asked him to be their spokesman, the first time the American hierarchy was so represented at the Council. Shehan sought the elimination not only of the unhappy expression but also that part of the text touching separation, it being too important a subject, he maintained, to be treated in passing.[31]

In mid-November a five-chapter schema on ecumenism was introduced, Cardinal Bea himself presenting the fourth chapter on the Jews and Bishop DeSmedt the fifth on religious liberty. In February 1964 Archbishop Shehan was recalled to Rome for a meeting of the Secretariat on Unity. There it became clear that a separate document on religious liberty was needed. A statement was hammered out largely by Bishop DeSmedt and the peritus John Courtney Murray, SJ.[32] The February meeting also produced a separate and more emphatic statement on the Jews than that of the schema.[33] The day he left for the third session Archbishop Shehan had a long interview with Jacob Blaustein, a spokesman for the Jewish community of Baltimore. Blaustein urged that the Council repudiate the word "deicide" and other terms offensive to the Jews found in Catholic prayers and writings. The archbishop promised to do what he could.[34]

With the opening of the third session in 1964 the American bishops formed a committee under the chairmanship of Archbishop Shehan to coordinate their presentations on the subject of religious liberty.[35] In an intervention on the decree on the Jews, which he submitted in writing, Shehan urged not only a repudiation "without ambiguity" of the charge of deicide but also the suppression of a statement advocating conversion of the Jews.[36]

In the third session he also planted seeds for an important statement in the fourth and final session. Room should be made in the decree on revelation, he told the Council fathers on October 1, for the role of the human mind in the interpretation of God's word. Then on October 22 he delivered what a Council historian would call "one of the most philosophically profound of all American observations."[37] In the encyclical *Ecclesiam Suam* of the new pope he found an acceptance of the basic thesis of Newman's *Essay on the Development of Christian Doctrine*. "A power of development is a proof of life," he quoted the English cardinal.[38] Before he could pursue this line of reasoning to its ultimate conclusion, the third session ended, to the exasperation of the Americans. A vote on religious liberty was postponed to the last session, a move Archbishop Shehan sought to avert by a handwritten letter to the pope.[39] The postponement, however, allowed him to speak to the subject with greater authority.

Shehan's reputation had grown as the Council advanced. In the fall of 1964 he was voted a member of the administrative board of the NCWC, episcopal chairman of its press department, and a member of the executive committee to study its reorganization. More significant was his election as chairman of the Committee for Ecumenical Affairs created by the American bishops.[40] He was the only American among the seventy consultors named for the Commission for the Revision of Canon Law.

On January 15, 1965, the apostolic delegate traveled to Baltimore to hand its archbishop a short letter from the pope. At the next consistory, it read, he would be made a cardinal "in order that we may be able to repay your goodness to the Church."[41] He was the only American among the twenty-seven new cardinals. The consistory was held on Washington's birthday. In a brief address, in which he took note of the unparalleled changes in the past twenty-five years, the new cardinal spoke of the great love for Baltimore he shared with the city's first cardinal.[42] His titular church, San Clemente, had been originally that of Cardinal Amleto Cicognani upon the latter's recall to Rome to become papal secretary of state. Shehan was certain it was not coincidental. "Since his arrival in Washington as Apostolic Delegate in 1933, he had taken an interest in me. . . ."[43]

As a cardinal, Shehan spoke directly to the Declaration on Religious Freedom on September 20. It was, he declared, the result of the development of a doctrine found in the writings of the modern popes from Leo XIII to Paul VI. In the line of reasoning he advanced, he successfully undermined the contentions of a conservative minority, including Cardinal Alfredo Ottaviani and Archbishop Marcel Lefebvre. As John Courtney Murray had observed at the beginning of the fourth session, it was not so much the concept of religious liberty that frightened the minority but the affirmation of the development of doctrine it entailed.[44] "It is obvious," the cardinal concluded, "that the whole world expects of this Council a declaration on religious liberty. The world needs such a declaration, for without the recognition of the right to religious liberty there can be no true and lasting peace among men."[45] The vote taken the next day registered 1,997 in favor and only 224 against.

Before the end of the Council other honors were heaped upon Baltimore's second cardinal. In the spring and summer of 1965 he was named to the Consistorial Congregation (now the Congregation of Bishops) and the Congregation of the Holy Office (now the Congregation of the Doctrine of the Faith), being one of only two non-Italians on the latter body. At the fourth session he was chosen one of the twelve Council presidents. On December 7, 1965, he headed the delegation named by the pope to meet with Patriarch Athenagoras in Istanbul, where in a ceremony similar to one held simultaneously in Rome with Paul VI the principal participant, the centuries-old mutual excommunications of the Roman and Orthodox churches were consigned to oblivion. At the concluding liturgy of the Council the following day the pope called Baltimore's cardinal to his throne to report on this symbolic event.[46]

Cardinal Shehan had spoken seven times in the course of Vatican Council II, more than any other member of the American hierarchy except Cardinals Spellman, Ritter, and Meyer. His quiet demeanor caught the attention of many but escaped headlines. To the redoubtable Paul Blanshard of the Protestants and Other Americans United for the Separation of Church and State (POAU) he was a "friendly compromiser" and a "mildly progressive leader."[47] None could deny that he was a prelate deeply concerned with the problems of ecumenism, a concern he would carry into the postconciliar years.

In 1964 the Archdiocesan Commission for Christian Unity and the Maryland Council of Churches had cosponsored a Christian Unity Week that featured ecumenical services in both Catholic and Protestant churches. The next month Archbishop Shehan issued a pastoral on unity in which he announced that the Archdiocesan Commission would conduct a national workshop on ecumenism in Baltimore, the first of its kind. In June some one hundred delegates from sixty-eight dioceses gathered at the Sheraton-Belvedere.[48] In March 1965 Cardinal Shehan chaired the first meeting of the American Bishops' Commission for Ecumenical Affairs. In December 1965 the National Conference of Christians and Jews bestowed upon the cardinal its highest honor, the National Brotherhood Award. A month later the Har Sinai Brotherhood presented him with a Bible and a birthday cake.[49] Eight weeks after the close of the Council the archdiocese of Baltimore hosted the first meeting between the Bishops' Commission for Ecumenical Affairs and the National Council of Churches, the main feature of which was an ecumenical prayer service at the Lyric Theater.[50]

Interfaith relations at the parish level developed as rapidly in the oldest archdiocese. Individual parishes reached out to the Protestant and Jewish congregations within their boundaries, sometimes forming neighborhood associations. St. Peter the Apostle, for example, and five other churches fashioned the Southwest Baltimore Citizens' Planning Council.[51] Catholic organizations also made friends with their non-Catholic counterparts. The Knights of Columbus cooperated with the Masons and B'nai B'rith in attempts to address urban and racial problems. The problems of the inner city, in fact, offered one of the most vital arenas for interfaith cooperation, as will be seen.

Persistence of Tensions

Despite the dramatically altered attitudes that ecumenism produced, some of the time-honored differences between Catholics and non-Catholics persisted. The archdiocese was still obliged to place itself in opposition to the City Health Department and the Maryland Public Welfare Board over birth control policies. Catholics, for the most part, continued to support state censorship of the movies. The American Civil Liberties Union took on the *Catholic Review* for its stand on obscenity.[52]

In 1960 Madalyn Murray and son sued the city of Baltimore and the local school board for allowing Bible reading in the public schools. When the case went to the Supreme Court, Maryland's attorney general, a Catholic, invited the attorneys general of the other forty-nine states to join him in petitioning the court to allow the Lord's Prayer or a verse from Scripture to be recited in the public schools.[53] When the Supreme Court upheld Mrs. Murray, Archbishop Shehan judged the decision "regrettable." In this he differed from the National Council of Churches, which saw prayer as the responsibility of the home.[54] The success of her celebrated case emboldened Mrs. Murray to sue the churches, unsuccessfully, on the matter of tax exemption. The *Catholic Review* took lightly her charge that the Catholic Church of Baltimore was behind a conspiracy to have her jailed to prevent the suit.[55]

Public aid for private schools remained a divisive issue in the postconciliar years. In 1964 the Horace Mann League tested state laws granting aid to four church-related colleges in Maryland: Hood College, Western Maryland College, the College of Notre Dame of Maryland, and St. Joseph College, Emmitsburg. The Maryland Court of Appeals blocked aid to all but the first as unconstitutional. In November 1966 the Supreme Court let the decision stand.[56] Five months before, Cardinal Shehan addressed the Baltimore Bar Association, urging its members to adhere to the traditional policy of cooperation between government and religion and eschew the "wall of separation" metaphor. "I take this opportunity, as my predecessors have done, to assert my devotion as a Catholic American citizen to the American church-state tradition and to affirm my conviction concerning the wisdom of the religion clauses of the First Amendment as they were historically intended, unclouded by the vagaries of rhetorical devices." In support of this affirmation he quoted Cardinal Gibbons as well as Archbishop McNicholas, who as head of the administrative board of the NCWC in 1948 had stated: "If tomorrow Catholics constitute a majority of our country, they would not seek a union of church and state."[57]

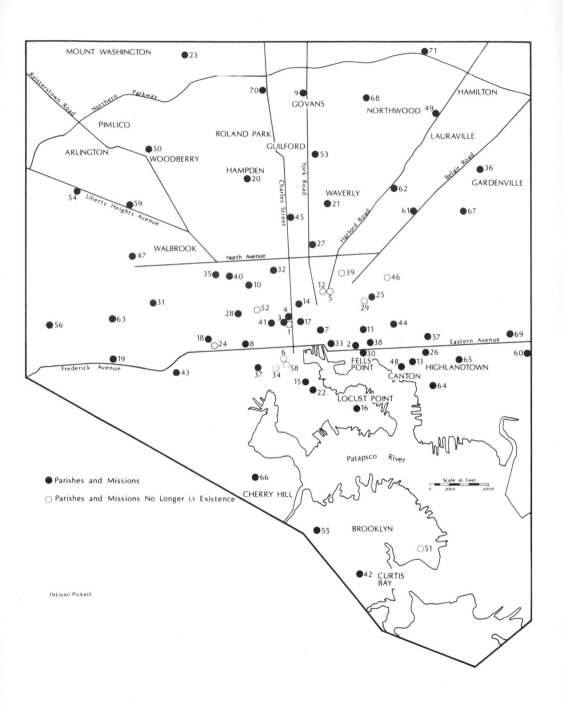

MOUNT WASHINGTON ●23

●71

Reisterstown Road

Northern Parkway

70●

9● ●68
GOVANS
NORTHWOOD 49● HAMILTON

PIMLICO

ROLAND PARK
GUILFORD
LAURAVILLE

ARLINGTON ●50 ●53
WOODBERRY

HAMPDEN
●20 ●36
GARDENVILLE

WAVERLY
●54 ●59 ●21 ●62 Belair Road
Liberty Heights Avenue ●61 ●67

Charles Street
York Road
Harford Road

WALBROOK ●45

●47 ●27
North Avenue

●32
35● ○39 ○46
●40
10● 12
○ ●25
●31 5 ○29
●14
28● ○52 4 ●44
41● 3 ●17 ●11
●56 ●63 1 7● ●57 ●69
18● ●8 33 2 ●38 Eastern Avenue
○24 30● ●26 60●
19● 6 ○ ○ 48 ●13 ●65
Frederick Avenue 37 34 58 FELLS CANTON HIGHLANDTOWN
43● POINT ●64
15●
●22 LOCUST POINT
●16

Patapsco River
Scale in Feet
0 2000 6000

●66
CHERRY HILL

● Parishes and Missions
○ Parishes and Missions No Longer in Existence

●55 BROOKLYN

○51

●42 CURTIS
BAY

DiLisio/Pickett

Map 3. Parishes and Missions of the City of Baltimore

NOTE: Italic entries indicate parishes no longer functioning.

1. *St. Peter Pro-cathedral, c. 1770–1842*
2. St. Patrick, 1792
3. *St. John*/St. Alphonsus (German), 1797 (1845)
4. Cathedral of the Assumption, 1821
5. *St. James (German), 1834–1986*
6. *St. Joseph, 1839–1962*
7. St. Vincent de Paul, 1841
8. St. Peter the Apostle, 1844
9. St. Mary of the Assumption, 1848
10. Immaculate Conception, 1850
11. St. Michael the Archangel (German), 1852
12. *St. John the Evangelist, 1853–1966*
13. St. Brigid, 1854
14. St. Ignatius, 1856
15. Holy Cross (German), 1858
16. *St. Lawrence O'Toole*/Our Lady of Good Counsel, 1859 (1889)
17. St. Francis Xavier (black), 1863
18. St. Martin, 1865
19. St. Joseph Monastery, 1867
20. St. Thomas Aquinas, 1867
21. *St. Bernard, 1867*
22. St. Mary Star of the Sea, 1868
23. Shrine of the Sacred Heart, 1868
24. *Fourteen Holy Martyrs (German), 1870–1964*
25. St. Wenceslaus (Bohemian), 1871
26. Sacred Heart of Jesus (German), 1873
27. St. Ann, 1873
28. St. Pius V, 1878
29. *St. Andrew, 1878–1974*
30. St. Stanislaus Kostka (Polish), 1879
31. St. Edward, 1880
32. Corpus Christi, 1881
33. St. Leo (Italian), 1881
34. *St. Monica (black), 1883–1959*

35. St. Gregory the Great, 1884
36. St. Anthony of Padua, 1884
37. St. Jerome, 1887
38. Holy Rosary (Polish), 1887
39. *St. Paul, 1888–1968*
40. St. Peter Claver (black), 1888
41. St. John the Baptist (Lithuanian/Italian), 1888
42. St. Athanasius (Polish), 1890
43. St. Benedict, 1893
44. St. Elizabeth of Hungary, 1895
45. SS. Philip and James, 1897
46. *St. Katharine of Sienna, 1902–86*
47. St. Cecilia, 1902
48. St. Casimir (Polish), 1902
49. St. Dominic, 1906
50. St. Ambrose, 1907
51. *St. Adalbert (Polish), 1907–67*
52. *St. Barnabas (black), 1908–31*
53. Blessed Sacrament, 1911
54. All Saints, 1912
55. St. Rose of Lima, 1914
56. *St. William of York, 1914*
57. Our Lady of Pompei (Italian), 1923
58. *Our Lady of Sorrows (Italian), 1924–35*
59. Our Lady of Lourdes, 1925
60. Sacred Heart of Mary (Polish), 1925
61. Shrine of the Little Flower, 1926
62. St. Francis of Assisi, 1927
63. St. Bernardine, 1928
64. St. Gerard Chapel, 1944
65. Holy Redeemer Chapel, 1944
66. St. Veronica (black), 1945
67. Most Precious Blood, 1948
68. St. Matthew, 1949
69. Our Lady of Fatima, 1951
70. Cathedral of Mary Our Queen, 1959
71. St. Thomas More, 1961

Misreading an item in the *Evening Sun*, the *Catholic Review* declared that Governor Spiro Agnew had "shocked and disappointed countless Maryland citizens" by precluding state aid to church-related schools. Hastily the governor attempted to set the record straight by saying that he favored granting nonpublic schools a wider share of services such as busing and athletics. The *Sun* accused the governor, as the *Review* read it, of "rekindling" an old controversy.[58] On the basis of the Catholic's need for state aid to exercise freedom of choice in the matter of schooling, the *Review* backed an amendment to the state constitution introduced by the archdiocese's attorney, Francis X. Gallagher, that restated the first amendment of the federal constitution.[59] After three hundred years and more Maryland was still a testing ground for questions of church and state.

The Liturgy

Ecumenism was significant for its implications for the future, but the liturgy constituted a more immediate concern. On February 23, 1962, Archbishop Shehan created a liturgical commission, one of the first in the country. It included Fathers Eugene Walsh and Joseph Connolly. After the promulgation of the Council's Constitution of the Liturgy, the archbishop placed Bishop Austin Murphy at the head of the commission and empowered him to act in his absence. The first version of the English mass was introduced into the parish churches in October 1964.

There was little or no opposition to the change until an angry voice was heard at Mount St. Mary's Seminary in Emmitsburg. Rev. Gommar DePauw, professor of canon law, issued a "manifesto" calling for the restoration of Latin in the liturgy. Toward this end he organized the Catholic Traditionalist Movement (CTM). Upset at this attack on the work of the Council by one of his own priests, Cardinal Shehan ordered DePauw in April 1965 to disassociate himself from the CTM or seek another bishop. DePauw sought incardination by the bishop of Tivoli in Italy, announcing later that it was with the encouragement and assistance of Cardinals Spellman and Ottaviani.[60] Cardinal Shehan had originally no objection to a transfer. In one of his frequent walks with Cardinal Cicognani during the Council, however, the latter exclaimed: "We have too many people like that over here."[61] Feeling himself obliged to keep the troublesome priest within his jurisdiction, he ordered his return from New York, where the CTM was headquartered. DePauw refused to obey. The cardinal revoked his faculties. When the public pronouncements of the disaffected priest became so outrageous as to discredit the CTM completely—in the fall of 1967 he delivered an ultimatum to the pope—the cardinal thought it best to ignore him.

The cardinal's stand discouraged all but a few of the irreconcilables within his jurisdiction from associating with the CTM. DePauw had a much larger following outside the archdiocese. The cardinal realized, nonetheless, that liturgical reform was the most urgent and potentially the most unsettling of the changes required by Vatican Council II. It became the focus, therefore, of his plans for implementing the decrees of the Council.

The evening following its close, Cardinal Shehan was back in Baltimore closeted with Bishop Austin Murphy and Monsignors Thomas Mardaga, Francis Murphy (his secretary) and Joseph Gossman (the vice chancellor). Well into the night they mapped out a program. The first year, it was decided, the cardinal would visit selected, or "stational," parishes with Monsignor Frank Murphy and Father Charles Riepe. Murphy would organize and Riepe, fresh from Innsbruck where he had studied under Joseph Jungmann, the renowned liturgist, would supervise the liturgy. Mass would be followed by an open meeting where the congregation would be encouraged to ask questions and to discuss the Council decrees. The next year all 129 parishes would be visited either by the cardinal, Bishop Murphy, or a second auxiliary bishop the cardinal would seek.[62]

The visitations continued through the spring of 1966 in the selected churches of greater Baltimore. In the fall the trio went west. By the end of the year the stational visits were completed. In only one parish had they encountered any stubbornness.[63] In the meantime Thomas Mardaga, director of the Confraternity of Christian Doctrine and executive secretary of the Charity Fund, was named the sixth auxiliary bishop of Baltimore. On January 25, 1967, Cardinal Shehan ordained him bishop. The visits of the three prelates to all the parishes, however, had to be postponed for a year.

Greater congregational participation with priests facing the people induced many pastors to undertake extensive renovations, even ill-advised guttings, which in turn led to minor crises in a few parishes. The liturgical reforms had a noticeable impact on church architecture. Even before the new liturgy went into effect architectural influences from outside were felt in the archdiocese. St. John's in Severna Park and St. Joan of Arc in Aberdeen represented striking departures from the traditional. At St. Philip Neri, the first octagonal church, no worshiper was more than fifty feet from the altar. Our Lady of Hope's church in Dundalk was the first designed with the liturgical directives of Vatican II in mind, though these were first tested in Manresa's chapel. Adverse comment was silenced when the Liturgical Arts Guild conferred its highest award upon the architect, William Gaudreau.[64]

The Laity

The cardinal's visitations convinced him of the importance of pursuing the third of his pastoral interests, an enlarged role for the laity. For Lawrence Shehan the most significant document that came from Vatican Council II was the Constitution on the Church, and among the parts he pondered long were the chapters on collegiality and on the laity. The Council had simply reinforced an already existing conviction. At the beginning of his administration he had placed lay consultors on the Archdiocesan Commissions for Christian Unity and the Liturgy. The laity was invited to send suggestions for the Tenth Synod and to participate in the work of the preparatory committees. Four businessmen were named to the Archdiocesan Board of Education. When one of them asked the archbishop to define the extent of the board's power, he responded: "Your decisions are my decisions."[65]

Lay organizations were experiencing a different kind of growth. The Confraternity of Christian Doctrine not only involved an increasing number of lay people in parish activities but afforded them at the same time a greater awareness of a developing theology. Monsignor Mardaga, its director, was probably not far from the mark when he called it in 1965 "the outstanding lay movement in the Church today." This he based upon the Baltimore experience, where more than sixteen hundred cathechists, six thousand active members, and six thousand associates were involved in a six-stage program that included such features as adult discussion clubs and the Apostolate of Good Will directed toward non-Catholics.[66] The decline of more venerable organizations, such as the Holy Name Society and the Sodality, was due in part to the increasing number of parishioners drawn to CCD work. Such was the case at St. Patrick's at Fells Point, which had introduced the CCD in 1962 and by 1967 had all six divisions going strong.[67]

On May 13, 1963, 153 corporate charters were filed with the Maryland Department of Assessments and Taxation, whereby all the parishes of the archdiocese were separately incorporated.[68] The corporators for each parish included two laymen chosen by the archbishop in consultation with the pastor. The lay corporators were to serve at the good pleasure of the archbishop. This, it was carefully explained, was to "guard against the danger of the lay trusteeship of the nineteenth century." In an editorial, however, the *Catholic Review* declared that historically trusteeism had "generated an excessive reaction" in the form of long years of little or no real cooperation between clergy and laity. "Happily this period seems to be at an end, and Archbishop Shehan's approach may well symbolize the arrival of a new era."[69] While the incorporation of the parishes was prompted by the numerous suits that came out of a fire at the St. Rose of Lima oyster roast in 1956 and the consequent need to shield the corporate sole, it did signal the reentry of the layperson into a leadership role at the parish level.

On April 3, 1964, the archbishop announced the formation of the Archdiocesan Council of Catholic Men (ACCM). Its purpose, he explained, was to coordinate the work of existing parish and diocesan organizations of Catholic laymen and to promote a better understanding and more effective approach to "the demands of the modern world."[70] Within a year units had been formed in more than half the parishes of the archdiocese. In the spring of 1965 the archbishop, now a cardinal, set forth as emphases for the ACCM foster homes, juvenile delinquency, the liturgy, housing for the elderly, and federal aid to education.

At the conclusion of Vatican II Cardinal Shehan repeated his intention to hold the Tenth Synod, to which the preparatory committees had applied themselves in 1962. Work on the liturgy and ecumenism was well advanced; it was now important to acquaint the laity with other teachings of the Council.[71] It was not long, however, before the attempt to formulate a definitive body of laws was abandoned. The cardinal and his advisers concluded that at a time of sweeping change it would be wise to wait until the revision of canon law was completed.

On April 15, 1966, the cardinal announced his decision to create an archdiocesan pastoral council. The Archdiocesan Council of Clergy, Religious, and Laity that he brought into being counted thirty-three members chosen by himself. These included five pastors, five assistant pastors, five religious priests, one brother, two sisters, fourteen laymen, and five laywomen. Among the laymen were John C. Evelius and Charles A. Fecher, both prominent in the ACCM. The council was asked to study its counterparts in the few sees where they existed and to devise a suitable government for itself. At a meeting in December 1967 a constitution drawn up by Evelius and Fecher was adopted.

When he announced the creation of this archdiocesan body, the cardinal also urged that pastoral councils be formed in each parish, citing as examples those already in existence at St. Lawrence in Woodlawn and St. Joseph Monastery. St. Lawrence was the first to develop a parish council. When it became a parish in 1962, the new pastor, Rev. Anthony Dziwulski, who had allowed teenagers to plan the CYO programs, was eager to have the whole parish membership involved in building a new parish. When separate men's and women's guilds proved unsatisfactory, he sent out a letter to all parishioners in May 1964. "I want you," he told them, "to help me run this parish. I want to hear your opinions. I want you to help me make the decisions which have to be made for the good of the parish. . . . In other words, I am trying to bring the laymen into greater participation in all phases of the parish activity, not just at Sunday Mass." The gatherings of the Parish Guild resembled town meetings.[72]

At St. Joseph Monastery parish John Evelius, one of the two lay corporators, wrote the pastor in June 1964 that the CCD program "would be a natural starting point in launching a lay apostolate parish program that could set the pace for the rest of the parishes in the Archdiocese." A meeting of the parish corporators was held in August to authorize the plan worked out by Evelius and two other laymen. It began with the organization of the Serra Club, the Legion of Mary, and study clubs.[73]

Attending a Holy Name convention not long after, Evelius was impressed by Bishop Murphy's call for a parish "superstructure." In June 1965 he presided over a meeting of the heads of the various parish societies to create what soon came to be called a parish council and also an advisory board. The council was made up of the presiding officers of the twelve parish organizations then in existence, namely, the Sodality, CCD, Holy Name, St. Vincent de Paul, Choir, Mothers Club, Ushers, Legion of Mary, CYO, Serra Club, Bingo Committee, and Boy Scouts. Its purpose was to coordinate, but not to control, the various goals and activities of the parish. To the advisory board were named parishioners with a professional expertise that could be utilized by the parish council, namely, a judge, a member of the state legislature, an attorney, and the personnel manager for the Hecht-May Company. The parish council would meet monthly.[74]

In October 1966 the Archdiocesan Council of Clergy, Religious, and Laity determined upon a pilot program of parish councils to run for eight months or a year in selected parishes of greater Baltimore, namely, St. Joseph Monastery, St. Lawrence, St. Rose of Lima, St. Clare, and St. Martin's. In September 1967 the Archdiocesan Council created a committee of seven under the chairmanship of John Evelius to draw up guidelines for the establishment of parish councils and advisory boards based upon the experience of the pilot program. The *Guidelines* were ready for a clerical conference held in April 1968. The chairman explained the procedures. Some of the pastors of the parishes of the pilot program responded to questions that often reflected a palpable uneasiness.

The pastor, the *Guidelines* were careful to explain, surrendered neither authority nor responsibility but simply became a better executive by using the talents of the laity. The parish council would consist of a representative, normally the president, of each parish organization, the superior of the sisters' community, the parish representative of the ACCM, and five members at large. Its purpose was to coordinate all lay activity. The advisory board would consist of the chairmen of five committees, namely, Finance, Maintenance, Education, Liturgy, and Parish and Community Relations. The members would be persons of professional competence, cleric or layperson, appointed by the board of corporators, which would also authorize the creation of the parish council.[75]

Some confusion and much apprehension persisted. It would not be until the Senate of Priests, created in 1967, addressed the question of councils and collegiality that parish councils would multiply and develop the potential that lay energies and talents offered. The important achievements of the priests' senate, however, fell within the last six years of Cardinal Shehan's administration and will be treated as a whole in that period. It was clear by the late '60s nonetheless that "the People of God" was a concept to be taken seriously.

Racial Justice

Of the four emphases and areas of concern, racial justice would be the one the twelfth archbishop agonized about the most.[76] He was not wanting for priests and laypeople ready to battle racism. If anything, he would have to moderate their zeal. But whether the majority of Catholics were ready to move was another matter.

In early 1962 the Catholic Interracial Council merged with the newly created Clergymen's Interfaith Committee on Human Rights. Father Joseph Connolly, president of the board, and five other members of the committee, in the company of the executive director of the Urban League, were denied entrance to Miller Brothers' restaurant. In March the archbishop came out publicly for a state accommodations law. A week later the Interfaith Committee deplored the Assembly's failure to pass such a law.[77]

In the early spring the superintendent of Catholic education required the integration of all parochial grammar and archdiocesan high schools. In the late spring the archbishop summoned the heads of all the Catholic hospitals of the archdiocese and persuaded them to adopt simultaneously policies of integration in admission and staffing.[78] In June 1963 he directed that a prevailing wage and nondiscrimination clause be written into all archdiocesan contracts. With the opening of the new St. Vincent Infants Home and Villa St. Louise Maternity Home for unwed mothers in April 1965 segregation officially vanished in the archdiocese of Baltimore. There was no more than the normal amount of foot-dragging in implementing the official policy.

The task of uprooting prejudices and patterns of segregation, however, was infinitely less difficult in diocesan institutions than in Catholic neighborhoods, fraternal and social organizations, and the hearts and heads of Catholics long accustomed to a social condition that was largely southern. To address these deep-rooted attitudes in Maryland, the archbishop determined upon a Lenten pastoral in 1963 that would be as outspoken and forceful as he could make it.

"In this, the oldest and most venerable See in the United States," he wrote, "it should be particularly disconcerting to all of us to know that last year an equal accommodations ordinance then before the Baltimore City Council failed to receive the support of some Catholic legislators who represented districts heavily Catholic in population. Does this mean that many of our own people have failed to recognize the serious duty of justice which flows from the basic equality of men of all races?" Prejudice should be erased in all relationships, "at work and at play." Catholics should not succumb to disreputable real estate brokers and join the flight from the city. "With humility and regret, we Catholics should acknowledge that we have been all too slow in the correction of our shortcomings, although in the light of the experience of many of our forefathers, we should have been particularly sensitive to the unjust inequalities suffered by other groups. For this reason, we have a special obligation to place ourselves in the forefront of movements to remove the injustices and discriminations which still remain." Prudence should not serve as a pretext for inaction or "unnecessary gradualism." Instead patience, understanding, planning, and cooperation were needed.[79]

The *Evening Sun* found the pastoral "eloquent, forthright, and even urgent," while the *Nation* suggested that it be recommended reading for President Kennedy.[80] When the American Communist Party attempted a rapprochement with the Catholic Church in the United States in 1963, Father John Cronin of the NCWC sent the party secretary a copy of the pastoral as a clear statement of the Catholic position on racial justice.[81]

The pastoral was a call to action. Not long after its appearance the inner-city program was launched. Father Joseph Connolly's dream of a small core of dedicated priests free to pursue inner-city work was outlined for the archbishop the year before. A board of priests was created that included Connolly, William Lee, SS, and Henry Offer, SSJ. But the man chosen, at Connolly's suggestion, to head the board and direct the program was Monsignor Austin J. Healy, pastor of St. Stephen's, Bradshaw. Respected by all, son of the author of the Healy Report on Racial Problems in Curley's time, he would be more acceptable to most than Connolly, Lee, or Offer. In the summer he was named pastor of St. Martin's and established the headquarters of the inner-city program near the church.[82]

On the eve of the launching of the inner-city program, the archbishop's commitment to racial justice would be tested in another way. The Gwynn Oak amusement park was chosen by the Congress of Racial Equality (CORE) for a Fourth of July demonstration in which the arrest of prominent churchmen, Eugene Carson Blake and Episcopal Bishop Daniel Corrigan among them, was planned. Father Connolly asked the archbishop if it could be taken as a principle that Monsignor Healy and himself should remain with Blake whatever happened, and Healy phoned the archbishop to tell him an arrest situation was developing and to ask his advice. "Do whatever the others are doing," the archbishop replied.[83] Connolly and Healy were among the thirty-six clergymen arrested under the Maryland Trespass Act. Seven priests, including the pastors of St. James, St. Pius, and St. Peter Claver, led 175 parishioners and 50 members of the Catholic Interracial Council in a picket line outside the park. Father Joseph Gallagher distributed copies of the archbishop's pastoral.[84]

The demonstration released a shock wave. The New York Times pronounced it the most important gesture to date on the part of churchmen. The Catholic Review editorialized that the country was in the throes of "an acute moral crisis."[85] Gwynn Oak, wrote Trueblood Mattingly, the pen name for a Baltimore layman, had thrown the Catholic body of that city into "appalling confusion." Catholic life there would "never be quite the same again."[86] One of the most disturbing aspects for many was the archbishop's apparent endorsement of the actions of his "rabble rousing" priests. On August 28, 1963, the archbishop, his auxiliary, 55 priests, 26 seminarians, and 450 lay Catholics of the archdiocese of Baltimore marched to the Washington Monument to hear Rev. Martin Luther King tell his countrymen that he had a dream.

The clergy and laity of Baltimore became increasingly involved in public protests against racial injustice. The ACCM, Holy Name Society, Archdiocesan Women's Committee for Civil Rights, the Christian Family Movement, and the Catholic Interracial Council all participated in a march for fair housing in Baltimore organized by CORE in November. CORE also made Baltimore a target city in the summer of 1966. In August, when segregationist rallies threatened to trigger riots, fifty-five priests and ministers fanned out over the danger zones to dampen the anger that was building. Their efforts kept Baltimore from becoming one of the combustible cities in a summer of urban riots.[87]

The year 1966 was critical in other ways. It began with Baltimore's spiritual leader's being jeered in public for his plea against racism in housing and ended with the resignation of the editor of the *Catholic Review* following a controversial letter against racism in politics. On January 13 Cardinal Shehan spoke in favor of an open housing ordinance introduced in the City Council by its president, Thomas D'Alesandro III. About half the audience at the War Memorial Building uttered boos and catcalls as he began to speak. The other half rose and clapped. Crosses were later burned in front of the War Memorial and the Cathedral of Mary Our Queen.[88] The measure was defeated by a vote of thirteen to eight. Of the thirteen Catholics on the Council, Father Connolly observed in an angry sermon, only one voted in favor. The failure of open housing was due in large measure, he claimed, to the "negligent attitude" of pastors in heavily Catholic wards, a sentiment echoed by the president of the City Council.[89]

When he went to Washington for the bishops' meeting in November, Cardinal Shehan excused himself from one of the sessions to visit Monsignor George Higgins and Father John Cronin at the Social Action Department. He felt that the bishops should not leave without issuing statements on the war in Vietnam and racial justice. Higgins agreed to do the one on the war and Cronin that on "Race Relations and Poverty," a large part of which was devoted to the problem of housing.[90]

In the fall campaign for governor, George P. Mahoney, a Catholic, ran on the Democratic ticket and Spiro Agnew, the future vice president, on the Republican. "Your Home is Your Castle" blared the Mahoney sound trucks in an obvious attempt to capture the anti-integrationist vote. Monsignor Gallagher, executive editor of the *Catholic Review*, in an "Open Letter" to Mahoney said bluntly: "I am sadly convinced . . . that your election would mean a victory for forces which are hostile to everything honorable which being Catholic, American, Democrat, and Irish should mean."[91] Many attributed Mahoney's defeat to the stand of the *Catholic Review*, which they saw as reflecting that of the cardinal archbishop. Less than a month after the election, the *Review* denied emphatically that Gallagher had resigned as a result of the cardinal's displeasure.[92]

More important than the protests and the politics were the quiet achievements of the inner-city program under Monsignor Healy. The initial unbudgeted grant for the program was $2,000, an amount that would in a few years expand to six figures.[93] A visitation program was started with regional meetings of priests of all inner-city parishes. Healy himself addressed the seminarians of St. Mary on Paca Street and several religious communities in an effort to get them involved in the visitation program, a house-to-house effort largely for data-gathering purposes, and in other activities. In time lay volunteers from suburban parishes were also recruited. Liturgical and catechetical programs were developed early as part of the larger program, as were day care and kindergarten centers and vacation schools. Food cooperatives were set up at Oella, largely black, near Ellicott City and in one or two inner-city parishes.

Monsignor Healy was approached by others to help launch projects that would become adjuncts to the inner-city program. Dismas House, a half-way house for ex-convicts, was opened in the empty rectory of Fourteen Holy Martyrs in June 1965 over the objections of many. Sister Beverly Bell, SND, proposed an instruction center for blacks. Healy helped her locate the Martin de Porres Center in the unused buildings of the former St. John's parish.

Some of the inner-city projects were a result of the Great Society and War on Poverty legislation and were supported by federal funds. A VISTA training program was based at Fourteen Holy Martyrs, and Catholic parishes and institutions were frequently used for field work. Even more successful were the Head Start programs of several inner-city parishes, the first in Baltimore in June 1965 at St. Francis Xavier. The responsibility for Operation Champ, a summer recreational Community Action project, was assumed by the archdiocese and made a part of its inner-city program.

In the summer of 1965 Philip Berrigan, SSJ, assistant at St. Peter Claver, sought the approval of Monsignor Healy to marshal seminarians and college students in a survey of slum conditions below North Avenue and west of Pennsylvania Avenue. Conditions were found to be worse than in Los Angeles' strife-torn Watts, the median income being $3,000, unemployment 25 percent, families on welfare 42 percent, and families without fathers 53 percent. Also uncovered were 1,078 housing code violations on the part of landlords. Berrigan opened in 1966 a storefront mission that directed block meetings and offered a variety of services such as adult education.[94] Not to be outdone, the Jesuits of St. Ignatius opened a storefront mission on Whitelock Street. St. Francis Xavier parish in July 1965 established a social services office with a drug abuse program and entrusted it to Barbara Mikulski, who had just obtained a master's degree in social work at the University of Maryland.

The cardinal remained vitally interested in the inner-city program, and supported it. In an effort to broaden it even more, he created in May 1966 an Urban Commission to replace the inner-city board. It initially included five priests, among them Healy, now in poor health, and Connolly, and three laymen, including Charles G. Tildon, a black, who would become chairman of the commission the following year. "If we don't save the city, we can forget about the Church in the Archdiocese," the cardinal told his priests in June 1966.[95]

His genuine distress over the deterioration of his native city prompted the cardinal to funnel considerable sums into urban renewal and other projects designed to revitalize Baltimore. At the suggestion of an inner-city volunteer, a corporation was erected called Home Ownership Plan Endeavor, or HOPE, in the fall of 1965. HOPE was an interfaith project that included renovation and lease or ownership of homes for low-income families. The first debenture was issued in February 1966. In 1967 the archdiocese awarded grants to Project Equality, an ecumenical endeavor, and to the Strategic Planning Corporation, while the finance committee voted $100,000 to the Urban Commission.

In the fall of 1965 the cardinal called in city planning specialists—the Rev. Robert G. Howes, chairman of the Program of City and Regional Planning at the Catholic University, William Lee, SS, who held a doctorate in economics, Edward W. Wood, Jr., head of the community planning for Providence, and Jack Ladd Carr, city planner for Annapolis—to do an urban parish study. It was the first of such magnitude under Catholic auspices in the United States.[96] Early in the study the specialists recommended the creation of an Office of Planning and Development. This was effected in 1966 with Carr as director. Baltimore was the first archdiocese with such an office in the United States. The consolidation of St. James and St. John and of St. Adalbert and St. Athanasius and the creation of an Interfaith Corporation in May 1967 were recommendations likewise effected before the *Baltimore Urban Parish Study* was released in December 1967.

The creation of the Office of Planning and Development reflected the study's concern for the coordination of efforts needed for any large-scale endeavor. There was little intercommunication between the inner-city board, Catholic Charities, and Education. The study urged that the Urban Commission serve as a focus of commitment, that all educational agencies be concentrated in one office, and that there be a closer cooperation, especially between Catholic Charities and the inner-city office. A large part of the study was given to a critical analysis of the fifty-one urban parishes, whose outlook ranged from "embattled inertia" to "outright heroism." Only St. Martin's received a superior rating for its response to the challenge of change. The *Study* received high praises nationally. *Commonweal* found it a "model" and was taken by the recommendation to place the church in the middle of urban renewal in housing. A full implementation of the study would accomplish "something close to an Archdiocesan revolution," the magazine believed and had reason to hope that "the will for that revolution exists."[97]

The years 1962 to 1968 witnessed the most extensive demographic changes in the city of Baltimore. A number of parishes went the way of St. Gregory the Great, St. Pius V, and the Immaculate Conception with startling rapidity. By 1968 St. Martin's, St. Katharine of Sienna, St. Andrew's, St. Ann's, St. Paul's, St. Edward's, St. Cecilia, St. Bernardine, Our Lady of Lourdes, and St. Ambrose were largely black parishes. Almost as many others saw black penetration at the edges. Hardly any parish in the city did not feel threatened by a drastic population shift.

Though habituated to unquestioning obedience to the expressed wishes of their ordinary, Catholics of the archdiocese could now display a stony intransigence and on rare occasions articulated anger and defiance. J. Michael Arisman in a series of essays written for the *Catholic Review* read Catholic prejudice in Baltimore as a product of the immigrant experience as well as the city's southern heritage and the defeat of open housing the result of cultural separation as much as racial prejudice. Many Catholics refused to follow the cardinal's lead in the belief that he had violated the ethnic values traditionally upheld by parish churches as well as neighborhood bars.[98]

Criticism on the other side came from those who deplored a lack of concern and overall leadership. One reader of the *Review*, reflecting a widespread attitude, saw in the removal of the Little Sisters, the Good Shepherd Home, the Bon Secours provincialate, and St. Joseph Hospital to the suburbs, plus the closing of several downtown parishes, an abandonment of the struggle for racial justice. "Millions for Catholic Centers," he said, "suburban Retreat Houses, and dinners at the Maryland Club, but not one cent for the Inner City."[99] Though misinformed on the last point, the complaint underscored the fact that the hundreds of thousands spent on the inner city could not match the millions invested in suburban growth.

Despite the critics of the right and of the left, however, the years prior to 1968 were characterized by a spirit of optimism and a sense of movement and achievement in the struggle with the social devil. Baltimore's overall record could be rivaled by few other sees in the tumultuous era of the '60s.

Vietnam

In one area, however, uncertain trumpets sounded. As early as July 26, 1963, the *Catholic Review* editorialized about the "remarkable confusion" and "complexity of the situation" in southeast Asia.[100] Not until 1965, however, did this concern sharpen on the editorial pages. "As Catholics," an offering of July 16 read, "our reaction should bear some relationship to the abiding concern of the Popes of the century for world peace." Yet on July 30 the *Review* insisted that the nation honor its pledge to help the South Vietnamese in their fight against enslavement. As late as March 11, 1966, it still thought the president's policy "substantially right," but on April 8 mused about the conspicuous silence of the American Catholic bishops on the Vietnam War. It concluded that they were generally too cautious in speaking out on the moral issues of modern warfare.

That summer the editor, Monsignor Gallagher, offered what he had intended as a Fourth of July editorial to the cardinal as a possible pastoral. With but a slight addition, the cardinal accepted it in toto. The pastoral found in the documents of Vatican Council II a legitimate role for patriotism but also a justification for conscientious objection to war. Its principal emphasis, however, was on the dangers and moral limitations of modern warfare. "Even though our hands are embattled," it concluded, "our hearts must remain steadfastly peace-loving. Otherwise, at the peril of an escalation which could end in mutual annihilation, we may fail to be responsive to the possibilities of reasonable and honorable negotiations." The cardinal's addition read: "That our president has earnestly sought such negotiations in the past, we do not doubt. That he and our national leaders would gladly enter into such negotiations now we firmly believe."[101] The pastoral was dated June 28, however, because American planes had bombed the Hanoi-Haiphong area for the first time on June 29. The cardinal did not want the pastoral to be seen as a response to this event.

It was the first statement by a Catholic bishop in the United States on the war in Vietnam. The *New York Times* gave it front page coverage. It was reprinted in full by the *Catholic World*, the *Catholic Mind*, and *Ave Maria*. *Commonweal* was heartened that the concern of the American church about the "peculiar madness of modern war" had surfaced. It was considered a breakthrough by groups like the American Pax Association. Three months later Archbishop Hallinan of Atlanta and his auxiliary, Joseph L. Bernardin, issued an even more forceful pastoral on "War and Peace." "You know your own Cardinal's pastoral was the inspiration for that of JLB & me," Hallinan wrote Gallagher.[102]

A month before the pastoral was issued, however, the Catholic War Veterans had decided to give the Celtic Cross, its award to an outstanding clergyman, to Cardinal Shehan and its Honor et Veritas award to an outstanding layman to General William G. Westmoreland, leader of the American forces in Vietnam. Though unable to attend the ceremony because of an airline strike, the cardinal wrote the national commander of the CWV thanking him for the opportunity to correct misstatements about his pastoral. Those who interpreted it as a condemnation of the American presence in Vietnam were misguided. Withdrawal, he felt, could have catastrophic results. "Cardinal Supports War" was the unfortunate headline sent out by the Catholic news service. The press in general read the cardinal's statement to the CWV as a retreat from the position of the pastoral.[103] In November, nevertheless, the American bishops' statement on the war prompted by Shehan followed closely his summer pastoral.

The Vietnam war more than any other issue produced an uneasy strain between the ordinary and his diocesan organ. Its editor, Joseph Gallagher, had been honored with the title of Monsignor (papal chamberlain) in the spring of 1965 largely because of his contribution to journalism. The previous fall the archbishop of Baltimore had been elected episcopal chairman of the Press Department of the NCWC largely because of his own balanced views on current affairs. The two events seemed to augur well for a harmonious relationship. At no time did Cardinal Shehan consider that the *Catholic Review* had exceeded the bounds of responsible journalism.[104] At times, however, he expressed displeasure at the appearance of certain items.

In August 1966 the cardinal informed the editor of his wish to establish a parish coverage plan for the *Review*. To assure the good will and cooperation of pastors and people, he believed, the *Review* should be circumspect in its treatment of race relations, the war in Vietnam, and the question of admitting Red China to the UN. At the end of August Gallagher wrote an editorial on "The Horror of Napalm," to which the cardinal took exception for its "sniping at the president," refusing to allow its publication.[105] A showdown of sorts over editorial policy came not over the war but over the "Open Letter" to George Mahoney already mentioned. When the cardinal asked that Gallagher subscribe to a policy statement that editorial opinion should reflect the mind of the publisher (the cardinal), Gallagher asked for a leave of absence to work for a Catholic publishing firm. It was granted.[106]

The *Review* continued its antiwar position but, in the summer of 1967, took exception to some of the antiwar remarks expressed by Philip Berrigan in a speech in Atlanta, which the Josephite answered in a letter to the editor.[107] Berrigan had attracted a following in Baltimore by his radical pacifism. He had organized in the fall of 1966 the Baltimore Interfaith Mission, an admixture of Catholic and Protestant clergy and laypeople who had been active in both civil rights and pacifist groups. It soon became one of the most active peace organizations in the country, ultimately earning for Baltimore the distinction of being "The Christian Guerrilla Capital of the United States."[108]

The Interfaith Mission spent its first year pressing its views upon assorted congressmen. On December 29, 1966, twenty of its members drove to Washington to picket the homes of Secretary of State Dean Rusk and Secretary of Defense Robert McNamara. Rusk phoned St. Peter Claver the next morning to invite Berrigan over to hear his views. Berrigan returned quoting the secretary, "I leave all morality up to you clergymen." A few weeks later the Baltimore pacifists escalated their protests at Fort Meyers, Virginia. On their third visit to Generals' Row they were hustled onto a bus and dumped unceremoniously outside the fort. That night, back in Baltimore, the peace group in an eight-hour "gut session" decided upon a drastic escalation—a nonviolent destruction of government property.[109]

In the meantime other antiwar activities attracted an increasing number of Catholic protesters. On October 21, 1967, Monsignor Gallagher and a group of seminarians went to the Pentagon to join one of the largest antiwar demonstrations to date. Berrigan and his Jesuit brother were there. Six days later Philip Berrigan, James Mengel, a minister of the United Church of Christ, Thomas Lewis, a young Catholic artist, and David Eberhardt, an agnostic son of a Presbyterian minister—the Baltimore Four—strolled casually into the United States Customs House near the Inner Harbor and poured a mixture of human and animal blood over records in the Selective Service office.[110] The *Catholic Review* pronounced the gesture a "disgusting act, repulsive in its disregard for orderly government."[111]

The blood-splattering event was a turning point, a moment in time when the liberal optimism of the Kennedy-Johnson era and of the Vatican II and post-Vatican II years began to collapse before the radical onslaught of the Berrigan followers, black power advocates, and others. The archdiocese of Baltimore had up to this point moved as easily as any into an altered world, shrugs, scowls, scoffs, and jeers notwithstanding. It had handled its recalcitrants of the old order with becoming firmness. But it was ill prepared to deal with the spiritual children who moved rapidly and well beyond the new consensus. Optimism, even exhilaration, would yield to uncertainty, even disenchantment, in the years to come.

17 Aftershocks

THE AFTERSHOCKS OF Vatican Council II seemed unremitting. On May 20, 1968, the *National Catholic Reporter* carried an "Open Letter to the U.S. Catholic Bishops" written by Monsignor Joseph Gallagher, who was still smarting from his clash with the cardinal over editorial policy. It professed to reflect the views of the seminarians he taught as well as of the "best young Catholics" generally. "In a few harsh words," he told the bishops, "you seem to them almost hopelessly remote, institutional, establishment, bureaucratic, bourgeois, defensive, legalistic, real-estated." The bishops, he claimed, refused to face up to the "dilemma" of birth control. "The Church is obviously sweating blood in a new Gethsemane," he concluded, "but Easter is still possible."[1]

In 1968 the metaphor of the "new Gethsemane" seemed not inappropriate. The murder of Martin Luther King, Jr., on April 4 triggered violence, arson, and looting in Baltimore, until then exempt from the ghetto riots of the long, hot summers. Nine Catholics with a passion for peace were arrested on May 17 for the destruction of draft records in Catonsville. A week after the publication on July 29 of the papal encyclical *Humanae Vitae* on birth control, seventy-two priests of the archdiocese, nine of them pastors, endorsed the statement of dissent of eighty-seven theologians, five of them of the faculty of St. Mary's Seminary.

For Cardinal Shehan this last event constituted the most painful episode of "the tragic year" of 1968. "The darkest aspects of the years following upon 1968," he recalled in his memoirs, "were caused not by racial tensions and conflicts, nor by the growing financial burden of the archdiocese, nor by the grave social problems that marked that period, but by the phenomenon that came to be called 'crisis of faith.' "[2] The cardinal would devote four chapters to the first six years of his regime in Baltimore but only one to "The Years of Crisis."

Continued Advances

The painful memories of the latter half of his administration be-clouded for him its solid accomplishments. On the four fronts confidently advanced in the first six years—ecumenism, liturgical renewal, lay involve-ment, and racial justice—the momentum slackened hardly a whit, and fresh successes outnumbered setbacks.

The steady advance on the ecumenical front was conspicuous. Conver-sations among an Episcopal priest, a Sulpician, and a professor at the Johns Hopkins University ended in a joint announcement by Bishop Harry Lee Doll of the Episcopal diocese and Cardinal Shehan in 1968 of the opening of the Ecumenical Institute of Theology at St. Mary's Seminary.[3]

The cooperation between church-related social agencies that led to regular meetings of representatives of Protestant, Jewish, and Catholic bodies—judicatories, they called themselves—produced, besides the joint projects already described, an agreement to create a permanent cooperative body. On October 30, 1970, the Interfaith Council of Metropolitan Balti-more came into existence. It included the Archdiocese of Baltimore, the Baltimore Jewish Council, and most of the Protestant bodies that had be-longed to the Maryland Council of Churches, which quietly dissolved itself to make way for the larger council.

On September 20, 1970, the $1.1 million Interfaith Center of Columbia was dedicated. Owned by the Columbia Religious Facilities Corporation, of which the archdiocese was a charter member, the center served several denominations besides the Catholic congregation of St. John the Evangel-ist. The principal Protestant denominations and the archdiocese worked out a "Covenant of Ecumenical Effort"—the basic principles for interfaith services and Bible studies.[4] In general Catholic parishes accustomed them-selves to easy participation in community and ministerial associations, many Catholic pastors developing close friendships with Protestant minis-ters and Jewish rabbis.

On the liturgical front, the bulk of Catholic worshipers responded warmly to the promptings of the cardinal and his two auxiliaries, Bishops Murphy and Mardaga, who in January 1968 began in earnest the postcon-ciliar parish visitations anticipated by the stational visits of 1966. The liturgy remained the focus of their efforts to enlighten the faithful on the signifi-cance of Vatican Council II. It was the overture that made other changes easier. The handshake of peace in the revised rite of 1970 was readily ac-cepted. Folk masses were well attended. Communions increased dramat-ically as confession lines dwindled. A few recalcitrant pastors notwithstanding, the Liturgical Commission was satisfied with the pace of liturgical renewal.

Lay involvement, the third of the four principal concerns of the first six years, enlarged in notable ways. In increasing numbers laypeople were named to advisory bodies, whose recommendations the cardinal rarely disallowed. Well aware that he was more in need of the advice of laypeople than his predecessors had been, he was more willing to suffer the "discomforts" of collegial procedures, allowing any group affected by a decision to play a part in making it. Religious institutions likewise opened their board rooms and executive offices to lay persons. In 1968 the governing board of Mount St. Mary's Seminary and College welcomed its first lay members, Henry Knott and James Keelty, Jr. In 1970 Alvin Powers became the first lay director of a Catholic hospital, namely Bon Secours. Lay involvement at the parish and diocesan levels was also assured by the creation of collegial structures in the second six years. These will be considered later.

The advance along the broad front of racial justice, the fourth concern, continued in spite of the "backlash" of the second six years. In September 1968 the Urban Commission reorganized itself and committed ever larger sums to inner-city projects. At the beginning of 1970 it appropriated $100,000 for thirteen neighborhood self-help associations. The League of the Little Flower, originally an agency for directing aid from large downtown parishes to small country missions, now reversed the flow, the former beneficiaries now becoming the benefactors. In 1968 a Catholic Worker house of hospitality called Viva House was opened in West Baltimore by Brendan Walsh and Willa Bickham, his wife, and in no time was feeding and clothing seventy to a hundred people a day. In 1971 Bon Secours Hospital opened a community health center and launched several outreach programs, including a drug abuse clinic and halfway house for alcoholics.[5] The Josephites and Jesuits also opened drug treatment and rehabilitation centers. A "Lively Learning" outdoor Bible program begun at St. Peter Claver was copied in several American cities.

The continued commitment of the archdiocese to the inner city was symbolized by the creation of an urban vicar. Vice Chancellor F. Joseph Gossman was chosen to replace Bishop Mardaga as auxiliary bishop when the latter was transferred to the see of Wilmington in 1968. On June 6, 1970, Bishop Gossman was named the first urban vicar, "an advocate for the needs of the Church in the city."[6]

The new vicar gave special encouragement to the work of urban organizations created to stabilize neighborhoods threatened by racial antagonisms. One such was the Northeast Community Organization, or NECO, designed by a committee representing fourteen churches and seven denominations and chaired by Monsignor Clare O'Dwyer of St. Matthew's. When NECO was officially launched in 1969, it set as its principal goal investigation of the scare tactics of real estate agents in the northern sector and housing shortages in the southern part of an area that ran from 25th Street to the northern boundary of the city. A year later the Southeast Community Organization was launched. Originally organized to block the construction of an expressway through southeast Baltimore, SECO soon began to play the same stabilizing role as NECO. The director, a professional community organizer, was a Marianist brother.

Baltimore was well represented at a National Housing Conference in Chicago in March 1972 with NECO, SECO, and Activists, Inc., playing conspicuous roles. The black president of NECO and chairman of the conference brought the message from Baltimore that racial problems tended to "take a back seat" when issues were clearly identified and that the Catholic Church had become a leader in the drive for fair housing in that city.[7] Out of the Housing Conference came a strategy to pressure banks and other lending institutions to offer more but smaller loans to city residents. At the forefront of the movement in Baltimore was Vincent Quayle, SJ, prominent in Activists, Inc., and founder of the St. Ambrose Housing Aid Center. The latter organization was funded by Catholic Charities, the Urban Commission, and the Jesuits. In 1973 the St. Ambrose Center, Activists, Inc., and other groups picketed six major lending firms, and held meetings with bankers and city officials. Baltimore Federal Savings and Loan Association was the first to capitulate.[8]

Except for the merger of St. Paul's and St. Francis Xavier in June 1968, not a parish of the inner city was suppressed in the second six years. Despite a continued shrinkage many of the inner-city congregations evidenced a new vitality that sprang largely from the conviction that parishes were not "plants" but communities. The same conviction could be detected in over half the new parishes in the suburbs, where simple, adaptable multipurpose buildings were erected instead of the traditional and more costly church, school, and hall that presumed unchanging roles and populations.

The continued multiplication of suburban parishes was for Cardinal Shehan one of the gratifying developments of the second half of his administration. Nine new parishes were established and two missions raised to parish status. St. Isaac Jogues, Annunciation, and Nativity at Timonium were all created in 1968 to fill the gap between congregations at the northeast boundaries of Baltimore and the old but now burgeoning parishes of exurbia, such as St. Joseph's, Texas, and St. John's, Long Green.[9] By 1971 all three boasted multipurpose buildings. In 1968 Resurrection Parish was created for the Catholics of Laurel who spilled into Anne Arundel County and St. Mark's, Fallston, swelled by families drawn to Aberdeen and Edgewood Arsenal, was awarded parochial status. In 1971 the venerable St. Ignatius, Hickory, closed since 1967 for a shoring up, reopened its doors as a full-fledged parish.[10] In 1972 three of the administrative units of Holy Trinity, Glen Burnie, were made parishes: Good Shepherd, Crucifixion, and St. Bernadette's at Severn. In 1974 a second parish named Resurrection was begun in the new school originally built for St. Paul's in Ellicott City, and Our Lady of Grace was created for the 250 Catholic families around Hereford (Parkton) at the northern end of Baltimore County.

In 1968 the calamity-prone St. Rose of Lima replaced the church whose roof had collapsed the year before. The mishap prompted the inspection of churches of the archdiocese for structural weaknesses and hastened the decision of several parishes to rebuild. Nine other church buildings were supplanted by sound ones in the second six years, stretching from St. John's in Westminster to Immaculate Conception in downtown Baltimore.

The Senate of Priests

Without doubt the most positive and important achievements of the second six years were the creation of collegial bodies, or pastoral councils at several levels, and a restructuring of Central Services. The first six years had seen only a groping toward collegial bodies. Sweeping changes were not possible until the clergy was organized and energized. This did not occur until 1967.

At the end of 1966, when speculation about clergy labor unions and priests' strikes seemed not at all preposterous, Cardinal Shehan had sought feedback on a possible senate of priests, a body recommended by Vatican Council II. In the first months of 1967 the diocesan clergy elected twelve of their number, four each from three peer groups, to represent them. Eventually the number would be enlarged to twenty or more, including religious priests. Members of the third, or youngest, peer group were the most active in promoting change and initially carried the other two groups with them.

The initial meeting of April 1967 took as its first order of business the approval of a proposal of the Urban Commission for shared or team ministries in the parishes. By the spring of 1968 teams had replaced the traditional pastor-curate arrangement in the city parishes of St. Ann's, St. Peter the

Apostle, and St. Ambrose, as well as the suburban parish of Holy Trinity. By 1973, however, all but St. Ambrose had reverted to the traditional arrangement. Parish teams did not work well in the archdiocese of Baltimore.

A more important accomplishment of the first years of the priests' senate was the personnel board for diocesan priests created by the cardinal in September 1968 with Monsignor Austin Healy as executive director. The board was the forerunner of a larger Department of Personnel. The senate was also responsible for the creation of the Clergy Education Committee, which provided workshops and other programs for professional development.

In one of its earliest proposals the senate demonstrated its power to effect drastic changes. In 1968 it drew up a list of a dozen pastors who in its view frustrated archdiocesan efforts at renewal by their inability to accept the mandates of Vatican Council II in such areas as the liturgy and lay involvement. The senate submitted the list to the cardinal, who with little hesitation requested their resignation.[11] The following year Monsignor F. Joseph Manns, pastor of St. Anthony's, Gardenville, was also asked to resign. The aggrieved pastor took his case to his parishioners, among whom he found unexpected and vocal support. The secular papers covered the dispute.[12]

The whole affair made for much uneasiness among the older clergy, many of whom were convinced that the cardinal favored his young and active priests. The cardinal was asked to explain his action at a meeting of the older priests. When Monsignor Manns got up to explain his side of the dispute, he received a standing ovation.[13] The resentment was further evidenced in 1971 by the election of the monsignor to the senate by the first, or oldest, peer group. The senate, nevertheless, established seventy as the age for mandatory, and sixty-five for optional, retirement. Most pastors resigned ungrudgingly, some even with relief. In the years 1967–69 more than a fifth of the parishes of the archdiocese lost their pastors through retirement, including such parochial giants as Monsignors Vaeth, Wachowiak, Slade, and Joseph A. Ells, a close friend of the cardinal from his seminary days.

Affiliation of the senate with the National Federation of Priests' Councils (NFPC) was a source of even greater polarization between older and younger members of the clergy. Because of the adversarial stance of some of its affiliates, the NFPC won less than overwhelming acceptance among American bishops. Such was his relationship with the senate in Baltimore, however, that Cardinal Shehan readily agreed to address the second annual convention of the NFPC in New Orleans in June 1969, despite the pointed refusal of other leading prelates to do so. When in 1971 he welcomed the federation to Baltimore, he was given a prolonged ovation. The Baltimore convention, however, passed a resolution in favor of optional celibacy for the priesthood, the Baltimore delegation, including the president of its senate, voting with the majority. In February 1972 the senate opened its meeting to those who wished to air their concern that it had distanced itself from parish matters. A straw vote a year later showed a majority of priests (181–160) in favor of withdrawal from the NFPC. The senate, nevertheless, voted 9–7 to continue affiliation for one year more and then review the question.[14] Disaffiliation, in fact, was stayed for another five years.

Collegial Structures

Differences of opinion within the senate hampered in no way its most significant accomplishment: the creation of collegial bodies. In March 1971 it created a Committee of Collegial Structures with Monsignor J. Francis Stafford, president of the senate, as chairman. Under this umbrella committee were three subcommittees: the first for the creation of an archdiocesan pastoral council under Father James R. Schaefer, the second for the fashioning of vicariates or area councils under Father Brian M. Rafferty, and the third for the modification of parish councils already in existence under Monsignor P. Francis Murphy. Religious and laypeople were named to the subcommittees. Surveys concerning structures and procedures were distributed at the clergy conference and at a meeting of the Archdiocesan Council of Catholic Men before the year was out.

The work of the subcommittee on area councils under Father Rafferty was hastened by the need to reorganize the Urban Commission. That part of the city embraced by the commission was divided into four area councils, each of which would be represented on the commission by four elected members. Area, or intermediate, councils, it was believed, would not only provide a more democratic means of representation but would create localities of common interest and facilitate information flow. The first election above the parish level in which priests, religious, and the laity alike participated was held April 18, 1971. By the end of 1972 twelve area councils had been created and grouped into three larger areas, the urban area counting four councils, the suburban five, and the rural three. Each of the twelve area councils, comprising about twelve parishes each, would elect three members to the archdiocesan council, only one of whom could be a priest.[15]

The subcommittee on parish councils under Monsignor Murphy had to revitalize and reshape already existing parish bodies. Confusion existed over the role of the corporators and advisory boards created in response to the guidelines of 1967. Corporators controlled by pastors could and often did negate parish council decisions simply by their failure to act. As a result of the subcommittee's report, issued in 1973, the role of corporators was restricted to legal matters and advisory committees were created by and made responsible to the parish council. Arbitration boards were provided to mediate disputes between pastor and parish council.

Several pastors expressed their concern to the cardinal about certain features of the new guidelines, particularly the provision that a two-thirds vote of the council could override the pastor's veto. The cardinal requested further consultation on these features. The process proved salutary. The polarization that had developed within the clergy began to ease. Older priests were, for the most part, appeased.[16]

The subcommittee on the archdiocesan council under Father Schaefer studied a number of diocesan constitutions, including that of the Episcopal Diocese of Maryland, and fashioned a document it deemed suitable to the archdiocese. The cardinal asked that the body's power be termed "consultative" rather than "deliberative," not because he feared a diminution of his own power but because he believed deliberative power an uncanonical grant. The issue was skirted by the use of the term "highest collegial body."[17] Some of the senate priests felt that the council would have no real power unless it had control of the archdiocesan budget. This the chairman viewed as "not politically feasible."[18] The cardinal nevertheless agreed that the council should review the budget before publication and should have a voice in the establishment of new parishes. The senate approved the constitution in June 1972.

In January 1973 the constitution of the archdiocesan council was sent to the area and parish councils for the required two-thirds approval of both, which it received.[19] In the fall the senate supervised elections to the council. Each of the area councils sent two laypersons and a priest to the archdiocesan council. The elected sisters plus appointed and ex officio members raised its total to a little more than fifty. The four members the cardinal could choose were all laywomen. An organizational meeting was held November 10–11 to establish procedures and elect officers. Laypeople swept the field. The president (William L. Clark), vice president, secretary, and treasurer were a lawyer, housewife, public school teacher, and banker respectively.

The first business meeting of the Archdiocesan Pastoral Council (APC) was held six weeks later. Uncertainty concerning real power and relationships with other bodies surfaced in debate over a motion to prod the school board to action on the matter of standard tuition rates for parochial schools.[20] Though the cardinal praised the council in a meeting of January 1974 for the way in which it had handled the tuition question, dubiety still hung over the highest collegial body at the time of his retirement in the spring. Not only the APC but also area councils would pose problems that his successor would have to address.

Central Services

Development of the APC coincided deliberately with the restructuring of Central Services because APC committees corresponded to the larger divisions fashioned for central services.[21] Well before the collegial structures were created, steps were being taken to reorder the maze of departments, boards, and bureaus lodged in the Catholic Center which had grown like Topsy under the twelfth archbishop, producing problems of communication and economy. In 1969 the cardinal created an Interdepartmental Communications Committee to devise a more streamlined and more accountable bureaucracy. The head of this committee was the person later chosen to chair the Committee on Collegial Structures, Monsignor J. Francis Stafford.

Central Services was restructured on a cabinet model. The forty-eight agencies were grouped under seven administrative offices or departments. The agencies would report to the secretaries of these offices instead of to the cardinal. The secretaries would hold monthly meetings with the cardinal. The seven offices and their secretaries were the Office of Administrative Services under Monsignor Porter White, Office of Financial Services under Monsignor Joseph Nelligan, Office of Research, Planning and Development under Jack Ladd Carr, Office of Legal Services under Francis X. Gallagher, the Tribunal under Monsignor Paul L. Love, Department of Christian Education under Monsignor William C. Newman, and Department of Community Services (Catholic Charities) under Monsignor Francis Stafford.

The plan was approved in April 1971 and implemented over the next two years by Rev. Thomas J. Bauernfeind, vice chancellor and coordinator of Central Services. As with the collegial structures, problems arose, necessitating occasional reshufflings and modifications. Nor did reorganization bring a reduction of personnel in Central Services. The two hundred or more employed in 1971 increased rather than diminished in the years that followed. It was a far cry from the days of Archbishop Curley, who shared two secretaries with his chancellor and knew by name everyone on the slender staffs of the Department of Education, Catholic Charities, and *The Catholic Review*.

Unequaled Turmoil

Despite the continued momentum and impressive gains of the period January 1968 to June 1974, when Cardinal Shehan welcomed a successor, it was a time of unequaled turmoil. In the "Years of Crisis" jolt followed jolt with unnerving insistence. Unexpected setbacks occurred on every front, including the four whose advance was recorded earlier in the chapter.

Though the ecumenical front occasioned the least anxiety, the sentiment of a clerical correspondent in the *Catholic Review*, who deplored the "Protestantization" of the Catholic schools, was, perhaps, more pervasive than the archdiocesan authorities were prepared to admit. "Let Protestants be Protestants," he wrote, "and the hell with them (with their religion anyway). Let Catholics be Catholics and the heaven with them."[22]

The Divisive Issues

While the time-honored animus toward Catholics had all but disappeared in the oldest archdiocese by 1968, certain issues continued to cause tension between Catholics and their non-Catholic neighbors. The two most publicized in the years 1968–74 were abortion and state aid for parochial schools.

The Maryland Catholic Conference (MCC), the legal counsel and lobbying body created jointly by the archdioceses of Baltimore and Washington and the diocese of Wilmington to represent them at Annapolis, had been organized in March 1967 to address a bill before the Assembly that would allow limited abortions. Largely as a result of Catholic opposition, the bill was tabled.[23] Catholic lobbying also caused the modification of a bill in 1968. In 1970, however, when the MCC failed to block an act to repeal all state abortion laws, the archdiocese mounted a campaign to prevent its acceptance. The cardinal urged a mass protest, and the MCC begged the governor to veto the bill, which he did.[24] In the fall the cardinal wrote a pastoral on abortion and in January asked that Right-to-Life committees be organized in all parishes in anticipation of the next battle in the Assembly. A bill that would have removed most restrictions on abortion was defeated in March 1971 after prolonged debate and intensive lobbying.

That summer the first of five pregnancy testing and counseling centers of Birthright, a national organization, was opened in Baltimore by Catholic Social Services. The pro-life movement accelerated after the Supreme Court decision of January 1973 liberalizing abortion. In May a committee gathered signatures in a vain effort to stop abortions at Baltimore County General Hospital. The following year pro-life leaders challenged even Associated Catholic Charities when ACC did not break with the United Fund after the latter's merger with an organization that included Planned Parenthood. The objection to Planned Parenthood now was that it gave abortion counseling.[25] More serious was the withdrawal of state certification for Bon Secours Hospital to build a 200-bed hospital and "health park" in Howard County because, as many believed and publicly stated, of its refusal to allow abortions. The certification went instead to Lutheran Hospital. When Bon Secours contested the decision, the dispute received nationwide attention. Eventually permission was given for the health park but not the hospital.[26]

As a result of the financial crisis that occurred in these years, state aid for parochial schools was considered crucial. In June 1968, a month after the archdiocese was asked for a $700,000 subsidy for inner-city schools, a Maryland chapter of Citizens for Educational Freedom was organized to call attention to this need. Even more active and influential was the grassroots organization founded by John Jicha of St. Joseph's Parish, Fullerton, called State Aid Group for Education or SAGE. By early 1969, when it claimed fifty coordinators in touch with two hundred organizations, SAGE was pushing hard for an $11 million aid bill for teachers' salaries and nonreligious texts. Governor Marvin Mandel named a blue-ribbon commission to study the "very difficult question" of state aid to nonpublic schools.[27] In the meantime the head of the American Civil Liberties Union formed a Maryland committee of PEARL (Public Education and Religious Liberty), which found ready support among such groups as Americans United for Separation of Church and State (POAU under a new name), the Maryland State Teachers Association, the Baltimore Teachers Union, the American Jewish Congress, and the Legislative Committee of Unitarians and Universalists. The battle lines were tightly drawn.

In January 1971 the Mandel commission recommended a $12 million aid bill to cover tuition vouchers. The bill provoked the heaviest lobbying of any session dealing with aid to education. When it passed, PEARL started a petition for a referendum, thereby deferring action until the November election of 1972. Though the bill had the endorsement of the AFL-CIO and the Sunpapers, and SAGE outspent its opponents ten to one, its cause was seriously damaged by Supreme Court decisions that placed the constitutionality of the bill in question. It was rejected by 53.5

percent of the voters, winning only in Baltimore City and St. Mary's County.[28]

Disappointed but undaunted, SAGE had a $6 million bill for auxiliary services allowed by the Supreme Court introduced the following March. This was killed in the House by a last-hour filibuster. The following year a similar bill for $9.7 million was successfully shepherded through the legislature only to be thwarted in a November referendum by 56 percent of the voters.[29] Catholic primary and secondary education, it seemed at this point, would have to be sustained by the conviction and generosity of the Catholic community alone. Some questioned whether the same conviction and same generosity that had carried the Catholic school system for a century and more still existed.

Liturgy and the Laity

In spite of Catholic opposition to abortion and push for public funds for parochial schools, ecumenism survived. Liturgical change brought greater problems. Allusion has been made to the pastors who refused to change and the parishioners who supported them. Other Catholics were impatient with mechanical masses and vapid homilies. The latter took their cue from the National Liturgical Conference, whose annual meetings in 1968 and 1969 under the presidency of Father Joseph Connolly, now pastor of St. Katharine of Sienna in Baltimore, were so controversial that they were suspended indefinitely. The "antics" of the "Anawim Community" in the chapel of Loyola College were another source of controversy as the result of an article in the *Sun* in the spring of 1971.[30] A "Pilgrim Community" of disaffected worshipers from St. John's in Severna Park after four years won a quasi-official recognition from the archdiocese. Many blamed lackluster liturgies for a decline in Sunday attendance. Yet fewer than half the parishes actually registered a decline even as late as 1974, the Liturgical Commission found, though almost all noted a worrisome absence of the sixteen to thirty age group.[31]

Lay involvement, the third goal of the first six years, was characterized more by apathy than by excess, though an occasional complaint about lack of power was heard. When parish councils found a voice in policy-making, it was sometimes a conservative one preoccupied with the power of the purse. Conservative pastors could be removed; conservative parishioners could not. The powers accorded the laity in the collegial structures represented an act of faith that remained to be tested under the cardinal's successor.

Racial Conflict

Pursuit of the fourth goal of the first six years, racial justice, together with the peace movement, produced the most painful jolts of the years after 1967. There was little destruction of church property in the riot that followed the murder of Martin Luther King in April 1968. Catholic priests and sisters, in fact, seemed pointedly immune from attack. A week after the riot whites organized a "processional of penance" at the Cathedral of Mary Our Queen. In the spring and fall, seven-week programs called Project Commitment and devoted to racial justice were conducted in almost every parish. The Baltimore riot nevertheless uncovered an uncompromising militancy in the black Catholic community.

At the beginning of 1970 a Baltimore chapter was organized of the Black Catholic Lay Caucus, a national organization born of the belief that the church was inherently racist and that real change could be effected only by blacks themselves. This body would soon be joined by the Black Clergymen's Caucus and the Black Sisters' Caucus to form the Baltimore Black Catholic Caucus. The Lay Caucus split for a time into two factions, the more militant, under Leo Burroughs, head of the Holy Name Society at St. Edward's and member of the Urban Commission, being also the more vocal. For two years and more indictment followed indictment and demand demand.

In the summer of 1970 some twenty-five blacks, including the principal and faculty of St. Frances Academy, picketed the Catholic Center demanding funds for a project that would save the school and enhance the surrounding black community, creating an "Oasis in the Desert."[32] In September the Lay Caucus charged the archdiocesan elementary and secondary schools with racism and in October the *Catholic Review* with slighting black activities.[33] In November Burroughs claimed that the cardinal had suppressed a report done by the staff of the Urban Commission because it clearly demonstrated the failure of Catholic hospitals in Baltimore to comply with the Civil Rights Act of 1964.[34] In June 1971 the Lay Caucus complained that one of the oldest black communities in the country had not one black diocesan priest to serve it and that the Josephite Fathers kept their black members hidden except for Philip Linden, the only black priest active in parish work in Baltimore.[35]

The following month Linden himself, as spokesman for a number of black leaders, charged the Baltimore Police Department with "overt racism and insensitivity." Forty policemen, mostly Catholic, descended upon the cardinal to protest the charge. Twenty-one Josephites came to Linden's defense and condemned the police for their intimidating tactics with the cardinal. Shehan, while he deplored "confrontational rhetoric" generally, upheld Linden's action.[36] In February 1972 the Senate of Priests approved a declaration rejecting the "plantation mentality" of the institutional church and endorsed the more moderate faction of the Black Catholic Lay Caucus.[37]

The Caucus when it complained of a lack of black priests had also called for a less intellectualized seminary, where black seminarians would not be "whitewashed." A special program was soon developed for the black seminarians of the archdiocese, who were allowed to live in a black parish (St. Ann's) rather than at the seminary. In May 1974 the first two blacks were ordained for the archdiocese of Baltimore: Donald A. Sterling and Maurice J. Blackwell.

Black militancy alienated many white Catholics. After the riot of 1968, whites disappeared entirely from the worshiping community of St. Gregory the Great and fewer seminarians volunteered to work in the inner city. The first collection for the Campaign for Human Development, an appeal begun by the Catholic bishops in 1970 in behalf of the poor, in Baltimore totaled $113,000, a record for any single collection in the archdiocese, but in 1971 the see's contribution dropped by 36 percent. United Fund, of which the archdiocese had been a participant since 1969, experienced a similar setback in 1971. Police spokesmen made no bones of the fact that the drop in contributions by the force to the United Fund was due largely to the radical programs conducted at the Martin de Porres Center, a beneficiary, particularly the free breakfasts offered by the Black Panthers.[38]

Many of the projects funded by the Urban Commission foundered. HOPE was phased out. Project Equality was an even more discouraging failure. Begun as an interfaith endeavor in June 1968, its object was to bring collective pressure to bear on Baltimore businesses to hire blacks. John Cronin, SS, now back at St. Mary's Seminary, was its first president. In 1972 Project Equality boasted a notable success: it induced the city's dairies to agree to a timetable for minority employment. In 1973, however, it dissolved itself for want of financial support. The director, a non-Catholic, made it clear that the archdiocese of Baltimore had come to bear half the operating budget. No one, he insisted, had "done more for equal opportunity in Maryland than Cardinal Shehan."[39]

Baltimore's twelfth archbishop never faltered in his promotion of racial justice, not even in the face of threats and insults from left and right alike. The new cathedral, for example, was emptied in December 1970 on the occasion of the celebration of his twenty-fifth anniversary as bishop by a voice on the telephone: "Would you tell the nigger-lover there's a bomb in the cathedral and it's going off in fifteen minutes."[40] If occasionally the cardinal responded to pressure from the left, it was because he perceived truth in many of its jeremiads.

The Peace Movement

Even more radical than black activists, though perhaps less effective, was the "Catholic Resistance" that developed in Baltimore in response to the war in Vietnam. Philip Berrigan, after his conviction but before sentencing for the blood-pouring episode in the fall of 1967, persuaded his Jesuit brother, Daniel, and six others—three former Maryknollers, a Christian Brother, a social activist, and a nurse—to join Tom Lewis and himself in another symbolic action.

On May 17, 1968, the nine drove to the Knights of Columbus building in Catonsville, took the draft records kept there outside, and burned them with homemade napalm. "All of us identify with the victims of American oppression all over the world," the statement they handed to the press read in part. "We submit voluntarily to their involuntary fate."[41] Even the sympathetic were uneasy. Baltimore's cardinal supported the message but deplored the method.[42] "Come to Baltimore," Daniel Berrigan begged in an invitation to the trial of the Catonsville Nine, "for an event that will blow your minds and open your hearts." And so it did for many. At emotion-laden rallies held in St. Ignatius Hall in October, nuns, seminarians, and college students jostled the veterans—Dorothy Day, Rabbi Abraham Heschel, Bishop James A. Pike, Harvey Cox, Rennie Davis, Noam Chomsky, and others. *United States* v. *Philip Berrigan et al.* was theater of protest at its best.[43]

The trial of the Catonsville Nine radicalized and redirected the energies of a not inconsiderable number of those engaged in inner-city work in Baltimore—secular priests, Josephites, Jesuits from Woodstock, seminarians from St. Mary's, sisters from the Martin de Porres Center, students from local colleges, and others. Baltimore and later the prison cell of Philip Berrigan served as the nerve center of a network of antiwar activists that stretched from Washington to Boston and westward to Milwaukee and beyond. Over the next two years members of the Catholic Resistance under various names conducted some thirty raids on draft boards in scattered cities.[44]

Five of the eleven members of the East Coast Conspiracy to Save Lives were from Baltimore. The group was named by J. Edgar Hoover in a statement that led to the arrest on January 12, 1971, in Baltimore of two secular priests and a former Josephite. Joseph Wenderoth was a curate at St. Vincent's and Neil McLaughlin at St. Bernardine's until they were removed for their participation in draft raids, and Anthony Scoblick was a Josephite at St. Francis Xavier until his marriage to Mary Cain, a former nun connected with the Martin de Porres Center. The three men were accused of conspiring to kidnap Henry Kissinger, National Security Council advisor, and blow up tunnels under the national capital.[45] Cardinal Shehan went to the Baltimore jail soon after the arrest, taking with him the archdiocesan attorney and the president of the priests' senate. By way of explanation, he offered the press the simple scriptural verse that begins: "I was in prison and you visited me." The three were released to his custody. Bail was raised by private donations mostly from the diocesan clergy.[46]

The visit proved the most controversial act of his life. The reaction—protest or praise—was loud and swift. "You are a follower of the devil!" screamed one of the outraged. A supporter expressed regret that there were not "more leaders in the Church like you." Well into March messages of condemnation or encouragement flowed into the cardinal's office.[47]

The trial in Harrisburg for the conspiracy above mentioned of the so-called Harrisburg Seven—Phil Berrigan, Wenderoth, McLaughlin, Scoblick and his wife, plus Sister Elizabeth McAlister of Tarrytown, New York, and Eqbal Ahmad, a Pakistani drawn to these "good primitive Christians"—was even more of a media event than that of the Catonsville Nine.[48] Its effect on the Catholic Resistance, however, was almost the opposite—a disenchantment intensified by the announcement of the secret marriage of Philip Berrigan and Elizabeth McAlister. After Berrigan's release from prison the couple returned to Baltimore to establish a war resistance center called Jonah House.

In the spring of 1972 an archdiocesan Commission for World Justice and Peace was established with the Sulpician William Lee its first chairman. That summer the cardinal wrote a pastoral on the Blessed Mother, a significant part of which was devoted to the "cancerous" war and its baneful effect on the nation. An unhappy reader remarked that "Christ was no wishy-washy pacifist."[49] This, however, may have already become a minority view among Maryland Catholics, as with Americans generally.

Probably not a minority view, and one at variance with the expressed concern of the cardinal, was Catholic sentiment in the see city against gun control. Two incidents in January 1973 allowed Shehan to make a more forceful appeal for Catholic support of gun-control laws. An armed high-jacker at the Baltimore airport demanded to see the cardinal. The small figure in black calmly boarded the plane and persuaded the one-time parishioner of St. William of York to surrender.[50] Two weeks later the pastor of St. Mary Star of the Sea was robbed and shot in the back. At the cardinal's retirement banquet the warm applause that would greet his censure of crimes of violence in a tribute to his native city would cease abruptly when he proposed a remedy: gun control.

The Years of Crises

The crises in race relations and the peace movement accompanied a series of crises the cardinal and other Catholic officials found even more unsettling—a crisis in Catholic education, a crisis in religious life and the priesthood, and a crisis in faith. To these were added a financial crisis of unprecedented proportions.

THE CRISIS IN EDUCATION

In 1968 there were 108 parochial schools; by 1974 there were 87. Parochial school enrollment had peaked in 1964 at 61,500, a year before it did so nationwide. By 1974 enrollment was down to 35,000. Private high school enrollment declined from 9,900 in 1962 to 6,500 in 1973 but began to climb back thereafter. Private high schools had, of course, lost students to the new diocesan high schools, whose numbers had grown to about 7,000 in 1965. There they hovered for five years, then slipped to 5,300 in 1974 for reasons that will become clear. Catholic college enrollment had risen from 4,500 in 1962 to 6,500 in 1968 but fluctuated uncertainly thereafter. The number of sisters, brothers, priests, and scholastics engaged in teaching fell from 2,122 in 1962 to 1,328 in 1974, while the number of lay teachers—with salaries double those of religious— grew from 605 to 1,530. At every level traditional Catholic education in the archdiocese was clearly in trouble.

The last new parish to build a school was St. Philip Neri, Linthicum Heights, in 1966. Most of the parishes established in the second six years incorporated religious education centers in multipurpose buildings with no intention of ever having a parish school. The number of grammar school students in CCD programs increased from 15,000 in 1962 to some 35,000 by 1974. The long-felt need for a traditional Catholic education waned as ecumenism waxed, but this change was rarely offered in justification of the failure to build. More often the financial burden was blamed. When in 1972 it was found that the annual parish school subsidy at Holy Trinity, Glen Burnie, would exceed $100,000, a task force recommended that the school be closed.[51] In 1973, however, the Arthur Slade Regional School was opened at Holy Trinity for its own children and those of its three daughter parishes—Crucifixion, Good Shepherd, and St. Bernadette's—as well as two neighboring parishes—Our Lady of the Fields and St. Joseph's, Odenton.

If suburban schools felt financially constrained, those of the city found their burden insupportable. While new parishes were unwilling to build schools, old ones were reluctant to lose them. Parishioners believed, and not without reason, that if the school went the parish would soon follow. To conserve resources and to save as many of the inner-city schools as possible, a Coalition of Pastors and Principals devised a system of "clustering." The first cluster was tried, successfully, in South Baltimore. The Catholic Community School, under a board drawn from the three parishes of the area, maintained grades one through five at St. Mary Star of the Sea and six through eight at Our Lady of Good Counsel, while closing the school at Holy Cross.

When the proposal was extended to other parts of the city in 1973, the ethnic parishes of southeast Baltimore were shocked and angry and the black parishes in northwest Baltimore complained. Bishop Gossman's attempt at explanation was drowned out by jeers at Our Lady of Pompei, and a bomb threat broke up a meeting at Holy Rosary.[52] Compromises had to be made. By the opening of the 1974 school year, however, six additional clusters counting sixteen school facilities were in operation in the inner city. The new schools were named Holy Spirit Community, Queen of Peace, Rosa Parks, Father Charles Hall, Bishop John Neumann, and Madonna. In the process seven inner-city schools were closed entirely.

The costly diocesan high schools failed to draw the numbers expected, especially Bishop Walsh in Cumberland and Martin Spalding in Severn. Enrollment, in fact, dropped precipitously with the tuition increases necessitated by the financial crisis. Subsidies for the diocesan high schools constituted the most serious drain on the archdiocese. Martin Spalding was made a coeducational school in 1973 to save it. A private high school, three parish high schools, and three business schools closed in the crisis years.

Catholic higher education likewise suffered a setback, the result of a cycle of operating deficits, tuition hikes, and shrinking student bodies. Three Catholic colleges ceased to exist. Mount Providence Junior College in 1968 was the first. On July 1, 1971, Mount St. Agnes College merged with Loyola. In June 1973 St. Joseph College, Emmitsburg, closed its doors after a strenuous effort of friends and alumnae to keep them open. Not long after the announcement of the closing, nearby Mount St. Mary's College went coed.

By 1970 nearly a quarter of all Catholic children of grade school age and more than two-thirds of those of high school age were receiving no form of religious instruction. There was, moreover, a growing need for adult education in Catholic doctrine. To study the manifold problems a fifty-six-member Archdiocesan Planning Commission for Total Christian Education was named in February 1971. In June 1973 it presented a comprehensive report with twenty-seven recommendations requiring a response from each of the now nine divisions of the newly reorganized Department of Education.[53] There were some bright spots. Suburban schools, where they existed, were generally healthy. The CCD program was one of the best in the country, its director, Monsignor Paul G. Cook, being twice elected president of the National Conference. While the report called for no major overhaul, it did in its totality offer a new vision of Catholic education that was more than the sister in the classroom. Its implementation would be attempted under Shehan's successor.

A CRISIS IN VOCATIONS

The crisis in education was, of course, due in part to the crisis in religious life and the priesthood. Vocations, particularly to the sisterhoods, declined alarmingly. The number of sisters in the archdiocese had peaked at 3,267 in 1963, three years before it did so nationwide. By 1968 it was down to 2,268 but rose slightly in 1969 and held for the next five years. The number of religious priests fell from a high of 530 in 1965 to 397 in 1974. The number of brothers remained at about 150. By 1974 religious orders were looking for other uses for empty novitiates, many of them built in the early 1960s in anticipation of unprecedented growth. Diminishing numbers were due also to a startling leap in dispensations and laicizations, a source of greater disquietude because more publicized than in the past. Maryland Catholics were unaccustomed to major superiors leaving the religious life for the married one.

Though the number of diocesan priests remained steady in the crisis years, more than 350, the number of seminarians studying for the archdiocese slid steadily downward, from a high of 283 in 1961 to 80 in 1974. Smaller student bodies were due in part to altered perceptions of seminary formation. A short-lived experiment was St. Paul Latin School begun as a day school for junior seminarians in 1962. In 1969 its few students were transferred to Gibbons High School and the program was phased out. The high school at St. Charles College was also discontinued in 1969 and the seminarians in philosophy at Paca Street were moved to St. Charles to become the junior and senior classes of St. Mary's Liberal Arts College, an institution doomed also to eventual extinction. The venerable building on Paca Street stood empty for five years before being demolished. Not all the bishops who patronized St. Mary's Seminary were happy with the changes there. As the Baltimore seminary lost students, Mount St. Mary's Seminary in Emmitsburg gained them, largely because of its more traditional theology, discipline, and rural isolation.

The problem of fewer priests was lessened a bit in Baltimore by the success of the permanent diaconate program. On June 12, 1971, Cardinal Shehan ordained six permanent deacons to serve in their own parishes. It was, the *Catholic Review* boasted, "the first ordination of men in a diocesan program [for the diaconate] to be held in the American Church."[54] In 1972 more than twenty were ordained permanent deacons. Thereafter the numbers would be fewer but substantial. Though the candidates were well prepared, the congregations they served often were not. To many the office seemed an anomaly, even the *Review* on more than one occasion using the term "lay deacon."

THE CRISIS IN FAITH

Confusion was a major factor in the crisis of faith. In pinpointing the reaction to *Humanae Vitae* as a turning point in Catholic attitudes, the cardinal was correct. Never within memory when the Holy Father spoke on a matter of import had a significant number of his priests differed, many openly, more, perhaps, in quiet places. The laity wavered. Many began to think for themselves. Some began to think the unthinkable.

The cardinal himself never wavered in his support of the pope, however difficult the intellectual exercise it demanded. As a member of the papal commission on birth control appointed at the end of the Council, he had done his homework well. He had consulted theologians and had taken a confidential poll of all the pastors of the archdiocese. At the meeting of the commission in Rome in 1966, he had asked its members to recognize that the church had always followed two laws, one of continuity, the other of progress. "The church grows," he said. "The church develops. And the *sensus fidelium* plays a big role in that development. The church must recognize how marriage is lived today." He reported on the poll he had taken. "The most intelligent answers," he insisted, "were on the side of change. Many spoke about the anxiety of their good couples." Ten percent had expressed no opinion, 70 percent had spoken for change, and 20 percent believed there could be no change because of the magisterium's consistent position in recent times.[55]

When the decision came from Rome in 1968, however, he acquiesced unhesitatingly. A headline in 1973 would push him finally to offer what was in effect an explanation of his compliance. Upset at being quoted as saying, "artificial birth control will never be approved," he wrote an article in which he had recourse once more to Cardinal Newman. In the latter's concept of concurring and converging probabilities he found a way to defend the papal dictum, but in the development of doctrine he still perceived the possibility of change.[56]

The cardinal was deeply pained, nevertheless, when fifty-five diocesan priests plus fifteen Jesuits and two Sulpicians in the archdiocese endorsed the statement of dissent of eighty-seven theologians, five of the latter being on the faculty of St. Mary's Seminary. The priests were also pained that the press put them in conflict with their archbishop. Without publicity the cardinal in private interviews won the priests' acceptance of a series of position statements requiring them to uphold *Humanae Vitae* in the pulpit, the confessional, and the classroom as "the sole authentic doctrine of the Church" on birth control.[57] Baltimore's cardinal won almost universal praise for his handling of the controversy.

One of the yardsticks of the crisis of faith that followed *Humanae Vitae* was the national decline in the Catholic population, Cardinal Shehan wrote in his memoirs.[58] In his own archdiocese the number fell from 480,000 in 1965 to 404,000 in 1971 but rose again to 455,000 in 1974. Not all was the result of leakage. Some of the losses were due simply to more scientific methods in data gathering, some to a decline in Catholic births. Baptisms in the archdiocese fell from 13,547 in 1962 to 7,938 in 1974 despite an increase in marriages from 3,831 to 4,213. Yet decidedly some Baltimore Catholics were "out of the church," by which they meant that they no longer went to mass. Intellectual leavetakings were probably few.

More overt than the quiet questionings of confused Catholics was the polarization that beset the archdiocese, itself a symptom of insecurity. Not only was there a polarization within the ranks of the clergy but between clergy and laity and within the laity itself. A poll taken by the *Catholic Review* in 1969, for example, revealed a gap in social awareness between priests and people. While 14 percent of the clergy thought there was too much civil rights activity and 43 percent too little, 43 percent of the laity felt there was too much and 16 percent too little.[59]

The *Catholic Review* maintained its mildly progressive stance, but its letters to the editor reflected clearly the growing polarization. While a photograph of a dancing nun sent some readers into a frenzy, a social worker found the endless debate over nuns' garbs "utterly absurd" in a nation that spent more on pet food than on food stamps.[60] One issue in 1971 carried a page and a quarter of conflicting statements on beards, abortion, drugs, *Jesus Christ Superstar*, GIFT (of which more later), and priestly celibacy, prompting a reader to suggest the following week: "If the world seems to be changing too rapidly for you, I recommend a visit to the Old Cathedral where you can find the Latin Mass and various publications that will bring back memories of the good old days when things were simpler."[61]

The postconciliar pastoral visits conducted by the cardinal and his two auxiliaries proved instructive. In every parish they held, in addition to an open forum, private meetings with individuals requesting them, with the parish council, and with sisters and priests. The uncertainties and antagonisms that surfaced convinced the cardinal and his advisers of the need for a program such as the one that came to be called GIFT, an acronym for Growth in Faith Together.

At Cardinal Shehan's request the Senate of Priests through a committee worked out a program that involved three stages: research, reflection, and response. The research would take the form of questionnaires designed to uncover the principal areas of concern in a parish. Reflection would be accomplished in small group discussions aided by facilitators in homes. Response would involve a catechetical week, to which noted speakers would be invited, and a liturgical week. The program would be under Father James Schaefer, archdiocesan director of adult education. Two pilot parishes, Immaculate Conception, Towson, and St. Joseph's, Texas, were chosen to try the three-month program beginning in September 1970. Participation would be voluntary, but GIFT was heralded by billboards, television spots, and newspaper stories.

Intended to unify as well as to enlighten, its initial effect was almost the opposite. Charges of manipulation, liberal bias, lack of participation, polarization, and "confusion compounded" had to be answered by Father Schaefer and other defenders.[62] At a clergy conference in January, after reports from the pilot parishes, 115 voted to continue the program but 101 to drop it. Even the cardinal wavered. In the spring, however, GIFT was introduced into three more parishes. To the speakers the cardinal sent a letter of caution warning against a one-sided presentation that could polarize and insisting on a strict adherence to the magisterium.[63]

Some of the most vocal critics of GIFT were members of Catholics United for the Faith (CUF), an organization formed to resist the excesses, as its members perceived them, emanating from Vatican Council II. The Mater Dei Chapter was established at the Cathedral of Mary Our Queen soon after the founding of the national body in August 1968. It held monthly meetings and maintained active committees on decency in the media, abortion, catechetics, and spirituality. One of its principal targets was sex education in the parish schools. Never large, the Baltimore chapter of CUF was outspoken and persistent enough to induce caution in the ranks of the liberals.

Also small but even more vocal, though perhaps less cerebral, than CUF was Catholics Concerned, a local group organized at the time of the cardinal's visit to the trio in the Baltimore jail. Its goal was to rid the church of "leftist trends." Every Sunday its members would stand before a score of Baltimore churches and distribute leaflets bearing such messages as "We are sick of the Social Gospel! Return to the word of God!" It called for a stoppage of financial support until priests returned to the "true" ministry.[64]

Though most of the membership of Catholics Concerned came from the Parkville and Hamilton areas of northeast Baltimore, Catholic conservatism was also strong in the ethnic areas of southeast Baltimore and in the Catonsville area to the west. Both Catholic right and Catholic left were as visible in Baltimore as in any great metropolis. But 1971 represented, perhaps, a climactic year for both. Signs of abatement could be detected even before the twelfth archbishop retired. Not all were distressed at the existence of divergent views, seeing in them the seeds of a healthy pluralism.

There appeared at the peak of polarization a phenomenon puzzling to liberal and conservative alike, but one that apparently had the blessing of the church. In Baltimore as elsewhere it was almost entirely a lay movement. Beginning in the home of Thomas Swartz of All Saints Parish in 1970, small groups of Catholics in search of a more intense spiritual life met weekly in private homes for prayer. The charismatics in time filled churches and halls. By 1974 fifteen distinct communities, many of them offshoots of All Saints, could be found in Baltimore, Bel Air, Aberdeen, and Hagerstown. Diverse in age, sex, race, and sometimes even in religious affiliation, all attributed their "gift" to baptism in the spirit. Like the Pentecostals many spoke in tongues and healed.[65]

THE FINANCIAL CRISIS

It was ironic, perhaps, that in the archdiocese of Baltimore things of the spirit reached a breathless intensity just as worldly concerns intruded with unequaled insistence. The financial crisis was unprecedented. No one knew quite how to handle it.

When Lawrence Shehan came to Baltimore as coadjutor archbishop, he was assured that he would have no financial problems. Some $16.3 million still remained from the O'Neill legacy to be used in any way, and the

Consolidated Fund, or archdiocesan investments, amounted to more than $10 million.[66] In the end the O'Neill legacy proved less than a blessing, imparting an unshakable sense of limitless largesse. With the conclusion of Vatican Council II the cardinal had begun to make important financial changes in anticipation of new programs that needed funding. In 1965 he had named a new chancellor and inaugurated the first archdiocesan audit since 1948. In 1966 indebtedness had been internalized by the archdiocese's acting as banker for parishes, and institutional purchasing had been centralized. At the time Baltimore was judged "light-years ahead of most sees."[67]

In 1967, however, subsidies for high schools and inner-city parishes passed the million dollar mark. The cardinal created a Finance Committee of outstanding businessmen with Bishop Mardaga the chairman until 1968 and then Monsignor Nelligan. Its collective expertise notwithstanding, the committee was no match for pleaders of special causes and persuasive department heads. By 1969, when Monsignor Newman, superintendent of education, announced a substantial jump in tuition for diocesan high schools, the archdiocese was caught in a web of ambitious projects, spiraling costs, highly salaried personnel, and dwindling revenues.

So sharp was the reaction to the tuition hike that it was deemed necessary to publish a complete disclosure of archdiocesan finances. This would become an annual affair. The projected deficit for the fiscal year 1969–70 was $2.1 million, double that of the previous year. An increase in the cathedraticum, or parish tax, from 5 to 10 percent and an across-the-board reduction imposed on all departmental budgets brought the projected deficit for the following year down to $1.4 million, but for the next three years the actual annual deficit hovered at about $1.8 million.

In his annual reports Monsignor Nelligan spoke ominously of the rapid depletion of the Consolidated Fund but as often as not blamed the deficit on "extraordinary funding requirements" that would not be repeated. In 1972, nevertheless, the Finance Committee approved a $4.9 million priests' retirement fund. Lesser amounts were forthcoming for equally compelling needs.

The sense of urgency apparent in these reports spurred no swell of Catholic generosity. Contributions to some charities, in fact, decreased in the crisis years. Two developments kept the financial strain from reaching a critical point under the twelfth archbishop. In 1969 Associated Catholic Charities joined with Associated Jewish Charities and the United Appeal to form the United Fund, thus ending the separate annual drive begun under Archbishop Curley. Not only were threatened cuts in ACC funding thereby averted, but the power of ACC under Monsignor Stafford was enlarged. Acting as liaison for such beneficiaries as Catholic Social Services, the Urban Commission, and the Martin de Porres Center, it also gained control over them. Not all were happy with this new arrangement. In 1970 the first annual collection was made for the American Bishops' Campaign for Human Development. Besides the 25 percent retained by the archdiocese, the CHD responded readily to applications for grants of the kind usually bestowed by the Urban Commission.

Though his inability to refuse worthwhile causes was a contributing factor, the financial crisis for which the cardinal tended to blame himself was in large measure beyond his control, given the unpredictability of the national economy as well as the magnitude of postconciliar demands upon the church. If he was unable to balance the budget, however, this shortcoming was one of the few dim spots in a career filled with coruscating moments. Not the least of Cardinal Shehan's accomplishments were the services he continued to render to the church at large.

The Outside Tasks

Unfortunately, in his second six years the American bishops began to look elsewhere for leadership as a conservative reaction swept both church and state. Still the bishops valued the talents and the conciliatory approach of Baltimore's cardinal and assigned him several tasks. They placed him at the head of a subcommittee charged with redrawing the statutes of the Catholic University of America.

In 1966 the Middle States Association had threatened to withdraw accreditation if substantial changes were not made by 1970. To Cardinal Shehan fell the impossible task of refashioning the university structure to please not only the MSA but also the federal government, the American bishops, the Congregation for Catholic Education in Rome, and the faculty and student body. An incident in 1967 underscored the kind of problem that concerned the MSA—a faculty and student boycott of the board's dismissal of Father Charles Curran for what it considered objectionable teachings. Cardinal Shehan himself as a member of the board of trustees broke the impasse by sending a telegram from Rome urging a reconsideration of the case.[68]

With the aid of Francis X. Gallagher and others the cardinal redrew the statutes and bylaws. He got the changes accepted in Rome and approved at the university in 1969 despite powerful opposition on the board by those who perceived them as a loss of pontifical status and episcopal control.[69]

The cardinal attended faithfully the meetings of the Roman Congregations to which he had been assigned. As president of the Commission of the International Eucharistic Congresses he was chosen papal legate to preside at the Fortieth Congress in Melbourne, Australia, in March 1973. It was, he would write in his memoirs, "a unique and inspiring experience. Coming as it did, almost at the end of my administration, after a period of so much distress and so many disappointments and discouragements . . . it seemed like a special dispensation of God's goodness and mercy to me." The cardinal devoted more pages to the Melbourne Congress than to any other episode in his life.[70]

Retirement

Upon his return to Baltimore on March 18, 1973, his seventy-fifth birthday, he sent a letter of resignation to Rome in conformity to papal directives. Asking for a month's delay so as not to complicate a change in administration at Good Samaritan Hospital, he was granted a full year's extension. Prior to this, however, he had acceded to a request of the Senate of Priests to petition the Holy See for a coadjutor with right of succession as a means of assuring a continuation of the work he had begun. When he learned of the possibility of outside intrusion into the process, he withdrew the petition.[71]

Henry Knott organized a testimonial dinner at the Civic Center, which netted $450,000 for the Cardinal Shehan Scholarship Fund to pay the tuition of needy children in inner-city schools. The banquet of May 21, 1974, was, the toastmaster boasted, the largest ever served in Baltimore. A month and five days later Cardinal Shehan presided at the installation of his successor, William D. Borders, former bishop of Orlando, Florida.

For the first time in its history the premier see had a former archbishop still much in evidence and increasingly a father figure. The cardinal continued to live at the rectory of the old cathedral, say the seven o'clock mass, and hear confessions. He readily responded to Archbishop Borders' requests to confirm and to preside at functions but scrupulously distanced himself from the administration of the archdiocese. He remained active and alert until a few months before his death, giving much of his time to study and writing and eventually composing his memoirs at the suggestion of his successor.[72]

In the course of painful radon treatments in 1967, when he thought he might be dying, he told his secretary, Monsignor P. Francis Murphy: "I wish a simple funeral without any fuss, and I want you to give the homily but don't exaggerate!" Bishop Murphy recalled the incident in his homily of August 31, 1984, five days after the death of the twelfth archbishop. A close association of almost twenty years allowed the bishop to characterize the cardinal with authority. "He was a man of inexhaustible energy and perennial youth, marvelously typified by his spritely gait. He had the capacity to transcend societal bias and distinctions by accepting the dignity of each person regardless of position or station in life. He was a man of intelligence and wit, reflecting a scholarly bent; a quiet and contemplative man, at home with solitude and reflection but also happy in the company of others; a man who was fully human, able to acknowledge doubts about his adequacy as bishop yet of no uncertain convictions and strength of character; caring for the needs of others; never vindictive, always ready to forgive; a true pontifex—bridge builder—between one person and another, between different groups, between people and God."[73] The homilist did not exaggerate. "He was a priest's priest, a gentleman's gentleman, and the essence of kindness and gentleness," Cardinal Krol was moved to tell reporters at the funeral.[74]

A Mind at Peace

Cardinal Shehan was eighty-six when he died, the same age as Cardinal Gibbons. In many ways he resembled Baltimore's first cardinal, his model. He had not the warmth of Gibbons, however, nor his ability to size up individuals, nor his inclination to befriend the mighty. Shehan shunned the fanfare that was Gibbons' nurture. He spent longer hours at his desk and more days in parish visitations. He made more decisions in a month than Gibbons in a year and was more willing to accept the responsibility, even odium, for unpopular ones. Lawrence Shehan was his own lightning rod.

An aspect of his life he shared with several of his predecessors was his scholarly bent. Stirred in the eighth grade by Bishop Russell's *Maryland: Land of Sanctuary*, he acquired a love for reading that never flagged, even in his busiest years. In Wilfred Ward's biography of Cardinal Newman, devoured in the seminary in a period of despondency, he found the intellect that shaped his own. He read and retained for his personal library the complete set of Newman's works and hung his portrait in his office at the Catholic Center. Yet he could not bring himself to quote Newman's famous counsel, "To live is to change," as such, rewording it to say, "To live is to grow."[75]

And grow intellectually he did until *Humanae Vitae*, when his focus shifted. Thereafter he felt compelled to defend the pope, not only in his traditional stand on birth control but also on priestly celibacy and the ordination of women. In 1972 he defended all three in perhaps his severest public reprimand. In a letter to the editor of the *Sun*, he criticized a column by Garry Wills as one of a number of "ill-tempered and savage attacks" upon the pope, in this case by one of "his own sons."[76] A more benign but ambitious and perhaps misguided effort was his rebuttal of the views of the Scripture scholar, Raymond E. Brown, SS, of St. Mary's Seminary, when the cardinal expanded his defense of traditional Catholic doctrine in his retirement years.[77] He began in the last year of his life a work then well beyond his capabilities: a history of the modern papacy.

Lawrence Shehan was basically a conservative with the American Catholic's ingrained respect for authority and reverence for the papacy. Like most American bishops he accepted *aggiornamento* initially because it was the pope's wish. But more than most he felt the need to make intellectual adjustments to the changes it demanded. This is most evident in his pastoral letters, remarkable for their range as well as their reconciliation of the traditional and the progressive. Though the pastoral on racism was his most powerful, the odyssey of an intellect can best be seen in his pastorals on papal primacy (1967), the Blessed Mother (1971), and the priesthood (1972), all essentially defenses of controverted doctrines but filled with the insights of a mind alert to changing needs. The quiet leadership that Cardinal Shehan brought to noisy times was rooted in an equanimity that came from a mind at peace with itself.

The twelve and a half years of the twelfth archbishop witnessed more rapid and radical changes than any other period in the history of the archdiocese except the decade and a half of the American Revolution. What may in truth be termed the see's second revolution was a time of institutional disintegration, an almost precipitate dismantling of the ghetto church. It was a moment of testing of time-honored beliefs and practices, of rapid maturation in new forms, attitudes, and relationships. At times it was planned. At times it happened. There was no wall-size blueprint. The genius of the twelfth archbishop was to pick the right vision from the right brain at the right moment and somehow make the congeries of visions meld. While not a man of deep prophetic insight nor of unequaled administrative ability, he was, all in all, as admirably suited for the second revolution as John Carroll was for the first.

Epilogue, 1974–1994

ON SEPTEMBER 14, 1975, Elizabeth Ann Seton was canonized, and the United States had its first native-born saint. The Roman officials were pleased to announce that the president of Mother Seton's Daughters was the first woman to read a lesson at a papal mass at the Vatican. They also proclaimed September 14 "Woman's Day."[1] In less than a month, however, Archbishop Joseph L. Bernardin, president of and spokesman for the National Conference of Catholic Bishops, reaffirmed the church's teaching that women could not be ordained priests. The *Catholic Review* editorialized: "One thing is certain about [the archbishop's] statement on the ordination of women: It will not be the last word on the subject."[2] The ordination of women was but one of a number of controversies that refused to be put to rest under Cardinal Shehan's successor.

The Indiana-born William Donald Borders, age sixty at the time of his arrival in Baltimore in 1974, was not only willing to continue his predecessor's efforts at consultation and collaborative involvement of the laity and clergy in search of workable solutions and structures but was temperamentally more disposed to do so. His experiential approach and style of leadership was signaled by the motto he chose as archbishop of the oldest see: "I will listen that I may serve" (*Auscultabo ut serviam*). The search began as soon as he arrived. It was still in progress as retirement neared. In his last pastoral he would write: "One of the challenges facing us today is to learn from the successes and failures of the past . . . and attempt to formulate a comprehensive vision for the future development of the church's ministry."

The comprehensive vision entailed changes in structures. Under the thirteenth archbishop there occurred, first of all, a thoroughgoing overhaul of Central Services. The process had already begun in Catholic Charities and the Department of Education before his arrival, but the new archbishop had in mind a larger blueprint, one that encompassed even the laity at the parish level.[3] For this he persuaded Father Canice Connors, OFM Conv., an expert in pastoral planning, to come to Baltimore to be chief architect of the reordering he desired. As it turned out, Central Services occupied most of the Franciscan's time before he was recalled by his superiors in 1979.

In the restructuring of 1976 an Executive Office of the Archbishop was created and the seven departments (formerly offices) at the Catholic Center were reduced to four. Administrative Services and the Tribunal were placed in the Executive Office and Fiscal Services under the Department of Pastoral Planning and Management. The latter under Father Canice himself and then Rev. Thomas J. Donnellan, the Department of Personnel under Rev. John F. Kinsella, the Department of Christian Formation under Rev. Nicholas P. Amato, and the Department of Associated Catholic Charities under Harold A. ("Hal") Smith attained a high degree of efficiency, expertise, and professionalism. The Department of Personnel in fact attracted national attention.

At the recommendation of Father Canice, the cabinet model was enlarged in 1976 with the establishment of the Committee of Vicars and Secretaries, or COVAS as it was usually called. COVAS consisted of the three vicar bishops and the four secretaries of the departments of Central Services. With the archbishop and chancellor they met twice a month until 1984 and then monthly thereafter, the vicar bishops and secretaries meeting separately once a month.

The creation of vicar bishops was one of the most serviceable of the new archbishop's innovations. Soon after Bishop Gossman, the urban vicar, was named bishop of Raleigh, North Carolina, Archbishop Borders persuaded the Roman authorities to name two assistant bishops. On February 29, 1976, J. Francis Stafford, head of Catholic Charities, and P. Francis Murphy, head of Personnel, were raised to the episcopacy. Bishop Stafford replaced Bishop Gossman as urban vicar. Bishops Frank Murphy and Austin Murphy were named to the two new vicariates, namely, the western vicariate and the eastern vicariate. In 1982, however, Bishop Stafford was named bishop of Memphis (and in 1986 archbishop of Denver) and Bishop Austin Murphy after twenty-two years of quiet and able service was ready to retire. To replace them Archbishop Borders ordained another pair of vicar bishops on July 2, 1984: William C. Newman, pastor of the new cathedral, and John H. Ricard, SSJ, pastor of Our Lady of Perpetual Help in Washington. Bishop Newman was appointed eastern vicar and Bishop Ricard, who had joined the growing number of black bishops in the country, urban vicar. The vicar bishops were more than auxiliaries; they were, in effect, deputies empowered by the archbishop to act in his stead.

Even more significant than the creation of the vicariate system was the further development of collegial bodies. These included not only the pastoral councils at three levels but also the Priests' Council, which in 1982 replaced the Senate of Priests, and the Forum, collectively the major superiors of the religious bodies that worked within the archdiocese, who in 1977 began to meet twice a year with the archbishop. In the restructuring of the pastoral councils particularly did Archbishop Borders demonstrate the seriousness with which he called the laity to share in the ministry of the church.

In 1975 the Archdiocesan Pastoral Council (APC) finished a mission statement begun under Cardinal Shehan. It represented a call "to proclaim and teach the Word, to build and model community, and to advocate and serve one another." For each of these three major responsibilities a series of five-year policy statements, three-year strategic goals, and one-year action goals were formulated in turn. These were to be used by the departments in Central Services and by the parishes in the preparation of their budgets. With the application of these goals a more structured system of accountability was made possible.[4]

Dissatisfaction with the APC, however, developed both within the body and without. It was too large, many believed. It tended to be more oriented to Central Services than to parishes. It seemed more preoccupied with procedural than substantive matters. In July 1979 the APC itself called for a six-month suspension of activities so that a "radical and creative" reorganization might be effected. This was one of its few resolutions the archbishop disallowed, calling upon it instead to study the concept of collegiality and to fashion a more effective and responsive government. A multistage process of study and consultation finally produced in 1986 a new Archdiocesan Pastoral Council. Its membership was reduced by half (from forty-nine to twenty-five) and its meetings from once a month to once every two months. The standing committees that corresponded to the departments of Central Services were abolished. Its elected members had to be elected first to the parish councils and then to the new regional councils, thus assuring a more effective linkage and representation.

The establishment of the new APC was delayed partly by the need to effect a change in the old area councils, the weakest link in the archdiocesan chain of collegial bodies. New regional councils were drawn along civil boundaries and parceled out among the three vicariates. The urban vicariate now encompassed the entire city of Baltimore, the eastern the counties of Baltimore, Harford, and Anne Arundel, the western all the rest. The vicar bishops were to preside over the meetings of the regional councils, the feature that gave the greatest assurance of success to these new middle-level bodies. The parish councils at the base of the collegial pyramid improved with age and as a result of workshops conducted by the Division of Collegial Services of the Department of Planning and Management.

Archbishop Borders' collaborative style of leadership became proverbial. His desire to see important changes broad based and deep rooted was best realized through the collegial bodies. His success in working with them was recognized by the American bishops. In 1984 he delivered the keynote address to a regional meeting of the hierarchy entitled "Perspectives on Diocesan Pastoral Councils." Alluding to the church as "a mystery that unfolds in each generation," he told his fellow bishops: "In our attempts to effectively use our resources, we must accept that we do not know all the answers. . . . We learn and grow a step at a time. Occasionally we step backward. Yet, we work to involve all members of the church. This involvement calls for a leadership that is collegial; it calls forth; it enables; it sums up accurately; it articulates the dreams of the whole community; it sets direction. Leadership must presume that everyone in some way is gifted, and the gifts are given to be shared and integrated for the building up of the whole body."[5]

The last of a number of teaching pastorals the archbishop would entitle "You Are a Royal Priesthood: A Pastoral Letter on Ministry." The distillation of a two-year effort at consulting the faithful, it was essentially the call to ministry he had issued in many guises throughout his episcopacy. The New Testament understanding of the priesthood, he told his readers, was "focused primarily on the priesthood of the entire community of the baptized." The future development of the church, he believed, would encompass "officially recognized and commissioned lay ministries," who with ordained ministers and religious would serve as catalysts in the empowerment of the laity in general to develop the gifts they could offer to the mission and ministry of the church. "If we are to pursue seriously the vision of a community of collaborative ministry," he wrote, "we must be willing to take risks and to learn from experience."

Solving the problems that carried over from the administration of his predecessor involved a great deal of risk taking. One problem was the financial crisis that had resulted from a continuing deficit of one to two million dollars a year. In 1976, when the APC called for a balanced budget, the cathedraticum was raised from 10 to 12.5 percent and an annual Stewardship Campaign was inaugurated. Rev. Richard T. Lawrence was persuaded to be fiscal director until the archdiocese climbed into the black again. This happy event occurred as early as 1978. The temporary fiscal director also introduced Central Services to the computer.

Another problem that carried over was not so easily resolved: the shortage of priests and religious. From 1979 to 1988 the number of pastors remained at 122 while associate pastors dropped from 124 to 76.[6] A committee on alternative parish staffing proposed nonordained pastoral leaders for some parishes and shared pastors for others. Both alternatives were tried before the archbishop's retirement. For many the clerical shortage underscored the need to take seriously the possibility of married priests—the archdiocese already had one active in parish work—and even of ordained women.[7]

Still another problem that carried over, one that related to the shortage of sisters, was the plight of the parochial schools. There was a tension both within the Department of Christian Formation and within the parishes themselves between the school people and the supporters of newer forms of Christian formation. The former were unhappy with the recommendations of a task force that in 1985 called for regional schools and tuition at cost. After a series of regional meetings and further studies, the archbishop finally declared himself in 1988 in favor of interparochial schools and school boards and tuition at cost but with financial assistance for parents unable to pay full tuition.

The problems of the inner city persisted but took new forms. The appointment of a black bishop for the urban vicariate came at a time when the focal concerns of Maryland's major city shifted from racial injustice to a powerlessness resulting from poverty and hunger that was more encompassing. In the Borders years the work of Catholic Charities expanded tremendously. From a budget of less than $2 million and fewer than two hundred employees in 1974, it would grow to $29 million (not including the $12 million outlay for Stella Maris Hospice) and a thousand employees by 1989.[8] About half of its income was from federal, state, and local governments and a fourth from service fees. The rest came from donations, including those of the United Way (formerly United Fund). Increasingly its beneficiaries were the homeless, the hungry, and the helpless elderly. Among the shelters and soup kitchens it opened were My Sister's Place, Sarah's House, and Our Daily Bread. Its Aging Division would find affordable apartments for the old. St. Ambrose Housing Aid Center broadened its renovation of houses and tenant counseling. Bread and Water offered bulk food and Charities Oil fuel at minimal cost. In all Associated Catholic Charities conducted some forty institutions, organizations, or programs.

Despite its many services, however, ACC could not begin to meet all the needs as government cutbacks in programs for the poor and powerless grew apace. Among the many independent Catholic enterprises was the Catholic Workers' Viva House, which in 1980 began to take in homeless mothers with children.⁹ A large number of these enterprises were the work of sisters. Among them would be the Franciscan Center of the Franciscan Sisters of Baltimore, a food and clothing distribution center, the Julie Community Center of the Sisters of Notre Dame de Namur, designed to develop a more self-reliant neighborhood, and the House of Hope of the School Sisters of Notre Dame in distant Oakland, a shelter for battered wives, victims of disasters, and others. Not a few parishes conducted shelters, kitchens, or centers for tutoring, counseling, or recreation.

Most of the major institutions built under Catholic auspices in the Borders years were for the elderly and the elderly ill. Basilica Place, an $8 million seventeen-story apartment building was erected not far from the old cathedral. The Sisters of Bon Secours gradually expanded Heartlands, their health park near Ellicott City. De Paul House was built by Associated Catholic Charities next to Jenkins Memorial. In 1978 the archbishop persuaded the six Catholic hospitals and four extended-care facilities of greater Baltimore to form a health consortium.

Though hardly as angry and insistent as in the Shehan years, voices of protest continued to be heard. The most persistent were the traditionalists, pro-life advocates, gays, feminists, and peace activists. The traditionalists were granted the Tridentine mass they demanded. The pro-life advocates, who continued to protest the archdiocesan involvement with United Way, were encouraged to apply a "negative designation" to their contributions. Though the archbishop opposed a gay rights ordinance in 1980 and again in 1988, when the measure passed despite his objections, he created in 1981 the Archdiocesan Gay/Lesbian Outreach (AGLO), one of the few such diocesan programs in the country, and said mass for the members of Dignity.

The archbishop's reaction to the demands of feminists was typical of his collaborative and consultative style. In 1977, after the Vatican's seemingly definitive pronouncement that women could not be priests, he issued a pastoral, "Women in the Church," in which he acknowledged the need to heal the pain caused by injustices and espoused equality in principle (though not ordination). In 1979, in response to concerns expressed at the Second National Women's Ordination Conference held in Baltimore in late 1978, he convoked a seminar to probe the place of women in the church in the light of ecclesiology, Christology, and missiology. In 1983 an ad hoc committee on women engaged the archbishop in dialogue and at its conclusion asked that he form a women's commission. After consulting the APC and the Priests' Council, he had a professional survey conducted, requested a series of hearings in each of the twelve regions, and submitted the results to a special committee for its recommendation. Only then did he create a women's commission and place it in the Executive Office.

Officially the archdiocese was not in sympathy with the radical pacifism of Jonah House and Viva House. From Jonah House in Baltimore Philip Berrigan and Elizabeth McAlister his wife masterminded the symbolic disablings of the Plowshares movement and took turns serving time in prison for their involvement.[10] It was not unreasonable to expect the archdiocese to respond to such witness in the light of its own involvement in the peace movement. In 1980 the somnolent Peace and Justice Commission was revived, budgeted, and placed under the chairmanship of Bishop Frank Murphy. That same year Bishop Murphy, with the support of other episcopal members of Pax Christi, proposed to the bishops at their annual meeting a pastoral on peace and war, the starting point for the bishops' *Challenge of Peace* issued in 1983.[11] In 1983 Archbishop Borders and Bishop Murphy joined twelve other prelates in deploring the deployment of the MX missiles. In 1985, on the fortieth anniversary of Hiroshima, and again on the fifth anniversary of *Challenge of Peace*, the archbishop and his three vicars issued statements seriously questioning whether "the Church in this country can continue to teach a Catholic ethic of war and peace based on the expectation of progress in the present system of arms control."[12]

The questions of peace and racial justice had not the ability to stir Catholics of the oldest archdiocese as in the days of Cardinal Shehan, whether liberal or conservative, but old attitudes persisted. Much of the old church survived healthy and hopeful and, for the most part, in peaceful coexistence with the new. Many still fingered their rosaries at masses reminiscent of the old. The traveling statue of Our Lady of Fatima still attracted crowds. Bingo nights remained popular; at least forty parishes in 1988 held them to help defray the costs of grammar schools. The creation of thirty-three monsignori in 1982, the first in a decade and a half, stirred memories of a nearly forgotten age. There was a modern day O'Neill and Furst in the person of Henry J. Knott, one-time director of the Arundel Corporation, whose multimillion dollar benefactions took such forms as the Marion Burk Knott Scholarship Fund and the Knott Athletic, Recreational, and Convocation Center at Mount St. Mary's College.

While many of the old organizations, such as the Holy Name Society and the Sodality, declined, the Knights of Columbus could still boast in 1988 eighty-two councils with twenty-one thousand active members and the renamed Catholic Daughters of the Americas forty-one courts with thirty-five hundred members. A juxtaposition of old and new could be found in many parishes. St. Dominic's in the 1980s, for example, could still count some fifty organizations. Among the old were the Holy Name Society, Altar Society, St. Vincent de Paul Society, and the Boy and Girl Scouts; among the new were the Breath of God prayer group, Senior Citizens, Singles Again, Suicides Anonymous, and ministries to shut-ins and the ill.[13]

Parish societies of the postconciliar church would increasingly fall into four categories: collegial bodies, prayer and Bible study groups, mutual support groups, and social outreach groups. Collegiality and coresponsibility brought into existence parish councils, finance committees, liturgical committees, and others, usually elected and usually organizational in function. Charismatic prayer groups continued to multiply—there were some forty-five by the late 1980s—but Bible study groups were a new phenomenon. Scripturally oriented programs such as Genesis 2 and Renew proved popular, as did such person-oriented programs as Cursillo and Marriage Encounter. Those attracted to the mutual support groups ranged from the bereaved to the lonely. SWORD (Separated, Widowed, or Divorced), launched at St. Joseph's, Cockeysville, in 1973, spread throughout the archdiocese. The Catholic Alumni and Pace Setters were active singles clubs. Social outreach groups took many forms. One would be those who volunteered to supply and serve Our Daily Bread and other such centers. Another would be those organized to visit hospitals, nursing homes, and shut-ins on a regular basis. There were also the Legislative Education Groups (LEG) which lobbied for social goals.[14]

The old survived in ethnic neighborhoods. While the last services in German were conducted at St. Michael's shortly after the outbreak of World War II, daily mass was still said in Polish at Holy Rosary as the bicentennial year of the archdiocese approached. "The Polish feeling remains," a future pope told the parishioners during a visit there in 1977.[15] The immigrants of the old church, nevertheless, were giving place to a new kind of immigrant. As early as 1963 an Hispanic Center had been organized, but no Spanish-speaking parish would follow. Originally dispersed and heterogeneous, Hispanics began to increase rapidly about 1986—to some fifteen or twenty thousand in the city and ten thousand in surrounding counties. They were mostly Caribbean and Central American, poor, young, and fertile.[16] In 1976 Korean Catholics organized a branch of the Legion of Mary and soon began to worship at St. Bernard's, where a Korean priest was stationed. In 1976 Catholic Charities opened the Indochina Center for the settlement of Vietnamese refugees. Both the Catholic Koreans and Vietnamese could claim about 250 families in the archdiocese. As the numbers would indicate, however, Baltimore attracted but a fraction of the Hispanics and Asians who represented a new epoch in the history of an immigrant nation.

The Catholic total did not increase appreciably in the Borders years, but significant shifts in population occurred. The days of counting steeples on the city's skyline to find the greatest concentration of Catholics were, of course, long gone. Baltimore City and Allegany County, once the Catholic strongholds, continued to decline in both Catholic and total populations. The younger and fastest growing bodies of Catholics could be found under new and often steepleless roofs in Anne Arundel and Howard counties, which looked as much to Washington as to Baltimore for their economic sustenance. Most impressive were the new parishes in Anne Arundel County, especially those created along the Chesapeake Bay and Route 50. The county's last four missions became parishes: Our Lady of Perpetual Help at Edgewater, Our Lady of Sorrows at Owensville, St. Andrew by the Bay (formerly Our Lady of the Cape) at Cape St. Claire, and Holy Family at Davidsonville. St. Elizabeth Ann Seton was created at Crofton in 1976 and Our Lady of the Chesapeake at Lake Shore in 1981.

Elsewhere an independent congregation developed at Relay from the body of worshipers at the University of Maryland Baltimore County. In Harford County a new parish was organized, which voted in 1977 to call itself Prince of Peace. In the western vicariate six of seven missions were still unable to achieve parochial status, the exception being St. Ignatius at Urbana in Frederick County. In the same county, however, St. Timothy's at Walkersville became a parish in 1983 and an independent mission at Middletown in no hurry for a name was awarded parochial status on January 4, 1989. In Garrett County St. Stephen's at Grantsville and St. Ann's at Avilton were merged to become a totally new parish called St. Ann's at Grantsville. In the fall of 1988 independent missions were created at Hunt Valley in Baltimore County and near Laurel in Howard County.

About 1985 a "phenomenal burst" of church building followed a "phenomenal low" caused by high interest rates. By 1988 some $8 million had been spent on ten church buildings—two of them, St. Patrick's at Fells Point and St. Stephen's at Bradshaw, necessitated by fire—and about twenty-five more projects were on the drawing board. Two more parishes, however, joined the list of inner-city closings: St. James and St. John (the merger did not save it) and St. Katharine of Sienna, both in 1986. Historically the most regrettable closing was the parish school of St. Patrick's in

1987, the oldest parochial school in the archdiocese. It signified the continuing decline in the number of parochial school students, from thirty-five thousand in 1974 to about twenty thousand in 1989.

The school question was but one of a number of problems facing the archdiocese as described in a "Report of the Committee on the Selection of Bishops" of the APC. The report was drawn in anticipation of the resignation of Archbishop Borders on October 9, 1988, his seventy-fifth birthday. During his *ad limina* visit in June of that year, he presented the report to the proper authorities at the Vatican for their enlightenment as to the state of the archdiocese, its needs and concerns, as well as the type of successor best calculated to meet them.

The list of ten problems the fourteenth archbishop would have to address was not intended to be exhaustive. Besides the school question they were a shortage of priests, loss of the young, a need for competent teachers, the role of women, the range of socioeconomic problems, sexual promiscuity, parish demographics, inner-city prospects, and the moral implications of medical advances. Not mentioned, surprisingly, except by inference in the case of the young, was a rather dramatic decline in church attendance. In 1984, when the national average for registered Catholics at Sunday mass was polled at 52 percent, that of the oldest archdiocese was computed to be 41.7 percent. By 1987 it was down to 38.9 percent and considerably lower in the age groups that fell between fifteen and forty-four.

The next archbishop, the report observed, would "find a long and rich tradition," of which he would be expected to be a part while placing his own stamp upon it. He should be a spiritual man, an administrator willing to listen, a man who relates well to civil authority. "In sum, the next archbishop should be a man of broad and noble vision and yet of a simple lifestyle. He should be an intellectual man, though there is no need for him to be a scholar in any particular field. He should be firmly rooted in tradition, and at the same time open and receptive to change when change is needed, and when it adds a new and vital element to the tradition. Above all he should have a firm commitment to the principles of collegiality and shared responsibility, since it is only by these means that he can offer genuine leadership to his people." In sum, the framers of the report would like their next leader to be as much like the outgoing one as possible.

The tradition in which the next archbishop should be "firmly rooted" was indicated in the mission statement offered by the APC a dozen years before and now appended to the report. "The Church in the Archdiocese of Baltimore," it read, "is a local Church in the Church Universal, united with our Bishop and the Bishop of Rome and also with other Christians, believers, and people of good will. It is made unique by its setting in space and time, and has the responsibility to interpret its mission in light of this setting for the realization of the Kingdom of God."

Locating the "Mother Church of the United States," the statement continued: "Our tradition, both as a people and a Church, begins as a colony established to be a haven for Catholics, where the first laws guaranteeing religious liberty in the new world were enacted. This tradition at its noblest is one of leadership: seen in the early collegiality of Bishop Carroll's election; the leadership of Cardinal Gibbons in social justice for working man and the blacks; the works of the Councils of Baltimore; and in our day, leadership in ecumenism, racial justice and revived collegiality."

Whatever one may say of their grasp of history, it is obvious that the framers of the statement had an appreciation of a development that was unique, that they had a basic understanding of the Maryland tradition, and that they were conscious that something had been lost that was now revived. Clearly "our day" was an allusion to the achievements of the second cardinal, whom they saw in the tradition of John Carroll and James Gibbons.

In 1789 Carroll had commenced the work of constructing a unique tradition. By 1889 Gibbons had begun the task of restoring it. By 1989 the restoration promoted by Shehan in his reponse to the mandates of Vatican II approached completion. And yet it cannot be said that in two hundred years the local church, much less the church in America, had come full circle. In broad outline the postconciliar church resembled the Carroll church in striking ways: in its dedication to American principles, its ecumenism, its sense of public service, its reimmersion in the mainstream. In some ways, however, it had gone beyond or broadened the Maryland tradition. In others it had failed to reclaim what Carroll, Gibbons, and others in that tradition had promoted.

Catholics in the oldest see, at the prompting of the twelfth and thirteenth archbishops, had gone beyond most others in their nation in restoring the vital role that Carroll—but not Gibbons—had envisioned for the laity. This was largely the result of their having pushed to its ultimate conclusion the concept of collegiality (though the thirteenth archbishop had warned them it did not mean democracy). In this they had gone even beyond Carroll, who saw the principal tasks of the laity as being performed by a Catholic elite. By 1989 the Maryland Catholic elite had become little more than a historical memory. Under the thirteenth archbishop the inclusion of the laity in the priestly role of the church was an advance that even Carroll, with his sharp distinction between the temporal and the spiritual, had not envisioned.

The sense of obligation to the whole, moreover, so much a part of Carroll's thinking, would be carried well beyond his circle of concerns by the dedication of the postconciliar church to issues of justice and peace. There was nothing in the life of the first archbishop, nor even that of the first cardinal, resembling the twelfth archbishop's preoccupation with racial justice.

In some ways the American bishops of the postconciliar church failed to resemble Carroll, Gibbons, and other bishops in the Maryland tradition. Only on rare occasions did they manifest publicly the latter's qualified acceptance of Roman leadership. They also displayed little of the missionary fervor of the Maryland tradition. Even Martin Spalding, the most "Roman" of the nineteenth-century archbishops of Baltimore, believed that the Universal Church had much to learn from his native land in respect to freedom, openness, and democratic procedures.

The ultimate consequences of a reclamation of the Maryland tradition and dismantling of the ghetto are not readily apparent. It may be questioned whether the embracement of the values of mainstream America represented the providential turn that Gibbons was sure it was. Even Carroll would have been more cautious. The memories of the more ardent champions of the Maryland tradition may focus on the defensive and benighted character of the immigrant church, forgetting that it produced the most loyal, devout, observant, generous, and active body of Catholics in the Catholic world. The task of the next hundred years may be to reclaim what was of value in that tradition.

On March 1, 1989, some 3,500 well-wishers attended a farewell banquet for Archbishop Borders at Baltimore's Convention Center. A gift of $1 million was presented to him by the Catholics of the archdiocese for youth programs. The business community promised another million dollars for capital needs. These tokens of esteem and gratitude and the many kind words said on the occasion afforded a satisfying conclusion to the fifteen years the smiling, courteous, considerate, busy archbishop had given the oldest see. In the previous month he had had to make one of the most painful decisions of his episcopacy, one he refused to leave to his successor. Mounting expenses had again created an alarming deficit, one that demanded a $1.1 million slash in the 1990 budget. This in turn necessitated the layoff of twenty-eight employees and the termination or curtailment of a number of programs, none of which was considered expendable. Small comfort could be taken by the fact that the financial bind was not peculiar to the archdiocese of Baltimore.

On April 11, some seven months after Archbishop Borders had sent his letter of resignation to the pope, it was announced that William Henry Keeler, until then bishop of Harrisburg, Pennsylvania, had been named his successor. Texas-born but raised in Lebanon, Pennsylvania, the fourteenth archbishop of Baltimore had been created an auxiliary bishop of Harrisburg in 1979 and its bishop in 1983. Catholics of the oldest archdiocese were pleased to learn that he had long been active in ecumenical affairs. Having served as chairman of the National Conference of Catholic Bishops' Committee on Ecumenical and Interreligious Affairs from 1983 to 1987, he had in 1988 been named episcopal moderator of Catholic-Jewish relations for the U.S. bishops. The previous November, the same bishops had elected him secretary of their national conference. Baltimore would install its next archbishop at the Cathedral of Mary Our Queen on May 23, 1989.

The same issue of the *Catholic Review* (April 12) that carried the news of Border's successor also published, after five and a half years of study, consultation, and controversy, the report on the Catholic Schools Project with its policy directives for implementation. Whatever discomfort may have been occasioned by what many saw as the passing of an era—when a Catholic parish measured its vitality by the size of its school—optimism could only have followed the reading of three other news items; ground had been broken for a new $1.4 million church at St. Mark's in Fallston; the parishioners at St. Joseph's in Sykesville were debating whether to erect a new church or enlarge the one built in 1868; and two parishes in the Baltimore–Washington corridor, St. Joseph's in Odenton and Resurrection in Laurel, were bracing for explosive growth.

When he hosted the celebration of the bicentennial of the archdiocese in November 1989, Archbishop Keeler was elected vice president of the National Conference of Catholic Bishops and three years later (1992) president. In the spring of 1994, Baltimore's fourteenth archbishop was appointed to the Synod for the Church in Africa and in the fall was elected by his fellow bishops to attend the Synod on Consecrated Life. At the same time he was appointed to the Pontifical Council for Promoting Christian Unity. On November 26, 1994 he was elevated by Pope John Paul II to the College of Cardinals and named soon after to the Congregation for Eastern Churches. As leader of the local church, he has continued to bolster the educational and social outreaches and pastoral programs of the premier see. He has also continued to promote ecumenical and interfaith collaboration in the solution of major societal issues.

Notes

Abbreviations

AAB	Archives of the Archdiocese of Baltimore
AANY	Archives of the Archdiocese of New York
APF	Archives of the Propaganda Fide
Acta	Acta Sacrae Congregationis
Cong. Generali	Scritture originali riferite nelle Congregazioni Generali
Congressi	Scritture riferite nei Congressi, America Centrale dal Canada all'Istmo di Panama
Lettere	Lettere e Decreti della Sacra Congregazione
AUND	Archives of the University of Notre Dame
BCR	*Baltimore Catholic Review*
CHR	*Catholic Historical Review*
CM	*Catholic Mirror*
CR	*Catholic Review*
HRS	*Historical Records and Studies*
Hughes, *Documents*	Thomas Hughes, *History of the Society of Jesus in North America: Colonial and Federal. Documents* (2 parts, New York, 1908, 1910)
JCP	Thomas O'Brien Hanley, ed., *The John Carroll Papers* (3 vols., Notre Dame, Ind., 1976)
MHM	*Maryland Historical Magazine*
RACHSP	*Records of the American Catholic Historical Society of Philadelphia*
SAB	Sulpician Archives, Baltimore
USCM	*United States Catholic Magazine*
USCH	*U.S. Catholic Historian*
WL	*Woodstock Letters*

Prologue, 1634–1789

1. Clifford M. Lewis and Alfred J. Loomie, *The Spanish Jesuit Mission in Virginia, 1570–1572* (Chapel Hill, N.C., 1953).

2. E. I. Watkin, *Roman Catholics in England from the Reformation to 1950* (London, 1950), p. 56.

3. See David Mathew, *Catholicism in England, 1535–1935: Portrait of a Minority, Its Culture and Tradition* (London, 1936); M. D. R. Leys, *Catholics in England, 1559–1829: A Social*

History (New York, 1961); John Bossy, *The English Catholic Community, 1570–1850* (New York, 1976).

4. Dan Herr and Joel Wells, eds., *Through Other Eyes: Some Impressions of American Catholicism by Foreign Visitors from 1777 to the Present* (Westminster, Md., 1965), pp. 153–54.

5. Clayton Colman Hall, ed., *Narratives of Early Maryland* (New York, 1910), p. 16.

6. Copley to Baltimore, St. Mary's, April 3, 1638, in *Calvert Papers*, 1 (Fund Publication No. 28, Baltimore, 1889), pp. 157–69. For the *Bulla Coenae* see *New Catholic Encyclopedia*, 14: 481.

7. William Hand Browne et al., eds., *Archives of Maryland* (83 vols. to date, Baltimore, 1883–   ), 1: 31–86 (hereafter *AM*); Thomas O'Brien Hanley, *Their Rights and Liberties: The Beginnings of Religious and Political Freedom in Maryland* (Westminster, Md., 1959), pp. 93–108.

8. Hughes, *Documents*, 1: 166–68.

9. *AM*, 1: 244–47; John Tracy Ellis, ed., *Documents of American Catholic History* (2 vols., Chicago, 1967), 1: 112–14.

10. Charles M. Andrews, *The Colonial Period of American History* (4 vols., New Haven, 1934–39), 2: 328–29, 376–78; Edward C. Papenfuse et al., eds., *A Biographical Dictionary of the Maryland Legislature, 1635–1789* (2 vols., Baltimore, 1979, 1984). The Brent family moved to Virginia but would continue to look to Maryland for spouses and spiritual succor.

11. A good account of the social history of the early Catholic families can be found in Michael James Graham, "Lord Baltimore's Pious Enterprise: Toleration and Community in Colonial Maryland, 1634–1724" (doctoral dissertation, University of Michigan, 1983), which indicates that Catholics were more generous in their benefactions to their church than were Protestants (pp. 97–98, 104–5, 213–14).

12. *AM*, 30: 375–79, 33: 58–59, 287–89; Bernard C. Steiner, "The Restoration of the Proprietary of Maryland and the Legislation against the Roman Catholics during the Governorship of Capt. John Hart (1714–1720)," *Annual Report of the American Historical Association* 1 (1899): 262–68.

13. Francis X. Curran, *Catholics in Colonial Law* (Chicago, 1963), passim.

14. Edward B. Carley, *The Origins and History of St. Peter's Church, Queenstown, Maryland, 1637–1976* (Baltimore, 1976), pp. 148–53.

15. "An Account of the Conditions of the Catholic Religion in the English Colonies of America," *CHR* 6 (1921): 520–24. Challoner's estimate of the Catholic population was probably a little high.

16. [Michael J. Riordan], *Cathedral Records from the Beginning of Catholicity in Baltimore to the Present Time* (Baltimore, 1906), pp. 5–9.

17. Peter Guilday, *The Life and Times of John Carroll, Archbishop of Baltimore (1735–1815)* (New York, 1922), pp. 151–56, Carroll's letter dated July 16, 1765.

18. *JCP*, 1: 32, John Carroll to [Daniel] Carroll, (Bruges, September 11, 1773).

19. Thomas O'Brien Hanley, *Charles Carroll of Carrollton: The Making of a Revolutionary Gentleman* (Washington, D.C., 1970), p. 138.

20. David Curtis Skaggs, *Roots of Maryland Democracy, 1753–1776* (Westport, Conn., 1973), p. 132.

21. Albert W. Werline, *Problems of Church and State in Maryland during the Seventeenth and Eighteenth Centuries* (South Lancaster, Mass., 1948), p. 135.

22. Charles H. Metzger, *Catholics and the American Revolution: A Study in Religious Climate* (Chicago, 1962), pp. 188–96.

23. Quoted in Annabelle M. Melville, *John Carroll of Baltimore: Founder of the American Catholic Hierarchy* (New York, 1955), p. 44.

24. The correct dates of Carroll's birth and ordination are given in Thomas W. Spalding, "John Carroll: Corrigenda and Addenda," *CHR* 71 (1985): 505–10. John's relationship to Charles can be established only on his mother's side.

25. *JCP*, I: 29, Carroll to Ellerker, n.p., February 3, 1773.

26. Mary Virgina Geiger, *Daniel Carroll: A Framer of the Constitution* (Washington, D.C., 1943).

27. *JCP*, I: 66, Carroll to Plowden, Maryland, February 20, 1782.

28. Ibid., pp. 59–63, 71–77; Hughes, *Documents*, 2: 617–19.

29. *JCP*, I: 78, Carroll to Plowden, Maryland, September 27, 1783.

30. Ibid., pp. 68–69, to Pius VI (undated).

31. Ibid., pp. 80–81, and AAB, C-A-4, Carroll to Vitaliano Borromeo [?], Maryland, November 10, 1783.

32. Ibid., p. 146, and Hughes, *Documents*, 2: 619n., Carroll to Plowden, Maryland, April 10, 1784. The parenthetical expression and concluding sentiment are inexplicably omitted from *JCP*. A vicar apostolic was usually invested with a titular see *in partibus infidelium*.

33. The extent of the four-way diplomacy involved is indicated in Finbar Kenneally et al., eds., *United States Documents in the Propaganda Fide Archives: A Calendar* (8 vols. to date, Washington, D.C., 1966–   ), Series I, Vol. I, nos. 32–69 (hereafter cited as Kenneally, *Calendar*).

34. Melville, *John Carroll*, p. 68.

35. Guilday, *John Carroll*, pp. 203–4.

36. *JCP*, I: 169–75, Carroll to Antonelli, Maryland, February 27, 1785.

37. Ibid., pp. 82–144, *An Address to the Roman Catholics of the United States of America by a Catholic Clergyman* (Annapolis, 1784).

38. Ibid., pp. 147–49, Carroll to Berington, Maryland, July 10, 1784. Italics are Carroll's.

39. Ibid., p. 253, Carroll to Plowden, Rock Creek, June 4, 1787.

40. Guilday, *John Carroll*, p. 130.

41. *JCP*, I: 168, Carroll to Plowden, Rock Creek, February 27, 1785.

42. Ibid., pp. 208–9, Carroll to Antonelli, Maryland, March 13, 1786.

43. *Votes and Proceedings of the Senate*, December 9, 13, 21–23, 29, 1788.

44. *JCP*, I: 204, Carroll to Lynch and Stoughton, Rock Creek, January 24, 1786.

45. Ibid., p. 214, Carroll to Nugent, Rock Creek, July 18, 1786.

46. Guilday, *John Carroll*, pp. 291–95.

47. Patrick W. Carey, *People, Priests, and Prelates: Ecclesiastical Democracy and the Tensions of Trusteeism* (Notre Dame, Ind., 1987), pp. 7–16.

48. *JCP*, I: 279–80.

49. Ibid., pp. 363, 370, 389, Carroll to Plowden, Baltimore, May 8[?], July 12, October 23, 1789.

50. Ibid., pp. 316–20, dated July 15, 1788.

51. Ibid., p. 461, Carroll to Plowden, King's Street [London], September 13, 1790.

52. Guilday, *John Carroll*, p. 352.

53. *JCP*, 1: 362, Carroll to Plowden, Baltimore, May 8[?], 1789.
54. Ibid.

Part I. Introduction

1. Martin E. Marty, *Religion and Republic: The American Circumstance* (Boston, 1987), pp. 31–50.
2. Carey, *People, Priests, and Prelates*, p. 17.
3. Jay P. Dolan, *The American Catholic Experience: A History from Colonial Times to the Present* (New York, 1985), pp. 101–24.
4. Christopher J. Kauffman, *Tradition and Transformation in Catholic Culture: The Priests of Saint Sulpice in the United States from 1791 to the Present* (New York, 1988), pp. xiv, 30, 70–73, and passim.

Chapter 1. Founding Father

1. A translation of the brief is given in John Gilmary Shea, *The History of the Catholic Church in the United States* (4 vols., New York, 1886–92), 2: 337–43.
2. Edward Norman, *Roman Catholicism in England from the Elizabethan Settlement to the Second Vatican Council* (New York 1986), pp. 60ff.
3. *JCP*, 1: 453, Carroll to Petre, London, August 31, 1790.
4. Guilday, *John Carroll*, pp. 377–79; Melville, *John Carroll*, pp. 117–18.
5. Joseph W. Ruane, *The Beginnings of the Society of St. Sulpice in the United States, 1791–1829* (Washington, D.C., 1935), pp. 21–32; Kauffman, *Saint Sulpice*, pp. 33–40.
6. *JCP*, 1: 466, Carroll to Plowden, London, September 25, 1790.
7. *JCP*, 1: 490, Carroll to Plowden, White Marsh, February 3, 1791.
8. Ibid., pp. 476–78, Sermon of December 12, 1790.
9. Ibid., p. 505, Carroll to Plowden, Boston, June 11, 1791.
10. Ibid., p. 514, Carroll to Hancock, Baltimore, August 28, 1791.
11. Robert H. Lord, John E. Sexton, and Edward T. Harrington, *History of the Archdiocese of Boston in the Various Stages of Its Development, 1604–1943* (3 vols., New York, 1944), 1: 479–631.
12. Charles G. Herbermann, *The Sulpicians in the United States* (New York, 1916), pp. 21–23, 39ff; Ruane, *St. Sulpice*, pp. 33–41; *JCP*, 1:523.
13. John M. Daley, *Georgetown University: Origin and Early Years* (Washington, D.C., 1957), pp. 1–63; *JCP*, 1: 516, Carroll to Plowden, Baltimore, September 3, 1791.
14. *JCP*, 1: 526–34.
15. Ibid., 2: 29, Carroll to Antonelli, Baltimore, April 23, 1792.
16. Ibid., pp. 43–52, Pastoral Letter, May 28, 1792.
17. AAB, 7-O-1, Sewall to Carroll, St. Thomas Manor, December 1, 1794 (hereafter AAB will not be indicated unless the document is unclassified).
18. *JCP*, 2: 390–91, Carroll to Wilson, Washington, May 8, 1802.
19. Though Charles Carroll of Carrollton wished all his grandchildren reared as Catholics, at least one, Charles Carroll Harper was buried in the Protestant Episcopal faith of his father. A prenuptial agreement in 1806 between Roger Brooke Taney, a devout Catholic, and Anne Phoebe Key, an equally devout Episcopalian, to raise their sons Catholic and daughters Episcopalian is doubtful. See Carl Brent Swisher, *Roger B. Taney*

(New York, 1935), pp. 50–51, and "Did Taney Make a Pre-Nuptial Agreement with His Wife?" *American Catholic Historical Researches* 29 (1912): 88ff. None of the Taneys' six daughters was brought up Catholic, though the first was baptized by the Catholic priest at Taneytown. Taneys' wife was sister of Francis Scott Key, author of "The Star-Spangled Banner," at whose death the Sulpician Louis Deluol would note in his diary, "very bigoted Protestant." SAB, Record group 1, Box 1a, Deluol diary, January 13, 1843. Deluol's diary suggests that the requirement to raise all children of interfaith marriages as Catholics came to be more strictly enforced during the episcopacy of Archbishop Samuel Eccleston.

20. *JCP*, 2: 40, Carroll to Plowden, Baltimore, April 30, 1792.

21. Hughes, *Documents*, 2: 720–26, 732–39, 768–70.

22. Ibid., pp. 738–39.

23. *JCP*, 1: 73.

24. Ibid., p. 230.

25. Ibid., pp. 154–55, Carroll to the Vestry of Charleston, n.p., September 1811; Carey, *People, Priests, and Prelates*, pp. 61–62.

26. *JCP*, 2: 499–500, Financial formula (1806); Carey, *People Priests, and Prelates*, pp. 229–30.

27. William Kilty, Thomas Harris, and John A. Watkins, compilers, *The Laws of Maryland*, Vols. 1–4 (Annapolis, 1792–1818), 1795, Ch. 15; 1796, Ch. 38; 1799, Ch. 53; and 1801, Ch. 51.

28. Ibid., 1801, Ch. 111.

29. Trustees of the Catholic Cathedral Church of Baltimore Minutes of Meetings (hereafter Cathedral Trustees Minutes), 1: 1–5.

30. Ibid., pp. 6–7.

31. Fillmore Norfleet, ed., "Baltimore as Seen by Moreau de Saint-Mery in 1794," *MHM* 35 (1940): 221–40.

32. Edward Felix Jenkins, *Thomas Jenkins, 1670: His Descendants and Allied Families* (Baltimore, 1985), pp. 49–55.

33. "The Maryland Tiernans," *American Catholic Historical Researches* 12 (1895): 189–91.

34. Sherry H. Olson, *Baltimore: The Building of an American City* (Baltimore, 1980), pp. 26–31; Walter Charlton Hartridge, "The Refugees from the Island of St. Domingo in Maryland," *MHM* 28 (1943): 103–22.

35. J. Thomas Scharf, *History of Baltimore City and County* (Philadelphia, 1881), pp. 573–89.

36. Terry D. Bilhartz, *Urban Religion and the Second Great Awakening: Church and Society in Early National Baltimore* (Rutherford, N.J., 1986), pp. 19–20, 149.

37. Riordan, *Cathedral Records*, p. 109.

38. Bilhartz, *Urban Religion*, pp. 22–25. Unskilled workers would decrease from 51 percent in 1800 to 39 percent in 1830 while white-collar members would increase from 17 percent to 28 percent (p. 27).

39. In addition to Riordan, *Catholic Records*, other good histories of the first cathedral are Cornelius M. Cuyler, "The Baltimore Cathedral: A Historical and Descriptive Sketch," the original study for a condensed *The Baltimore Cathedral* (Baltimore, 1951), in the SAB; John W. Bowen, "A History of the Baltimore Cathedral to 1876" (master's thesis, Catholic University of America, 1963).

40. John S. Ezell, "The Church Took a Chance," *MHM* 43 (1948): 266–79.

41. William D. Hoyt, Jr., "Land for a Cathedral: Baltimore, 1806–1817," *CHR* 36 (1951): 441–45.

42. For the correspondence between Carroll and Latrobe see Riordan, *Cathedral Records*, pp. 30–44. The nineteen sketches of Latrobe in the AAB were in 1975 valued at $27,000 each.

43. Cathedral Trustees Minutes, 1: 7, January 9, 1796.

44. Ibid., pp. 14–15, September 4, 1797.

45. Ibid., pp. 41, November 8, 1805.

46. *Sesquicentennial: St. Patrick's Parish* (Baltimore, 1942), pp. 11–25, 45–63.

47. Ibid., pp. 25–31, 98–103.

48. *JCP*, 3: 43, Carroll to Maréchal, Baltimore, February 7, 1808.

49. *Sesquicentennial: St. Patrick's*, p. 103.

50. Scharf, *Baltimore City and County*, p. 540n.

51. *JCP*, 2: 13–20.

52. Vincent J. Fecher, *A Study of the Movement for German National Parishes in Philadelphia and Baltimore (1787–1802)* (Rome, 1955), pp. 35–60.

53. Actually Carroll sent two letters to Rome of the same tenor by different routes. The second was stronger. *JCP*, 2: 263–65, 270–73, Carroll to Brancadoro, Baltimore, February 9, 1799, and August 20, 1799.

54. Fecher, *German Parishes*, pp. 61–65; *JCP*, 2: 255–56, 268–69, Memorandum and Reuter's faculties.

55. APF, Congressi 3: 104r–15v, Baltimore trustees to Propaganda, October 11, 1799, and Philadelphia trustees to Propaganda, October 30, 1799.

56. Bilhartz, *Urban Religion*, pp. 49–50.

57. Ibid., pp. 124–25; Fecher, *German Parishes*, pp. 83–87; Shea, *History*, 2: 242–25.

58. *JCP*, 3: 273, Carroll to Fenwick, Washington, June 11, 1814.

59. Bilhartz, *Urban Religion*, p. 135.

60. Cathedral Trustees Minutes, passim. As pewholders women were sometimes listed among the electors.

61. Whereas pews in the old cathedral in 1797 rented for $6.00, $5.00, and $4.00 a year, a quarterly rent of $40.00, $28.00, and $16.00 would be set in 1820 for pews in the new cathedral (ibid., 1: 12, 167–71).

62. *JCP*, 2: 3.

63. Constance McLaughlin Green, *Washington: Village and Capital, 1800–1878* (Princeton, N.J., 1962), p. 5.

64. Margaret Brent Downing, "The Earliest Proprietors of Capitol Hill," *Records of the Columbia Historical Society* 21 (1918): 1–23.

65. Geiger, *Daniel Carroll*, pp. 166–80.

66. Laurence J. Kelly, *History of Holy Trinity Parish, Washington, D.C., 1795–1945* (Baltimore, n.d.), pp. 13–14, 17–19.

67. *JCP*, 2: 122, Carroll to Caffry, n.p., July 15, 1794.

68. Green, *Washington: Village and Capital*, pp. 37–38.

69. Parishes in the United States, said the Propaganda, were conferred *"ad nutum ordinarii"* and not *"ad titulum"* as were canonical parishes in Europe. Kenneally, *Calendar*, 3: 220, no. 1340.

70. Thomas J. Stanton, *A Century of Growth, Or the History of the Catholic Church in Western Maryland* (2 vols., Baltimore, 1900), 2: 132.

71. 2-F-2, Cahill to Carroll, Hagerstown, January 24, 1795, which Stanton, *Century of Growth*, 1: 10, incorrectly dates as 1791.

72. Rita Clark Hutzell, *Mother of Churches: A History of St. Mary's Church, Hagerstown, Maryland* (n.p., 1976), pp. 8–14.

73. *USCM* 2 (1844): 673–76.

74. Stanton, *Century of Growth*, 2: 58–59.

75. Richard Shaw, *John Dubois: Founding Father* (New York, 1983), pp. 17–36.

76. 8A-G-3, Dubois to Carroll, Frederick Town, March 14, 1807.

77. J. Thomas Scharf, *History of Western Maryland* (Philadelphia, 1882), pp. 730–31; 8A-G-4, Dubois to Carroll, Frederick Town, July 17, 1807.

78. 11-O-3, Trustees to Carroll, Taneytown, February 6, 1797.

79. Scharf, *Western Maryland*, p. 937.

80. Clarence V. Joerndt, *St. Ignatius, Hickory, and Its Missions* (Baltimore, [1972]), pp. 52–72.

81. Kauffman, *Saint Sulpice*, pp. 44–45; Ruane, *St. Sulpice*, pp. 36–39.

82. Born 1770 in the Netherlands, where his father was the Russian ambassador, Gallitzin eventually converted to the Catholic faith of his mother, the Countess Amalie von Schmettau. He came to America as a tourist and was immediately drawn to the Sulpicians.

83. Ruane, *St. Sulpice*, pp. 40–43.

84. 7-O-2, Sewall to Carroll, St. Thomas Manor, January 30, 1797.

85. *JCP*, 2: 189, Carroll to Plowden, Baltimore, September 24, 1796.

86. Annabelle M. Melville, *Louis William DuBourg: Bishop of Louisiana and the Floridas, Bishop of Montauban, and Archbishop of Besançon, 1766–1833* (2 vols., Chicago, 1986), 1: 1–74; Melville, *John Carroll*, pp. 144–46.

87. Kauffman, *Saint Sulpice*, pp. 45–47; Ruane, *St. Sulpice*, pp. 81–85.

88. Ruane, *St. Sulpice*, pp. 105–7.

89. Ibid., p. 107, quoting a letter of October 16, 1800.

90. *JCP*, 2: 318, Carroll to Plowden, Washington, September 3, 1800.

91. 7-O-5, Sewall to Carroll, St. Thomas Manor, December 15, 1800.

92. *JCP*, 2: 359 61, Carroll to Trustees of the Clergy, n.p., September 1, 1801.

93. Carey, *People, Priests, and Prelates*, p. 71.

94. Hughes, *Documents*, 2: 785–89. Hughes surmises that the second was William Pasquet, who had no previous connections with the Jesuits.

95. Ibid., pp. 708–12.

96. *JCP*, 2: 343, Carroll to Emery, n.p., January 6, 1801.

97. Melville, *DuBourg*, 1: 92–122; Ruane, *St. Sulpice*, pp. 120–34.

98. *JCP*, 3: 37, Carroll to Plowden, Baltimore, January 10, 1808.

99. Daley, *Georgetown*, pp. 112–15; Melville, *John Carroll*, pp. 152–55.

100. Hughes, *Documents*, 2: 778–80, 813–19.

101. *JCP*, 2: 463–65, Carroll to Stone (1805).

102. Robert Emmett Curran, *American Jesuit Spirituality: The Maryland Tradition, 1634–1900* (New York, 1988), p. 38.

103. *JCP*, 2: 489–91.

104. Hughes, *Documents*, 2: 826–27.

105. 6-D-4, Pasquet to Carroll, Baltimore, September 9, 1805.

106. Gerald Fogarty, Joseph Durkin, and R. Emmett Curran, *The Maryland Jesuits, 1634–1833* (Baltimore, 1976), pp. 47–49.

107. Hughes, *Documents*, 2: 978: *JCP*, 3: 74–75, Carroll to Strickland, Baltimore, December 8, 1808.

108. Sarah M. Brownson, *Demetrius Augustine Gallitzin, Prince and Priest* (New York, 1873), p. 109.

109. Sp. A-F-1, Cahill to Carroll, Winchester, January 21, 1796.

110. *JCP*, 2: 166–67, 183–84, Carroll to Cahill, n.p., March 2 and June 11, 1796.

111. Ibid., p. 415, notation of June 4, 1803.

112. Sp. A-A-5, Ashton to Carroll, White Marsh, July 2, 1801.

113. Sp. A-B-1, same to same, Port Tobacco, January 10, 1806.

114. Sp. A-B-2, same to same, Port Tobacco, November 24, 1806; Hughes, *Documents*, 2: 705–19.

115. 5-P-9 and 5-Q-9, Neale to Carroll, Georgetown, August 25 and September 8, 1809.

116. Sp. A-B-10, Ashton to Carroll, Port Tobacco, November 20, 1809.

117. 5-P-1, Neale to Carroll, Philadelphia, August 12, 1795.

118. *JCP*, 2: 258, Carroll to Gallagher, Baltimore, January 23, 1799.

119. Ibid., 3: 29, Carroll to Neale, n.p., June 20, 1807[?]. The year is undoubtedly incorrect. On June 3, 1807, Edward Lynah wrote from Charleston to express the hope to Carroll that Gallagher would "continue to persevere in a virtuous & pious life" (5-B-13). The most likely year is 1801.

120. *JCP*, 2: 354–55, Carroll to Gallagher, Baltimore, July 14, 1801; 10-M-6, Gallagher to Carroll, Charleston, August 19, 1801.

121. 5-B-12 and 13, Lynah to Carroll, Charleston, October 23, 1806, and June 3, 1807.

122. APF, Congressi 5: 147r–48r, 618r–19r, Carroll to Gallagher, Baltimore, May 30, 1809, and August 23, 1808.

123. Though Guilday, *John Carroll*, p. 738, maintains that in 1805 began a schism that "lasted during the remainder of Carroll's episcopate," there was never a schism strictly speaking in Charleston in the Carroll years.

124. *JCP*, 2: 377, Carroll to Brancadoro, Baltimore, February 10, 1802.

125. Dolan, *American Catholic Experience*, p. 123. One may question, however, how many of the "many of his contemporaries . . . were eager to fashion a uniquely American Roman Catholic Church" (p. 124).

Chapter 2. Metropolitan

1. *JCP*, 2: 26–33, Carroll to Antonelli, Baltimore, April 23, 1792.

2. Guilday, *John Carroll*, pp. 569–71.

3. Ibid., pp. 572–73.

4. Garrett Sweeney, "The 'Wound in the Right Foot': Unhealed?", in Adrian Hastings, ed., *Bishops and Writers: Aspects of the Evolution of Modern English Catholicism* (Wheathampstead, Hertfordshire, 1977), pp. 207–19, especially pp. 215–17. Outside the Papal States, and excepting the United States, in only twenty-four dioceses (in the Russian territories, Greece, and Albania) were bishops appointed by Rome in 1829. Of the

646 ordinaries of the Latin church in 1829, 555 owed their appointments to the state and the rest, minus those mentioned above, to cathedral chapters or their equivalents. By 1918 nearly 700 dioceses would be subject to appointment by Rome with only 170 left to state patronage (ibid., pp. 218–19, 228). See also Robert F. Trisco, "An American Anomaly: Bishops without Canons," *Chicago Studies* 9 (1970): 143–57.

5. *JCP*, 2: 33, Carroll to Antonelli, Baltimore, April 23, 1792.

6. Ibid., pp. 95–96, same to same, Baltimore, January 17, 1793.

7. 1-K-5, Barry to Carroll, Washington, June 10, 1807.

8. According to the national census, in the period 1790–1810 St. Mary's County lost 25 percent of its white population. In the decade 1800–1810 Charles and Prince George's Counties experienced comparable losses.

9. Mary Ramona Mattingly, *The Catholic Church on the Kentucky Frontier (1785–1812)* (Washington, D.C., 1936), pp. 1–39; Clyde F. Crews, *An American Holy Land: A History of the Archdiocese of Louisville* (Wilmington, Del., 1987), pp. 27ff.

10. Melville, *DuBourg*, 1: 186–87, 259ff.

11. Joseph G. Daley, "Archbishop John Carroll and the Virgin Islands," *CHR* 53 (1967): 305–27; *JCP*, 2: 449–52, 455–56.

12. Guilday, *John Carroll*, pp. 579–81.

13. APF, Atti di Cong. Particolari 145: 106r–12r, Carroll to Di Pietro, Baltimore, November 23, 1806, and June 17, 1807; AAB, Letterbook III, pp. 71–75.

14. 3-H-10, Egan to Carroll, Philadelphia, September 14, 1810.

15. Joseph Bernard Code, *Dictionary of the American Hierarchy (1789–1964)* (New York, 1965).

16. 11-I-2, "Decisions of the Arch Bishop & Bishops of the Ecclesiastical Province established in the United States, in Council assembled in Baltimore"; *JCP*, 3: 130–35.

17. *JCP*, 3: 128–30; Pastoral of November 15, 1810, and pp. 35–39, Letter and report to Pius VII, n.p., November 17, 1810.

18. The absence of correspondence is indicated in Kenneally, *Calendar*.

19. *JCP*, 3: 207–8, Bishops to Pius VII (1813).

20. Ibid., p. 67, Carroll to Kohlmann, Baltimore, August 15, 1808.

21. Ibid., pp. 230–32, Carroll to Grassi, Washington, September 24, 1813.

22. Guilday, *John Carroll*, pp. 658–74.

23. Melville, *DuBourg*, 1: 281–348.

24. Daley, "Carroll and the Virgin Islands," pp. 318–27.

25. 11-H-5, undated subscription list.

26. AAB, Letterbook III, p. 105, Carroll to Tiernan and Walsh, Baltimore, July 6, 1813.

27. Richard C. Madden, "Joseph-Pierre Picot de Limoelan de Clorivière (1768–1826)" (master's thesis, Catholic University of America, 1938).

28. 5-N-8, Neale to Carroll, Mount Carmel, September 18, 1810.

29. Hughes, *Documents*, 2: 969–95.

30. *JCP*, 3: 247, Carroll to Plowden (December 12, 1813).

31. 6-U-8, Bitouzey to Carroll, n.p., n.d.

32. *JCP*, pp. 235–36, Carroll to Grassi, Baltimore, October 16, 1813.

33. Ibid., pp. 254–56, Carroll to Stone, Baltimore, January 31, 1814.

34. Ibid., pp. 308–11, Carroll to Grassi, Baltimore, December 10–27, 1814.

35. Robert Emmett Curran, "From Saints to Secessionists," in Nelson H. Minnich

et al., eds., *Studies in Catholic History in Honor of John Tracy Ellis* (Wilmington, Del., 1985), pp. 249–51.

36. *JCP*, 3: 323–26, Carroll to Grassi, Baltimore, February 21, 1815.

37. Ibid., p. 338, Carroll to Plowden, n.p., June 25, 1815.

38. Ibid., p. 335, Carroll to Grassi, Baltimore, May 19, 1815.

39. Ruane, *St. Sulpice*, pp. 158–73; Shaw, *Dubois*, pp. 37–42.

40. Mary M. Meline and Edward F. X. McSweeny, *The Story of the Mountain: Mount St. Mary's College and Seminary, Emmitsburg, Maryland* (2 vols., Emmittsburg, Md., 1911) 1: 17–58.

41. Barbara Misner, "A Comparative Social Study of the Members and Apostolates of the First Eight Permanent Communities of Women Religious within the Original Boundaries of the United States, 1790–1850" (doctoral dissertation, Catholic University of America, 1980), pp. 14–17; Charles Warren Currier, *Carmel in America* (Baltimore, 1890), pp. 95ff.

42. Misner, "Comparative Study of Women Religious," pp. 18–23; Eleanore C. Sullivan, *Georgetown Visitation since 1799* (n.p., 1975), pp. 48–52.

43. Melville, *DuBourg*, 1: 147ff; Joseph I. Dirvin, *Mrs. Seton: Foundress of the American Sisters of Charity* (New York, 1962), p. 221.

44. Annabelle M. Melville, *Elizabeth Bayley Seton* (New York, 1951), pp. 129–83.

45. Shaw, *Dubois*, pp. 43–58.

46. *JCP*, 3: 84, Carroll to his sisters, Baltimore, April 20, 1809.

47. Ibid., p. 295, Carroll to David, n.p., September 17, 1809.

48. [Sister John Mary Crumlish], *1809–1859* (Emmitsburg, Md., 1959), pp. 1–9; Dirvin, *Mrs. Seton*, pp. 350–54.

49. *Heads of Families at the First Census of the United States Taken in the Year 1790: Maryland* (Washington, D.C., 1907). The four other Catholics who owned 150 or more slaves were Notley Young, the archbishop's brother-in-law, with 265, Bennett Darnall with 157, Richard Darnall with 153, and Thomas Sim Lee with 150. Other Catholics who owned more than 100 slaves were Henry Rozer and George Digges.

50. Melville, *John Carroll*, pp. 266–68.

51. Whitman H. Ridgeway, *Community Leadership in Maryland, 1790–1840: A Comparative Analysis of Power in Society* (Chapel Hill, N.C., 1979), pp. 214–40.

52. *JCP*, 3: 460.

53. Ellis, *Documents*, 1: 174–75.

54. *JCP*, 3: 70, Carroll to Troy, Washington, September 28, 1808.

55. Ibid., 2: 297–308, Discourse of February 22, 1800.

56. Bilhartz, *Urban Religion*, p. 122.

57. William Gribbin, *The Churches Militant: The War of 1812 and American Religion* (New Haven, 1973), p. 110.

58. Bilhartz, *Urban Religion*, pp. 41, 100ff.

59. Ibid., p. 59; Melville, *John Carroll*, pp. 151–52; J. Thomas Scharf, *Chronicles of Baltimore* (Baltimore, 1874), pp. 277, 291; Scharf, *Baltimore City and County*, pp. 594–95, 658.

60. *JCP*, 3: 200, Carroll to Fenwick, n.p., September 23, 1812.

61. Ibid., p. 317, Carroll to Plowden, Washington, September 3, 1800.

62. Stuart C. Sherman, "The Library Company of Baltimore," *MHM* 39 (1944): 6–24.

63. Joseph T. Durkin, *William Matthews: Priest and Citizen* (New York, 1963), pp. 57–77.

64. Bilhartz, *Urban Religion*, pp. 102; AUND, Baltimore papers, a printed brochure.

65. Bilhartz, *Urban Religion*, pp. 100–102; Olson, *Baltimore*, pp. 61–66.

66. Bilhartz, *Urban Religion*, pp. 83–99, 117–22.

67. Ibid., p. 122; Melville, *DuBourg*, 1: 246–52.

68. Melville, *DuBourg*, 1: 250.

69. AAB, "Records of Confraternities." This notebook is mostly a roster of members, some recorded as late as the 1840s. "Coloured" with first names only, presumably slaves, predominated at the beginning, but increasingly well-to-do whites enrolled.

70. Ann Taves, *The Household of Faith: Roman Catholic Devotions in Mid-Nineteenth-Century America* (Notre Dame, Ind., 1986), p. 16.

71. Ibid., pp. 14–16, 72–73, 165–66.

72. Bilhartz, *Urban Religion*, p. 66.

73. Ibid., pp. 70, 94.

74. *JCP*, 3: 152–53, Carroll to Fenwick, Washington, June 25, 1811.

75. Bilhartz, *Urban Religion*, pp. 54–56.

76. *JCP*, 3: 95, Carroll to Garnier, Baltimore, August 31, 1809.

77. Kauffman, *Saint Sulpice*, pp. xiv, 57–63.

78. *JCP*, 3: 279–83, Pastoral of July 7, 1814.

79. Guilday, *John Carroll*, p. 829, quoting Robert Walsh.

80. *JCP*, 3: 22, Carroll to Seton, Baltimore, May 23, 1807.

81. Ibid., p. 318, Carroll to Plowden, n.p., January 5, 1815.

82. Ibid., pp. 338–39, same to same, n.p., June 25/July 24, 1815.

83. 5-A-5, Litta to Carroll, Rome, March 11, 1815.

84. *JCP*, 3: 256–57, Carroll to Plowden, Baltimore, February 3, 1814.

85. Ibid., p. 339, same to same, n.p., June 25/July 24, 1815.

86. Ibid., p. 313, Carroll to Troy, n.p., n.d.

87. Ibid., p. 345, Carroll to Litta, July 17 [20?], 1815.

88. Ibid., pp. 291–92, Carroll to bishops and administrators, Baltimore, August 23, 1814.

89. Ibid., pp. 301–304, Carroll to Litta, Baltimore, November 28, 1814/January 5, 1815.

90. Melville, *DuBourg*, 1: 351.

91. Quoted in *CM*, December 25, 1858.

Chapter 3. That Pernicious System

1. Quoted in M. Bernetta Brislen, "The Episcopacy of Leonard Neale, Second Archbishop of Baltimore," *HRS* 34 (1945): 54.

2. Ibid., pp. 20–47; Shea, *History*, 3: 25–26.

3. Kenneally, *Calendar*, 3: 232, no. 1418.

4. 21-P-8, Neale to Maréchal, Georgetown, January 24, 1817.

5. Brislen, "Leonard Neale," p. 56.

6. 16-G-2, Edelen to Maréchal, Newton, August 23, 1817.

7. For these changes and the trustee controversy they provoked see Peter Guilday,

The Catholic Church in Virginia, 1815–1822 (New York, 1924), pp. 1–62; Guilday, *England*, 1: 164–207; Brislen, "Leonard Neale," pp. 59–93.

8. APF, Congressi 5: 36r–37r, Cosslett to Neale, Charleston, February 5, 1816.

9. 12-R-2, Neale to Lucas, Georgetown, March 6, 1817 (copy). The underscoring for emphasis was Neale's.

10. 12-U-8, *Letter Addressed to the Most Reverend Leonard Neale, Archbishop of Baltimore* (Norfolk, [1816]); Guilday, *Virginia*, pp. 28–32.

11. Thomas T. McAvoy, *A History of the Catholic Church in the United States* (Notre Dame, Ind., 1969), p. 95. See also Carey, *People, Priests, and Prelates*, pp. 128, 179–89.

12. Guilday, *Virginia*, pp. 35–38; Brislen, "Leonard Neale," pp. 101–3.

13. 12-Q-3, Litta to Neale, Rome, October 5, 1816.

14. Quoted in Shea, *History*, 3: 33–34.

15. APF, Congressi 5: 192r–99v, Neale to Litta, Georgetown, March 12, 1817.

16. Kenneally, *Calendar*, 1: 77–78, nos. 467–468, 470–72.

17. 12-Y-6, Lucas to Neale, Norfolk, May 4, 1817.

18. APF, Congressi 3: 533r–36v; Guilday, *Virginia*, pp. 45–53.

19. APF, Congressi 3: 580r–87v.

20. 12-S-2, Pius VII to Neale, Rome, July 9, 1817.

21. 12-Q-6, Litta to Neale, Rome, June 11, 1817.

22. Cathedral Trustee Minutes, 1: 87ff; Riordan, *Cathedral Records*, pp. 47–48, 99.

23. Hughes, *Documents* 2: 952–53.

24. Ibid., pp. 949–50.

25. Ibid., pp. 960–62; 22-I-19, a list of missions.

26. All of the above are taken from the Neale-Grassi agreement of 1816 and in the order given. The Carmelite monastery is also listed as a mission of St. Thomas Manor. There were actually two or three other small churches on the Eastern Shore that were not mentioned.

27. Martinsburg and Shepherdstown in (West) Virginia are listed as missions of Frederick. Arnold's Settlement is not listed as such but is probably the "Batto-Church" coupled with Cumberland. Two unidentified missions, Hardy's and Hawack, were possibly in Virginia. They are included with Liberty Town "et aliae."

28. Hughes, *Documents*, 2: 886–87.

29. Joerndt, *St. Ignatius*, pp. 84–86.

30. 12A-T-2, Malevé to Rev. Father, Boonsboro, June 29, 1816.

31. 12A-L-6, Redmond to Neale, Georgetown College, November 18, 1816; 20-B-2, Redmond to Maréchal, Rockville, December 8, 1817.

32. Brislen, "Leonard Neale," pp. 43–44; Sullivan, *Georgetown Visitation*, pp. 53–54.

33. Dirvin, *Mrs. Seton*, pp. 389, 398.

34. Neale's body would later be moved to the crypt of the convent chapel completed in 1820, where it still reposes. The sisters turned down a request of the cathedral trustees of Baltimore that his body be transferred to the new cathedral completed in 1821.

35. Quoted in Shea, *History*, 3: 37–38.

36. Carey, *People, Priests and Prelates*, p. x.

37. Ibid., pp. 154–72; Patrick Carey, "The Laity's Understanding of the Trustee System, 1785–1855," *CHR* 64 (1978): 357–76.

38. In a report to Rome in 1818, Archbishop Maréchal claimed: "For a number of

years he [Carroll] defended the system. However so many dissensions and schisms resulted from it, that shortly before he died he regretted very much that he had ever permitted it" (Ellis, *Documents*, 1: 216). Neale, who knew the mind of Carroll better, never made such a claim. In his last year, in fact, Carroll said that he did not consider the "refractory opposition" of the "Jacobinised" trustees of St. John's "of much moment, or at all formidable in itself, if it be met with calm and dignified fortitude" (*JCP*, 3: 273).

39. 12-A-12, Lynah to Neale, Charleston, October 7, 1816.

40. APF, Congressi 5: 261r–70r, Lynah to Litta, Charleston, May 4, 1819.

41. Olson, *Baltimore*, pp. 54–58 and passim.

Chapter 4. Chosen for Trials

1. Ronin John Murtha, "The Life of the Most Reverend Ambrose Maréchal: Third Archbishop of Baltimore, 1768–1829" (doctoral dissertation, Catholic University of America, 1965), pp. 1–10.

2. 14-U-5, Concanen to Maréchal, Naples, June 15, 1810.

3. Shea, *History*, 3: 41–42.

4. "Diary of Archbishop Maréchal, 1815–1825," *RACHSP* 11 (1900): 417–54, from two small notebooks in the AUND, hereafter "Maréchal Diary" with pages from the published version.

5. Ibid., p. 425.

6. Ibid., pp. 430, 432.

7. 18-N-3 and 5, Malevé to Maréchal, Frederick Town, January 9, April 23, 1818.

8. "Archbishop Maréchal's Report to the Propaganda, October 15, 1818," in Ellis, *Documents*, 1: 202–20.

9. Gerald Shaughnessy, *Has the Immigrant Kept the Faith?* (New York, 1925), still the most reliable source historically for numbers, gives 195,000 for 1820 (p. 73).

10. Maréchal said fifty-two priests, of whom twelve Americans and eleven Irish, but the actual list with the nationalities indicated beside each name shows otherwise. See Edward I. Devitt, "The Clergy List of 1819, Diocese of Baltimore," *RACHSP* 22 (1911): 238–67, and Hughes, *Documents*, 2: 956–57.

11. APF, Congressi 5: 447r–80r, Petition of the vestrymen to Pius VII, May 13, 1818 (printed).

12. For the priest and trustee problems of Norfolk and Charleston under Maréchal, see Murtha, "Maréchal," pp. 50–69; Guilday, *Virginia*, pp. 63–115; and Guilday, *England*, 1: 208–82.

13. APF, Lettere 298: 540r–42r, Litta to Oliveira Fernandez, Rome, September 20, 1817.

14. Guilday, *Virginia*, pp. 93–101.

15. APF, Cong. Generali 921: 346r–52v, Petition of January 4, 1819, and Carbry to Hayes, New York, February 17, 1819.

16. 22B-L-1, *Pastoral Letter . . . of Archbishop Maréchal to the Congregation of Norfolk* (Baltimore, 1820).

17. Sp. C-K-2, Jefferson to Maréchal, Monticello, January 17, 1820.

18. APF, Cong. Generali 921: 444r–45v, Trustees to Pius VII, Philadelphia, May 1, 1819.

19. Code, *Dictionary*, pp. 49, 84, 151.

20. APF, Cong. Generali 926: 102r–11r, Maréchal to Fontana, Baltimore, October 16, 1820.

21. Guilday, *Virginia*, p. 134.

22. Ibid., pp. 145–47; Murtha, "Maréchal," pp. 219–24.

23. SAB, Record Group 1, Box 1A, Diary of Louis Regis Deluol (hereafter Deluol diary), October 22, 1821.

24. Hughes, *Documents*, 2: 891–92, 899–901.

25. 17-W-42, Kohlmann to Maréchal, Georgetown College, March 13, 1820.

26. Hughes, *Documents*, 1: 455–58.

27. Ibid., 2: 903–5.

28. Murtha, "Maréchal," pp. 131–37; Melville, *DuBourg*, 2: 644–77.

29. 16-A-3, DuBourg to Maréchal, Bordeaux, October 14, 1816.

30. Shaw, *Dubois*, pp. 82–83; Ruane, *St. Sulpice*, pp. 175–85.

31. 18-C-4, Latrobe to Latrobe, Baltimore, October 4, 1818.

32. Murtha, "Maréchal," p. 74. See also Riordan, *Cathedral Records*, pp. 50–51.

33. Murtha, "Maréchal," pp. 224, 233–34. The first doctorates were conferred on James Whitfield, Edward Damphoux, and Louis Deluol, Bruté apparently refusing the honor.

34. APF, Congressi 7: 167r–70v.

35. See Shaughnessy, *Immigrant*, p. 72, who estimates 195,000 for 1820.

36. APF, Cong. Generali 927: 341r–52v.

37. APF, Congressi 7: 745r–52v, Maréchal to Consalvi, Rome, June 4, 1822.

38. APF, Acta 185: 210(a)–230(b).

39. Murtha, "Maréchal," pp. 231–32.

40. 22-B-9, Pius VII to Maréchal, suffragans, trustees, and faithful, Rome, August 24, 1822; Carey, *People, Priests, and Prelates*, pp. 258–61.

41. 22-M-6, Consalvi to Maréchal, Rome, July 27, 1822.

42. For the Roman phase of the Jesuit controversy, see Murtha, "Maréchal," pp. 257–64; Hughes, *Documents*, 1: 403–82; 2: 1031–68.

43. For the final phase of the controversy, see Murtha, "Maréchal," pp. 268–87; Hughes, *Documents*, 1: 483–582, 2: 1069–1103.

44. 22B-V-2, Neale to Maréchal, Mount Carmel, December 23, 1822.

45. 22B-W-2, Fesch to Maréchal, Rome, August 27, 1823.

46. Hughes, *Documents*, 2: 1071–77.

47. 16-F-27 and 28, Dzierozynski to Maréchal, Georgetown College, October 12, 15, 1826.

48. 16-F-30, same to same, Georgetown College, September 28, 1827.

49. 20-N-20, Sewall to Maréchal, n.p., April 21, 1824. Maréchal had asked for English Jesuits for Georgetown College.

50. R. Emmett Curran, "From Mission to Province," in *The Maryland Jesuits, 1634–1833* (Baltimore, 1976), pp. 53–58.

51. Joerndt, St. Ignatius, pp. 92–95.

52. Patrick J. Dignan, *A History of Legal Incorporation of Catholic Church Property in the United States, 1784–1932* (Washington, D.C., 1933), p. 119; Cathedral Trustee Minutes, 1: 184–93.

53. Hughes, *Documents*, 1: 509–10.

54. *Sesquicentennial: St. Patrick's*, pp. 104–105.

55. 19-B-19, Matthews to Maréchal, Washington, February 1, 1825.

56. 15-Q-5, De Vos to Maréchal, Rockville, January 22, 1820.

57. For the Philadelphia troubles see James F. Connelly, ed., *The History of the Archdiocese of Philadelphia* (Philadelphia, 1976), pp. 83–104; Francis E. Tourscher, *The Hogan Schism and Trustee Problems in St. Mary's Church, Philadelphia, 1820–1829* (Philadelphia, 1930).

58. For the New York troubles see Kenneally, *Calendar*, 5: 273–82, nos. 1608–1664; Florence D. Cohalan, *A Popular History of the Archdiocese of New York* (Yonkers, N.Y., 1983), pp. 29–37.

59. Guilday, *England*, 1: 11–16, 299–379, 453–516; A good treatment of England's democratic ideas is Patrick Carey, *An Immigrant Bishop: John England's Adaptation of Irish Catholicism to American Republicanism* (Yonkers, N.Y., 1982).

60. Archives of the English College, Maréchal to Gradwell, Baltimore, July 14, 1825.

61. 16-J-5, England to Maréchal, Charleston, March 1, 1821.

62. Guilday, *England*, 2: 98–107.

63. Ibid., 1: 344.

64. 21A-U-1, Conc[ilium] Prov[inciale].

65. Melville, *DuBourg*, 2: 751–53.

66. Murtha, "Maréchal," pp. 149–53.

67. Cheverus in 1826 was named archbishop of Bordeaux, DuBourg in 1833 archbishop of Besançon. He died that same year. Melville, *DuBourg*, 2: 919–62.

68. Ruane, *St. Sulpice*, pp. 184–85; Kauffman, *Saint Sulpice*, pp. 82–84.

69. "The First Generation of American-born Sulpicians," *Whence*, Autumn 1982, p. 17.

70. Ruane, *St. Sulpice*, pp. 189–200.

71. Deluol diary, November 15, 1823.

72. Ibid., June 10, 1823, December 13, 1826.

73. Daley, *Georgetown*, pp. 203–18.

74. Quoted in Mary Xavier Maloney, "The Catholic Church in the District of Columbia (Earlier Period: 1790–1866)" (master's thesis, Catholic University of America, 1938), p. 74.

75. Daley, *Georgetown*, pp. 195–97; 17-P-3, Keily to Maréchal, Washington, December, 1827.

76. 20-N-8, Seton to Maréchal, n.p., January 1, 1819.

77. Crumlish, *1809–1959*, pp. 12–14.

78. 18-N-3, Malevé to Maréchal, Frederick Town, January 9, 1819. The map showed that Frederick Town had 100 Catholic families, Turkey Foot 40, Hagerstown 30, Fifteen Mile Creek 10, Sinking Creek 10, Cumberland 8, and Maryland Tract "200 Peoples." No numbers were given for Carroll Manor and Liberty, and the single digit for Hancock is illegible. The map shows also seven churches attended by Malevé in Jefferson and Berkeley Counties in Virginia. The church at Liberty was blessed by Maréchal September 28, 1823 ("Maréchal Diary," p. 440).

79. Stanton, *Century of Growth*, 2: 85–86, maintains that the land was given by a Mr. West, a Protestant, for a church for his slaves. "Maréchal's Diary," p. 440, indicates that the land was given by members of the family of Governor Thomas Sim Lee and the church planned by Messrs. Lee, Horsey, Belt, and Jamison.

80. Joerndt, *St. Ignatius*, pp. 100, 251–56, 267–73.

81. Maloney, "Church in the District," pp. 28–42.

82. "Maréchal Diary," pp. 422, 449.

83. 16-G-8, Edelen to Maréchal, Newton, November 13, 1820.

84. 18-N-3, Malevé to Maréchal, Frederick Town, January 9, 1818.

85. 20-B-14, Redmond to Maréchal, Hagerstown, July 27, 1818.

86. 20-C-27, same to same, Hagerstown, May 22, 1821.

87. 20-C-4, same to same, Hagerstown, August 8, 1820.

88. 21A-B-4 and 5, Edelen to Maréchal, Newtown, June 13, 27, 1819; 22A-M-2, *Faithful Statement of the Correspondence* . . . (Washington, 1819); Shea, History, 3: 54.

89. Ellis, *Documents*, I: 208.

90. 20-O-1, Maréchal to Matthews, Baltimore, March 12, 1824; 19-A-16, 17, and 18, Matthews to Maréchal, Washington, March 19, 27, 31, 1824. The Mattingly cure was followed by a number of such "miracles." Robert Emmett Curran, " 'The Finger of God Is Here': The Advent of the Miraculous in the Nineteenth-Century Catholic Community," *CHR* 73 (1987): 41–61.

91. Deluol diary, February 26, 1824.

92. "Maréchal Diary," passim.

93. Deluol diary, December 6, 8, 1827.

Chapter 5. No Noisy Stirring Course

1. Guilday, *England*, 2: 115–16.

2. Matthew Leo Panczyk, "James Whitfield, Fourth Archbishop of Baltimore, the Episcopal Years: 1828–1834," *RACHSP* 75 (1964): 227–28. This first part of Whitfield's episcopacy, pp. 222–51, will hereafter be designated "Whitfield" 1. The second part, *RACHSP* 76 (1965): 21–53, will be designated "Whitfield" 2.

3. Whitfield's early years are covered in Bosco David Cestello, "James Whitfield, Fourth Archbishop of Baltimore: The Early Years, 1770–1828," *HRS* 45 (1957): 32–78. Whitfield was ordained July 24, 1809, by the bishop of Grenoble.

4. Panczyk, "Whitfield" 1: 248–49.

5. Rosati was also administrator of the vacant see of New Orleans.

6. 23-G-2, Eccleston to Whitfield, Charleston, December 26, 1828.

7. Peter Guilday, *A History of the Councils of Baltimore, 1791–1884* (New York, 1932), pp. 81–99; Thomas F. Casey, *The Sacred Congregation de Propaganda Fide and the Revision of the First Plenary Council of Baltimore* (Rome, 1957).

8. 23-Q-13, Capellari to Whitfield, Rome, October 16, 1830.

9. *Annales de l'association de la propagation de la foi* (hereafter *Annales*) 4 (1830–31): 243.

10. Ibid., pp. 233–42.

11. Ibid., pp. 243–46.

12. 23A-Q-1, undated draft.

13. "Churches, Pious and Charitable Institutions, &c. of Baltimore," *Metropolitan* 1 (1830): 31–33, 63–67.

14. Thomas W. Spalding, *Martin John Spalding: American Churchman* (Washington, D.C., 1973), p. 10.

15. *Annales* 5 (1831–1832): 714–23.

16. Archives of the Leopoldine Society, Whitfield to the Society, March 8, 1832, and March 8, 1833; 23A-Q-3, undated English draft of the first. From 1828 through 1832 the Society for the Propagation of the Faith allocated about 5,500 francs a year for the archdiocese of Baltimore or approximately $5,500 in all. *Annales*, passim.

17. AUND, Baltimore collection, "Priests under Archbishop Whitfield in November 1831 in Maryland, District of Columbia, and Virginia." Of the seventy-two, twenty-seven were native born, nineteen French, sixteen Irish, and the rest Belgian, German, English, Polish, and Italian.

18. Robert K. Judge, "Foundation and First Administration of the Maryland Province," *WL* 88 (1959): 376—79.

19. Hughes, *Documents*, 2: 1104—18.

20. Ibid., pp. 1118—32.

21. Kauffman, *Saint Sulpice*, pp. 116—21.

22. Deluol diary, September 10, 26, 29, October 7, 1829.

23. Panczyk, "Whitfield" I: 244.

24. Meline and McSweeny, *Story of the Mountain*, I: 264—77.

25. John J. Tierney, "St. Charles College: Foundation and Early Years," *MHM* 43 (1948): 294—300.

26. AUND, Baltimore collection, Hickey to Whitfield, Emmitsburg, February 5, 1830.

27. Crumlish, *1809—1959*, pp. 12, 15—25.

28. Sullivan, *Georgetown Visitation*, pp. 79—84.

29. Grace H. Sherwood, *The Oblates' Hundred and One Years* (New York, 1931), pp. 3—11.

30. Ibid., pp. 11—30.

31. Herbermann, *Sulpicians*, p. 235.

32. Archives of the Oblates of Providence, Annals, Volume I and Register. The Annals are in Joubert's hand until September, 1838.

33. George R. Taylor, *The Transportation Revolution, 1815—1860*, (New York, 1951), pp. 3ff.

34. 23-M-3, Marshall to Whitfield, Friends Post Office, September 27, 1831; *USCM* 3 (1844): 673 76.

35. Stanton, *Century of Growth*, I: 244—58, 295—304.

36. Shea, *History*, 3: 422—32.

37. 24-E-8, Dzierozynski to Whitfield, Georgetown, April 8, 1829.

38. Riordan, *Cathedral Records*, pp. 58—60.

39. James Henry Bailey, *A History of the Diocese of Richmond, the Formative Years* (Richmond, 1956), pp. 65, 75—78; 23-J-7, Van Horsigh to Whitfield, Norfolk, November 20, 1832.

40. Olson, *Baltimore*, pp. 86—88.

41. Carl Brent Swisher, *Roger B. Taney* (New York, 1935), pp. 40ff. In 1804, for example, Taney helped to run the lottery for the completion of the first St. John's Church in Frederick. Ibid., p. 49n; Stanton, *Century of Growth*, 2: 66—67.

42. Shea, *History*, 3: 104.

43. Ridgeway, *Community Leadership in Maryland*, pp. 241—320, tabular listings of members of the elites of Baltimore City and Frederick and St. Mary's Counties, which indicate party allegiances.

44. Ibid., pp. 210–11.

45. Olson, *Baltimore*, pp. 77–79.

46. Ibid., pp. 83, 91.

47. Taylor, *Transportation Revolution*, pp. 32ff, 74ff.

48. Katherine A. Harvey, *The Best Dressed Miners: Life and Labor in the Maryland Coal Region, 1835–1910* (Ithaca, N.Y., 1969), pp. 7–8.

49. Purcell to Jameson, July 1, 1831, in Meline and McSweeny, *Story of the Mountain*, I: 256.

50. *U.S. Catholic Miscellany*, August 27, 1831.

51. Stanton, *Century of Growth*, I: 104–110.

52. Currier, *Carmel in America*, pp. 180–94.

53. R. Emmett Curran, " 'Splendid Poverty': Jesuit Slaveholding in Maryland, 1805–1838," in Randall M. Miller and Jon L. Wakelyn, eds., *Catholics in the Old South: Essays on Church and Culture* (Macon, Ga., 1983), pp. 125–41.

54. Ibid., pp. 141–46; Judge, "Foundation of the Maryland Province," pp. 390–401.

55. Penelope Campbell, *Maryland in Africa: The Maryland State Colonization Society, 1831–1857* (Urbana, Ill., 1971), p. 178.

56. Olson, *Baltimore*, p. 96; Campbell, *Maryland in Africa*, pp. 15–38.

57. Swisher, *Taney*, pp. 148–49.

58. Richard K. McMaster, "Bishop Barron and the West African Missions," *HRS* 50 (1964): 83–90.

59. 23A-Q-1, a partial draft of APF, Congressi 10: 428r–32v, Whitfield to Capellari, Baltimore, August 27, 1830.

60. Ray Allen Billington, *The Protestant Crusade, 1800–1860: A Study of the Origins of American Nativism* (New York, 1938), pp. 32–55.

61. Quoted in Mary St. Patrick McConville, *Political Nativism in the State of Maryland* (Washington, D.C., 1928), pp. 94–96.

62. Quoted in *U.S. Catholic Miscellany*, September 3, 1831.

63. Sherwood, *Oblates*, pp. 55–61.

64. Quoted in *U.S. Catholic Miscellany*, July 13, 1833.

65. Billington, *Protestant Crusade*, pp. 68–76.

66. Archives of the Oblates of Providence, Annals, Volume I, October 1834.

67. Deluol diary, May 14, 18, 20, 1835.

68. Frederick Jackson Turner, *The United States, 1830–1850* (New York, 1935), p. 17.

69. Thomas Bevan, *220 Years . . . A History of the Catholic Community in Frederick Valley* (Frederick, Md., 1977), pp. 16–17.

70. In addition to the standard histories of these institutions already cited, much information can be found in the prospectuses published in the *United States Catholic Miscellany* and *Catholic Almanac and Laity's Directory*.

71. Herr and Welles, *Through Other Eyes*, pp. 23–25.

72. 23A-Q-1, undated draft but first part touching events of 1829.

73. Dignan, *Legal Incorporation*, pp. 145–46, 158; *Mode of Tenure: Roman Catholic Church Property in the United States*, a survey by the Legal Department of the NCWC (Washington, D.C., 1941), pp. 7–11, 69–70.

74. AUND, Baltimore collection, "The U. States Catholic Book Society," undated but a page of revision calls for the appointment of active members before October 1829.

75. M. Eulalia Teresa Moffatt, "Charles Constantine Pise (1801–1866)," *HRS* 24 (1931): 64–77. Pise was elected chaplain of the United States Senate in 1832, the only Catholic priest to have ever been so.

76. Richard J. Tommey, "Fielding Lucas, Jr., First Major Catholic Publisher and Bookseller in Baltimore, 1804–1854" (master's thesis in Library Science, Catholic University of America, 1952), pp. 1ff; David Francis Sweeney, "A Survey of Catholic Americana and Catholic Book Publishing in the United States, 1831–1840" (master's thesis in Library Science, Catholic University of America, 1950), pp. 40–47. Though a pewholder in the cathedral Lucas was baptized only on his deathbed.

77. Eugene P. Willging and Herta Hatzfeld, *Catholic Serials of the Nineteenth Century in the United States: A Descriptive Bibliography and Union List*, 2nd Series, Part II, *Maryland and the District of Columbia* (Washington, D.C., 1965), pp. 5–8; see also Joseph H. Meier, "The Official Catholic Directory," CHR 1 (1915): 299–304.

78. Guilday, *England*, 2: 233–35.

79. Hugh J. Nolan, *The Most Reverend Francis Patrick Kenrick: Third Bishop of Philadelphia, 1830–1851* (Washington, D.C., 1948), pp. 102ff.

80. Robert Frederick Trisco, *The Holy See and the Nascent Church in the Middle Western United States, 1826–1850* (Rome, 1962), pp. 27–44 and passim.

81. 23-V-5, Whitfield to England, n.p., December 27, 1831 (copy).

82. Quoted in Panczyk, "Whitfield" 2: 37–38.

83. Shea, *History*, 3: 428.

84. APF, Congressi II: 47r–50v, Kenrick to England, Philadelphia, January 29, 1833.

85. Guilday, *Councils*, pp. 104–111.

86. Guilday, *England*, 2: 260–66.

87. Quoted in Nolan, *Kenrick*, pp. 170–71.

88. Deluol diary, October 29, 1833.

89. Ibid., October 14–19, 1834.

Part II. Introduction

1. George E. Bell, "Emerson and Baltimore: A Biographical Study," *MHM* 65 (1970): 343.

2. Thomas T. McAvoy, "The Formation of the Catholic Minority," in Philip Gleason, ed., *Catholicism in America* (New York, 1970), p. 11, an essay first published in 1948.

3. John Cogley, *Catholic America* (New York, 1973), p. 168.

4. Hugh McLeod, *Religion and the People of Western Europe, 1789–1970* (Oxford, 1981), p. 36.

Chapter 6. Native Born and Newcomers

1. Kenrick to Cullen, quoted in Nolan, *Kenrick*, pp. 171–72.

2. Columba E. Halsey, "The Life of Samuel Eccleston, Fifth Archbishop of Baltimore, 1801–1851," *RACHSP* 76 (1965): 70.

3. Deluol diary, February 4, 1819.

4. Ibid., October 18, 19, 1819.

5. Halsey, "Eccleston," pp. 78–92.

6. Ibid., pp. 93–104.

7. Deluol diary, March 12, 1838.

8. In 1839 Eccleston sent Bishop Anthony Blanc a copy of the catechism he and Damphoux had prepared for corrections, which he had published at his own expense. AUND, New Orleans papers, Eccleston to Blanc, Baltimore, April 8, 1839.

9. *U.S. Catholic Miscellany,* May 27, 1843.

10. Guilday, *Councils,* pp. 112–63; Halsey, "Eccleston," pp. 117–22, 127–28, 131–35, 138–41, 146–49.

11. Deluol diary, October 29–November 1, 1835.

12. Nolan, *Kenrick,* pp. 193ff.

13. Richard Shaw, *Dagger John: The Unquiet Life and Times of Archbishop John Hughes of New York* (New York, 1977), pp. 127–33; 27-M-1, Fransoni to Eccleston, Rome, June 1, 1839.

14. Trisco, *Nascent Church,* pp. 344–84.

15. AUND, New Orleans papers, Eccleston to Blanc, Baltimore, November 10, 1837, April 26, 1838, October 8, December 13, 1842, November 20, 1843.

16. Halsey, "Eccleston," pp. 149–53.

17. Deluol diary, November 3, 1841.

18. Ibid., October 28, 1839, January 13, 1840, December 21, 1840.

19. Meline and McSweeny, *Story of the Mountain,* 1: 362–81.

20. Edward J. Power, *A History of Catholic Higher Education in the United States* (Milwaukee, 1958), p. 276.

21. Owen B. Corrigan, *History of the Catholic Schools in the Archdiocese of Baltimore* (Baltimore, 1924), pp. 63–64; *Catholic Almanac, 1837,* pp. 92–97; *BCR,* May 7, 1937.

22. Sullivan, *Georgetown Visitation,* pp. 86, 91; *CM,* October 5, 1850, May 31, 1851.

23. *USCM* 8 (1849): 478–79.

24. Ridgeway, *Community Leadership,* p. 122. These percentages are probably too low since they do not include those Catholics in the sampling whose religious affiliation the author was unable to discover.

25. Maldwyn Allen Jones, *American Immigration* (Chicago, 1960), p. 94.

26. Kathleen Neils Conzen, "Germans," in *Harvard Encyclopedia of American Ethnic Groups* (Cambridge, Mass., 1980), p. 413.

27. William J. Evitts, *A Matter of Allegiance: Maryland from 1850 to 1861* (Baltimore, 1974), pp. 67–68.

28. Shaughnessy, *Immigrant,* p. 112.

29. Green, *Washington: Village and Capital,* p. 138.

30. The number of Catholics for the archdiocese of Baltimore in the *Metropolitan Catholic Almanac* remained at 100,000 for the last three years of Eccleston's episcopacy but jumped to 120,000 in 1851, as reported in the 1852 *Almanac.*

31. Jean H. Baker, *Ambivalent Americans: The Know-Nothing Party in Maryland* (Baltimore, 1977), p. 18.

32. Ibid., p. 17.

33. David Baird, "Violence Along the Chesapeake and Ohio Canal, 1839," *MHM* 66 (1971): 121–34.

34. Billington, *Protestant Crusade,* pp. 85–141.

35. McConville, *Nativism in Maryland,* pp. 90–94.

36. 27A-L-7, Eccleston to Kenrick, Baltimore, February 20, 1835.

37. Deluol diary, August 18–21, 1839.

38. Joseph G. Mannard, "The 1839 Baltimore Nunnery Riot. An Episode in Jacksonian Nativism and Social Violence," *Maryland Historian* 11 (1980): 13–23.

39. Shea, *History*, 3: 450.

40. Ibid., pp. 457–59; *Religious Cabinet* 1 (1842): 357–58.

41. Billington, *Protestant Crusade*, pp. 220–34; Deluol diary, May 9, 12, 1844.

42. Mannard, "Baltimore Nunnery Riot," p. 22.

43. McConville, *Nativism in Maryland*, pp. 1–9.

44. Ibid., pp. 14–20.

45. *CM*, October 12, 1850.

46. Ibid., May 25, 1850.

47. AAB, Coskery papers, J.P.K. to trustees, Baltimore, "Monday the 12th," 1849.

48. Olson, *Baltimore*, pp. 123–26.

49. *U.S. Catholic Miscellany*, May 13, 1837.

50. Helene, Estelle, and Imogene Philibert, *St. Matthew's of Washington, 1840–1940* (Baltimore, 1940), pp. 14–25.

51. Ibid., pp. 35–41.

52. Deluol diary, December 14, 1839; *U.S. Catholic Miscellany*, January 4, 1840.

53. *U.S. Catholic Miscellany*, May 30, 1840; the church was consecrated by Bishop Chanche November 14, 1841.

54. Michael J. Curley, *The Provincial Story: A History of the Baltimore Province of the Congregation of the Most Holy Redeemer* (New York, 1963), pp. 1–55.

55. Archives of the Leopoldine Society, Eccleston to "each and all," Baltimore, July 26, 1840.

56. Ibid., Eccleston to Milde, Baltimore, November 13, 1841. In the three years 1841–1843 the Society at Lyons sent $30,000 (*Annales*, passim).

57. *Religious Cabinet* 1 (1842): 356–57; *USCM* 2 (1843): 297–304.

58. Archives of the Leopoldine Society, Neumann to Milde, Baltimore, December 6, 1843.

59. John F. Byrne, The *Redemptorist Centenaries* (Philadelphia, 1932), pp. 93–94.

60. Charles L. Boehmer, *History of St. Mary's Church of the Mother of God, Washington, D.C., 1845–1945* (n.p., 1945), pp. 13–18; Curley, Provincial Story, pp. 91–92, 110.

61. Archives of the Leopoldine Society, Neumann to Milde, Baltimore, December 6, 1843.

62. Stanton, *Century of Growth*, 1: 43–52.

63. *The Story of St. Michael the Archangel Church, 1852–1977* (Hackensack, N.J., 1978), p. 8.

64. Byrne, *Redemptorist Centenaries*, pp. 116–17.

65. Curley, *Provincial Story*, pp. 99–100, 113–19.

66. *USCM* 2 (1843): 121–22, 378–79, 636–37; 3 (1844): 673.

67. *Sesquicentennial: St. Patrick's*, p. 73.

68. Ibid., pp. 72–73; Olson, *Baltimore*, p. 118.

69. Paul E. Meyer, *History of St. Mary's Church, Govans* (Baltimore, 1942), pp. 15–27.

70. *USCM* 3 (1844): 673–75.

71. Ibid.; Stanton, *Century of Growth*, 1: 17–22.; *CM*, November 20, 1851.

72. Harvey, *Best Dressed Miners*, pp. 4ff, and frontispiece map.

73. Stanton, *Century of Growth*, 1: 138–43.

74. Deluol diary, May 9, 1837; Brother Fabrician of Jesus, *St. Paul's Church and Parish, Ellicott City, Maryland: Its Origin and Development* (Baltimore, 1910), pp. 20−22. The cornerstone was laid May 9, 1837, and the dedication performed December 13, 1838.

75. *USCM* 4 (1845): 333−34.

76. Joerndt, *St. Ignatius*, pp. 294−307.

77. *USCM* 3 (1844): 742; 4 (1845): 333−34.

78. Edward P. McAdams, *History of Saint Charles Borromeo Parish, Pikesville, Maryland, 1849−1949* (n.p., 1949), pp. 15−23. The cornerstone was laid July 16, 1848, and the dedication performed September 9, 1849.

79. In addition to those already noted, the *Catholic Almanac* before 1851 also listed congregations, presumably with churches, at Keyser's Ridge, Lonaconing, Oldtown, and Pinewood, all in western Maryland.

80. *Religious Cabinet* 1 (1842): 536.

81. Owen B. Corrigan, "Model Country Parish," *RACHSP* 35 (1924): 218−20, 239−41. "It is worthy of remark," Bishop Corrigan writes, "that there is no evidence any time of controversy or conflict between the trustees and the clergy" of the "model" parish of Bryantown (p. 218).

82. Joerndt, *St. Ignatius*, pp. 92−93. 210−11, and passim.

83. *Metropolitan Catholic Almanac, 1851,* pp. 104−6; *CM,* March 8, 1851; Corrigan, *Catholic Schools,* passim.

84. Until 1847 free schools in the archdiocese of Baltimore were included under the title of "Charitable Institutions" in the *Catholic Almanac.*

85. [Sister Dymphna Flynn], *Mother Caroline and the School Sisters of Notre Dame in North America* (2 vols., St. Louis, 1928), 1: 31−33.

86. Ibid., pp. 46−52; Curley, *Provincial Story,* pp. 114−15; Deluol diary, August 30, 1847. Curley's account receives little support in M. Hester Valentine, ed., *The North American Foundations: Letters of Mother M. Theresa Gerhardinger* (Winona, Minn., 1977).

87. Brother Angelus Gabriel, *The Christian Brothers in the United States, 1848−1948* (New York, 1948), pp. 73−80; *USCM* 4 (1845): 660, 662−64.

88. Angelus Gabriel, *Christian Brothers,* pp. 83−84.

89. *USCM* 5 (1846): 686.

90. Riordan, *Cathedral Records,* p. 106. Some dates given by Riordan would seem to be contradicted by the *United States Catholic Magazine,* which indicates that the Metropolitan Temperance Society was founded in 1842 (1 [1842]: 536) and the Catholic Library Association in 1845 (4 [1845]: 63). A number of societies, however, went through one or more reorganizations.

91. Meyer, *St. Mary's Church,* pp. 23−24.

92. Olson, *Baltimore,* pp. 117, 400.

93. Archives of the Leopoldine Society, Neumann to Milde, Baltimore, December 3, 1843.

94. *CM,* November 24, 1877, March 26, 1881, September 1, 1883.

95. *USCM* 3 (1844): 67.

96. Hugh J. Nolan, ed., *Pastoral Letters of the American Hierarchy, 1792−1970* (Huntingdon, Ind., 1971), pp. 100−1, 111−12.

97. SAB, Record Group 26, Box 13, copies of the *Sun,* February 12, 14, 1844.

98. *Metropolitan Catholic Almanac, 1850,* p. 85.

99. Taves, *Household of Faith*, pp. 21–45, 113–33; Dolan, *American Catholic Experience*, pp. 210–14.

100. Nearly all of the Catholic prayer books that were published in the 1840s came from the presses of Fielding Lucas or John Murphy of Baltimore. See Taves, *Household of Faith*, pp. 135–36 and pp. 4–10.

101. Ibid., pp. 89–100.

102. Jay P. Dolan, *Catholic Revivalism: The American Experience, 1830–1900* (Notre Dame, Ind., 1978), pp. 19–21; R. Emmett Curran, "Troubled Nation, Troubled Province, 1833–1880" (unpublished manuscript), pp. 19–22.

103. *Religious Cabinet* 1 (1842): 190, 253–55.

104. *USCM* 3 (1844): 673.

105. 27A-G-1, Piot to Eccleston, Ellicott Mills, February 8, 1848.

106. Curley, *Provincial Story*, pp. 116–17.

107. SAB, Record Group 26, Box 9, a bound volume of some forty tracts, the last published in 1844.

108. Willging and Hatzfeld, *Catholic Serials: Maryland*, pp. 46–50.

109. Among his writings was the first biography of Mother Seton and the first history of the Catholic Church in the United States in the form of a concluding chapter to a translation of Darras' *History of the Catholic Church*.

110. Carl Wittke, *The German Language Press in America* (Lexington, Ky., 1957), pp. 178–79. Willging and Hatzfeld, *Catholic Serials: Maryland*, pp. 3, 29–32.

111. Willging and Hatzfeld, *Catholic Serials: Maryland*, pp. 14–15.

112. *CM*, October 12, 26, November 9, 16, 1850, January 4, 1851.

113. Deluol, who in his diary supplies almost no information on Eccleston's episcopal visitations, notes almost all of these visits. On November 16, 1841, he recorded that a visiting priest had remarked that there was much talk in town about the archbishop's frequent trips to Georgetown.

114. Archives of the Archdiocese of Boston, Eccleston to Fenwick, Baltimore, November 8 (no year is given but the internal evidence indicates 1841).

115. 24-U-10, Fenwick to Eccleston, Boston, December 2, 1841.

116. Deluol diary, July 24, 25, 1843.

117. Ibid., August 24, 1843.

118. APF, Congressi 13: 787r–881, Fornari to Fransoni, Paris, September 27, 1843.

119. Ibid., 13: 894r–95r, Kenrick to Fransoni, Philadelphia, January 25, 1844.

120. Halsey, "Eccleston," pp. 137–38, 141–42.

121. 25-F-17, Kenrick to Eccleston, Philadelphia, October 23, 1846.

122. APF, Congressi 14: 392rv, Kenrick to Fransoni, Philadelphia, December 7, 1846.

123. Ibid., 399r–400v, Eccleston to Fransoni, Baltimore, December 16, 1846.

124. Kauffman, *Saint Sulpice*, pp. 126–27, 132.

125. Sherwood, *Oblates*, pp. 107–109.

126. Deluol diary, October 7, 1847.

127. Sherwood, *Oblates*, pp. 115–21.

128. Joseph B. Code, "Brief Sketch of the Community of the Sisters of Charity (1821–1927)," an appendix to Madame [Helene] de Barbery, *Elizabeth Seton* (New York, 1940), pp. 480–81; Crumlish, *1809–1959*, pp. 55–59.

129. Deluol diary, March 26, 27, April 2, May 9, 1844.

130. *USCM* 6 (1847): 486–92; 7 (1848): 196–200.

131. Code, "Brief Sketch," pp. 467–80; Shaw, *Dagger John*, pp. 209–212.

132. From the Sisters of Charity of New York came also the Sisters of Charity of Halifax in 1855 and the Sisters of Charity of Convent Station in 1859.

133. Code, "Brief Sketch," pp. 480–91; Crumlish, *1809–1959*, pp. 59–73.

134. From the Sisters of Charity of Cincinnati came also the Sisters of Charity of Greensburg.

135. Deluol diary, February 26, 28, 1848.

136. Ibid., September 26, 1848.

137. Ibid., January 1, 1849.

138. Kauffman, *Saint Sulpice*, pp. 126–27; Herbermann, *Sulpicians*, pp. 245–51.

139. Kauffman, *Saint Sulpice*, pp. 127–28.

140. Ibid., pp. 128–29.

141. 24-M-12, Chanche to Eccleston, Natchez, March 14, 1850.

142. Guilday, *Councils*, pp. 154–63.

143. 24-M-14, Chanche to Eccleston, Natchez, April 30, 1851.

144. AUND, New Orleans papers, Purcell to Blanc, [Rome], Low Sunday [April 27, 1851]. "Entre nous," Purcell also wrote, "Deluol tells me alarming things of certain propensities of Abp. Ec[cleston] which I have not breathed here."

145. Ibid., Chanche to Blanc, Natchez, April 30, 1851.

146. AUND, Cincinnati Papers, Kenrick to Purcell, Philadelphia, April 29, 1851; Carriere to Purcell, Vienna, May 15, 1851.

147. APF, Cong. Generali 974: 77r–78r, Kenrick to Fransoni, Philadelphia, May 13, 1851, copy of document dated May 12, 1845, enclosed.

148. AUND, New Orleans papers, Chanche to Blanc, Natchez, June 2, 1851.

149. Halsey, "Eccleston," pp. 85–86.

Chapter 7. Prerogative of Place

1. Quoted in John P. Marschall, "Francis Patrick Kenrick, 1851–1863: The Baltimore Years" (doctoral dissertation, Catholic University of America, 1965), p. 44.

2. Nolan, *Kenrick*, passim.

3. Quoted in Marschall, "Kenrick," p. 84.

4. Archives of the Irish College (hereafter AIC), Kenrick to Kirby, Baltimore, November 4, 1852.

5. APF, Congressi 16: 276r, Kenrick to O'Connor, Baltimore, October 2, 1852.

6. Marschall, "Kenrick," p. 89.

7. Guilday, *Councils*, pp. 167–86.

8. Marschall, "Kenrick," pp. 102–3, 114–15.

9. APF, Atti 215: 184r–210r.

10. APF, Congressi 16: 146r–47v, Kenrick to O'Connor, Baltimore, July 12, 1852; AAB, Acta Episcopalia, p. 3, August 11, 1852.

11. APF, Congressi 16: 276r, Kenrick to O'Connor, Baltimore, October 2, 1852; AIC, Kenrick to Kirby, Baltimore, November 4, 1852.

12. APF, Atti 214: 403r; Atti 215: 211rv.

13. APF, Acta 220: 391r–92v, 431r.

14. Michael J. Curley, *Venerable John Neumann, C.SS.R.: Fourth Bishop of Philadelphia* (Washington, D.C., 1952), pp. 267ff.

15. Henry A. Szarnicki, *Michael O'Connor, First Catholic Bishop of Pittsburgh, 1843–1860* (Pittsburgh, 1975), passim.

16. AUND, Cincinnati papers, Kenrick to Purcell, Baltimore, April 18, 1855.

17. Francis X. Gartland was first bishop of Savannah from 1850 to 1854 and John Barry second bishop from 1857 to 1859.

18. APF, Atti 214: 400r, 404r–406r.

19. 32C-J-6, Fransoni to Kenrick, Rome, September 28, 1852.

20. APF, Acta 221: 92r–96v; Kenneally, *Calendar* 6: 192, nos. 1112–13.

21. APF, Congressi 18: 97rv, Kenrick to Barnabò, Baltimore, February 26, 1858.

22. APF, Congr. Generali 983: 622rv, Kenrick to Pius IX, Baltimore, May 9, 1858.

23. 32C-P-3, Barnabò to bishops, Rome, August 15, 1858.

24. APF, Acta 225: 1r–11r. On the matter of obligation of residence, the cardinals were concerned about the frequent trips of American bishops abroad. In this they evidenced, perhaps, a lack of appreciation of their need to beg.

25. Robert F. McNamara, *The American College in Rome, 1855–1955* (Rochester, 1956), pp. 16ff.

26. Spalding, *Spalding*, pp. 74–75.

27. 29-I-7 and 8, Hughes to Kenrick, New York, October 22, December 23, 1855.

28. McNamara, *American College*, pp. 63–88.

29. 29-I-3, Hughes to Kenrick, New York, December 28, 1852.

30. Shaw, *Dagger John*, pp. 195–97, 201–2.

31. Ibid., pp. 267, 288, 351; Marschall, "Kenrick," pp. 71–73, 360–63.

32. AIC, Kenrick to Kirby, Baltimore, March 15, 1851.

33. Congr. Generali 987: 204r, undated note found with Kenrick letters of August, 1860, but 1862 seems the more likely year. Shaw, *Dagger John*, p. 325n, gives no credence to the rumors that Hughes had a drinking problem.

34. Marschall, "Kenrick," pp. 186–200.

35. Vincent F. Holden, *The Yankee Paul: Isaac Thomas Hecker* (Milwaukee, 1858), p. 391.

36. Marschall, "Kenrick," pp. 236–61.

37. 29-J-11, Hughes to Kenrick, New York, July 3, 1861.

38. APF, Congressi 19: 496rv, Kenrick to Barnabò, Baltimore, December 6, 1861.

39. *CM*, October 18, 1862, quoted in the New York *Metropolitan Record*, October 25, 1862.

40. A table in the *Metropolitan Catholic Almanac, 1860*, p. 27, gives the archdiocese of Baltimore 98 churches and chapels and 127 priests and the archdiocese of New York 78 churches and chapels and 124 priests. The diocese of Philadelphia, however, could claim 153 churches and chapels and 142 priests.

41. *Freeman's Journal*, January 13, 1855.

42. Willging and Hatzfeld, *Catholic Serials: Maryland*, pp. 20–21, 36–42.

43. In the period 1856–1860 New York publishers recorded 245 Catholic imprints and Baltimore publishers 205, of which 109 could be claimed by John Murphy and Company alone. Catherine Ignatius Dodd, "A Survey of Catholic Americana and Catholic Book Publishing in the U.S., 1856–1860" (master's thesis in Library Science, Catholic University of America, 1953), pp. 33–37, 157–58.

44. Willging and Hatzfeld, *Catholic Serials: Maryland*, pp. 32–36, 45–46; *CM*, March 14, 1874, July 13, 1878.

45. Sydney E. Ahlstrom, *A Religious History of the American People* (New Haven, 1972), Ch. 38.

46. Nolan, *Kenrick*, pp. 372–73.

47. AIC, Kenrick to Kirby, Baltimore, November 4, 1852.

48. Nolan, *Kenrick*, pp. 373–80.

49. Baker and Lyman entered the Catholic Church as a result of the conversion of Henry Edward Manning in England.

50. AIC, Kenrick to Kirby, Baltimore, August 28, 1853.

51. Marschall, "Kenrick," pp. 160–65; Spalding, *Spalding*, pp. 65–66.

52. 31-B-10, Purcell to Kenrick, Newark, September 17, 1853.

53. Marschall, "Kenrick," pp. 166–67.

54. 34-J-20, Kenrick to Spalding, Baltimore, April 29, 1854.

55. Brownson's conversion was not a result of the high church movement but of the romantic impulse in transcendentalism. See Arthur M. Schlesinger, Jr., *Orestes A. Brownson: A Pilgrim's Progress* (Boston, 1939).

56. 32A-N-18, Spalding to Kenrick, Louisville, October 9, 1855.

57. Michael Moran, "The Writings of Francis Patrick Kenrick, Archbishop of Baltimore (1797–1863)," *RACHSP* 41 (1930): 230–62.

58. Quoted in Marschall, "Kenrick," p. 180.

59. Ibid., pp. 179–80.

60. Gerald Fogarty, *American Catholic Biblical Scholarship: A History from the Early Republic to Vatican II* (San Francisco, 1989), pp. 7–34.

61. At the Second Plenary Council (1866), Kenrick's brother, Peter Richard Kenrick, prevented acceptance by his refusal as literary executor to allow any modification of his brother's work. Spalding, *Spalding*, pp. 220–21.

62. John Joseph Lardner, "Kenrick's Moral Theology—Its Adaptation to American Conditions" (Licentiate dissertation, Catholic University of America, [n.d.]), pp. 30–34. One of the reasons, Lardner explains, is that Kenrick's Latin was too classical.

63. *Concilium Baltimorense Provinciale VIII habitum anno 1855* and *Concilium Baltimorense Provinciale IX habitum anno 1858* in *Acta et Decreta Sacrorum Conciliorum Recentiorum: Collectio Lacensis* (Freiburg, 1875), Vol. 3, Cols. 155–62, 169–75.

64. *Synodus Diocesana Baltimorensis, Mense Junio 1853 Habita* (Baltimore, 1853). Among the decrees of the plenary council having no corresponding statutes in the synod were those concerning trustees and the establishment of parish schools.

65. *Synodus Dioecesana Baltimorensis, Mense Junio 1857 Habita* (Baltimore, 1857); *Synodus Dioecesana Baltimorensis, Mense Maii 1863 Habita* (Baltimore, 1863). No information on the council and chancery was given for Baltimore in the *Catholic Almanac* until 1859, though presumably Kenrick created these offices at the time of his first synod. New York in 1854 was the first to supply such information.

66. 29-J-5, Hughes to Kenrick, Baltimore, May 3, 1860.

67. These annual reports, due November 1, are unclassified in the AAB.

68. The 1853 synod required that stole fees be placed in a common fund, from which two-thirds would go to the parish priest (pastor) and one-third to his assistant.

69. *CM*, March 7, 1857.

70. The number 130,000 supplied to the *Metropolitan Catholic Almanac* in 1857

(p. 75) was the last reported until 1880, when 200,000 was supplied to *Sadlier's Catholic Directory* (p. 60).

71. 32B-V-10, "Relatio Status Ecclesiae Baltimorensis 1862."

72. Baltimore's population in 1860 was 212,418 and Washington's 75,080. The population of Maryland was 687,049.

73. *St. John the Evangelist Church, 1853–1953* (Baltimore, 1953), pp. 17–54.

74. Scharf, *Baltimore City and County*, pp. 539–40.

75. *Holy Cross Centennial, 1858–1958* (Baltimore, 1958), unpaginated.

76. John A. Ryan, *Chronicle and Sketch of the Church of St. Ignatius of Loyola, Baltimore, 1856–1906* (Baltimore, 1907), pp. 1–3, 72–74.

77. Ibid., pp. 5, 15; *St. Francis Xavier Church Centennial: The first Negro Parish Established in the United States, 1863–1963* ([Baltimore], 1963), unpaginated.

78. 30-K-9, Lynch to Kenrick, Washington, May 1, 1858.

79. "Gonzaga High School and St. Aloysius Church," *WL* 62 (1933): 378–79. Senator Stephen A. Douglas rented pew No. 1.

80. V. F. O'Daniel, *Historical Souvenir of the Consecration of St. Dominic's Church, Washington, D.C., October 12, 1919* (Baltimore, 1919), pp. 11–20, 29–32.

81. Byrne, *Redemptorist Centenaries*, pp. 118–19.

82. *History of the Redemptorists at Annapolis, Md., from 1853 to 1903* (Ilchester, Md., 1904), pp. 12ff.

83. Albert E. Smith, *The Diamond Jubilee of St. Joseph's Parish, Maryland (1852–1927)* (Baltimore, 1927), pp. 15–51.

84. *Our Celebration: St. Agnes Church, 1852–1977* (Hackensack, N.J., 1977), pp. 7–27.

85. Stanton, *Century of Growth*, 1: 118–19, 139–43, 170–71, 267–72, 291–92; Scharf, *Western Maryland*, pp. 1463, 1484, 1541.

86. Stanton, *Century of Growth*, 2: 93–94, 156; *CM*, passim; Acta Episcopalia, passim.

87. Joerndt, *St. Ignatius*, pp. 308–9, 316–26.

88. *CM*, November 3, 1860.

89. Ibid., August 25, 1855, May 30, December 12, 1857; Litterarum Registrum I, p. 124, Kenrick to Clarke, June 22, 1857.

90. Mary Loretto Costello, *The Sisters of Mercy of Maryland (1855–1930)* (St. Louis, 1931), pp. 1–52.

91. *Sesquicentennial: St. Patrick's*, pp. 111, 115.

92. Corrigan, *Catholic Schools*, pp. 45–47; Crumlish, *1809–1959*, pp. 31, 77–94; *CM*, September 1, 1860, July 25, 1862.

93. Sherwood, *Oblates*, pp. 126–36.

94. Nicholas Varga, *Baltimore's Loyola, Loyola's Baltimore: A History of Loyola College, Baltimore, Maryland, 1851–1986* (Baltimore, in press).

95. Power, *Catholic Higher Education*, pp. 280, 285, 288.

96. *CM*, February 26, March 5, April 16, December 3, 1853.

97. Daniel T. McColgan, *A Century of Charity: The First One Hundred Years of the Society of St. Vincent de Paul in the United States* (2 vols., Milwaukee, 1951), 1: 212–15.

98. *CM*, March 10, 1860.

99. Marschall, "Kenrick," pp. 175–79.

100. 34-K-53, Kenrick to Spalding, Baltimore [November 1], 1861.

101. *CM*, October 24, 1863.

102. Swisher, *Taney*, pp. 470–73.

103. Olson, *Baltimore*, pp. 141–42.

104. Douglas Bowers, "Ideology and Political Parties in Maryland, 1851–1856," *MHM* 64 (1969): 202–3.

105. *CM*, October 25, 1852; McConville, *Nativism in Maryland*, p. 23.

106. *CM*, April 16, 23, 1853.

107. Ibid., June 4, 1853.

108. Ibid., June 11, 1853.

109. James F. Connelly, *The Visit of Archbishop Gaetano Bedini to the United States of America, June, 1853—February, 1854* (Rome, 1960).

110. Litterarum Registrum I, p. 59, Kenrick to Marcy, Baltimore, January 1, 1854.

111. *CM*, January 21, 1854.

112. Connelly, *Bedini*, pp. 211–12, 163, 231, 235.

113. Richard Walsh and William Lloyd Fox, eds., *Maryland: A History, 1632–1974* (Baltimore, 1974), pp. 303–12.

114. Laurence Frederick Schmeckebier, *History of the Know Nothing Party in Maryland* (Baltimore, 1899), p. 11.

115. Baker, *Ambivalent Americans*, pp. 63, 77.

116. She soon disavowed the book. *CM*, May 12, 19, 1855. See also Billington, *Protestant Crusade*, pp. 310–11.

117. *CM*, February 16, March 8, 15, 1856.

118. McConville, *Nativism in Maryland*, pp. 112–27; Baker, *Ambivalent Americans*, pp. 126–27.

119. In 1856 the counties that registered the lowest number of Know Nothings were St. Mary's with 19 percent and Charles with 37.8 percent, while Baltimore City counted 63.1 percent. Baker, *Ambivalent Americans*, p. 130.

120. *CM*, May 19, 1855.

121. Ibid., May 22, 1858.

122. Ibid., January 1, 1859.

123. Ibid., May 22, 1858. Joseph D. Brokhage, *Francis Patrick Kenrick's Opinion on Slavery* (Washington, D.C., 1955), concludes that Kenrick's principles were drawn from European theologians who addressed milder forms of slavery and that he failed, therefore, to treat the problem in the United States as it deserved.

124. *Metropolitan* 1 (1853): 88; *CM*, March 31, 1855.

125. *CM*, January 9, 1858; Acta Episcopalia, p. 189, June 14, 1856.

126. *CM*, November 3, 1860.

127. Ibid., December 1, 1860.

128. Benjamin J. Blied, *Catholics and the Civil War* (Milwaukee, 1945), pp. 70–82; Judith Conrad Wimmer, "American Catholic Interpretations of the Civil War" (doctoral dissertation, Drew University, 1980), pp. 107–9 and passim.

129. *CM*, October 10, 1863, June 4, 11, 1864.

130. Quoted in John Tracy Ellis, *The Life of James Cardinal Gibbons, Archbishop of Baltimore, 1834–1921* (2 vols., Milwaukee, 1952), I: 46–47.

131. APF, Congressi 20: 213r–14v, Kenrick to Barnabò, Baltimore, May 11 [?], 1863.

132. 32-O-18, Young to Kenrick, Baltimore, March 8, 1861.

133. Marschall, "Kenrick," pp. 163–64; Thomas J. Peterman, *The Cutting Edge: The Life of Thomas Andrew Becker* (Devon, Pa., 1982), pp. 41–52.

134. *CM*, September 27, 1862.

135. Sullivan, *Georgetown Visitation*, pp. 102–3.

136. Virginia Walcott Beauchamp, "The Sisters and the Soldiers," *MHM* 81 (1986): 117–33.

137. Ellen Ryan Jolly, *Nuns of the Battlefield* (Providence, R.I., 1927), pp. 57–84, 141, 240–57.

138. AUND, New Orleans papers, Dubreul to Odin, Baltimore, July 13, 1863.

Chapter 8. The Lion of Baltimore

1. Spalding, *Spalding*, pp.147–50.

2. APF, Acta 228: 80r–84r.

3. Quoted in the *CM*, August 13, 1864.

4. Spalding, *Spalding*, pp. 5ff.

5. Ibid., Ch. 4. His best-known works were his *Life of Flaget* (1852), *Miscellanea* (1855), and *History of the Protestant Reformation* (1860). See also Adam A. Micek, *The Apologetics of Martin John Spalding* (Washington, D.C., 1951).

6. Acta Episcopalia, p. 200.

7. *CM*, September 17, October 1, 1864; McColgan, *Century of Charity*, 1: 268–72.

8. Acta Episcopalia, p. 1, August 16, 1864.

9. Ibid., pp. 8–9, October 21, December 20, 1864; *CM*, December 24, 1864.

10. Spalding, *Spalding*, pp. 161–65; Michael V. Gannon, *Rebel Bishop: The Life and Era of Augustin Verot* (Milwaukee, 1964), pp. 110–14.

11. 39B-A-2, printed circular.

12. 34-D-10, Hardie to Spalding, Washington, April 16, 1865.

13. Letterbook 1, p. 141, Spalding to Timon, Baltimore, July 21, 1865.

14. Mrs. Surratt ran a boarding house in which the conspirators, including her son, met. Though evidence of her complicity was tenuous, she was convicted July 5 and hanged two days later. See Guy W. Moore, *The Case of Mrs. Surratt* (Norman, Okla., 1954).

15. Jacob A. Walter, *The Surratt Case* (New York, 1891), a printed address delivered before the United States Historical Society on May 25, 1891.

16. Spalding, *Spalding*, pp. 167–68, 170.

17. Letterbook I, p. 246, Spalding to O'Kean, Baltimore, July 11, 1866.

18. 39B-G-10, Lynch to Spalding, Charleston, January 26, 1866.

19. Spalding, *Spalding*, p. 173.

20. Acta Episcopalia, p. 21; *CM*, January 6, 13, 1866.

21. *CM*, June 17, 1865.

22. *Acta Synodi Diocesanae Sextae [sic]; una cum Constitutionibus, ab illustrissimo ac reverendissimo Martino Joanne Spalding, Archiepiscopo Baltimorensi; Latis ac promulgatis; in feria quarta Rogationum, Die 24 Maii, A.D. MDCCCLXV* (Baltimore, 1865). This and subsequent synods were misnumbered because Spalding was apparently unaware of the synod held under Eccleston that was never published. This was the seventh synod held in Baltimore. Kenrick did not number his.

23. APF, Congressi 20: 1463rv, Spalding to Barnabò, Baltimore, May 20, 1865.

24. Letterbook I, pp. 27–28, Spalding to Wood, Baltimore, February 29, 1865.

25. 36-K-1, Walter to Spalding, Washington, September 9, 1864; 36-0-5, White to Spalding, Washington, October 11, 1864.

26. Maloney, "Catholic Church in the District, 1790–1866," pp. 62–64; Mary Loretta McHale, "The Catholic Church in the District of Columbia (Later Period: 1866–1938)" (master's thesis, Catholic University of America, 1938), pp. 34–37; Lawrence P. Gatti, *Historic St. Stephen's* (Washington, D.C., [1952]), pp. 27–31.

27. Scharf, *Chronicles of Baltimore*, p. 660; *CM*, July 15, 1865.

28. *CM*, July 8, 1865.

29. Ibid., April 13, 20, May 18, August 24, October 5, December 7, 28, 1867; Acta Episcopalia, passim.

30. Stanton, *Century of Growth*, 1: 87–88; *CM*, May 6, 1865.

31. Olson, *Baltimore*, p. 189.

32. Aaron I. Abell, *American Catholicism and Social Action: A Search for Social Justice* (New York, 1950), pp. 19–23, 34–36.

33. Letterbook I, pp. 730–31, Spalding to Duchess of Leeds, Baltimore, April 20, 1866.

34. Cyril Marcel Witte, "A History of St. Mary's Industrial School for Boys in the City of Baltimore, 1866–1950" (doctoral dissertation, University of Notre Dame, 1955), pp. 8–28.

35. Ibid., pp. 29–36; Spalding, *Spalding*, pp. 178–79.

36. Felix Ward, *The Passionists: Sketches Historical and Personal* (New York, 1923), pp. 297–99.

37. Spalding, *Spalding*, pp. 179–80.

38. Byrne, *Redemptorist Centenaries*, pp. 116–23.

39. Patrick J. Dooley, "Woodstock and Its Makers," WL 56 (1927): 3–25.

40. Costello, *Sisters of Mercy*, pp. 56–58.

41. Spalding, *Spalding*, pp. 182–85.

42. Kauffman, *Saint Sulpice*, pp. 143–51.

43. Letterbook I, pp. 725–26, Spalding to Caval, Baltimore, February 1, 1866.

44. Herbermann, *Sulpicians*, p. 308; Spalding, *Spalding*, p. 183.

45. SAB, Record Group 5, Box 10, Spalding to Debreul, Baltimore, May 14, 1868.

46. Spalding, *Spalding*, pp. 180–81.

47. Ibid., pp. 194–95.

48. AUND, Cincinnati and New Orleans papers, Spalding to Purcell, Spalding to Odin, Baltimore, October 1, 2, 1865; Letterbook I, p. 163, Spalding to Kenrick, Baltimore, October 2, 1865.

49. Spalding, *Spalding*, pp. 202–3.

50. Ibid., pp. 204–5.

51. AANY, A-22, Spalding to McCloskey, Baltimore, October 9, 1865.

52. Spalding, *Spalding*, pp. 194–216.

53. *CM*, October 13, 1866.

54. Archives of the Archdiocese of Indianapolis, Purcell to Chatard, Montreal, October 26, 1866.

55. There are two sets of minutes for this discussion, 39A-D-5 and APF, Acta 232: 406r–407v, the latter a somewhat softened version. Both Kenrick and Archbishop John

Odin of New Orleans strongly opposed the creation of a special prefect apostolic. When collections in all dioceses for work among the blacks were proposed, Archbishop Mc-Closkey insisted that "in no way was the conscience of the Bishops of the North burdened."

56. Spalding, *Spalding*, pp. 222–23, 225.

57. Archives of the Archdiocese of Dublin, Spalding to Cullen, Baltimore, December 10, 1866.

58. Letterbook I, p. 312, Spalding to McCloskey, Baltimore, February 13, 1868; AUND, Cincinnati papers, Spalding to Purcell, Baltimore, February 13, 1868.

59. Outside the province of Baltimore little was done for the blacks before the Third Plenary Council. Edward J. Misch, "The American Bishops and the Negro from the Civil War to the Third Plenary Council of Baltimore (1865–1884)" (doctoral dissertation, Gregorian University, 1968).

60. See Joseph Chinnici, "Organization and the Spiritual Life: American Catholic Devotional Works, 1791–1866," *Theological Studies* 40 (1979): 229–55.

61. Guilday, *Councils*, pp. 201–14.

62. 36-A-11, Foley to Spalding, Baltimore, July 23, 1867.

63. Walsh and Fox, *Maryland*, pp. 377–92; Scharf, *Baltimore City and County*, pp. 720–22.

64. *The Sun*, February 3, 1868.

65. Acta Episcopalia, p. 34, March 25, 1868.

66. Letterbook I, p. 195, Spalding to Morgan, November 24, 1867.

67. *Synodus Diocesana Baltimorensis Septima [sic]* . . . (Baltimore, 1868).

68. *CM*, October 3, 1868.

69. 39C-D-13, report; SAB, Record Group 5, Box 10, Dubreul to Spalding, Baltimore, January 16, 1868.

70. *CM*, February 20, March 6, 1869.

71. McHale, "Church in the District," pp. 38–40.

72. Spalding, *Spalding*, pp. 310–11.

73. Louise Callan, *The Society of the Sacred Heart in North America* (London, 1937), pp. 601–3.

74. Corrigan, *Catholic Schools*, pp. 39–40, 47–48.

75. Acta Episcopalia, pp. 42–45, February 1, April 7, August 10, September 1, 1869. In 1854 the Roman Catholic Asylum for Widows, the first Catholic home for the aged in the archdiocese of Baltimore, was founded but did not last many years.

76. Joan Marie Donohoe, *The Irish Catholic Benevolent Union* (Washington, D.C., 1953), p. 4n.

77. Misch, "Bishops and the Negro," pp. 357–70; *CM*, May 15, 1869 (bishop's pastoral).

78. 33-F-9, Boyle to Spalding, Washington, May 23, 1871.

79. Sherwood, *Oblates*, pp. 152–56.

80. Richard H. Steins, "The Mission of the Josephites to the Negro in America" (master's thesis, Columbia University, 1966); John T. Gillard, *The Catholic Church and the American Negro* (Baltimore, 1929), and *Colored Catholics in the United States* (Baltimore, 1941).

81. Quoted in Spalding, *Spalding*, p. 343.

82. *Pastoral Letter of the Most Rev. Martin John Spalding, D.D., Archbishop of Bal-*

timore, to the Clergy and Laity of the Archdiocese: Promulgating the Jubilee, together with the Late Encyclical of the Holy Father, and the Syllabus of Errors Condemned (Baltimore, 1865).

83. Letterbook I, p. 504, Spalding to Antonelli, Baltimore, February 21, 1865.

84. Spalding, *Spalding*, p. 245.

85. Ibid., pp. 245–51; Fergus McDonald, *The Catholic Church and the Secret Societies in the United States* (New York, 1946), Ch. 2.

86. 35-Q-11, Purcell to Spalding, Cincinnati, September 7, 1864.

87. Spalding, *Spalding*, pp. 201, 205, 216, 251.

88. Letterbook I, p. 748, Spalding to Baillargeon, Baltimore, January 28, 1867.

89. APF, Congressi 22: 1116r, Spalding to Barnabò, Baltimore, August 15, 1869.

90. Spalding, *Spalding*, p. 252.

91. Ibid., p. 256.

92. APF, Congressi 22: 284r–87r, Spalding et al, to Barnabò, Emmitsburg, June 24, 1868; *CM*, July 4, 1868.

93. 43B-H-14, Barnabò to Spalding, Rome, July 22, 1868.

94. Acta Episcopalia, p. 41, November 30, 1868. The donors of the three full burses were William Kennedy, Charles Dougherty, and (anonymously) C. Oliver O'Donnell. *CM*, December 5, 1868.

95. McNamara, *American College*, pp. 149ff; Spalding, *Spalding*, pp. 260–64.

96. For a thorough treatment of this problem see Robert Trisco, "Bishops and Their Priests in the United States," in John Tracy Ellis, ed., *The Catholic Priests in the United States: Historical Investigations* (Collegeville, Minn., 1971), pp. 111–292.

97. New York *Tribune*, October 23, 1868.

98. Nelson J. Callahan, ed., *The Diary of Richard L. Burtsell, Priest of New York: The Early Years, 1865–1868* (New York, 1978), passim; John Talbot Smith, *The Catholic Church in New York* (2 vols., New York, 1908), I: 297–302.

99. Spalding, *Spalding*, pp. 274–79.

100. Trisco, "Bishop and Their Priests," pp. 150–94.

101. Spalding, *Spalding*, pp. 272–73.

102. Ibid., pp. 280–82, 329–31; Nelson J. Callahan, *A Case for Due Process in the Church: Father Eugene O'Callaghan, American Pioneer of Dissent* (Staten Island, N.Y., 1971).

103. Spalding, *Spalding*, pp. 331–39; Clyde F. Crews, "American Catholic Authoritarianism: The Episcopacy of William George McCloskey, 1868–1909," *CHR* 70 (1984): 560–80.

104. AUND, Cincinnati papers, McCloskey to Purcell, Louisville, February 8, 1873.

105. 39C-B-4, Bayley to Spalding, Newark, June 12, 1868.

106. James J. Hennesey, "James A. Corcoran's Mission to Rome," *CHR* 48 (1962): 161–62.

107. APF, Congressi 22: 1115r, August 15, 1869 (covering letter); 39-M-6, Memoranda pro Concilio Oecumenico.

108. Twenty-one American bishops signed the inopportunist petitions, ten the infallibilist, and five Spalding's petition for compromise, while ten remained uncommitted. James Hennesey, *The First Council of the Vatican: The American Experience* (New York, 1963), 91–101.

109. Ibid., pp. 110–16; Spalding, *Spalding*, pp. 297–303.

110. Eight American bishops presented lengthy critiques of the *schema* (Hennesey, *First Vatican*, pp. 133–410).

111. Spalding, *Spalding*, pp. 304–5.

112. Ibid., pp. 305–10.

113. Ibid., pp. 312–14.

114. *CM*, June 25, 1870.

115. Kenrick's *Concio* is translated in full in Raymond Clancy, "American Prelates in the Vatican Council," *HRS* 28 (1937): 93–131.

116. See Martin John Spalding, *Lectures on the Evidences of Catholicity*, 4th ed. (Baltimore, 1870), pp. 263–68.

117. Spalding, *Spalding*, pp. 308–9, 319–20.

118. Ibid., pp. 320–22.

119. Quoted in ibid., p. 326.

120. Scharf, *Chronicles of Baltimore*, pp. 684–85.

121. APF, Congressi 23: 1377r–78r, Spalding to Barnabò, Baltimore, October 8, 1871.

122. Acta Episcopalia, p. 57, May 3, 1871.

123. 37-F-17, Spalding to Hecker, Baltimore, December 2, 1871.

124. Spalding, *Spalding*, pp. 345–46.

125. *Brownson's Quarterly Review*, Last Series, 2 (1874): 107–21.

Chapter 9. No Lasting City

1. 42-O-12, Spalding to Bayley, Baltimore, June 13, 1868.

2. 72-J-8, Bayley to Gibbons, Newark, August 18, 1872.

3. 44-B-17, Bayley to Barnabò, Newark, August [1872].

4. AUND, Seton papers, Bayley to Seton, Paris, September 15, 1842.

5. M. Hildegarde Yeager, *The Life of James Roosevelt Bayley, First Bishop of Newark and Eighth Archbishop of Baltimore: 1814–1877* (Washington, D.C., 1947), pp. 1–42.

6. Ibid., p. 747.

7. *CM*, September 7, 1872.

8. Ibid., October 19, 1872.

9. Yeager, *Bayley*, pp. 346–47, quoting the *Herald* of October 15, 1872.

10. AANY, C-2, Bayley to Corrigan, Baltimore, January 11, 1873.

11. APF, Congressi 24: 648r–49r, Bayley to Chatard, Seton Hall, January 9, 1873.

12. 43-G-19, Roosevelt to Bayley, Watch Hill, R.I., August 25, 1872.

13. Constance McLaughlin Green, *Washington: Capital City, 1879–1950* (Princeton, N.J., 1962), pp. 85–88.

14. Memorandum book, January 28, 1876.

15. Ibid., April 13, 1874.

16. Episcopal Diary of Archbishop Bayley (hereafter Bayley diary), p. 13.

17. *CM*, July 5, 1873.

18. Memorandum book, September 77, 1873.

19. AANY, C-2, Bayley to Corrigan, Baltimore, March 7, 1876.

20. In 1875, for example, Bayley distributed $8,000 in Baltimore and $7,000 in Newark.

21. Quoted in Yeager, *Bayley*, p. 441.

22. Quoted in ibid., p. 442.

23. Ibid., pp. 403–4.

24. Ibid., p. 403; Felicitas Powers, "Archives of the Archdiocese of Baltimore: History and Content" (unpublished paper), pp. 4–8.

25. *Synodus Diocesana Baltimorensis Septima [sic], quae antecedentium etiam complectitur Constitutiones, die 27 Augusti 1875 ad BVM in Seminario S. Sulpitii Baltimorae habita ab illustrissimo Jacobo Roosevelt Bayley, Archiepiscopo Baltimorensi* (Baltimore, 1875).

26. *CM*, September 8, 1877.

27. Yeager, *Bayley*, Ch. 6.

28. 40-P-5 to 8, Shea to Bayley, July 12, October 31, 1875, February 11, August 31, 1876.

29. Yeager, *Bayley*, pp. 392–96; 41-B-12, Bennett to Bayley, New York, November 15, 1874.

30. Yeager, *Bayley*, pp. 432–33; *CM*, February 27, 1876.

31. *CM*, January 11, 1873.

32. SAB, Record Group 5, Box 9, Bayley to Dubreul, Madison, N.J., July 13, 1875.

33. Ibid., same to same, Cumberland, October 1, 1875.

34. 40-L-13, McQuaid to Bayley, Rochester, April 9, 1876.

35. 73-D-2, Bayley to Gibbons, Vichy, July 3, 1877.

36. *CM*, October 5, 1872, March 27, 1875; Milton E. Smith, *History of St. Patrick's Church*, Washington, D.C. (n.p., 1904), pp. 38–39.

37. *CM*, September 6, 1873, May 23, 30, 1974; *History of Sacred Heart of Jesus Parish, Baltimore, Maryland, 1873–1948* (n.p., 1948), pp. 25–36.

38. *CM*, January 8, 1873, February 7, 1874. According to tradition, the church was the result of a vow made when Captain Kennedy's ship was foundering in a storm. The anchor that held the ship was preserved at St. Ann's. *Church of St. Ann: 1873 Centennial 1973* (n.p., 1973), pp. 9–10.

39. *CM*, November 29, 1873, May 26, 1877.

40. Ibid., June 13, 1874, June 17, 1876.

41. Albert Sidney Foley, "The Catholic Church and the Washington Negro" (doctoral dissertation, University of North Carolina, 1950), pp. 60–61.

42. Steins, "Josephites," pp. 20–22, 25–27. The AAB contains extensive correspondence on this quarrel.

43. Stanton, *Century of Growth*, 1: 68ff.

44. SAB, Record Group 5, Box 9, Bayley to Dubreul, Frederick, October 8, 1875.

45. *CM*, March 23, 1873.

46. Memorandum book, March 27, 1876; *CM*, May 6, 1876.

47. Corrigan, *Catholic Schools*, pp. 135–38. In 1874–75 they went to Hagerstown, Westernport, and Star of the Sea Parish in South Baltimore.

48. 40-E-5 and 6, Sister Euphemia to Bayley, Emmitsburg, May 5, 12, 1876; *CM*, June 10, 1876.

49. Costello, *Sisters of Mercy*, pp. 93–95.

50. *CM*, August 21, 1875, April 13, 1878.

51. Bayley diary, p. 38.

52. Memorandum book, June 13, 1876; 40-I-2, Mother Ildephonsa to Bayley, Baltimore County, May 20, 1876.

53. 40-K-7 and 8, Lyman to Bayley, Govanstown, August 1, 4, 1876. Sister Dorothy Daiger, SSND, Maryland archivist of the School Sisters of Notre Dame, could find little evidence of Mother Caroline's displeasure.

54. *CM*, November 25, 1876, September 1, 1877.

55. Ibid., February 5, June 3, 1876.

56. Donohoe, *Irish Catholic Benevolent Union*, p. 4.

57. *CM*, December 1, 8, 15, 1877. On October 27, 1877, the *Catholic Mirror* began a series of histories of the Catholic societies of the archdiocese, which ran for several years.

58. Ibid., May 18, 1872.

59. Ibid., November 16, 1872, January 18, 1873.

60. Donohoe, *Irish Catholic Benevolent Union*, p. 211.

61. At least two versions of the address were published, that of the *Catholic Mirror*, October 31, 1874, quoted in Yeager, *Bayley*, pp. 386–88, and that of the Boston *Pilot*, October 31, 1874, quoted by Aaron I. Abell, "The Reception of Leo XIII's Labor Encyclical in America, 1891–1919," *Review of Politics* 7 (1945): 464–95, with whose interpretation Yeager differs.

62. *CM*, December 15, 1877.

63. Ibid., January 26, 1878.

64. Ibid., January 23, 1875.

65. Ibid., February 8, 1875.

66. *Diamond Jubilee Celebration and the 74th Annual Convention of the Catholic Central Verein of America* (Baltimore, 1930), p. 19.

67. *CM*, October 23, 1875, September 30, 1876.

68. Donohoe, *Irish Catholic Benevolent Union*, p. 211.

69. Joan Bland, *Hibernian Crusade: The Story of the Catholic Total Abstinence Union of America* (Washington, D.C., 1951), pp. 45–55.

70. *CM*, December 2, 1871.

71. Bland, *Hibernian Crusade*, pp. 63–72.

72. Ibid., p. 75.

73. Ibid., pp. 77–80.

74. *CM*, June 28, 1873.

75. For the temperance movement in western Maryland in general, see Harvey, *Best-Dressed Miners*, pp. 117–18.

76. *CM*, July 12, 1873.

77. Ibid., January 12, 1878.

78. Ibid., passim. See especially the lists of societies that marched for the laying of the cornerstone of St. Pius V Church in the issue of May 11, 1878.

79. 72-H-5, Bayley to Gibbons, Newark, January 10, 1872.

80. *CM*, November 9, 1872.

81. Ibid., March 22, 1873.

82. Ibid., September 14, 1872, January 24, 1874.

83. Yeager, *Bayley*, pp. 362, 369, 408; *CM*, December 6, 16, 1873.

84. *CM*, September 18, 1875.

85. Smith, *St. Patrick's*, pp. 41–42.

86. *CM*, June 15, 1878.

87. Ibid., October 14, 1876.

88. Patrick Henry Ahern, *The Life of John J. Keane: Educator and Archbishop, 1839–1918* (Milwaukee, 1954).

89. *CM*, December 11, 1875.

90. Ibid., January 16, February 27, 1875.

91. Ibid., March 13, 1875.

92. Ibid., May 18, 1872.

93. Ibid., February 1, 1879.

94. Smith, *St. Patrick's*, p. 44.

95. *Synodus Diocesana . . . 1875*, no. 104.

96. *CM*, April 24, 1875.

97. Fabrician of Jesus, *St. Paul's*, pp. 114–23.

98. Edwin Warfield Bietzell, *The Jesuit Missions of St. Mary's County, Maryland* (Abell, Md., 1976), pp. 282–83; Joerndt, *St. Ignatius*, pp. 335–36; Carley, *St. Peter's*, pp. 124–31.

99. Joerndt, *St. Ignatius*, p. 151.

100. *CM*, December 23, 1876.

101. Ibid., October 14, 1876.

102. Ibid., September 1, 1877.

103. Olson, *Baltimore*, pp. 161–75.

104. *CM*, June 8, 1872.

105. Olson, *Baltimore*, pp. 179–83.

106. Ibid., pp. 151–52, 175–79; Scharf, *Baltimore City and County*, pp. 382, 403–4, 447, 838–39.

107. Scharf, *Baltimore City and County*, p. 472; *CM*, July 18, 1874.

108. *CM*, July 21, 28, 1877; Olson, *Baltimore*, pp. 195–97.

109. *CM*, July 28, 1877.

110. Quoted in Olson, *Baltimore*, p. 197.

111. *CM*, October 2, November 6, 1875.

112. Walsh and Fox, *Maryland*, pp. 592–96.

113. Yeager, *Bayley*, pp. 419–23.

114. *CM*, December 14, 1875; Witte, "St. Mary's Industrial School," pp. 59–60.

115. *CM*, June 23, 1877.

116. Ibid., June 2, July 28, 1877.

117. Ibid., February 8, 1879; Gibbons diary, p. 126, July 6, 1879.

118. *CM*, November 11, 1876.

119. Ibid., March 17, 1877.

120. APF, Congressi 24: 964r–65v, Bayley to Barnabò, Baltimore, July 25, 1873.

121. 43-K-1, Barnabò to Bayley, Rome, August 27, 1873.

122. AUND, Cincinnati papers, Bayley to Purcell, Baltimore, December 23, 1873.

123. Yeager, *Bayley*, pp. 375–78.

124. Thomas T. McAvoy, "Public Schools vs. Catholic Schools and James McMaster," *Review of Politics* 28 (1966): 19–46.

125. Quoted in Yeager, *Bayley*, p. 381.

126. 43-I-7, "Copy of letter to Card. Franchi," n.d.

127. Peter J. Rahill, *The Catholic Indian Missions and Grant's Peace Policy, 1870–1884* (Washington, D.C., 1953), pp. 3–28.

128. *CM*, November 18, 1876.

129. Ibid., November 11, 18, 25, 1876; Rahill, *Indian Missions*, pp. 29ff; 44-B-11, printed circular of May 30, 1876.

130. Yeager, *Bayley*, pp. 444–48; McNamara, *American College*, pp. 218–21.

131. 44-B-10, Bayley to McCloskey, Baltimore, March 31, 1875 (copy). The original is not in the AANY.

132. 43-F-10, Roosevelt to Bayley, New York, March 17, 1875.

133. Quoted in Yeager, *Bayley*, p. 412.

134. *CM*, January 13, 1877.

135. AANY, C-2, Bayley to Corrigan, Baltimore, November 1, 1876.

136. A fact that would probably have occurred to none of the curious in America but might have raised questions in Rome is suggested by a letter from Ella Edes to Bayley congratulating him on his elevation to Baltimore. "In strictest confidence," she advised him to write Julia Beers, a close friend living in Rome, not to be so "expansive" when talking about him. "You know they do not understand *the Platonics* where Bishops and priests are concerned and she may well end by compromising you seriously." Barnabò had inquired about the relationship. 41-P-4, Edes to Bayley, Rome, July 22, 1872.

137. 40-N-4, Purcell to Bayley, Cincinnati, March 26, 1876.

138. Yeager, *Bayley*, pp. 448–51; Ellis, *Gibbons*, I: 152–54. The other two names placed on the terna were Bishops Foley of Chicago and Becker of Wilmington.

139. Quoted in Yeager, *Bayley*, p. 463n.

140. Quoted in ibid., pp. 462–63.

Part III. Introduction

1. James Gibbons, *A Retrospect of Fifty Years* (2 vols., Baltimore, 1916), I: 248–49.

2. Cogley, *Catholic America*, p. 222.

Chapter 10. A Masterly Inactivity

1. Ellis, *Gibbons*, I: 3.

2. Ibid., pp. 3–43

3. Ibid., pp. 47–163

4. AAB, Gibbons diary, p. 94.

5. *Sadlier's Catholic Directory, 1878*, pp. 61–65.

6. The northern counties include Anne Arundel, Baltimore, Harford, and Howard; the southern, Calvert, Charles, Montgomery, Prince George's, and St. Mary's; and the western, Allegany, Carroll, Frederick, Garrett, and Washington. Several of the churches of the northern counties would be absorbed by Baltimore with the extension of its boundaries in 1886.

7. The Sulpicians, six at St. Mary's Seminary and ten at St. Charles, were not religious strictly speaking but, as members of a distinct society of priests, were usually considered such.

8. These and the following data are taken from *Sadlier's Catholic Directory, 1878*, pp. 67–72, with corrections and additions from Corrigan, *Catholic Schools*, passim.

9. *CM*, April 8, 1882. The largest colleges and academies were Georgetown College with 255 students, St. Joseph's Academy (Calvert Hall) with 250, St. Catherine's Normal School with 170, St. John's College (formerly St. Matthew's Institute of Washington) with 150, Rock Hill College with 130, and Notre Dame of Maryland with 112. St. Charles College, the minor seminary, had 185 students and St. Mary's Seminary 130. The rounded figures suggest some inflation.

10. 73-Q-8/1, Keane to Gibbons, Washington, April 9, 1878.

11. 75-Q-5, Walter to Gibbons, Washington, February 15, 1881.

12. Gibbons diary, p. 125.

13. 75-K-4, Videnka to Gibbons, Luxemburg, Wis., October 2, 1880.

14. 76-R-12, Foley to Gibbons, Baltimore, June 14, 1882.

15. Curley, *Provincial Story*, pp. 189—91.

16. Thomas L. Cholochwast, "Baltimore's Polish Pioneers," *Maryland Magazine of Genealogy* 5 (1892): 3—7. I am indebted to Thomas Hollowak (Cholochwast) for much of my information on Baltimore's Polish community, especially in this chapter to his "The Emergence of a Baltimore Polonia," an unpublished paper. As early as 1865 Polish Jews formed a Hebrew congregation on Gay Street. Scharf, *Baltimore City and County*, p. 598.

17. St. Stanislaus was dedicated June 26, 1881. Marie Giza, *The History of Stanislaus Kostka Parish, 100th Anniversary* (Baltimore, 1981), unpaginated.

18. 76-Q-10, Polish Catholics to Gibbons, Baltimore, May 29, 1882.

19. 77-E-10, Wdrzynski to Gibbons, Baltimore, March 30, 1883.

20. 78-L-4, Koncz to Gibbons, Baltimore, August 18, 1884.

21. Hollowak, "Baltimore Polonia," p. 34 and n. 95; *The Sun*, February 9, 1886.

22. Enrico Causici and Antonio Cappellano respectively.

23. For much of my information on the Italians of Baltimore I am indebted to Vincenza Scarpaci and her "*Ambiente Italiano*: Origins and Growth of Baltimore's Little Italy" (unpublished paper). See also Gilbert Sandler, *The Neighborhood: The Story of Baltimore's Little Italy* (Baltimore, 1974).

24. 74-R-4, Andreis to Gibbons, Baltimore, September 11, 1879.

25. *The Church of St. Leo the Great, 1881–1981: The Heart of Little Italy* (Baltimore, 1981), pp. 3—7.

26. 75-Y-10, Didier to Gibbons, Baltimore, June 24, 1881.

27. 76-H-14, same to same, Baltimore, November 15, 1881.

28. 76-S-7, Andreis to Gibbons, Baltimore, July 28, 1882.

29. *CM*, September 9, 1882.

30. Dieter Cunz, *The Maryland Germans, A History* (Princeton, N.J.), pp. 393, 437.

31. Paul C. Crovo, *St. Anthony of Padua Parish, Baltimore, Maryland, 1884–1984* (n.p., 1984), pp. 17—18.

32. The percentage of foreign born in the District of Columbia dropped from 12.3 in 1870 to 9.7 in 1880. Green, *Washington: Capital City*, p. 89.

33. 73-K-7, Didier to Gibbons, Baltimore, December 26, 1877.

34. Frances Meginnis, "A History of Corpus Christi-Jenkins Memorial Church" (unpublished paper), pp. 1—20.

35. *CM*, May 31, 1884, September 19, 1885; *St. Gregory the Great Celebrates 100 Years* (n.p., 1984), p. 14.

36. Meyer, *St. Mary's*, pp. 75—78.

37. *WL* 9 (1880): 50—53; 10 (1881): 69—70.

38. Beitzell, *Jesuit Missions*, p. 238; *CM*, May 28, 1881.

39. Stanton, *Century of Growth*, 2: 96—97

40. Ibid., 1: 230—31.

41. *CM*, December 9, 1882, January 27, 1883.

42. 73-R-4, Harthman et al. to Gibbons, Washington, April 22, 1878.

43. *CM*, September 8, October 16, 1886.

44. Ibid., August 7, 1880, April 1, 1882.

45. Ibid., November 6, 20, 1886, February 19, 1887.

46. Gibbons Diary, p. 95, October 23, 1878.

47. Mary Cecilia O'Sullivan, *The Sisters of Bon Secours in the United States, 1881–1981: A Century of Caring* (n.p., 1982), pp. 1–45.

48. *CM*, June 29, 1878, June 21, 1879.

49. Ibid., December 8, 1877, February 23, March 2, November 9, 1878.

50. Ibid., August 7, October 18, 25, 1879.

51. Ibid., July 3, 10, 1880.

52. Ellis, *Gibbons*, I: 445–46.

53. Ibid., p. 452.

54. *CM*, December 18, 1880, June 4, 1881.

55. Ibid., June 22, 29, 1889.

56. Ibid., February 18, 1882.

57. For such law suits see ibid., March 22, August 16, December 13, 1879, January 10, 1880, May 7, 1881.

58. Donohoe, *Irish Catholic Benevolent Union*, pp. 6–13.

59. Branches of the EBA were numbered in the order in which they were founded in a given state.

60. *CM*, August 6, 1887.

61. Branches of the CKA were numbered in the order in which they were founded nationally.

62. Donohoe, *Irish Catholic Benevolent Union*, pp. 9–10.

63. *CM*, August 18, 1883.

64. Ibid., March 6, 1886.

65. Ellis, *Gibbons*, I: 444, 449–51.

66. Ibid., pp. 451–54.

67. *CM*, September 17, 1887.

68. Carl Bode, *American Lyceum*, (New York, 1956).

69. *CM*, December 3, 1887. The four from Baltimore were St. John's Institute, St. Patrick's Lyceum, St. Peter's Lyceum, and Star of the Sea Lyceum; the three from Washington were the Carroll Institute, the Georgetown Union, and St. Aloysius Literary Society.

70. Ibid., March 29, 1884.

71. Ibid., June 19, 1883. Athletics were not limited to the literary societies and colleges. In 1883 the Sacred Heart Sodality of St. Patrick's, Baltimore, also furnished a gymnasium.

72. *CM*, July 28, 1883.

73. Ibid., June 12, 1886.

74. Ibid., November 16, 1878, April 12, 1879.

75. Ibid., November 16, 1878.

76. O'Sullivan, *Bon Secours*, p. 24.

77. O'Daniel, *St. Dominic's*, pp. 46–50.

78. To Archbishop John Ireland in 1888, quoted in Mary Adele Gorman, "Federation of Catholic Societies in the United States, 1870–1920" (doctoral dissertation, University of Notre Dame, 1962), pp. 25–26.

79. Ellis, *Gibbons*, I: 204.

80. 75-P-5, McCaffrey to Gibbons, Mount St. Mary's, January 7, 1881.

81. Ellis, *Gibbons*, 1: 204.

82. *CM*, December 29, 1883, January 5, 1884.

83. Ellis, *Gibbons*, 1: 222–63."

84. Guilday, *Councils*, pp. 221–49; McAvoy, History, pp. 254–62.

85. *Synodus Dioecesana Baltimorensis Nona [sic] quae antecedentium etiam complectitur Constitutiones; die 24 Septembris, AD. 1886 ad BVM in Seminario S. Sulpitii, Baltimorae habita ab Eminentissimo ac Reverendissi:::o Jacobo Cardinali Gibbons, Archiepiscopo Baltimorensi* (Baltimore, 1886).

86. Kenrick had requested that Damphoux receive this honor for his faithful service as secretary to the first seven councils. APF, Congressi 16: 146r–47v, Kenrick to O'Connor, Baltimore, July 12, 1852.

87. *CM*, September 10, 1887.

88. Ibid., January 27, 1883.

89. John Tracy Ellis, *The Formative Years of the Catholic University of America* (Washington, D. C., 1946), pp. 87–146.

90. Gerald P. Fogarty, *The Vatican and the Americanist Crisis: Denis J. O'Connell, American Agent in Rome, 1885–1903* (Rome, 1974), pp. 42–45.

91. Robert Emmett Curran, *Michael Augustine Corrigan and the Shaping of Conservative Catholicism in America, 1878–1902* (New York, 1978), pp. 109–10, 164.

92. Henry J. Browne, *The Catholic Church and the Knights of Labor* (Washington, D.C., 1949), pp. 182–227.

93. Ibid., pp. 34–69, 127.

94. Ellis, *Gibbons*, 1: 494, quoting a letter of May 6, 1886.

95. *CM*, January 19, 1878.

96. Harvey, *Best-Dressed Miners*, pp. 205–6.

97. 74-J-6, Schmitt to Gibbons, Frostburg, February 9, 1879.

98. 76-R-7, Mayer to Foley, Cumberland, June 1, 1882.

99. 76-R-9 and 10, Schmitt to Gibbons, Frostburg, June 8, 9, 1882.

100. Harvey, *Best-Dressed Miners*, pp. 228–52, 385–87.

101. *CM*, July 11, 1885.

102. Ibid., April 24, 1886.

103. Ibid., March 13, 1886; Richard T. Ely, *Ground under Our Feet; An Autobiography* (New York, 1938), pp. 78–79.

104. *CM*, May 15, 1886.

105. Ellis, *Gibbons*, 1: 547–54; Curran, *Corrigan*, pp. 259–60.

106. Ellis, *Gibbons*, 1: 291–304.

107. Colman J. Barry, *The Catholic Church and the German Americans* (Milwaukee, 1953), pp. 1–65.

108. 82-G-4, Keane to Gibbons, Rome, December 4, 1886.

109. 82-J-4, same to same, Rome, December 29, 1886.

110. Ellis, *Catholic University*, pp. 222–27.

111. Ellis, *Gibbons*, 1: 358–60.

112. Ibid., pp. 554–85.

113. The memorial is given in full in Browne, *Knights of Labor*, pp. 365–78.

114. Ellis, *Gibbons*, 1: 511–13.

115. Ibid., pp. 307–9; Fogarty, *O'Connell*, pp. 96–97.

116. *CM*, April 1, 1887.

117. It was, according to his principal biographer, "by all odds the most popular work in apologetics ever published by an American Catholic" (Ellis, *Gibbons*, 2: 591).

118. 85-W-13, Ireland to Gibbons, St. Paul, April 20, 1889.

119. AAB, unclassified, Gibbons' own draft; *CM*, December 25, 1886.

Chapter 11. *Prince of the Church*

1. *CM*, June 11, 1887.

2. Ellis, *Gibbons*, 1: 316–21, 325–30.

3. AANY, C-16, McQuaid to Corrigan, Rochester, October 9, 1887.

4. Thomas W. Wangler, "The Birth of Americanism: Westward the Apocalyptic Candlestick," *Harvard Theological Review* 65 (1972): 415–23.

5. Ibid., p. 432.

6. Curran, *Corrigan*, p. 320. Corrigan also named Archbishop Patrick W. Riordan of San Francisco, Bishop John S. Foley of Detroit, and Bishop John Lancaster Spalding of Peoria. Spalding, however, remained aloof from both factions.

7. Robert D. Cross, *The Emergence of Liberal Catholicism in America* (Cambridge, Mass., 1958), pp. 22ff.

8. Kauffman, *Saint Sulpice*, pp. 163–64.

9. Ellis, *Gibbons*, 1: 375–78.

10. *CM*, November 1, 1884; "Some Defects in Our Political and Social Institutions," *North American Review* 145 (1887): 345–54. The other two evils were divorce (coupled with Mormonism) and the desecration of the Christian Sabbath.

11. Daniel F. Reilly, *The School Controversy, 1891–1893* (Washington, D.C., 1943), pp. 1–49.

12. *CM*, July 19, 1890

13. 88-D-9, O'Connell to Gibbons, Rome, November 29, 1890; 88-E-1, Ireland to Gibbons, St. Paul, December 11, 1890.

14. Reilly, *School Controversy*, pp. 242–47 (appendix).

15. Ibid., pp. 75–133.

16. 88 S 3, Ireland to Gibbons, St. Paul, July 2, 1981.

17. 91-J-6, Gibbons to Vaughan, Baltimore, April 17, 1893 (copy).

18. The arrangement at Texas lasted from 1856 to 1926. See Smith, *St. Joseph's*, pp. 98–99. The Hampden arrangement lasted from 1874 to 1896, as indicated in the parish Notitiae.

19. 90-A-3, Gibbons to Mathews, Baltimore, July 2, 1982 (copy).

20. *CM*, January 21, 1893.

21. Gerald P. Fogarty, *The Vatican and the American Hierarchy from 1870 to 1965* (Wilmington, Del., 1985), pp. 114–20.

22. Ibid., pp. 120–24; Ellis, *Gibbons*, 1: 618–26.

23. Ellis, *Gibbons*, 1: 634–35.

24. 91-A-7, Ireland to Gibbons, St. Paul, January 8, 1893.

25. 93-J-7, Keane to Gibbons, Pegli, July 31, 1894.

26. 94B-A-1; Ellis, *Documents*, 2: 499–511.

27. *CM*, December 9, 1893.

28. The sermon was carried in full in the Baltimore *Katholische Volkszeitung*. See Ellis, *Gibbons*, I: 648–50.

29. Fogarty, *Vatican*, p. 136.

30. Fogarty, *O'Connell*, pp. 252–53. The black aristocracy was that created by the pope.

31. Ahern, *Keane*, pp. 178–85.

32. Fogarty, *Vatican*, pp. 147–48.

33. Cross, *Liberal Catholicism*, pp. 189–95.

34. Thomas T. McAvoy, *The Great Crisis in American Catholic History, 1895–1900* (Chicago, 1957), pp. 154ff.

35. Fogarty, *O'Connell*, pp. 317–26 (appendix).

36. Kauffman, *Saint Sulpice*, p. 165.

37. McAvoy, *Great Crisis*, p. 207.

38. 97-B-7/1; Ellis, *Documents*, 2: 537–47.

39. Ellis, *Gibbons*, 2: 71–72

40. Ibid., p. 74.

41. Ahern, *Keane*, p. 263.

42. *CM*, April 1, 1899.

43. Richard M. Linkh, *American Catholicism and European Immigrants (1900–1924)* (Staten Island, N.Y., 1975), pp. 1–19.

44. *CM*, June 13, 1891.

45. Ellis, *Gibbons* I: 691.

46. *Church News* (Washington), February 1, 1896.

47. 87-D-8, Schmitt to Gibbons, Washington, February 12, 1890.

48. Charles Hirschfeld, *Baltimore, 1870–1900: Studies in Social History* (Baltimore, 1941), pp. 19–26.

49. Ibid., pp. 32–65; Olson, *Baltimore*, pp. 166, 198–203, 228–29, 285–86; Walsh and Fox, *Maryland*, pp. 397–509; Scarpaci, "Ambiente Italiano," pp. 1–25.

50. James B. Crooks, *Politics & Progress: The Rise of Urban Progressivism in Baltimore, 1895–1911* (Baton Rouge, La., 1968), pp. 4–5; Olson, *Baltimore*, pp. 271–73.

51. Hirschfeld, *Baltimore*, p. 65.

52. *CM*, October 19, 1895.

53. 84-P-5, Starr to Gibbons, Baltimore, June 21, 1888.

54. *CM*, January 21, 1882.

55. 105-D-1, Kerr to Gibbons, Baltimore, February 2, 1907.

56. Accounts of these two churches can be found in [Ernesto Begni, ed.], *The Catholic Church in the United States; Undertaken to Celebrate the Golden Jubilee of His Holiness, Pope Pius X* (3 vols., New York, 1914), 3: 89–90, 110.

57. Dolan, *American Catholic Experience*, p. 299.

58. Thomas Hollowak, "The Church as Landmark in the Formation of a Polish-American Community" (unpublished paper).

59. Thomas Hollowak, *Faith, Work, and Struggle: A History of Baltimore Polonia* (Baltimore, 1988; to commemorate the 90th anniversary of Holy Cross Polish National Catholic Church), pp. 21–35.

60. The *Przyjaciel Domu* ran from 1895 to 1905. Willging and Hatzfeld, *Catholic Serials: Maryland*, pp. 44–45.

61. Hollowak, *Baltimore Polonia*, pp. 35–48; *CM*, March 5, 26, 1898.

62. *Church News*, July 30, 1898.

63. *CM*, May 20, 1905; *Seventy-Fifth Anniversary of Holy Rosary Church* (Baltimore, 1964), pp. 18–20.

64. 101-P-2, Morys to Gavan, Baltimore, October 5, 1904; information from the *Dziennik Chicagoski* supplied by Thomas Hollowak.

65. Quoted in John Quentin Feller, "The Public Character of Cardinal Gibbons in His Archdiocese" (master's thesis, Catholic University of America, 1965), pp. 75–77.

66. Begni, *Catholic Church*, 3: 70; *CM*, February 16, 1889, April 24, 1897.

67. William Wolkovich-Valkavicius, "Religious Separatism Among Lithuanian Immigrants in the United States and Their Polish Affiliation," *Polish American Studies* 40 (1983): 102, and other information from Rev. William Wolkovich.

68. 103-M-3, Mackall to Gavan, Midland, May 4, 1906.

69. 89-U-6.1, Andreis to Gibbons, Baltimore, April 19, 1901.

70. 101-C-15 and 16, Falconio to Gibbons, Washington, March 2, 1904, and clipping from the *Washington Times* of February 29, 1904.

71. 101-D-2, Gibbons to Falconio, Baltimore, March 3, 1904 (copy).

72. *CM*, December 28, 1889, February 4, 1891.

73. Ibid., April 11, 1891.

74. Owen B. Corrigan, "Catholicity in Allegany and Garrett Counties, Maryland," *RACHSP* 36 (1925): 240. In 1912 it was reported that there were only 950 Italians in Allegany County, mostly in Cumberland.

75. *St. Peter Claver Catholic Church, 1888–1963* (Baltimore, 1963), pp. 11–12.

76. *CM*, August 1, 1891.

77. Beitzell, *Jesuit Missions*, pp. 287–88.

78. Begni, *Catholic Church*, 3: 60–79 and passim; *St. Benedict Church, Baltimore, Maryland* (Hackensack, N.J., 1968); *Golden Jubilee: St. Elizabeth's Parish* (Baltimore, 1945), pp. 11–23.

79. Begni, *Catholic Church*, 3: 112–20 and passim; *CM*, passim.

80. Joerndt, *St. Ignatius*, pp. 290–91, 339–40, 352–54.

81. Corrigan, "Catholicity in Allegany and Garrett Counties," pp. 209–10, 240–41, 245–48. St. Dominic's at Hoyes in Garrett County also replaced the older mission of St. James at Cross Roads in this period.

82. Philibert, *St. Matthew's*, pp. 57ff.

83. Corrigan, *Catholic Schools*, passim.

84. Costello, *Sisters of Mercy*, pp. 96–98.

85. Steins, "Josephites," pp. 72–85.

86. Joseph T. Durkin, *Georgetown University: The Middle Years, 1840–1900* (Washington, D.C., 1963), pp. 215–26.

87. *CM*, June 17, 1899.

88. Angela Elizabeth Keenan, *Three against the Wind: The Founding of Trinity College, Washington, D.C.* (Westminster, Md., 1973).

89. *CM*, June 2, 1888, November 22, 1889; Lawrence H. Larsen, *The Rise of the Urban South* (Lexington, Ky., 1985), pp. 139–40.

90. *CM*, November 16, 1889.

91. Ibid., March 1, 1890, March 18, 1893.

92. Ibid., August 26, 1893.

93. Ibid., January 14, 1899.

94. Ibid., January 21, 1899.

95. Ibid., January 12, 1901.

96. Ibid., September 22, 1883.

97. Ibid., March 21, 1891.

98. Ibid., December 19, 1896; [Louis O'Donovan], *Diamond Jubilee: St. Martin's Church* (n.p., [1940]), p. 147.

99. *CM*, February 18, 1893.

100. Ibid., December 14, 1895, January 25, 1896.

101. Christopher Kauffman, *Faith and Fraternalism: The History of the Knights of Columbus, 1882–1982* (New York, 1982), pp. 1–94, 132–43.

102. John P. Bauernschub, *Fifty Years of Columbianism in Maryland* (Baltimore, 1949), pp. 30–34.

103. Ibid., pp. 34–54, 185–97.

104. Kauffman, *Knights of Columbus*, pp. 143–47; *Church News*, January 28, July 1, 1899.

105. *CM*, June 16, 1900.

106. Ibid., September 15, 1900.

107. V. F. O'Daniel, *Very Rev. Charles Hyacinth McKenna, O.P., P.G.: Missionary and Apostle of the Holy Name Society* (New York, 1917), pp. 108–10, 179–81, 277.

108. *BCR*, September 20, 1924, an account by Bishop Owen Corrigan, the first archdiocesan chaplain. The second branch was at St. Martin's in 1892 and the third at St. Gregory's in 1893.

109. *CR*, June 18, 1937.

110. *CM*, July 16, 1892.

111. Scarpaci, "Ambiente Italiano," pp. 33–34.

112. *CM*, September 28, 1907.

113. Ibid., November 2, 1901. The CWBL had a limit of $1,000 in benefits compared to the CBL's $5,000.

114. *Church News*, January 21, 28, May 13, 20, 1899.

115. *CM*, November 2, 9, 16, 1895.

116. Ibid., June 6, 1896, January 23, 1897.

117. Rasin was converted to the Catholic Church on his deathbed in 1907. Mary Anne Dunn, "The Life of Isaac Freeman Rasin, Democratic Leader of Baltimore from 1870–1907" (master's thesis, Catholic University of America, 1949).

118. *CM*, November 23, 1895.

119. Crooks, *Politics & Progress*, pp. 59–60, 66–67, 90, 170–71, and passim.

120. Ibid., p. 68. See also Margaret Law Callcott, *The Negro in Maryland Politics, 1870–1912* (Baltimore, 1969), pp. 129–30.

121. 100-H-1.2, statement of February 11, 1903. Crooks, *Politics & Progress*, p. 189, is mistaken in saying that Gibbons was opposed to local option.

122. Crooks, *Politics & Progress*, pp. 224–34, provides a profile of 108 men and 28 women outstanding for their progressivism, of whom there were eight Catholic men but no Catholic women.

123. Feller, "Public Character," p. 56.

124. Callcott, *Negro in Maryland Politics*, pp. 84–85, 96–98.

125. Gorman, "Federation of Catholic Societies," pp. 26–37; Cross, *Liberal Catholicism*, pp. 169–70.

126. Gorman, "Federated Catholic Societies," p. 53.

127. *CM*, December 30, 1894.

128. *Putnam's Monthly* 2 (1907): 62–67.

129. 106-K-7, Kelly et al. to Gavan, Washington, October 16, 1908.

130. 106-M-5, Gavan to Gilmore, Baltimore, December 21, 1908 (copy).

131. 127-M-9, Rollman to Gibbons, Baltimore, July 26, 1919.

132. 121-F-5, Gibbons to Schwab, Baltimore, March 12, 1918 (copy).

133. *CM*, May 7, 1892. On more than one occasion the *Catholic Mirror* quoted approvingly gibes of the English Jesuit and future modernist, George Tyrrell, against the "new woman," an "abomination to Catholic instincts" in Tyrrell's eyes (ibid., November 9, 1895, August 7, 1897).

134. Ibid., February 10, 1900.

135. David Spalding, "The Negro Catholic Congresses, 1889–1894," *CHR* 55 (1969): 337–57; Cyprian Davis, "Black Catholics in Nineteenth Century America," *USCH* 5 (1986): 12–17.

136. *CM*, January 5, 1889.

137. *The Sun*, June 29, 1894.

138. Spalding, "Negro Catholic Congresses," pp. 351 52.

139. 96-D-3, Griffith to Gibbons, Washington, March 1, 1898.

140. *CM*, May 10, 17, 24, 1890, and several later issues. Among the contributors to the debate was the unblushing racist James Ryder Randall, who wrote as "A Southern Catholic Layman."

141. Ibid., September 20, 1890.

142. 124-C-4, Turner et al. to Gibbons, Washington, December 23, 1918.

143. *CM*, January 12, 1895.

144. Ibid., copied from *Donahoe's Magazine*.

Chapter 12. A Twilight Aura

1. No records of meetings earlier than February 26, 1920, were preserved except for those of November 10, 1916, inserted in a book entitled "Consultors Meetings" (AAB). These concern a request of the founders of Maryknoll to establish a second house of training in the archdiocese of Baltimore for Christian but missionary lands, which was declined. The first minutes in the book itself were of a "special meeting to comply with requirements of the new code."

2. Ellis, *Gibbons*, 2: 428–29.

3. Fogarty, *Vatican*, p. 205.

4. See Thomas T. McAvoy, "Liberalism, Americanism, Modernism," *RACHSP* 62 (1952): 225–31, and Margaret Mary Reher, "Americanism and Modernism—Continuity or Discontinuity," *USCH* 1 (1981): 87–103.

5. *CM*, February 29, March 7, 1908.

6. Albert Houtin, *Histoire du modernisme catholique* (Paris, 1913), pp. 113–14, 240–42.

7. William L. Portier, "Modernism in the United States: The Case of John R. Slattery, 1851–1926" (unpublished paper).

8. Kauffman, *Saint Sulpice*, pp. 160-77, 199-223, 226-28.

9. Michael De Vito, *The New York Review, 1905-1907* (New York, 1977).

10. Ellis, *Gibbons*, 2: 172-82, 447-78.

11. Peter E. Hogan, *The Catholic University of America, 1896-1903: The Rectorship of Thomas J. Conaty* (Washington, D.C., 1949).

12. Colman J. Barry, *The Catholic University of America, 1903-1909: The Rectorship of Denis J. O'Connell* (Washington, D.C., 1950).

13. Ibid., pp. 71-108.

14. Blaise Dixon, "The Catholic University of America, 1909-1928: The Rectorship of Thomas Joseph Shahan" (doctoral dissertation, Catholic University of America, 1972).

15. Kauffman, *Saint Sulpice*, pp. 270-73.

16. *CM*, November 18, 1905.

17. Ellis, *Gibbons*, 2: 343-45, 379-88.

18. *CM*, June 13, 1908.

19. Washington also had a Catholic weekly, the *Church News*, under a talented lay editor, Milton E. Smith, from 1886 to 1900. Its successor, the *New Century*, operated by a Milwaukee firm, carried little of local interest. See Willging and Hatzfeld, *Catholic Serials: Maryland and the District of Columbia*, pp. 18-19, 84-87. *Baltimore* would be dropped from the *Baltimore Catholic Review* in 1936. It was issued by the Metropolitan Publishing Company under a board of six priests and two laymen. Its first editor was the Rev. Cornelius F. Thomas.

20. Ellis, *Gibbons*, 2: 108.

21. Ibid., pp. 547-53; Allen Sinclair Will, *Life of Cardinal Gibbons, Archbishop of Baltimore* (2 vols., New York, 1922), 2: 688-710.

22. Ellis, *Gibbons*, 2: 433-37.

23. Ibid., pp. 84-85.

24. *CM*, June 2, 1906.

25. Ibid., March 5, 1898.

26. Ibid., January 26, 1901.

27. Ellis, *Gibbons*, 2: 232-38.

28. Ibid., p. 239. See Dorothy Dohen, *Nationalism and American Catholicism* (New York, 1967), pp. 146-55.

29. Ellis, *Gibbons*, 2: 254.

30. Ibid., pp. 121-39. The Jones Act was passed in 1916.

31. Ibid., pp. 314-19.

32. Ibid., pp. 243-46.

33. Ibid., pp. 205-21.

34. *BCR*, February 24, 1916.

35. 136-H-1, O'Sullivan to Gibbons, Bardstown, October 4, 1920.

36. 108-Q-4, Gibbons to Baker, n.p., August 21, 1910 (copy).

37. Ellis, *Gibbons*, 2: 343.

38. Ibid., p. 236.

39. Gorman, "Federation of Catholic Societies," pp. 72-73, 92-93.

40. Hirschfeld, *Baltimore*, pp. 76-81; Olson, *Baltimore*, pp. 237-91.

41. Linkh, *Catholicism and Immigrants*, pp. 23-31.

42. Ellis, *Gibbons*, 2: 464-65.

43. Francesco Guglielmi, *The Italian Methodist Mission in the Little Italy of Baltimore, Md.: Seven Years of Evangelical Christian Work* (Baltimore, 1912).

44. *CM*, July 14, 1906.

45. *The Church of St. Leo*, pp. 15–19.

46. 117-C-8, Russell to Gibbons, Washington, May 15, 1916.

47. 127-P-11, Answers to questionnaires on Italian priests, August 26, 1919.

48. 111-Q-10, Bladzinski et al. to Gibbons, Baltimore, February 14, 1913.

49. *Golden Jubilee: SS. Peter and Paul Ukranian Church* (n.p., 1963), unpaginated.

50. Gerald P. Fogarty, "The American Hierarchy and Oriental Rite Catholics, 1890–1907," *RACHSP* 85 (1974): 17–28.

51. In 1923 Sandalgi would be called to Rome as an authority on the Ruthenians. In 1924 the Ruthenians and the Ukranians would be given separate bishops in the United States.

52. John LaFarge, *The Manner Is Ordinary* (New York, 1954), pp. 178–80, 381–84.

53. Olson, *Baltimore*, pp. 285–86.

54. In 1920 the pastor of St. Stanislaus had almost $10,000 on deposit from twelve parish societies and $65,000 from sixty-seven individual members of the congregation.

55. Scarpaci, "Ambiente Italiano," pp. 46–49.

56. *BCR*, March 7, 1914.

57. Olson, *Baltimore*, p. 270.

58. Ibid., pp. 266–71.

59. 100-V-5.1, Gibbons to Kerby, Baltimore, December 7, 1903 (copy).

60. McColgan, *Century of Charity*, 2: 210–17.

61. Ibid., pp. 218–20; John O'Grady, *Catholic Charities in the United States: History and Problems* (Washington, D.C., 1930), pp. 426–27; Aaron I. Abell, *American Catholicism and Social Action: A Search for Social Justice, 1865–1950* (Garden City, N.Y., 1960), pp. 167–68; *BCR*, January 10, 1914.

62. *BCR*, December 1, 1917.

63. McColgan, *Century of Charity*, 2: 226–27; Abell, *Social Action*, pp. 159–60; *Church News*, October 15, 1898.

64. *BCR*, July 11, 1914.

65. O'Grady, *Catholic Charities*, pp. 324–26.

66. *BCR*, May 1, September 11, 1920.

67. Ibid., April 27, 1918.

68. Begni, *Catholic Church*, 2: 436–40; Marie Elizabeth Spellacy, "The Evolution of the Catechetical Ministry Among the Mission Helpers of the Sacred Heart, 1890–1980" (doctoral dissertation, Catholic University of America, 1984).

69. Begni, *Catholic Church*, 2: 262–63; 125-J-10, Mother de Sales to Gibbons, Forest Park, March 14, 1921; 125-K-5, Smith to Mother de Sales, Baltimore, March 16, 1921 (copy).

70. *BCR*, July 4, 1914.

71. Ibid., February 26, 1916; O'Grady, *Catholic Charities*, pp. 316, 409–10.

72. McColgan, *Century of Charity*, 2: 294–313; Abell, *Social Action*, pp. 167–68.

73. *BCR*, May 1, 1920.

74. Ibid., March 25, 1916.

75. Ibid., February 15, 1916.

76. O'Grady, *Catholic Charities*, p. 219.

77. Mary Elenora Smith, "The Jenkins Family of Baltimore" (master's thesis, Catholic University of America, 1941), p. 75.

78. Eleanor Stephens Bruchey, "The Business Elite in Baltimore, 1880–1914" (doctoral dissertation, Johns Hopkins University, 1967), pp. 338–39.

79. Ibid., pp. 223–24.

80. Prominent in the *Society Visiting List or "Blue Book"* for 1920 were such Catholic families as the Abells, Boones, Brents, Chatards, Elders, Jenkinses, McSherrys, O'Donovans, and Shrivers. The socially acceptable Catholic churches were the cathedral, the chapel of the Visitation, Corpus Christi, Immaculate Conception, St. Ann's, St. Ignatius, and St. Martin's.

81. Olson, *Baltimore*, pp. 263–65; *BCR*, January 26, 1934; *Evening Sun*, January 23, 1934.

82. 120-M-7, Will of Thomas O'Neill. Loyola was originally bequeathed $500,000, but $200,000 of it was given before O'Neill died.

83. *St. Rose of Lima Church, 1914–1974*, (Baltimore, 1974), pp. 6–7.

84. McHale, "Catholic Church in the District," pp. 56–60; Foley, "Catholic Church and the Washington Negro," pp. 63–66.

85. Foley, "Catholic Church and the Washington Negro," pp. 64–65, 82–83.

86. St. Paul's had a revenue of $116,000, but $65,000 of this was in loans.

87. Consultors Meetings, p. 12, November 15, 1920.

88. Corrigan, *Catholic Schools*, pp. 25–27.

89. LaFarge, *The Manner Is Ordinary*, p. 157.

90. Ibid., pp. 155ff.

91. O'Sullivan, *Bon Secours*, pp. 101–13.

92. *BCR*, September 11, 1915.

93. Bauernschub, *Columbianism*, pp. 50–90; *BCR*, December 18, 1915.

94. *BCR*, November 23, 1913, January 10, 1914.

95. Ibid., October 9, 16, 1915, January 29, April 30, 1921.

96. Ibid., May 20, 1916.

97. Kauffman, *Knights of Columbus*, pp. 125–26.

98. Joseph J. Burns, *The Educational Influences of the International Federation of Catholic Alumnae* (Washington, D.C., 1937), pp. 1–9.

99. AAB, Corrigan papers, Corrigan et al. to Gibbons [April 10, 1912].

100. 99-H-6, Gibbons to O'Connell, Baltimore, December 17, 1901 [*sic*: 1911] (copy).

101. 113-M-1 through Q-1, Gibbons to Pius X and Gibbons to De Lai, Baltimore, May 1, 1914 (copies); SAB Record Group 26, Box 10, same to same. In both archives there are several drafts of both letters.

102. 98-V-9, Gibbons to Mother Marie Verger, n.p. [May 1901] (copy); Ellis, *Gibbons*, 2: 470–71.

103. Will, *Gibbons*, pp. 422–29.

104. 74-A-4, McCaffrey to Gibbons, Mount St. Mary's, October 11, 1878.

105. Ellis, *Gibbons*, 1: 46, 178, 320; 2: 526, 547.

106. Ibid., 2: 496–98; Feller, "Gibbons," pp. 69–71.

107. B. H. Hartogensis, "Christian Prelates of Baltimore on Russo-Jewish Persecution," *MHM* 28 (1933): 4–7; 123-R-11, statement of November 18, 1918; 124-M-4, Gibbons to Epstein, Baltimore, May 28, 1919 (copy).

108. Gibbons and Mendes Cohen, president of the Maryland Historical Society,

were charter members of an otherwise "perfect male Wasp bastion," the University Club. *Evening Sun*, October 29, 1974.

109. 94B-D-1, Rectors to Gibbons, Washington, January 1, 1896, and Gibbons to rectors, Baltimore, January 14, 1896 (copy).

110. AAB, Unclassified and undated statement.

111. 125-R-13, Whitman to Gibbons, New York, April 17, 1919.

112. 131-C-13, Smith to Thomas, Baltimore, February 21, 1920 (copy).

113. 125-H-4, Sister A. Clare to Gibbons, St. Mary of the Woods., Ind., March 5, 1919; 125-N-6, Myers to Gibbons, Chicago, April 1, 1919.

114. *CM*, January 18, 1908.

115. *BCR*, February 25, 1919.

116. Ibid., April 5, 19, 1919.

117. 107-O-2, Gibbons to Vives, Baltimore, September 16, 1909 (copy); 107-O-3, Sullivan to Gibbons, aboard the Adriatic, September 17, 1919.

118. 112-B-12, Bonzano to Gibbons, Washington, April 28, 1913.

119. 100-T-1, Sartori to Gibbons, Midland, November 3, 1903; 100-T-5, Jones to Sartori, Lonaconing, November 11, 1903.

120. 100-U-2, Sartori to Gibbons, Midland, November 18, 1903.

121. 111-Q-4, Manley to Gibbons, Baltimore, February 6, 1913.

122. 112-M-6, Schmitt to Gibbons, Washington, October 30, 1913.

123. AAB, Corrigan papers, Schmitt to Gibbons, Washington, October 30, 1914. Gibbons entrusted this well documented case to his vicar general, Bishop Corrigan.

124. Ibid., same to same, Washington, March 11, 1914.

125. 113-F-3, Schmitt to Gibbons, Baltimore, March 24, 1914 (apology and promise of reform).

126. AAB, Corrigan papers, newspaper clippings.

127. 109-G-4, Devine to Gibbons, Baltimore, April 18, 1911.

128. Ellis, *Gibbons*, 2: 293–98.

129. *BCR*, November 24, 1917.

130. Olson, *Baltimore*, p. 300.

131. *BCR*, February 2, 1918.

132. Ellis, *Gibbons*, 2: 298–309.

133. Francis L. Broderick, *Right Reverend New Dealer: John A. Ryan* (New York, 1963), pp. 104–8.

134. Secret Vatican Archives, Secretary of State, Apostolic Delegation of the U.S., Bonzano to De Lai, n.p., May 12, 1921 (courtesy of Gerald Fogarty, SJ).

135. Will, *Gibbons*, p. 1056, quoting the New York *Herald*.

136. John W. Bowen, "Loyal Son and Father," *The Borromean* 16 (1953): 3–5, 27–29.

137. *A Blessing of Years: The Memoirs of Lawrence Cardinal Shehan* (Notre Dame, Ind., 1982), pp. 51–52.

138. *The Sun*, June 8, 1916.

Part IV. Introduction

1. *BCR*, July 9, 1921.

2. William M. Halsey, *The Survival of American Innocence: Catholicism in an Era of Disillusionment, 1920–1940* (Notre Dame, Ind., 1980), p.2.

3. Constantine E. Maguire, ed., *Catholic Builders of the Nation* (5 vols., Boston, 1923).

4. Garry Wills, *Bare Ruined Choirs: Doubt, Prophecy, and Radical Religion* (Garden City, N.Y., 1972), p. 18.

5. Cogley, *Catholic America*, pp. 143–45.

Chapter 13. Who Is Like God

1. Vincent de Paul Fitzpatrick, *Life of Archbishop Curley: Champion of Catholic Education* (Baltimore, 1929), pp. 5–10.

2. In his recommendation to Cardinal De Lai of the Consistorial Congregation in May 1921, Bonzano reasoned that the archbishops of St. Louis, San Francisco, and St. Paul should not be transferred to Baltimore. Of the Baltimore suffragans he proposed Curley and Bishop William Russell of Charleston but indicated an obvious preference for the former, citing a letter of the senior suffragan, Bishop Benjamin J. Keiley of Savannah, who praised Curley as "a man of true administrative ability and truly a man of God." Secret Vatican Archives, Secretary of State, Apostolic Delegation of the United States, Bonzano to De Lai, n.p., May 12, 1921 (courtesy of Gerald Fogarty, SJ).

3. Fitzpatrick, *Curley*, pp. 26–34.

4. Both quoted in the *BCR*, July 30, 1921.

5. Fitzpatrick, *Curley*, pp. 46–55.

6. *BCR*, April 1, 1922.

7. A biography of Father Bishop, founder of the Glenmary Home Missions, is being prepared by Christopher J. Kauffman.

8. Fitzpatrick, *Curley*, pp. 102–3.

9. Mc-716, Curley to McGuire, January 23, 1925 (copy).

10. B-869, Curley to Biggs, November 22, 1922 (copy).

11. W-271.1, Walsh to Curley, Portland, April 9, 1922. See also Fogarty, *Vatican*, p. 221.

12. T-814, Turner to Curley, American College, May 29, 1922.

13. T-815, same to same, Bagni di Montecatini, June 6, 1922.

14. P-794, on the reverse of a blessing from the pope. The first item was "Cooperation of priests and people."

15. W-272, Walsh to Curley, Portland, October 2, 1922.

16. SAB, Record Group 9, Box 6, Curley to Walsh, October 2, 1922.

17. H-1601, Curley to Hull, April 15, 1935 (copy).

18. G-1382, Curley to Guilday, February 14, 1927 (copy); *BCR*, June 10, 1927.

19. *BCR*, February 12, 1926.

20. Ibid., November 27, 1931.

21. Ibid., January 22, 1932.

22. Costello, *Sisters of Mercy*, pp. 182–200.

23. P-379, 380, 382, Curley to Sister Paula, April 5, May 31, October 5, 1926 (copies); *BCR*, August 27, 1926.

24. The archdiocesan *Official Catholic Directory* did not give figures for these schools in the "Recapitulation" (p. 79), but they are given in the data supplied for each parish.

25. Beitzell, *Jesuit Missions*, pp. 290–91.

26. Witte, "St. Mary's Industrial School," pp. 113–26.

27. Fitzpatrick, *Curley*, pp. 76–78; *BCR*, November 23, 1928.

28. Roman Letters, Curley to Bisleti, October 24, 1932 (copy). For this and other points of interest I am indebted to Joseph M. White, who is preparing a history of seminary education in the United States.

29. John J. Lardner, "Forever a Friend," *The Voice* (March 1947), p. 5.

30. *BCR*, June 14, 1924.

31. Quoted in Dixon, "Catholic University," p. 214.

32. H. Warren Willis, "The Reorganization of the Catholic University of America during the Rectorship of James H. Ryan, 1929–1935" (doctoral dissertation, Catholic University of America, 1972), pp. 1–141, 228–46.

33. Ibid., pp. 249–53; Roy J. Deferrari, *Memoirs of the Catholic University of America, 1918–1960* (Boston, 1962), pp. 26–33.

34. M-404, Curley to Marella, November 7, 1935 (copy).

35. L-621, Curley to Leonard, March 13, 1923 (copy); M-1900, Moore to Curley, Baltimore, April 4, 1923; B-881, Biggs to Curley, Baltimore, April 20, 1923. The contest was in part one between laity and clergy. See B-874, Biggs to Sullivan, Baltimore, March 16, 1923; M-781 and 784, Mattfeldt to Curley, Catonsville, May 5, 1923, and n.d.

36. O-653 and 668, O'Grady to Curley, Washington, November 28, 1925, and May 21, 1929.

37. M-1321, Curley to Miles, March 11, 1926 (copy).

38. O'Grady, *Catholic Charities*, pp. 442–46.

39. *BCR*, November 9, 1934.

40. Ibid., February 8, 1929.

41. Fitzpatrick, *Curley*, pp. 80–84.

42. *BCR*, May 30, 1930.

43. [J. Frank Griffin, Jr.], *A Story of the Parish, 1926–1951: Shrine of the Little Flower* (Baltimore, 1951), pp. 12–17; *The Story of St. Francis of Assisi Church* (South Hackensack, N.J., 1977), pp. 5–6; *St. Bernardine's Church: Silver Anniversary 1928–1953* (n.p., 1953), pp. 3–16; *St. Rita's Church, Baltimore, Maryland* (South Hackensack, N.J., 1972), pp. 5–12; *St. Clement's, Rosedale: A Memoir 1925–1975* (n.p., 1975), unpaginated.

44. *BCR*, November 27, 1931.

45. Philibert, *St. Matthew's*, p. 84.

46. Bauernschub, *Columbianism*, pp. 92–122, 171–74.

47. Mc-631, Curley to McGreevy, November 9, 1926 (copy); M-333, Curley to Manley, January 12, 1927 (copy).

48. *BCR*, January 10, 17, 1930.

49. Ibid., January 25, 1929, January 17, 1935.

50. Ibid., January 21, 1937.

51. See Gerald P. Fogarty, ed., *Patterns of Episcopal Leadership* (New York, 1988), pp. 167–70 and passim.

52. B-2028, Curley to Burke, May 29, 1934 (copy).

53. Roman Letters, Cicognani to Curley, Rome, October 6, 1927.

54. K-841, Curley to Kiley, January 27, 1928 (copy).

55. C-1412, Curley to Conroy, February 9, 1923 (copy).

56. C-1473, same to same, September 1, 1939 (copy).

57. S-1180, Curley to Sheen, November 5, 1935 (copy).

58. M-1316, Curley to Mihm, June 15, 1933 (copy).

59. M-314, Manley to Curley, Baltimore, April 10, 1931.

60. M-316, Curley to Manley, April 13, 1931 (copy).

61. M-322, same to same, May 3, 1934 (copy).

62. T-323, Curley to Thomas, April 6, 1928 (copy).

63. G-1376, Curley to Guilday, March 13, 1926 (copy).

64. W-24, Undated address.

65. W-5, Curley to Wachowiak, April 7, 1924 (copy).

66. O-1272, Curley to McNamara, June 6, 1935 (copy); O-1273, Curley to Wikarski, June 5, 1935 (copy).

67. Roman Letters, Sandalgi to Curley, Baltimore, December 1, 1931; Curley to Fumasoni-Biondi, December 3, 1931 (copy).

68. *BCR*, April 25, 1930.

69. A-420, Arena to Curley, Baltimore, December 13, 1929.

70. H-6, Curley to Haarpainter, June 11, 1927 (copy).

71. M-651, Curley to Martini, December 9, 1927 (copy).

72. Marilyn Wenzke Nichols, "The Federated Colored Catholics: A Study of Three Variant Perspectives on Racial Justice as Represented by John LaFarge, William Markoe, and Thomas Turner" (doctoral dissertation, Catholic University of America, 1975), pp. 41–43.

73. Quoted in ibid., p. 107.

74. C-874, Curley to Clark, March 28, 1933 (copy).

75. T-804, Curley to Turner, February 4, 1933 (copy).

76. R-594, Curley to Riordan, November 1, 1924 (copy).

77. O-225, Curley to O'Connell, June 10, 1942 (copy); W-411, Curley to Walsh, November 9, 1942 (copy).

78. *BCR*, February 3, 10, 17, 1933.

79. *CR*, October 8, 1937.

80. Ibid., October 22, 1937.

81. *BCR*, July 19, 26, August 2, 16, 1929.

82. L-811, Curley to Lillis, February 20, 1933 (copy).

83. George Seldes, *The Catholic Crisis* (New York, 1939), pp. 202–205.

84. K-243, Curley to Kelley, November 5, 1934 (copy).

85. *BCR*, June 29, 1934.

86. Ibid., July 20, 1934. One estimate set the *Sun's* circulation loss at 50,000, out of 137,000 (Seldes, *Catholic Crisis*, p. 204). Concerning Mencken, Curley told Kelley that "he doesn't mean half of what he says. He abuses everybody in sight, but has not yet openly attacked the Catholic Church" (K-243, Curley to Kelley, November 5, 1934 [copy]). Mencken never did.

87. Presidential file, Coolidge to Curley, Washington, January 31, 1925.

88. John Whitney Evans, *The Newman Movement: Roman Catholics in Higher Education, 1883–1971* (Notre Dame, Ind., 1980), pp. 78–81.

89. O-50, Curley to O'Brien, February 8, 1926 (copy).

90. Ibid., March 11, April 1, 1927.

91. Roman Letters, Curley to Fumasoni-Biondi, [March 29, 1927] (copy); M-1219, Curley to Merry del Val, April 23, 1927 (copy).

92. Ibid., Fumasoni-Biondi to Curley, Washington, April 20, 1927.

93. John B. Sheerin, *Never Look Back: The Career and Concerns of John J. Burke* (New

York, 1975), pp. 108–110. Burke was wrong about the date. *BCR*, February 19, 26, 1927. For background to the Mexican question see James P. Gaffey, *Francis Clement Kelley & The American Catholic Dream* (2 vols., Bensenville, Ill., 1980), 2: 3–73, and Robert E. Quirk, *The Mexican Revolution and the Catholic Church, 1910–1929* (Bloomington, Ind., 1973).

94. L-492, Curley to Ledvina, March 6, 1926 (copy); Mc-734, Curley to McGuire, April 9, 1926 (copy).

95. B-1328, Curley to Boylan, April 9, 1926 (copy).

96. Quirk, *Mexican Revolution*, pp. 162–64.

97. Sheerin, *Burke*, pp. 111–12. Caruana wrote to Curley from Mexico to explain that he had not confided in him at the apostolic delegation in Washington before he left for Mexico because of a message he carried under seal from the Holy Office, but he called Curley his "best ally and backer" (Roman Letters, Caruana to Curley, Mexico D. F., April 14, 1926). Caruana was expelled in May. Referring to the Mexican situation, Fumasoni-Biondi expressed his "sincere appreciation" for Curley's "ready and constant cooperation in all that makes for the welfare of the Church" (ibid., Fumasoni-Biondi to Curley, Washington, March 17, 1926).

98. Roman Letters, Curley to Fumasoni-Biondi, March 19, 1926 (copy).

99. Roman Letters, Curley to Perosi, December 17, 1929 (copy).

100. *BCR*, October 12, 1934.

101. The book drawn from these essays, *No God Next Door* (New York, 1935), was more inflammatory than Bishop Francis Kelley's *Blood-Drenched Altars* (Milwaukee, 1935).

102. W-131, Walsh to Curley, Washington, February 23, 1935.

103. H-228, Curley to Hanna, March 9, 1935 (copy).

104. Roman Letters, Curley to Cicognani, February 26, 1935 (copy).

105. *BCR*, March 29, 1935.

106. Ibid., April 19, 1935.

107. AAB, Mexico I, Walsh to Curley, Washington, April 30, 1935.

108. K-255, Curley to Kelley, December 5, 1935 (copy); Roman Letters, Curley to Cicognani, January 20, 1936 (copy).

109. Sheerin, *Burke*, p. 169. It is not altogether clear what Cicognani meant. He also told Burke that he would not break with Curley "as his predecessor had done." When a new rector was named for the Catholic University, Cicognani also remarked, he would "leave the University alone." There is no evidence that Fumasoni-Biondi broke with Curley. There can be little doubt, however, that Cicognani was well aware of Curley's displeasure at the role he had played in the dismissal of James H. Ryan as rector.

110. Gaffey, *Kelley*, 2: 92–94.

111. K-640, Curley to Kenny, February 25, 1936 (copy); M-1687, Mooney to Curley, Washington, February 26, 1936; B-2097, Burke to Curley, Washington, February 27, 1936; K-257, Curley to Kelley, March 2, 1936 (copy).

112. B-2098, Curley to Burke, February 28, 1936 (copy).

113. Gaffey, *Kelley*, 2: 94–103.

114. *CR*, August 14, 1936.

115. The *Catholic Review*, December 15, 1939, would take exception to Seldes, *Catholic Crisis*, pp. 204–5, which cited the *Nation* to this effect. With the exception of Mencken, the *Catholic Review* claimed with some truth, the *Sun* was always pro-Loyalist.

116. *CR*, February 19, 1937.

117. Seldes, *Catholic Crisis*, pp. 137–38; *Treasure in Clay: The Autobiography of Fulton J. Sheen* (Garden City, N.Y., 1980), pp. 81–90. In an interview with Fulton J. Sheen, Roosevelt expressed his private annoyance that the man sitting in the chair once occupied by his cousin should use such words about a public servant (p. 83).

118. CR, January 13, 20, 1939.

119. L-892, Lloyd to Curley, Annapolis, January 27, 1937.

120. *CR*, March 18, 1932.

121. This was the Hebrew meaning of the name Michael.

122. B-788, Bergin to Curley, Champaign, Ill., April 7, 1927.

123. *BCR*, October 14, 1922.

124. Hennesey, *American Catholics*, p. 258.

125. Edwin Rothman, "Factional Machine Politics, William Curran and the Baltimore City Democratic Organization, 1929–1946" (doctoral dissertation, Johns Hopkins University, 1949).

126. Rita Marie Helldorfer, "The Gubernatorial Career of Albert Cabell Ritchie, Governor of Maryland, 1920–1935" (master's thesis, Catholic University of America, 1955).

127. R-716 and 717, Ritchie to Curley, Annapolis, December 15, 1925, January 5, 1926; R-718, Curley to Ritchie, January 7, 1926 (copy).

128. Harry W. Kirwin, *The Inevitable Success: Herbert R. O'Conor* (Westminster, Md., 1962), pp. 226–27.

129. *BCR*, September 24, 1921.

130. David Roberts, "St. Mary's Elects the President, 1840–1980," *Chronicles of St. Mary's* 28 (1980): 226–28.

131. *BCR*, November 9, 1929.

132. Ibid., October 26, November 1, 1924.

133. Ibid., February 11, 1927.

134. Ibid., October 30, November 14, 1930, February 13, 20, March 6, June 19, 1931, May 25, 1934, and others.

135. Mc-1208, Curley to McNicholas, January 22, 1934 (copy); L-995, Lord to Curley, St. Louis, May 31, 1934.

136. F-648, Fitzpatrick to Curley, Baltimore, January 26, 1935.

137. The Novena of Grace dated from the early seventeenth century as a private devotion promoted by the Jesuits. In the late nineteenth century it flourished in Jesuit churches in America, and in the twentieth was extended by Pius XI to any church. See Curran, *American Jesuit Spirituality*, pp. 19–20, 161–68.

138. *CR*, October 16, 1981.

139. O'Donovan, *St. Martin's*, p. 77.

140. G-476, Memorandum of WLG [Galvin], March 2, 1935.

141. Olson, *Baltimore*, p. 338.

142. G-476, Memorandum of WLG, March 2, 1935.

143. Shehan, *Blessing of Years*, pp. 86–91.

144. *Washington Post*, December 20, 1978 (obituary).

145. Thomas J. Harte, *Catholic Organizations Promoting Negro-White Race Relations in the United States* (Washington, D.C., 1947), pp. 62–116; Foley, "Catholic Church and Washington Negro," pp. 257–80.

146. S-1368, Curley to Sheridan, May 6, 1933 (copy).

147. O'Donovan, *St. Martin's*, pp. 53, 77–83.

148. Olson, *Baltimore*, p. 347.

Chapter 14. The War Years

1. Mc-1093, McNamara to Curley, Washington, October 13, 1939.

2. Roman Letters, Curley to Cicognani, March 6, 1939 (copy).

3. Ibid., same to same, March 13, 1939.

4. M-2201, Murphy to Curley, Washington, October 11, 1939 (telegram).

5. T-858, Tydings to Curley, Washington, October 12, 1939.

6. I-170, Ireton to Curley, Richmond, October 14, 1939.

7. R-1243, Curley to Ryan, November 1, 1939 (copy). Curley frequently visited friends and relatives in New York and rode the subway there.

8. Roman Letters, Cicognani to Curley, Washington, February 27, 1940.

9. Ibid., Curley to Cicognani, February 28, 1940 (copy).

10. Ibid., same to same, March 20, 1940 (copy).

11. Mc-1094, Curley to McNamara, March 1, 1940 (copy).

12. Roman Letters, draft of address; *CR*, March 29, 1940.

13. *The Secret Diaries of Harold L. Ickes* (3 vols., New York, 1954), 3: 382–83.

14. Elliott Roosevelt, ed., *F.D.R.: His Personal Letters, 1928–1945*, (New York, 1950), p. 997.

15. Ibid., p. 999, memorandum of February 13, 1940.

16. AAB, "Apostolic Delegation" in Curley papers, especially reports of 1931 and November 15, 1937.

17. *CR*, May 23, 1947.

18. W-983, Curley to Winter, November 27, 1936 (copy).

19. *CR*, October 30, 1936; *New York Times*, October 26, 1937, 7:3.

20. *CR*, January 15, 1937.

21. S-2320, Curley to Sullivan, December 3, 1937 (copy).

22. *CR*, January 28, 1938.

23. AAB, Chancery papers of Monsignor Joseph Nelligan (hereafter Nelligan papers), "School of Social Action for Baltimore Clergy" folder; *CR*, September 16, 30, December 30, 1938; S-586, Curley to Schrembs, January 31, 1939 (copy).

24. C-2025, Curley to Curran, April 8, 1937 (copy).

25. S-2306, Curley to Sullivan, February 17, 1937 (copy).

26. Green, *Washington: Capital City*, pp. 355–56.

27. Mc-239, Curley to McCormack, February 11, 1937 (copy).

28. S-2317, Curley to Sullivan, October 11, 1937 (copy).

29. *CR*, June 13, 1941.

30. AAB, "Statement on Communism 1941" box contains clippings from the Chicago *Tribune*, *New York Times*, Los Angeles *Examiner*, Denver *Post*, and other papers dated December 3 or 4, 1941.

31. Ibid., Beckman to Curley, Dubuque, December 4, 1941.

32. S-2340 and 2343, Curley to Sullivan, March 26, April 1, 1939 (copies).

33. S-2345, Sullivan to Curley, Washington, January 17, 1939, leaflet enclosed.

34. S-2349, Curley to Sullivan, January 21, 1939 (copy).

35. J-194, Curley to editor of *Jewish Times*, January 25, 1923 (copy).

36. *CR*, May 25, 1934; T-518, Curley to *Jewish Times*, May 7, 1935 (copy).

37. Nelligan diary, November 13, 1938; *New York Times*, November 14, 1938, 7:3.

38. L-1120, Curley to Ludlow, April 18, 1935 (copy).

39. L-1126, Ludlow to Curley, Washington, September 16, 1937; L-1127, Curley to Ludlow, September 18, 1937 (copy).

40. Charles De Benedetti, *The Peace Reform in American History* (Bloomington, Ind., 1980), p. 132.

41. R-1308, Curley to Ryan, March 13, 1936 (copy).

42. Patricia F. McNeal, *The American Catholic Peace Movement* (New York, 1968), pp. 14ff; William A. Au, *The Cross, the Flag, and the Bomb* (Westport, Conn., 1985), pp. 3ff.

43. *CR*, June 27, July 11, 1941.

44. B-505, Bazinet to Curley, Baltimore, July 1, 1941.

45. B-545, Curley to Beckman, September 18, 1941 (copy).

46. George Q. Flynn, *Roosevelt and Romanism: Catholics and American Diplomacy, 1937–1945* (Westport, Conn., 1976), pp. 170–73.

47. W-1045, Wood to Curley, Chicago, November 3, 1941 (telegram).

48. R-19, Curley to Radcliffe, November 6, 1941 (copy).

49. Nelligan diary, December 7, 1941; C-1993, clipping from the *Evening Sun*, December 8, 1941.

50. *CR*, December 12, 1941.

51. Nelligan diary, January 9, 1942.

52. Flynn, *Roosevelt and Romanism*, p. 189.

53. Roman Letters, Curley to Cicognani, January 14, 1941 (copy).

54. Ibid., Cicognani to Curley, Washington, January 18, 1942.

55. John Tracy Ellis, *Catholic Bishops: A Memoir* (Wilmington, Del., 1983), p. 52.

56. *CR*, December 12, 1942.

57. George H. Callcott, *Maryland & America: 1940–1980* (Baltimore, 1985), Ch. 2; Olson, *Baltimore*, pp. 347–50.

58. Green, *Washington: Capital City*, pp. 469–74, 481–82.

59. Nelligan papers, "Defense Program" folder, Nelligan to Stryock, August 8, 1941.

60. *CR*, January 9, 23, July 3, August 28, 1942, January 29, March 19, 1943, November 10, 1944, and passim; Nelligan papers, "War Production Board" folder.

61. Nelligan papers, "Auxiliary Chaplains" folders.

62. *CR*, January 2, October 3, 1942, December 15, 1944, November 2, 1945.

63. Morris L. Radoff, *The Old Line State* (Annapolis, Md., 1971), pp. 264–65. Many Baltimore Catholics were killed in the Battle of the Bulge.

64. *The Long Loneliness: The Autobiography of Dorothy Day* (New York, 1952), pp. 245–50.

65. Curley refused, however, to allow a chapel at St. Anthony's.

66. *Catholic Worker* 8 (December 1940): 1; 8 (January 1941): 5; 9 (January 1942): 7.

67. *CR*, March 27, 1942.

68. Gordon Zahn, *Another Part of the War: The Camp Simon Story* (Amherst, Mass., 1979), pp. 209ff.

69. Z-14, Curley to Zahn, February 6, 1945 (copy).

70. *CR*, November 10, 1939, November 15, 1946.

71. Lawrence J. Shehan, "Current Problems in Catholic Agencies," *Catholic Charities Review* 27 (1943): 60–61, 91.

72. Nelligan papers, "Catholic Charities" folders, report.

73. Ibid., Nelligan to O'Brien, June 27, 1940 (copy).

74. Nelligan papers, "Campaign for Charity and Education" folder 1; Nelligan diary, January 5–April 15, 1941. Catholic Charities of Washington had long been affiliated with the Community Chest.

75. *CR*, May 2, 9, 1941.

76. Ibid., May 23, 30, 1941; Nelligan papers, "Campaign for Charity and Education" folder 2.

77. *CR*, May 21, June 4, 25, 1943; Nelligan diary, May 31, June 27, 1943.

78. *CR*, May 5, 19, June 9, 1944.

79. Ibid., June 30, 1944, November 29, 1946.

80. J-285, Curley to Johnson, June 22, 1944 (copy).

81. N-645, Curley to Noll, December 21, 1942 (copy).

82. The sketch, which appeared on the first page of the *Catholic Review* of January 20, 1933, bears little resemblance to the present Cathedral of Mary Our Queen.

83. N-276, Nelligan to Curley, April 26, 1932.

84. Nelligan diary, August 23, 1936; J-285, Curley to Johnson, June 22, 1944 (copy).

85. Nelligan diary, May 4, 1937.

86. Nelligan papers, "Good Samaritan Hospital" folder.

87. Ibid.

88. Peter E. Hogan, "Archbishop Curley and the Blacks" (unpublished paper), pp. 19–21.

89. Beitzell, *Jesuit Missions*, pp. 254–55, 306–7.

90. *CR.*, June 29, 1945.

91. Ibid., September 17, 1943.

92. Ibid., September 27, 1946; Varga, *Loyola* (in press).

93. Nelligan papers, "Catholic Youth Organization of Baltimore" folder.

94. W-282, Walsh to Curley, New York, November 19, 1941.

95. Nelligan papers, "Catholic War Veterans" folder, Bowman to Nelligan, Washington, October 4, 1947.

96. Ibid., "Legion of Mary" folder. Bishop McNamara had established a praesidium at St. Gabriel's in Washington in 1938.

97. Nelligan diary, September 19, October 28, 1943.

98. Nelligan papers, "Baltimore Community Fund" folder.

99. Ibid., "National Conference of Christians and Jews" folder, Nelligan to Spence, May 30, 1940 (copy); Nelligan to Furfey, July 6, 1942 (copy).

100. Ibid., Nelligan to Healy, June 28, 1944 (copy).

101. S-193, Curley to Sands, November 24, 1944 (copy).

102. Interview with Rev. John F. Cronin.

103. Nelligan diary, December 15, 1941.

104. *Sign* 22 (May 1943): 583–86.

105. C-1871, Cronin to Curley, Baltimore, May 2, 1944.

106. AUND, Cronin papers, "The Problem of American Communism in 1945: Facts and Recommendations" [1945], pp. 16–18, 46.

107. Ibid., pp. 61–80.

108. Peter Irons, "America's Cold War Crusade," p. 177, a doctoral dissertation done at Boston State College, a portion of which is in the Cronin papers.

109. Interview with Rev. John F. Cronin; Garry Wills, *Nixon Agonistes: The Crises of the Self-Made Man* (Boston, 1970), pp. 24–29; Allen Weinstein, *Perjury: The Hiss-Chambers Case* (New York, 1978), pp. 7–8, 347.

110. *CR*, April 4, 1947.

111. C-1503, Curley to Coogan, November 25, 1942 (copy); "Timely Message," *Catholic Missions* 20 (January/February 1943): 16–17.

112. Nelligan papers, "Negro Reports" folders, Gillard to Curley, Baltimore, February 15, 1940.

113. Hogan, "Curley and the Blacks," pp. 12–19.

114. Nelligan diary, May 16, 1942.

115. *The Sun*, December 10, 1943.

116. L-420, LaFarge to Curley, New York, December 27, 1943.

117. Nelligan papers, "NCWC" folders, Curley to Ryan, January 8, 1944 (copy).

118. N-135, Curley to Nelson, November 1, 1943 (copy).

119. Interview with Miss Anita Williams.

120. W-835, Williams to Curley, n.d.; M-2175, Murphy to Curley, Baltimore, February 6, 1945; J-44, Jackson to Curley, Baltimore, February 8, 1945.

121. Archives of the Josephite Fathers, transcript interview with John A. McShane, SSJ, and undated clipping from "St. Peter Claver" folder; *CR*, March 3, 1942.

122. Mary Catherine Taylor, "Color Harmony in Baltimore," *Interracial Review* 19 (September 1946): 186–88.

123. Nelligan papers, "Interracial Relations" folder.

124. John J. O'Connor, "A Man's a Man for A' That," *Interracial Review* 20 (January 1947): 86–89; *CR* February 23, 1945; *Interracial Review* 18 (December 1945): 190–91.

125. Ibid., "Sodality Union" folder, Nelligan to Mattingly, May 15, 1947 (copy).

126. R-1314, Curley to Ryan, June 21, 1941 (copy).

127. R-1315, same to same, January 12, 1943 (copy).

128. N-56, Curley to Nee, January 12, 1943 (copy).

129. P-907, Curley to Probey, April 16, 1940 (copy).

130. R-235, Curley to Ready, December 6, 1944 (copy).

131. M-1696, Mooney to Curley, Detroit, November 17, 1946.

132. Mc-1241, Curley to McNicholas, March 30, 1942 (copy).

133. Mc-1242, McNicholas to Curley, Norwood, Oh., April 11, 1942.

134. Mc-1243, Curley to McNicholas, April 22, 1942 (copy).

135. Nelligan papers, "Catholic University" folder, Curley to Alter, July 14, 1942 (copy).

136. Fitzpatrick, *Life of Curley*, p. 24.

137. The Nelligan diary contains much detail concerning Curley's health.

138. Ibid., January 5 to March 16, May 12, 15, 22, 1941, and Varga, *Loyola*, (in press).

139. Interview with Cardinal Shehan.

140. Nelligan diary, October 17 to December 19, 1946.

141. There are two boxes in the Curley papers filled with messages of condolence.

142. L-896, Lloyd to Hoover, April 28, 1939 (copy).

143. S-1289, Curley to Shehan, November 27, 1941 (copy).

144. Nelligan diary, March 4, 1942.

145. J-417, Curley to Sister M. Joseph, February 5, 1934 (copy).

146. C-2073, Curley to Curry, March 6, 1942.

Chapter 15. Breezes in the Storied Land

1. Jack Harrison Pollack, "The Cobbler and the Archbishop," *Catholic Digest* 22 (June 1958): 15–18.

2. This and other episodes well known to the clergy and laity of Baltimore will not be documented.

3. Interview with Monsignor Porter White.

4. Quoted in *CR*, December 12, 1947.

5. *CR*, May 7, 1948.

6. Ibid., April 22, May 6, 1949.

7. Ibid., April 27, 1951.

8. The lay chairmen of the annual appeals were Joseph P. Healy (1949), Henry P. Irr (1950), William C. Rogers (1951), James Keelty, Jr. (1952, 1953, 1954), Herbert R. O'Conor (1955, 1956), John F. Eyring (1957, 1958), and Rodney J. Brooks (1959, 1960, 1961). In 1958 all (but Brooks) were named Knights of St. Gregory for their services to the appeals.

9. *CR*, April 15, 1955.

10. O'Sullivan, *Bon Secours*, pp. 257–58.

11. Shehan, *Blessing of Years*, pp. 105–7.

12. *The Story of Baltimore's New Cathedral: The Cathedral of Mary Our Queen* [1959], a handsome souvenir volume.

13. Even more costly and controversial was the National Shrine of the Immaculate Conception dedicated in Washington five days later.

14. Interview with Monsignor Porter White.

15. *Our Lady of Victory Church: Silver Anniversary* (Baltimore, 1977).

16. *Silver Anniversary: Immaculate Heart of Mary Church* (n.p., [1973]).

17. The Josephites would also lose St. Monica's, which was suppressed in 1959. Its mission of St. Veronica, however, had been made a parish in 1951.

18. Beginning in the fall of 1948 the *Catholic Review* gave often an entire page to such events.

19. O'Sullivan, *Bon Secours*, pp. 123–24.

20. *CR*, February 20, 1959.

21. U.S. Bureau of Census, *The Statistical History of the United States from Colonial Times to the Present* (New York, 1976), G-226.

22. Bishop John J. Russell's stricture, made at a Catholic Charities convention in New York, appeared in the *CR*, September 30, 1960.

23. Callcott, *Maryland & America*, p. 117.

24. Bauernschub, *Columbianism*, pp. 135–37; Kauffman, *Knights of Columbus*, pp. 359–64.

25. Callcott, *Maryland & America*, p. 118.

26. *CR*, January 10, April 4, May 9, 1947.

27. Callcott, *Maryland & America*, p. 118.

28. Much information on the Maryland Action Guild can be found in the Bazinet papers, SAB, Record Group 13, Box 4.

29. *CR*, July 14, August 4, 11, 1950.

30. When in 1952 O'Conor demanded an investigation of the involvement of Hungary's new minister to the United States in the Mindszenty case, the *Review* supplied the ammunition that would effect, it claimed, the minister's departure from the country. Ibid., February 15, 29, July 18, 1952.

31. Bazinet papers.

32. *CR*, June 9, 1950.

33. Ibid., November 17, 1950; Nolan, *Pastoral Letters*, pp. 431–32.

34. *CR*, December 18, 1953.

35. Ibid., August 7, 14, 28, 1953.

36. Ibid., August 28, September 4, 11, 1953.

37. Ibid., January 1, 1954. Under pressure from the committee Mayor Thomas D'Alesandro in 1957 created his own ten-member Committee on Decency, to which he appointed the president of the archdiocesan Holy Name Society and the Maryland commander of the Catholic War Veterans, two organizations as outspoken on obscenity as the K of C. While Archbishop Keough was urging parishes to cooperate with the mayor's committee, the NCWC, of which he was again chairman of the board, issued its statement on censorship and obscenity. Nolan, *Pastoral Letters*, pp. 498–503.

38. *CR*, January 18, 1957.

39. Ibid., January 24, February 7, 28, March 7, 1958.

40. Ibid., July 17, 1959. The film version of the D. H. Lawrence novel was released at the same time the unexpurgated version of the novel itself was banned from the U.S. mails. *America* 101 (August 1, 1959): 576.

41. *CR*, September 4, 1953.

42. Ibid., February 27, 1959; *The Sun*, February 22, 1959. A Baltimore suburban store was party to the blue laws case before the Supreme Court.

43. Lenora Heilig Nast et al., eds., *Baltimore: A Living Renaissance* (Baltimore, 1982), pp. 36–45; Harold A. Williams, "Baltimore's Way of Life," *Catholic Digest* 24 (May 1960): 36–42; Callcott, *Maryland & America*, pp. 81–91.

44. Kirwin, *O'Conor*, p. 228.

45. Ibid., p. 519.

46. This was particularly true of the presidential election year 1952, when the *Review* was accused of being partial to Eisenhower. See *CR*, January 18, February 15, March 28, May 2, November 7, 1952. Maryland Catholics voted for Eisenhower in both 1952 and 1956 in significantly greater numbers than for the Republican candidate in any previous election except, perhaps, 1920.

47. Nast, *Baltimore*, pp. 229–33. The importance of D'Alesandro in Maryland politics is indicated in Walsh and Fox, *Maryland*, pp. 773–845.

48. Interviews with Cardinal Lawrence Shehan and Rev. Joseph Gallagher. For information on his brother, see Joseph Gallagher, *The Pain and the Privilege: Diary of a City Priest* (Garden City, NY, 1983), pp. 53–55 and passim.

49. *CR*, July 27, 1956.

50. Ibid., October 26, 1956.

51. Ibid., August 15–September 18, 1958 (six installments).

52. Ibid., March 11, 1960. See also *Jubilee* 6 (August 1958): 22.

53. Gallagher, *Pain and Privilege*, pp. 187–89.

54. *CR*, September 16, November 25, 1960.

NOTES TO PAGES 403–413

55. Ibid., November 3, 17, 1961.

56. Timothy Leonard, *Geno: A Biography of Eugene Walsh, S.S.* (Washington, D.C., 1988).

57. Walsh contributed frequently to the *Proceedings* of the Liturgical Week and to *Worship*. He also wrote the introduction for the *People's Hymnal*.

58. Interview with Miss Anita Williams.

59. David L. McManus, "A Parish Profile," *Worship* 34 (1960): 332–38. Connolly himself contributed articles on Bible vigils and other liturgical experiments to Catholic journals, to one of which the Congregation of the Holy Office eventually took exception. Interview with Rev. Joseph Connolly.

60. YCW groups were being organized in Baltimore by other priests, one of the most successful being Casimir Pugevicius, assistant at St. Alphonsus and another disciple of Gene Walsh. See *Jubilee* 6 (August 1958): 22–23.

61. *CR*, June 19, 1970.

62. Interview with Rev. Joseph Connolly.

63. *CR*, January 15, 1960.

64. Interview with Cardinal Lawrence Shehan.

65. Interview with Rev. Joseph Connolly.

66. Interview with Cardinal Lawrence Shehan.

67. According to Monsignor Porter White, his secretary at the time, Keough spoke in Latin when he called from Connecticut to inform him of his first heart attack.

68. *CR*, July 14, 1961.

Part V. Introduction

1. McAvoy, *History of the Catholic Church*, p. 291.

2. Walter M. Abbott and Joseph Gallagher, eds., *The Documents of Vatican II* (New York, 1966), p. 209. The translation editor, Monsignor Joseph Gallagher, recruited a number of prominent priests of the archdiocese of Baltimore to help in the preparation of this standard English translation of the documents of Vatican II (see p. xii).

3. Ibid., p. xvii.

4. Ibid., pp. 179–80.

5. Ibid., p. xvii.

6. Peter Hebblethwaite, *The Runaway Church: Post-Conciliar Growth or Decline* (New York, 1975), p. 43.

Chapter 16. The Council

1. A census conducted by the archdiocese in November 1963 almost a year later, counted 480,653 Catholics, or 23.20 percent of the population. Baltimore City contained 213,327 Catholics, or 21.71 percent of its population. Of the counties Baltimore had the highest ratio with 30.86 percent, followed by Howard with 25.83 percent, Allegany with 21.14 percent, Anne Arundel with 19.79 percent, Harford with 13.63 percent, Frederick with 9.86 percent, Carroll with 8.54 percent, Washington with 7.59 percent, and Garrett with 5.52 percent. Holy Trinity, Glen Burnie, with 15,734 Catholics was the largest parish in the archdiocese, St. Anthony of Padua with 14,624 the largest in the city. *CR*, March 20, 1964.

2. Shehan, *Blessing of Years*, pp. 109–27; Gerard E. Sherry, "The Bridge-Building Cardinal," *Sign* 44 (May 1965): 13–14.

3. Shehan, *Blessing of Years*, pp. 224–26.

4. Ibid., pp. 226–29.

5. *CR*, May 13, 1966.

6. Ibid., December 13, 1965.

7. Ibid., January 12, 1962.

8. Ibid., May 13, 1966.

9. *America* 110 (April 4, 1964): 478–81.

10. *CR*, April 17, 1964. The NCEA proposed raising $40,000 for a scholarly answer to Mrs. Ryan's book.

11. *CR*, March 22, 1963.

12. Sullivan, *Bon Secours*, pp. 267–70. The Bon Secours Sisters withdrew after a year and were replaced by the Daughters of Charity.

13. Shehan, *Blessing of Years*, pp. 216–17.

14. Ibid., pp. 217–22. The names of all who pledged more than $15,000 are given.

15. Ibid., p. 222.

16. Ibid., pp. 229–31.

17. See Callcott, *Maryland & America*, pp. 66–68.

18. Shehan, *Blessing of Years*, p. 230.

19. Ibid., pp. 230–31.

20. Ibid., p. 231.

21. *CR*, February 20, 1967.

22. Thomas Matthews, "New City, New Church," *Commonweal* 86 (August 25, 1967): 518–22.

23. Information supplied by Miss Elizabeth Sweeney, the cardinal's secretary.

24. *CR*, December 9, 1966.

25. Interview with Cardinal Shehan.

26. "Baltimore's Initiative," *America* 106 (January 20, 1962): 493–94.

27. Interview with Monsignor Porter White.

28. Shehan, *Blessing of Years*, pp. 142–50.

29. Xavier Rynne, *Vatican Council II* (New York, 1968), pp. 109–46. Archbishop Shehan had been elected to the Commission on Discipline of the Clergy but surrendered his seat when the Secretariat for Christian Unity was raised also to a commission.

30. Vincent A. Yzermans, *American Participation in the Second Vatican Council* (New York, 1967), pp. 34–35, 59–61; Michael Novak, *The Open Church* (New York, 1967), p. 115; *CR*, October 11, 18, 1963.

31. Yzermans, *American Participation*, pp. 38–39, 66–67.

32. Archbishop Shehan and Monsignor White worked more closely with DeSmedt in the formulation of the decree. Interview with Monsignor White.

33. Rynne, *Vatican II*, pp. 303–5.

34. Shehan, *Blessing of Years*, p. 169.

35. Yzermans, *American Participation*, p. 625.

36. Shehan, *Blessing of Years*, pp. 174–76; *CR*, October 2, 16, November 25, 1964.

37. Yzermans, *American Participation*, p. 196.

38. Shehan, *Blessing of Years*, pp. 181–82.

39. Interview with Monsignor Porter White.

40. *CR*, November 20, 1964.

41. Shehan, *Blessing of Years*, p. 188.

42. *CR*, February 26, 1965.

43. Shehan, *Blessing of Years*, p. 192.

44. Rynne, *Vatican II*, pp. 460, 462, 479.

45. Shehan, *Blessing of Years*, pp. 197–99.

46. Ibid., pp. 203–5.

47. *Paul Blanshard on Vatican Council II* (Boston, 1966), pp. 16, 117.

48. *CR*, February 14, June 12, 1964.

49. Ibid., November 26, 1965, January 7, 28, 1966.

50. Ibid., January 28, 1966.

51. Ibid., November 17, 1967.

52. Ibid., June 10, 1966. By 1966 Maryland was the only state that still had a censorship system for movies. The state attorney general, a Catholic, drafted a bill in the early part of the year to keep the forty-nine-year-old censorship board alive. Ibid., February 4, 1966.

53. Ibid., August 3, November 2, 1962, February 8, 1963.

54. Ibid., June 21, 1963.

55. Ibid., October 22, 1966.

56. Ibid., November 27, December 11, 1964, November 18, 1966. Western Maryland College at Westminster was a Methodist foundation, and Hood College German Reformed.

57. Ibid., June 11, 1965. The cardinal quoted Gibbons' Trastevere speech in 1887 and an article written for the *North American Review* in 1909.

58. *CR*, October 6, 13, 1967.

59. Ibid., November 3, 1967.

60. Ibid., January 14, 21, 1966.

61. Interview with Cardinal Shehan.

62. Shehan, *Blessing of Years*, pp. 206–8

63. Ibid., pp. 209, 213–14.

64. Ibid., p. 231.

65. Interview with Monsignor Austin Healy.

66. *CR*, October 29, 1965.

67. Ibid., March 17, 1967.

68. Much of the following is from an interview with, and papers supplied by, John C. Evelius.

69. *CR*, April 12, 1963.

70. Ibid., April 3, 1964.

71. Ibid., December 17, 1965.

72. Interview with Monsignor Anthony Dziwulski.

73. Interview with, and papers supplied by, John Evelius.

74. Ibid. St. Matthew's also developed a parish council before the fall of 1966.

75. *Guidelines for Parish Councils and Advisory Boards* (1968).

76. Interview with Cardinal Shehan.

77. *CR*, February 7, March 9, 16, 1962.

78. "The Baltimore Story," *America* 109 (September 14, 1963): 256.

79. *CR*, March 1, 1963; Shehan, *Blessing of Years*, pp. 236–38.

80. Quoted in the *CR*, March 8, 22, 1963.

81. AUND, Cronin papers.

82. Interviews with Rev. Joseph Connolly and Monsignor Austin Healy.

83. Ibid.

84. *CR*, July 12, 1963; Gallagher, *Pain and Privilege*, pp. 212–14.

85. *CR*, July 12, 1963.

86. *America* 109 (August 10, 1963): 136–37.

87. *CR*, August 10, 1966: *Afro-American*, August 6, 1966.

88. *CR*, January 21, 1966; *News American*, January 24, 1966.

89. *CR*, January 28, 1966; *The Sun*, January 24, 1966.

90. Gerald M. Costello, *Without Fear or Favor: George Higgins on the Record* (Mystic, Conn., 1984), p. 235; Nolan, *Pastoral Letters*, pp. 604–7, 613–15.

91. *CR*, October 28, 1966.

92. Ibid., December 30, 1966. See also *The Sun*, December 28, 1966; S. J. Adamo, "Baltimore Blues," *America* 115 (December 24–31, 1966): 837.

93. Much of the information that follows is from an interview with Monsignor Austin Healy.

94. *CR*, March 18, October 28, 1966; *The Sun*, November 5, 1965.

95. *Baltimore Urban Parish Study*, p. 8.

96. Robert G. Howes, "The Baltimore Urban Parish Study: The Changing Church in the Changing City," *Catholic World* 207 (July 1968): 153–57.

97. "Baltimore's Parishes," *Commonweal* 87 (February 2, 1968): 520–21.

98. *CR*, June 3, 1966. See also March 4 and July 8, 1966.

99. *CR*, February 11, 1966.

100. Gallagher, *Pain and Privilege*, pp. 122–25, summarizes the editorials he composed for the *Review* on the Vietnamese War. Outspoken criticism of the war appeared in several letters to the editor. See especially those of Ruth Von Bramer, May 31, August 6, 1965, and Brother Louis Doherty, CFX, November 5, 1965, October 21, 1966.

101. Gallagher, *Pain and Privilege*, pp. 204–5; *CR*, July 1, 1966.

102. Gallagher, *Pain and Privilege*, pp. 205–7.

103. Ibid., p. 206.

104. Interview with Cardinal Shehan.

105. Gallagher, *Pain and Privilege*, pp. 248–249, 258–261.

106. Ibid., pp. 299–307, 319–23; interview with Rev. Joseph Gallagher.

107. *CR*, August 11, 25, 1967.

108. Francine du Plessix Gray, *Divine Disobedience: Profiles in Catholic Radicalism* (New York, 1970), pp. 109–11.

109. Ibid., pp. 111–16.

110. Ibid., pp. 116–23.

111. *CR*, November 3, 1967.

Chapter 17. Aftershocks

1. Text given in full in Gallagher, *Pain and Privilege*, pp. 371–74.

2. Shehan, *Blessing of Years*, pp. 243, 248.

3. Kauffman, *Saint Sulpice*, p. 302.

4. *CR*, September 18, 1970.

5. O'Sullivan, *Bon Secours*, pp. 126–34.

6. *CR*, June 5, 1970.

7. Ibid., March 31, 1972.

8. Ibid., July 13, August 3, 1973; *The Sun*, June 28, August 17, 1973.

9. Shehan, *Blessing of Years*, pp. 232–33.

10. Joerndt, *St. Ignatius*, pp. 225–50.

11. Interview with Bishop Francis Murphy.

12. *CR*, February 21, 1969.

13. Interview with Monsignor Joseph Manns.

14. *CR*, March 30, 1973.

15. Ibid., April 23, July 9, 1971, December 8, 1972.

16. Interview with Bishop Francis Murphy.

17. Shehan, *Blessing of Years*, pp. 215–16; interview with Bishop Francis Murphy.

18. *CR*, June 23, 1972.

19. Ibid., July 13, 1973.

20. Ibid., December 21, 1973.

21. Interview with Bishop Francis Stafford.

22. *CR*, March 29, 1974.

23. Ibid., March 3, 10, 1967.

24. Ibid., April 3, 10, 17, May 29, 1970; Walsh and Fox, *Maryland*, p. 884.

25. In *Blessing of Years*, pp. 267–72, the cardinal offers a detailed explanation of the difficulty presented by the merger of United Fund and the Commerce and Industry Combined Health Appeal and how it was resolved to the satisfaction of all but the pro-life people.

26. *CR*, July 20, 17, August 3, 1973; O'Sullivan, *Bon Secours*, pp. 134–35.

27. *CR*, February 14, March 21, 1969.

28. Ibid., November 3, 10, 1973; Walsh and Fox, *Maryland*, pp. 894–95.

29. *CR*, September 28, 1973, April 12, November 8, 1974.

30. *The Sun*, May 24, June 1, 2, 1971; *CR*, May 28, June 11, 1971.

31. *CR*, January 18, 1974.

32. *The Sun*, July 1, 1970.

33. Ibid., September 30, 1970; *CR*, September 11, October 2, 1970.

34. *The Sun*, November 7, December 17, 1970.

35. *CR*, June 11, 18, 1971.

36. Ibid., July 30, August 6, 1971.

37. Ibid., February 25, 1972.

38. *The Sun*, December 27, 1971.

39. *CR*, May 8, 1970, February 25, 1972, September 28, 1973.

40. *The Sun*, December 13, 1970.

41. Gray, *Divine Disobedience*, pp. 123–33.

42. *CR*, May 31, 1968.

43. Gray, *Divine Disobedience*, pp. 153–228; Richard Curtis, *The Berrigan Brothers: The Story of Daniel and Philip Berrigan* (New York, 1974), pp. 93–108.

44. Charles A. Meconis, *With Clumsy Grace: The American Catholic Left, 1961–1975* (New York, 1979); William O'Rourke, *The Harrisburg 7 and the New Catholic Left* (New York, 1972); interviews with two of those actively involved. Meconis supplies an "incomplete" list of 232 of those who preferred calling themselves the "action community" (pp. 153–66).

45. Jack Nelson and Ronald J. Ostrow, *The FBI and the Berrigans: The Making of a Conspiracy* (New York, 1972), pp. 11ff.

46. The stern attitude the cardinal ascribed to himself in *Blessing of Years*, pp. 272–74, is belied by the sympathy and concern remembered by those he visited. The episode is detailed as part of a tribute to the attorney, Francis X. Gallagher, who died of a heart attack during the trial at age forty-two.

47. Nelson and Ostrow, *FBI and Berrigans*, pp. 155–56; *The Sun*, January 24, 1971. Almost every issue of the *Catholic Review* from January 15 to March 19 carried messages of support.

48. For its larger significance see John C. Raines, ed., *Conspiracy: The Implications of the Harrisburg Trial for the Democratic Tradition*, (New York, 1974).

49. *The Sun*, June 1, 1972; *CR*, June 16, 1972.

50. *CR*, January 5, 19, 26, 1973; Shehan, *Blessing of Years*, pp. 275–78.

51. *CR*, January 14, 1972.

52. *The Sun*, January 30, February 3, May 8, 1973.

53. *CR*, June 15, August 31–September 14, 1973.

54. Ibid., June 18, 1971.

55. Robert Blair Kaiser, *The Politics of Sex and Religion: A Case History in the Development of Doctrine* (Kansas City, 1985), p. 164.

56. "Humanae Vitae: 1968–1973," *Homiletic and Pastoral Review* 74 (November and December 1973): 14ff, 20ff.

57. Shehan, *Blessing of Years*, pp. 248–52. Shehan allowed the teachers to respond truthfully to questions on the statement of dissent. See Kauffman, *Saint Sulpice*, p. 304.

58. Shehan, *Blessing of Years*, pp. 257–58.

59. *CR*, April 11, 1969.

60. Ibid., April 26, May 3, October 4, 1968.

61. Ibid., April 16, 23, 1971.

62. Ibid., October 2, 1970, January 15, 22, February 12, 19, 1971.

63. Ibid., June 4, 1971.

64. Ibid., January 29, 1971; *The Sun*, January 25, February 7, 1971.

65. *CR*, February 8, 1974.

66. Interview with Monsignor Porter White.

67. James Gollin, *Worldly Goods: The Wealth and Power of the American Catholic Church, the Vatican, and the Men Who Control the Money* (New York, 1971), p. 215.

68. Interview with Bishop Francis Murphy.

69. Shehan, *Blessing of Years*, pp. 258–66; interviews with Monsignor Porter White and Brother Nivard Scheel, CFX, former acting rector of the University.

70. Shehan, *Blessing of Years*, pp. 279–89.

71. Interview with Bishop Francis Murphy.

72. Interview with Archbishop Borders.

73. Text supplied by Bishop Murphy.

74. *News American*, September 1, 1984.

75. "To Live Is to Grow," *The Priest* 21 (June 1965): 478–88, an address delivered at St. Mary's Seminary.

76. *The Sun*, September 28, 1972. In 1974 Wills, who had contributed to the *Catholic Review* in the 1960s, was again criticized by the cardinal as well as a former editor of the *Review* for his disparagement of the new cathedral and his reference to bishops assembled

there as "high muck-a-mucks of hocus-pocus." Ibid., July 12, 22, 1974.

77. "The Priest in the New Testament: Another Point of View" and "Apostles and Bishops: Still Another Point of View," *Homiletic and Pastoral Review* 76 (November 1975): 10–23, and (January 1976): 8–23.

Epilogue, 1974–1994

1. *CR*, September 12, 19, 1975. The president of the six religious congregations that recognized Mother Seton as their founder was that year the superior general of the Sisters of Charity of Convent Station.

2. Ibid., October 10, 1975.

3. Interview with Archbishop Borders.

4. Interview with Sister Rosalie Murphy, SND, head of the Division of Collegial Services.

5. From *Journeying Together: Proceedings of Three Regional Convocations of Shared Responsibility in America* (Bishops Committee on the Laity, 1985).

6. Information supplied by Miss Sheila Kelly, secretary of the Department of Personnel.

7. Rev. Stephen R. Sutton, a former Episcopal priest and both husband and father, was ordained in the Latin rite August 4, 1984.

8. Interview with Harold Smith, secretary of Associated Catholic Charities.

9. A study of their plight, *The Long Loneliness in Baltimore: A Study of Homeless Women*, coauthored by its director, Brendan Walsh, sent others to their assistance.

10. See Daniel Berrigan, *To Dwell in Peace: An Autobiography* (San Francisco, 1987), pp. 290–93, 336–37.

11. Au, *The Cross, the Flag, and the Bomb*, pp. 203ff.

12. *CR*, August 7, 1985, May 4, 1988.

13. Ibid., March 11, 1983.

14. LEG, a network of lobbyists, looked for direction to the Maryland Catholic Conference, which focused on such issues as capital punishment, handgun control, abortion, and welfare coverage.

15. *CR*, August 7, 1977.

16. Interview with Ms. Laurie Lomba Vega, who also revealed that about 74 percent are Catholic and 12 to 23 percent Pentecostals, the latter increasing at the expense of the former.

Sources

Until now the oldest American archdiocese has not had a history. A number of works, such as Riordan's *Cathedral Records* and Stanton's *Century of Growth*, have served to fill the gap, and all the archbishops up to Michael J. Curley have been accorded scholarly biographies. But the need to examine one of the richest diocesan archives, to peruse the longest run of diocesan monthlies and weeklies, and to consult the mass of secondary material bearing upon a see that until well into the twentieth century played a pivotal role in the history of American Catholicism as a whole has deterred sensible historians.

For the history of the archdiocese of Baltimore, I have chosen to examine virtually piece by piece the papers of the archbishops and administrators and the Roman correspondence through Curley, some 165 file boxes. This does not include the voluminous chancellor files of Monsignor Joseph Nelligan, which I also examined. I have perused every issue of the *United States Catholic Magazine* (1840–50), *Catholic Mirror* (1850–1908), and *Catholic Review*, originally called the *Baltimore Catholic Review* (1913 to the present). I have also examined a number of other archives. Those of the University of Notre Dame are the most important. They contain not only the original papers of such early dioceses as New Orleans, Cincinnati, and Detroit, but also in microfilm form the American material in the Archives of the Propaganda Fide in Rome, Propagation of the Faith in Lyons and Paris, the Leopoldine Society of Vienna, the English College in Rome, and the Irish College in Rome. I have also examined personally the archives of the archdiocese of New York, the Sulpicians of Baltimore, the Maryland Province of the Society of Jesus at Georgetown University, Mount St. Mary's Seminary and College at Emmitsburg, the Josephite Fathers in Baltimore, and the Oblate Sisters of Providence in Baltimore.

I have also made an attempt to examine all important secondary works and periodical literature touching the archdiocese of Baltimore. Much of this was repetitive or derivative; much had been superseded. I therefore, will not attempt to present an exhaustive bibliography. What follows is simply a list of the works that have proved the most serviceable for the story

I have tried to tell. Almost every parish has its commemorative history, but I have listed only the few of those I remember as having special merit. A large number of parish histories of the archdiocese of Baltimore can be found not only in the archdiocesan archives but also in the collection of parish histories at the Cushwa Center of the University of Notre Dame. The following works are listed by author, or by title when the author is not known, with no attempt to sort them by books, articles, dissertations, or otherwise.

Agonito, Joseph Anthony. "The Building of an American Catholic Church: The Episcopacy of John Carroll." Doctoral dissertation, Syracuse University, 1973.

Ahern, Patrick H. *The Life of John J. Keane: Educator and Archbishop, 1839–1918*. Milwaukee, 1954.

Angelus Gabriel (Brother). *The Christian Brothers in the United States, 1848–1948*. New York, 1948.

Au, William A. *The Cross, the Flag, and the Bomb: American Catholics Debate War and Peace, 1960–1983*. Westport, Conn., 1987.

Baker, Jean H. *Ambivalent Americans: The Know-Nothing Party in Maryland*. Baltimore, 1977.

Bauernschub, John P. *Fifty Years of Columbianism in Maryland*. Baltimore, 1949.

[Begni, Ernesto]. *The Catholic Church in the United States of America: Undertaken to Celebrate the Golden Jubilee of His Holiness, Pope Pius X*. 3 vols. New York, 1912.

Beitzell, Edwin Warfield. *The Jesuit Missions of St. Mary's County, Maryland*. Abell, Md., 1976.

Bevan, Thomas. *220 Years . . . A History of the Catholic Community in Frederick Valley*. Frederick, Md., 1977.

Bilhartz, Terry D. *Urban Religion and the Second Great Awakening: Church and Society in Early National Baltimore*. Rutherford, N.J., 1986.

Billington, Ray Allen. *The Protestant Crusade, 1800–1860: A Study of the Origins of American Nativism*. New York, 1938.

Bowen, John W. "A History of the Baltimore Cathedral to 1876." Master's thesis, Catholic University of America, 1963.

Brislen, M. Bernetta. "The Episcopacy of Leonard Neale, Second Archbishop of Baltimore," *Historical Records and Studies* 34 (1945): 20–111.

Bruchey, Eleanor Stephens. "The Business Elite in Baltimore, 1880–1914." Doctoral dissertation, Johns Hopkins University, 1967.

Callcott, George H. *Maryland & America: 1940–1980*. Baltimore, 1985.

Carey, Patrick W. *People, Priests, and Prelates: Ecclesiastical Democracy and the Tensions of Trusteeism*. Notre Dame, Ind., 1987.

Carley, Edward B. *The Origins and History of St. Peter's Church, Queenstown, Maryland, 1637–1976*. Baltimore, 1976.

The Catholic Red Book of Baltimore-Washington and Environs: A Catholic Directory, Alphabetically Arranged, under Parochial Classification. Baltimore, 1908.

The Catholic Red Book of Western Maryland. Baltimore, 1909.

Cestello, Bosco David. "James Whitfield, Fourth Archbishop of Baltimore: The

Early Years, 1770–1828," *Historical Records and Studies* 45 (1957): 32–78.

Code, Joseph B. "Brief Sketch of the Community of the Sisters of Charity (1821–1927)," an appendix to [Helene] de Barbery, *Elizabeth Seton*. New York, 1940.

Gogley, John. *Catholic America*. New York, 1973.

Corrigan, Owen B. "Catholicity in Allegany and Garrett Counties, Maryland," *Records of the American Catholic Society of Philadelphia* 36 (1925): 113–54, 209–53.

———. *History of the Catholic Schools in the Archdiocese of Baltimore*. Baltimore, 1924.

———. "Model Country Parish," *Records of the American Catholic Historical Society of Philadelphia* 35 (1924): 197–241.

Costello, Mary Loretto. *The Sisters of Mercy of Maryland (1855–1930)*. St. Louis, 1931.

Crooks, James B. *Politics & Progress: The Rise of Urban Progressivism in Baltimore, 1895–1911*. Baton Rouge, La., 1968.

[Crumlish, Sister John Mary]. *1809–1959*. Emmitsburg, Md., 1959.

Curley, Michael J. *The Provincial Story: A History of the Baltimore Province of the Congregation of the Most Holy Redeemer*. New York, 1963.

Curran, Robert Emmett. *American Jesuit Spirituality: The Maryland Tradition, 1634–1900*. New York, 1988.

———. " 'Splendid Poverty': Jesuit Slaveholding in Maryland, 1805–1838," in Randall M. Miller and Jon L. Wakelyn, eds., *Catholics in the Old South: Essays on Church and Culture*. Macon, Ga., 1983.

———. "Troubled Nation, Troubled Province, 1833–1880." Unpublished manuscript.

Cunz, Dieter. *The Maryland Germans, A History*. Princeton, N.J., 1948.

Currier, Charles Warren. *Carmel in America*. Baltimore, 1890.

Cuyler, Cornelius M. *The Baltimore Cathedral*. Baltimore, 1951.

Daley, John M. *Georgetown University: Origin and Early Years*. Washington, D.C., 1957.

Devitt, Edward I. "The Clergy List of 1819, Diocese of Baltimore," *Records of the American Catholic Historical Society of Philadelphia* 22 (1911): 238–67.

"Diary of Archbishop Marechal, 1815–1825," *Records of the American Catholic Historical Society of Philadelphia* 11 (1900): 417–54.

Dignan, Patrick J. *A History of the Legal Incorporation of Catholic Church Property in the United States, 1784–1932*. Washington, D.C., 1933.

Dirvin, Joseph I. *Mrs. Seton: Foundress of the American Sisters of Charity*. New York, 1962.

Dolan, Jay P. *The American Catholic Experience: A History from Colonial Times to the Present*. New York, 1985.

Durkin, Joseph T. *William Matthews: Priest and Citizen*. New York, 1964.

Ellis, John Tracy, ed. *Documents of American Catholic History*. 2 vols. Chicago, 1967.

———. *The Life of James Cardinal Gibbons, Archbishop of Baltimore, 1834–1921*. 2 vols. Milwaukee, 1952.

Fabrician of Jesus (Brother). *St. Paul's Church and Parish, Ellicott City, Maryland: Its Origin and Development*. Baltimore, 1910.

Fecher, Vincent J. *A Study of the Movement for German National Parishes in Philadelphia and Baltimore (1787–1802)*. Rome, 1955.

Feller, John Quentin. "The Public Character of Cardinal Gibbons in His Archdiocese." Master's thesis, Catholic University of America, 1965.

Fitzpatrick, Vincent de Paul. *Life of Archbishop Curley: Champion of Catholic Education*. Baltimore, 1929.

Fogarty, Gerald, Joseph Durkin, and R. Emmett Curran. *The Maryland Jesuits, 1634–1833*. *Baltimore, 1976*.

Fogarty, Gerald P. *The Vatican and the American Hierarchy from 1870 to 1965*. Wilmington, Del., 1986. Paper.

Foley, Albert Sidney. "The Catholic Church and the Washington Negro." Doctoral dissertation, University of North Carolina, 1950.

Gallagher, Joseph. *The Pain and the Privilege: Diary of a City Priest*. Garden City, N.Y., 1983.

Geiger, Mary Virgina. *Daniel Carroll: A Framer of the Constitution*. Washington, D.C., 1943.

Gorman, Mary Adele. "Federation of Catholic Societies in the United States, 1870–1920." Doctoral dissertation, University of Notre Dame, 1962.

Green, Constance McLaughlin. *Washington: Capital City, 1879–1950*. Princeton, N.J., 1962.

———. *Washington: Village and Capital, 1800–1870*. Princeton, N.J., 1962.

Guilday, Peter. *A History of the Councils of Baltimore, 1791–1884*. New York, 1932.

———. *The Life and Times of John Carroll: Archbishop of Baltimore, 1735–1815*. New York, 1922.

———. *The Life and Times of John England: First Bishop of Charleston, 1786–1842*. 2 vols. New York, 1927.

Halsey, Columba E. "The Life of Samuel Eccleston, Fifth Archbishop of Baltimore, 1810–1851," *Records of the American Historical Society of Philadelphia* 76 (1965): 69–156.

Hanley, Thomas O'Brien. *Charles Carroll of Carrollton: The Making of a Revolutionary Gentleman*. Washington, D.C., 1970.

———. *The John Carroll Papers*. 3 vols. Notre Dame, Ind., 1976.

Harvey, Katherine A. *The Best Dressed Miners: Life and Labor in the Maryland Coal Region, 1835–1910*. Ithaca, N.Y., 1969.

Hennesey, James. *American Catholics: A History of the Roman Catholic Community in the United States*. New York, 1981.

Herbermann, Charles G. *The Sulpicians in the United States*. New York, 1916.

Herr, Dan, and Joel Wells, eds. *Through Other Eyes: Some Impressions of American Catholicism by Foreign Visitors from 1777 to the Present*. Westminster, Md., 1965.

Hirschfeld, Charles. *Baltimore, 1870–1900: Studies in Social History*. Baltimore, 1941.

Hogan, Peter E. "Archbishop Curley and the Blacks." Unpublished manuscript.

Hollowak, Thomas. *Faith, Work, and Struggle: A History of Baltimore Polonia*. Baltimore, 1988.

Hughes, Thomas. *History of the Society of Jesus in North America: Colonial and Federal*. 4 vols. New York, 1907–1917.

Hutzell, Rita Clark. *Mother of Churches: A History of St. Mary's Church, Hagerstown, Maryland*. N.p., 1976.

Joerndt, Clarence V. *St. Ignatius, Hickory, and Its Missions*. Baltimore, [1972].

Judge, Robert K. "Foundation and First Administration of the Maryland Province." *Woodstock Letters* 88 (1959): 376–406.

Kauffman, Christopher J. *Faith and Fraternalism: The History of the Knights of Columbus, 1882–1982.* New York, 1982.

———. *Tradition and Transformation in Catholic Culture: The Priests of Saint Sulpice in the United States from 1791 to the Present.* New York, 1988.

Kelly, Mary Almira. "A History of the School Sisters of Notre Dame in Maryland." Master's thesis, Catholic University of America, 1944.

Kenneally, Finbar, et al. *United States Documents in the Propaganda Fide Archives: A Calendar.* 9 vols. to date. Washington D.C., 1966–

LaFarge, John. *The Manner Is Ordinary.* New York, 1954.

Linkh, Richard M. *American Catholicism and European Immigrants (1900–1924).* Staten Island, N.Y., 1975.

McAvoy, Thomas T. *A History of the Catholic Church in the United States.* Notre Dame, Ind., 1969.

McColgan, Daniel T. *A Century of Charity: The First One Hundred Years of the Society of St. Vincent de Paul in the United States.* 2 vols. Milwaukee, 1951.

McConville, Mary St. Patrick. *Political Nativism in the State of Maryland, 1830–1860.* Washington, D.C., 1928.

McCormick, Leo J. *Church-State Relationships in Education in Maryland.* Washington, 1942.

McHale, Mary Loretta. "The Catholic Church in the District of Columbia (Later Period: 1866–1938)." Master's thesis, Catholic University of America, 1938.

Maloney, Mary Xavier. "The Catholic Church in the District of Columbia (Earlier Period: 1790–1866)." Master's thesis, Catholic University of America, 1938.

Marschall, John P. "Francis Patrick Kenrick, 1851–1863: The Baltimore Years." Doctoral dissertation, Catholic University of America, 1965.

Meline, Mary M., and Edward F. X. McSweeny. *The Story of the Mountain: Mount St. Mary's College and Seminary, Emmitsburg, Maryland.* 2 vols. Emmitsburg, Md., 1911.

Melville, Annabelle M. *Elizabeth Bayley Seton.* New York, 1951

———. *John Carroll of Baltimore: Founder of the American Catholic Hierarchy.* New York, 1955.

———. *Louis William DuBourg: Bishop of Louisiana and the Floridas, Bishop of Montauban, and Archbishop of Besançon, 1766–1833.* 2 vols. Chicago, 1986.

Micek, Adam A. *The Apologetics of Martin John Spalding.* Washington, D.C., 1951.

Moran, Michael. "The Writings of Francis Patrick Kenrick, Archbishop of Balimore (1797–1963)," *Records of the American Catholic Historical Society of Philadelphia* 41 (1930): 230–62.

Murtha, Ronin John. "The Life of the Most Reverend Ambrose Maréchal: Third Archbishop of Baltimore, 1768–1828." Doctoral dissertation, Catholic University of America, 1965.

Nast, Lenora Heilig. "The Role of the Clergy in Jewish-Christian Relations in Baltimore from 1945 to 1975." Doctoral dissertation, St. Mary's Seminary and University, 1978.

Nast, Lenora Heilig, et al. *Baltimore: A Living Renaissance.* Baltimore, 1982.

O'Grady, John. *Catholic Charities in the United States: History and Problems.* Washington, D.C., 1930.

Olson, Sherry H. *Baltimore: The Building of an American City.* Baltimore, 1980.

O'Sullivan, Mary Cecilia. *The Sisters of Bon Secours in the United States, 1881–1981: A Century of Caring.* N.p., 1982.

Panczyk, Matthew Leo. "James Whitfield, Fourth Archbishop of Baltimore, The Episcopal Years: 1828–1834," *Records of the American Historical Society of Philadelphia* 75 (1964): 222–51; 76 (1965): 21–53.

Phillips, Hugh J. "The Catholic Settlement in the Monocacy Valley." Unpublished manuscript.

Radoff, Morris L. *The Old Line State: A History of Maryland.* Annapolis, Md., 1971.

Ridgeway, Whitman H. *Community Leadership in Maryland, 1790–1840: A Comparative Analysis of Power in Society.* Chapel Hill, N.C., 1979.

[Riordan, Michael J.] *Cathedral Records from the Beginning of Catholicity in Baltimore to the Present Time.* Baltimore, 1906.

Ruane, Joseph W. *The Beginnings of the Society of St. Sulpice in the United States, 1791–1829.* Washington, D.C., 1935.

Scarpaci, Vincenza. "*Ambiente Italiano*: Origins and Growth of Baltimore's Little Italy." Unpublished manuscript.

Scharf, J. Thomas. *Chronicles of Baltimore.* Baltimore, 1974.

———. *History of Baltimore City and County.* Philadelphia, 1881.

———. *History of Western Maryland.* Philadelphia, 1882.

Schlegel, Laurence. "The Publishing House of John Murphy of Baltimore: The First Forty Years, with a List of Publications." Master's thesis in Library Science, Catholic University of America, 1961.

Schmeckebier, Laurence F. *History of the Know Nothing Party in Maryland.* Baltimore, 1899.

Sesquicentennial: St. Patrick's Parish. Baltimore, 1942.

Shaw, Richard. *John Dubois: Founding Father.* New York, 1983.

Shea, John Gilmary. *The History of the Catholic Church in the United States.* 4 vols. New York, 1886–92.

Shehan, Lawrence J. *A Blessing of Years: The Memoirs of Lawrence Cardinal Shehan.* Notre Dame, Ind., 1982.

Sherwood, Grace H. *The Oblates' One Hundred and One Years.* New York, 1931.

Smith, Mary Eleanora. "The Jenkins Family of Baltimore." Master's thesis, Catholic University of America, 1941.

Spalding, Thomas W. "John Carroll: Corrigenda and Addenda," *Catholic Historical Review* 71 (1985): 505–18.

———. *Martin John Spalding: American Churchman.* Washington, D.C., 1973.

Stanton, Thomas J. *A Century of Growth, Or the History of the Catholic Church in Western Maryland.* 2 vols. Baltimore, 1900.

Steins, Richard H. "The Mission of the Josephites to the Negro in America." Master's thesis, Columbia University, 1966.

Swanson, Mary Laura. "A Study of the Polish Organizations in the Polish Community of Baltimore." Master's thesis, Johns Hopkins University, 1925.

Taves, Anne. *The Household of Faith: Roman Catholic Devotions in Mid-Nineteenth-Century America.* Notre Dame, Ind., 1986.

Tierney, John J. "St. Charles College: Foundation and Early Years," *Maryland Historical Magazine* 43 (1948): 294–311.

Tommey, Richard J. "Fielding Lucas, Jr., First Major Catholic Publisher and Bookseller in Baltimore, 1804–1854." Master's thesis in Library Science, Catholic University of America, 1952.

Trisco, Robert. "Bishops and Their Priests in the United States," in John Tracy Ellis, ed., *The Catholic Priest in the United States: Historical Investigations*. Collegeville, Minn., 1971.

Varga, Nicholas. *Baltimore's Loyola, Loyola's Baltimore: A History of Loyola College, Baltimore, Maryland, 1851–1986*. Baltimore, in press.

Walsh, Richard, and William Lloyd Fox, eds. *Maryland: A History, 1632–1974*. Baltimore, 1974.

Willging, Eugene P., and Herta Hatzfeld. *Catholic Serials of the Nineteenth Century in the United States: A Descriptive Bibliography and Union List*, 2nd Series, Part II, *Maryland and the District of Columbia*. Washington, D.C., 1965.

Witte, Cyril Marcel. "A History of St. Mary's Industrial School for Boys in the City of Baltimore, 1866–1950." Doctoral dissertation, University of Notre Dame, 1955.

Yeager, M. Hildegarde. *The Life of James Roosevelt Bayley, First Bishop of Newark and Eighth Archbishop of Baltimore, 1814–1877*. Washington, D.C., 1947.

Index

About the Author **Thomas W. Spalding,** C.F.X., is professor of history at Spalding University in Louisville, Kentucky. He is the author of *Martin John Spalding: American Churchman,* awarded the John Gilmary Shea award of the American Catholic Historical Association